CW00945006

OXFORD
TWENTY-FIRST CENTURY
APPROACHES TO LITERATURE

OXFORD
TWENTY-FIRST CENTURY
APPROACHES TO LITERATURE

Late Victorian into Modern

Edited by

LAURA MARCUS
MICHÈLE MENDELSSOHN
AND
KIRSTEN E. SHEPHERD-BARR

OXFORD
UNIVERSITY PRESS

OXFORD
UNIVERSITY PRESS

Great Clarendon Street, Oxford, OX2 6DP,
United Kingdom

Oxford University Press is a department of the University of Oxford.
It furthers the University's objective of excellence in research, scholarship,
and education by publishing worldwide. Oxford is a registered trade mark of
Oxford University Press in the UK and in certain other countries

Published in the United States of America by Oxford University Press
198 Madison Avenue, New York, NY 10016, United States of America

British Library Cataloguing in Publication Data

Data available

Library of Congress Control Number: 2016946639

ISBN 978–0–19–870439–3

Printed in Great Britain by
CPI Group (UK) Ltd, Croydon, CR0 4YY

This volume is dedicated to Sally Ledger (1961–2009)

ACKNOWLEDGEMENTS

We are very grateful to Alex Bubb for his invaluable editorial assistance. We would like to thank the Faculty of English at the University of Oxford for generous research support and our anonymous readers for their timely and helpful suggestions. At Oxford University Press, Jacqueline Norton, Rachel Platt, and Lowri Ribbons have expertly guided this project through to fruition. Thanks are also due to St Catherine's College for providing the perfect surroundings and environment in which to do our collaborative work as editors. Our greatest thanks go to our contributors for their commitment and intellectual energy.

CONTENTS

LIST OF ILLUSTRATIONS

EDITORS AND CONTRIBUTORS

Faith Binckes, Senior Lecturer in English Literature, Bath Spa University, UK

Elleke Boehmer, Professor of World Literature in English, Wolfson College, University of Oxford, UK

Alexander Bubb, Leverhulme Early Career Research Fellow, Department of English, King's College London, UK

Vincent J. Cheng, Shirley Sutton Thomas Professor of English, University of Utah, USA

Rachel Crossland, Senior Lecturer in English, University of Chichester, UK

Santanu Das, Reader in English Literature, King's College, London, UK

Dennis Denisoff, McFarlin Professor of Victorian Literature and Culture, University of Tulsa, USA

Kamilla Elliott, Professor of Literature and Media, Lancaster University, UK

Sos Eltis, Associate Professor; Tutorial Fellow in English, Brasenose College, University of Oxford, UK

Stefano Evangelista, Associate Professor; Tutorial Fellow, Trinity College, Oxford, UK

Anne Fernihough, University Lecturer in English, and Fellow of Girton College, University of Cambridge, UK

Penny Fielding, Grierson Chair of English Literature, University of Edinburgh, UK

Kate Flint, Provost Professor of Art History and English, University of Southern California, USA

Jana Funke, Advanced Research Fellow, Department of English, University of Exeter, UK

David Glover, Emeritus Professor of English, University of Southampton, UK

William Greenslade, Professor of English Literature, University of the West of England, Bristol, UK

Marah Gubar, Associate Professor of English, University of Pittsburgh, USA

Christos Hadjiyiannis, Research Fellow in English Literature, Wolfson College, University of Oxford, UK

Sam Halliday, Senior Lecturer in Nineteenth-Century American Literature, Department of English, Queen Mary University of London, UK

Adrian Hunter, Senior Lecturer, English Studies, School of Arts and Humanities, University of Stirling, UK

Benjamin Kohlmann, Assistant Professor, Englisches Seminar, University of Freiburg, Germany

Tatiana Kontou, Senior Lecturer in Nineteenth-Century Literature, Oxford Brookes University, UK

Ruth Livesey, Reader in Nineteenth-Century Literature and Thought, Department of English, Royal Holloway University of London, UK

Laura Marcus, Goldsmiths' Professor of English Literature, New College, University of Oxford, UK

Michèle Mendelssohn, Associate Professor and Tutorial Fellow, Mansfield College University of Oxford, UK

Adam Parkes, Professor of English, University of Georgia, USA

Angelique Richardson, Associate Professor, English, University of Exeter, UK

Max Saunders, Director, Arts and Humanities Research Institute and Professor of English, King's College, London, UK

Laurence Scott, College of Global Studies, Arcadia University, USA

Kirsten E. Shepherd-Barr, Professor of English and Theatre Studies; Tutorial Fellow, St Catherine's College, University of Oxford, UK

Hannah Sullivan, Associate Professor, English, New College, University of Oxford, UK

Matthew Taunton, Lecturer, School of Literature, Drama and Creative Writing, University of East Anglia, Norwich, UK

Olga Taxidou, Professor of Drama, Department of English Literature, University of Edinburgh, UK

Marcus Waithe, University Senior Lecturer in the Faculty of English, University of Cambridge, UK

Tiffany Watt Smith, Lecturer in Theatre, Drama and Performance, School of English and Drama, Queen Mary University of London, UK

Michael H. Whitworth, University Lecturer, English, and Tutorial Fellow, Merton College, University of Oxford, UK

Daniel G. Williams, Professor of English Literature and Director of the Richard Burton Centre for the Study of Wales, Swansea University, UK

James Williams, Department of English and Related Literature, University of York, UK

Jarad Zimbler, Lecturer in Modern English Literature, University of Birmingham, UK

INTRODUCTION

Our volume's title, *Late Victorian into Modern*, emphasizes the in-between: not one period or the other, but the 'into', the gradual changeover from one to the next. When was the modernist moment set in motion? And when does the Victorian era end? The 1880s make a sensible beginning, inaugurating as they did so many of the cultural, aesthetic, scientific, social, and political tendencies that later find full expression as modernism. Stopping in 1920 may seem a restrictive move, since the decade of the 1920s has traditionally been seen as the apex of literary modernism. Our focus, however, is on the crossroads in this journey, 'the middle way' in T. S. Eliot's phrase. We aim to map the forking paths taken in these four decades, and to record their numerous intersections. This approach enables us to examine the developments shared by these two periods, rather than drawing absolute boundaries between them. By challenging the dominant teleological story of the *fin de siècle*, the narratives shift.

Focusing on this literary and cultural nexus, we have been concerned to point out continuities more than ruptures. To do so we have sought out both established and emerging scholars on literature published between 1880 and 1920. Some of our contributors concentrate more fully on the earlier part of the period we cover, while others look forward to the decades more clearly associated with modernism.

In questioning traditional generic and period categories, the volume proposes to explore and exploit an understanding of the decades as a cultural moment in which new knowledges were forming with particular speed and intensity. The late nineteenth to the early twentieth centuries thus function as a hinge that opens out into the central paradoxes of a period constructed as at once radically new and very old, as modern and archaic, as a beginning and a *fin*. Our project is therefore less preoccupied with precise beginnings or endings than with the midpoint of the period's life: the multiple centres around which this dynamic period constructed and constituted itself. While the critical works on modernist literature and culture that have proliferated since the mid-twentieth century have helped shape our understandings of the period, we have not reached too readily for modernism as an umbrella category, preferring instead the exploration of multiple literary and cultural modes and phenomena in their own particular terms.

Today literary periodization is a prominent issue in critical discourse, as well as in the classroom. As our title suggests, *Late Victorian into Modern* is particularly concerned to accentuate the continuities between the end of one century and the beginning of the next while also taking on board the models of radical rupture that distinguish modernist self-fashioning and manifesto making. *Late Victorian into Modern* suggests that there are crucial continuities across this period and that focusing on these can be more productive than adopting traditional, compartmentalized models. Nothing is lost, but much is transformed. Taken as a whole, the volume emphasizes the connections across four crucial decades. It examines the changes produced by what Yeats called 'the widening gyre': the gaps created between old and new, as well as the bridges built between them. While wishing, for example, to give due recognition to the rupture effected by the First World War (which broke, among many other persons and things, the burgeoning English avant-garde of the early 1910s), we have not made 1914 a cut-off point, instead exploring ways of writing through the war years.

We are not alone in the task of spanning the late nineteenth century and the twentieth. Michael Saler's *The fin-de-siècle World* throws open the geographical boundaries usually imposed on the study of these decades, bringing a welcome globalism to bear that complements our own focus. Recent interventions by Kirstin Mahoney and Vincent Sherry have signalled the necessity of thinking about 1880–1920 as a continuous, unbroken period. Mahoney's *Literature and the Politics of Post-Victorian Decadence* demonstrates how much the twentieth century's avant-gardism was invested in the *fin de siècle*'s developments, disappointments, and dilemmas including queer culture, pacifism, elitism, occultism, dandyism, and feminism. In *Modernism and the Reinvention of Decadence,* Sherry reaches back to the Decadence of Baudelaire and Poe to trace modernism's long trajectory. Before Sherry and Mahoney, Regenia Gagnier's studies of Oscar Wilde and of turn-of-the-century literature and culture, and monographs such as Rachel Teukolsky's *The Literate Eye: Victorian Art Writing and Modernist Aesthetics* had located the beginnings of 'long modernism' in the early decades of the nineteenth century.

Writing from the perspective of what we might call the long Decadence, David Weir's *Decadence and the Making of Modernism* argues that Decadence is 'a dynamics of transition': a dialectic that synthetized its components (including romanticism) in modernism. Still other critics have taken an even longer view. Matei Calinescu's *Five Faces of Modernity* considered the variations on the theme of modernity represented by modernism, the avant-garde, Decadence, kitsch, and postmodernism. Aris Mousoutzanis's *Fin-de-siècle Fictions, 1890s–1990s: Apocalypse, Technoscience, Empire* and, before him, John Stokes's *Fin de siècle, fin du globe: Fears and Fantasies of the Late Nineteenth Century* have prompted renewed thinking about century endings and especially about the late Victorian era and the 1990s *fin de siècle*, our own nineties before the noughties. We share with these studies the concern to work across the period and the desire to look beyond a traditional canon and absorb a broad range of modes and genres of writing.

When, in 1890, Oscar Wilde used the expression '*fin de siècle*' in *The Picture of Dorian Gray*, he described the spirit of his age. The phrase became synonymous with his world-weary circle who, like Dorian himself, wished 'it were *fin du globe*' because their lives were such 'a great disappointment'. Writing in 1893, Arthur Symons alerted readers to the view that the Decadent movement had no wish to be considered as 'healthy'; instead, it revelled in having contracted the *fin-de-siècle* malady, because it made it feel more alive. By the 1920s, the period of the *fin de siècle* had taken on an entirely different association. When Eliot wrote 'A Preface to Modern Literature', he post-dated the beginning of modern literature to 1895. The trial of Oscar Wilde, Eliot argued, struck the death knell for liberal, cosmopolitan culture: its chastening result was to return English (by which he meant British) culture to its most puritanically and parochially vulgar forms. The 1890s were admirably irresponsible, Eliot claimed, while the 1920s were so staid they were 'already dead'. Eliot's elegiac version of the 1890s is very different from that of Symons, and his tribute equally different from Henry James's 1904 description of Aestheticism as a 'bad smell' that had to be accounted for. Today, the term '*fin de siècle*' retains strong associations with decline, degeneration, and disease. Literary-critical definitions are for the most part negative and tend to emphasize its end of days weariness and *je-m'en-foutisme*. Yet this commonplace is at odds with Eliot's perspective and, indeed, with the points of view of several of the authors included in this volume, who argued that the *fin de siècle* was generative for their generation.

Many of the women and men we think of as having made it new in the first decades of the twentieth century—including T. S. Eliot, James Joyce, D. H. Lawrence, Wyndham Lewis, Katherine Mansfield, Ezra Pound, Lytton Strachey, Virginia Woolf—were children of the 1880s. The writers we most often constitute as 'modernist' were thus formed in and by the values of the late nineteenth century, and while they frequently sought, and fought, to break with the immediate past, their identities were, at least in part, shaped by it. The moderns were also very aware of themselves as 'transitional', and our volume remains attentive to the question of what it means to perceive oneself as living in a transitional age. *Transition* was indeed the title the poet and literary critic Edwin Muir gave his 1926 study of contemporary literature: in his introduction he explored the 'modern' concern with 'the spirit of the age', writing that 'it is he who wrestles with the age who finally justifies both it and himself'. 'What we feel', Muir argues, 'as the contemporary Zeit Geist [sic] . . . is a raw potentiality whose crystallizations in art are less clearly recognizable by us the more completely we are under the influence of that potentiality'.

Muir's concern was with the relationship between his present and the future, but nearly a century later, we find that twilights interest us as much as new dawns. We consider a sense of exhaustion with the novelty of the modern. Our volume intervenes in debates about the concept of lateness in modern culture, brought to prominence by Theodor Adorno, among others, and recently developed by a number of theorists, art historians, and literary critics. Lateness, and its corollary, 'late style', can refer to the stages of an artist's work (as in Adorno's discussion of late Beethoven) but, as Andrew Goldstone has suggested, it becomes as significantly implicated in models of aesthetic autonomy (from the 'art for art's sake' doctrines of the late nineteenth century through to concepts of 'impersonality' in the early twentieth). Here art is perceived to stand apart from the forces that surround it, as the ageing self stands outside the life that has gone before.

Many narratives of the modern have made strong associations between individual and cultural life stages. This can be seen in the focus not only on 'the fatal aging of the modern', in Adorno's phrase, but also in the attention to 'adolescence' as an awkward and transitional age. It is one that defines much turn-of-the-century literature, including the work of Henry James and, into the 1910s, the *Bildungsromane* of Virginia Woolf (as with the unformed heroines of her first novels *The Voyage Out* and *Night and Day*), as well as James Joyce (*Stephen Hero* and *A Portrait of the Artist as a Young Man*) and D. H. Lawrence (*Paul Morel, Sons and Lovers*, and *The Rainbow*). Adolescence and old age stand at opposite ends of the individual's lifespan, but the focus on their states and temporalities—transition and lateness respectively—are further pointers towards the profound time-awareness characterizing the decades covered by this volume.

We have also been concerned with concepts of space and with spatial and geographical boundaries. The metropolis is, for many commentators, the condition of modernity, the 'fourth dimension' of scientific discovery and occult thought. Many of our chapters acknowledge the internationalist dimensions and aspirations of literary movements such as Decadence, Aestheticism, and modernism. The volume is primarily, but by no means exclusively, concerned with British literature and includes discussions of nationalism, regionalism, and Celticism. We point outwards when the topic demands such expansion, and have been concerned to give due weight to questions of cosmopolitanism, imperialism, and colonialism.

The organizing principle of this volume is to retain a key focus on literary texts—broadly understood to include familiar categories of genre as well as extra-textual elements such as press and publishing history, performance events, and visual culture—while remaining keenly attentive to the interrelations between text and context in the period. We have avoided author-based chapters, because the volume's overarching strategy is to frame the period in terms of its networks, genres, and intellectual and cultural formations. This informs our concept of the literary, which is not a bounded concept but sits within much broader cultural intersections. We draw attention to 'minor' genres such as parody and self-portrait that were familiar in their own time but from which recent criticism has become more estranged; here they are granted a new legibility.

The volume also rethinks and expands the categories that have tended to dominate criticism of the period, such as 'the New Woman', 'Aestheticism and Decadence', 'Degeneration', the 'New Drama', 'Empire', and, of course, 'the *fin de siècle*'. Alongside these well-established classifications, the volume proposes newer or less familiar ones, with chapters focusing on topics including early cinema and telephony; motherhood and reproduction; sexualities; bodies and the machine; visual culture; race and biology; authorship; reading and transmission; primitivism; time and space; selenography; and technology. We also foreground performance and theatricality—concepts that permeate a wide range of discourses and practices but that are rarely given enough attention in other books on the period. Many chapters in the volume take as their core preoccupation the interplay between the literary and other modes of expression and forms of knowledge, such as psychological writings (theories of consciousness, psychoanalysis); scientific knowledge (evolutionary theory, physics, popular science writing, and scientific fantasies); political and social discourses (Fabianism, liberalism, social anthropology); and para-scientific or unofficial knowledge (spiritualism and the occult). The volume as a whole is not intended as a comprehensive history, or survey, of the period: our intention is rather that it should open up, in new and innovative ways, a range of dimensions, some familiar and some more obscure, of the late Victorian into the modern.

The chapters in Part I, Twilights, explore those aspects of literary and cultural thought at the turn of the nineteenth century that have traditionally been understood as part of that period's embrace of nostalgia, decline, and closure. All four chapters engage and, at times, argue with this received idea. In 'Medievalism and Modernity', Marcus Waithe points to the variety of 'aesthetic effects and political tendencies' which made up nineteenth- and early twentieth-century medievalism, and the phenomenon of medievalism's survival: its sheer and unlikely 'staying power'. Through his examination of work by William Morris, Thomas Hardy, Bram Stoker, C. R. Ashbee, and David Jones, and in his discussion of art and architecture as well as literature, Waithe suggests that medievalism should be characterized 'less as a sentimental reversion than as a distinctive outgrowth of modernity, and ultimately a constituent of modernism'. Medievalism does not merely look back to old materials, but reveals an 'enduring capacity for [their] adaptation and reformulation': reshaping the future rather than returning to the past.

The centrality of 'adaptation' emerges in a rather different context in Jarad Zimbler's 'Mythology, Empire, and Narrative'. Zimbler explores the ways in which novelists of empire and colonialism, including Olive Schreiner, Rudyard Kipling, and Joseph Conrad, negotiated the inherited generic and narrative conventions of the novel at a time of intense debates about the art of fiction and the relationship between realism and romance. Schreiner, for one, refused the association between romance and the colonies so dear to the 'imperial spirit'. We find a similar wariness towards romance in Kipling. It is, in Zimbler's phrase, 'generic irregularity' that replaces romance in Schreiner's *The Story of an African Farm* and Kipling's *Kim*, as well as an engagement with mythology that transcends both romance and realism. 'The margins of empire', Zimbler argues, 'are revealed, or rather constituted, as the proper testing grounds of the self, indeed of the spirit': the place of existential truth and metaphysical insight.

Stefano Evangelista's 'Death Drives: Biology, Decadence, and Psychoanalysis' suggests that the conventionally held view that Freud's theory of the death drive arose out of the context of the First World War risks overlooking its earlier roots in late nineteenth-century biological theories, including the work of the German scientist August Weismann. Evangelista argues that both Weismann (in whose theories biological death is to be understood as a by-product of evolution) and Freud participate in a much broader cultural debate on death—a debate that crossed national and disciplinary boundaries as well as the period boundaries of the nineteenth and twentieth centuries. Freud's scientific formulation of the death drive is in direct dialogue with Decadence, with its intrinsic concepts of decay and death, as demonstrated in the writings of Charles Baudelaire, Walter Pater, Algernon Charles Swinburne, W. B. Yeats, A. E. Housman, and the poetic duo 'Michael Field' (Katharine Bradley and Edith Cooper) whose poetics of morbidity and death encode a lesbian sexuality. The chapter explores the imbrications of a Decadent world view with homoeroticism and a queer poetics, as well as the 'productive synergy' between Decadent aesthetics and psychoanalytic theory.

Daniel Williams's 'Celticism' also takes up the topic of Aestheticism. Williams, critiquing the post-colonial view, most powerfully proposed by Edward Said, that late nineteenth-century and early twentieth-century Celticism was 'an internally inflected variant of imperial Orientalism', suggests (through a reading of the twentieth-century poet Edward Thomas's *Beautiful Wales*) that 'Celticism emerges from moments of disorientation rather than of straightforward subjugation'. The chapter engages with writings by Matthew Arnold, W. B. Yeats, Ernest Rhys, and William Sharp to examine the complex and diverse relations to Celticism in Irish, Welsh, and Scottish contexts, opening out from Celtic literatures (with 'The Celtic Twilight' understood as 'a regional variation of aestheticism') to broader questions of race, nation, and language.

The chapters in Part II, Making it New, pursue the question of periodization, and the continuities and discontinuities between the late nineteenth and the early twentieth centuries. In the case of the modernist and avant-garde groupings discussed by Christos Hadjiyiannis in 'Cultures of the Avant-Garde', we see a strongly performative dimension to the claims for 'newness' that dominate the period. Poetry, in particular, becomes the 'advance guard of language' for T. E. Hulme, Ezra Pound, and others of their London-based circle. In calling for experimentation with 'regular' forms and a new, modern mode of composition, these avant-gardists sought to capture the changing 'spirit' of their time, which they felt existing forms and techniques could no longer accommodate. What unites the different avant-garde practices of the time is the belief that poetry ought to spearhead all means of communication. This conviction underlies the avant-garde distinction between 'prose' (or conventional language) and 'poetry' (direct, immediate language), an opposition which, in turn, at least in the case of Hulme and Pound, carries serious ideological implications. Hadjiyiannis connects Imagist poetics, exemplified by Pound, H.D., and F. S. Flint, to both modernist visuality and Bergsonian anti-positivism. His chapter opens up the complex aesthetic and political stances taken by the avant-garde poets of the period.

As Hadjiyiannis acknowledges, 'the modern spirit', so strongly identified with the modernist movements of the early twentieth century, was a phrase deployed by the Victorian Matthew Arnold, who, in writing of nineteenth-century intellectuals, observed the 'awakening of the modern spirit'. Hannah Sullivan, in her chapter on 'Emerging Poetic Forms', fastens on the 'first moment in literary history when poetry was not expected to follow fixed, inherited, generically specific rules about scansion, line length, syllable weight, or rhyme'—a moment when poetry blossomed in a remarkable efflorescence of prosodic and musical experiment, as represented by Eliot, Dobson, Dowson, Pound, Whitman, and others. The First World War invigorated the writing and reading of poetry but it also had a recursive effect on form and diction. By the 1920s, Sullivan contends, poetry was at a three-way stand-off between modish *vers libre*, the consoling traditional poetic forms of the soldier poets, and the increasingly complex experiments and pastiches of the avant-garde.

Michael Whitworth's 'When *Was* Modernism?' considers the dates at which modernism might be taken to have started and ended, and the ideological and aesthetic judgements we implicitly make when we periodize the movement. To open the story in 1890 is to make Aestheticist and symbolist works an essential part of the movement; to start in 1908 is to privilege those avant-garde groupings on which Hadjiyiannis's chapter focuses; to date modernism's beginnings 'on or around . . . 1910' invokes Virginia Woolf and, with her, Bloomsbury culture. In investigating modernisms' chronologies, Whitworth argues, there is a need 'to remain sensitive to modernism's self-conceptions, and [to] be sceptical about their limits'. The chapter examines the history of the idea of 1922 as modernism's *annus mirabilis*, and its consequences for the modernist canon. It asks about the value of tying aesthetic modernism to socio-historical modernity, and taxonomizes the different modernities currently in use. It also opens up the contested relations between 'modernism' and 'modernity', as well as new apprehensions of global and transnational modernisms and modernities.

Sos Eltis and Kirsten Shepherd-Barr's 'What *Was* the "New Drama"?' shifts from the question of when to the question of what. The much-touted 'new drama' defies easy categorization as it straddled—and indeed obliterated—the line between popular and avant-garde theatre, encompassing 'a huge range of theatrical activity'. Through examples such as George Bernard Shaw, John Galsworthy, Elizabeth Robins, and Susan Glaspell, Eltis and Shepherd-Barr show that social reform and aesthetic innovation were not mutually exclusive but could go hand in hand. This in turn has profound implications for definitions of modernism that have tended to privilege exclusivity and rupture as the prime requirement for inclusion in the modernist canon. A deeper exploration of the theatre of this period breaks down the binaries of 'new' and 'old', high and low, 'mainstream and coterie' and reveals that 'bold stylistic experimentation coexisted with active social engagement'.

Like the 'new drama', the 'New Woman' was, in many ways, an avatar of 'the modern spirit', with her origins in the last decades of the nineteenth century. In 'Who *Was* the "New Woman"?' Angelique Richardson explores the coining of the term and the identification of the figure, while noting that those women writers and political campaigners to whom the label was applied at the turn of the century frequently resisted its implications and simplifications. Olive Schreiner, discussed by Jarad Zimbler in relation to narrative and empire, took exception to the very 'notion of newness', proclaiming 'We are not new!'. Richardson explores the different political and cultural stances taken by so-called New Women, contrasting, for example, the 'social purity' platform of Sarah Grand with the radically reformist stance on marriage of the novelist and polemicist Mona Caird. She also points to male writers such as Hardy, Gissing, Ibsen, and Granville-Barker who put women's lives and predicaments, including 'the marriage question', centre stage. Richardson suggests that the figure of the New Woman, for all its constructed nature, 'earned a remarkable place in literary and social history, giving rise to modernist consciousness and setting a feminist agenda for the twentieth century'.

A slightly later version of the 'New Woman' was 'the Freewoman', a figure closely connected to the socialist and gender politics and the new philosophies developing at the turn of the nineteenth and twentieth centuries. These are discussed in Anne Fernihough's 'Utopian Thought and the Way to Live Now', which examines the socialisms of the period, 'ideal' and 'practical' and (in ways that intersect with Christos Hadjiyiannis's chapter, Chapter 5) philosophical vitalism and 'free verse'. Throughout her chapter, Fernihough notes the temporal complexities that lie at the heart of our volume as a whole: D. H. Lawrence's utopianism harks back to the rhetoric of 'a new heaven on earth' characteristic of early nineteenth-century millenarianism, while Wells's version of the good society 'brought realism and modernism together in unexpected ways'. Fernihough's arguments further suggest that questions of literary form and style connect in the most profound ways to those of ideology, culture, and ways of living.

The chapters in Part III, Modes and Genres, pursue the exploration of literary style and form at the turn of the century, and examine genres of popular fiction, including scientific romances and adventure and detective stories. In 'Naturalism, Realism, and Impressionism', Adam Parkes traces the emergence, from the legacy of nineteenth-century realism, of specifically *literary* notions of naturalism and impressionism in British and Irish writing of the long *fin de siècle*. While noting theoretical differences between naturalism and impressionism, Parkes pays special attention to how often they overlap in the literary practice of such authors as Henry James, George Moore, John Galsworthy, Virginia Woolf, Ford Madox Ford, Jean Rhys, and James Joyce. Impressionists and naturalists often use the same metaphors and settings, while some works usually associated with impressionism are governed by naturalistic plots. At the same time, realism never really dissolves; it persists and renews itself even in some of modernism's most experimental narratives. In tracking the numerous ways in which the aesthetics of these modes 'would imprint them-selves . . . on the literature of the long *fin de siècle* and beyond', Parkes argues for the continuous and often contested relationships among the different fictional modes he discusses.

Adrian Hunter's 'The Rise of Short Fiction' points to the fact that, by contrast with histories of the novel, discussion of short fiction has been, to an overwhelming and limiting extent, formal and aesthetic rather than cultural and historical. Furthermore, he suggests that the problematic homogenizing of the years 1880-1920 within the modernist paradigm (a tendency that this volume as a whole questions and subverts) has been in large part responsible for the critical failure to understand the short story's rise to prominence in the period. It was, Hunter argues, in the 1890s and not the 1910s 'that the short story became aligned with values and prac-tices of a literary avant-garde and entered into a distinctively modernist phase'. There are, for example, significant connections between the 'plotless' short story (as produced by Arthur Morrison, among many others) and 'the representational demands of urban modernity'. Hunter turns to women writers such as George Egerton (also discussed in Angelique Richardson's chapter, Chapter 9) to point up the relationship between 'the interrogative short story form' and the focus on gen-der and women's selfhood at the turn of the century and beyond.

The last two chapters in this part explore the genres of scientific romance and of adventure and detective fiction. Matthew Taunton's 'Moon Voyaging, Selenography, and the Scientific Romance' explores the genre of the scientific romance and its relationship with scientific knowledge and with literary modernism. Depictions of the moon by Mark Wicks, H. G. Wells, Garrett P. Serviss, Charles Hannan, and G. H. Ryan are situated within a broader context of literary and scientific thinking about the moon in order to interrogate the idea—put forward by Jean-Paul Sartre and Marjorie Nicholson—that increasing scientific knowledge of the moon tends to dispel its mythical and poetic power. Taunton argues instead that scientific knowl-edge and the literary imagination coexist and at times feed one another. Moreover, despite a tendency in conventional literary histories to position the scientific romance outside modernism, Taunton shows how the depiction of the moon in a modernist text—in this case, the 'Ithaca' episode of Joyce's *Ulysses*—reveals essen-tial similarities with the scientific romances under discussion.

The close of the Victorian era is often regarded as marking the inception of the modern system of popular genres. But as David Glover's 'Superniches? Detection, Adventure, Exploration, and Spy Stories' shows, an examination of some conspicuous anomalies in recent histories of the nineteenth-century literary field suggests that the emergence of the kinds of generic labels by which readers oriented themselves to the market for popular fiction was a messy, uneven, and never fully completed process. Tracing the pivotal role played by Robert Louis Stevenson in the modernization of romance novels, particularly his influence on the rise of the single-volume imperial adventure story, this chapter looks at the latter's eclipse by two overlapping yet frequently competing domestic subgenres: the spy thriller and the detective story. Genres seldom comprise neat self-contained narrative structures, but are best understood as loose clusters of literary devices, branching off in a variety of rival directions, and creating what the critic Franco Moretti has called 'super-niches'.

Part IV, Sites and Spaces of Knowledge, brings new perspectives on three domains that are essential for study of the period—science, the city, and empire— and rethinks the literary–critical currency of these terms. In 'Scientific Formations and Transformations' Rachel Crossland probes the ways in which writers registered the new scientific ideas that made 1880–1920 'one of the most turbulent and revolutionary periods of scientific discovery to date', especially for the field of physics. Conrad, Madox Ford, Eliot, Wells, Lawrence, and Woolf in particular embraced such discoveries as X-rays and radioactivity, Brownian motion, the electron, the birth of quantum theory, and the theory of relativity. The chapter explores writers' contacts with the new scientific thinking and with the ways in which they transformed ideas through their engagements with them. The radical break with the past that has become one of the definitive attributes of modernism emanates, Crossland argues, as much from these scientific developments, ushering in new ways of conceptualizing the physical world, as from aesthetic imperatives; the one cannot be separated from the other. Recent work by Peter J. Bowler and others has illuminated the role of the periodical press in feeding the wider public's appetite for popular science; Crossland offers two specific examples, the *Cornhill Magazine* and the *New Quarterly* (edited by Desmond MacCarthy), and considers the emergence of a new 'interdisciplinary matrix' to which literary writers and scientists alike contributed.

In 'Spirit Worlds', Tatiana Kontou addresses the allure of the supernatural and the para-scientific. Psychical researchers were dedicated to the rigorous and scientific investigation of manifestations that often seemed to defy natural laws. They were eager to remove the connotations of sensational, gothic, or supernatural genre writing from their reports and framed their experiments within contemporary scientific and technological developments. The empirical terminology employed by the Society for Psychical Research, for example its re-categorizations of 'ghosts' as 'phantasms' and 'mediums' as 'sensitives', fuelled the period's literary imagination, as in works by Oscar Wilde and Florence Marryat. Popular writers such as Algernon Blackwood and William Hope Hodgson were captivated by the figure of the scientifically minded and disinterested psychical researcher, leading to fictionalized psychic detectives who operate at the margins of legal and natural order. Kontou examines a variety of short stories alongside SPR reports and proceedings to discuss the complicated relationship between genre writing and psychical research.

In his chapter on 'Cityscapes', Laurence Scott expands the concept of the urban by bringing it in relation to hyperspace (the idea of a fourth dimension) and hypostatization (the process of converting abstractions into physical objects), showing how these notions inflected literary representations of the metropolis and gave them 'a precarious physicality'. London by the end of the century was 'an ambiguous site, at once abstract and material', as shown by writers like Wells, Conrad, Madox Ford, Edwin A. Abbott, Arthur Morrison, Arthur Machen, and Thomas Burke. Taking London as its main example, the chapter seeks to draw a connection between late-Victorian interest in the fourth dimension and contemporaneous literary representations of the cityscape, as writers repeatedly show a troubling concern about the failures of permanent escape through time travel to other dimensions and ultimately reveal 'the seemingly inevitable solipsism of transcendence'.

Penny Fielding, in 'Regionalisms', challenges the long-held impression that a residual romanticism, local and rural, suddenly gave way in the late Victorian period to the new national and transnational forces of modernism. As her chapter shows, the literary geographies of the period are considerably more complex. Fielding discusses a range of authors and genres that reveal national geography as a fluid, interactive network rather than, as Benedict Anderson would have it, as a 'homogenous empty space'. The chapter examines, in these contexts, the work of Hardy, Conan Doyle, and George Douglas Brown; popular narratives of invasion like *The Thirty-Nine Steps*; poetry including Edward Thomas's 'Chalk Pit' that set the old certainties of rural localities against a new, modernist sense that no locations can be bearers of communal or continuous history. Examining the late work of Robert Louis Stevenson, Fielding also shows that in a globalized world, the local becomes a site of memory. The literature of the period often foregrounds the need to think of the global *from* somewhere, or to recognize oneself as a global subject by using memory to measure the distance from one position to another.

Pursuing the question of modernity, globalism, and space, Elleke Boehmer's 'The View from Empire' explores how the large-scale technological networking of the planet that accompanied empire at the turn of the nineteenth into the twentieth century brought a marked new preoccupation with international exchange and cross-border interaction into literary writing worldwide, including in Britain. Writers in the period around 1900 question the wealth of empire and paradoxically reflect 'an awareness of at-once-uneven and heterogenous globalization'. Boehmer asks what forms and structures writers of the periphery like Rudyard Kipling, Joseph Conrad, Leonard Woolf, Solomon T. Plaatje, and Olive Schreiner (as well as metropolitan writers such as T. S. Eliot) deployed to express their critiques of exploitative and unbalanced migratory and commodity flows under empire.

The chapters in Part V, Minds and Bodies, signal the lively interdisciplinarity of the period and foreground the current innovative work on contemporary psychology and physiology. The recent and growing interest in the somatic and sensory dimensions of literary production and reception has important antecedents in the scientific and cultural endeavours of the *fin de siècle* writ large, including the fascination with psychophysiology and psychophysical parallelism. William Greenslade in 'Race and Biology' reminds us that amid the surge of interest in eugenics were the 'countervailing' voices of writers such as Mona Caird, William James, and the anthropologist Franz Boas. These thinkers contested biological and racial determinism's apparent hegemony, even while many of their contemporaries like Ibsen, Hardy, and Gissing were 'creatively entangled' in deterministic discourses around heredity, race, and biology. The chapter examines the centrality of these widely circulating discourses to the development of eugenic ideas in this period. It also explores the typological resources granted to writers, both to voice such deterministic ideas and to offer points of resistance through the different subject positions that their texts could adopt.

Much research has been done in recent decades on issues having to do with memory, trauma, remembrance, memorials and monuments, truth and reconciliation; indeed, memory studies are a notable presence in 'twenty-first-century approaches to literature' and culture. But, as Vincent Cheng argues in 'The Will to Forget: Amnesia, the Nation, and *Ulysses*', hardly anyone—in medicine and neuroscience, in psychology and psychiatry, in studies of ethnicity and identity, in cultural and literary studies—considers the desirability or usefulness of forgetting. Cheng probes the mechanisms of amnesia in relation to nationhood, taking Joyce's *Ulysses* as his case study in productive forgetting—an impulse that runs deliberately counter to the cultural imperative to remember. Among Cheng's chief advocates of forgetting are the nineteenth-century thinkers Nietzsche, Marx, and Renan, whom he situates suggestively in relation to Joyce's 'nightmare' of history, showing how in *Ulysses* the processes of individual forgetting and remembering become symptomatic of the collective amnesia and cultural dynamics involved in a conquered people's struggle to imagine a national identity, reconstitutes it and keeps it from fossilizing.

If the act of forgetting helps ultimately to keep us human/humane, at the other end of the spectrum is the concept of the post-human, explored by Dennis Denisoff in 'The Post-Human Spirit of the Neopagan Movement'. Though most often regarded negatively as an aspect of British Decadence, the neopagan movement was in fact the product of diverse interests including archaeological discoveries, modernist philosophy, new spiritualities often rooted in hermeticism and theosophy, and debates in nationalist and socialist politics. Neopaganism was sustained primarily by individuals who felt a deep, personal investment in these ecological faiths and their seemingly uninhibited philosophies and respect for diversity. Authors such as A. E. Benson, Edward Carpenter, Aleister Crowley, and Michael Field explored the place of the humanist individual in a nature-centred belief system that stands in opposition not only to scientific materialism, but also to the industrialism and consumerism of the age. In so doing, they offered an early queer formulation of what today might be recognized as a post-human eco-spirituality.

Tiffany Watt Smith in 'Theatre and the Sciences of Mind' investigates scientists' attempts to understand the workings of the mind through an exploration of mimicry, the near-universal urge to imitate, which has natural affinities with the stage. She explores the relationship between the scientific interest in mimicry in 1890–1914 and the practices and problems of theatre, showing how scientific experimentation and theatrical performance mutually informed one another. At this time, psychologists ventured forth from their laboratories into music halls, circuses, and other theatrical venues, interviewed actors, and adopted performance techniques in their own experiments, while theatre itself was assimilating and reflecting scientific ideas about the processes of mind and thought. Tracing the connections running back and forth between theatre and scientific psychology at the *fin de siècle*, Watt-Smith argues that, despite increased codification and professionalization, the sciences of mind remained embedded in their wider cultural context.

The late nineteenth century saw detailed exploration not only of 'mimicry' but also of the 'new' concept of 'empathy' (*Einfühlung*). The capacity to share the feelings and bodily sensations of another or others is a central topic of Santanu Das's 'The Theatre of Hands: Writing the First World War'. The chapter also opens up, though in very different contexts, the terms of 'touching, feeling, flinching', which have been the subject of Watt Smith's research on nineteenth-century spectacle and physiology. Extending his work on 'touch and intimacy' in First World War literature, Das focuses on the significance of hands and gestures in a range of First World War poems, memoirs, and short stories, including D. H. Lawrence's 'The Blind Man' and Claire Goll's 'The Hand of Wax'. In the texts he discusses, the focus is at times on the 'limits of empathy' in the face of the other's pain and the body's destruction: in all his instances, the reader is implicated, as a 'witnessing subject', in the experiences of war, psychological and physiological, that writers took it upon themselves to narrate and describe.

This part of the volume then turns to the prevalent preoccupations and anxieties surrounding the sexual body, including the construction of the category of the homosexual and of the stages of childhood and adolescence in relation to sexuality. In 'The Cult of the Child Revisited', Marah Gubar challenges head-on the assumptions that lie behind the enduring 'cult of the child' that supposedly dominated the late Victorian scene. Far from being idealized for their innocence and remoteness from adulthood, children were often enlisted to solve the problems of modern society, 'from the rocky state of turn-of-the-century gender and race relations to widespread worries about class conflict and rising materialism'. Gubar explores key examples such as Hodgson Burnett's *Little Lord Fauntleroy*, a transatlantic stage hit on the scale of Stowe's *Uncle Tom's Cabin* and Barrie's *Peter Pan*. While often ridiculed for their sentimentality, the cult narratives and the parodies they inspired alike express concern about the excesses and inhumanities engendered by capitalism, even as both cashed in on the popular appeal of the figure of the child. As Peter Pan remarks, 'Children know such a lot now'.

Jana Funke's 'Intersexions: Dandyism, Cross-Dressing, Transgender' examines late nineteenth- and early twentieth-century literary and scientific constructions of ambiguous and cross-gendered figures, such as the New Woman and the New Man, the male and female dandy, the cross-dresser and transvestite, and the sexual invert. Exploring the shifting relation between literature and sexual science across the period from 1880 to 1920, the chapter highlights frequently overlooked continuities between *fin-de-siècle* and modernist understandings of gender and sexuality. It challenges previous scholarship in demonstrating that the scientific and medical views that increasingly shaped literary production in the first decades of the twentieth century did not result in more rigid or limiting understandings of gender and sexuality. On the contrary, scientific and medical debates emerged in tandem with literary writing and, in turn, shaped modernist understandings of the gendered and sexual self, subjectivity, and creativity.

Part VI, Political and Social Selves, opens with a focus on the radical political movements of the period. The 'isms' in Ruth Livesey's 'Political Formations: Socialism, Feminism, Anarchism' might seem to invoke collective change, in relation to economic organization, social institutions, or gender. Yet one of the distinctive aspects of radicalisms in the period 1880-1920—and what makes such politics so visible in the arts—is the manner in which these movements shook up comfortable preconceptions about the self. While many enduring historical accounts stress the anti-aesthetic aspects of late-nineteenth political radicalism, particularly in relation to the Fabian Society, Livesey traces the relations between anti-capitalist politics, feminism and literary experiment in the era of mass culture. The work of Olive Schreiner and William Morris, explored in detail in the chapter, shows how late nineteenth-century literature, in its repudiation of Naturalism, could become a means to explore alternative futures for sexual relations, for social equality, and for the individual's rejection of capitalist modernity. Livesey also examines the role played by the figure of the anarchist in turn-of-the-century literature as the 'dark double' of the cultural critic and artist. The anarchist takes centre stage even in the work of writers, such as Joseph Conrad and Henry James, who distanced themselves from the era's political groupings and activities.

In 'The End of Laissez-Faire: Literature, Economics, and the Idea of the Welfare State', Benjamin Kohlmann begins by noting how literary scholars writing in the wake of recent financial crises tend to associate economic discourse with an uncritical promulgation of (neo)liberal ideology. This tendency can produce myopic assessments of the role that turn-of-the-century economists played in early critiques of laissez-faire. The chapter pays attention to early critiques that emerged within the discipline of economics, and it places them in relation to a range of literary works, including novels by Anthony Trollope, Joseph Conrad, H. G. Wells, and E. M. Forster. Taken together, these case studies suggest that we need to rethink the dominant literary-historical account according to which the theorization of consumerism in marginal utility economics was the single most significant intellectual contribution by economists to the development of British literature around 1900.

In 'Representing Work', Sos Eltis takes as her starting point the concern of literature and the arts of the late Victorian and Edwardian period to show work not as a problem to be solved but as an experience, a key element of life in the mechanized industrial society, as captured cheerfully in the burgeoning subgenre of the 'shop-girl musical'. But equally, novels and plays focused on the plight of the white-collar worker caught up in and oppressed by larger systems and institutions and the alienating conditions of modern labour. A range of writers such as Hardy, Shaw, Wells, and Galsworthy remained unconvinced that modern industry and commerce had necessarily improved social mobility or eroded the traditional power of the property-owning classes. A more ambivalent response to the new employment opportunities that accompanied an expanding commercial economy can be found in the writings of late-Victorian and Edwardian feminists like Cicely Hamilton and Elizabeth Baker, who weighed the trials of workplace harassment, low wages, and long hours against the opportunities and self-respect offered by the working woman's economic independence.

Part VII on Authorship, Aesthetics, and Print Cultures encompasses reading practices as well as genres, ranging from parodies, spoofs, and satires to biography, self-portraits, and 'autobiografiction' to periodicals and the illustrated book. It also attends to key movements including cosmopolitanism, aestheticism, and Decadence. In 'Reading Aestheticism, Decadence, and Cosmopolitanism', Michèle Mendelssohn traces the development of cosmopolitan, transnational sensibilities later emphasized by early twentieth-century writers such as E. M. Forster. Ranging from Anglo-American aesthetes including Wilde, James, Pater, and Michael Field to French decadents like Baudelaire and Huysmans, the chapter demonstrates how the *Zeitgeist* depended on the development of connections or what Conrad called 'the latent feeling of fellowship with all creation'. Style, synaesthesia, and ekphrasis, Mendelssohn argues, were among the tools writers employed to emphasize the multivalent nature of their politics and aesthetics. In doing so, however, they hearkened back to the politicized aesthetics underscored earlier in the nineteenth century in the works of Ruskin, Marx, and Engels. Current critical practice shares many of the concerns of these writers: we therefore need to preserve modes of reading that attend to stifled, marginalized voices because of the salutary socio-political lessons they can teach our discipline.

In 'Parodies, Spoofs, and Satires', James Williams uses the proliferation of these genres to show how they grapple with modernity and 'with an art which seems to be "peering . . . into the immediate future"' (as Max Beerbohm said of Henry James). Williams argues that though parody was largely conservative in the nineteenth century, by the early twentieth century writers such as G. K. Chesterton used satire to critique the new literary culture. There is, Williams concludes, a rich parodic undercurrent coursing through Anglophone modernism: from Pound's 'kulchur', to T. S. Eliot's petit-bourgeois Prufrock (in conversation with *The Diary of a Nobody* [1892]), and *Blast*'s implicit dialogue with *Punch*.

In 'Life Writing: Biography, Portraits and Self-Portraits, Masked Authorship, and Autobiografictions', Max Saunders explores the form's vital connections with portraiture, noting in particular the late nineteenth century's disintegration of earlier forms of life writing. Starting with Wilde's *The Picture of Dorian Gray*, the chapter argues that the mimetic concept of portraiture is disturbed at the *fin de siècle* as it becomes increasingly subjectivized: portraits come to be read as autobiographical; as expressing the artist as well as the sitter. Saunders's intervention takes up the question of literary impressionism, explored by Adam Parkes in Chapter 11, this volume, but this time with an emphasis on the relationship between literary portraiture and new concepts of subjectivity. Using Stephen Reynolds's 1906 coinage 'autobiografiction', Saunders nuances the narrative strategies undertaken in fictionalized autobiographical writings by A. C. Benson, George Gissing, and Mark Rutherford in order to demonstrate that this hybrid genre recast its data into metafictions that anticipate postmodernism.

Faith Binckes's 'Journalism and Periodical Culture' probes the centrality of periodicals and 'little magazines' to modernism. 'In the years between 1880 and 1920', Binckes argues, 'periodicals both told the story and were the story'. Binckes's chapter extends to the twenty-first century, when digitization projects have reconfigured the way that we engage with periodicals as media. By examining a number of creative bibliographic interventions, she considers how interpretations of these media function as proto-modernist or, alternatively, as eccentric to the principal modernist narratives. Throughout, this chapter attends to the 'interrelated modernities, sharing the same temporal and textual space' that emerged within the period's print culture and which carry on in contemporary research.

Between 1880 and 1920 the illustrated book was a prime locus for contesting the relative roles of literature and art, authors and artists, and their representational abilities. Kamilla Elliott in 'The Illustrated Book' shows that in spite of (or rather because of) the power and popularity of illustrated books, their discourses contained the seeds of illustration's subsequent neglect in literary studies, though eventually segueing into debates over literary film adaptation, where they have continued to the present day. Elliott reveals that despite the scarcity of paper during the First World War, this was the golden age of Anglo-American book illustration, thanks to photomechanical engraving and the proliferation of styles. From William Morris's Kelmscott Press to Aubrey Beardsley's *Yellow Book* and Macmillan's Illustrated Classics and periodicals, the period saw literary classics illustrated in new ways, and contemporary authors join hands with artists. These changes diversified realism's challenges and interventions, as well as reviving the age-old rivalry between literary and visual artists. The competition between picture and text was, Elliott reveals, won by the literary critic who stepped in with magisterial 'commentaries' that displaced visual interpretation.

With the entry of photography into the fray, debates intensified. Some, like James, considered photography supportive of prose and therefore preferred it for his New York editions. But, as Elliott shows, James was wrong to underestimate the new medium because 'photoplay editions' put pictures and texts side by side in service of the medium that would rival them both: the moving picture. Film fiction *replaced* illustrated fiction. As Laura Marcus argues in Part VIII, Technologies, 'The Coming of Cinema' at the end of the nineteenth century had a powerful impact not only on a number of writers but also on broader conceptions of literary representation. Connections with the turn-of-the-century short story were particularly marked, as in works by Rudyard Kipling, H. G. Wells, and less familiar writers, such as the American author J. Brander Matthews, whose story 'The Kinetoscope of Time' was published in 1895, the year in which the Lumière brothers gave the first public exhibition of their Cinématographe. The chapter explores early commentaries on the new medium of film as well as the entry of cinema into literary texts, including those by Wells, Joseph Conrad, and Virginia Woolf.

The approaches of writers and early commentators towards film were often ambivalent, as the new medium presented both a threat and a promise to the established arts. These divergent responses had also been present at the birth of photography some decades earlier. Kate Flint, in her chapter on 'Literature and Photography', pursues the terms of this ambivalence and the question of photography as an art. Her chapter charts the ways in which photography became a theme in literary texts from the late nineteenth century onwards, in works by, among many others, Amy Levy, Thomas Hardy, and Arthur Conan Doyle, through to E. M. Forster and D. H. Lawrence. The chapter also discusses the significance of the photograph's actual inclusion in literary texts, such as the New York editions of works by Henry James and, relatedly, of the photographic work of Alvin Langdon Coburn, whose images of writers forged important connections between the spheres of literature and photography.

Sam Halliday's 'Electricity, Telephony, and Communications' charts material and conceptual relationships between the three, both as they appear historically and as they are represented in literary texts. It shows how the telephone and other electrical technologies are part of 'media ecologies', some of which are older than and extrinsic to electrical technology itself. Among the authors looked at who reveal how media technologies both enable and impede communications are D. H. Lawrence, Bram Stoker, and Henry James. In addition to these figures, the chapter looks at telephony's depiction by Theodore Dreiser, Wyndham Lewis, Mark Twain, Ford Madox Ford, and Robert Frost, and the theory of 'communication' advanced in 1894 by American sociologist Charles Horton Cooley. The chapter concludes with analyses of postal and other communications in novels by James and E. M. Forster, and in Oscar Wilde's *De Profundis*.

In 'The Residue of Modernity: Technology, Anachronism, and Bric-à-Brac in India', Alexander Bubb investigates the British presence in India through the prism of broken or obsolete technology. Focusing on Rudyard Kipling, Flora Annie Steel, and Edmund Candler, and with additional reference to Jules Verne and Rabindranath Tagore, Bubb looks at how these writers use a certain literary trope in episodes in which modern inventions are introduced to, and find a tenuous niche within, discrepant Indian settings. They stage the appearance of foreign products as *anachronism*—the trappings of the European future displaced into the Asian past. This pattern raises two questions: why are the three writers often drawn not to the railway and telegraph, but to everyday manufactures like the bicycle, sewing machine, and gramophone? And why do these objects frequently appear misplaced, discarded, or left to rust? Rather than underlining Britain's superiority, its residue is used to critique and cast doubt on the imperial project.

One of the strengths of our volume is the space it gives to theatre and performance. In 'Actors and Puppets: From Henry Irving's Lyceum to Edward Gordon Craig's Arena Goldoni', Olga Taxidou explores the 'aesthetics of catastrophe' that inform the stage experiments of the period, epitomized by Edward Gordon Craig's essay manifesto of 1909, 'The Actor and the Übermarionette', one of many anti-theatrical tracts of early modernist theatre whose aim, paradoxically, was to 'retheatricalize' an art form that many felt had been dulled by realism. Anti-theatrical stage experiments, frequently located within the physical, semantic/representational, and ideological contours of the performing body, were deeply influenced by puppets, masks, robots, and automata. These are the focus of Taxidou's discussion as she charts writing on puppets by Arthur Symons, Walter Pater, and Oscar Wilde, in conjunction with the work of Heinrich von Kleist, Charles Baudelaire (on dolls), and the actual puppet theatres of France and Italy that were so influential at the end of the nineteenth century. The human-or-marionette debate within modernist theatre helps not only to redefine modernist theatricality but, as this chapter claims, also rehearses the oldest debate in aesthetic theory: that between poetry/theatre and philosophy, placing the issue of theatricality at centre stage within the project of modernity.

PART I

TWILIGHTS

CHAPTER 1

MEDIEVALISM AND MODERNITY

MARCUS WAITHE

The history of nineteenth-century medievalism presents a dizzying array of aesthetic effects and political tendencies.[1] Confronted with the sheer variety of possible forms—some purely stylistic, others decidedly structural, or moral—we may quickly abandon any ambition to speak of it as a coherent movement or set of values. Yet a striking feature of nineteenth-century medievalism was the tendency of its different strands to cross-fertilize and re-emerge in new combinations. While the young John Ruskin disapproved of neo-Catholicism, he nevertheless shared A. W. N. Pugin's conception of functional ornament as a challenge to Renaissance aesthetics.[2] And while Gerard Manley Hopkins can have had little sympathy for the anti-Catholic leaning of Charles Kingsley's Saxonism, his experiments in linguistic and poetic Saxonism indicate the subtle connections between what might seem incompatible parts of the mix.[3] William Morris's socialism, equally, was informed by the neo-feudalism of Charlotte Yonge, and indirectly influenced by Disraeli's Young England.[4] Yet its equalitarian emphasis drew on medievalism in its Teutonic forms, and on the proto-commercial world of the guilds.[5] Eric Gill would inherit Morris's concern with guilds and artistic communities, but laid aside Morris's

---

[1] The forms of medievalism ranged from Romantic Gothic and anti-rationalism, to poetic Arthurianism, Tractarianism, Ruskinian Gothic, Disraelian conservatism, Celticism, Saxonism, Teutonism, Guild Socialism, and the Arts and Crafts Movement.

[2] Ruskin chastised Pugin for deducing 'the incompatibility of Protestantism and art'. See E. T. Cook and Alexander Wedderburn (eds), *The Stones of Venice: The Library Edition of the Works of Ruskin*, 39 vols (London: George Allen, 1903–12), IX, 439.

[3] Kingsley expressed his Saxonism in *Hereward the Wake: 'Last of the English'*, 2 vols (London: Macmillan, 1866), and attacked the Roman clergy in the pages of *Macmillan's Magazine* 9/51 (January 1864), 217.

[4] For Morris's early affection for Yonge's *The Heir of Redclyffe*, and the probable influence of Disraeli's Young England, see Fiona MacCarthy, *William Morris: A Life for Our Time* (London: Faber and Faber, 1994), 63–5.

[5] Morris discussed guilds and 'the equality of freemen' in 'Art and Industry in Fourteenth Century', in May Morris (ed.), *The Collected Works of William Morris*, 24 vols (London: Longmans, 1910–15), XXII, 380.

socialism in preference for a new iteration of the monastic ideal.[6] Thus one potential indicator of incoherence—medievalism's sheer variety and historical longevity—
actually highlights its enduring capacity for adaptation and reformulation of old
materials.

This chapter is concerned precisely with the unlikely 'staying power' of medievalism. Its focus is on that period in the late nineteenth century and early twentieth
century when one is conventionally asked to accept that its resources were running
down, or if not, that it was heading for the cataclysmic disillusionment of the Great
War.[7] Such assumptions draw on the unexamined notion that, by looking into the
past, medievalism was in some respect, *of* it. They depend, too, on the debatable
notion that medievalism constituted a 'dream of order', such that the turmoil of real,
or mechanized, armed encounter could not be accommodated.[8] By accepting the
multifariousness of medievalism, and its robust quality of survival, we are better
placed to appreciate its methods of coping with the peculiar challenges of modernity. This means characterizing it less as a sentimental reversion, than as a distinctive outgrowth of modernity, and ultimately a constituent of modernism.

Towards a more rounded medievalism

Approaches to a more rounded conception of medievalism are obscured by assumptions operating at the level of reception. New Left rehabilitations of Victorian social
criticism stopped short of reappraising the medievalism that informed its cultural
position. E. P. Thompson founded his biography of Morris on a narrative of transformation, from *Romantic to Revolutionary*.[9] Though not strictly inaccurate, the
title's prepositional movement implies that these terms are mutually exclusive, as if
there could be no overlap between the elaborate yearning of *The Earthly Paradise*
(1867–70) and the settled socialism of *News from Nowhere* (1890). Raymond
Williams offered a more balanced view in *Culture and Society, 1780–1950* (1958).
Catching the directional insistence of Marxist teleology, he noted that 'regressive
elements are present in Morris, as they were in Ruskin', before acknowledging
that 'their concern is with the present and the future'.[10] The radical potential that
Morris saw in the romance form goes largely unacknowledged in his casual verdict
that Morris's romances were 'compensatory', 'sentimental', and 'a product of a

---

[6] Eric Gill, 'Responsibility, and the Analogy between Slavery and Capitalism', in *Art-Nonsense and
Other Essays* (London: Cassell, 1929), 137.

[7] Alice Chandler, *A Dream of Order: The Medieval Ideal in Nineteenth-Century English Literature*
(London: Routledge & Kegan Paul, 1971), 11.

[8] Ibid., *A Dream of Order*, 7.

[9] E. P. Thompson, *William Morris: Romantic to Revolutionary*, 2nd edn (London: Merlin Press, 1976).

[10] Raymond Williams, *Culture and Society* (Harmondsworth: Penguin, 1968), 159.

fragmentary consciousness'. Similar views were aired in *The Country and the City* (1973), where Williams alluded complacently to 'the dreaming and often backward-looking Morris'.[11]

These conclusions have been challenged in recent years by scholars keen to propound a more expansive conception of the potential in dreams.[12] In this way, a Marxist language that insists on distinguishing 'reactionary' from 'progressive' has given way to less rigid categorizations of past and present modes. A more enduring obstacle has been the implicit reliance of post-war critics on the apocalyptic historicism of modernism, a legacy routinely attributed to the technology worship of futurism. Selective quotation from Wyndham Lewis's *Blast* (1914–15) feeds into this discourse. Readers are invited to 'BLAST years 1837 to 1900', and to target 'good-for-nothing Guineveres'.[13] Lewis had broken with the Omega Workshops of Roger Fry in 1913, so it is likely that he had their Arts and Crafts, or 'greenery-yallery', sensibility in mind.[14] But a nuanced reading must register *Blast*'s simultaneous targeting of 'the sentimental Future', and the 'gush' of 'AUTOMOBILISM'.[15] The implication is that medievalism had no monopoly on emotional flaws. Especially revealing is the perception that 'Wilde gushed twenty years ago about the beauty of machinery'.[16] Not simply a provocation, this remark usefully locates the debate about medievalism's 'pastness' in the period of its late Victorian flourishing.

A further Victorian source for these attitudes is Walter Pater's account of 'medieval religion' in *The Renaissance* (1873).[17] Characterized as a faith hostile to the senses, a stultifying disease of the mind, it engendered an arrested state broken only by the Renaissance's 'rehabilitation of human nature, the body, the senses, the heart, the intelligence'.[18] Though Pater's attack on 'medievalism' was limited by a relatively circumscribed attention to asceticism, his vision of fruitless self-denial proved influential. Drawing on his own youthful adherence to Ruskinian Gothic as an apprentice architect,[19] Thomas Hardy restaged the drama of these competing standpoints in *Jude the Obscure* (1895). Pugin's equation of the Gothic with 'Christian architecture' makes its way into the novel in Jude's vision of Oxford as an 'ecclesiastical romance in stone'.[20] As the drama develops, the forces of convention and obsolete

---

[11] Williams, *The Country and the City* (London: Hogarth Press, 1985), 272.

[12] See, for instance, Ruth Levitas, 'Marxism, Romanticism and Utopia: Ernst Bloch and William Morris', *Radical Philosophy* 51 (1989), 27–36.

[13] Wyndham Lewis, ed., *Blast: Review of the Great English Vortex* 1 (1914), 18, 19.

[14] Lewis, 'A Review of Contemporary Art', *Blast* 2 (1915), 46.

[15] Lewis, 'Long Live the Vortex!', *Blast* 1 (1914), n. p.   [16] Ibid., n. p.

[17] Walter Pater, *The Renaissance*, ed. Adam Phillips (Oxford: Oxford University Press, 1998), 27.

[18] Pater, *The Renaissance*, 27.

[19] For evidence of Ruskin's architectural influence on Hardy, see C. J. P. Beatty (ed.), *The Architectural Notebook of Thomas Hardy* (Dorchester: Dorset Natural History and Archaeological Society, 1966).

[20] Augustus Welby Pugin, *The True Principles of Pointed or Christian Architecture: Set Forth in Two Lectures Delivered at St. Marie's, Oscott* (London: John Weale, 1841); Thomas Hardy, *Jude the Obscure*, ed. C. H. Sisson (Harmondsworth: Penguin, 1985).

morality are confused with this, Jude's favoured architectural style. The sight of Oxford's 'porticoes, oriels, doorways of enriched and florid middle-age design' prompts the reflection, in free indirect speech, that 'it seemed impossible that modern thought could house itself in such decrepit and superseded chambers'. That seed of doubt is corroborated by the proleptic aside that Jude 'did not at that time see that mediaevalism was as dead as a fern-leaf in a lump of coal', while a final verdict is delivered by the observed 'deadly animosity of contemporary logic and vision towards so much of what he held in reverence'. Ironically, the subsequent history of medievalism suggests a relationship between 'reverence' and modernity that is closer to a veiled symbiosis than a fatal conflict.[21]

Hardy softens these oppositions in the figure of Sue Bridehead, whose self-proclaimed aestheticism looks less to the future than to an alternative past. Her competing retrospect is signalled by the taunt that 'You ought to have learnt classic. Gothic is barbaric art, after all. Pugin was wrong, and Wren was right'.[22] The allusion to jockeying pasts, and the possibility that both sides might be missing the point, allows Hardy to present his most searching response to contemporary historicism. What he does not quite articulate is the extent to which aestheticism, as a curious amalgam of classical lightness, medievalist colour, and emergent Decadence, defined itself not in relation to the real past, but to the *function* of looking back. The poignant, 'out-worn' time to which W. B. Yeats alluded in the *Celtic Twilight* (1893, 1902) is illustrative.[23] If the 'waning' spirit in that case referred to Celticism, it was equally a preoccupation of late nineteenth-century aestheticism and medievalism.[24] At the same time, one should distinguish between this function of looking back, and the vitality of the cultural phenomenon itself. In new forms, and often conjoined to the discipline of classicism, medievalism continued to influence artistic life well beyond the Great War, and in some cases right up to the brink of the Second World War.[25] In what follows, I will explore some resonant cases of this 'modern' medievalism, first as it concerns modernity, and then in relation to modernism as a cultural movement.

A symptom of modernity

If medievalism is often understood as a matter of order, feudal hierarchy, chivalry, the festive calendar, craftsmanship, and pilgrimage, then 'modernity' has stood

---

[21] Ibid., 125, 131.   [22] Ibid., 376.

[23] W. B. Yeats, 'Into the Twilight', *The Celtic Twilight* (London: A. H. Bullen, 1902), 235.

[24] See, for instance, Morris's lyric 'Love is Enough', in *Collected Works*, IX, 5: 'LOVE IS ENOUGH: though the World be a-waning / And the woods have no voice but the voice of complaining'.

[25] For the 'pre-eminent rationality and dignity' of classical letter forms, see Gill, *An Essay on Typography* (1931), ed. Christopher Skelton (London: Lund Humphries, 1988), 24.

more or less in opposition to it, as restless, equalitarian, liberal, individualistic, urban, secular, profane, and atomistic. The problem with this way of proceeding is that it assumes medievalism to be something miraculously outside modernity. This assumption makes sense to the extent that medievalism represents the longed for 'other' of modernity, with characteristics configured in polar opposition to the experience of life in an increasingly urban, and possibly post-revolutionary, Europe. But the thrill of the Gothic Novel depends upon the element in modernity's constitution that welcomes a controlled witnessing of something supposedly beyond itself. Similarly, that genre's view of European travel as a version of time-travel to a pre-Reformation world indicates a dual awareness based on a fragmented sense of place.

Medievalism, in short, was a symptomatic awareness best understood in relation to the modernity of the present. Dickens knew this well. The neo-Gothic residence occupied by Wemmick in *Great Expectations* (1861) is at one level a satire on the excesses of medievalism.[26] The fortified state of mind evoked by the house's castellations, by its flag-pole and canon, are comic details reminiscent of the drawbridge and 'military ideas' of Uncle Toby in Laurence Sterne's *Tristram Shandy* (1759).[27] But more than that, they are tokens of an artistic movement translated out of its experimental element, so as to seem absurdly at odds with the peaceable character of urban surroundings. At the same time, Dickens makes us feel that the Walworth property stands in direct relation to the circumstances of modern life. He reminds us that there is something feudal about the walls that divide the modern commuting man's home from the world beyond. And the medievalism is double edged: for all its air of Wardour Street fancy dress, and Wemmick's boasts of self-sufficiency, the Walworth property evokes the pattern-book mentality of modern manufacturing, and the inauthentic privileging of architectural styles over functional purpose.

Bram Stoker's *Dracula* (1897) presents similar complexity in its dealings with medievalism. Critics have noted that the novel dramatizes the mobilization of a technological apparatus against a supernatural threat.[28] Modern secretarial principles, and the new inventions of the typewriter and rifle, show the fruits of middle-class civilization defeating the undead perpetuity of central European feudalism. The problem with this reading is that it ignores the Count's comfortable relationship with the modern world. While the fixed hierarchy of his Romanian village imposes constraints on operations, the anonymous networks of modern trade and distribution are perfectly suited to his purposes. Established imperial sea routes enable him to land at Whitby without ceremony, and his decision to deposit

[26] Charles Dickens, *Great Expectations*, ed. David Trotter (Harmondsworth: Penguin, 1996), 204–10.
[27] Laurence Sterne, *The Life and Opinions of Tristram Shandy, Gentleman* (Oxford: Oxford University Press, 1983), 168–9.
[28] See Jennifer Wicke, 'Vampiric Typewriting: *Dracula* and its Media', *English Literary History* 59/2 (1992), 467–93.

coffins at suburban residences shows his delight in the principles of privacy and 'minding one's own business' that characterize the Englishman's home, or 'castle'. As Van Helsing observes, the Count 'may have many houses which he has bought', and 'Of them he will have deeds of purchase, keys and other things'.[29] By observing the correct legal procedure, the Count avoids suspicion, yet also reminds us that there is something about liberal individualism and the sanctity of private property that suits the personal empire building of a feudal robber baron very well.

This possibility—that there is something medieval about modernity—was registered at an early stage in the development of the Marxist tradition. In *The Condition of the English Working Class* (1844), Friedrich Engels dwelt on the state of 'social warfare' in Manchester, with 'every man's house in a state of siege'.[30] The suggestion that industrial civilization is merely another version of feudal tyranny satisfies the notion that the middle-class revolution has been a partial affair. Marx and Engels's declaration that a 'spectre is haunting Europe' contains a similar suggestion of recurrence, though one that accords better with Sigmund Freud's later description of analeptic haunting in 'The Uncanny' (1919).[31] There are also hints of parasitism, related to the lurking anti-Semitism of the vampire myth, where a bourgeois consciousness apparently settled around the concept of respectability is reconceived as a threat to the collective social health.[32] Engels is a useful case because he saw how the element of Gothic sensation could be reconfigured to serve an alternative and largely positive vision of the past, closer in his case to the Dark Ages. In *The Origin of the Family, Private Property, and the State* (1884), he demonstrated the historical contingency of the modern nuclear family, drawing on Andreas Heusler's research into the primitive unit of 'the old communistic household', which was based on cross-generational forms of association.[33] The possible 'modernity' of this model depends on Engels's insistence that the new era of communism would return to these principles after the decline of the proprietorial capitalist family.[34]

Engels was not alone in discovering a source of alternative values in this late nineteenth-century turn towards the Middle Ages. W. H. Hudson, in *A Crystal Age* (1887), imagined a communal and matriarchal household living in circumstances

---

[29] Bram Stoker, *Dracula*, ed. Maud Ellmann (Oxford: Oxford University Press, 1996), 292.

[30] Friedrich Engels, *The Condition of the Working Class in England* (Harmondsworth: Penguin, 1987), 69.

[31] Karl Marx and Friedrich Engels, *Manifesto of the Communist Party*, in *Collected Works*, 49 vols (London: Lawrence & Wishart, 1975–2001), VI, 481; Sigmund Freud, 'The Uncanny', in James Strachey (ed.), *The Standard Edition of the Complete Psychological Works of Sigmund Freud*, 24 vols (London: Hogarth Press, 1981), XVII, 245.

[32] See Judith Halberstam, 'Technologies of Monstrosity: Bram Stoker's *Dracula*', *Victorian Studies* 36/3 (Spring, 1993), 346; see also Ken Gelder, *Reading the Vampire* (London: Routledge, 1994), 13–17.

[33] Friedrich Engels, *The Origin of the Family, Private Property and the State, in the Light of the Researches of Lewis H. Morgan*, trans. Alick West (London: Lawrence & Wishart, 1940), 62, 78–9; Heusler published *Institutionen des deutschen Privatrechts* in 1886.

[34] Engels, *The Origin of the Family*, 204.

that come *after* modern history, rather than before it. Even Pater, whose aestheticism usually leant towards the classical, explored the possibility of a 'medieval Renaissance'. Perhaps influenced by the quaintly aesthetic medievalism of Morris's *The Earthly Paradise*, he identified it with the period's 'antinomianism', a term which he glosses as 'its spirit of rebellion and revolt against the moral and religious ideas of the time'. The result is a search after pleasure, and a 'worship of the body', that impels people 'beyond the bounds of the Christian ideal', making love 'a strange idolatry, a strange rival religion'. Though this indicates a 'return' of Venus, and the 'old pagan gods', the revisionism does not work in favour of classicism alone: 'this element of the middle age', Pater notes, has been 'for the most part ignored by those writers who have treated it pre-eminently as an "Age of Faith" '.[35] Among 'those writers' we might count Ruskin, whose tolerance of medieval gargoyles, and early championing of 'grotesqueness', stopped short of celebrating the sexually sportive poses of the lofty cathedral imp.[36]

The past, it turns out, was the most reliable source of alternative values for the reforming consciousness of the younger generation. Edward Carpenter saw 'a cosmic self' holding sway in the deeper past, when 'men instinctively felt and worshipped the great life coming to them through Sex'.[37] Though he associated 'homogenic', or homosexual, attachment with the classical and Renaissance periods, rather than with the 'chivalric love' of the Middle Ages, his 1908 chapter *The Intermediate Sex* acknowledged Pater's account of the 'story of Amis and Amile (thirteenth century)'.[38] Morris mounted his own challenge to the force of conventional morality in *News from Nowhere*. Influenced by the triangulation of his own personal life, and its ongoing imbrication with the Arthur–Guinevere myth, he sought to accommodate, rather than repress, the unruly currents of sexual desire.[39] After Clara finds a new lover, she lives apart from Dick for a year without prompting a collapse of the wider social structure, or any repeat of the proclamation issued by Tennyson's Arthur, that 'My house has been my doom'.[40] While this may seem to reject the Arthurian notion that bonds, romantic and knightly, depend on fidelity, Morris's inspiration was drawn from the kind of medieval counter-discourse celebrated by Pater. It was a 'rival religion' of love that rested on the Chaucerian precept that 'Whan maistrie comth, the God of Love anon / Beteth his wynges'.[41]

---

[35] Pater, *The Renaissance*, 16.

[36] John Ruskin, 'The Nature of Gothic', in *The Stones of Venice*, in *Works*, X, 184.

[37] Edward Carpenter, *Civilization—Its Cause and Cure, and Other Essays* (London: Swan Sonnenschein, 1891), 44–5.

[38] Carpenter, *The Intermediate Sex: A Study of Some Transitional Types of Men and Women* (New York and London: Mitchell Kennerley, 1921), 43.

[39] Morris's wife, Jane, began an affair with Dante Gabriel Rossetti in the 1860s.

[40] Morris, *Collected Works*, XVI, 55; see 'The Passing of Arthur', *Idylls of the King* in Christopher Ricks (ed.), *The Poems of Tennyson*, 3 vols (London: Longmans, 1987), III, 551.

[41] Geoffrey Chaucer, 'The Franklin's Tale', in Christopher Cannon (ed.), *The Riverside Chaucer*, 3rd edn (Oxford: Oxford University Press, 1987), 179.

A lineage of values

From this discussion of 'modernity'—construed variously in relation to historicism, industrial civilization, and alternative approaches to personal morality—I now move to address the ways in which modernism made use of medievalism. The most influential early effort to instal medievalism in the programme of modernist design and reform was effected by Nikolaus Pevsner in *Pioneers of the Modern Movement* (1936).[42] Instead of viewing attitudes to the machine as the touchstone of modern reform, or to style per se, he focused on the 'plea for functionalism'.[43] Pevsner traced the origins of this 'modern' design principle to the architectural medievalism of Pugin, who contended, as Ruskin did later, that architectural decoration should never flout the underlying truths of honest structure and use.[44] Arguing that '[Walter] Gropius regards himself as a follower of Ruskin and Morris', Pevsner completed the circle in claiming that the design principles of the experimental Staatliches Bauhaus were owing to this aspect of the Arts and Crafts tradition.[45] While Pevsner's thesis has been disputed, critics tend to focus on variables that he openly excluded, namely the medievalist attitude to machines and the question of historical style.[46] Moreover, the passage of ideas from England to Germany— perhaps as counter-intuitive as the leap from medievalism to modernism—is credibly substantiated by his indebtedness to the work of Hermann Muthesius. After working as cultural and technical attaché to the German Embassy in London, Muthesius had developed his concept of *Sachlichkeit* (practicality, or sincerity), and contributed to founding the Deutscher Werkbund in 1907.[47] In *Das englische Haus* (1904), he wrote of 'a new departure in the tectonic arts', one 'that had originated in England and spread across the whole field of our European culture'.[48] By this, he meant 'the modern movement' of the Arts and Crafts, a 'primitive' vernacular to be distinguished from the 'fantastic, superfluous and, often, affected quality' of the Continental Art Nouveau.[49]

Pevsner's focus on a lineage of values, or spirit, is itself a German Romantic conception, and as such is open to challenge. More compelling is the possible 'modern-

---

[42] The revised edition was retitled as Nikolaus Pevsner, *Pioneers of Modern Design: From William Morris to Walter Gropius* (Harmondsworth: Penguin Books, 1960).

[43] Pevsner, *The Sources of Modern Architecture and Design* (London: Thames and Hudson, 1968), 9.

[44] Pugin, *True Principles*, 1.   [45] Pevsner, *Pioneers of Modern Design*, 39.

[46] See, for instance, Sir Hugh Casson, 'Red House: The Home of William Morris', *The Listener* 50 (1 October 1953), 536, and Mark Girouard, 'Red House, Bexleyheath, Kent', *Country Life* 127 (16 June 1960), 1383.

[47] Stanford Anderson, *Style-Architecture and Building-Art: Transformations of Architecture in the Nineteenth Century and its Present Condition* (Santa Monica, CA: The Getty Center, 1994), 5.

[48] Hermann Muthesius, *The English House*, ed. Dennis Sharp, trans. Janet Seligman (Oxford: BSP Professional Books, 1987), 13.

[49] Ibid., 63.

ism' of such design in the minds of its practitioners. The common emphasis, in this case, was on futurity. Williams's characterization of Morris as 'backward looking' responds to the medieval form of the buildings in the utopian land of Nowhere. While reasonable in itself, that verdict does not pry very far into the historical rationale for this style of building. In a lecture on 'The Arts and Crafts of To-day' (1889), Morris proposed that if, in the immediate future, 'we may have to recur to ideas that to-day seem to belong to the past only, that will not be really a retracing of our steps, but rather a carrying on of progress from a point where we abandoned it a while ago'.[50] There is self-consciousness in the phrase, 'seem to belong to the past'. It indicates that this is not an unthinking or sentimental position. Rather, he is making the searching proposal that Gothic architecture is a flexible, 'rational', and structurally frank approach to buildings and space, and that of all historical styles, it is best suited to meeting the needs of the future. In his lecture on 'Gothic Architecture', Morris insisted that 'In the future . . . our style of architecture must be Gothic Architecture'.[51] The explanation offered is that 'an organic style cannot spring from an eclectic one'. Morris was speaking from a position not yet able to imagine the complete break with historicism that would follow. This places obvious limits on his alignment with modernism proper. But it remains true that he was rejecting isolated gestures based on a moving historical target in favour of a future coherence. In its scope, its rationalism, and its collective emphasis, if not in its appearance, there are surprising affinities with the International Style of Le Corbusier.[52] So often conceived as the destroyer of Arts and Crafts principles, this champion of 'profile and contour' as 'pure creation of the mind'[53] had been a keen reader of Ruskin in his youth.[54]

This conception of medievalism as a set of structural principles, rather than an historical reference point, was developed in the Edwardian period by the Garden City Movement. Ebenezer Howard's *Tomorrow: A Peaceful Path to Real Reform* (1898) combined explicit indebtedness to Ruskin and Robert Blatchford with an emphasis on rational planning.[55] Its millenarian rhetoric of future states pre-empted the phraseology of the modernist manifestos. Before the First World War interrupted building work, the new town of Letchworth powerfully combined the adapted medievalism of Parker and Unwin's domestic architecture with the overall planning ethos of Howard's diagrammatic vision.

---

[50] Morris, 'The Arts and Crafts of To-day', in *Collected Works*, 371.

[51] Morris, 'Gothic Architecture', in May Morris (ed.), *William Morris: Artist Writer Socialist*, 2 vols (Oxford: Blackwell, 1936), I, 285.

[52] See Maiken Umbach and Rüdiger Hüppauf, *Vernacular Modernism: Heimat, Globalisation and the Built Environment* (Stanford, CA: Stanford University Press, 2005), 20.

[53] Le Corbusier, *Towards a New Architecture* (1931; repr. New York: Dover, 1986), 200.

[54] Giovanni Cianci and Peter Nicholls (eds), *Ruskin and Modernism* (Basingstoke: Palgrave, 2001), xi; Le Corbusier, *L'Art décoratif d'aujourd'hui* (Paris: Arthaud, 1925), 134–7.

[55] *Tomorrow* was revised and reissued as *Garden Cities of To-morrow* (1902). See Ebenezer Howard, *Garden Cities of To-morrow*, ed. F. J. Osborn (Cambridge, MA: MIT Press, 1965), 50, 57, 133–5.

A fictional example of this 'future medieval' style is apparent in H. G. Wells's *A Modern Utopia* (1905), which sets the scene by describing an inn, structured as a 'quadrangle after the fashion of an Oxford college'. Its architect, we learn, was 'happily free from the hampering traditions of Greek temple building, and of Roman and Italian palaces'; instead of imitation, the focus again is on values, in this case 'simple, unaffected, gracious'.[56] The Arts and Crafts philosophy of social, domestic, and professional integration is apparent in its combination of apartments with 'dining-room, writing-room, smoking and assembly rooms, a barber's shop, and a library'. And yet the modernity of this inn is inescapable: it is 'perhaps forty feet high, and with about five storeys of bedrooms above its lower apartments', and as such is reminiscent of C. F. A. Voysey's balanced efforts to combine vernacular and Queen Anne Revival with modern scale.[57]

The concern with medieval structure was also organizational. The leading lights of the Arts and Crafts Movement put Morris's ideas into practice by founding guilds of handicraft. Notable among them was C. R. Ashbee, whose move from Whitechapel to Chipping Campden staged a rustication or flight from the social problems that the East End settlements had originally confronted in their breeding ground.[58] While the beauty of these new surroundings appealed to Ashbee, his work in the Cotswolds was a further chapter in a process of institutional experiment, according to which the well-tried principles of association and worker participation were translated into a wider field of outdoor sports (especially swimming), amateur dramatics, and pageant. In this respect, Ashbee's Guild of Handicraft was reverting to type, and falling into line with Ruskin's Guild of St George, whose activities entered a new era between 1889 and 1914, when members of the Liverpool Ruskin Society moved south to begin a new life of agriculture and rural crafts on the Guild's land at Bewdley, in Worcestershire.[59] It would be a mistake to regard these activities as the last vestiges of the Romanticism that modernism was destined to replace, for they exercised a powerful influence on the next generation of artists and writers. The main representatives of the British tradition, in Eric Gill and David Jones, took medievalism away from socialism and returned it to the religious premise of monasticism and Catholicism. The neo-Thomist theology of Jacques Maritain was an inspiration in this respect. It understood the creative process less as a re-channelled communal spirit, than as the incarnation of a divine spirit, whereby 'art is collaboration with God in creating'.[60]

[56] H. G. Wells, *A Modern Utopia* (London: Penguin Books, 2005), 146–7.

[57] Ibid., 146; see, for instance, Voysey's unexecuted design for a 'tower house' at Bognor (1903) in John Brandon-Jones and Others, *C.F.A. Voysey: Architect and Designer, 1857–1941* (London: Lund Humphries, 1978), 53.

[58] Alan Crawford, *C.R. Ashbee: Architect, Designer & Romantic Socialist* (New Haven, CT: Yale University Press, 2005), 110.

[59] Stuart Eagles, *After Ruskin: The Social and Political Legacies of a Victorian Prophet, 1870–1920* (Oxford: Oxford University Press, 2011), 190.

[60] For Maritain's comment that 'artistic creation does not copy God's creation, but continues it', see *Art and Scholasticism* (Sheed & Ward, 1930), 63; Gill, 'Apology', *Art-Nonsense and Other Essays*, p.v.

This ascetic turn explains why the social principle remained dominant even where the socialism receded, as in most forms of 'high' modernism. Where the socialism was retained, a medieval structure moved to the fore. According to S. T. Glass, the Guild Socialism of the early twentieth century was the inheritor of 'the medievalist reaction against the nineteenth century, particularly as it related to the industrial system'.[61] This makes sense as an indication of lineage, but it would be more accurate to conceive Guild Socialism as an ongoing preoccupation than to see it as a belated instance of Victorian thought.

The medievalism of Ezra Pound is illustrative. It was inherited from nineteenth-century precedents, but was also one of the routes he took to becoming 'modern', enabling him to sidestep tired poetic diction and formal constraint. In the pages of *The New Age* (1907–1922), Pound published chapters and medievalist poems, among them renderings of the Provençal troubadour Arnaut Daniel, and a translation of *The Seafarer* from the Anglo-Saxon.[62] The magazine itself reinforced the forward vision implied by these fragments of a distant past. Edited by two enthusiastic proponents of Guild Socialism, Holbrook Jackson and A. R. Orage, it was also the forum in which A. J. Penty and S. G. Hobson proposed a restoration of the guild system, arguing that competition over quality rather than price would rescue the idea of a popular art.[63]

Major C. H. Douglas's entrance on the scene in 1918 signalled a cross-fertilization of Guild Socialism's Edwardian world view with Italian Fascism's syndicalist roots. The result was a marked shift away from organizational issues towards the financial and collectivist preoccupations of the 'Social Credit' movement.[64] Pound's anti-Semitism, and his subsequent foray into fascist propagandizing, are too often treated as something 'not easy to explain', an unaccountable obsession corroborated by his own admission late in life to 'that stupid, suburban prejudice of anti-Semitism'.[65] Though informed by paranoia and other disorders of personality, it was also an ideology and an intellectual commitment, explicable as a result of this late convergence between Guild Socialism's medievalism and the racialized economics of fascism.[66] According to it, usury was regarded as a social evil that 'rusteth the

[61] S. T. Glass, *The Responsible Society: The Ideas of the English Guild Socialist* (London: Longmans, 1966), 6.

[62] Ezra Pound, 'I Gather the Limbs of Osiris: I. The Seafarer', *The New Age* 10/5 (November 1911), 107–8; Pound, 'I Gather the Limbs of Osiris: VIII. Canzon: of the Trades and Love', *The New Age* 10/12 (January 1912), 274–5.

[63] Penty's articles on this subject began with 'The Restoration of the Guild System. The Collectivist Formula I', *The New Age* 8/14 (July 1913), 388–9; the following year, S. G. Hobson published *National Guilds; An Inquiry into the Wage System and the Way Out*, ed. A. R. Orage (London: G. Bell & Sons, 1914).

[64] Glass, *The Responsible Society*, 53.

[65] Peter Ackroyd, *Ezra Pound and his World* (London: Thames and Hudson, 1980), 77; Pound quoted in Barry Miles, *Ginsberg: A Biography* (London: Virgin, 2000), 398.

[66] Robert Casillo notes that Pound praised 'Ruskin's and Morris's guild and craft ideals in his [Fascist] radio broadcasts' in *The Genealogy of Demons* (Evanston, IL: Northwestern University Press, 1988), 50. See also Clive Wilmer, 'Sculpture and Economics in Pound and Ruskin', *PN Review* 24/6 (1998), 46.

chisel', a threat to craft-based community so insidious that it required a visible scapegoat.[67] The uncomfortable implication is that anti-Semitism reached deep into Pound's broader conception of the poet as a figure whose craft practice and apprenticeship were imperilled by the modern financial system.

Destructive novelty

I have focused so far on modernism's concern with rebuilding and re-describing society, whether architecturally, organizationally, or economically. The contrary tendency in modernism—its yearning for destructive novelty—will now be addressed. It emerged in the self-conscious barbarism of the futurist desire to level Venice and clear Italy of medieval buildings.[68] It is also associated with Pound's injunction to 'make it new', according to which the palimpsestic artwork was reconceived as a clean slate.[69] Still, the desire to start from scratch does not necessarily imply a uniquely 'modern' attitude, nor confirm the inherent 'modernity' of modernism. This much is clear from the ancient Chinese origin of Pound's dictum, attributed in *Canto* 53 to writing on the side of the Emperor Tching Tang's bath tub.

In a different context, Peter Mandler has demonstrated the extraordinary boldness of Victorian railway building, especially as it remodelled existing urban areas. 'Most Victorians', he notes 'would have been bemused by the preservation of St. Pancras Station', because 'they thought that "creative destruction" was a constant process that would eventually demolish them as they had demolished others.'[70] One might add that the railway's division of neighbourhoods engendered social divisions and fortified 'embankments' that were feudal in their way. In the surviving photographs that depict these mammoth efforts of construction, we glimpse a boldness and scale of destruction not matched until aerial bombardment destroyed large parts of London's East End during the Second World War.

Tony Pinkney contributes to this debate when discussing critical complaints about the feudality of Morris's *News from Nowhere*. He notes in particular the perception that the 'values of modernity, of "fire" in a positive sense, have been too thoroughly abolished' from this medievalist vision of the future. He offers the qualifying consideration that '*News from Nowhere* itself suspects that something of this sort has happened', and the text is even 'beginning to muster certain narrative

---

[67] Pound, Canto XLV, *The Cantos of Ezra Pound* (London: Faber and Faber, 1989), 229.

[68] Filippo Tommaso Marinetti, 'Manifesto against Past-Loving Venice' (July 1910). See Christine Poggi, *Inventing Futurism: The Art and Politics of Artificial Optimism* (Princeton, NJ: Princeton University Press, 2009), 67.

[69] Pound, Canto LIII, *The Cantos of Ezra Pound*, 265.

[70] Peter Mandler, 'The Creative Destruction of the Victorian City', unpublished paper.

resources to do something about this situation'.[71] The implication is that the pastoralism should not be taken at face value: something is stirring, and the dynamic forces that precipitated a revolution may not be dormant forever. 'Who knows?' remarks Ellen, 'Happy as we are, times may alter; we may be bitten with some impulse towards change.'[72] Subsequent clauses warn against this alteration, as 'but phases of what has been before; and withal ruinous, deceitful, and sordid'. All the same, the word 'impulse' allows us to read against the text. It rises above the dampening effect of political discipline, to suggest an intrinsic capacity for new futures.

Another form of medievalist self-consciousness arises from the new society's relationship with the past, in this case the past of the nineteenth century. Only certain characters are gifted with this awareness, perhaps because it supplies the dangerous knowledge that Nowhere is the product of another kind of 'fire', an emboldened erasure of past forms. The reader is repeatedly reminded that many of the 'medieval' buildings in evidence are in fact 'new'. By the same token, William Guest learns from his guide, Dick, that Walthamstow is 'a very jolly place, now that the trees have had time to grow again since the great clearing of houses in 1955'.[73] This casual reference to what would have been a seismic demolition is made to seem inevitable, an act of good housekeeping; but it is ruthless in its way, and as such marks a limit on the new society's extension of aesthetic and social tolerance.

In Nowhere, the Houses of Parliament are retained, though they function in the new age as a Dung Market. The reference to 'a queer antiquarian society' having campaigned to save it humorously invokes Morris's own grudging protection of Wren's City Churches as part of his work for the Society for the Protection of Ancient Buildings. In other cases, the approach is less forgiving: we know, for instance, that the iron bridge at Hammersmith has not survived the revolution.[74] The scale of the transformation is underpinned by Morris's confidence in the rectitude of his own aesthetic judgements, though there is also an element of pastiche about this wholesale reordering. He had himself witnessed, and lamented, the destructive side of medievalism, brought home to him repeatedly by acts of insensitive 'restoration'.[75] The work of the French architect Viollet-le-Duc, with its privileging of structure over surface detail, had executed bold refashionings of the past on the canvas of the original.[76] His remodellings of the fortress at Carcassonne, and of Sainte-Chapelle in Paris, were every bit as daring, experimental, and presentist, as the most lurid imaginings of the futurists, in that they used the architectural

[71] Tony Pinkney, 'Versions of Ecotopia in *News from Nowhere*', in Phillippa Bennett and Rosie Miles (eds), *William Morris in the Twenty-First Century* (Bern: Peter Lang, 2010), 98.

[72] Morris, *Collected Works*, XVI, 194.

[73] Ibid., 9, 16.   [74] Ibid., 41, 32, 8.

[75] See Morris, 'To the Editor of *The Athenaeum*', 4 April 1877, in Norman Kelvin (ed.), *Collected Letters of William Morris*, 4 vols (Princeton, NJ: Princeton University Press, 1984–96), I, 362.

[76] Eugène Emmanuel Viollet-le-Duc outlined his theories of structural rationalism in *Dictionnaire raisonné de l'architecture française du XIe au XVIe siècle* (Paris: B. Bance, 1854).

record as the quarry for a reordered, and in many respects, entirely new composition.

My last example addresses an aspect of the supposed disillusionment of chivalry, associated with the development of trench warfare and mechanized killing in the First World War. That thesis is convincing when focused on the recruitment posters of 1914, and the 'knights of the Empire' rhetoric, as surveyed by Mark Girouard in *The Return to Camelot*.[77] But as a report on the fortunes of medievalism, it is not adequate. Undoubtedly, the propaganda machine and the fictions of 'boy's own' literature drew heavily on a crudely adapted version of Tennyson's imperial Arthurianism. But the idea of a cosmic check on heroism ignores what Victorian literature had already achieved in this respect. One thinks of George Osborne 'lying on his face, dead, with a bullet through his heart' in Thackeray's *Vanity Fair* (1847–8), and of Tennyson's more ambiguous portrait of the sacrificial calculus in 'The Charge of the Light Brigade' (1854).[78] Both works scrutinized the terms of heroism and the fruits of battle in ways that queried merely dutiful action.[79]

Medievalism itself mustered a considered response to this theme of devastated landscapes and devastated lives. Morris's descriptions of the Hundred Years War in *The Defence of Guenevere and Other Poems* (1858), of awkward poses in fickle or dubious landscapes, are strikingly reminiscent of the ways in which artists of the First World War reimagined the angles of a body undergoing physical realignment. The medieval notion of the waste land was a key part of this concern with landscapes of destruction.[80] Adapted from Malory by Morris in his story 'The Hollow Land' (1856),[81] and famously reprised by T. S. Eliot in *The Waste Land* (1922), it establishes a precedent for the modern tendency to understand pollution and environmental spoliation as an existential threat, if not a moral verdict.[82] A notable transposition of this principle was attempted by Richard Jefferies, in his romance of the primitive future, *After London* (1885). That novel's questing hero, Felix, discovers a miasmic terrain on the site of London's ruins. While a mythic implication is carried by the skeletal remains of previous questers, the adaptability of these tropes is conveyed by a vaguer atmosphere of threat, which evokes Bunyan's Slough of

[77] Girouard, *The Return to Camelot: Chivalry and the English Gentleman* (New Haven, CT: Yale University Press, 1981), 276–93.

[78] William Makepeace Thackeray, *Vanity Fair*, ed. John Sutherland (Oxford: Oxford University Press, 1993); Ricks (ed.), *The Poems of Tennyson*, II, 510–13.

[79] See, for instance, Trudi Tate, 'On Not Knowing Why: Memorializing the Light Brigade', in Helen Small and Trudi Tate (eds), *Literature, Science, Psychoanalysis: Essays in Honour of Gillian Beer* (Oxford: Oxford University Press, 2003), 160–80; see also the essays on Victorian war poetry in *The Oxford Handbook of British and Irish War Poetry* (Oxford: Oxford University Press, 2007).

[80] Sir Thomas Malory, *Le Morte d'Arthur*, 2 vols (Harmondsworth: Penguin, 1986), II, 335.

[81] Morris, *Collected Works*, I, 254–90.

[82] See Barbara Everett, *Times Literary Supplement*, 3 March 1972, 249; see also Robert Macfarlane, 'At the World's Waning: William Morris and the Sources of *The Waste Land*', *Times Literary Supplement*, 16 November 2001, 114–15; see also Ingrid Hanson, *William Morris and the Uses of Violence, 1856–1890* (London: Anthem, 2013), 10.

Despond, while prefiguring some future equivalent that modern readers are likely to associate with a landscape polluted by nuclear fallout.[83]

A mythical transfiguring of landscape is apparent in certain of Wilfred Owen's poems, but it is to David Jones's *In Parenthesis* (1937) that we must look for the most searching convergence between medievalism and trench warfare.[84] Discussing the ' "medievalizing" of the memory of the Great War', Stefan Goebel interprets acts of commemoration among survivors as an unconscious search for a shared European culture. It is an analysis that applies readily to Jones, who joined Eric Gill's Roman Catholic Guild of St Joseph and St Dominic after he was demobbed, and participated in its memorial work.[85] The nature of the backward glance in his work has generated some critical disquiet. Michael Alexander notes a refusal among the previous generation of critics to accept 'the analogy Jones offers with earlier wars, some of them heroic or chivalric', on the basis that 'to accept it would deny the traumatic claim of the literature which protested that the First World War was absolutely unprecedented'.[86] One might add to Alexander's defence of Jones, that the possibilities of horror are not governed by precedent. Indeed, it was precisely by harnessing the resources of medievalism that *In Parenthesis* discovered an enhanced potential for conveying terror and discord. As Eliot later demonstrated, and the Gawain poet made amply clear before him, it was possible to stage a fertility rite without glibly satisfying a civilizational need.

Jones's great theme is 'misadventure'.[87] In this respect he draws on the Arthurian story of Balin and Balan, two brothers who slay each other under a misapprehension brought about by Balin's decision to fight with an unknown shield.[88] The dedication of *In Parenthesis* to the 'ENEMY FRONT-FIGHTERS, WHO SHARED OUR PAINS' is moving precisely because it hangs on to a heightened awareness of brotherhood brought to blows by a perverse fate. The effect is no sentimental recourse to outmoded values or affinities, and the ensuing reference to 'MISADVENTURE' is no simple negation of a primary value. Rather, the horror is sharpened and made poignant by the conflict between the deep mythic resonance of a ruptured bond, and its intrusion upon a modern system of values that has no use for bonds at all. This occurs within a martial context whose senselessness is enhanced, rather than diminished, by comparison with the anarchic quagmire of the Hundred Years War.

[83] John Bunyan, *The Pilgrim's Progress* (Oxford: Oxford University Press, 1984), 13.

[84] See, for instance, the descent into hell in Owen's 'Strange Meeting', in Jon Stallworthy (ed.), *Wilfred Owen: The Complete Poems and Fragments* (London: Chatto & Windus, 1983), 148–50.

[85] Goebel notes Gill's use of a Jones design on the Cross he erected in Trumpington, Cambridge, in 1921. See Stefan Goebel, *The Great War and Medieval Memory: War, Remembrance and Medievalism in Britain and Germany, 1914–1940* (Cambridge: Cambridge University Press, 2007), 1, 61.

[86] Alexander refers to comments made by Paul Fussell and Jon Silkin. See Michael Alexander, *Medievalism: The Middle Ages in Modern England* (New Haven, CT and London: Yale University Press, 2007), 242.

[87] David Jones, 'Dedication' to *In Parenthesis* (London: Faber and Faber, 1978), n. p.

[88] Malory, *Le Morte d'Arthur*, I, 88–9.

Precedents for this emphasis could be found in the vivid bloodiness of Morris's *The Defence of Guenevere and Other Poems*, itself inspired by the arbitrary smiting and hewing of heads in *Le Morte d'Arthur*.[89]

Reshaping the future

While demonstrating the remarkable 'staying power' of medievalism, I have avoided characterizing it as a coherent or continuous cultural phenomenon. Instead, a loose kind of lineage is suggested, apparent in the recurrence of interdependent preoccupations in altered contexts. Medievalism, I have argued, is not so much an alternative to modernity, or a 'backward looking' strategy of avoidance, than a way of facing, and reshaping, the future. There is even something about the modern world that is medieval, as suggested by writers as diverse as Engels, Dickens, and Stoker. Ironically, it is just at that point when medievalism is regarded as a declining force that it feeds most directly into plans for the reorganization of life and economy. The formation of artists' communities, and of workers' 'guilds' in the Edwardian period channelled medievalism's concern with fraternal relations, bonds, and non-monetary craft ideals.

Pevsner's notion of a non-stylistic lineage based on functional structure is too counter-intuitive to carry the point alone, but the personal links between Morris, Muthesius, and Gropius demonstrate a convincing passage of values, just as the connections between Morris, Penty, Orage, Hobson, Douglas, and Pound evoke a lineage for Guild Socialism that leads eventually, if not inevitably, to fascism. This unwholesome link may explain why the influence of medievalism on social policy declined in the Britain of the 1930s. The forces of 'fire' and destruction already contained within nineteenth-century medievalism should also be acknowledged. Ranging from the more aggressive forms of architectural 'restoration' to a visceral approach in representing human conflict, medievalism granted access to the dark heart of modernity and supplied an uneasy awareness of ongoing 'misadventure'.

FURTHER READING

Alexander, Michael. *Medievalism: The Middle Ages in Modern England* (New Haven, CT: Yale University Press, 2007).

Banham, Joanna and Jennifer Harris (eds). *William Morris and the Middle Ages: A Collection of Essays, Together with a Catalogue of Works Exhibited at the Whitworth Art Gallery, 28 September–8 December 1984* (Manchester: Manchester University Press, 1984).

Biddick, Kathleen. *The Shock of Medievalism* (Durham, NC: Duke University Press, 1998).

---

[89] See Hanson, *William Morris and the Uses of Violence*, 31–63.

Chandler, Alice. *A Dream of Order: The Medieval Ideal in Nineteenth-Century British Literature* (London: Routledge & Kegan Paul, 1971 [1970]).

Girouard, Mark. *The Return to Camelot: Chivalry and the English Gentleman* (New Haven, CT: Yale University Press, 1981).

Glass, S. T. *The Responsible Society: The Ideas of the English Guild Socialist* (London: Longmans, Green, 1966).

Goebel, Stefan. *The Great War and Medieval Memory: War, Remembrance and Medievalism in Britain and Germany, 1914–1940* (Cambridge: Cambridge University Press, 2009).

Hanson, Ingrid. *William Morris and the Uses of Violence, 1856–1890* (London: Anthem, 2013).

Muthesius, Hermann. *The English House* (*Das englische Haus*, 1904), ed. Dennis Sharp, trans. Janet Seligman (Oxford: BSP Professional Books, 1987).

Palmgren, Jennifer A. and Lorretta M. Holloway. *Beyond Arthurian Romances: The Reach of Victorian Medievalism* (Basingstoke: Palgrave, 2005).

Pevsner, Nikolaus. *Pioneers of Modern Design: From William Morris to Walter Gropius*, 2nd edn (Harmondsworth: Penguin Books, 1960).

Robichaud, Paul. *Making the Past Present: David Jones, the Middle Ages, and Modernism* (Washington, DC: The Catholic University of America Press, 2007).

Saler, Michael T. *The Avant-Garde in Interwar England: Medieval Modernism and the London Underground* (New York: Oxford University Press, 1999).

Shippey, Tom and Richard Utz (eds). *Medievalism in the Modern World: Essays in Honour of Leslie J. Workman* (Turnout, Belgium: Brepols, 1998).

Simpson, Roger. *Camelot Regained: The Arthurian Revival and Tennyson, 1800–1849* (Cambridge: D. S. Brewer, 1990).

Wilmer, Clive. 'Sculpture and Economics in Pound and Ruskin', *PN Review* 24/6 (July–August 1998), 43–50.

Wilmer, Clive. 'Ruskin, Morris and Medievalism', *The Ruskin Review and Bulletin* 6/1 (Spring 2010), 21–42.

CHAPTER 2

MYTHOLOGY, EMPIRE, AND NARRATIVE

JARAD ZIMBLER

How are we to understand the confluence of empire and narrative? Here is one course: European imperialism gives definitive form to the world system during the nineteenth and early twentieth centuries; all-encompassing, it conditions metropolitan cultural production, especially the novel; all the same, it breeds a desire, even a compulsion, to mask its effects. Our task, then, would be to unmask, demystify, demythologize. Or, we might follow a different path: considering the challenges of writing in a specific time and place, we could think about decisions regarding technique and subject matter in relation to a literary field and literary material; and, by thus locating literary practice in its context of intelligibility, seek to articulate its truth content.[1]

This chapter develops the latter approach; it asks: how did empire complicate and circumscribe the novelist's craft? What generic and narrative modifications did it entail? And what do works produced in this moment tell us about empire itself? The works in question here are Olive Schreiner's *The Story of an African Farm* (1883) and Rudyard Kipling's *Kim* (1901), which, along with Joseph Conrad's *Almayer's Folly* (1895) and *An Outcast of the Islands* (1896), will be considered in light of ideas about narrative fiction published contemporaneously with them.

Histories of narrative theory tend to begin with Russian formalism, and in particular with Vladimir Propp's *Morphology of the Folktale* (1928). This is a mistake: the swell that generates the late wave of Propp's work is the comparative philology and mythology of the nineteenth century. In the writings of Jacob Grimm, F. Max Müller, E. B. Tylor, and James Frazer one finds already that distinction between story and narration which eventually grounds the narratologies of Genette and

---

[1] For Pierre Bourdieu's theory of the 'literary field', see *The Rules of Art: Genesis and Structure of the Literary Field*, trans. Susan Emanuel (Cambridge: Polity Press, 1996). For 'aesthetic material' and 'truth content', see Theodor W. Adorno, *Aesthetic Theory*, ed. Gretel Adorno and Rolf Tiedemann, trans. Robert Hullot-Kentor (London: Continuum, 2004).

Todorov. The claims made by Müller and Frazer—that various Aryan and Semitic myths could be re-described as stories of the sun's rising, or of spring's renewal—depended upon the same kind of comparison and abstraction implicit in Propp's reduction of Russian folk tales to seven characters and thirty-one functions.[2] Tylor identified the myths of Cyrus and Romulus and Remus as 'specimens of a widespread mythic group...in which exposed infants are saved to become national heroes'.[3] Müller spoke of 'stories...identical in form and character whether we find them on Indian, Persian, Greek, Italian, Slavonic or Teutonic soil'.[4] What do we see here if not incipient recognition of *fabula* and *syuzhet*, *récit* and *discours*?

In the present context, we should note that these new branches of knowledge—comparative philology and mythology—were themselves nourished by the expansion of European imperial formations. If narratology is therefore entangled with empire at its roots, it is at least as important that a real concern with narrative began in this moment to inflect the views of European writers and readers of novels, prompting debates about the 'art of fiction' and the relative merits of realism and romance, which were conducted in the British periodical press of the 1880s and 1890s. Mythology informed these debates only indirectly, but certain ideas about myth were important to them, as well as to the novels with which we are concerned.

Difficult subjects

In an early essay, South African novelist J. M. Coetzee looks back to a local predecessor, Sarah Gertrude Millin, and attempts to explain her metaphorics of blood degeneration. Largely concerned to show how this metaphorics draws on *fin-de-siècle* racial science, Coetzee also considers Millin's 'interest in blood and race' in relation to 'her vocation as a novelist' and especially her need to adapt 'whatever models and theories lie to hand to make writing possible'. It is by taking up 'the mainstream English novel of class', and then extending 'its operations to a mixed field of race, class, and caste' that Millin is able to solve problems precipitated by her position, and faced 'by every colonial novelist of her generation: the problem of deciding which elements of the European novel were relevant to the colonial situation; and the problem of locating in the colony a social field rich enough to support the transplanted European novel'.[5]

---

[2] See James G. Frazer, *The Golden Bough: A Study in Comparative Religion*, 2 vols (London: Macmillan, 1890); F. Max Müller, *Selected Essays on Language, Mythology and Religion*, 2 vols (London: Longmans, Green and Co., 1881).

[3] Edward B. Tylor, *Primitive Culture: Researches into the Development of Mythology, Philosophy, Religion, Art and Custom*, 2 vols (London: John Murray, 1871), i, 255.

[4] Müller, *Selected Essays*, i, 309.

[5] J. M. Coetzee, *White Writing: On the Culture of Letters in South Africa* (New Haven, CT: Yale University Press, 1988), 161–2.

Coetzee says these problems are 'closely intertwined'. In fact, they are two sides of the same coin, that of literary practice: on the one side, inherited genres and techniques developed elsewhere and for different purposes; on the other, subject matters and themes that seem infertile ground for certain kinds of narrative. This is not to resort to any facile distinction between form and content, but to recognize that there are different questions that can be put to any literary work. From both perspectives, the novelist of empire's margins is in a peculiar quandary: 'Because the texture of colonial society is typically thin, rather than dense, and does not permit the play of social nuance on which the novel of manners is built, the colonial novelist has to look beyond the field of purely social interaction'. There is an option of turning to 'Emily Brontë rather than Jane Austen' and adopting the 'Romantic novel, with its emphasis on solitary destinies,' but this presents the difficulty of making narratives from 'the careers of people outside society'.[6]

Is it true that colonial life could not easily be made into novels of a familiar kind; that its social fabric was too threadbare, and existence beyond its boundaries hard to imagine? Henry James thought so, writing of Nathaniel Hawthorne:

> [T]he coldness, the thinness, the blankness, to repeat my epithet, present themselves so vividly that our foremost feeling is that of compassion for a romancer looking for subjects in such a field. It takes so many things, as Hawthorne must have felt later in life, when he made the acquaintance of the denser, richer, warmer European spectacle—it takes such an accumulation of history and custom, such a complexity of manners and types, to form a fund of suggestion for a novelist.[7]

Of course, within a generation, as James's novels attest, this fund was better supplied, at least for the American writer.

For authors elsewhere, however, a difficulty with subject matter persisted. Evidence is found in Schreiner's Preface to her novel's second edition, published in 1887: 'should one sit down to paint the scenes among which he has grown, he will find that the facts creep in upon him. Those brilliant phases and shapes which the imagination sees in far-off lands are not for him to portray. Sadly he must squeeze the colour from his brush, and dip it into the gray pigments around him.'[8] The world presented is indeed monotonous—something emphasized in repeated descriptions of arid landscapes—though the drabness of her surroundings was hardly Schreiner's only problem. As several reviewers observed, when the novel first appeared in 1883 under the pseudonym 'Ralph Iron', *The Story of an African Farm* put before its readers 'unfamiliar scenes and circumstances', 'a sort of life not yet made familiar by books of travel and scarcely touched at all by fiction'.[9]

[6] Ibid., 161.
[7] Henry James, *The Critical Muse: Selected Literary Criticism* (Harmondsworth: Penguin, 1987), 132.
[8] Olive Schreiner, *The Story of an African Farm* (Oxford: Oxford University Press, 1992), xxxix–xl.
[9] 'An African Novel', *Spectator* (2 June 1883), 713; 'Recent Novels', *Daily News* (6 March 1883), 3.

Undomesticated and dull, life at the Cape seemed an unlikely subject to all concerned. A reviewer for the *Morning Post* thought the situation still worse:

> The author has been a little unfortunate, perhaps, in his choice of a subject, for his characters do not possess the least tinge of romance, and the scenes among which the action of the story takes place are as uninteresting as could well be imagined. The chief fault of the book is that the persons represented are for the most part degraded and coarse, so much so as to be often repulsive. Many charming novels have been written describing life among the humbler classes, but the Boer women and Hottentots in the present instance awake no sympathy and inspire no interest whatever … he would have done better to have written a simple narrative of farm life, and not have endeavoured in vain to make a 'novel' out of such unsuitable material.[10]

But Schreiner was not unduly troubled. On the contrary, she seems to have confronted the restriction on her subject matter at the level of narration itself. After all, the narrator hardly strays beyond the bounds of the farm. Although significant events occur elsewhere, a return is required if they are to be narrated: only when restored to the farmhouse can Waldo recount his experiences by writing his letter to Lyndall, news of whose own fate must first be carried back by Gregory Rose. Nothing can happen, it seems, without being folded into the existence of the farm, which becomes the very nexus of life and death, at its centre standing not the homestead but the small hill for which it is named: Kopje Alone. The furthest the narrator gets, apart from the brief excursion to Lyndall's death-bed, is to a neighbouring farm, where Tant Sannie is married, and here the departure is only brief—a night—and then we are back; so that the novel is, after all, nothing *but* what its title claims, and the curtailment of subject matter is embraced as the very condition of narration.

What then of Kipling? He provides no direct statement of difficulty, and his problem was hardly thinness or lack, when India was a place of proverbial richness. Yet, in addressing himself to the subcontinent, he needed to know what lay beyond the spectacle of daily life well enough to write of it; or at least to write of it as something other than spectacle. A measure of Kipling's failure is the insistence with which reviewers acknowledged the 'kaleidoscopic quality' of *Kim*'s prose, while straining to see the narrative as anything more than a series of vignettes, loosely assembled.[11] The prominence of colourful description becomes especially noticeable when *Kim* is compared with Kipling's previous short stories, the best of which are withering pencil-sketches of a colonial society found wanting precisely in its narrowness, to which the caustic narrator is matched. Whether or not such a society could sustain a novel of character and manners we cannot say, because Kipling did not attempt it. Instead, he turned to the rich and varied world beyond

---

[10] 'An African Farm', *Morning Post* (12 February 1883), 3.
[11] See, for example, 'Recent Fiction', *Blackwood's Edinburgh Magazine* 170/1034 (December 1901), 793–6.

the confines of colonial society, a world unknown to him in any detail, and certainly not from the inside.

Intensification of description is not the only indicator of Kipling's problem with subject matter. Ostensibly concerned with cultural difference and subject formation, *Kim* is notable for keeping aloof from interiors and interiority. Very seldom does the narrator penetrate the outer limits of person or place. We get from Kim, it is true, laments about his solitude and singularity, but otherwise we are largely shut out, and the burden of insight into character is placed on dialogue. Nor are the kaleidoscopic descriptions of domestic or private spaces, but of train compartments, mountain passes, and the Grand Trunk Road.

Indeed, *Kim* is a novel in which narrator and focalizer are ever on the threshold: in the courtyard of the Jullunder cultivator's brother, outside Creighton's home, around the Kulu woman's palanquin, at the gates of St Xavier's. To the rooms themselves, entry is barred, as in the Kashmir Serai, where they are 'guarded by heavy wooden doors and cumbrous native padlocks'.[12] Much of Indian life, then, lies beyond the scope of this narrative, and this provokes momentary anxiety, as in the defensive disavowal of Kim's schooling: 'you would scarcely be interested in Kim's experiences as a St Xavier's boy'; 'The record of a boy's education interests few save his parents, and, as you know, Kim was an orphan'.[13]

Novel forms

In different ways, then, we find evidence of a difficulty with colonial subject matter in both *The Story of an African Farm* and *Kim*. Yet limits are imposed as much by particular forms as by particular themes, as Coetzee states clearly, and as several early reviews imply—including the *Morning Post*'s, where the subject matter of the Cape Colony is considered problematic not for narrative in general, but for the novel, and even particular kinds of novel.

But which kinds? Are 'charming novels' and 'tinge of romance' allusions to the genres Coetzee identifies as the 'mainstream English novel of class' and the 'Romantic novel' of Brontë? This is unlikely: until the 1870s, it is true, the field had been divided between manners and character (the former traced to Fielding, the latter to Richardson, in line with Samuel Johnson's judgement on the two authors), but this distinction seems largely to have dissolved by the 1880s. In the *Saturday Review* of July 1876, the novel of character was already understood to have subsumed the novel of manners, insofar as customs and social codes were valued for the access they gave to the deepest recesses of the self.[14] Even in a late defence of the novel of

[12] Rudyard Kipling, *Kim* (Oxford: Oxford University Press, 1998), 17.   [13] Ibid., 123, 164.
[14] 'The Limits of Fiction', *Saturday Review* (29 July 1876), 132–3.

manners, published in 1885, the exemplary fictions of this kind—Austen's and Thackeray's—were praised for illuminating thought and feeling.[15]

As the opposition between character and manners faded, an opposition between character and incident became prominent, leading to a series of debates regarding the relative merits of plot, on the one hand, and portrayal, on the other. Even in Henry James's 'The Art of Fiction' (1884), which rejected any distinction as valid except that between good and bad, the direction of the prevailing winds was clear: the notion that James resisted was that only some novels had stories. Stevenson's 'Gossip on Romance' (1882) and 'A Humble Remonstrance' (1884), and Andrew Lang's 'Realism and Romance' (1887), offered stirring counterclaims, championing incident against character, or rather romance against realism.[16]

Here, then, we begin to see certain of the parameters within which English-language novelists of the late nineteenth century operated. For the opposition of romance to realism was not simply a convenient means for dividing literary territory. Rather, it identified two poles according to which serious novelists charted a course: the novel of incident-and-adventure on the one hand, and the novel of character-and-manners on the other. Together, these structured a space of position-takings in which only certain practices became feasible, at least to authors committed to the 'art of fiction'. Of course, it is always possible for a work to change the terms of the debate; but even then, the nature of the change will be determined by the field. Literary genres do not emerge *ex nihilo*; they are products of history, of changing practices and the values attached to those practices.

The state of the field is thus the context of a work's intelligibility, the basis for its meaning, and for particular expectations. So, in the present case, each kind of novel implied a set of techniques as well as a certain thematics. *Realism* meant detailed description of manners, moments, places, and minds; but also encounters with the difficult or unseemly elements of social and psychological reality; and thus a commitment to the novel as vehicle of analysis. *Romance*, on the other hand, meant narrative that was compelling, fascinating, enchanting; but also, for reasons easily understood, distant either in place or time. Since the present was somehow inimical to it, adventure ought to happen elsewhere, in the past that was another country, or in another country that might as well have been the past. Thus Stevenson observed that the stories of highwaymen he had enjoyed as a boy began inevitably 'in the year 17 –', as those beloved of his 'friend' took place always on a far island or an empty coast.

This emphasis on distance, and so on the exotic, ensured a firm association between the novel of incident and the far territories of empire. Indeed, the

---

[15] H. D. Traill, 'The Novel of Manners', *The Nineteenth Century: A Monthly Review* 18/104 (October 1885), 561–76.

[16] R. L. Stevenson, 'A Gossip on Romance', *Longman's Magazine*, 1/1 (November 1882), 69–79; Stevenson, 'A Humble Remonstrance', *Longman's Magazine*, 5/26 (December 1884), 139–47; Andrew Lang, 'Realism and Romance', *The Contemporary Review*, 52 (November 1887), 683–93.

link was such that the imperial spirit itself explained the English preference for romance:

> The English is a colonizing race that seeks adventures and finds them in every quarter of the globe... Fighting fevers and famines in India, or toiling for a livelihood on the frozen plains of Manitoba; seeking gold amid the rain-storms of Mashonaland, or on the sun-baked waterless wastes of West Australia, the Briton's life is apt to be one of great vicissitudes... It is not to be wondered at that the race that most loves adventures and perils, and feels more keenly than others the fascination of the unknown, should prefer works of art that render its peculiar passion... The novel of adventure is still, as it has always been, the chief type of English creative work in prose.[17]

Of course, the association between particular subject matters and forms runs both ways: if romance dwelt on the colonies, the colonies evoked romance. This helps to explain the *Saturday Review*'s denigration of Schreiner's novel:

> [W]e fancied that we should have a story of South African speculation and adventure on the borderland between savagery and civilization. We had hoped to hear of encounters with ravening lions, and of hairbreadth escapes from raiding Zulus; of oxen dropping in their tracks on long journeys through waterless deserts, or driven by Bechuanas or Bushmen into inaccessible *kranzes*... For we love, by way of variety, a novel of wild incident. As a matter of fact, we have nothing of the kind.[18]

But nor was *The Story of an African Farm* realist, in any obvious sense: its art seemed one of caricature, rather than character; its figures were too idiosyncratic to be believable.

We find similar tensions in the reception of *Kim*. Though it approached romance more closely, reviewers found it disappointing: 'The story, as a story, is not much. But it is a thread upon which are strung many bright and vivid pictures';[19] 'The story which gives unity to these pictures serves its purpose well, but will not enhance Mr. Kipling's reputation as a novelist. It is mechanical and a trifle forced';[20] 'The construction of the plot is wretchedly defective'. Yet, on the grounds of psychological and social insight, *Kim* hardly fared better: 'The boy Kim and the Lama are the only two characters in the story that have the slightest resemblance to human beings.'[21] Which made it difficult to say what *Kim* was, exactly, even for sympathetic reviewers: 'Were it judged by the common canons applied to novels of plot and circumstance or of character, much could be said against it.'[22]

---

[17] 'Romanticism and Realism', *Saturday Review* (8 December 1894), 615.
[18] 'The Story of an African Farm', *Saturday Review* (21 April 1883), 507–8.
[19] 'Some Notable Books of the Month', *Review of Reviews* (November 1901), 537.
[20] 'Fiction', *The Speaker* (5 October 1901), 23.
[21] Review of *Kim*, 'Belles Lettres', *Westminster Review*, 156/6 (December 1901), 708–14.
[22] Review of *Kim*, *Athenaeum*, 3861 (26 October 1901), 552–3.

Half-breed books

The problem of subject matter, then, was hardly straightforward. It was easy enough to write novels about colonial life, in spite of its lack of nuance or inaccessibility; to do so one needed only to embrace romance. But if the notion of fiction as simple pleasure or as a means of escape seemed unpalatable, and one preferred to write of complex reality, then the lure of romance must have induced anxiety, and a degree of caution.

That its exoticism was anathema to Schreiner is apparent in her Preface, which responded directly to the *Saturday Review*:

> It has been suggested by a kind critic that he would better have liked the little book if it had been a history of wild adventure; of cattle driven into inaccessible 'kranzes' by Bushmen...This could not be. Such works are best written in Piccadilly or in the Strand: there the gifts of the creative imagination, untrammelled by contact with any fact, may spread their wings.[23]

Schreiner's taste was clearly for realism, in which light we ought, surely, to understand her commitment to a grey palette, to the truth of life as it was lived, no matter how disagreeable. And Schreiner's Preface in any case only confirmed what was already apparent in the novel, where the charms of imaginative narrative were undercut by allusions to the fairy-tale romances beloved of Otto and also of Em; the ludicrous stories of adventure told by Bonaparte Blenkins; and the clerk's tales of colonial erotica discovered by Waldo. In each case, a genre of 'wild incident' is associated with characters either naïve or depraved, and is marked by a desire to escape reality or confound it.

In *Kim*, the curtailment of romance was not as direct. Nevertheless, of the many marvellous tales we hear *about*, there are few we ever *hear*. Kim narrates prodigiously: 'Kim told the older children tales of the size and beauty of Lahore'; 'he varied his tale, or adorned it with all the shoots of a budding fancy'; 'then, Kim told his adventures between coughs'; 'he...was cheering his neighbours with a string of most wonderful yarns.'[24] But he is hardly alone: the old cavalry officer tells 'tales of the Mutiny', and the Kulu woman 'of some old local Gods'; the boys of St Xavier's thrash 'through the hot nights telling tales till the dawn', reciting 'their adventures, which...would have crisped a Western boy's hair'; even the lama has his moments: 'Whereupon he told it: a fantastic piled narrative of bewitchment and miracles that set Shamlegh agasping.'[25] And when Hurree Babu returns from his exploits, he announces: 'I will tell you all my tale at Lurgan's. It was splendid...And I told the common people – oah, *such* tales and anecdotes!'[26] But, time and again, the details of fantastic adventure are only indicated, never revealed, though, by their nature,

---

[23] Schreiner, *The Story of an African Farm*, xxxix–xl.
[24] Kipling, *Kim*, 45, 127, 132, 186.   [25] Ibid., 50, 77, 123, 124, 258.   [26] Ibid., 280.

they clearly lay within Kipling's grasp. Thus the narrative seems to repudiate the pleasures of fancy, indeed of romance, in spite of the fact that these are precisely the pleasures in which Kim has indulged.

Is this intended? It hardly matters: literary craft is a practical knowledge, which does not require theoretical reflection for judgement. It does seem, however, that Schreiner and Kipling were aware of their predicaments; or, at least, that the truth of their predicaments emerged in and through writing. At the very least, both novels express a wariness of romance, and both, at the level of narration and style, confront the limitations of recalcitrant colonial literary material, which, again, comprehends both subject matter and technique.

But the consequence is a compromise of sorts, which perhaps explains why each seemed 'one of those half-breed books that are neither novels in the ordinary acceptation of the term nor descriptive narratives, but partake of some of the characteristics of each'.[27] This is most obviously the case in *Kim*, which has multiple plot interests and trajectories: the excitement of the Great Game, with its secrets, disguises, and intrigues, feels like romance; yet the novel is also an account of its eponymous hero's emergence into adulthood; of the lama's spiritual quest; and of regional life and customs. A novel can, of course, have many themes, but here we are dealing with more than thematics: each strand implies a particular pattern, and these do not always coincide. The chief incident of *Kim*'s adventure plot, for example, the encounter with the Russian spies, is only vaguely anticipated and then too swiftly resolved to be considered the proper climax of the novel. The conversion of Kim from impish meddler to spy has required a break of so many years that the connection of this incident to Kim's first meeting with Mahbub Ali feels forced, not because the chain of events rests too much on coincidence, but because there is hardly a chain of events. Cutting the other way, the episodic structure associated with romance must in itself inhibit any detailed exploration of Kim's self-discoveries at St Xavier's, which transform boy into man.

In *The Story of an African Farm*, the romance proper may be kept at bay, but generic irregularity is nevertheless apparent, particularly in the transition from the first part of the novel to the second: the often jaunty, picaresque narration of Bonaparte Blenkins's rise and fall gives way to strange and sombre monologues, as Waldo, Lyndall, and Em emerge into adulthood, making passionate speeches, holding weighty dialogues. Some of the differences are narratological: in the novel's first part, the chapters advance chronologically, and each is clearly related to a particular incident; in the second, narrative and plot diverge, noticeably in Chapters XI and XII, which are largely constituted of analepsis. Moreover, while the structure of the first part recalls the episodic narratives of the eighteenth century—we have a young hero (Waldo), a craven villain (Bonaparte), a wicked stepmother (Tant Sannie), a kind uncle (Otto), and in Lyndall and Em, two potential love interests—the second

---

[27] 'An African Farm', *Morning Post*, 3.

part's rectangular complexity suggests a narrative closer to *Adam Bede* than *Roderick Random*. Much the same can be said about characterization: rough lines, approaching caricature, give way to greater nuance. The difference is clearest in the treatment of Tant Sannie, who becomes, towards the end, something other than the villain of farce and fairy tale.

'The solution that emerges in colonial practice', Coetzee says of Millin and her predecessors, 'tends to be a mixed one: an ethnic typology for those parts of the novel set in the wilderness, a class typology for those parts set in society'. I am suggesting of Schreiner and Kipling that their own response was more a mixing of genres than a mixing of character typologies. Since the fund of subject matter was either lacking or inaccessible, and the novel of character and manners therefore impossible, recourse was had to incident, or at least episodic structure and the excitement it promised, as well as to the painterly description of scene.

Enter mythology

So we return to mythology. For if both novels seemed uneven, they were nevertheless successful, which had much to do with the atmosphere of mysticism and mythic profundity they attained. The experience of such an atmosphere is attested in early reviews. The *Athenaeum*, for example, thought *Kim* contained 'evidence of a higher quality of observation and divination, of something more of spiritual beauty and aspiration underlying phenomena'. It conveyed 'a large, an almost overwhelming feeling of life, of space, and background', and was somehow imbued with a 'curiously suggestive quality, the aspect of infinity'.[28] Similarly, *The Story of an African Farm* indicated 'in a profound way, a religious conception which is emerging above the chaos and undiscriminating toleration of the present day, and which prepares a broad convergence on the things and themes of perennial import to mankind'.[29]

These impressions were hardly accidental. Schreiner's novel might have staged doubts about the value of orthodox religion, but it also offered an explicit account of 'souls' years', asserting that the 'most material life is not devoid of them; the story of the most spiritual is told in them'.[30] The sense of universal longing and deep time was communicated also in those passages in which stones and stars look upon transient human suffering; as well as in moments that reflect on transcendent human needs. An example of the latter is the narrator's reflection on Waldo's dream:

[28]   Review of *Kim*, *Athenaeum*, 552.
[29]   Thomas F. Husband, '*The Story of an African Farm*: A Reflection', *Westminster Review*, 141 (January 1894), 637.
[30]   Schreiner, *The Story of an African Farm*, 101.

[T]he sweetness was all there, the infinite peace, that men find not in the little can-
kered kingdom of the tangible. The bars of the real are set close about us; we cannot
open our wings but they are struck against them, and drop bleeding. But, when we
glide between the bars into the great unknown beyond, we may sail for ever in the
glorious blue, seeing nothing but our shadows . . . Without dreams and phantoms man
cannot exist.[31]

If such moments suggest a certain mysticism, the parable told by Waldo's stranger
is properly mythological. It configures the desire for truth as atavistic quest: the
hunter-hero glimpses a magical bird; goes in search of it, though warned of dangers; is tested, but overcomes exile, temptation, and despair; and, though his aim is
frustrated, is given a sign at last that his struggle has not been wholly in vain. The
appearance of this embedded myth is surprising, marked by a shift in style and
narration, but also somehow necessary, since it is proleptic of and gives meaning to
the lives and careers of Waldo and Lyndall, both seekers after truth. Indeed, it is the
novel's means of counterbalancing the pessimism of the epigraph appended to its
second part (quoted from its first): 'And it was all play, and no one could tell what it
had lived and worked for. A striving and a striving, and an ending in nothing'.

In *Kim*, the atmosphere of mythology and air of mysticism are introduced with
the lama. Unlike those religious beliefs exposed as superstitious—their magic dissipated by the narrator's cool reason, much as Lurgan Sahib's illusions are dispelled by
Kim's command of English and his multiplication tables—his quest for the River of
the Arrow is treated as integral to the narrative, and the possibility of its success
must therefore remain open till the very end, when the lama is given the final
thought: 'He crossed his hands on his lap and smiled, as a man may who has won
Salvation for himself and his beloved.'[32]

Moreover, at the origin of this quest lies the mythic 'tale of the Arrow', a tale the
lama tells many times over, much as he repeats the mythological drawing of the
wheel of life, and as Kim recounts to all those who will listen the story of his origin
and destiny, which in the perpetual retelling and elaboration, comes in itself to
resemble myth. And not only for this reason, since there is a mystery surrounding
Kim's destiny that is never resolved: it is accurately foretold by the Brahmin at
Umballa whose 'rude horoscope' is made of 'mysterious signs' scratched in dust.[33]

The meaning of myth

How then are these briefly sketched mythological elements related to the challenges
of colonial material? Do they structure narratives that would otherwise prove too
expansive and fragmentary, as T. S. Eliot suggested of modernist myths?[34] If we wish

---

[31] Ibid., 260.   [32] Kipling, *Kim*, 289.   [33] Ibid., 40.
[34] T. S. Eliot, 'Ulysses, Order and Myth', *The Dial* 75 (November 1923), 480–3.

to claim Kipling and Schreiner as proto-modernists, the idea is appealing. But it is without much substance: their works are threatened by a thinness of subject matter, not by expansiveness.

To see the proper purpose of these elements it is helpful to know something of the fascination exerted by mythology on Schreiner and Kipling's contemporaries, who not only collected and analyzed myths, but speculated fervently as to their origins. Among leading scholars, there were real disagreements: Müller believed myth the product of a disease of language, 'the dark shadow that language throws on thought', whereas Tylor understood it as early science.[35] But, whatever its origins, *myth* intimated: semantic density (evidenced by competing interpretations); aspiration to metaphysical truth; and an attempt to know and produce the world by mimesis. For the religious and even ritual purpose of myth, and its association with sympathetic magic, was generally acknowledged. Finally, myth was identified with the past, or at least an earlier stage of man's development, and continued to exist, according to scholars such as Lang and Frazer, only among native peoples on the margins of empire, or, as survivals of primitive thought, among the European peasantry.

There was, then, a skein of associations to which *myth* belonged, so that we might well speak of a *mythological register*, the use of which was prompted by the material. Myth was at home in the colonies, and offered a means of compensating for the inadequacy of subject matter. As mythological register, it made the worlds of *Kim* and *The Story of an African Farm* more profound. Indeed, for colonial novelists sceptical of romance but denied access to the most familiar varieties of realism, a turn to mythology was a great boon. Existential depth would make up for social detail and psychological precision.

In fact, this mythological register was something considerably greater than supplement or compensation. For myth was also opposed to science, the progress of which, scholars agreed, would soon make the former redundant. 'Enlightenment's program [sic] was the disenchantment of the world. It wanted to dispel myths, to overthrow fantasy with knowledge.'[36] And the opposition of myth to science, refracted in the sphere of the novel, became the opposition of romance to realism. Zola's celebration of experiment made the association with science explicit, but it was no less apparent in the belief that realism entailed 'the unrelenting minute portraiture of modern life and analysis of modern character, the unrelenting exclusion of exciting events and engaging narrative'.[37] Romance, on the other hand, shared with myth an emphasis on plot and on enchantment, as well as an imbrication with metropolitan past and colonial present. Indeed, the mythologist and literary critic Andrew

[35] Müller, *Selected Essays*, i, 590.
[36] Max Horkheimer and Theodor W. Adorno, *Dialectic of Enlightenment: Philosophical Fragments*, ed. Gunzelin Schmid Noerr, trans. Edmind Jephcott (Stanford, CA: Stanford University Press, 2002), 2–3.
[37] Lang, 'Realism and Romance', 688.

Lang had argued that it was precisely to a person's primitive parts that romance appealed. The rise of romance was thus in itself concomitant with the disenchantment of the world: myth was recuperated from science as the novel of incident.

But if there are clear grounds for discerning a parallel between romance and myth, and between realism and science, the transposition to the literary field occurred only under the sign of the triumph of instrumental reason. For the recuperation of myth as fiction required that both were deprived of access to truth: the story as story was justified on the grounds of simple pleasure; and while realism resisted the claims of science to knowledge as its exclusive preserve, the novel of character and manners tended to restrict itself to details proliferating on the surface of life, the social nuances and personal struggles produced by the advance of scientific rationalism in league with commerce. In its crude materialism, it shied away from deeper truths; truths that were associated with myth, not least by Friedrich Nietzsche, whose *Birth of Tragedy* (1872) offered the period's most concerted defence of myth and indeed of art. Myth, Nietzsche said, is dream, the Apollonian vision whose beauty makes an encounter with the truth of existence bearable.[38]

In this light, the use of a mythic register in the novels of Schreiner and Kipling can be seen not only as a compromise necessitated by the limits of the material, but also as a means of transcending those limits by sublating realism and romance. The necessity of a restricted scope becomes a virtue; mysticism and enchantment are brought within the ambit of the novel, not as exotic adornment, but as avenues to metaphysical insight. An atmosphere produced by mythological elements, as well as by description—almost ekphrastic—negates the priority both of story and of character. And, what is more, the margins of empire are revealed, or rather constituted, as the proper testing grounds of the self, indeed of the spirit. Away from the commotion of metropolitan business and bustle, the truth of existence can emerge. But, since empire itself will liquidate its margins—something acknowledged in both novels, and even celebrated in *Kim*—the possibility of this emergence is written as always already threatened. For it is conditional on a form of life on the verge of extinction, if not already extinguished.[39]

Conrad's contribution

Here we might consider very briefly Joseph Conrad's first two novels, *Almayer's Folly* and *An Outcast of the Islands*, which took as their subject matter the colonial

[38] Friedrich Nietzsche, *The Birth of Tragedy and Other Writings*, ed. Raymond Geuss and Ronald Speirs, trans. Ronald Speirs (Cambridge: Cambridge University Press, 1999), 46–7.
[39] I am grateful to Ben Etherington for this insight. For his related argument, see 'Literary Primitivism: Essence, Aesthetics, Politics' (unpublished doctoral thesis, University of Cambridge, 2010).

world of the Malay Archipelago. The proximity of *Almayer's Folly* to romance has been remarked by several critics, who adduce as evidence its colonial setting, its 'love story with a happy ending', and such 'adventure-story motifs' as hidden treasure, pirates, political intrigue, 'mistaken identity', and 'the heroine's dauntless self-sacrifice'.[40] Yet Conrad disliked exotic adventure, and distanced himself from the likes of Rider Haggard in several ways, not least by framing the triumph of love within a narrative of dissolution and torpor. Indeed, in the Author's Note written for the novel, but not published with it, Conrad objected to the presumption that 'in those distant lands all joy is a yell and a war dance, all pathos is a howl and a ghastly grin of filed teeth, and that the solution of all problems is found in the barrel of a revolver or on the point of an assegai.'[41]

It was in any case only 'during some relatively late stage of composition', Ian Watt reports, that 'Conrad was constrained to add to the story of Almayer . . . an invented romantic intrigue'. And he did so, in all likelihood, because his 'knowledge of Olmeijer's past was too sketchy to supply the action for a whole novel' and because he 'had been ashore much too briefly to have anything but the most superficial understanding of Malay life'.[42] Clearly, this relates Conrad's practice to Schreiner's and Kipling's, as does the distinctive intensity of his descriptive passages. For, if Watt claims that romance 'afforded Conrad an opportunity of developing . . . his power to describe the outside world', we might instead explain both romance and description as means of compensating for a lack in the material.[43] This avoids Watt's teleology, but it also makes better sense of the changes in practice discernible in *An Outcast of the Islands*, where romance elements are stripped out while description is further intensified.

Conrad's descriptions, moreover, are not of manners or customs, or even of the struggles of interiority, but of the world itself, made pregnant with significance by the meditative and incantatory intensity of his prose. Thus description ceases to supplement the story, and instead usurps it, and we return once more to the question of mythology. Neither *Almayer's Folly* nor *An Outcast of the Islands* incorporates mythological elements in the manner of *Kim* and *The Story of an African Farm*, but they do attain, precisely through this meditative description complemented by a concern with existential truth, that atmosphere of semantic density associated with myth. And if Conrad's novels are mythological in this broader sense, they are mythological also because style becomes a means of enchantment, a vehicle for sympathetic magic; and because both novels associate enchantment, mystery, storytelling, sublime insight, and the margins of empire with a way of life in the process of being liquidated.

[40] Ian Watt, *Conrad in the Nineteenth Century* (London: Chatto & Windus, 1980), 44, 46–7, 43.

[41] Joseph Conrad, *Almayer's Folly: A Story of an Eastern River*, ed. Floyd Eugene Eddleman and David Leon Higdon (Cambridge: Cambridge University Press, 1994), 3.

[42] Watt, *Conrad in the Nineteenth Century*, 38, 44.   [43] Ibid., 44.

These claims, admittedly speculative, can be grounded in an early passage from *An Outcast of the Islands*:

> The sea, perhaps because of its saltiness, roughens the outside but keeps sweet the kernel of its servants' *soul*. The old sea; the sea of many years ago, whose servants were devoted slaves and went from youth to age or to a sudden grave without needing to open the *book of life*, because they could look at *eternity* and reflect on the element that *gave the life and dealt the death*. Like a beautiful and unscrupulous woman, the sea of the past was glorious in its smiles, irresistible in its anger, capricious, enticing, illogical, irresponsible; a thing to love, a thing to fear. It **cast a spell**, it gave joy, it lulled gently into boundless *faith*; then with quick and causeless anger it killed. But its cruelty was redeemed by the **charm** of its *inscrutable mystery*, by the immensity of its promise, by the supreme **witchery** of its possible favour. Strong men with childlike hearts were *faithful* to it, were content to live by its *grace* – to die by its will. That was the sea before the time when the French mind set the Egyptian muscle in motion and produced a dismal but profitable ditch. Then a great pall of smoke sent out by countless steam-boats was spread over the restless mirror of the *Infinite*. The hand of the engineer tore down the *veil of the terrible beauty* in order that greedy and *faithless* landlubbers might pocket dividends. The *mystery* was destroyed. Like all *mysteries*, it lived only in the hearts of its *worshippers*. The hearts changed; the men changed. The once *loving and devoted servants* went out armed with fire and iron, and conquering the fear of their own hearts became a calculating crowd of cold and exacting masters.[44]

Here, the agents of enlightenment become destroyers of access to the ineffable. The distribution of words related to aesthetic experience, the past, magic (in bold) and religiosity (italicized), suggests precisely the skein of associations we have identified with the mythological register. Myth itself might be missing, but its lexical signals are abundant. And what this passage proposes, in its own power and fluidity, is that the prose itself—which becomes as enchanting, indeed mesmerizing, as the 'sea of the past'—may be the only means of recovering these losses, or at least knowing their truth.

With this in mind, we might consider a question posed by Conrad: 'what is a novel if not a conviction of our fellow-men's existence strong enough to take upon itself a form of imagined life clearer than reality?'[45] To Watt, who prefers to understand 'fellow-men' in biographical terms, Conrad here conceived the novel as a means of authenticating his own memories. In light of the preceding discussion, I think it better to read this question as evidence of an emergent belief that fiction was powerful not because it allowed escape from the world, but because it could know the world, and in its own right, not by the borrowed light of analytical clarity.

In his Preface to *The Nigger of the 'Narcissus'*, Conrad said as much, disavowing the 'gods' of 'Realism, Romanticism, Naturalism' while insisting that the 'glimpse of

[44] Conrad, *An Outcast of the Islands* (Oxford: Oxford University Press, 2002), 14 (emphases added).
[45] Conrad, *A Personal Record*, ed. Zdzisław Najder and J. H. Stape (1912; repr. Cambridge: Cambridge University Press, 2008), 27–8.

truth' was fiction's ultimate end and task, and that—echoing the passage from *An Outcast of the Islands*—it was 'only through an unremitting never-discouraged care for the shape and ring of sentences' that one could bring 'the light of magic suggestiveness... to play for an evanescent instant over the commonplace surface of words: of the old, old words, worn thin, defaced by ages of careless usage'.[46]

Colonial novelists

In offering this account of mythology, narrative, and empire, I have largely taken for granted the designation of Kipling, Schreiner, and Conrad as colonial authors. Yet *Kim* and *The Story of an African Farm* were published originally in England, where both authors resided. Schreiner, it is true, was recently arrived, and her novel mostly written at the Cape, but Kipling had been absent from India for almost a decade when *Kim* was published, and Conrad's knowledge of the Malay Archipelago was gleaned from brief visits.

If the category of 'colonial author' holds good it must therefore be on grounds other than residence or place of publication and reception; I would suggest the nature of the problems they faced and the manner in which these were resolved. That is, Schreiner, Conrad, and Kipling are colonial authors insofar as their subject matter was of the colonies, understood *not* as locations of adventure and romance, but of the emergence of existential truth. We must recognize nevertheless that the techniques and genres available to all three were bequeathed almost exclusively by a European tradition. If their literary material was thus colonial in a limited sense, their literary field was basically metropolitan. Their predecessors and rivals were other European novelists, and, as I have tried to show, the debates that shaped their literary practices and gave them meaning were precisely those of the British literary field of the late nineteenth century, a space of relational position-takings which structured reception as much as it did production, ensuring confusion on the part of reviewers, who misrecognized inventive narratives in which genres were blended and mythology was infused as a way of refusing the lure of romance and responding to the principles of realism, without access to its means.

FURTHER READING

Brantlinger, Patrick. *Victorian Literature and Postcolonial Studies* (Edinburgh: Edinburgh University Press, 2009).

Brennan, Timothy. *Borrowed Light: Vico, Hegel and the Colonies* (Stanford, CA: Stanford University Press, 2014).

---

[46] Conrad, *The Nigger of the 'Narcissus': A Tale of the Sea* (London: Heinemann, 1921), x–xi.

Chrisman. Laura. *Rereading the Imperial Romance: British Imperialism and South African Resistance in Haggard, Schreiner, and Plaatje* (Oxford: Oxford University Press, 2000).

Cooper, Frederick. *Colonialism in Question: Theory, Knowledge, History* (Berkeley, CA: University of California Press, 2005).

Daly, Nicholas. *Modernism, Romance and the Fin de Siècle* (Cambridge: Cambridge University Press, 1999).

Dryden, Linda. *Joseph Conrad and the Imperial Romance* (Basingstoke: Palgrave-Macmillan, 2000).

Esty, Jed. *Unseasonable Youth: Modernism, Colonialism and Fiction of Development* (Oxford: Oxford University Press, 2013).

Etherington, Ben and Jarad Zimbler. 'Field, Material, Technique: On Renewing Postcolonial Literary Criticism', *Journal of Commonwealth Literature* 49/3 (September 2014), 279–98.

Jameson, Fredric. *The Antinomies of Realism* (London and New York: Verso, 2013).

McDonald, Peter D. *British Literary Culture and Publishing Practice 1880–1914* (Cambridge: Cambridge University Press, 1997).

Osterhammel, Jürgen. *The Transformation of the World: A Global History of the Nineteenth Century*, trans. Patrick Camiller (Princeton, NJ: Princeton University Press, 2014).

Parry, Benita. *Postcolonial Studies: A Materialist Critique* (London and New York: Routledge, 2004).

Poole, Adrian. 'Henry James and Charm', *Essays in Criticism* 61/2 (April 2011), 115–36.

Sergeant, David. *Kipling's Art of Fiction 1884–1901* (Oxford: Oxford University Press, 2013).

CHAPTER 3

DEATH DRIVES

Biology, Decadence, and Psychoanalysis

STEFANO EVANGELISTA

Written in 1920, Freud's landmark work *Beyond the Pleasure Principle* (*Jenseits des Lustprinzips*) looks back to the evolution of psychoanalysis over its relatively short life. This retrospective journey brings him to formulate an extremely important revision: for the first time he postulates the existence of a death drive, envisaged as a powerful desire to turn away from life in order to return to an original inanimate state that preceded birth. Freud had formerly believed that self-preservation and the pursuit of pleasure were the unconscious goals of all living beings. But that theory was now displaced by the realization that, in actual fact, 'the organism wants only to die in its own particular way' and therefore that the life drives, including the all-important sex drive, are ultimately ways of managing this unconscious desire for death.[1] Freud was deeply aware of the disturbing philosophical implications of this idea, and repeatedly warned readers to take it with due caution, stressing the provisionality of his hypothesis and alerting them to his inevitable recourse to figurative language. Nonetheless, his assertion here that *'the goal of all life is death'*[2] would have deep repercussions both on psychoanalysis and on twentieth-century cultural history more broadly.

Traditionally, Freud's discovery of the death drive has been read as an indirect product of the First World War. This is mainly due to the fact that *Beyond the Pleasure Principle* builds on a study of war neurosis: proceeding from clinical observations of former soldiers' compulsion to repeat traumatic experiences and thereby actively procure themselves un-pleasure, Freud weaves together psychology and philosophy, examining mortality as both an individual fear and a broader cultural concern. Historically, *Beyond the Pleasure Principle* therefore belongs to the same

---

[1] Sigmund Freud, *Beyond the Pleasure Principle and Other Writings*, trans. John Reddick (London and New York: Penguin, 2003), 79.

[2] Ibid., 78 (emphasis in original).

post-war moment that gave rise to other classics of twentieth-century cultural pessimism such as Oswald Spengler's *The Decline of the West* (*Der Untergang des Abendlandes*, 1918) and T. S. Eliot's *The Waste Land* (1922).

For the purposes of this volume, however, it is important to take into consideration another, often overlooked archive that lies behind Freud's theorization of the death drive: late nineteenth-century biology, and in particular the work of the German scientist August Weismann (1834-1914). Although his name is relatively obscure outside scientific circles today, Weismann is widely regarded as the most important nineteenth-century evolutionary biologist after Darwin.[3] He was the author of a series of influential works which were translated into English as *Studies in the Theory of Descent* (with a preface by Charles Darwin, 1882) and *Essays upon Heredity and Kindred Biological Problems* (1889). Starting from the close observation of cells, Weismann concluded that death is not the universal *telos* of all organic life, but rather an acquired condition of what were once immortal, unicellular forms of life. In other words, death was to be understood as a by-product of evolution—a phenomenon that came about as increasingly complex organisms adapted to the external conditions of life. Moreover, Weismann postulated that, while all multicellular organisms were naturally bound to biological death, unicellular organisms could still be regarded as potentially immortal, as their germ-plasm was passed on from generation to generation, sidestepping the laws of natural death. The titles of chapters such as 'The Duration of Life' and 'Life and Death' already show that Weismann's research raised fundamental questions that went beyond science, and that could find philosophical and metaphorical applications in literature and the arts.

It is easy to see why in 1920 Freud went back to Weismann, in whose theories he found an 'unexpected similarity' to his own. The connection with Weismann, though, reveals more than a link between psychoanalysis and late-Victorian science, a link that Freud himself partly disputes later in the same chapter. It shows that Weismann and Freud participated in an extensive cultural debate on death that took place across national and disciplinary boundaries. In other words, rather than responding to a specific condition of modernity brought about by the Great War, Freud's theory of the death drive crystallizes a body of thinking about death that spans science, psychology, philosophy, literature, and the arts, and that connects intellectuals writing on either side of 1900.

In particular, this chapter will suggest that Freud's scientific formulation of the death drive is in dialogue with aesthetic and philosophical experiments carried out in literary works linked to Decadence, a literary movement that originated with

---

[3] See for instance Ernst Mayr, 'Weismann and Evolution', *Journal of the History of Biology* 18/3 (1985), 295–329. On Freud's debt to Weismann, see also Suzanne Raitt, 'Freud's Theory of Metaphor: *Beyond the Pleasure Principle*, Nineteenth-Century Science and Figurative Language', in Helen Small and Trudi Tate (eds), *Literature, Science, Psychoanalysis: Essays in Honour of Gillian Beer* (Oxford and New York: Oxford University Press, 2003), 118–30. Raitt's focus is on Freud's use of metaphor and scientific language.

Charles Baudelaire in the French mid-nineteenth century and peaked (in France and across Europe) in the 1880s and 1890s, the decades that also saw the publication and diffusion of Weismann's experiments in cell biology. Tracing the genealogy of the death drive in Decadent writing enables us to tease out an often overlooked link between the literature of the *fin de siècle* and modernism. It also enables us to reposition Freud as, in the words of Charles Bernheimer, both 'a diagnostician of Decadence' and 'a decadent diagnostician'.[4] Like Max Nordau and Friedrich Nietzsche, Freud was a detached observer of Decadence as a set of cultural practices but his works are also bound up with its mentality, and broadcast its sensibility into the new century. To put it a different way, if Freud's psychoanalysis is deeply implicated in the modernist revolution, the modernity of the early twentieth century is also fundamentally Decadent in its ways of thinking about issues such as aesthetics, sexuality, and the idea of time.

Notions of decay and death are intrinsic to nineteenth-century Decadence, a literary movement that was widely defined by analogy with the last stages of the Greek and Roman civilizations. In his influential essay, 'The Decadent Movement in Literature' (1893), Arthur Symons for instance claimed that, if classical art is chiefly characterized by sanity and proportion, modern Decadence, 'this representative literature of today', should be understood as 'a new and beautiful and interesting disease'.[5] Like Symons's, canonical definitions repeatedly mobilized concepts of belatedness, old age, decrepitude, collapse, and posterity. The most famous of these, by the French critic Paul Bourget (here in the English translation by Havelock Ellis) pushes Decadence right into the territory of the *post mortem*.

> A style of decadence is one in which the unity of the book is decomposed to give place to the independence of the page, in which the page is decomposed to give place to the independence of the phrase, and the phrase to give place to the independence of the word.[6]

Deploying a repulsive imagery of decomposition, Bourget asks readers to conjure not only books and pages, but also language itself, and ideas, values, and moral certainties rotting away under the touch of the Decadent writer. It is as though the thematic fascination with decay infiltrates the very fabric of the Decadent text, which Bourget, playing on images of literary composition and organic decomposition, sees as subjected to the same natural cycles that regulate living organisms. This vision of literature as organic matter stands in sharp contrast to classical ideas of

---

[4] Charles Bernheimer, *Decadent Subjects: The Idea of Decadence in Art, Literature, Philosophy, and Culture of the Fin de Siècle in Europe* (Baltimore, MD and London: Johns Hopkins University Press, 2001), 185.

[5] Arthur Symons, 'The Decadent Movement in Literature', *Harper's New Monthly Magazine* 87 (1893), 859.

[6] Havelock Ellis, 'A Note on Paul Bourget', in *Views and Reviews: A Selection of Uncollected Articles, 1884–1932* (Boston and New York: Houghton Mifflin, 1932), 52. The essay originally appeared in the *Pioneer* (London) in October 1889, signed HE.

writing as a process of monumentalization, i.e. of turning the fleeting and historically bound into the inorganic and hence immortal.[7] The image of an organic Decadence resistant to the proper laws of literature, physics, and ethics appears again and again in late-Victorian criticism, where it is used to particularly good effect by conservative voices. Thus, for instance, in 1895, in the aftermath of the Oscar Wilde trials, the critic Hugh Stutfield speaks of Decadence as 'an exotic growth unsuited to British soil', hoping that it might never 'take permanent root' on this side of the Channel.[8] Such rhetoric is typical of anti-Decadent criticism, where Decadence is repeatedly described as spreading, multiplying, infecting, and contaminating, like a cancer in an otherwise healthy social body.

Even in the midst of his reactionary exaggerations, Stutfield is of course right in diagnosing Decadence as a foreign import. By 1895, though, it was as well rooted in Britain as it was in France; and so was its interest in morbidity. Baudelaire's *Les fleurs du mal* (1857), a volume that is generally regarded as foundational for Decadent literature, is populated with images of death and decay. In one of its most famous poems, 'Une charogne' (A Carcass), for instance, Baudelaire lingers on the description of the corpse of an animal, providing an archetypal image of the aesthetics of decomposition identified by Bourget. The carcass, lying legs-up on the gravel, appears to Baudelaire 'like a lecherous whore' ('comme une femme lubrique') and he takes a perverse pleasure in describing the foul gases, sounds, flies, and maggots that emanate from it.[9] Inverting commonplace associations, this spectacle of death evokes in the poet flowers, music, and the thought of his lover, to whom the poem is addressed, and who is herself envisioned as a putrefying corpse, which the worms will devour with kisses ('vous mangera de baisers'). 'Une charogne' exemplifies a characteristic feature of Baudelaire's poetry that will be much imitated in the following decades: the combination of beauty of form (here represented by the carefully wrought poetic language) with an ugly or corrupt subject matter. The implication is that literature should be able to deal with death and, by extension, with other challenging or even shocking themes without recourse to the sentimental register or other moralizing gestures.

The poems in *Les fleurs du mal* repeatedly come back to visions of tombs and corpses, depicting the modern city as a landscape of death and decay. In several poems, moreover, the poet imagines himself as a dead man or a ghost. This is the

[7] In her recent study of Decadence, individualism, and liberalism, Regenia Gagnier also alerts us to the importance of organic imagery derived from late nineteenth-century biology. She shows that in the same essay Bourget describes the individual's relation to society, at the heart of many Decadent works, as functioning like that between the cell and the organism (Gagnier, *Individualism, Decadence and Globalization* (Basingstoke and New York, NY: Palgrave Macmillan, 2010), 2–3).

[8] Hugh E. M. Stutfield, 'Tommyrotics', *Blackwood's Edinburgh Magazine* 157 (1895), 834.

[9] Quotations from Baudelaire are taken from the bilingual edition, Baudelaire, *The Flowers of Evil*, trans. James McGowan (Oxford and New York, NY: Oxford University Press, 1998); 'Une charogne' is on pp. 58–63.

case in 'Le mort joyeux' ('The Joyful Corpse'), which opens with a playful, characteristic variation on what Freud would later call the death drive: 'In a rich land,
fertile, replete with snails / I'd like to dig myself a spacious pit / Where I might
spread at leisure my old bones / And sleep unnoticed, like a shark at sea' ('Dans une
terre grasse et pleine d'escargots / Je veux creuser moi-même une fosse profonde /
Où je puisse à loisir étaler mes vieux os / Et dormir dans l'oubli comme un requin
dans l'onde').[10] These verses express more than a macabre taste: Baudelaire celebrates
death as a heightened state of feeling, only paradoxically figured through images
of absence and negativity ('l'oubli'). Death, in actual fact, is full of vital energies—
grotesquely figured here as maggots and snails—while being alive means being part
of the undistinguished mass of humanity, depressingly unintelligent and unfeeling.
The poet therefore prefers death to life because it enables him to remove himself
from all that is banal and frustrating in the world of the living. As a violent oblit-
eration of the commonplace, death works just like poetry, and in these verses it
figures repeatedly as a startling symbol for the poetic or the aesthetic: death is a
privileged space that confers distinction and superiority on the individual; it is,
paradoxically, a state that ennobles organic life by dissolving and perverting its
fabric, liberating it from social habits and moral schemata.

Baudelaire's poetics of death will become one of the most visible hallmarks of
Decadent writing, crossing the generic boundaries of poetry to short stories (indeed,
Baudelaire had himself been heavily influenced by Edgar Allan Poe), fiction, and
criticism. In his poems Baudelaire suggests that death is not separate from life but
at the very heart of it; or, to put it another way, that death and life should not be
understood as opposites, but rather as contiguous, porous dimensions. On the aesthetic plane, by insisting that there is no fixed boundary between the organic and
inorganic, light and darkness, plenitude and emptiness, the known and the
unknown, meaning and its negation, this Decadent poetics of death is a cry against
binary logic and semantic closure.

But Baudelaire's attempt to rethink the stark differentiation between life and
death also calls to mind Weismann's biological experiments, which, at the time of
the publication of Les fleurs du mal, were still some years in the future. This overlap
between the literature and science of death helps us to dispel the persistent myth
that Decadence operates in antithesis to the positivist mentality.[11] We only need to
zoom forwards to J. K. Huysmans's Against Nature (À rebours, 1884), which appeared
at the height of Weismann's success, to find an example of how the Decadent text
tests the limits of knowledge by enacting a fantastic scientific experiment, and to

---

[10] Ibid., 140–1.

[11] On the alliance of Decadence and scientific positivism, see Christine Ferguson, 'Decadence as
Scientific Fulfillment', Publications of the Modern Language Association of America (PMLA) 117/3 (2002),
465–78. More generally, on repositioning Decadence within nineteenth-century culture, see editors'
introduction to Liz Constable, Dennis Denisoff, and Matthew Potolski (eds), Perennial Decay: On the
Aesthetics and Politics of Decadence (Philadelphia, PA: University of Pennsylvania Press, 1999).

see that the Decadent fascination with systems and taxonomies is heavily indebted to scientific methodology.

Going back to Baudelaire, in English literature his poetry left a particularly strong legacy among writers linked to Aestheticism and the followers of the doctrine of art for art's sake (A. C. Swinburne was his first critic and imitator), although his lure would still be very powerful on T. S. Eliot, who praised Baudelaire as a prophet of modernity. One of the key figures of the aesthetic movement, Walter Pater, thought that 'aesthetic poetry', by which he meant the best modern poetry, worked by contrasting the seduction of the material world to the suggestion of 'the shortness of life'. His own writings are full of this complex sentiment, which he glosses as 'the desire of beauty quickened by the sense of death'.[12] In the short story 'The Child in the House' (1878), for instance, Pater examines how an early encounter with death affects the aesthetic education of his young protagonist, Florian Deleal. Florian remembers how, as a child, rambling around in a churchyard on a beautiful summer morning, he came upon 'an open grave for a child - a dark space on the brilliant grass - the black mould lying heaped up round it, weighing down the little jewelled branches of the dwarf rose-bushes in flower'.[13] While Florian is repulsed by this sight which, for the first time, triggers in him 'the physical horror of death', it is clear that fear is mingled with elements of aesthetic desire, conveyed by Pater through the striking image of the rose blooms, whose memory is inseparable from that of the open grave. This epiphany forms Florian's consciousness of death, and its peculiar compound of sensations and emotions repeatedly comes back to him in adult life, at unexpected times, casting a shadow on moments of happiness and companionship, just as its buried memory compels him to go and seek out the faces of the dead in cemeteries and morgues.

The subtle psychological treatment of the death drive in 'The Child in the House' shows Pater at his most proto-modernist and proto-psychoanalytic, as he studies the workings of childhood memories on adult consciousness and develops his story along a pattern of trauma and compulsion to repeat. In his best-known book, *The Renaissance* (1873), the aesthetic lure of death is particularly prominent in the chapter on Leonardo, a work on which Freud would later draw in his psychoanalytic study of the Renaissance painter. Pater emphasises Leonardo's ability to understand death and to convey the 'fascination of corruption' in his art.[14] Given what has been said so far about Decadence and science, it is important to remember that Leonardo was a scientist as well as an artist, a double identity that Pater glosses in the chapter as a double pull towards 'curiosity', on the one hand, and 'desire of beauty' on the other.[15] It is the

---

[12]   Walter Pater, 'Aesthetic Poetry', in *Appreciations* (London: Macmillan, 1889), 227.

[13]   Pater, 'The Child in the House', in *Imaginary Portraits*, ed. Lene Østermark-Johansen (London: MHRA, 2014), 94.

[14]   Pater, *The Renaissance: Studies in Art and Poetry*, ed. Donald L. Hill (Berkeley and Los Angeles: University of California Press, 1980), 83.

[15]   Ibid., 86.

spirit of science that drives Leonardo to penetrate deeper and deeper into the secrets of the physical world, up to the ultimate boundary of knowledge—death, 'the last curiosity'.[16] A similar attraction towards death can be seen in his art. Pater wants to show his readers that Leonardo's paintings represent the human body as inhabiting a dimension suspended between life and death. This characteristic is especially true of his portraits, which Pater sees as a window into what lies beyond reality and the visible. In the portrait of Beatrice d'Este, for instance, 'Leonardo seems to have caught some presentiment of early death, painting her precise and grave, full of the refinement of the dead, in sad earth-coloured raiment, set with pale stones'.[17] Pater's impressionistic description works to translate Leonardo's macabre vision into language, as words such as grave, dead, earth, and stones pile up to evoke death and burial, creating a Baudelairean dissolution of organic and inorganic matter. In this painting Pater discovers a shocking commingling of human body and earth which in fact expresses, in perverse terms, a universal condition of portrait painting, an artistic genre that achieves life-likeness through the use of pigments and other substances.

Pater, in other words, traces the theme of death in Leonardo's Renaissance art in order to broadcast French Decadence to British readers, instructing them not only in how to read Leonardo as a Decadent *avant la lettre*, but also in how to reread the history of art through the Decadent sensibility in order to discover there new and perhaps perverse meanings. Nowhere are these aims more successfully met than in the famous ekphrasis of the Mona Lisa, whom Pater describes as a 'vampire, [who] has been dead many times, and learned the secrets of the grave', and as at once reincarnation and mythic synthesis of the dead women of biblical and classical antiquity, St Anne and Helen of Troy.[18] The Mona Lisa is a compendium of ancient and modern theories of death, from metempsychosis to evolution. Paradoxically, although she is in closer contact with death than any other image in the chapter, Pater's Mona Lisa is far from being a dead end: with its lyric cadences and sepulchral undertones, Pater's description will become iconic of the new aesthetic sensibility of the *fin de siècle* and, as such, it will have a productive afterlife in the form of quotations, homages, and rewritings in the decades on either side of the turn of the century, from Oscar Wilde's playful take in 'The Critic as Artist' (1891) to W. B. Yeats's verse rendition in *The Oxford Book of Modern Verse* (1936), where Pater's ekphrasis features as the point of origin and foundational text of modern English poetry.

Yeats's use of Pater helps us to see the long history of the reception of Baudelaire's original yoking of morbid poetics and transgressive aesthetics that goes from the early days of English Aestheticism to the inter-war period. The crucial middle step in this history is in the 1890s, with the work of poets such as Ernest Dowson, Lionel Johnson, and John Davidson. Yeats famously dubbed these figures the 'tragic generation', referring both to the prevalence of dark themes in their works and, on

---

[16] Ibid., 101.   [17] Ibid., 88.   [18] Ibid., 99.

the biographical plane, to the early or violent deaths of these poets, brought about by self-destructive habits such as alcohol abuse. Like Freud, Yeats was a diagnostician of Decadence. In his autobiography his assessment of the tragic generation is at once an act of homage and marker of distance: he acknowledges the importance of these 'minor' poets of the 1890s, with whom he was closely associated, ascribing to them a distinctive chapter in British literary history; but, at the same time, he makes it clear that their culture was doomed, and destined to be superseded by a full-fledged, healthier version of modernity which Yeats surveys from the vantage point of the new century. Employing a mythic pattern of thought to which he was strongly drawn in his work, Yeats presents his involvement in Decadence as a kind of temporary death or *katabasis*: a descent into the underworld that was the necessary precondition for regeneration and rebirth.

Yeats believed that what helped him to turn his back on the self-destructive culture of Decadence was his discovery of Irish nationalism. In this sense, his diagnosis of the tragic generation contains a broader reflection on the relationship between Decadence and the late-Victorian idea of the nation: while economically successful and politically powerful nations such as France and England spiralled into the type of cultural pessimism that generated a perverse fascination with decay and death as existential conditions, emergent nations such as Ireland embraced modernity optimistically, profiting from its ethos of youth, intellectual energy, and promises of renewal. This analysis is not unproblematic, as it shares some of the assumptions behind Nordau's *Degeneration* (*Entartung*, 1892) and other conservative critiques of late nineteenth-century Decadence as a social disease. It does however help us to see another important aspect of the Decadent death drive: the belief that, like individual organisms, societies and nations are also subjected to biological cycles of birth, growth, decline, and death. This idea according to which the more advanced is a culture in the march towards civilization, the closer it gets to collapse and extinction, had a strong purchase for intellectuals at the time, especially as it became compounded with theories of cultural entropy in the final decades of the century. The *fin de siècle* in particular abounds with sensational proclamations of the death of civilization as we know it: these range from popular fictional treatments, in dystopian and gothic settings, in H. G. Wells's *Time Machine* (1895) and Bram Stoker's *Dracula* (1897), to Friedrich Nietzsche's famous cry about the death of God, which heralds the arrival of a post-Christian order that calls for a complete revision of our moral codes.[19]

In this context, the death of the civilizations of classical antiquity—Egypt, Greece, and Rome—could be read as a powerful *memento mori* to the great imperial capitals of the modern world such as Paris and London, where choice remnants of the classical past, shipped from the South and the East, filled museums that were meant to proclaim the political triumph of the colonial superpowers. In this age of unparalleled

---

[19] Nietzsche pronounced the death of God for the first time in the parable of the madman in *The Gay Science* (*Die fröhliche Wissenschaft*, 1882).

activity in classical archaeology, the earth was being dug up more than ever before in order to excavate the material remains of civilizations that had lain buried in it for centuries. The return of these objects had a ghostly appeal about it—an unnatural crossing of the boundary between death and life—captured in literature in an international revival of the archaeological fantastic, a genre populated with images of reincarnated gods, cursed objects, and animated statues that goes from Henry James's 'The Last of the Valerii' (1874) to Pater's *Imaginary Portraits* (1887), Vernon Lee's *Hauntings* (1890), Arthur Machen's *The Great God Pan* (1890, 1894), E. M. Forster's 'The Story of a Panic' (1904), and Wilhelm Jensen's 'Gradiva' (1907), the novella on which Freud would base a well-known essay in which he sets up a parallel between psychoanalysis and archaeology as sciences for the excavation of mysteries.

The notion of a defunct, decomposed, and re-exhumed classicism exercised an especially strong appeal on Decadent taste. In *Against Nature*, Des Esseintes looks with enthusiasm to the collapse of the Roman Empire as an historical analogue for his own times. Huysmans's Decadent (anti)hero is a student of ancient Decadence who amasses an impressive collection of late Latin literature in his library. By a process of *mise en abyme*, the Decadent novel itself works as a collection or archive of Decadent taste: it preserves and displays the death of other civilizations for the benefits of a modernity that understands itself as the end of history. In *Against Nature* the relationship between a dead but generative classicism and modernity is conceived of in perverse terms, like that between the carcass and the maggots in Baudelaire's 'Une charogne'. Like individual death, the Decadent death of history is never simple closure, though: it is not the final triumph of the inorganic over life, the consigning of meaning to silence and oblivion; rather, it produces new and aggressive organic mutations, new combinations of organic and inorganic matter— like violets springing from the grave, according to Pater's favourite variation on Baudelaire's maggot-ridden carcass.

Where Decadent theories of the death of civilization diverge most sharply from the positivist mentality is not so much that they insist on death as an inevitable fact of the past and the future, but that they regard it as a condition of the present: revising traditional ideas of time, Decadence thus sees death not as the negation of life but as inseparable and coterminous with it. This paradox goes to the heart of the problem of the death drive as conceptualized by Weismann's biology and Freud's psychoanalysis. One of its major consequences is that it entails a radical rethinking of the instinct of reproduction, which can no longer be understood simply as a force for the preservation and renewal of life. When dealing with the question of sex, both Freud and Weismann look back to another late nineteenth-century biologist, the embryologist Alexander Götte, who had argued that death should be seen as the direct consequence of reproduction.[20] Although Freud (like Weismann before him) is sceptical of this hypothesis, he is nonetheless forced to question the fundamental

[20] See Freud, *Beyond the Pleasure Principle*, 86.

relationship between sexual desire, as prime manifestation of the pleasure princi-ple, and death, postulating for the first time a psychological link between the two.

Once again the scientific and literary canons of these years operate in parallel. We have already seen how Baudelaire, comparing his lover to a corpse, depicts death as a sexual temptress in 'Une charogne' (the same is also true in several other poems in *Les fleurs du mal*). In Britain similar themes come to the fore in a large literary and visual oeuvre that goes from the Pre-Raphaelite art of the mid-century to the Decadent and Symbolist works of the *fin de siècle*, where death is provoca-tively coupled with physical beauty and eroticism or even staged as a moment of sexual ecstasy. Swinburne's *Poems and Ballads* (1866) is marked by a persistent, deliberately shocking fusion of macabre and erotic themes that did not fail to attract the opprobrium of contemporary critics. In one of the most widely criticized poems in the volume, 'Anactoria', Swinburne channels Sappho's voice as she indulges in a violent fantasy that has as its object a former female lover.

> I would my love could kill thee; I am satiated
> With seeing thee live, and fain would have thee dead.
> I would earth had thy body as fruit to eat,
> And no mouth but some serpent's found thee sweet.
> I would find grievous ways to have thee slain,
> Intense device, and superflux of pain;
> Vex thee with amorous agonies, and shake
> Life at thy lips, and leave it there to ache;
> Strain out thy soul with pangs too soft to kill,
> Intolerable interludes, and infinite ill;
> Relapse and reluctation of the breath,
> Dumb tunes and shuddering semitones of death.[21]

In these verses death is depicted as the culmination of the erotic game: the con-summation and *telos* of sexual desire. The open sadomasochism of 'Anactoria' makes apparent a universal condition that is explored with various degrees of clarity in Swinburne's early poetry, which is populated with scenes that blur the lines between death, sex, and violence, and which repeatedly stage the poet's eroticized desire to die by the hand of dominatrices, *femmes fatales*, and ghostly Venuses. Death for Swinburne is the secret side of sex: it reveals the uncomforta-ble truths of sexuality—first and foremost that libido works to destroy life rather than affirm it—when viewed outside the euphemistic and sentimental trappings of bourgeois culture.

The sensation caused by Swinburne's dark *eros* sent ripples across late-Victorian and Decadent poetry; but the work that more than any other set out to unmask the destructive and self-destructive energies of sexual desire is Oscar Wilde's drama *Salomé* (1893), in which it is easy to see the influence both of Swinburne and of the

---

[21] A. C. Swinburne, *Poems and Ballads* (London: Penguin, 2000), 48.

French Decadent and Symbolist traditions. In this rewriting of the biblical story teeming with proto-Freudian tropes, the heroine has the ascetic John the Baptist beheaded as a punishment for turning down her sexual advances. The play climaxes with a memorable necrophiliac encounter in which Salomé kisses the severed head of the prophet. Sexual desire, in other words, generates the desire to kill and then, more perversely still, to taste death and mingle with it—a fantasy that is destined to become reality in this text that is set on breaking every last taboo, as, after the kiss, Herod orders the execution of his step-daughter, disgusted by the spectacle of her perverse sexual ecstasy. *Salomé* is a bridge between the avant-gardes of the nineteenth and twentieth centuries not only for its psychosexual interests but because its distinctly *fin-de-siècle* Symbolism will be successfully translated into musical modernism by Richard Strauss in his operatic setting of the play (1905), which renewed its topicality all over Europe at a time when Wilde's Decadent aesthetics were otherwise starting to lose their power to shock.

Since Mario Praz's groundbreaking *Romantic Agony* (*La carne, la morte e il diavolo nella letteratura romantica*, 1930)—a study that leans heavily on Freudian psychoanalysis—scholars have explored various aspects of the overlap of death and *eros* in the literature of this period. In particular, critics have drawn attention to a misogynistic taste at work in many of these texts, which are explicitly or implicitly invested in controlling and degrading the female body and eroticizing female suffering. In most recent years, as Foucauldian and queer criticism have established the *fin de siècle* as a pivotal period in the history of homosexuality, the interest has shifted to same-sex desire, which was deemed socially unacceptable and criminalized at the time, and therefore could only be represented indirectly and by allusion. Indeed, looking at the canon of homosexual writing of the late-Victorian years, it is impossible not to be struck by the insistence with which same-sex eroticism is associated with death and morbidity. Pater, for instance, consistently sublimates homosexual desire in the form of macabre imagery. In his novel *Marius the Epicurean* (1885)—a work that is punctuated with philosophical disquisitions on the meaning and aesthetics of death in the classical and Christian traditions—we are given a vivid description of how Marius, the young protagonist, nurses his friend Flavian through the latter's terminal illness and tends to his corpse after his untimely death. Perhaps as a result of this episode, Marius himself will always feel a morbid curiosity towards death (not unlike Leonardo in *The Renaissance*) and at the end of the novel he deliberately takes on the identity of his Christian friend Cornelius knowing that he would be martyred by Roman soldiers in his place. These narrative and plot devices give Pater the licence to represent physical intimacy and emotional intensity between men, associating same-sex desire with purity and heroism, and thus lifting it from the pejorative connotations of transgression, base instincts, and libidinal excess that were prevalent at the time.

A similar poetics of morbidity pervades A. E. Housman's *A Shropshire Lad* (1896), a collection that, albeit outside the Decadent canon in terms of form and cultural allegiance, assimilates aspects of its perverse aesthetics. In *A Shropshire Lad* death is systematically presented, with bitter matter-of-factness, as the inevitable consequence of desire and *eros*. Like Pater, Housman makes no explicit reference to homoeroticism; but it is easy to see how the lyrics of *A Shropshire Lad*, set in a very bleak present, offer a stark, pessimistic reflection on the impossibility of same-sex relationships in modern England. Suicides and violent deaths of young men—many of them for the love of un-gendered subjects—take the place of healthy natural relationships. Updating classical pastoral poetry (including its free acceptance of homosexual eroticism) in a macabre key, Housman populates the collection with images of deaths, burials, graves, suicides, and executions, and of dead, mutilated, and punished male bodies.[22] Politically, the poems can be read as a cry against social prejudice and the injustice of the criminal system with regards to male homosexuality. But, as with Pater, it is also possible to detect in them elements of internalized homophobia which works in the opposite direction, by policing same-sex desire, especially when the dead male body becomes an eroticized spectacle, as it often does, and when death is problematically equated with happiness and emotional fulfilment.

Outside the male canon, the poetic duo Michael Field (Katharine Bradley and Edith Cooper) makes use of a similar poetics of morbidity and death in order to represent lesbian sexuality and female same-sex desire. Michael Field's work has come to prominence in recent years both for its imaginative use of the lyric and as the rare instance of a Victorian open treatment of female homoeroticism. The influence of Baudelaire and the Decadent tradition is strong on Michael Field, whose lyrics often present death as a space of intimacy and secrecy—a desirable state that enables the poets to escape the social constraints of the actual, lived reality of the late nineteenth century. Their collection *Underneath the Bough* (1893) contains many instances of poems that represent eroticism by means of macabre imagery, the most extreme of which is a hymn to Thanatos—the personification of death in ancient Greek mythology. The poets invoke Thanatos to transport them to the realm of the dead, where they imagine themselves in 'endless revellings' among 'unpolluted things'.[23] Michael Field's mythic voyage beyond the grave is a voyage of exploration—an aesthetic or intellectual journey into the Decadent world view— but also a performance of *eros*, conveyed in the poem through a vocabulary of mystic ecstasy. The 'unpolluted' communion they visualize in death is set up as an implicit antitype to the view of queer sexuality as impure and unnatural prevalent

---

[22] See especially lyrics IX and XVI, in A. E. Housman, *Collected Poems and Selected Prose* (London and New York, NY: Penguin, 1989). Joseph Bristow reads the poetics of death explored by Housman and other 1890s writers as linked to the way these lyrics historicize their own modernity in relation to the Greek and Latin classics. See Bristow, 'How Decadent Poems Die', in Jason David Hall and Alex Murray (eds), *Decadent Poetics: Literature and Form at the British Fin de Siècle* (Basingstoke and New York: Palgrave Macmillan, 2013), 26–45.

[23] Michael Field, *Underneath the Bough* (London: George Bell and Sons, 1893), 59–60.

among the living. In representing themselves as worshippers of death the two women therefore tap into a Decadent sensibility that allows them to encode homo-eroticism in the public sphere, bypassing moral censorship; but, like their male contemporaries, their acts of queer resistance, with their striking readiness to relinquish the world, risk degenerating into philosophical pessimism and self-destructive gestures.

Later in the twentieth century, critics would routinely refer to Thanatos as a byword for the Freudian death drive, in order to stress its mythic matrix. Freud himself would go back to the relationship between *eros* and the death drive in his late works, especially in *Civilization and its Discontents* (*Das Unbehagen in der Kultur*, 1930), where the dialectic of these two forces is given supreme importance as the prime meaning of civilization and 'essential content of all life'.[24] What emerges from this brief survey of the Decadent prehistory of the Freudian theory of the death drive is that in the late nineteenth century the ambition to revise the boundaries between life and death emerges in parallel in the fields of science and literature, creating a productive dialogue between the two and paving the way for psychoanalysis. In writings associated with Decadence in particular, the death drive leads to daring experiments that challenged contemporary artistic and social norms and, in its coupling with sexual desire, facilitated the articulation of a distinctly queer perverse poetics. Like Pater's and Housman's, Michael Field's representations of homosexual desire would of course not have been legible as such to all readers. Indeed they would become so in the twentieth century largely thanks to the interpretative tools made available by psychoanalysis, completing the productive synergy between Decadent aesthetics and psychoanalytic theory that this chapter has attempted to sketch.

FURTHER READING

Bernheimer, Charles. *Decadent Subjects: The Idea of Decadence in Art, Literature, Philosophy, and Culture of the Fin de Siècle in Europe* (Baltimore, MD and London: Johns Hopkins University Press, 2001).

Bronfen, Elisabeth. *Over Her Dead Body: Death, Femininity, and the Aesthetic* (Manchester: Manchester University Press, 1992).

Davis, Whitney. *Queer Beauty: Sexuality and Aesthetics from Winckelmann to Freud and Beyond* (New York: Columbia University Press, 2010).

Dowling, Linda. *Language and Decadence in the Victorian Fin de Siècle* (Princeton, NJ: Princeton University Press, 1986).

Downing, Lisa. *Desiring the Dead: Necrophilia and Nineteenth-Century French Literature* (Oxford: Legenda, 2003).

---

[24] Freud, *Civilization and its Discontents*, trans. David McLintock (London and New York: Penguin, 2002), 58.

Edelman, Lee. *No Future: Queer Theory and the Death Drive* (Durham, NC: Duke University Press, 2004).

Freud, Sigmund. *Beyond the Pleasure Principle and Other Writings*, trans. John Reddick (London and New York: Penguin, 2003).

Gagnier, Regenia. *Individualism, Decadence and Globalization* (Basingstoke: Palgrave Macmillan, 2010).

Raitt, Suzanne. 'Freud's Theory of Metaphor: *Beyond the Pleasure Principle*, Nineteenth-Century Science and Figurative Language', in Helen Small and Trudi Tate (eds), *Literature, Science, Psychoanalysis: Essays in Honour of Gillian Beer* (Oxford and New York: Oxford University Press, 2003).

Stewart, Garrett. *Death Sentences: Styles of Dying in British Fiction* (Cambridge, MA: Harvard University Press, 1984).

Weir, David. *Decadence and the Making of Modernism* (Amherst, MA: University of Massachusetts Press, 1995).

CHAPTER 4

CELTICISM

DANIEL G. WILLIAMS

Before 'entering Wales' in his 1905 travelogue *Beautiful Wales*, the poet Edward Thomas assesses the impact of other writers on his conception of the Welsh. The first group he identifies are 'lovers of the Celt'. These individuals are 'fine flowers of sounding cities' who prefer '*crême de menthe* and *opal hush* to metheglin or stout, and Kensington to Eryri and Connemara'.[1] The influence of these metropolitan Celtophiles seems largely negative, for they are 'a class of "decadents" not unrelated to Mallarmé, and the aesthetes' who wish to 'go about the world in a state of self-satisfied dejection, interrupted, and perhaps sustained, by days when they consume strange mixed liquors to the tune of all the fine old Celtic songs which are fashionable'.[2] Thomas is usefully drawing our attention to the fact that what Holbrook Jackson would refer to in 1913 as the 'discovery of the Celt' was closely linked to aestheticism in art, and to metropolitan perceptions of the 'Celtic fringe'.[3] 'If you can discover a Celtic great-grandmother, you are at once among the chosen', notes Thomas of these aesthetes.

Thomas himself was London-born, with strong familial connections to Wales and to the Welsh community in Swindon, and while he registers the influence of the London Celtophiles, he notes that there are alternatives to their conceptions of the Celt. 'The typical Celt is seldom an imperialist', he notes before expressing his preference for 'the kind of Celt whom I met in Wales' on a stormy August night, who possessed 'a fair-skinned, high-cheek-boned face, wizened like a walnut, with much black hair about it, that yet did not conceal the flat, straight, eloquent mouth'. Once Thomas had demonstrated his ability to pronounce 'Bwlch-y-Rhiw', the two men proceeded to share a beer and the Celt revealed 'that he had played many parts – he was always playing – before he took to the road: he had been a booking-office clerk,

---

[1] Edward Thomas, *Wales* (Oxford: Oxford University Press, 1983), 10. First published as *Beautiful Wales* (London: A & C Black, 1905).

[2] Ibid., 11.

[3] Holbrook Jackson, *The Eighteen Nineties: A Review of Art and Ideas at the Close of the Nineteenth Century* (London: Pelican, 1950), 147.

a soldier, a policeman, a gamekeeper,' and traced 'what he called his variability' to 'the feminine gender'.[4] Thomas's critique of the 'lovers of the Celt' anticipates, as Andrew Webb has noted, post-colonial responses to 'the ways in which a colonizing power maintains the myth of its own supremacy', and his description of the Welshman's role-playing 'anticipates (without fully articulating) postcolonial insights into the hybridity and gendering of those in colonial situations'.[5] But even in his rejection of metropolitan distance for immersion in Wales itself, and despite his sympathetic account of the Welshman and his language, the facial descriptions and gendered terms deployed seem to reinforce rather than to undermine the terms of Victorian Celticism.

It is by now common to consider late nineteenth-century Celticism a highly influential discourse which was an internally inflected variant of imperial Orientalism. Joep Leerssen for example notes that the classification 'Celtic' was imposed from outside and is similar to 'the construction of concepts like "the Negro" or "the Oriental" as analyzed in its hegemonistic intent by critics such as Frantz Fanon and Edward Said', while Simon Brooks has suggested that Celticism amounts to an intellectual fraud, sustained by academia, but ultimately reliant on an irrelevant and spurious connection between the 'Celtic' peoples and their diverse literatures and historical experiences.[6] In *Orientalism* (1978) and *Culture and Imperialism* (1993), Said argued that Western empires constructed 'the Orient' through discourses—scientific, rational, analytic—that reinforced hierarchical relationships, subjugated colonized cultures, and legitimated Western authority. While Said's theory has been critiqued from several directions, its application to minorities within Western societies is particularly problematic.[7] In Edward Thomas's *Beautiful Wales* the apparent coexistence of identification and distance, of sympathetic engagement and withdrawn observation, of respect for an individual coupled with sweeping generalizations about his 'race', suggests that Celticism emerges from moments of disorientation rather than of straightforward subjugation—moments in which the metropolitan or imperial mind, far from dominating and categorizing a pliable native environment to the scientific and epistemological categories of the

---

[4] Thomas, *Wales*, 10, 13–14.

[5] Andrew Webb, *Edward Thomas and World Literary Studies: Wales, Anglocentrism and English Literature* (Cardiff: University of Wales Press, 2013), 143–4.

[6] Joep Leerssen, 'Celticism', in Terence Brown (ed.), *Celticism* (Atlanta, GA: Rodopi, 1996) 4, 6; Simon Brooks, *Yr Hawl i Oroesi* (Llanrwst: Gwasg Carreg Gwalch, 2009) 105–7.

[7] Edward Said, *Orientalism: Western Conceptions of the Orient* (London: Penguin, 1995); Said, *Culture and Imperialism* (London: Vintage, 1994); Daniel G. Williams, *Ethnicity and Cultural Authority: From Arnold to Du Bois* (Edinburgh: Edinburgh University Press, 2006), 9–10. Gregory Castle draws on Said in examining the impact of anthropology on the Irish Revival in his *Modernism and the Celtic Revival* (Cambridge: Cambridge University Press, 2001). 'Celtic' is unfortunately equated with 'Irish' throughout Castle's study. His argument that the clash between 'civilized observers' and 'primitive society' existed in 'no other context save that of the Anglo-Irish revival' (29) is only sustainable if Wales and Scotland are ignored.

centre, finds itself being relativized, at a loss, disoriented, and being forced to turn back on itself. The Celt's ability to 'play roles' leads one to question the authenticity of his presumed identity, and while the anxieties in Thomas's descriptions may be traced to his own national allegiances and background, they are typical of responses towards the Celt in the late Victorian and early modernist eras. The encounter with the Celt tends not to culminate in an act of English epistemological mastery and political domination, but rather in a sense of uncertainty, scepticism, and self-questioning. This chapter seeks to explore the tensions and ambivalences that characterized the construction of Celticism in the late nineteenth and early twentieth centuries, and which have continued to be prevalent in analyses of the movement's cultural and political consequences ever since.

Constructing the Celt

Joep Leersen's argument that Celticism was 'imposed from outside' the Celtic countries is widely accepted. Several critics and commentators have analyzed the influence that the Victorian men of letters Ernest Renan (in France) and Matthew Arnold (in Britain) had on Victorian constructions of the Celt.[8] Arnold's lectures *On the Study of Celtic Literature* (1867) drew on Renan's *La poésie des races celtiques* (1859), and had a profound influence on the idea of the Celt that emerged in the 1890s. In introducing *Lyra Celtica*, a comprehensive anthology of ancient and modern poetry from the Celtic countries published in 1896, the Scot William Sharp noted that Arnold, writing 'with the true instinct of genius', was 'the most sympathetic and penetrating critic of the Celtic imagination'.[9] Similarly, in his 'Introduction' to the 1910 Everyman edition of *On the Study of Celtic Literature*, the Welshman Ernest Rhys noted that while Arnold 'appears confused by the thickets of Welsh and Irish philology...his account, after forty years and more of research by later explorers, is still a highly stimulating one to read'.[10]

Arnold envisaged a Celt characterized by certain enduring visible traits. 'The Celtic genius', he noted, has 'sentiment as its main basis, with love of beauty, charm, and spirituality for its excellence...ineffectualness and self-will for its deficit'.[11] The Celt is 'always ready to react against despotism of fact', is 'sensual', and is 'particularly

---

[8] Robert J. C. Young, *Colonial Desire: Hybridity in Theory, Culture, and Race* (London: Routledge, 1995), 67–9; Williams, *Ethnicity and Cultural Authority*, 126–33.

[9] William Sharp, 'Introduction', in Elizabeth A. Sharp (ed.), *Lyra Celtica: An Anthology of Representative Celtic Poetry* (Edinburgh: Patrick Geddes, 1896), xliii.

[10] Ernest Rhys, 'Introduction', in Matthew Arnold, *On the Study of Celtic Literature and Other Essays* (London: Everyman Library, 1910), vii.

[11] R. H. Super (ed.), *The Complete Prose Works of Matthew Arnold*, 11 vols (Ann Arbor, MI: University of Michigan Press, 1962), III, 311.

disposed to feel the spell of the feminine idiosyncrasy; he has an affinity to it; he is not far from its secret'.[12] This inevitably, and crucially, makes the Celt 'ineffectual in politics', a notion that is developed further:

> The bent of our time is towards science, towards knowing things as they are; so the Celt's claims towards having his genius and its works fairly treated, as objects of scientific investigation, the Saxon can hardly reject, when these claims are urged simply on their own merits, and are not mixed up with extraneous pretensions which jeopardize them.[13]

The desire to observe the Celts scientifically while denying them any hope of national self-determination is made explicit. The Saxons are the agents of history, who have the power to 'reject' or accept the Celt's claims to genius as they like. The relatively benevolent Arnold is prepared to accept that claim, as long as it is not part of a wider political agenda. He thus goes on to produce a contributionist argument in which the Celts are flattered into accepting a subsidiary position for themselves. The Celts can contribute their sensuality, femininity, and natural magic in counterbalancing the Teutonic, instrumental, and culturally philistine tendencies which coexist within the historically emergent Englishman. The Celt is being invited to assimilate.

Ironically, Arnold's chapters had little impact upon that 'Philistine' English society for whom he wrote—indeed he was lambasted for being a Celtophile by *The Times*— but his lectures cast a long shadow over the emergent cultures of the Celtic nations themselves.[14] It is within the early writings of William Butler Yeats that we encounter the most profound engagement with Arnold's ideas. As early as his chapter on 'The Celtic Element in Literature' (1897), Yeats sought to 'restate' Arnold's views on the Celts 'and see where they are helpful and where they are hurtful'.[15] His unambiguous conclusion that 'I do not think any of us who write about Ireland have built any argument upon them' sits uneasily beside Yeats's attempts at defining the unique characteristics of Celtic culture in the 1890s.[16] Yeats argued, for instance, that the Irish cultural revival was 'the revolt of the soul against the intellect', and in an article on Ernest Rhys's *Welsh Ballads* he noted that 'were it not for one or two delicate and musical translations in "The Study of Celtic Literature", Welsh poetry would not even be a great name to most of us'.[17]

---

[12] Ibid., III, 344, 345, 347.

[13] Ibid., III, 299. It is worth stressing the originality of Arnold's analysis within the context of the period's anti-Celticism. A sense of English views of the Celts in the 1860s can be sensed from the reviews of Arnold's lectures that appeared in *The Times* and the *Daily Telegraph*, where critiques of Arnold's views give way to attacks on Wales and the Welsh. These are reprinted in Carl Dawson and John Pfordresher (eds), *Matthew Arnold: Prose Writings: The Critical Heritage* (London: Routledge, 1995), 159–66. See also L. P. Curtis, *Anglo Saxons and Celts: A Study of Anglo-Irish prejudice in Victorian England* (Bridgeport, CT: Conference on British Studies, 1968).

[14] See note 13.

[15] W. B. Yeats, *Essays and Introductions* (London: Macmillan, 1961), 174.

[16] Ibid., 174.

[17] John Kelly et al. (eds), *The Collected Letters of W. B. Yeats*, 4 vols (Oxford: Clarendon Press, 1986–), I, 303; John P. Frayne and Colton Johnson (eds), *Uncollected Prose by W. B. Yeats*, 2 vols (London:

Even when anxiously rejecting Arnold's observations on Celticism, Yeats's critique is little more than a subtle change of emphasis, as opposed to the wholesale revision of Arnold's views that the polemical thrust of Yeats's own argument may lead us to expect. Where Arnold explains the 'turn for natural magic' by invoking the 'Celtic strain' in English literature, Yeats placed Celtic primitivism within an internationalist context noting that 'literature dwindles' if it is not 'constantly flooded with the passions and beliefs of ancient times', such as 'the Slavonic, the Finnish, the Scandinavian and the Celtic'. Of these, 'the Celtic alone has been for centuries close to the main river of European literature' and 'has again and again brought the vivifying spirit of excess into the arts of Europe'.[18] It is difficult to see how this analysis modifies Arnold's argument in any way. Indeed, it is not difficult to imagine this passage appearing in Arnold's Celtic essays. Arnold himself noted that the Celtic contribution to English philistinism derived from the fact that 'there is something Greek in them', and spoke of the Celtic peoples as a 'primitive race'.[19] Indeed, his earlier analysis of the absorption of ancient minority cultures into the emergent nation states of Europe made connections between the Irish absorption into England, the Breton absorption into France, and the Polish absorption into Russia.[20]

Indeed, the Arnoldian basis of Yeats's 'Celt' has been regarded as an example of the way in which a colonized author appropriates the stereotypes ascribed to his people by an imperial power and turns them into positive attributes.[21] Robert Welch talks of Yeats 'completely transforming' Arnold's 'intellectual strategy', and Edward Said makes a similar point in broader terms when discussing Yeats as a poet of 'decolonization'.[22] Yet, in looking at Yeats's response to Arnold, what we note is that nothing is inverted, nothing is transformed. The reason for this lies, interestingly, not in Yeats's own writings—where the positive appropriation of Celtic spirituality and imagination fits the colonial model—but in the evaluation of the Celtic temperament offered by Arnold himself.

Arnold's *On the Study of Celtic Literature*, despite arguing for bringing Celtic culture fully into the political and cultural system of England, 'reinforced an interpretation of Celticism that strengthened irreconcilable ideas of separatism,' as R. F. Foster notes.[23] Yeats's use of Arnold's ideas as the basis for Irish cultural independence derives, as Foster implies, from a tension embedded within Arnold's argument

Macmillan, 1975), II, 92. John Kelleher notes Yeats's reliance on Arnold's essays as a source for quotations from Celtic writings in 'Matthew Arnold and the Celtic Revival', in Harry Levin (ed.), *Perspectives of Criticism* (Cambridge, MA: Harvard University Press, 1950), 204–5.

[18] Yeats, *Essays and Introductions*, 185.

[19] Super, *Complete Prose Works*, III 296, 384.

[20] In 'England and the Italian Question' (1859). See ibid., I, 73.

[21] For example, see Robert Welch, 'Introduction' in his edited *W. B. Yeats: Writings on Irish Folklore, Legend and Myth* (London: Penguin, 1993), xxiii. For an account of this appropriation of colonial stereotypes, see Ania Loomba, *Colonialism/Postcolonialism* (London: Routledge, 1998), 212–15.

[22] Welch, 'Introduction', xxiii; Said, *Culture and Imperialism*, 265.

[23] R. F. Foster, *Paddy & Mr Punch: Connections in Irish and English History* (London: Penguin, 1993), 9.

itself. Arnold's Celtic essays are based on a contributionist argument in which the Philistinism of the English middle classes can only be alleviated by accessing the Celtic strain within the English hybrid character. However, this argument for the control of one's racial constituents is developed in terms of distinctive racial characteristics. This leads to a tension in the argument of the final lecture:

> [I]n the spiritual frame of us English ourselves, a Celtic fibre, little as we may have ever thought of tracing it, lives and works...of the shrunken and diminished remains of this great primitive race, all, with one insignificant exception, belongs to the English empire; only Brittany is not ours; we have Ireland, the Scotch Highlands, Wales, the Isle of Man, Cornwall. They are part of ourselves, we are deeply interested in knowing them, they are deeply interested in being known by us.[24]

This final attempt at synthesis foregrounds the contradictions within Arnold's argument. For not only is there a 'Celtic fibre' within the English composite self, this 'great primitive race' also continues to reside on the western and northern peripheries of the British Isles. Rather than 'interested in knowing us', the active verbs refer only to the English, with the static, visualized, Celtic residue welcoming the scholarly interest of the English ethnographer and philologist. Yet the very existence of a 'diminished remnant' with its own racial characteristics as defined by Arnold implies the possibility of separation. If a 'Celtic residue' has the potential to reinvigorate English cultural life, then it is a small step for an emergent nationalism to adopt this argument as a basis for making the case that the Celts have the potential to lead their nations to cultural and political self-determination. Despite Arnold's assimilationist intentions, the argument can potentially go in two directions. Thus, rather than subjugating the Celt to the omnipotent and omniscient logic of English imperialism, Arnold's thinking contains two contradictory impulses: an explicit assimilationism and an implicit (and unintentional) separatism.

Celtic cosmopolitanism

Given his broadly positive evaluation of Celtic literature and the ambivalent and contradictory nature of his thought, it may therefore be misleading to impose a Foucauldian model on Arnold's work, by which the English man of letters embodies the imperial imposition of power through an intellectual and discursive superiority that energizes, directs, and legitimizes the imperial project. Within Irish historical studies, R. F. Foster is the most prominent figure to warn against viewing the complexities and contradictions of Irish history through what he sees as the distorting and simplifying lens of post-colonial theory.[25] In recovering the forgotten

---

[24] Super, *Complete Prose Works*, III 384.
[25] Foster, *The Irish Story: Telling Tales and Making it up in Ireland* (London: Penguin, 2001), xii.

voices of Irish history, Foster and other Irish historical revisionists, sceptical of nationalist narratives, tend to offer positive accounts of Victorian Celticism. In the late nineteenth century the long-standing and multifaceted discourse on Celticism, described earlier, comes to inform a more organized Pan-Celtic cultural movement. Ruth Dudley Edwards speaks of the 'Pan-Celts' as attracting 'the more broad-minded' members of the Irish revival, and argues that 'their more cosmopolitan attitudes were seen as a threat to a purely Irish political stance'.[26] Foster draws on Dudley Edwards to argue that Pan-Celticism was identified with the Protestant Ascendancy and aristocracy, and was held in considerable suspicion by nationalists in general and prominent members of the Gaelic League in particular.[27] Thus where Edward Said viewed Yeats as a poet of 'decolonization', Foster emphasizes Yeats's shifting political views, his mobile life, and his engagement with a range of literary, cultural, and occultist societies in the 1890s. Neither, however, pays much attention to the 'Celtic' activities of the early Yeats.

Throughout the 1890s, before and after the fall of Parnell, Yeats was active in forming various literary groups as a means of pooling resources in the formation of various cultural movements, and in developing an audience for his own work. The Hermetic Order of the Golden Dawn, the Irish Literary Society, the National Literary Society, the putative Celtic Order of Mysteries, and the Irish Literary Theatre were among the nationalist and occult groups with which Yeats was involved, if not actively leading, during the 1890s. In an article of 1892 Yeats seemed to suggest that the tendency to form into groups was indeed a characteristic of the Celtic peoples. Describing England as 'a land of literary Ishmaels', Yeats remarked that 'it is only among the sociable Celtic nations that men draw nearer each other when they want to think and dream and work'.[28] The various movements in which Yeats was involved often cross-fertilized each other, creating a circle of poets and intellectuals with whom to discuss work and ideas. When, in 1894, W. P. Ryan published a history of the Irish literary revival, he revealed that a good number of the London-based Irish Literary Society were drawn from the Rhymers' Club, a heterogeneous group of poets labelled by their detractors as decadents. As Ryan recalls, a Fleet Street tavern was 'the little Parnassus of the "Rhymers", [who] mean, I hope, to "hammer the ringing rhyme" on a Celtic anvil henceforward'.[29] Yeats and Ernest Rhys—described as the Welshman 'whose mind runs in the direction of schools'— founded the Rhymers' Club in 1890.[30] Famously preserved as 'The Tragic Generation'

---

[26] Ruth Dudley Edwards, *Patrick Pearse: The Triumph of Failure* (London: Gollancz, 1977), 31–2.

[27] Foster, *Irish Story*, 99.

[28] Yeats, *Letters to the New Island*, ed. George Bornstein and Hugh Witemeyer (London: Macmillan, 1989), 57. Leerssen discusses Yeats's Celticism in *Remembrance and Imagination: Patterns in the Historical and Literary Representation of Ireland in the Nineteenth Century* (Cork: Cork University Press, 1996), 208–10.

[29] Quoted by Karl Beckson in 'Yeats and the Rhymers' Club', *Yeats Studies* 1/1 (1971), 20.

[30] Kelly, *Collected Letters of W. B. Yeats*, I, 128.

in Yeats's *Autobiographies*, the Club's marked Celtic tinge induced Victor Plarr to describe it erroneously as a 'rediscovered and reconstituted' grouping of Dublin poets in London.[31]

The poetry collected in the two 'Books' of the Rhymers' Club is generally characterized by a rejection of politics, a repudiation of realist and naturalist tendencies in literature, and the espousal of a doctrine of 'art for art's sake' derived from Walter Pater and soon to be given a fuller expression by the Rhymer Arthur Symons in his *The Symbolist Movement in Literature* (1899).[32] Seamus Deane usefully regards the trend that came to be termed 'The Celtic Twilight' as 'a regional variation on aestheticism', a view reinforced by the fact that 'Into the Twilight' (one of Yeats's most characteristically aestheticist poems in its emphasis on transcendence from earthly concerns into the realm of art) initially appeared in 1893 under the title 'The Celtic Twilight'.[33]

> Out-worn heart, in a time out-worn,
> Come clear of the nets of wrong and right;
> Laugh, heart, again in the grey twilight,
> Sigh, heart, again in the dew of the morn.

In the second stanza, the invocation of 'Eire' makes explicit the poem's Celtic credentials. The emphasis on emotion, on the sense of decline and world-weariness, already strikes the characteristic tones of Twilight verse and suggests that many of the techniques and imagery of late nineteenth-century poetry were easily compatible with the 'Celtic note' that Yeats encouraged writers to strive for in their works.

Indeed, in his 1898 review of Ernest Rhys's *Welsh Ballads* Yeats considers the rise of an aestheticism of 'dreams and passions' to be connected to the 'sudden importance' accorded to the Celtic nations. 'Because a great portion of the legends of Europe, and almost all of the legends associated with the scenery of these islands, are Celtic,' he wrote, 'this movement has given the Celtic countries a sudden importance, and awakened some of them to a sudden activity.'[34] In referring here to the 'sudden importance' now bestowed upon the Celtic nations, Yeats seems to be writing from a London-based, metropolitan, perspective. London proved to be an important setting not only for the emergence of the poetic societies such as the Rhymers' Club, but also for the development of the Pan-Celtic consciousness that influenced Yeats's writing throughout the 1890s. Yeats's close associations with Rhys and the Scottish writer Fiona Macleod (the pseudonym of William Sharp) proved

[31] Quoted by Beckson, 'Yeats and the Rhymers Club', 24.

[32] *The Book of the Rhymers' Club* (London: Elkin Matthews, 1892); *The Second Book of the Rhymers' Club* (London: Elkin Matthews and John Lane, 1894).

[33] Seamus Deane, *Field Day Anthology of Irish Writing*, 5 vols (Derry: Field Day Company, 1991), II, 720. The transition from 'The Celtic Twilight' to 'Into the Twilight' is noted by R. K. R. Thornton in *Decadent Dilemma* (London: Edward Arnold, 1983), 169.

[34] Frayne and Johnson, *Uncollected Prose of W. B. Yeats*, II, 91.

that the Celtic message had spread to the other Celtic nations, thus fostering the 'mutual understanding and sympathy of the Scotch, Welsh and Irish Celts' that was, he noted in 1896, 'a matter I have myself much at heart'.[35] There were, however, significant differences between the idea of Celticism developed by each of these figures.

Whereas Yeats developed Arnold's descriptions of Celtic uniqueness into an argument for the preservation of Irish cultural difference, both Rhys and Sharp follow the contributionist logic of Arnold's argument in seeing the Celtic peoples' ultimate fulfilment within a British context. Writing from Scotland, where home rule was primarily the concern of a grouping within the Liberal party and had largely failed to fire the interest of the people, Sharp's Celtic contributionism reflected the unionist views of the majority. Sharp's Celticism was deeply anti-nationalist, as his conclusion to the introduction of *Lyra Celtica* suggests:

> No, it is no 'disastrous end': whether the Celtic peoples be slowly perishing or are spreading innumerable fibres of life towards richer and fuller, if less national and distinctive existence... The Celt falls, but his spirit rises in the heart and the brain of the Anglo-Celtic peoples, with whom are the destinies of the generations to come.[36]

The creation of his female alter ego, the Celtic recluse Fiona Macleod, can be considered a means for Sharp, the well-travelled cosmopolitan, to enter the Celtic debates of the period in the spirit of 'disinterestedness' so valued by Matthew Arnold.[37] While Macleod's novels were regarded by Yeats as part of the Celtic movement and 'she' was invited to write plays for the Abbey theatre, Sharp consistently used his alter ego to reject emphatically any association with a nationalist movement. Writing as Fiona Macleod in an article titled 'Celtic' he pressed for a Celtic movement 'that is not partisan, but content to participate in the English tradition'.[38] That Arnoldian argument was again repeated in the article 'Prelude' where the tenor and method of argumentation follow Arnold's example, but Macleod significantly emphasizes that she is speaking from a non-English perspective:

> I am not English, and have not the English mind or the English temper, and in many things do not share the English ideals; and to possess these would mean to relinquish my own heritage. But why should I be irreconcilably hostile to that mind and that temper and those ideals?[39]

---

[35] Kelly, *Collected Letters of W. B. Yeats*, II, 37.

[36] Sharp, 'Introduction', li.

[37] Sharp's adoption of a feminine Celtic persona also follows Arnold's argument that 'no doubt the sensibility of the Celtic nature, its nervous exaltation, have something feminine in them, and the Celt is peculiarly disposed to feel the spell of the feminine idiosyncrasy; he has an affinity to it; he is not far from its secret'; Super, *Complete Prose Works*, III, 347.

[38] Fiona Macleod, 'Celtic', in *The Winged Destiny: Studies in the Spiritual History of the Gael* (London: Chapman and Hall, 1904), 200.

[39] Macleod, 'Prelude', in *The Winged Destiny*, 177.

Macleod's writing underlines the centrality of Arnold's example in the development of nineteenth-century Celticism, and also alerts us to the complexity of a British identity that cannot be wished away, nor simply equated with Englishness.

Ernest Rhys—born in Islington but identifying with an idealized, pastoral, and 'Celtic' Wales—was more ambivalent about following Arnold's argument to the point where Celtic national distinctiveness would be eradicated. As Rhys noted in his revealingly titled autobiography *Wales England Wed*:

> Yeats's imagination of Ireland set me wondering whether I could not give Wales, country of the Druids and the Mabinogion, her new deliverance. But I was complicated in ways he was not. A Londoner born as well as a Welshman in exile, I suffered from the mixed sympathies that are bound to affect a man of mixed race.[40]

This explanation of cultural schizophrenia will clearly not do when we consider Yeats's own well-documented feelings of cultural duality as a nationalist poet and member of the Protestant Ascendancy. Rhys did in fact contribute to the nationalist journal *Young Wales* in 1895, and invited Yeats to accompany him to 'Cymru Fydd' meetings in London.[41] Nevertheless, given that the most radical wing of the 'Cymru Fydd' movement desired no more than greater autonomy within the British Empire, Rhys's Celticism was fundamentally connected to an idea of Britain, with his poems idealizing a generalized and romanticized Celtic past that would appeal to a London audience. Typical of much of his work is the lyric 'On a Harp Playing in a London Fog', which begins:

> What Ariel, far astray, with silver wing
> Upborne with airy music, silver-sweet,
> Haunts here the London street? –
> And from the fog, with harping string on string,
> Laughs in the ear, and spurs the lagging feet,
> While Caliban-like, London sulks, though all the stars should sing.[42]

The image of the 'laughing' Celtic harp offering a much needed source of revitalization for a foggy imperial city reconstitutes the Arnoldian relationship between an idealized Celtic periphery and a 'sulking' English centre. This very same structure of feeling forms the subject matter for many of the poems that Rhys collected as *Welsh Ballads* in 1898. The tone and content of his work is representative of the poetry of the 1890s, and there is little to distinguish Rhys's work from the kinds of poems collected in anthologies such as the *Book of the Rhymers' Club* and *Lyra Celtica*. The writings of Rhys and Sharp can broadly be regarded as examples of what Seamus Deane has called, in the Irish context, 'literary unionism', and their reactions to

[40] Rhys, *Wales England Wed* (London: Dent, 1940), 104.
[41] Kelly, *Collected Letters of W. B. Yeats*, II, 77.
[42] Rhys, *A London Rose & Other Rhymes* (London: Elkin Matthews and John Lane, 1894), 9.

Yeats's poetry reinforces this point.[43] For Rhys, the significance of Yeats's work was that it was 'surcharged with imagination and...Celtic glamour', and while Macleod also stressed that Yeats was a poet who could 'see and dream in a reality so vivid that it is called imagination', the true significance of his work lay in the fact that he was 'too wise, too clear-sighted, too poetic, in fact, to aim at being Irish...at the expense of being English in the high and best sense of the word'.[44] That Sharp could consider Yeats a fellow worker in the field of anti-nationalist Celticism supports Seamus Deane's observation that Yeats's compositions were regarded by an English audience as 'essentially picturesque manifestations of the Irish sensibility'.[45] This should guard us against considering Yeats's works of this period as unambiguously anti-colonial, for Celticism did not entail a commitment to nationalist politics.

Celticism, race, and language

Roy Foster offers an account of late nineteenth-century Irish cultural politics in which the positive connections encouraged by 'the Celtic Revival' were frustrated by the politicization of the movement as it became transformed into the more narrow-minded 'Gaelic Revival'. Like Ruth Dudley Edwards, he embraces Celticism for its cosmopolitanism, and resistance to linguistic and nationalist politics. There are good reasons, however, for questioning this narrative. Drawing on the work of Hannah Arendt, Walter Benn Michaels sees the pan-movements of the late nineteenth and early twentieth centuries as underlining the centrality of 'race' in the 'constitution of a community' in that era.[46] In *The Origins of Totalitarianism* (1951), Arendt identified the rise of modern European racism with the 'decline of the European nation-state' and the rise of movements that sought to transcend 'the narrow bounds of a national community' by asserting the primacy of 'a folk community that would remain a political factor even if its members were dispersed all over the earth'.[47] 'Nationalism', Arendt writes, 'has been frequently described as an emotional surrogate of religion, but only the tribalism of the pan-movements offered a new religious theory and a new concept of holiness...Nazism and

---

[43] Deane, 'Heroic Styles: The Tradition of an Idea', in Deane (ed.), *Ireland's Field Day* (London: Hutchinson, 1985), 49.

[44] A. Norman Jeffares (ed.), *W. B. Yeats: The Critical Heritage* (London: Routledge & Kegan Paul, 1977), 94, 117. Sharp (ed.), *Lyra Celtica*, 399.

[45] Deane, 'Heroic Styles', 49.

[46] Walter Benn Michaels, *Our America: Nativism, Modernism, Pluralism* (Durham, NC: Duke University Press, 1995), 102. Michaels notes erroneously that there 'were no plausible parallel "pan-movements" in Britain'. On the connections between Pan-Celticism and other Pan-movements see Marion Löffler, 'Agweddau ar yr Undeb Pan-Geltaidd, 1889-1914', *Y Traethodydd* 155/652 (January 2000), 43–59.

[47] Hannah Arendt, *The Origins of Totalitarianism* (New York: Harcourt Brace, 1973), 232.

Bolshevism owe more to Pan-Germanism and Pan-Slavism (respectively) than to any other ideology or political movement.'[48] Writing in response to the mass murders of the Second World War, Arendt argued bravely that race and nation were distinct and could be separated. While R. F. Foster and Dudley Edwards see Pan-Celticism as a cosmopolitan movement seeking to transcend the narrow boundaries of political nationalism, Pan-Celticism could equally validly be placed within the context of Arendt's reading of pan-movements where the 'decline of the nation state' is to be regretted as this results in a shift from a political concept of *national* identity to a transnational concept of *racial* identity. Arendt's discussion of the 'pan-movements' forces us to consider the costs of abandoning the 'nation' as the primary form of social organization and allegiance.

It is notable that many of the figures debating in the 1890s the merits and limitations of Pan-Celticism were aware of the distinctions that needed to be made between conceptions of identity rooted in race and language. The question as to whether Pan-Celticism was a progressive cultural movement that sought to move beyond the nation state in creating a transnational network of allegiances, or a dangerous movement that replaced the civic space of the modern nation state with a racial and wholly discriminatory account of identity, was itself debated in the late nineteenth century. Hannah Arendt's arguments were anticipated by those Irish nationalists who rejected Pan-Celticism as it was perceived to entail a dangerously racial definition of identity, as opposed to a national definition, which was seen to transcend divisions of race and religion. An anonymous Gaelic Leaguer commented in 1907 that:

> We are not Pan-Celts ourselves – and for this reason. We are working for the building up of the Irish nation … The Irishman of Saxon or Norman or Danish blood is of vastly more importance to the Gaelic League than the man of Celtic origin who belongs to any other nation. Our objects are national, not (in the narrow sense of the word) racial.[49]

The movement did, however, have considerable support among influential figures within the Gaelic League, such as Patrick Pearse, who visited the National Eisteddfod of Wales on its behalf in 1899, and Douglas Hyde. If Wales and Scotland generally followed Ireland in politics, the cultural influence travelled both ways. Scottish Gaelic books were frequently reviewed in Irish journals, aided by the similarities between the two languages, and Welsh cultural events were widely reported in the Gaelic press. The Welsh Eisteddfod was admired by cultural revivalists in both Scotland and Ireland. The Scots established their equivalent festival, the *Mod* (Assembly), in 1892, and if it was difficult in 1892 to imagine any Irish organization capable of arranging such an institution, that changed with the birth of *Connradh na Gaeilge* (the Gaelic League) in 1893. By 1897, the *Oireachtas* had been born, and the editor of the journal *Irisleabhar na Gaedhilge* (the *Gaelic Journal*) paid tribute to

[48] Ibid., 161, 232, 222.
[49] Quoted in Philip O'Leary, ' "Children of the Same Mother": Gaelic Relations with the other Celtic Revival Movements, 1882-1916', *Proceedings of the Harvard Celtic Colloquium* 6 (1986), 109.

the inspiration of the Welsh Eisteddfod: 'We hope to see the Oireachtas, in course of time, do for Irish what the Eisteddfod has done for Welsh'. While not all Gaelic nationalists were as interested in Pan-Celtic connections, there was a pragmatic awareness of similar objectives and shared obstacles among those embracing what Philip O'Leary describes as a 'lower-case pan-celticism'.[50] *Fainne an Lae* (lit. 'the rise of day'), the official organ of the Gaelic League, was Pan-Celtic in its sympathies, committing its allegiance to a vision of 'Celtia' in its edition of January 6th, 1899:

> 'Celtia' or 'Keltia' is the name adopted at Cardiff last year for the aggregate territory of the Five Celtic Nations, i.e., those nationalities whose surviving, or rather reviving, national language belongs to the Celtic family of Indo-European languages. That definition leaves the question of blood-relationship, of historical connection, of racial purity, and of present political status altogether on one side.[51]

As these examples suggest, the basis for this 'lower-case pan-celticism' was not 'racial'; it was linguistic. Thus if Pan-Celticism represented a dangerously racial definition of identity for some, it offered a model of a multinational movement for others, thus providing a space in which support for the Irish language could be expressed without that inevitably entailing a commitment to the goals of Irish nationalism. Whereas no one can change their ancestors, languages can be learnt. A living language, as Etienne Balibar notes, 'immediately naturalizes new acquisitions'.[52] This is not to say that racism does not exist in minority language communities, but is to suggest that the implications for multicultural tolerance are very different for forms of identity rooted in language, and those rooted in race. Indeed, if the Celtic idea has any relevance today it is primarily as a linguistic category for it is, as John Koch notes, 'the scientific fact of a Celtic family of languages that has weathered unscathed the Celtosceptic controversy'.[53]

Conclusion

Any convincing account of Celticism must register its diversity. From one perspective Celticism is a product of English epistemological mastery and political domination, an internal form of Orientalism in which the feminine, superstitious, and poetic Celt could be easily accommodated as a junior partner in the British Imperial adventure. From another, Celticism offers a radical reconceptualization of national

---

[50] O'Leary, *The Prose Literature of the Gaelic Revival 1881–1921: Ideology and Innovation* (University Park, PA: Penn State University Press, 1994), 376.

[51] Quoted in ibid., 378.

[52] Étienne Balibar and Immanuel Wallerstein, *Race, Nation, Class: Ambiguous Identities* (London: Verso, 1995), 98–9.

[53] John T. Koch, *An Atlas for Celtic Studies* (Oxford: Oxbow Books, 2007), 3.

identities within the British Isles, fostering new avenues of dialogue and artistic and political collaboration. For some it is a cosmopolitan movement gesturing at structures of feeling that transcend the moribund category of the nation state. For others it is a dangerously atavistic movement which, in rejecting territorial nationhood, relies on a conception of race for its basis. If the Welshman evoked by Edward Thomas at the beginning of this chapter was always playing many parts—from clerk, to soldier, to policeman—then he may offer a useful embodiment for the Celtic movement itself. He is able to locate himself within the structures of the British state, but is not wholly of it. He is 'always playing', questioning, and at times radically undermining the categories of nation, race, and language.

FURTHER READING

Beckson, Karl. 'Yeats and the Rhymers' Club', *Yeats Studies* 1/1 (1971), 20-41.

Brown, Terence (ed.). *Celticism* (Amsterdam: Rodopi, 1996).

Castle, Gregory. *Modernism and the Celtic Revival* (Cambridge: Cambridge University Press, 2001).

Curtis, L. P. *Anglo Saxons and Celts: A Study of Anglo-Irish Prejudice in Victorian England* (Bridgeport, CT: Conference on British Studies, 1968).

Foster, R. F. *Paddy & Mr Punch: Connections in Irish and English History* (London: Penguin, 1993).

Harvey, David. *Celtic Geographies: Old Cultures, New Times* (London: Routledge, 2002).

Kelleher, John. 'Matthew Arnold and the Celtic Revival', in Harry Levin (ed.), *Perspectives of Criticism* (Cambridge, MA: Harvard University Press, 1950), 197–221.

Koch, John T. *An Atlas for Celtic Studies* (Oxford: Oxbow Books, 2007).

Nagai, Kaori. ' " 'Tis Optophone which Ontophanes": Race, the Modern and Irish Revivalism', in Len Platt (ed.), *Modernism and Race* (Cambridge: Cambridge University Press, 2011), 58-76.

O'Leary, Philip. ' "Children of the Same Mother": Gaelic Relations with the other Celtic Revival Movements, 1882–1916', *Proceedings of the Harvard Celtic Colloquium* 6 (1986), 101–30.

Regan, Stephen. 'W. B. Yeats and Irish Cultural Politics in the 1890s', in Sally Ledger and Scott McCracken (eds), *Cultural Politics at the Fin de Siècle* (Cambridge: Cambridge University Press, 1995).

Williams, Daniel G. *Ethnicity and Cultural Authority: From Arnold to Du Bois* (Edinburgh: Edinburgh University Press, 2006).

PART II

MAKING IT NEW

CHAPTER 5

CULTURES OF THE AVANT-GARDE

CHRISTOS HADJIYIANNIS

The opening years of the twentieth century saw the rise of the avant-garde. Taken as a general aesthetic category, 'avant-garde' indicates radical experimentation with literary or artistic norms. It is also a descriptive term, used here to refer specifically to the practices of a group of poets at work in the early twentieth century, whose questioning of poetic conventions contributed to the development of Anglophone modernism. Avant-garde coteries that flourished in Britain in the opening years of the century included T. E. Hulme's 'School of Images', Ezra Pound's *Imagistes*, and Pound and Wyndham Lewis's Vorticists. These literary–artistic groupings coincided with the emergence of avant-garde manifestations elsewhere in Europe: Futurism, *Der Blaue Reiter*, Cubism. Among those who, in the London of 1908-14, charged against poetic conventions were T. E. Hulme and Ezra Pound, the two figures examined most closely in this chapter. Together with their close associates F. S. Flint, Edward Storer, Joseph Campbell, H. D. (Hilda Doolittle), and Amy Lowell, and in tandem with continental *avant-gardistes* (Marinetti, Kandinsky, Apollinaire, and Shklovsky), Hulme and Pound campaigned for a distinctly 'modern' poetry. Free from formal restrictions and energized against clichés, this poetry was to be composed according to a new method of recording images in distinct lines. This modern method of poetic composition was advocated by Hulme as early as 1908; it went on to form the basis of the poetic doctrine of Imagism (formally launched by Pound and Flint in 1913), and found its way into Pound's Vorticist poetics soon thereafter.

In calling for experimentation with 'regular' forms and a new modern mode of composition, Hulme, Pound, and those in their circle wanted to capture the changing 'spirit' of their time, which, they felt, existing forms and techniques could no longer accommodate. Spurred by 'new' philosophies and inspired by developments in other cultural fields, they challenged long-standing literary and artistic conceptions and forms. And although they saw much in the past they wanted to conserve, they all felt it was imperative to present the 'modern spirit' in a way that necessitated an irreverent (sometimes polemical) approach to form and metric. Ultimately, what unites the different avant-gardes of the time is the shared belief that poetry (and art in general) ought to be at the *front* of all means of communication. This conviction underlies the avant-garde distinction between 'prose' and 'poetry'. 'Prose' or conventional language is to be contrasted to 'poetry', the 'advance guard' of language; the poet has a responsibility to break through language by presenting new images. The prose/poetry opposition feeds into the myth of the artist-as-genius, which, at least in the case of Hulme and Pound, carries a political valence. The ideological implications of this aspect of Hulme and Pound's avant-garde poetics are addressed in the final section of this chapter, 'Avant-garde visions'.

The 'modern spirit'

'A Lecture on Modern Poetry', delivered to the 'Poets' Club' in London in late 1908, presents Hulme's programme for a 'modern', 'relative', and 'Impressionistic' poetry. Composed in 'free verse', this poetry aims at presenting the poet's emotions through the juxtaposition of 'distinct images in distinct lines'.[1] The demands that Hulme makes on the modern poet follow from the lecture's double proposition: that in the early twentieth century a new 'spirit' could be detected; and that the modern poet had a duty to express this modern 'spirit' through devising a new method of composition and through searching for those verse forms that would best accommodate it. Whereas poetry since 'ancient' times had striven for permanence and perfection, poets at the beginning of the century, Hulme claims, finally came to 'frankly acknowledge the relative'.[2] The binary set up here is between 'absolute' philosophies (Platonism, mechanism, neo-Hegelianism) that present the world as a rigid and structured system in which a unified or absolute Truth can be found, and the anti-intellectualism of thinkers such as Henri Bergson. Bergson, whose work Hulme would soon begin to defend in various lectures and articles, held that it is wrong to try to quantify or organize experience according to any external standards. Mathematics, science, reason in general, Bergson insisted, cannot provide access into the deeper structures of reality, to which only instinct or intuition can lead us. As Hulme puts it in a later article, thinkers such as Bergson showed all attempts at understanding reality to be only 'elaborate means for the expressions of quite personal and human emotions'.[3] Modern thinkers, that is, had come to recognize that it was a folly and a fantasy to impose permanence or fixity on experiential flux. With regard to poetry, this 'ancient' desire to give the world fixity and

---

[1] Karen Csengeri (ed.), *The Collected Writings of T. E. Hulme* (Oxford: Oxford University Press, 1994), 53.

[2] Ibid., 53.   [3] Ibid., 101.

permanence explains the metric and rhythmic rigidity of 'old' regular forms. And it is precisely because the rigidity of these forms cannot accommodate the modern 'relative', personal, and 'imperfect' attitude towards the world that newer, more flexible forms and methods of composition must be sought.

Turning to contemporaneous developments in painting where the 'modern spirit' had already manifested itself as Impressionism, but also in music, where 'for the melody' that is one-dimensional music, was substituted harmony which moves in two', Hulme predicts that modern poetry will be 'impressionist'.[4] As well as establishing analogical alliances across the arts (a key feature of all avant-gardes) and embracing what was most modern in the arts at the time, Hulme's mention of 'Impressionism' reveals a lot about the method that he wanted modern poetry to follow. Modern poetry presents momentary impressions or images as these are received by the poet's mind, with these, in turn, temporarily uniting to suggest a new image. According to Hulme, this method of 'recording impressions by visual images in distinct lines' (which, as I argue in the following section, ' "Poetry" versus "prose" ', is best read through Bergson's intuitionist metaphysics) 'does not require the old metric system'; on the contrary, it leads to an unrestrictive form—hence the need to move from 'regular' to 'free' verse. Ultimately, the defining characteristic of Hulme's brand of modern poetry is that it is 'visual': rid of regular metre and rhythm, but also of 'clichés or tags of speech', it should above everything else aim at 'arresting the attention' of the reader through the presentation of intensely visual images.[5]

Hulme's early modernist manifesto alerts us to some of the key ideas shared by those in his immediate circle, especially Pound and the proto-Imagists who began to meet at the *Tour d'Eiffel* restaurant in Soho from late 1908 onwards. The poets who gathered there, and whom Pound later described as belonging to a 'School of Images', were a uniquely disparate group, united only in what Flint later described as their 'dissatisfaction with English poetry as it was then...being written.'[6] Edward Storer, expressing his discontent at the state of poetry as it was being written in the London of 1908, urged fellow poets to try new verse forms along similar lines to Hulme.[7] Flint voiced similar concerns, concurring with Storer that there was 'need for revaluation of all poetical values'. Flint's idea of revaluation involved a turn towards Japanese poetic forms and French *vers libre*, both of which he considered to be 'free' forms, allowing greater emphasis on individual rhythm and thus enabling the poet to capture the 'soul's music'.[8] Pound, who was already promoting himself as 'out of

[4] Ibid., 54.   [5] Ibid., 54–5.

[6] Ezra Pound, Preface to 'The Poetical Works of T. E. Hulme', in Pound, *Early Writings: Poems and Prose*, ed. Ira B. Nadel (London: Penguin, 2005), 54 [page numbers of all subsequent quotations from this edition of Pound's writings (abbreviated as *EW*) will follow in brackets]; F. S. Flint, 'The History of Imagism', *The Egoist* 2/5 (May 1915), 71.

[7] Edward Storer, 'An Essay', *The Mirrors of Illusion* (London: Sisley, 1908), 79, 107.

[8] 'Book of the Week, Recent Verse', *New Age*, 26 November 1908, 95; 'Book of the Week: Recent Verse', *New Age*, 11 July 1908, 213.

key with his time' and 'born/In a half savage country, out of date' (as he was to put it in *Hugh Selwyn Mauberley* twelve years later), was far more outspoken (*EW*, 127). With his trademark bravado, the young Pound berated 'the florid rhetorical bombast' (*EW*, 191) of much contemporary criticism and decried the 'ornate and approximate poetry' that resembled 'balderdash – a sort of embroidery for dilettantes and women'.[9] In *Personae* (1909), he vowed to 'Revolt' against 'the crepuscular spirit in modern poetry', to 'shake off the lethargy of this our time'. And Pound vowed, like Hulme, Storer, and Flint, to 'modernize' English poetry. He too held that it was the responsibility of poets to capture the spirit of their age—to make, as he put it in a letter to Floyd Dell in 1910, 'emotional translations of their time'.[10]

In 1914, with the publication of *Des Imagistes* under Pound's stewardship, various ideas emanating from the 'School of Images' crystallized in the Imagist doctrine. Imagism (or *Imagisme*, as it was first launched) inaugurated the triad of 'directness', precision (or poetic economy), and musical irregularity as the basis of a new, modern poetry. Combined together, these three tenets encouraged poets to break from the restrictions of regular forms and, what was more crucial, create 'visual' poems that conveyed in the mind of the reader intense, epiphanic evocations. As has been well documented, Imagism, which Pound modelled on continental avant-garde groupings, helped start the careers of Flint, Richard Aldington, and H.D. (Hulme never published as an 'Imagist'). It owed its success not only to Pound's formidable marketing skills, and subsequently the financial and editorial support of Amy Lowell, but also to the willingness of magazines such as Harriet Monroe's *Poetry*, Dora Marsden's *The New Freewoman* (later *Egoist*), and Harold Monro's *Poetry Review* to publish new experimental poetry. Indeed, it would be hard to overestimate the contribution of these magazines. Like periodicals such as Alfred Orage's *The New Age* and Ford Madox Ford's *The English Review*, they were important outlets for the early twentieth-century Anglophone avant-garde. As the editors of another important venue for the avant-garde, *Rhythm*, put it in an 'Advertisement' in the spring of 1912, the aim of the younger generation of writers and artists should be to 'unite…all the parallel manifestations of the modern spirit'.[11] The described aim of *Rhythm* can be read as a prospectus for many modernist magazines.

Meanwhile in London, Roger Fry's post-impressionists were campaigning for a new language in the visual arts through a return to 'pure', anti-representational forms. Reversing traditional hierarchies inherited from the Renaissance, Fry's hope was that the post-impressionists' 'primitive' emphasis on pure or significant form would rescue modern art 'from the hopeless encumbrance of its own accumulations

---

[9] Pound, *Selected Prose, 1909–1965*, ed. William Cookson (London: Faber, 1973), 41 [page numbers of all subsequent quotations from this edition (abbreviated as *SP*) will follow in brackets].

[10] Pound, 'Revolt', *Personae* (London: Elkin Matthews, 1909), 53; Pound quoted in Helen Carr, *The Verse Revolutionaries: Ezra Pound, H.D. and the Imagists* (London: Jonathan Cape, 2009), 322–3. See also Pound's praise of Walt Whitman as a poet who is 'his time and his people' (*EW*, 187).

[11] 'Advertisement', *Rhythm* 1/4 (Spring 1912), iv.

of science', enabling it to 'regain its power to express emotional ideas'.[12] In March 1912, a Futurist exhibition opened in London, with this group's impresario, Filippo Marinetti, introducing to the London-based audience the works of Severini, Boccioni, Carrà, and Russolo. Marinetti had been rejecting the past in uncompromising terms since June 1909, calling in manifestoes published in Italy and in France for art consistent with the 'emerging new sensibility'.[13] The Futurists celebrated the death of all conventional codes of communication and the birth of a new aesthetic alphabet. Extolling speed and simultaneity, they rallied against fixed forms and representation in favour of 'the man at the wheel, who hurls the lance of his spirit across the Earth'.[14] The Futurist aesthetic was welcomed by C. R. W. Nevinson and by some of the members of the Rebel Art Centre, including Edward Wadsworth and Frederick Etchells. Futurism's influence on the London avant-garde can be gauged from the catalogue of Frank Rutter's *The Post-Impressionist and Futurist Exhibition*, held at the Doré Gallery in London in 1913, which showcased art composed according to Futurist demands for movement and fragmentation. Despite his proclamations to the contrary, the Futurist emphasis on intensity and fragmentation can also be seen at play in the contemporaneous artwork of Wyndham Lewis. Lewis, blasting his way through the London literary and artistic scene, was seeking at this time to re-energize decrepit modernity and replace 'dead ideas and worn-out notions' via his 'intensive' geometric and semi-abstract art.[15] Elsewhere in Europe, the Russians Zdanevich and Larionov announced that the 'new life requires... a new way of propagation'; in Germany, the Russian-born Kandinsky made it a requirement that artists presented the new 'Creative Spirit'; and in France, Apollinaire was working through the 'New Spirit that is making itself felt today and that will certainly appeal to our best minds'.[16]

It was against this backdrop—London as a modern metropolis where aesthetic ideas collided and fused—that the British avant-garde took its shape. Raymond Williams has written cogently about the important part played by metropolises as centres of power in the development of modernism, noting how the 'complexity' and 'miscellaneity' of the city accommodates 'the whole range of cultural activity'. He has also noted how it was not only ideas that came together to form modernism, but also individuals 'from a variety of social and cultural origins'.[17] It is perhaps

[12] 'The Grafton Gallery – I', *Nation*, 19 November 1910, 331.

[13] Filippo Marinetti, 'The Variety Theatre', *Modernism: An Anthology of Sources and Documents*, ed. Vassiliki Kolocotroni, Jane Goldman, and Olga Taxidou (Edinburgh: Edinburgh University Press, 1998), 254.

[14] Marinetti, 'Manifesto of Futurism', *Modernism: An Anthology*, 251.

[15] Quoted in Jeffrey Meyers, *The Enemy: A Biography of Wyndham Lewis* (London: Routledge, 1980), 64.

[16] Ilya Zdanevich and Mikhail Larionov, 'Why We Paint Ourselves: A Futurist Manifesto'; Wassily Kandinsky, 'The Problem of Form'; Guillaume Apollinaire, 'On Painting', *Modernism: An Anthology*, 257, 270, 213.

[17] Raymond Williams, *The Politics of Modernism: Against the New Conformists*, ed. Tony Pinkney (London: Verso, 1989), 45.

significant that those associated with Imagism and Vorticism included artists, poets, and writers of different nationalities, backgrounds, socioeconomic class, and political persuasions: the royalist Storer, the American heiress Lowell, the working-class and life-long Socialist Flint, the Tory Hulme, the Irish nationalists Joseph Campbell and Desmond Fitzgerald, the anarchist and feminist Dora Marsden. Ford and H.D., both of whom were sympathetic to the suffragettes' cause, also crossed paths and exchanged ideas with these figures.

Thus understood, the kind of avant-garde experimentation with aesthetic norms with which Hulme, Pound, and their associates were involved at this time was motivated by a double desire: to break free from 'restrictive' and 'out-dated' norms and forms; and in doing so create poetry or art in tune with the 'modern spirit'. As I have already suggested, 'new' anti-intellectualist philosophies, such as the one presented by Bergson, were a key influence on the Imagist poetic. Already celebrated in France as a thinker whose philosophy conformed to the anti-positivist 'spirit' of the time, Bergson had by 1911 become hugely popular in England. Between 1909 and 1911, there appeared no fewer than two hundred articles on or about his work. In the spring and autumn of 1911, he toured the country, his lectures in London, Birmingham, and Oxford attracting large audiences.[18]

We can think of Bergson's philosophy as part of a broader intellectual shift away from rationalist modes of understanding the world, and as symptomatic of the general loss of confidence marking the early modernist period towards established ways of understanding the world and shared social practices. Christopher Butler has traced this modernist scepticism back to Nietzsche, Ibsen, and William James, three thinkers who challenged totalizing philosophical, religious, social, and political frameworks.[19] We may say, redeploying Edward Said's metaphor in a slightly different context, that these thinkers unlocked doors that led modern artists and writers further and further away from standard notions of 'reality' and from the cultural and social norms that followed from these.[20] To Butler's list we could add Bergson, with his emphasis on the power of instinct, who much like Freud questioned set ways of understanding the world, including narratives of progress that emphasized the human capability for rational thought. In Hulme's case, Bergson's anti-positivism released him from the 'nightmare' of determinism: 'If I compare my nightmare to imprisonment in a small cell', Hulme wrote in October 1911, then in

---

[18] For useful accounts of Bergson's reception in France and in England, see Mark Antliff, *Inventing Bergson: Cultural Politics and the Parisian Avant-Garde* (Princeton, NJ: Princeton University Press, 1993), 3; R. C. Grogin, *The Bergsonian Controversy in France 1900–1914* (Calgary, AB: University of Calgary Press, 1988), 2; Mary Ann Gillies, *Henri Bergson and British Modernism* (Montreal, QC: McGill-Queen's University Press, 1996), 33.

[19] Christopher Butler, *Early Modernism: Literature, Music, and Painting in Europe, 1900–1916* (Oxford: Clarendon Press, 1994), 1–2.

[20] See Edward Said, *Reflections on Exile and Other Literary and Cultural Essays* (London: Granta, 2012), 1.

reading Bergson he felt that 'the door of that cell was for the first time thrown open'.[21] Pound would credit 'newer psychologists' such as Bernard Hart for presenting new possibilities for artistic experimentation, while H.D. would eventually find the potential for a new language capable of giving the poet prophetic authority in the psychoanalysis of Freud.[22] Nietzsche, James, Bergson, and Freud interrogated religious and political institutions, creating what Butler has described as a generation of artists and writers who had come to see themselves as 'critics...divorced from, and marginal to, the society in which they lived'.[23] They also, however, equipped these moderns with new modes through which to understand, record, and present modern life. In the poetry of Hulme and Pound, as well as H.D., this amounted to the intuitive method of presenting images in distinct lines.

At the same time, however, for all their declared keenness to embrace the new, many of these early twentieth-century *avant-gardistes* were sceptical of modernity, at least its proliferation of mass culture and mass politics. As artists or intellectuals, they felt relegated to the margins, their conviction (inflected as it often was by cultural nostalgia and the myth of the artist as legislator) in the important status and function of art severely challenged. In this sense, to modernize poetry was also to make it, as Pound put it in 1912, a 'vital part of contemporary life' (*SP*, 41). We see a critique of modernity in Pound's 'Prolegomena' (1912), where it is expressed as nostalgia for the 'age of gold', the time when the poet was let alone to pursue his art without consideration for the law of the market or the machinations of mass politics (*EW*, 258). Although far less nostalgic, Hulme records his disaffection with Enlightenment values in his articles for *The Commentator*, where he justifies his support for hierarchical politics on the belief that 'the percentage of capable and disinterested people in any society is always the same and is always small'.[24]

Tracing such contradictions is, of course, a well-trodden path within modernist studies, as in John Carey's argument that high modernism emerged primarily as a reaction to democratic politics.[25] What is also registered in this account, however, is the alienation and disaffection felt by *avant-gardiste* artists more widely, who inscribed in their polemical art the aim of integrating art into the praxis of life.[26] Not that any single event, circumstance, or motivation could ever explain or account for the kind of radical experimentation in art or literature that characterizes the

[21] Csengeri (ed.), *Collected Writings of T. E. Hulme*, 127.

[22] Pound, 'A Few Don'ts by an Imagiste', in Peter Jones (ed.), *Imagist Poetry* (London: Penguin, 2001), 130. According to Polina Mackay, H.D. found in Freud's psychoanalysis the possibility for 'a new language'. See her 'H.D.'s Modernism', in Nephie J. Christodoulides and Polina Mackay (eds), *The Cambridge Companion to H.D.* (Cambridge: Cambridge University Press, 2011), 52.

[23] Butler, *Early Modernism*, 2.

[24] Csengeri (ed.), *Collected Writings of T. E. Hulme*, 230.

[25] See John Carey, *The Intellectuals and the Masses: Pride and Prejudice among the Literary Intelligentsia, 1880–1939* (London: Faber, 1992).

[26] See Peter Bürger, *Theory of the Avant-Garde* (Minneapolis, MN: University of Minnesota Press, 1984), 22.

early twentieth-century avant-garde and the disparate groups that formed it. Rather, it can only be for a confluence of reasons, idiosyncratic and ideological, that artists turned to new forms, methods, and techniques. It would similarly be inaccurate to put undue emphasis on the 'newness' of what I have described earlier as the modern condition or 'spirit'—or, indeed, the 'newness' of the poetic experiments we have come to associate with modernism. For not only, as Hannah Sullivan expertly shows in her contribution to this volume (see Chapter 6), was the move from metrical to free verse initiated in the nineteenth century, but in finding themselves in a precarious position, the early twentieth-century *avant-gardistes* were not much unlike their Victorian counterparts. Matthew Arnold described nineteenth-century intellectuals as living estranged in an 'immense system of institutions... which have come to them from times not modern'. For Arnold, the realization on the part of the Victorian moderns that they were no longer part of the social consensus constituted an 'awakening of the modern spirit'.[27]

'Poetry' versus 'prose'

Perhaps no other principle unites the early twentieth-century avant-garde as much as the idea that literature and art in general can (and ought to) break through conventional discourse. This principle, which lies at the basis of all forms of avant-garde experimentation, often manifests itself as a distinction between 'poetry' and 'prose' (or conventional discourse). 'Poetry', the domain of the artist, contains the new, the original, and the cutting-edge. It is a means of communication that has an intensity and 'directness' lacking in 'prose', which is the used, commodified language of the marketplace and of dated philosophical systems. We find a version of this distinction in the writings of a range of poets and thinkers, from Mallarmé and Hofmannsthal, through to Binyon, Apollinaire, Shklovsky, Stramm, and de Gourmont.[28] In Hulme and Pound, this distinction—read via Bergson—explains the Imagist/Vorticist emphasis on the use of images in poetry. It thus provides one way of reading the 'visual' poetry of the Imagists.

The distinction between 'poetry' and 'prose' forms the central theme of 'Notes on Language and Style', the set of rudimentary notes that, together with 'Cinders',

[27] Matthew Arnold, 'Heinrich Heine', *Lectures and Essays in Criticism*, ed. R. H. Super (Ann Arbor, MI: University of Michigan Press, 1962), 109.

[28] See, for example, Stéphane Mallarmé, 'Crisis of Verse', *Divagations*, trans. Barbara Johnson (Cambridge, MA: Belknap Press, 2007), 205–11; Lawrence Binyon, 'The Return to Poetry', *Rhythm* 1/4 (Spring 1912), 1; Apollinaire, 'Zone', in Garnet Rees (ed.), *Guillaume Apollinaire: Alcools* (London: Athlone Press, 1975), 39; Victor Shklovsky, 'Art as Technique', *Modernism: An Anthology*, 218; Remy de Gourmont, *Le problème du style* (Paris: Mercure de France, 1907), 37, 142. On the distinction as manifested in Stramm and Hofmannsthal, see Butler, *Early Modernism*, 9–10, 244–5.

represents Hulme's earliest known writings (1906-1907). In 'Notes', Hulme makes it clear that the two terms are not to be taken in their literal sense: 'prose', for instance, includes 'genteel poetry like Shelley's', while 'poetry' may refer to Morris's 'firm simple prose'. As it turns out, the crucial difference is that, while in 'prose' words are 'divorced from any real vision', with it being language that deals in 'counters' and whose 'intermediate terms have only counter value', 'poetry' is a language of 'images'. It is the place where 'phrases [are] made [and] tested', and where words 'are all glitter and new coruscation'. This is what makes 'Poetry always the advance guard in language'. Moreover, unlike in 'prose', where words are vague and superfluous, in 'poetry' 'each sentence should be a lump, a piece of clay, a vision seen'.

In 'A Lecture on Modern Poetry', Hulme casts this distinction into a theory for modern poetry. Here, the standard of 'true' poetry is whether it attests to 'direct' communication; true poetry, Hulme claims, is 'direct because it deals in images'. The modern poet must thus 'continually be creating new images, and his sincerity may be measured by the number of his images'.[29] Hulme redeploys the antithesis in 'Romanticism and Classicism' (1911-1912), now giving his early poetics an unmistakably political edge. The 'positive fundamental quality' of the 'classical' verse to which Hulme aspires in this piece is that it not be 'a counter language, but a visual concrete one'.

> It always endeavours to arrest you, and to make you continuously see a physical thing, to prevent you gliding through an abstract process. It chooses fresh epithets and fresh metaphors, not so much because they are new, and we are tired of the old, but because the old cease to convey a physical thing and become abstract counters.

Thus, as in his earlier lecture, the classical poet in 'Romanticism and Classicism' is assigned the task of searching within himself for that 'intense zest which heightens a thing out of the level of prose'.[30]

Pound upholds this distinction himself, also making it a central feature of his poetics. In 'I Gather the Limbs of Osiris', he explains that the main struggle of the poet is against ordinary language consisting of 'arbitrary and conventional symbols' (*SP*, 34). A similar distinction between pure and conventional language is drawn in 'The Wisdom of Poetry'. The function of poetry, Pound argues here, has always been to 'new-mint the speech, to supply the vigorous terms for prose'. In 'The Serious Artist', employing the terms in a more literal sense, Pound claims that, compared to prose, poetry is 'the more highly energized'. He explains that in our acquisition of language we progress from gestures to symbols, to ideas, and, finally, to emotions, with poetry always standing at the most advanced stage of communication. Elsewhere, Pound captures the distinction more pithily: 'if formed words, to literature; the image to poetry' (*EW*, 192, 242, 244, 278).

---

[29] Csengeri (ed.), *Collected Writings of T. E. Hulme*, 24–7, 55.   [30] Ibid., 69–70.

Unsurprisingly, and again in a similar way to Hulme, the standard for poetry for Pound turns out to be whether the poet 'who cares and believes in the pint of truth that is in him will work, year in and year out, to find the perfect expression'. The end result is poetry rid of conventional or indirect language, a form of communication that 'exalts the reader, making him feel that he is in contact with something arranged more finely than the commonplace' (*SP*, 34, 41). This is what Pound found so captivating in the Chinese poems he inherited from the art historian Ernest Fenollosa: they rely on 'natural suggestion', not convention, to gain sense, and are thus very much unlike the 'mental counters' of conventional speech, which Fenollosa conceived as bricks on a 'little checker-board' (*EW*, 309, 311). Pound told Harriet Monroe in 1915 that, like his Chinese ancestor, the modern poet must strive for 'poetry', not 'prose'. 'There must be no clichés, set phrases, stereotyped journalese'; and the only escape is 'by precision, a result of concentrated attention to what is writing'.[31]

In Hulme and Pound's discussion of the distinction between 'poetry' and 'prose', we see traces of the evolutionary account of language presented by Nietzsche in his 1873 essay 'On Truth and Lies in a Nonmoral Sense'. The antithesis can also be productively read via the evolutionary psychology of the French psychologist Théodule Ribot.[32] Here, I only have space to deal with how their distinction can be understood through Bergson. As already mentioned, Bergson's intuitive metaphysics proceeds on the idea that reason (or the intellect) alone always gives a false picture of the world, for we need instinct (or intuition) to reach the deeper structures of reality. A product of the intellect, conceptual language is useful and needed for practical purposes, but it prevents us from seeing the real 'flux' of experience, what Bergson calls 'real duration' or '*durée*'. In *An Introduction to Metaphysics*, Bergson explains that conceptual language consists of 'abstract, general, or simple ideas'; these concepts, he goes on to argue, 'have the disadvantage of being in reality symbols substituted for the object they symbolize, and demand no effort on our part', and are thus incapable of capturing the 'inner life'. Concepts, that is, are incapable of capturing the 'inner life' or the 'fundamental self', the latter of which remain always 'inexpressible'.[33] As Bergson puts it in *Time and Free Will*, 'language cannot get hold of [inner life] without arresting its mobility or fit it into its common-place forms without making it into public property'.[34] 'Intuition', Bergson's trademark philosophical

[31] D. D. Paige (ed.), *Selected Letters of Ezra Pound 1907–1941* (New York: New Directions, 1950), 49.

[32] See Christos Hadjiyiannis, 'T. E. Hulme and the Beginnings of Imagism', *Global Review* 1/1 (2003), 141–64.

[33] Henri Bergson, *An Introduction to Metaphysics*, trans. T. E. Hulme, ed. Thomas A. Goudge (Indianapolis, IN: Hackett, 1999), 27.

[34] Bergson, *Time and Free Will: An Essay on the Immediate Data of Consciousness*, trans. F. L. Pogson (London: Sonnenschein and New York: Macmillan, 1910), 129.

method, is precisely intended to help us reach the flux of experience that is pre-vented to us by conceptual language.

In *An Introduction to Metaphysics*, which Hulme (with significant help from Flint) translated for publication in 1914, Bergson argues further that, although real duration or the inner life 'cannot be represented by images [it] is even less possible to represent it by *concepts*':

> It is true that no image can reproduce exactly the original feeling I have of the flow of my own conscious life... [However,] the image has at least this advantage, that it keeps us in the concrete. No image can replace the intuition of duration, but many diverse images, borrowed from very different orders of things may, by the convergence of their action, direct consciousness to the precise point where there is certain intuition to be seized.

Bergson's suggestion here is that, because visual impressions are supra-rational and non-conceptual, they can carry us through to the point of intuition and, therefore, reveal to us duration, the *immédiatement donnée*. While Bergson is adamant that images alone cannot lead us directly to duration—for duration to be reached 'consciousness must...consent to make the effort'—he is, in a sense, allowing that images are the nearest thing to the original moment of intuition, and, further, that they provide the means through which we can reach a moment of intuition.[35] Translated in Hulme and Pound's terms, Bergson's language of images amounts to 'poetry'; conceptual language to 'prose'.

Bergson's method of intuition, according to which images are more 'direct' than conceptual language, is at work in all six of Hulme's proto-Imagist experiments. Take, for instance, 'Above the Dock':

> Above the quiet dock in midnight,
> Tangled in the tall mast's corded height,
> Hangs the moon. What seemed so far away
> Is but a child's balloon, forgotten after play.

Consider also 'Autumn':

> A touch of cold in the Autumn night –
> I walked abroad
> And saw the ruddy moon
> Like a red-faced farmer.
> I did not stop to speak, but nodded,
> And round about were the wistful stars
> With white faces like town children.[36]

In 'Above the Dock', the image of the hanging moon is swiftly followed by that of a balloon held by a child, with the poem achieving what Pound describes in 'I Gather

---

[35] Bergson, *An Introduction to Metaphysics*, 27–8.
[36] Csengeri (ed.), *Collected Writings of T. E. Hulme*, 1.

the Limbs of Osiris' as a 'resembling unlikeness' (*SP*, 41). The two images carry equal weight and, presented in juxtaposition, invite the reader to construct a new image, in accordance with the method Hulme advocated in his lectures. Likewise, 'Autumn' establishes analogies between the 'ruddy moon' and the 'red-faced farmer', and 'wistful stars' and the 'white faces' of 'town children'. The surprising links present new possibilities: in 1966 George Oppen, misquoting 'Autumn', told Serge Fauchereau that the poem's strength lies in its 'demand that one actually *look*'; its 'lucence, that emotional clarity', which Oppen found characteristic of Imagism, is what the 'objectivists wanted'.[37] As we read 'Autumn', our attention shifts suddenly from one image to the next, the poem guiding us to a moment where, in the terminology of *An Introduction to Metaphysics*, there is an 'intuition to be seized'. This is what is required by Bergson's intuitive method: we must make an effort, suspending any 'particular and clearly-defined disposition' we may have. Having first broken from conceptual language, the poet asks us to follow him to that fullness of experience that no intellectual or conceptual experience can match.

A similar process is at play in some of the poetry of other members of the 'School of Images'. In an early poem by Joseph Campbell, for example, images are swiftly juxtaposed as we are presented with the poet's impressions of a landscape when 'Darkness' descends: 'I stop to watch a star shine in a boghole – / A star no longer, but a silver ribbon of light'.[38] Flint's 'Four Poems in Unrhymed Cadence' are also built around arresting images, briefly evoked to convey the poet's mood, as is John Gould Fletcher's 'In the City of Night', a poem which, as Carr notes, works in 'imagist fashion' in that it projects the poet's emotion on to the city: 'Along the dismal, empty street, stretching endlessly away / The darkened houses stand, in mournful dull array / Like wretched starving folk'.[39] All of these poems adhere to Hulme's Bergsonian method of juxtaposition, but also to the symbolist techniques promoted by Amy Lowell. Lowell was one of the women who played an important part in the development of the London-based avant-garde, but whose contributions are somewhat obfuscated (others are Kate Lechmere and Helen Saunders). In *Six French Poets*, quoting de Gourmont, Lowell encourages the modern poet 'to write down himself, to unveil for others the sort of world which mirrors itself in his individual glass', adding that a true poet must always 'say things not yet said, and say them in a form not yet formulated'.[40]

The archetypal Imagist poem, Pound's 'In a Station of the Metro', superimposes images to convey an epiphanic evocation of an intense perception:

---

[37] Rachel Blau DuPlessis (ed.), *The Selected Letters of George Oppen* (Durham, NC: Duke University Press, 1990), 146.

[38] Joseph Campbell, *The Mountainy Singer* (Dublin: Maunsel, 1909), 3.

[39] Flint, 'Four Poems in Unrhymed Cadence', *Poetry* 2/4 (1913), 136–9; Carr, *Verse Revolutionaries*, 550; John Gould Fletcher, *The Dominant City* (London: Max Goschen, 1913), 23.

[40] Amy Lowell, *Six French Poets: Studies in Contemporary Literature* (New York: Macmillan, 1915), 120.

The apparition of these faces in the crowd:
Petals on a wet, black bough.[41]

Short and succinct, the poem eschews the 'ornate and approximate', as per Pound's demand in 'I Gather the Limbs of Osiris' (*SP*, 41). Using parataxis so that two apparently heterogeneous images are laid side by side, this haiku-like poem aspires to the condition of 'poetry': it is direct, precise, stirring in the mind of the reader images, not tokens. As well as Bergson's language of images leading to intuition, here we see put into practice what Pound called in 'The Spirit of Romance' in 1910 'primary apparition'. This is the apparition that aims to 'give vividness to description and stimulate conviction in the actual vision of the poet', and which Pound eventually made the ultimate aim of all Imagist and Vorticist poetry.[42] A similar principle is described in 'The Wisdom of Poetry', where 'perception by symbolic vision' is understood to be 'swifter and more complex than that by ratiocination' (*EW*, 191). This is the poetic ideal of 'Luminous Detail', a method which is 'most vigorously hostile to the...method of sentiment and generalization' and which gives us 'facts' that are 'hard to find', that suddenly illuminate, and that 'are swift and easy of transmission' (*SP*, 21, 23).

When Pound recharged Imagism as Vorticism in 1914, he kept the emphasis on the immediacy of impact but stressed 'super-position', the technique of the haiku he uses in 'A Station of the Metro', and also an extension of the method of juxtaposition recommended by Hulme six years earlier. When he introduced Vorticism in *Blast* in July 1914, Pound claimed H.D.'s 'Oread' as a paradigmatic Vorticist poem.[43] By this time, H.D. had already published three imagist poems: 'Hermes of the Ways', 'Orchard', and 'Epigram', all of which appeared in *Poetry* in 1913. In all three, she elaborates on a central image, swiftly juxtaposing images that are mediated through the poet's gaze. In 'Hermes of the Ways', for example, a complex image is created through the interaction of diverse images in an instant of time. The seashore, a liminal place in the poem, is undergoing transmutations, and with it the poem, too; as the wind that 'Piles little ridges', the poem stacks image on image: 'The hard sand breaks, / and the grains of it / are clear as wine'; 'the boughs of the trees / are twisted'; 'sea-grass tangles / with Shore grass'. 'Orchard' similarly presents a series of images in the poet's mind, this time the impressions that the garden makes on the poet: 'fallen hazel-nuts', 'grapes, red-purple', 'Pomegranates already broken', 'And shrunken figs / And quinces untouched'.[44]

H.D. included both 'Hermes of the Ways' and 'Orchard' in her first collection, *Sea Garden* (1916). The opening poem in *Sea Garden*, 'Sea Rose', presents a rose from multiple angles in a process during which we come to experience the

[41] *Poetry* 2/1 (1913), 12.
[42] Pound, *The Spirit of Romance* (London: Peter Owen, 1970), 159.
[43] *Blast* 1 (1914), 154.
[44] H.D., *Collected Poems 1912–1944*, ed. Louis L. Martz (Manchester: Carcanet, 1984), 37–8, 28–9.

significance that the rose has for the poet. According to Polina Mackay, the poet in 'Sea Rose' is engaged in an act of 'intellectual and emotional searching'.[45] The same can be said of 'Oread', with its two prevailing images (sea and forest) uniting to create one dynamic image, complex, or vortex:

> Whirl up, sea –
> whirl your pointed pines,
> splash your great pines
> on our rocks,
> hurl your green over us –
> cover us with your pools of fir.[46]

As the two images fuse to suggest a new one (as prescribed by Hulme), the sea merges with the forest, a unison achieved through the conflation of images, anaphora, and epistrophe. The poet breaks from conceptual language to achieve an intensity and directness not afforded to us through 'prose', and to become one with the outside world, as the outside world is at the same time internalized.

Avant-garde visions

My argument so far has been that the distinction between poetry (new, 'direct' language) and 'prose' (worn-out, 'indirect' language) is what lies at the basis of—indeed, unifies—the poetics of the pre-war London avant-garde. Insofar as this opposition is premised on the conviction that the artist possesses a unique, rare ability to break free from conceptual restrictions that allow him or her to perceive and present new images, it carries ideological implications. In the case of H.D., the poet she creates inaugurates woman as storyteller. As Mackay puts it, in her poetry H.D. 'draws attention both to the role of female authorship in the discovery and sustainment of literary tradition as well as to her new responsibilities as she writes her way through modernity'.[47] That is, H.D.'s break from conventional language may be seen as a move away from male-centred narratives.

With Hulme and Pound, the case is quite different. Comentale has argued with much gusto that Hulme's classicist poetics, with its emphasis on 'material tensions that define and delimit individuals, classes, and nations', ensures that his poet, despite possessing an extraordinary ability to break through conceptual language, never transcends either subject or object.[48] As Hulme puts it himself, the 'classic'

---

[45] Mackay, 'H.D.'s Modernism', 56.

[46] H.D., *Collected Poems 1912–1944*, 55.

[47] Mackay, 'H.D.'s Modernism', 60. Susan Stanford Friedman argued that it was only in her prose discourse that H.D. was able to find her voice as woman. See her *Penelope's Web: Gender, Modernity, H.D.'s Fiction* (Cambridge and New York: Cambridge University Press, 1990), 6, 128–32.

[48] Edward P. Comentale, *Modernism, Cultural Production, and the British Avant-Garde* (Cambridge: Cambridge University Press, 2004), 7.

poet 'never flies into the circumambient gas'. Yet Hulme's insistence on the autonomous logic of the poet creates the heavily ideologized cult of genius. For the
Hulmean poet, able as he is to put himself in 'a state of tension or concentration of
mind', follows his Poundian counterpart in becoming what Carey has described as
an 'intellectual aristocrat', whose mental prowess sets him apart from the 'masses'.[49]

Indeed, it is easy to see why so many so readily read into this kind of avant-garde
poetics a strong anti-democratic prejudice. In various places in his writings, Pound
describes the artist or poet as someone who perceives at a greater intensity than the
general reader, going so far as to call, in 1914, for the 'aristocracy of the arts' to 'take
over control' of 'Modern civilization [which] has bred a race with brains like those
of rabbits'.[50] Pound's later praise of Mussolini as an artist with 'passion for construction', and Hulme's staunch defence of a strong upper chamber of parliament well-
suited to rule (or, at the very least, keep in check) the disorderly 'masses', only add
credence to the well-rehearsed narrative that maps their modernist poetics onto
their anti-democratic politics. In the short space that I have left, I would like to very
briefly touch on another political implication emerging out of Hulme's and Pound's
poetics. This relates to the belief, shared by many *avant-gardistes*, that the effectiveness (and hence success) of poetry is to be measured not against any external or
communal standards, but against the inner 'sincerity' of the poet.

'An art is vital', Pound writes in 'Psychology and Troubadours', 'so long…as it
manifests something which the artist perceives at greater intensity, and more intimately, than his public'. Elsewhere, Pound compares his ideal poet to the 'abstract
mathematician' and the 'analytical geometer'—but the logic to which this mathematician–artist adheres is entirely his own. This is also the case with other *avant-
gardistes*, from Schoenberg and Kandinsky through to Picasso (*EW*, 195, 193).[51]
Hulme makes 'sincerity' the standard of poetry, too, most famously in 'Romanticism
and Classicism', where his demand for classical 'accuracy' is intriguingly metamorphosed into a call for 'sincerity', the inner unity of the artist with his own perceptions rather than with conventional forms. This reversal has led many critics to
question Hulme's purported classicism. Krieger, Kermode, and Howarth, for example, all find something distinctly 'romantic' in Hulme's theory of inspiration.[52] There
is, however, also another kind of 'romanticism' at work in Hulme's and Pound's

---

[49] Csengeri (ed.), *Collected Writings of T. E. Hulme*, 62, 69; Carey, *Intellectuals and the Masses*, 71.
For Poggioli, it is the withdrawal of the *avant-gardiste* into individual solitude or a circle of a select few
that gives the category 'avant-garde' its 'aristocratic quality'. See Renato Poggioli, *Theory of the Avant-
Garde* (Cambridge, MA: Belknap Press, 1968), 99.

[50] Pound, *Jefferson and/or Mussolini* (New York: Liveright, 1935), 33–4; Pound, 'The New Sculpture',
The Egoist 1/4 (February 1914), 68.

[51] On the avant-garde's emphasis on the inner vision of the artist, see Butler, *Early Modernism*,
55–6, 68.

[52] See Murray Krieger, 'The Ambiguous Anti-Romanticism of T. E. Hulme', *ELH* 20/4 (1953), 300–
14; Frank Kermode, *Romantic Image* (London: Routledge, 2002), 141–63; Peter Howarth, *British
Poetry in the Age of Modernism* (Cambridge: Cambridge University Press, 2005), 34–44.

theory of inspiration, in the sense of the term given to it by the political philosopher Isaiah Berlin in his 1952 lecture 'Two Concepts of Freedom'.[53]

Conceived and developed in the aftermath of the Second World War, at a time when the central ideological struggle was that between communism and liberal democracy, Berlin's discussion of romanticism is to a great extent politically driven. A passionate anti-communist, Berlin was keen to interpret contemporary political conflicts in light of the history of ideas; this means that, just as with his some-times-oversimplified view of the Enlightenment which he sees as a progenitor to authoritarianism, Berlin's account of romanticism may often be idiosyncratic.[54] Yet turning to his criticism of romanticism is useful for us here, because it provides an astute critical analysis of possible political implications attached to the blind belief in individual genius. It thus offers one entry point into the ideological poetics of Hulme and Pound.

Romanticism's most lasting political legacy according to Berlin is its inaugura-tion of the free-creating personality, which, crucially for Berlin, imposes itself on the world outside it.[55] The romantic personality creates works out of his own life, his own genius; art, society, and life more broadly become the expression of his inner vision; and the 'outside' becomes the 'inside' in a process of identification through creation of the external world by the self. As Berlin puts it, this process 'automatic-ally makes the world part of oneself'; in doing so, romanticism (in arts, morals, and politics) manages to subvert the view according to which an objective structure independent of human perception exists.

Read speculatively through Berlin, the anti-intellectualist, intuitive avant-garde poetics of Hulme and Pound gains a distinctly 'romantic' bearing. For the free-creating personality described by Berlin closely resembles the avant-garde artist envisaged by Hulme and Pound: modern *avant-gardiste* and his romantic predeces-sor alike discriminate in favour of the inner vision of the artist. In Berlin's reading, the romantic poet–politician 'does what he does at the moment of the highest ten-sion of his faculties... when the vision... "takes hold of him", and he becomes the sacred vessel through which the creative spirit makes its advance'.[56] In 'Romanticism

---

[53] 'Two Concepts of Freedom' was one of four Mary Flexner lectures delivered at Bryn Mawr in the spring of 1952. Key ideas from this lecture echo in Berlin's later writing, for example, 'Two Concepts of Liberty' and 'The Restrained Romantics'. See Henry Hardy's Preface to Isaiah Berlin, *Political Ideas in the Romantic Age: Their Rise and Influence on Modern Thought*, ed. Henry Hardy (London: Chatto & Windus, 2006), xviii.

[54] See Joshua L. Cherniss's introduction 'Isaiah Berlin's Political Ideas', in Berlin, *Political Ideas in the Romantic Age*, xxiii. For a useful account of Berlin's discussion of romanticism, see George Crowder, *Isaiah Berlin: Liberty, Pluralism and Liberalism* (Cambridge: Polity, 2004), 104–14.

[55] Despite his criticism of the political aspects of romanticism, Berlin does acknowledge the 'posi-tive...heritage of Romanticism'. See Claude Galipeau, *Isaiah Berlin's Liberalism* (Oxford: Oxford University Press, 1994), 57.

[56] Berlin, 'Two Concepts of Freedom: Romantic and Liberal', *Political Ideas in the Romantic Age*, 184, 177, 199.

and Classicism', Hulme presents his ideal poet as resembling 'a man employing all his fingers to bend the steel out of its own curve and into the exact curve which you want'.[57] In 'Affirmations', Pound describes how 'pattern-units' arise in the mind of the poet-receiver—'if the mind is strong enough'—and proceeds to explain how the mind of the poet works to internalize, and then externalize, the world (*EW*, 292-3). Both of their poets are engaged in a process during which we as readers rely on the self-legislating poet-perceiver to disclose his (our) world to us.

Ultimately, Berlin aims to show that such a 'romantic' act of rendering the outside into the inside (and vice versa) gives rise to the organic state shaped by a single mighty spirit, as embodied by Alexander the Great, Charlemagne, Frederick the Great, Napoleon—as well as Mussolini and Hitler. '[T]he inspired artist at the moment of creation, the inspired statesman or soldier or philosopher,' Berlin writes, 'is justified in acting as he does by his intuitive grasp of... inner connections'.[58] Although the Hulmean/Poundian artist is analogous in relying on his inner vision, my point here is not that Hulme's or Pound's avant-garde poetics (or indeed any other kind of art or literature, including romanticism) leads to, or contains in it a blueprint for, authoritarian politics. Even if Pound's politics did grow increasingly authoritarian as his career progressed, it can often be simplistic to read back from his politics into his early poetics. We need to be careful, that is, not to mistake accidental (i.e. not necessary) associations between certain avant-gardes and specific political beliefs for inevitable connections.[59]

My aim, rather, has been to emphasize the autonomous position that the avant-garde artist occupies as perceiver-creator, and speculate about some of the ideological implications that this might entail. To do so is only to renew a question that has reverberated within literary studies since at least the time of Hazlitt. In his chapter on Shakespeare's *Coriolanus*, Hazlitt wonders if poetry, insofar as it relies on imagination ('an exaggerating and exclusive faculty') is not always 'aristocratic'.[60] Building on Hazlitt in his own discussion of Philip Larkin's poetry, Mark Rowe returns to this question, pondering whether a poet's interest in realizing his own artistic vision will not inevitably make him reticent (uninterested?) in sacrificing his time or liberties to social democratic causes.[61] We may ask, after Hazlitt and Rowe: might it be that the avant-garde emphasis on the mental prowess and inner vision of the poet creates an irreparable distance between the realization of the *avant-gardiste*'s own vision and our social realities?

---

[57] Csengeri (ed.), *Collected Writings of T. E. Hulme*, 69.

[58] Berlin, 'Two Concepts of Freedom', 199.

[59] See Poggioli, *Theory of the Avant-Garde*, 95. As Carr rightly notes, citing the examples of H.D., Aldington, and Flint, not all *avant-gardistes* turned reactionary. See Carr, 'Introduction', in John Gery, Daniel Kempton, and H. R. Stoneback (eds), *Imagism: Essays on its Initiation, Impact and Influence* (New Orleans: UNO Press, 2013), xxi.

[60] William Hazlitt, *Selected Writings*, ed. Jon Cook (Oxford: Oxford University Press, 1991), 345.

[61] Mark Rowe, *Philip Larkin, Art and Self: Five Studies* (London: Palgrave, 2011), 64.

FURTHER READING

Beasley, Rebecca. *Ezra Pound and the Visual Culture of Modernism* (Cambridge: Cambridge University Press, 2007).

Bürger, Peter. *Theory of the Avant-Garde* (Minneapolis, MN: University of Minnesota Press, 1984).

Butler, Christopher. *Early Modernism: Literature, Music, and Painting in Europe, 1900–1916* (Oxford: Clarendon Press, 1994).

Carr, Helen. *The Verse Revolutionaries: Ezra Pound, H.D. and the Imagists* (London: Jonathan Cape, 2009).

Comentale, Edward P. *Modernism, Cultural Production, and the British Avant-Garde* (Cambridge: Cambridge University Press, 2004).

Levenson, Michael. *A Genealogy of Modernism: A Study of English Literary Doctrine, 1908–1922* (Cambridge: Cambridge University Press, 1984).

North, Michael. *The Political Aesthetic of Yeats, Eliot and Pound* (Cambridge: Cambridge University Press, 1991).

Perloff, Marjorie. *The Dance of the Intellect: Studies in the Poetry of the Pound Tradition* (Cambridge: Cambridge University Press, 1985).

Poggioli, Renato. *The Theory of the Avant-Garde* (Cambridge, MA: Belknap Press, 1968).

Williams, Raymond. *The Politics of Modernism: Against the New Conformists*, ed. Tony Pinkney (London: Verso, 1989).

CHAPTER 6

EMERGING POETIC FORMS

HANNAH SULLIVAN

A conventional but mistaken history of poetic form runs as follows: by the end of the nineteenth century, poets began working in progressive, freer forms, loosening themselves from the rules of ictus, accent, foot, and line that had dominated English poetics since the Renaissance. Then, in the period of high modernism, these experiments solidified into free verse, an open, unconstricted form that remains dominant today.

This is largely a story told by modernists, and by critics of modernism, and it has the ring of winner's history. Charles Hartman's influential book *Free Verse* begins with the idea that in 1908, poets wrote in a 'generally confident prosodic atmosphere', which exploded suddenly in 1912, when Ezra Pound formulated Imagism.[1] For Pericles Lewis, the prosodic fact is a given, and the important question is *why*: 'The victory of free verse over traditional meters, decisively won in English by Ezra Pound and his friends, was actually undertaken in the name of mimesis.'[2] Definitions of modernism often cite free verse as the prosodic change accompanying disjunctions of content and structure: 'modernism's stylistic ruptures—its disjointed syntax, free verse, unorthodox subjects, mythical superstructures, collage juxtapositions.'[3]

By refocusing on the period 1880-1920, I want to suggest that the conventional account dates the shift from metrical to free verse too late, attributes too much agency to modernist writers, and neglects the seriously important metrical changes that had already happened in nineteenth-century poetry. By drawing attention to five strategies for reforming poetry, I also want to draw attention to some unlikely, and neglected, affinities between writers we are prone sharply to demarcate:

[1] Charles O. Hartman, *Free Verse: An Essay on Prosody* (Princeton, NJ: Princeton University Press, 1980), 6.

[2] Pericles Lewis, *The Cambridge Introduction to Modernism* (Cambridge: Cambridge University Press, 2007), 7.

[3] Robert Bernard Hass, '(Re)Reading Bergson: Frost, Pound, and the Legacy of Modern Poetry', *Journal of Modern Literature* 29/1 (2005), 55–75, 67.

W. B. Yeats and T. S. Eliot; James Joyce and Ernest Dowson; Christina Rossetti and Gerard Manley Hopkins; late Tennyson and Walt Whitman.

A good place to start is with Pound's own famous but elliptical pronouncement of reform in *Canto* 81. The parentheses are usually omitted in citation. '(To break the pentameter, that was the first heave.)'[4] The line is memorable because it jumpily enacts the constraints it describes and, in doing so, it remains wedded to the form it decries. 'To break the metre, that was the first heave' would, after all, have *been* a line of iambic pentameter. And later, Canto 81 goes on, in some of the most devastating (and famous) lines in all of the Cantos, to resurrect the metre it claims to be 'broken'. 'What thou lov'st well shall not be reft from thee', 'Pull down thy vanity, I say pull down'. And finally it claims that error is not in the done, but in the not done, 'all in the diffidence that faltered'.

Like many conventional stories, like many Whig histories, 'the rise of free verse' is partly true. Before the late nineteenth century, very little poetry was written in a metre that could not be identified or, more importantly, copied; during the twentieth century, the majority of poems published were in unique, one-off forms. But almost everything else about the conventional prehistory of free verse—with its accommodating reading of Pound—is wrong. Free verse is, as many critics have noted, not easy to define, nor obviously free.[5] Free from what? Not free from convention, once freedom has become convention; nor from the fact that stress in English is fixed at the level of the word and constrained at the level of the phrase by focus and nuclear stress; nor from an aesthetic pull towards sonic repetition. Whitman's prosody (in 'The Song of Myself', 1855) may be looser, and his lines longer, than most verse written in this period, but freedom of versification leads to constraints in syntax. The near-constant anaphora is a constraint on thought, as well as sound. Sometimes it is a constraint on realism:

> Twenty-eight young men bathe by the shore;
> Twenty-eight young men, and all so friendly:
> Twenty-eight years of womanly life, and all so lonesome.[6]

Exactly twenty-eight? Really?

In fact, it isn't clear that Pound does not intend the parenthetical aside in Canto 81 to be an example of false belief—an idea that could have been entertained (notice also that he supplies no agent)—but which is actually, like many of the other ideas in this Canto, false dogma. He was certainly not sympathetic to the democratic principles that some of free verse's supporters have seen it as promoting. Indeed, the

---

[4] Ezra Pound, *The Pisan Cantos, The Cantos of Ezra Pound* (London: Faber, 1975), 553.
[5] Chris Beyers opens his study *A History of Free Verse* (Fayetteville, AR: University of Arkansas Press, 2001) by quoting T. V. F. Brogan, 'Useful ... so long as one does not enquire further into what it means', 13.
[6] Walt Whitman, *Leaves of Grass: A Textual Variorum of the Printed Poems*, ed. Sculley Bradley et al., 3 vols (New York: New York University Press, 1980), I, 12.

parenthesis occurs after a reported conversation between Thomas Jefferson and John Adams about monarchy versus aristocracy, 'You the one, I the few'. In this correspondence, both remain committed to a 'natural aristocracy'.[7] Nor does Pound represent himself as having any great agency over English prosody here or anywhere else; more often, in fact, he and Eliot present themselves as the metrically dispossessed, as victims. 'No verse is free', said Eliot, 'for the man who wants to do a good job' and 'there is no freedom in art'.[8] Pound was fond of misquoting this as 'no verse is libre'. The French term itself adds a note of suspicion, as Eliot perhaps also intended in his 'Vers Libre' essay. [9] Neither poet was hospitable to liberalism as a political idea.

Eliot and Pound both recognized that if modern English poetry was and had to be metrically different from its antecedents, this was because the language itself had changed. Barthes's dictum that 'it is language which speaks, not the author' may hold truer for prosody than most other parts of poetic composition. In the preface to his mother's dramatic poem *Savonarola*, Eliot commented elliptically: 'The next form of drama will have to be a verse drama but in new verse forms. Perhaps the conditions of modern life (think how large a part is now played in sensory life by the internal combustion engine) have altered our rhythms.'[10] In the late chapter 'Poetry and Drama', reflecting on his playwriting career, 'the rhythm of regular blank verse had become too remote from the movement of modern speech'.[11] What was new in modernist poetry was, at times, an attempt to codify these changes (Hopkins's doctrine of sprung rhythm, Eliot's hankering after a new prosody for verse drama) and at others, a conscious attempt to evade them (e.g. in Pound's and Eliot's experiments with quatrain poems, after Gautier) by returning to the 'hard' chiselled forms in use before the Romantic period. The major modernist poets—Eliot, Yeats, Pound, Auden, Stevens—all wrote verse that is much *less* free than many of their contemporaries, and between them they reprised (not always successfully) a number of forms that the nineteenth century had forgotten: Auden's trochaic catalectics for example ('Lay your sleeping head, my love'), or un-enjambed *abab* tetrameter quatrains reminiscent of eighteenth-century verse (the nineteenth century preferred *abac* or the 'In Memoriam' *abba*), or rhyme royal (Auden's 'Letter to Lord Byron'), and ottava rima ('Sailing to Byzantium').[12]

---

[7] See particularly the letter from Adams to Jefferson of 15 November 1813, in Lester J. Cappon (ed.), *The Adams–Jefferson Letters* (Chapel Hill, NC: University of North Carolina Press, 1959), 400.

[8] The first statement is introduced as a remark made twenty-five years ago in 'The Music of Poetry', in T. S. Eliot, *On Poetry and Poets* (London: Faber and Faber, 1957), 26–38, 36; the second is from the 1917 essay 'Vers Libre', *The New Statesman* 8/204 (3 March 1917), 518–19.

[9] Pound originally made this misquotation in his review of *Prufrock and Other Observations*, *Poetry* (August 1917), though it continued to be ascribed to Eliot in Pound's essay, 'T. S. Eliot', in Eliot's own edition: *Literary Essays of Ezra Pound* (London: Faber, 1954), 418–23, 421.

[10] T. S. Eliot, introduction to Charlotte Eliot's *Savonarola: A Dramatic Poem* (London: Cobden Sanderson, 1926), xi.

[11] T. S. Eliot, 'Poetry and Drama', *On Poetry and Poets*, 72–88, 80.

[12] Edmund Gosse distinguishes between Keats's couplets and those of classical versifiers as follows: 'the romantic class is of a loose and elastic kind, full of these successive overflows, while the classical is closely confined to the use of distich', *From Shakespeare to Pope: An Inquiry into the*

Compare the following two passages, written at either end of this long turn-of-the-century period. Which is freer? The first is from the end of the first part of Pound's *Hugh Selwyn Mauberley*, and was printed with the date 1919 above it.

> Tell her that sheds
> Such treasure in the air,
> Recking naught else but that her graces give
> Life to the moment,
> I would bid them live
> As roses might, in magic amber laid,
> Red overwrought with orange and all made
> One substance and one colour
> Braving time.

As an 'enigmatic pastiche' of Edmund Waller's 'Go, lovely rose', Pound's 'Envoi' has puzzled critics. He rated it highly enough to propose its inclusion in an anthology containing only two of his poems, but omitted it during a 1958 recording of *Mauberley*.[13] Sarah Davison has argued that it forms part of his attempt to 'resurrect the art of the lyric', and specifically the *classical* pre-romantic lyric—a project which continues in Canto 81 ('to break the pentameter'). And this was eminently a formal problem for Pound, who thought lyric could only be revived by going one step beyond Waller and Campion ('mere imitation of them won't do'): that is, by writing in new versions of their metres. In Canto 81, he produces another, even more lovely, virtuosic imitation of late Renaissance lyric, before quoting two lines attributed to Chaucer, and measuring out the gap: 'And for a hundred and eighty years almost nothing.'

A more typical example of the changes in nineteenth-century metrical norms is evident in the first stanza of Christina Rossetti's 'Song of Flight', published in 1881. Where Pound maintains the rule that there should be an equal number of stressed and unstressed syllables (allowing only for the possibility of a feminine rhyme, an extra unstressed at the end), Rossetti allows extra, unstressed syllables to creep in everywhere in her restless, leaping short lyric:

> While we slumber and sleep
> The sun leaps up from the deep–
> Daylight born at the leap!–
> Rapid, dominant, free
> Athirst to bathe in the uttermost sea.

How are we to hear or say (or sing) this lyric? The first line is made from two anapests; the second teases us. If it follows the pattern of the first, we should stress

---

Causes and Phenomena of the Rise of Classical Poetry in England (Cambridge: Cambridge University Press, 1885), 6.

[13] Sarah Davison, 'Pound's Esteem for Edmund Waller: A New Source for Hugh Selwyn Mauberley', *Review of English Studies* 60/247 (2009), 785–800.

'leaps', but, in that case, why didn't Rossetti write the perfectly possible 'The sun leaps from the deep'? The addition of the preposition 'up' leads to wilful metrical irregularity. And then the first line's pattern is repeated in the third, making the stress on the long vowel 'born' even heavier. The fourth line is irregular in a different way. The poem's ground rule, two anapests per line, has not been firmly enough established to stick, so the *possible* pronunciation 'rapid DOMinant FREE' falters, and the natural trochee of 'rapid', with the stress on the first syllable, swings against the notionally upward rhythm—turning, in the last line, into a pattern that seems more naturally dactylic, falling, than anapestic, rising ('bathe in the' and 'uttermost' are both, isolated, falling rhythms).

In one sense, this small poem is in free verse, because no pattern that is replicable can be discerned from it, and its form is unique. At the same time, it is also typical of a general tendency in later nineteenth-century poetry to agglutinate extra, unstressed syllables, while keeping the stresses constant, creating sound patterns that would traditionally be defined as anapestic or dactylic: one long, two shorts. If we allow that stresses can always be separated by one or two syllables, then the alternation between dimeter and tetrameter is, in an abstract sense, the same pattern as Waller's 'Go lovely rose', although the pacing and mood produced is very different.

Pound's uncertainty about 'Envoi' is testament to the fact that the English lyric never really had a codified form. In fact, poets' search for new forms at the turn of the twentieth century can be understood as part of a much longer search for a lyric metre. Traditionally, lyric's prestige was lower than that of dramatic, epic, or narrative verse, and the most ingenious and experimental of Renaissance versifiers devoted their metrical attention elsewhere. But during the long nineteenth century, this all changed. After romanticism, the abject lyric became the most privileged of poetic modes, for J. S. Mill, 'more eminently and peculiarly poetry than any other'.[14] *Palgrave's Golden Treasury*, first published in 1861, is often described as a watershed moment in this history; for Marjorie Perloff it is testament to 'the codification of Romantic theory, with its gradual privileging of lyric over other modes'.[15] Marion Thain has recently suggested that it inaugurates, in addition, a movement away from the self-aware lyric of Tennyson, Arnold, or Clough towards the pathological 'lyric solipsism' evident in the Decadent poetry of Swinburne and Symons.[16]

The metrical consequences of a turn to lyric are not so often discussed as the thematic and generic ones, but if English poetry had backed itself into a 'lyric

---

[14] John Stuart Mill, 'Thoughts on Poetry and its Varieties', *Dissertations and Discussions: Political, Philosophical, and Historical*, 4 vols (London: J. W. Parker, 1859), I, 63–94, 85.

[15] This important point is given attention by Scott Brewster in *Lyric* (Abingdon: Routledge, 2009), and in Marjorie Perloff, *The Dance of the Intellect: Studies in the Poetry of the Pound Tradition* (Cambridge: Cambridge University Press, 1985), 177–8.

[16] Marion Thain, 'Victorian Lyric Pathology and Phenomenology', in Thain (ed.), *The Lyric Poem: Formations and Transformations* (Cambridge: Cambridge University Press, 2013), 156–76.

ghetto' by 1900 (in Mark Jeffreys' memorable phrase) it is not surprising that it had also lost use of its most natural, conversational line, the pentameter.[17] A poem such as Tennyson's 'Ulysses' is a soliloquy in a blank frame, a remote, dramatized speaker, obviously not the poet himself, talking to a remote listener. Its lyricism lies in the surreptitious way we are asked to 'overhear', but the speaker himself, being quite solidly a dramatic character, inhabits blank verse easily. But, in Palgrave's first edition, there is not a single poem like this: nothing in blank verse. All of the poems rhyme. The most metrically irregular are the ballads in dialect, but even here an underlying, if flexible and variable, structure can be discerned.[18] Even the number of poems in rhyming iambic pentameter is fairly low (under 25 per cent). Take out Shakespeare's sonnets, and it would be much lower again. Traditionally, lyric used different forms: trochaic catalectics ('Fear no more the heat of the sun'), heavily rhymed, artificial iambic tetrameter ('When as in silks my Julia goes'), and structures describable only at the level of the strophe, not the line.

The turn to lyric was accompanied, as Rossetti's lyric shows, by a phonological or aural change in English poets' attitude towards unstressed syllables, 'quick rhythms', and trisyllabic feet. In fact, these changes, one of mode, one of phonology, may not be entirely unrelated. In his study of the English lyric, George Saintsbury tellingly observes that disyllabic feet had, from the beginning of English poetry, been problematic for lyricists, perhaps because of musical monotony: 'the deplorable heresy that there was in English "only a foot of two syllables" – from which it almost necessarily followed that lyric must be crippled or at least fettered.'[19] Lyric in English, he is saying, seems to encourage poetry written with different kinds of metrical base rhythms. Are there historical, linguistic reasons to explain why old forms might cease to work for modern English? It is tempting to say so, and changes in pronunciation would be a good, basic explanation for new prosodies. But there was no great vowel shift around 1880.

The deep causes—phonological or, as Eliot suggests, technological—of changes in the English ear in the nineteenth century require much more systematic investigation by scholars. But the solutions, the new forms, that poets found as a response to these pressures might be loosely categorized into five kinds, and I will discuss them in order of increasing metrical 'freedom'.

First, a classicist interest in preserving traditional forms: poems in isometric (equal-length) lines and with almost entirely trochaic or iambic feet. This, which is the solution of many of the high modernist poets, at least at points during their

---

[17] Mark Jeffreys, 'Ideologies of Lyric: A Problem of Genre in Contemporary Anglophone Poetics', *Publications of the Modern Language Association of America* (*PMLA*) 110/2 (1995), 196–205, 200.

[18] One of the most 'irregular' poems is CLII, 'Auld Robin Gray', attributed to Lady A. Lindsay. But even this poem is in quatrains rhyming *aabb*, with four stresses per line and a variable number of unstressed syllables. Francis Turner Palgrave, *The Golden Treasury of English Lyrical Poems and Songs* (London: R. Clay, 1861), 149–50.

[19] George Saintsbury, *The Historical Character of English Lyric* (London: British Academy, 1912), 5.

career, was accompanied by distaste for sentimental, personal, or effusive poetry—in fact, a distaste for lyric. The quatrain poems that Pound and Eliot wrote in the mid-teens, supposedly under the influence of Gautier, are some of the clearest examples; in fact, a poem like 'Sweeney Among the Nightingales', where clauses are contained within the unit of the line, is also reminiscent of eighteenth-century quatrain writing. When Yeats approved the ending of this poem as speaking 'in the grand manner', he was recognizing not its continental, but its English, ancestry. This solution, not always a success, was conservative both in its desire to preserve the traditional metres of English and, just as importantly, in its commitment to keeping the diegetic range of poetry as wide as possible. The combatant soldier poets, whose recourse to traditional poetic forms is usually read as nostalgic, comforting, and stylistically outmoded, also wrote largely in traditional metres. Rupert Brooke's sonnets and T. S. Eliot's quatrain poems are not, in terms of their sound and form, at quite such divergent ends of the poetic spectrum as Paul Fussell suggests.[20] The difference lies in the sonnets' plush lyricism and archaic diction, their lack of irony, and their voicing.

A related, though less successful, strategy was the importation of new forms into English, usually from French. The poets of the Rhymers' Club experimented with intricate, repetitious forms not seen much in English poetry before or (except as exercises in writing workshops) since: sestinas, villanelles, rondeaus, rondels. But however quickly poets threw up new structures, none seemed to stick. The villanelle that Stephen Dedalus writes on the back of a cigarette packet in *A Portrait of the Artist* seems intended, within its context, to be read ironically as an example of Stephen's aesthetic pretentiousness. The nagging repetitiousness of the form has a hollowing-out effect; like the diary with which the novel finishes, it suggests that Stephen, along with Joyce's other Dubliners, is destined to paralysis, to staying put. Pound's own 'Villanelle: The Psychological Hour' is *not* a villanelle, but it is a satirical take on the mood of these Decadent forms: 'I had over-prepared the event', 'So much barren regret!/So many hours wasted!' In fact, both Pound and Joyce had written poems of this kind in earnest in their early twenties, copying the examples of Symons and Dowson.[21] The impulse to produce new forms for lyric poetry to inhabit is essentially modernist; the problem was simply that these kinds of poems quickly became self-limiting and self-thematizing—studies of circularity, indifference, impotence. Dowson's 'Dregs', with its sense of everything gone leewards, is one typical example.

The third solution, already seen in Rossetti's song, was to keep the traditional rhyming, stress, and line structures of English poetry, but without insisting on

[20] The influential argument made in *The Great War and Modern Memory* (Oxford: Oxford University Press, 1975).

[21] See Robert Adams Day, 'The Villanelle Perplex: Reading Joyce', *James Joyce Quarterly* 25/1 (1987), 69–85, 71.

isosyllabism (the same number of syllables per line). Almost always in this period, the tendency is to keep the number of stresses constant, while increasing the number of syllables. Rossetti's poem is one example; another, more metrically consistent, would be Hardy's 'The Voice', written in 1912, which calls out in a predominantly dactylic metre:

> Woman much missed how you call to me, call to me
> Saying that now you are not as you were…

In his early poetry, Yeats was also fond of these triple rhythms. He presents the curious example of a versifier who becomes stricter, not freer over time; the Pound-influenced modernist poet of the 1920s was writing in more classical forms than the Celtic twilight poet of *The Rose*:

> I would that we were, my beloved, white birds on the foam of the sea!

Even Hopkins's notorious theory of sprung rhythm—described by recent critics as 'completely idiosyncratic',[22] 'puzzling',[23] 'peculiar', and badly described by Hopkins—can be understood as an attempt to drive this tendency in late nineteenth-century poetry to its codified extreme.[24] In her recent work on the cultural significance of the (surprisingly vehement) metrical debates at this period, Meredith Martin asks: 'What if Hopkins's prosody is part of a larger story about the instability of English meter in the nineteenth century?'[25] Her own focus is, however, more on the intellectual history of prosody than its comparative employment. This is Hopkins's description:

> Sprung Rhythm, as used in this book, is measured by feet of from one to four syllables, regularly, and for particular effects any number of weak or slack syllables may be used. It has one stress, which falls on the only syllable, if there is only one, if there are more, then scanning as above, on the first, and so gives rise to four sorts of feet, a monosyllable and the so-called accentual Trochee, Dactyl, and the First Paeon.[26]

The most important point here is that each foot has 'one stress', and that 'any number of weak or slack syllables may be used'. Hopkins also points out that these

---

[22] Paul Kiparsky cites Paul Fussell, *Poetic Meter and Poetic Form* (New York: Random House, 1965), noting that the comment is withdrawn in the second edition. See 'Sprung rhythm' in Paul Kiparsky and Gilbert Youmans (eds), *Phonetics and Phonology, Volume 1: Rhythm and Meter* (San Diego, CA: Academic Press, 1989), 305–40, 306.

[23] Peter L. Groves opens his discussion of Hopkins's metre by noting that the diacritics with which he peppered his poems have puzzled and even 'irritated' readers. See '"Opening the Pentameter": Hopkins's Metrical Experimentation', *Victorian Poetry* 49/2 (2011), 93–110, 93.

[24] For another version of this argument, see Elizabeth W. Schneider, *The Dragon in the Gate: Studies in the Poetry of G. M. Hopkins* (Berkeley, CA: University of California Press, 1968), 42–82. Paul Kiparsky notes that the standard assumption is that sprung rhythm is purely accentual, but that it has also been compared to spondaic verse (Fussell) and trisyllabic verse (Schneider).

[25] Meredith Martin, 'Hopkins's Prosody', *Victorian Poetry* 49/2 (2011), 1–30, 9.

[26] Gerard Manley Hopkins, 'Author's Preface', in Robert Bridges (ed.), *Poems of Gerard Manley Hopkins* (London: Humphrey Milford, 1918).

patterns are primarily strophic (phrasal) rather than stichic (line-based), for 'it is natural in Sprung Rhythm for the lines to be *rove over,* that is for the scanning of each line immediately to take up that of the one before'.

A huge amount of attention has been paid by both linguisticians and literary critics to the subtleties of Hopkins's metre, but many of these studies err by assuming that Hopkins's own *rules* for pronunciation, suggested in part by diacritical marks, show the actual pronunciation of the poems. In fact, it makes very little sense for poets to be prescriptive about metre, because readers don't follow their advice; we know by eye that 'prove' and 'love' must rhyme, in a Shakespeare sonnet, but the eye is not enough to persuade the ear. Hopkins's rhythms are largely falling with a stress every three or four syllables (often, emphatically, on syllables that are quantitatively long). His diacritics *overmark* the amount of stress we actually pronounce. Once they are removed, is the opening of 'Spring and Fall' so different from Hardy's 'The Voice'? The similarity is seen more clearly when two lines are written as one long dactylic line:

> Margaret, are you grieving over Goldengrove unleaving?[27]

Or compare this little lyric to Rossetti's 'the sun leaps up from the deep'.

> And I have asked to be
> Where no storms come,
> Where the green swell is in the havens dumb,
> And out of the swing of the sea.[28]

In the fifth volume of *Palgrave's Golden Treasury*, which was added to the others in 1926 and covered verse from the beginning of the Victorian period to Yeats, a very high proportion of the poems work with triple rhythms, from Tennyson's 'Break, Break, Break' and Browning's 'Love Among the Ruins' to the huntsman's chorus from *Atalanta in Calydon* and James Clarence Mangan's translation from Irish 'My dark Rosaleen' (Rosaleen's name itself forcing the metre).

A fourth, more visually surprising solution was long lines (sometimes combined, as in Hardy's case, with triple rhythms). Ten syllables, and five stresses, had traditionally been about as far as English could stretch. Even the alexandrine seemed too long; Samuel Johnson's observation that it 'invariably requires a break at the sixth syllable' illustrates that it was traditionally felt to be no more than two trimeters stuck together.[29] Was this increased tolerance for long lines the result of industrial time speeding things up? Tennyson claimed to have made the fifteen syllable

---

[27] The first two lines (minus diacritics) of 'Spring and Fall', in Robert Bridges (ed.), *Poems of Gerard Manley Hopkins,* 2nd ed. (Oxford: Oxford University Press, 1935), 50.

[28] Second and last stanza of 'Heaven-Haven', in Robert Bridges (ed.), *Poems of Gerard Manley Hopkins,* 2nd ed. (Oxford: Oxford University Press, 1935), 8.

[29] Dryden, however, is said sometimes to neglect this rule. See Samuel Johnson, *The Lives of the Most Eminent English Poets*, 4 vols (London: C. Bathurst et al., 1781), II, 192.

rollicking line of 'Locksley Hall', 'Let the great world spin forever down the ringing grooves of change', after travelling by rail for the first time: 'When I went by the first train from Liverpool to Manchester (1830), I thought that the wheels ran in a groove. It was a black night and there was such a vast crowd round the train at the station that we could not see the wheels. Then I made this line.'[30] It is a tempting correspondence, but I do not think it can be quite so simple; in the hands of other poets, particularly Decadent poets of the 1890s, excess length produces languor and diffuseness. The initial anapest in Tennyson's line gives the same kind of speedy upsurge that Rossetti uses in her leaping flight poem. The long initial iamb in Arthur Symons's 'Grey Hours: Naples' produces a very different effect.

> There are some hours when I seem so indifferent; all things fade
> To an indifferent greyness, like that grey of the sky;
> Always at evening-ends, on grey days; and I know not why,
> But life, and art, and love, and death, are the shade of a shade.[31]

The break after 'indifferent' is world-weary, and the overlong line's tendency to cluster nouns (life and art and love *and* death), repeat words (grey, indifferent), and dwell on long syllables creates intellectual flaccidity and enervation.

One might object, following Johnson, that the very long lines in 'Locksley Hall' are only superficially unusual, an experiment in lineation and pagination, rather than metrical form. As one handbook has it, the line 'readily breaks down into standard ballad metre of common measure of alternating three and four stress lines'.[32] By this argument, each of the couplets resolves into *abcb* ballad metre, so:

> Not in vain the distance beckons. Forward, forward let us range,
> Let the great world spin forever down the ringing grooves of change.[33]

has, as its underlying metrical or grammatical structure, this:

> Not in vain the distance beckons.
> Forward, forward let us range,
> Let the great world spin forever
> Down the ringing grooves of change.

This works in some cases, but not all, because polysyllables sometimes prevent the line from being broken up. We can scan the line trochaically as 'LET the GREAT world SPIN forEVer', but we tend to hear it more hurriedly, in an upward movement, 'let the GREAT world spin forEVer'.

---

[30] John Picker calls this an 'ambiguous' appeal to technological innovation, in *Victorian Soundscapes* (Oxford: Oxford University Press, 2003), 110.

[31] Arthur Symons, 'Grey Hours: Naples', dated 1897 in *Poems: Vol. 3* (London: Martin Secker, 1924), 39.

[32] Entry for 'heptameter' in J. A. Cuddon, *A Dictionary of Literary Terms and Theory*, 5th edn (Oxford: Blackwell, 2013), 327.

[33] The opening of Alfred Lord Tennyson's 'Locksley Hall', first published in *Poems, Vol. 2* (London: Edward Moxon, 1842), 92–111.

The *difference* between this line and a traditional common metre is even more apparent in the later poem, 'Locksley Hall Sixty Years After', published in 1886.[34] It is nominally in the same form as the original 'Locksley Hall'. But, somehow, it also is not. It is much closer to being 'free' verse. It is harder to turn these fifteen-syllable lines back into ballad metre, because the sense units do not fit so readily into line units. In fact, the second poem, which casts a seriously pessimistic look back over a century of progress, seems to display, in the way that the first poem did not quite, a more essential problem of formal entropy. Take these couplets, for example, from the opening of the poem's second section.

> Here is Locksley Hall, my grandson, here the lion-guarded gate.
> Not to-night in Locksley Hall – to-morrow – you, you come so late.
>
> Wreck'd – your train – or all but wreck'd? a shatter'd wheel? a vicious boy!
> Good, this forward, you that preach it, is it well to wish you joy?
>
> Is it well that while we range with Science, glorying in the Time,
> City children soak and blacken soul and sense in city slime?
>
> There among the glooming alleys Progress halts on palsied feet,
> Crime and hunger cast our maidens by the thousand on the street.

Here self-interruption and repair produce some of the free effects of a Browning monologue. 'Wreck'd – your train – or all but wrecked?' could be pronounced and stressed in many different ways. And the tendency of the fifteen-syllable line to split into two four-beat trochaic lines, the second catalectic, is denied by the strange break at 'to' in the word 'tomorrow', which gets broken into two. The effect is that of a stutter, as the speaker diagnoses some kind of *essential* breach between today and tomorrow, telling his interlocutor that he has come too late, the once aggressive train now wrecked and shattered, and Progress itself 'halting'. And in the second couplet, the vigorous travelling metre never quite gets going: the heavy consonants of 'range' and 'science', the late caesuara in line one, and the alliterative consonants in line two, produce a heavy, serious long line, one that seems on the verge of devolving into prose.

In fact, as Whitman recognized, this long-line poem sounds—via a different means—quite a lot like Whitman. The two poets are not usually grouped together, and Whitman's comment about 'finest verbalism' is usually understood to be disparaging. Significantly, it was made in a short, largely approving chapter written in response to this poem. 'Beautiful as the song was, the original "Locksley Hall" of half a century ago was essentially morbid, heart-broken, finding fault with everything'.[35] And then, after quoting ten lines from the just-out sequel, he moves on to the topic of Tennyson's conservatism: 'He shows how one can be a royal laureate, quite elegant and "aristocratic", and a little queer and affected, and at the

---

[34] Alfred Lord Tennyson, *Locksley Hall Sixty Years After, Etc.* (London: Macmillan, 1886).
[35] Whitman, *November Boughs* (Philadelphia, PA: David McKay, 1888), 65.

SIXTY YEARS AFTER 17

Envy wears the mask of Love, and, laughing sober
fact to scorn,
Cries to Weakest as to Strongest, 'Ye are equals,
equal-born.'

Equal-born? O yes, if yonder hill be level with
the flat.
Charm us, Orator, till the Lion look no larger than
the Cat.

Till the Cat thro' that mirage of overheated language loom
Larger than the Lion,—Demos end in working its
own doom.

Russia bursts our Indian barrier, shall we fight
her? shall we yield?
Pause, before you sound the trumpet, hear the
voices from the field.

C

Figure 1 Taken from the first edition of *Locksley Hall Sixty Years After, Etc.*

A WORD ABOUT TENNYSON.

BEAUTIFUL as the song was, the original ' Locksley Hall' of half a century ago was essentially morbid, heart-broken, finding fault with everything, especially the fact of money's being made (as it ever must be, and perhaps should be) the paramount matter in worldly affairs ;

> Every door is barr'd with gold, and opens but to golden keys.

First, a father, having fallen in battle, his child (the singer)

> Was left a trampled orphan, and a selfish uncle's ward.

Of course love ensues.   The woman in the chant or monologue proves a false one ; and as far as appears the ideal of woman, in the poet's reflections, is a false one—at any rate for America. Woman is *not* ' the lesser man.'   (The heart is not the brain.) The best of the piece of fifty years since is its concluding line :

> For the mighty wind arises roaring seaward and I go.

Then for this current 1886–7, a just-out sequel, which (as an apparently authentic summary says) ' reviews the life of mankind during the past sixty years, and comes to the conclusion that its boasted progress is of doubtful credit to the world in general and to England in particular.   A cynical vein of denunciation of democratic opinions and aspirations runs throughout the poem in mark'd contrast with the spirit of the poet's youth.' Among the most striking lines of this sequel are the following :

Envy wears the mask of love, and, laughing sober fact to scorn,
Cries to weakest as to strongest, ' Ye are equals, equal born,'
Equal-born !   Oh yes, if yonder hill be level with the flat.
Charm us, orator, till the lion look no larger than the cat:
Till the cat, through that mirage of overheated language, loom
Larger than the lion Demo—end in working its own doom.
Tumble Nature heel o'er head, and, yelling with the yelling street,
Set the feet above the brain, and swear the brain is in the feet.
Bring the old dark ages back, without the faith, without the hope
Beneath the State, the Church, the Throne, and roll their ruins down the
    slope.

5   (65)

Figure 2 Walt Whitman's quotation from 'among the most striking lines of this sequel'.

same time perfectly manly and natural. As to his non-democracy, it fits him well, and I like him the better for it.' At first sight, Tennyson and Whitman are ideological opposites, a conservative and a progressive but, in the more complex hinterland of form and the ideologies it inscribes, they seem to have shared similar instincts. To the question—how to get modernity into poetry?—they offer the same answer: by going long.

Notice that this act of misprision in quoting does three things: it gets rid of the allegorizing capitals, it moves the word 'Demos' to the other side of the en dash, as 'Demo', thus implicitly and bizarrely *naming* the lion, and, most importantly, it prints the rhyming couplets as continuous verse. These lines are also heavy in internal anaphora and parallelism—two of Whitman's own favourite techniques for holding long lines together. Whitman's reprinting is, in one sense, of course, an aggressive act of reformatting; any format he read the poem in would have maintained, on the page, the blank spaces between the couplets. But it is also an acknowledgment of a curious formal and syntactic kinship. Tennyson's views on social progress are very pessimistic, but his container-like, overlong poem, is also in instinct restitutive: it shows us what society, and poetry, have been omitting to notice.

The tendency to agglutinate unstressed syllables, and the willingness to craft longer lines with medial polysyllables, are both ways of allowing poetry to do *more*, to contain more (Tennyson's city children soak *and* blacken soul *and* sense). In *Leaves of Grass*, the lines' propensity to 'ride over' and their over-length is, even more obviously, a problem of describing the excess of modern city life:

I hear all sounds running together, combined, fused or following...
...The heave'e'yo of stevedores unlading ships by the wharves, the refrain of the anchor-lifters,
The ring of alarm-bells, the cry of fire, the whirr of swift-streaking engines and hose-carts with premonitory tinkles and color'd lights,
The steam-whistle, the solid roll of the train of approaching cars...[36]

Pound's strategies for Imagism, formulated in 1912, are in a perverse way an attempt to address the same problem: by refusing to admit superfluous adjectives or to follow the beat of the metronome, and by insisting on condensed focus on 'the thing', he was also calling for a poetry that could do more with the line length that it had, allowing for superpositions of unlike things, and for syntactical relations that are less predictable than those encouraged by traditional form.[37]

We can see some of the same formal strategies operating in the prose of the period, and this leads to my final 'new form' for the period 1880-1920: rhythmical prose, or the prose poem. In 1912, George Saintsbury published *A History of English Prose Rhythm* as a companion to his history of prosody. It begins by explaining the

[36] Whitman, 'Song of Myself', *Leaves of Grass: A Textual Variorum*, I, 36.
[37] Pound, 'A Few Don'ts by an Imagiste', *Poetry* (March 1913).

classical idea that good prose is well-written *as* prose precisely because it avoids 'poetic' rhythms (the hexameter ending, a dactyl and a spondee, being one).[38] In the same year, Pound 'invented' Imagism: 'Don't think any intelligent person is going to be deceived when you try to shirk all the difficulties of the unspeakably difficult art of good prose by chopping your composition into line lengths.'[37] What is he saying here? His useful suggestion is that unrhythmical prose chopped into arbitrary 'lines' is nothing at all—neither good prose nor good poetry; all good writing, for Pound, involves artifice and stylization. The common definition of free verse as 'nonmetrical, nonrhyming lines that closely follow the natural rhythms of speech' might in fact be regarded as the antithesis of many of Joyce's sentences in *Ulysses*, which are metrically analyzable, not 'natural', and yet not printed in lines. (And this is studied: we know that Joyce relied on Saintsbury's history of prose rhythms in writing *Oxen of the Sun*.)

The notebooks for Ulysses, which contain a semantically puzzling collection of rather ordinary phrases, are in fact rhythmically quite predictable: Joyce prized falling rhythms, both disyllabic (yahoo, bludgeon, Cusack, carcinoma—on a random page of the *Cyclops* notesheet) and trisyllabic ('good as gold', 'those things that', 'cuckoo clock', 'he is gone').[39] He also noted down phrases combining these two rhythms: 'Me have a nice pace' (in Milly's letter) 'hyacinth perfume', 'Bacon & Essex' in *Nausicaa*. This particular rhythm is as close an imitation as one can get in English of the hexameter ending that Saintsbury, in *his* study, tells us that classical prose avoided. Plugged into the final text, they produce sentences like these, neither of which can intelligently be described as 'free' from rhythmic, alliterative, or even rhyming constraints: 'Hyacinth perfume made of oil of ether or something. Muskrat.'

In English literature of this period there are far fewer attempts than in French to write *actual* prose poems, labelled as such—but some survive, mostly by Americans. Examples include Carl Sandburg's 1916 *Chicago Poems* (full of Whitmanian anaphora, as Michael Delville's useful study shows), Sherwood Anderson's *Mid-American Chants*, and Gertrude Stein's *Tender Buttons*. T. S. Eliot's 'Hysteria' is the lone example in *Prufrock and Other Observations*; I have seen students sometimes quote this *as* a poem, with the arbitrary last words of the lines preserved. Within the context of the original volume, and within a culture that regards Eliot's poems as 'free', and 'free verse' as no more than chopped-up prose, much about this mistake is forgivable. But it is also a mistake that *exactly* fails to see what is experimental about Eliot's account of an infectious, embarrassing moment of sexual panic, where 'her teeth were only accidental stars [iambic pentameter] with a talent for squad-drill' and 'the shaking of her breasts' refuses to be stopped. The banality of repetition as the

---

[38] Saintsbury, *A History of English Prose Rhythm* (London: Macmillan, 1912).
[39] Examples chosen almost at random from Philip Herring's *James Joyce's Ulysses Notesheets in the British Museum* (Charlottesville, VA: University Press of Virginia, 1972), 110, 131–2.

waiter invites the couple 'to take their tea in the garden', the nervous attempts at mastery of the situation by a simple 'I' speaker, and the uncontrolled engulfment of the hysteria itself are all enhanced by the careful formal choice. In the final poem of the volume, an antithetical situation—a melancholy hypothetical mood, regret for what wasn't—is weighed up in mournfully self-aware rhymes:

> I should have lost a gesture and a pose.
> Sometimes these cogitations still amaze
> The troubled midnight and the noon's repose.

Here Eliot is writing in iambic pentameter, and he does so with a degree of indebted virtuosity (his feel for Tennysonian vowel sounds; the elegant variation of the end-stoppped line and the syntactically enjambed one). What is new here is not a negative freedom from form, an absence of form, but the positive freedom to select critically from the prosody handbook, manipulating old forms for new ends.

FURTHER READING

Beyers, Chris. *A History of Free Verse* (Fayetteville, AR: University of Arkansas Press, 2001).

Delville, Michael. *The American Prose Poem: Poetic Form and the Boundaries of Genre* (Gainesville, FL: University Press of Florida, 1998).

Eliot, T. S. 'Vers Libre', *The New Statesman* 8/204 (3 March 1917), 518–19.

Eliot, T. S. 'Poetry and Drama' and 'The Music of Poetry', *On Poetry and Poets* (London: Faber, 1957).

Jeffreys, Mark. 'Ideologies of Lyric: A Problem of Genre in Contemporary Anglophone Poetics', *Publications of the Modern Language Association of America* (*PMLA*) 110/2 (1995), 196–205.

Martin, Meredith. *The Rise and Fall of Meter: Poetry and English National Culture, 1860–1930* (Princeton, NJ: Princeton University Press, 2012).

Perloff, Marjorie. *The Dance of the Intellect: Studies in the Poetry of the Pound Tradition* (Cambridge: Cambridge University Press, 1985).

Pound, Ezra. 'A Few Don'ts by an Imagiste', *Poetry* (March 1913).

Saintsbury, George. *A History of English Prose Rhythm* (London: Macmillan, 1912).

Thain, Marion. 'Victorian Lyric Pathology and Phenomenology', in Marion Thain (ed.), *The Lyric Poem: Formations and Transformations* (Cambridge: Cambridge University Press, 2013).

CHAPTER 7

WHEN *WAS* MODERNISM?

MICHAEL H. WHITWORTH

Declining an invitation to speak in a debate on 'modernist' poetry in December 1926, T. S. Eliot hinted at an instability in the term itself: 'If I were able to be present I should certainly protest against the pestilential word "modernist" for which I see no excuse...The word is almost as hopeless as "Futurist"...The term "Modernist" is a good ten years out of date.'[1] Just as 'futurist' attempts to lay claim to a future that is inexorably moving into the past, 'modernist' tries to refer to a present moment that cannot endure. Likewise, the 'avant-garde' presents itself as being ahead of the present moment. There are many reasons why the chronology of modernism is hard to pin down, but its simple insistence on defying conventional chronology is central to the problem. As Raymond Williams noted in his 1987 lecture 'When Was Modernism?', modernism's hold over 'the modern' has forced criticism to refer to later periods as 'contemporary' or 'post-modern'.[2] For Williams, this is not just an 'intellectual problem' but 'an ideological perspective'. To accede to modernism's own claims is to grant it normative power over us; but, we might add, to place it within temporal limits and to register its death may be to disregard some of its own profoundest claims.

Williams suggested that the dominant version of 'the modern' spanned the years 1890 to 1940. One influential introductory book took 1890–1930 as its dates; a more recent introduction has taken 1910–45.[3] A wider survey finds many critics dating the origins of the movement to 1857; others argue that it never ended, and continues to the present day.[4] Arguments about the chronological boundaries of the movement are important for pedagogical reasons as they can affect which texts are included on a given course or module. And they are important because the chronological frame

---

[1] Valerie Eliot, John Haffenden, and Hugh Haughton (eds), *The Letters of T. S. Eliot*, 5 vols (London: Faber, 1988–), III, 344.

[2] Raymond Williams, *The Politics of Modernism: Against the New Conformists*, ed. Tony Pinkney (London: Verso, 1989), 32.

[3] Malcolm Bradbury and James McFarlane (eds), *Modernism 1890–1930* (Harmondsworth: Penguin, 1976); Jane Goldman, *Modernism, 1910–1945* (Basingstoke: Palgrave Macmillan, 2004).

[4] Michael H. Whitworth (ed.), *Modernism* (Oxford: Blackwell, 2007), 272–96.

determines the kind of story we can tell about the movement, and that goes to the very heart of our analysis of what it was and why it mattered. The question about chronology opens up other important questions about the status of the individual writer, about modernity, and about location. The answers vary according to the arts involved; the debate about 'postmodernism' is deeply, perhaps distortingly, indebted to architectural history. This chapter focuses on fiction and poetry.

Those critics who date the origins of modernism to 1857 have usually done so because of two controversial French works published in that year, Gustave Flaubert's *Madame Bovary* and Charles Baudelaire's *Les fleurs du mal*. To identify Flaubert as a proto-modernist is to recognize the importance of verbal style and *le mot juste* for both novelists and poets; to identify Baudelaire is to make the city central to our account of modernism and modernity, and not only the city, but the *flâneur*'s characteristic urban consciousness. Flaubert's mastery of prose set an important example to James Joyce and to Ezra Pound; Baudelaire's understanding of the city is important to T. S. Eliot's poems from 'The Love Song of J. Alfred Prufrock' through to *The Waste Land*.[5] The controversial nature of both books—both were subject to legal proceedings—also anticipates the history of provocative subject matter and legal intervention in the history of modernism, whether Joyce's *Ulysses*, Wyndham Lewis's 'Cantleman's Spring Mate', or D. H. Lawrence's *The Rainbow*. Eliot's quotation in *The Waste Land* from Baudelaire's prefatory poem to *Les fleurs du mal* also serves as a reminder that Baudelaire had pioneered a revision in relations between author and reader, especially with regard to socially unacceptable subject matter. Writing of a personified 'ennui', Baudelaire challenges the reader: 'Tu le connais, lecteur, ce monstre délicat, / –Hypocrite lecteur,–mon semblable,–mon frère!'[6] The role of the poet, this suggests, is not to entertain, to reassure, or to offer sage wisdom: it is to confront, to unsettle, and to question.

Although *Madame Bovary* and *Les fleurs du mal* were significant works for many of the generation of writers born in the 1880s and early 1890s, seeing them as starting points for later works is very different from seeing them as actual modernist works. Later starting dates bring us closer to the core of what is usually considered modernism, but even these dates involve significant choices. Choosing between 1890 and 1900 involves deciding whether aestheticist and symbolist works in the 1890s might have enough in common with those of the 1900s to belong to the movement. The connection between the symbolists and the modernists, mediated by Arthur Symons's *The Symbolist Movement in Literature* (1899), has been well documented and widely discussed, particularly because it calls into question modernist rejections of Romanticism.[7]

---

[5] T. S. Eliot, 'What Dante Means to Me' (1950), in *To Criticize the Critic* (London: Faber, 1965), 126.

[6] Charles Baudelaire, *The Flowers of Evil*, trans. James McGowan (Oxford: Oxford University Press, 1993), 6.

[7] Frank Kermode, *Romantic Image* (London: Routledge and Kegan Paul, 1957), 107.

The choice between 1908 (the starting date of Michael Levenson's *The Genealogy of Modernism*) and 1910 (the date in Jane Goldman's book) is small in terms of years, but significant in terms of consequences. Beginning in 1908 places the focus on Ezra Pound's arrival in London, the launch of *The English Review* under Ford Madox Hueffer (later Ford), and T. E. Hulme's membership of the Poets' Club. It allows the inclusion of F. T. Marinetti's 'The Founding and the Manifesto of Futurism' (1909), and allows the later Imagist and Vorticist manifestos to be understood in a continental context. Beginning in 1910 places the emphasis more firmly on Bloomsbury: in 1924, Virginia Woolf declared that 'human character' had changed in 1910, and insofar as this somewhat tongue-in-cheek remark responds to earnest analysis, analysts have agreed that the Post-Impressionist Exhibition of 1910 was a crucial event.[8]

The identification of a peak moment is just as important to the question of modernism's history as the identification of initial and terminal dates. In 1960, Harry Levin established the dominant interpretation by suggesting that 1922 was the *annus mirabilis*: in Levin's account it merited attention for being the year of Marcel Proust's death, and the year of publication of the 'central volume' of *À la recherche du temps perdu*, *Sodom et Gomorrhe*. In the English-speaking world it was the year also of *Ulysses* and *The Waste Land*, and of Lawrence's *Aaron's Rod*, Woolf's *Jacob's Room,* and Katherine Mansfield's collection of stories, *The Garden Party*.[9] Levin's identification was echoed in Bradbury and McFarlane's widely distributed *Modernism 1890–1930* (though they amplify Levin's scepticism about the audacity needed to identify a single peak year), and the idea of 1922 as *annus mirabilis* has become taken as read in critical discourse.[10] It would be difficult to deny the impact of *Ulysses* and *The Waste Land* within Anglophone modernism, but to choose 1922 and to foreground those works is to create a teleology for all works before them, and to suggest that those that followed were doing so in the shadow of the masterpieces. The latter logic is particularly visible in hostile accounts of Woolf's *Mrs Dalloway* and its relation to *Ulysses*.[11] Attempts to revise the values associated with the year of wonders by emphasizing the importance of other works face the almost impossible task of displacing the critical work devoted to Joyce and Eliot.

It has become a commonplace within studies of Scottish modernism that the *annus mirabilis* also saw C. M. Grieve's creation of his pen-name Hugh MacDiarmid

---

[8] Virginia Woolf, 'Character in Fiction', in Andrew McNeillie and Stuart N. Clarke (eds), *Essays of Virginia Woolf*, 6 vols (London: Hogarth Press, 1986–2012), III, 420.

[9] Harry Levin, 'What Was Modernism?', *Massachusetts Review* 1/4 (Summer 1960), 618–19.

[10] Bradbury and McFarlane, 'The Name and Nature of Modernism', in Bradbury and McFarlane (eds), *Modernism 1890–1930*, 33. See, more recently, Michael North, *Reading 1922: A Return to the Scene of the Modern* (New York, NY: Oxford University Press, 1999).

[11] For sympathetic accounts, see Harvena Richter, 'The *Ulysses* Connection: Clarissa Dalloway's Bloomsday', *Studies in the Novel* 21/3 (Fall 1989), 305–19; Carolyn Heilbrun, *Hamlet's Mother and Other Women* (New York, NY: Columbia University Press, 1990), 58–88.

and the publication of his first poems in 'synthetic Scots'.[12] While such additions to the canon are salutary in reminding us that other kinds of experiment were being undertaken beyond the metropolitan centres, they supplement rather than reform the existing canon. Attempts to rethink modernism need at the very least to rethink when its high point came, as Bonnie Kime Scott has done by arguing for a female-authored canon with 1928 as its key year, or to rethink its moment of origin, as Peter Stansky and Jean-Michel Rabaté have done by focusing on 1910 and 1913 respectively.[13] More radically, such recent studies abandon the idea of a single narrative for the whole movement with a single peak, and understand modernism as a wider territory with a complex topography consisting of many peaks, ridges, and valleys.

Critics who believe that modernism came to some sort of end have also disagreed about when and why it did so. The Second World War has often been suggested, with both 1939 and 1945 appearing commonly as dates. The earlier of the two dates may also be used to suggest that the movement came to an end with the deaths of W. B. Yeats and James Joyce, or with the publication of *Finnegans Wake*: such an explanation places primary importance on the canonical artists. Another explanation is that the war against fascism brought into focus the right-wing politics of some modernist writers, and the apparent political indifference of others. The argument was influentially advanced by Archibald MacLeish in *The Irresponsibles* (1940) and reiterated by Van Wyck Brooks, and was given significant coverage by the New York-based *Partisan Review* in 1942.[14] Critics who believe that a modernist tradition continued after 1945 have argued usually on the basis of there being a 'late modernist' tradition in poetry which was brought into focus by Donald Allen's anthology *The New American Poetry, 1945–1960* (1960), and which continued thereafter in North America and Britain; or, as we shall see, on the basis of a 'transnational modernism', that extended beyond Europe and North America. In recent years, many novelists have also engaged with modernism and with the early twentieth-century cultural scene in their fiction, thereby ambivalently signalling a relation to the high modernist tradition.[15]

In the years after the end of the Second World War, the critics who established the modernist canon did not reflect on when modernism was; their concern was to win acceptance for writers and works that had been deemed controversial on aesthetic and legal grounds. Their question concerned not the dating of modernism, but the identification of the important figures; the dates of modernism followed by

[12] Alan Bold, 'Dr Grieve and Mr MacDiarmid', in P. H. Scott and A. C. Davis (eds), *The Age of MacDiarmid* (Edinburgh: Mainstream, 1980), 44.
[13] Bonnie Kime Scott, *Refiguring Modernism*, 2 vols (Bloomington, IN: Indiana University Press, 1995). Vol. I is subtitled 'The Women of 1928'.
[14] Various writers, 'On the "Brooks-MacLeish Thesis"', *Partisan Review* 9/1 (January–February 1942), 38–47.
[15] David James and Urmila Seshagiri, 'Metamodernism: Narratives of Continuity and Revolution', *Publications of the Modern Language Association of America (PMLA)* 129/1 (January 2014), 87–100.

default. In early critical accounts of modernism, it was an epic struggle in which great writers wrestled with outmoded literary forms and with a reading public that was largely unsympathetic to experimental writing. The rhetoric of struggle was derived uncritically from the modernist writers and artists themselves. The terms of the debate were largely aesthetic; the relation of literature to social and cultural movements beyond it was either ignored or packaged into a litany of great names.

For Hugh Kenner, whose efforts to win acceptance for modernism began with his *The Poetry of Ezra Pound* (1951), the key writers were those that Wyndham Lewis had identified as the 'men of 1914': Pound, Joyce, Eliot, and Lewis himself. Its great works are *Ulysses*, *The Waste Land*, and the first thirty *Cantos* (Pound's *Draft of XXX Cantos* was published in 1930); its last masterpiece was Samuel Beckett's *Waiting for Godot* (first performed as *En attendant Godot*, 1953). On the basis of Kenner's chosen masterpieces, modernism flourished from 1922 to 1953, but he acknowledges a phase of 'early modernism' from 1910–20.[16] Kenner's modernist canon was rooted in a specific analysis of what had happened to 'English' literature: it had ceased to be the literature of a political entity, England, and had become the literature of a language, English, which was being used in very different ways in the 'Three Provinces': England, Ireland, and America. Modernism brought a further development, in which literary English ceased to be attached to any place; the true modernism for Kenner is 'a supranational movement called International Modernism'.[17] Kenner's label owes much to the idea of the International Style in architecture, which had itself been named as early as 1932 by Henry-Russell Hitchcock and Philip Johnson. His distinction between the provincial and the international led to his making surprising exclusions from the canon: Virginia Woolf 'is not part of International Modernism; she is an English novelist of manners, writing village gossip from a village called Bloomsbury for her English readers'; similarly William Faulkner, William Carlos Williams, and Wallace Stevens are provincial American writers, 'craftily knowing, in a local place, about mighty things afar'.[18] Kenner's construction of Woolf as provincial village gossip echoes the misogyny of Wyndham Lewis, for whom Woolf was a timid writer, 'peeping' out from behind the curtains.[19]

The narrative of heroic individual geniuses has been modified in several ways since the 1980s. The feminist revisionary work of Gillian Hanscombe and Virginia Smyers, Shari Benstock, and Bonnie Kime Scott acknowledges a greater number of modernist writers and, more importantly, emphasizes their interconnectedness and mutual support.[20] To expand the list of writers identified as writers is not to claim importance

---

[16] Hugh Kenner, 'The Making of the Modernist Canon', *Chicago Review* 34/2 (Spring 1984), 49–61, 55.

[17] Ibid., 53.   [18] Ibid., 57.

[19] Wyndham Lewis, *Men without Art* (1934), ed. Seamus Cooney (Santa Rosa, CA: Black Sparrow, 1987), 139.

[20] Gillian Hanscombe and Virginia L. Smyers, *Writing for their Lives: The Modernist Women, 1900–1940* (London: Women's Press, 1987); Shari Benstock, *Women of the Left Bank* (Austin, TX: University

for a greater number; such work simultaneously calls into question the criteria and processes whereby a writer's value is produced. Many of the unfamiliar names recovered by such work are not those of writers or artists, but of publishers, editors, booksellers, and the hosts of literary and artistic salons. Such work reconceives modernism in terms of institutions rather than individuals. The institutional base of modernist literature has come under scrutiny from Lawrence Rainey, whose *Institutions of Modernism* (1998) focuses on publication and patronage; more recently, Jason Harding in his work on *The Criterion*, and the contributors to the *Oxford Critical and Cultural History of Modernist Magazines* (2009–13) have produced detailed accounts of the print institutions which published many of the key works of modernism, and which also began shaping the canon by reviewing them.[21]

The shift in focus from individuals to institutions can have various effects. Rainey's study, though it introduced an unprecedented level of detail into analysis of the mechanics of production, examined already canonical writers—Joyce, Eliot, Pound, H.D. (Hilda Doolittle), and F. T. Marinetti—even if the chapter on H.D. questions the process whereby she became canonical. However, by emphasizing the importance of the patron in literary modernism, Rainey makes a case for modernism having ended around 1929, or at least having suffered a significant change in its material base. In Rainey's account, the Wall Street Crash of October 1929 is the significant event: it inaugurated the great depression of 1929–34, and reduced the incomes available for private patronage; *The Little Review* and *The Dial*, publishers of *Ulysses* and *The Waste Land*, respectively, both ceased publication in 1929. The wider scope and multi-authored nature of the *Oxford Critical and Cultural History* means that it offers no single thesis. However, as some of the magazines had precedents before modernism (as does the very idea of the little magazine), and as many survived beyond Rainey's cut-off of 1929, as well as several beyond the widely observed chronological limit of 1945, the study encourages belief in a modernism that continually mutated in the face of external pressures, and that had many continuities with what came before and after.

If modernism was more than the aggregate of modernist artists and their works, then it must have either some inner logic or some significant relation to external circumstances, or both. To comprehend it only according to its aesthetics is a difficult task, given the diversity of modernist movements and the extent to which they differed on fundamental matters of aesthetics. While individual groups such as the futurists, the Imagists, and the Vorticists claimed that their works had distinct aesthetic programmes, and claimed to articulate them in their manifestos, there was

of Texas Press, 1986); Scott (ed.), *The Gender of Modernism* (Bloomington, IN: Indiana University Press, 1990).

   [21] Jason Harding, *The Criterion: Cultural Politics and Periodical Networks in Inter-War Britain* (Oxford: Oxford University Press, 2002); Peter Brooker and Andrew Thacker (eds), *The Oxford Critical and Cultural History of Modernist Magazines*, 3 vols (Oxford: Oxford University Press, 2009–13).

no manifesto for the modernists as such. As many critics have warned in recent years, modernism was a movement named in retrospect, and the terms 'modernism' and 'modernist' were never on the lips of the actual artists and writers.[22] (As T. S. Eliot's letter of 1926 suggests, the philological truth about the key terms is rather more complicated, but it is fair to say that 'modernism' had a very different status and function from group names such as 'Imagism'.)

It becomes easier, in one respect, to make sense of the diversity of modernist practices if we understand them in relation to the social world beyond modernism; but to do so inevitably raises a new set of questions. One approach, established by the New Criticism, is to see modernism as a fascinated but essentially hostile response to modernity. The important terminological distinction here—though it is not unproblematic—is that 'modernism' refers to an aesthetic movement, while 'modernity' refers to its social context. In recent years, in recognition of the need to think plurally of modernisms, this approach has been developed so that the various modernisms represent diverse reactions to modernity, some sympathetic, some hostile, others ambivalent. Establishing a divide between the aesthetic and the social allows space for reflection on the most shocking truths about the early twentieth century: that works of art of breathtaking emotional and intellectual sophistication could coexist with a European culture that could implement acts of unparalleled barbarism, whether in its colonies, or on its battlefields, or in the concentration camps.

If we raise the question of modernism's relation to modernity, we need to define what we mean by modernity; the question 'when was modernism?' becomes dependent on the question 'when was modernity?', though the answers need not be identical. Among the many modernities we might identify are:

(1) a Renaissance modernity in which a humanist conception of the universe supplants a theocentric one;
(2) an Enlightenment modernity in which rationalism supplants superstition; a pessimistic inflection of this modernity is one in which 'God is dead' and there is a crisis of 'values';
(3) a modernity in which instrumental reason—the belief that knowledge should always be subordinated to practical ends—comes to dominate over pure intellectual inquiry;
(4) a modernity shaped around the encounter of Europe with its colonial 'other';
(5) a modernity of the industrial revolutions: steam power, mechanization, and urbanization; and later, Fordism and Taylorization;
(6) an urban modernity: the city as a site of immigration, and of cross-cultural communication and confusion; the city as showcase of the newest technologies; the city as a place both of isolation and of community;

---

[22] Stan Smith, *The Origins of Modernism* (New York and London: Harvester Wheatsheaf, 1994), 1.

(7)   a modernity of intellectual specialization, in which no single way of seeing the world can comprehend the others; the scientific, the theological, the aesthetic, and the ethical struggle to communicate with each other;

(8)   a cyborgian modernity in which the human senses are supplemented by technology (the microscope, the telescope, the X-ray), and in which knowledge is dependent on technology;

(9)   a modernity of uneven development, one in which the essence of modernity lies in the disparities between locations: between the country and the city, and between the imperial metropolis and the colonial outpost;

(10) a democratic modernity, in which the electoral franchise is extended both to the lower classes and to women, and in which democratic socialism becomes a possibility; one in which political, social, and legal institutions are rationalized;

(11) a modernity shaped by the major thinkers of the late nineteenth and early twentieth centuries, such as Darwin, Marx, Nietzsche, Freud, Bergson;

(12) experiential modernities: a subcategory of many branches, each trying to frame modernity according to the experience of a particular social group; the most notable has been women's modernity.

These modernities are not necessarily mutually exclusive. The democratic modernity can be understood as a specific instance of Enlightenment modernity, especially if Enlightenment is seen not simply as an intellectual project but as a political one. The modernity of intellectual specialization can be interpreted as a subset of industrial specialization. The urban modernity described above includes elements of colonial modernity. Others, however, are harder to reconcile. The Enlightenment trust in reason is compromised by the specialization of intellectual discourses. Moreover, in the account given by Theodor Adorno and Max Horkheimer, the Enlightenment is itself unstable: the belief in reason itself reverts to a form of superstition.[23]

Many of these modernities developed over a timescale quite different from that usually attributed to aesthetic modernism: the Renaissance was well under way by the seventeenth century, the Enlightenment by the eighteenth; European encounters with its cultural 'others' could be dated to Christopher Columbus's voyages to the West Indies in the late fifteenth century. To note these long modernities is not to suggest that we need radically to extend the duration of modernism, but rather to suggest that some of what it responded to had been in train for several centuries. Stephen Toulmin has argued that modernity had 'two distinct starting points', 'a humanistic one grounded in classical literature' and 'a scientific one' that begins with seventeenth-century natural philosophy.[24] The one is the modernity of

---

[23] Theodor Adorno and Max Horkheimer, *Dialectic of Enlightenment*, trans. John Cumming (London: Allen Lane, 1972), 115.

[24] Stephen Toulmin, *Cosmopolis: The Hidden Agenda of Modernity* (New York: Free Press, 1990), 43.

Erasmus, Rabelais, Shakespeare, and Montaigne; the other the modernity of Galileo, Newton, and Descartes. In Toulmin's account these modernities were in competition from the outset. One might also argue that initially the scientific modernity answered to the humanistic one, and—to invoke Adorno and Horkheimer—the competition began when the scientific one became incomprehensible in its discourse, and its data became imperceptible to the human body. The moment of modernism then becomes the moment at which contradictions between different modernities become apparent. Some modernists then find themselves making a critique of modernity through the medium of art, while others find themselves attempting to resolve the contradictions. And of course many others do not decide which role to take.

Different accounts of modernism have, usually implicitly, taken different modernities as their starting points. The New Criticism rejected scientific and technological rationalism, and saw the modern city as its culmination. These ideas go to the heart of the New Critical account of poetic language: wit, irony, paradox, and connotative language were essential properties of poetry because scientific language dealt in direct statement.[25] As Kenner notes, such an account shapes the canon: it can find a place for the poetics of Pound's *Hugh Selwyn Mauberley* (1920) but not for his usual mode of 'lapidary *statement*'; it cannot find a place at all for William Carlos Williams.[26] The poetics of indirection owed something to symbolist poetics: the New Critical 'heresy of paraphrase' is a restatement of a key symbolist idea. In this regard, the New Critical antipathy to science indirectly shapes the starting date of modernism, because the symbolists take on the role as the first opponents of scientific rationalism. It also shapes the rise and fall narrative of modernism: for the New Criticism, *Hugh Selwyn Mauberley* might be something of a peak; for Kenner, it is an aberration, and the real peak comes with the *Draft of XXX Cantos*.

The diversity of feminist approaches to modernism has been such that there is no single feminist approach to modernity, but feminist critique has valuably questioned assumptions about modernity and its relation to modernist modes of writing. Shari Benstock has taken issue with narratives of modernism that locate its origin in a 'crisis of belief' and that see the First World War as the primary cause of that crisis.[27] The idea that modernism began from a state of despair at the 'shattering of cultural symbols and norms' should be called into question if those symbols and norms were perceived as oppressive by the writers in question: such a situation might occasion not despair, but celebration; more realistically, it might lead to cautious optimism informed by an awareness of 'the continuing hegemony of traditional

[25] Cleanth Brooks, *The Well-Wrought Urn: Studies in the Structure of Poetry* (1947; repr. London: Dennis Dobson, 1968), 1–7.
[26] Kenner, 'The Making of the Modernist Canon', 57.
[27] Susan Stanford Friedman, quoted by Benstock, 'Beyond the Reaches of Feminist Criticism: A Letter from Paris', in Benstock (ed.), *Feminist Issues in Literary Scholarship* (Bloomington and Indianapolis, IN: Indiana University Press, 1987), 12.

material values'.[28] Benstock singles out for particular criticism the view that the First World War was pivotal, and analyzes its consequences for feminism. Such a view roots modernism in what is usually presented as a predominantly male experience; most accounts of the First World War ignore or marginalize the home front. It treats pre-war texts as anticipating the war, while later ones 'live in its wake'.[29] Benstock's remark about the logic of anticipation is an important one. A history of modernism that gave its starting point as 1900 or 1910, but which found the value of the early years in their anticipation of post-war writing, or of the *annus mirabilis* of 1922, would be very different from one that tried to understand the texts of 1900 to 1914 on their own terms, without the benefit of hindsight. Those terms would include war and militarism (the Boer War, the Dreadnought Crisis of 1909, the place of the 'argument from force' in debate about women's suffrage), but would also include home rule, suffrage, Bergson, Post-Impressionism, and theosophy, to name but a few; to include them is to recover something of the optimism of pre-war modernity and its modernisms.

If, in literary-critical accounts of modernity, the city has been something of a constant, that may be simply because the major modernist writers were based in cities and took it as their subject matter, but may also be because the sheer scale and diversity of urban experience allow it to be interpreted selectively in accordance with different critical agendas. For the New Criticism, its trams and telephone lines are the most visible signs of the triumph of technological modernity. For the Marxist tradition derived from Walter Benjamin, its boulevards and shopping arcades produce a distinctive modern subjectivity, and its flows of vehicles and pedestrians are a cypher for the unseen flow of capital. In a post-colonial tradition, capital cities are the places where imperial power is concentrated, but they are also places to which immigrants are drawn and to which colonial administrators return, and in which, in consequence, diverse cultural codes are sharply juxtaposed.

As Raymond Williams noted some time ago, focusing exclusively on the city risks removing it from the contrastive relations that define it. Although Williams's 'Metropolitan Perceptions and the Emergence of Modernism' (1985) insists on the importance of the city, it also insists on the unoriginality of many modernist ideas about it. The city as a crowd of strangers and the city as a place of social unity are both seen in Wordsworth's *Prelude* (1850); the city as a maze is seen in Henry Fielding's prose in the mid-eighteenth century.[30] In Williams's analysis, what makes the city of the late nineteenth century different is its relation to all that lies beyond it. Drawing on the idea of 'uneven development' established by Leon Trotsky and Ernst Bloch, Williams notes the difference between capitals and provinces, socially,

---

[28] Ibid., 13, 14.

[29] Benstock, 'Expatriate Modernism: Writing on the Cultural Rim', in Mary Lynn Broe and Angela Ingram (eds), *Women's Writing in Exile* (Chapel Hill, NC: University of North Carolina Press, 1989), 21.

[30] Williams, 'Metropolitan Perceptions and the Emergence of Modernism', in *The Politics of Modernism*, 39–42.

culturally, and economically.[31] Moreover, as the city is a site of immigration, and is a place that is constituted by cultures that are alien to it, it constantly confronts and incorporates that which lies beyond it. Because of this, the city reveals the arbitrariness and strangeness of language and other cultural codes. In order to investigate the city 'with something of its own sense of strangeness and distance', Williams insists, we need to look at it 'from the deprived hinterlands, where different forces are moving, and from the poor world which has always been peripheral to the metropolitan systems'.[32] The consequences for a chronology of modernism are subtle but important. Williams's strategy of comparing modernist texts with eighteenth- and nineteenth-century ones is one means of looking at modernism from outside. Whatever chronological boundary we choose, he implies, we should look beyond it.

One way of pursuing the uneven development theory would be to see modernist literature as one of the means whereby the metropolis identifies itself as more sophisticated and more advanced than the periphery. However, Fredric Jameson has noted that modern art 'drew its power and its possibilities from being a backwater and an archaic holdover within a modernizing economy: it glorified, celebrated, and dramatized older forms of individual production which the new mode of production was elsewhere on the point of displacing and blotting out'.[33] The meaning of the work, in the largest sense, can only be understood in the larger cultural context. As Jameson wrote elsewhere, to understand 'the practice of language in the literary work', we must establish continuity between it and rationalizing practices of modernity, so that we understand how the former might have seemed to be the solution to the problem posed by the latter.[34] To understand the artisanal quality of modernist works, with their custom-made literary forms and unique visions, we must have some acquaintance with mass production, including, but not limited to, mass-produced cultural forms. Traces of such things can be found within the classics of high modernism—food in tins, skywritten advertising, 'Epps's massproduct, the creature cocoa'[35]—but they matter even when they are absent. As with Williams's use of uneven development theory, the consequences of Jameson's view are subtle: it might not change the chronological boundaries of modernism itself, but it suggests the imperative of looking beyond them.

The model of uneven development also leads to further questions that do not in themselves concern chronology. Recent work on modernism has broadened the canon to include writers from outside Europe and North America, and in doing so has been forced to reinterpret the relation of their work to the canon. Kenner's 'International' Modernism has been replaced by the 'transnational'. Kenner's model

---

[31] Ibid., 44.   [32] Ibid., 47.

[33] Fredric Jameson, *Postmodernism: or, The Cultural Logic of Late Capitalism* (London: Verso, 1991), 307.

[34] Jameson, *The Political Unconscious: Narrative as a Socially Symbolic Act* (London: Methuen, 1981), 42.

[35] James Joyce, *Ulysses: The 1922 Text*, ed. Jeri Johnson (Oxford: Oxford University Press, 1993), 629.

has been rejected for embodying a European ideology of 'diffusionism' in which originality can occur only at the centre, and in which works produced at the periphery can only be understood as imitative.[36] Though 'transnational' modernism is by no means a settled model, particularly as regards the concept of modernity, critics have agreed in recognizing that European modernism was not necessarily authoritarian or oppressive to readers and writers on the periphery, and that its linguistic, formal, and rhythmic qualities often spoke sympathetically to post-colonial subjects. As Kamau Brathwaite has written, T. S. Eliot was the primary influence on Caribbean poets 'moving from standard English' to creolized English, or 'nation language'.[37]

An immediate consequence for the chronology of modernism is the need to extend it beyond 1945, to take in writers from the colonies that became independent from 1945 to the 1960s. It can be argued that a new phase of modernity began for those countries with their independence; indeed, Laura Doyle has argued persuasively that the rhetoric of liberation is a key theme of modernity.[38] To extend the canon thus is not to forget what was at stake for non-European writers in looking to European texts. As Ramazani has written: 'The conditions of possibility for postcolonial hybridity are violent occupation and cultural imposition at home, across immense differences of power, topography, culture, and economics. Its non-West is primary and profoundly experiential, not the object of extraterritorial questing via tourism and museums, books and ethnography, friendships and translations.'[39] The modernism of transnational modernism is thus very different from the late modernism of Charles Olson and others.

Unresolved difficulties within the transnational model involve the status of modernity and the significance of uneven development within nation states. Building on the work of Dilip Parameshwar Gaonkar, Friedman speaks of multiple modernities and of the need to 'locate many centers of modernity across the globe'.[40] While she recognizes that a multiplication of the term 'beyond its conventional meaning of what happened in the West after 1500' might render it meaningless, her specification of what counts as modernity is very abstract, involving a 'powerful vortex of historical conditions', 'sharp ruptures', and 'velocity, acceleration, and dynamism'. 'Across the vast reaches of civilizational history,' she concludes, 'eruptions of different modernities often occur in the context of empires and conquest.'[41] Friedman's rhetoric of

---

[36] Friedman, 'Periodizing Modernism: Postcolonial Modernities and the Space/Time Borders of Modernist Studies', *Modernism/Modernity* 13/3 (September 2006), 429.

[37] Kamau Brathwaite, quoted by Jahan Ramazani, 'Modernist Bricolage, Postcolonial Hybridity', *Modernism/Modernity* 13/3 (September 2006), 446.

[38] Laura Doyle, 'Liberty, Race, and Larsen in Atlantic Modernity: A New World Genealogy', in Laura Doyle and Laura Winkiel (eds), *Geomodernisms* (Bloomington and Indianapolis, IN: Indiana University Press, 2005), 51–76.

[39] Ramazani, 'Modernist Bricolage, Postcolonial Hybridity', 449.

[40] Friedman, 'Periodizing Modernism', 427, 429.   [41] Ibid., 433.

dynamism, acceleration, and impressive magnitude is itself derived from European modernism, and has the flavour in particular of Italian futurism. Although Friedman acknowledges that our analytic tools might be indebted to the very thing we are trying to analyze ('modernity' itself might be a term generated, along with 'tradition', by modernity), she does not examine her own concepts.

Engaging critically with Gaonkar, Neil Lazarus has returned to Jameson and to a conception of modernity as an expression of the capitalist world system. This allows for a modernity that is singular but that is lived differently in each and every social situation.[42] While it can be granted that works of literature themselves may attempt to enact a rejection of a 'Western' modernity (for example, by advocating Afrocentrism or equivalent cultural traditions),[43] analytically such reactions can be understood as a compensatory gesture within an economic system that allows little room for national autonomy. In this account, there is no simple location for modernism or modernity. Brathwaite writing with T. S. Eliot's use of language in mind is both in the West Indies and in London, and, for that matter in the other places where he and Eliot lived and worked.

Questions of temporality, chronology, and synchronization are central to modernism itself, and much modernist writing forces us to reassess them, both through its internal form, such as non-chronological narratives, and through its relations to the tradition; as Jameson notes, Flaubert looks different after Joyce, becoming a modernist as well as a realist.[44] At the same time, the language of the decisive break and the revolutionary innovation is everywhere in modernist rhetoric. Investigations into the chronology of modernism—not just initial and terminal dates, but peaks and troughs—need reflexively to examine their own concepts and rhetoric; they need to remain sensitive to modernism's self-conceptions, and be sceptical about their limits. Placing modernism in relation to modernity enables such scepticism, especially when modernity is conceived as having a duration far exceeding that of modernism itself. Placing chronological limits on modernism helps to define a canon of texts, but it also helps to define positions outside, from which to view it with a renewed sense of its strangeness.

FURTHER READING

Anderson, Perry. 'Modernity and Revolution', *New Left Review* 1/144 (March–April 1984), 96–113.

Benstock, Shari. 'Beyond the Reaches of Feminist Criticism: A Letter from Paris' (1984), in Shari Benstock (ed.) *Feminist Issues in Literary Scholarship* (Bloomington and Indianapolis, IN: Indiana University Press, 1987), 7–29.

---

[42] Neil Lazarus, 'Modernism and African Literature', in Mark Wollaeger with Matt Eatough (eds), *The Oxford Handbook of Global Modernisms* (Oxford: Oxford University Press, 2012), 232–4.
[43] See ibid., 229–32.   [44] Jameson, *Postmodernism*, 302.

Benstock, Shari. 'Expatriate Modernism: Writing on the Cultural Rim', in Mary Lynn Broe and Angela Ingram (eds), *Women's Writing in Exile* (Chapel Hill, NC: University of North Carolina Press, 1989), 19–40.

Berman, Marshall. *All That Is Solid Melts into Air: The Experience of Modernity* (New York: Simon & Schuster, 1982).

Eysteinsson, Astradur. *The Concept of Modernism* (Ithaca, NY: Cornell University Press, 1990).

Felski, Rita. *The Gender of Modernity* (Cambridge, MA and London: Harvard University Press, 1995).

Friedman, Susan Stanford. 'Definitional Excursions: The Meanings of Modern / Modernity / Modernism', *Modernism/Modernity* 8/3 (September 2001), 493–513.

Friedman, Susan Stanford. 'Periodizing Modernism: Postcolonial Modernities and the Space/Time Borders of Modernist Studies', *Modernism/Modernity* 13/3 (September 2006), 425–43.

James, David and Urmila Seshagiri. 'Metamodernism: Narratives of Continuity and Revolution', *Publications of the Modern Language Association of America (PMLA)* 129/1 (January 2014), 87–100.

Jameson, Fredric. *Postmodernism: Or, the Cultural Logic of Late Capitalism* (London: Verso, 1991).

Levenson, Michael H. *Modernism* (New Haven, CT and London: Yale University Press, 2011).

Ramazani, Jahan. 'Modernist Bricolage, Postcolonial Hybridity', *Modernism/Modernity* 13/3 (September 2006), 445–63.

Sheppard, Richard. 'The Problematics of European Modernism', in Steve Giles (ed.), *Theorizing Modernism: Essays in Critical Theory* (London: Routledge, 1993), 1–51.

Shiach, Morag. 'Periodizing Modernism', in Peter Brooker, Andrzej Gasiorek, Deborah Longworth, and Andrew Thacker (eds), *The Oxford Handbook of Modernisms* (Oxford: Oxford University Press, 2010), 17–30.

Whitworth, Michael H. (ed.). *Modernism* (Oxford: Blackwell, 2007).

Williams, Raymond. *The Politics of Modernism: Against the New Conformists*, ed. Tony Pinkney (London: Verso, 1989).

CHAPTER 8

WHAT *WAS* THE 'NEW DRAMA'?

SOS ELTIS AND KIRSTEN E. SHEPHERD-BARR

In 1923, William Archer titled his survey of the theatre of the previous four decades *The Old Drama and the New*, signalling his sense of a clear division between mainstream conventional drama and a more innovative and politically engaged theatre that had emerged in the wake of Ibsen's revolutionary impact in the 1890s. The term 'New Drama' was common coinage at the turn of the twentieth century and has remained in use ever since, referring to the plays of George Bernard Shaw, St John Hankin, John Galsworthy, Harley Granville-Barker, Elizabeth Robins, and the other writers staged as part of the experimental repertory seasons of 1904–9 at the Court and Savoy theatres.[1] In more general terms, New Drama encompassed a huge range of theatrical activity including: private theatre societies such as J. T. Grein's Independent Theatre, the Incorporated Stage Society, and William Archer's New Century Theatre; the Irish Literary Theatre's productions of plays by Yeats, Synge, and Lady Gregory, among others; productions of European avant-garde plays by writers such as Maurice Maeterlinck, Gerhart Hauptmann, Hermann Sudermann, and Frank Wedekind; plays and sketches written and performed as part of the campaign for women's suffrage; and verse drama by a range of playwrights including Yeats, Laurence Housman, and John Masefield. Uniting this extraordinarily diverse body of plays is its distinction from 'old' drama: the extravagant and costly West End theatre of actor-managers like Henry Irving, Wilson Barrett, and Herbert Beerbohm Tree, which produced lavish spectacles complete with *haute couture* costumes and hundreds of extras, and the morally and sexually conservative society plays of playwrights such as Arthur Wing Pinero, Henry Arthur Jones, and Sidney Grundy.

But these binaries of 'new' and 'old', high and low, mainstream and coterie break down under a deeper exploration of the theatre of this period. The borderline was

---

[1] See for example Jan McDonald, *The 'New Drama' 1900–1914: Harley Granville-Barker, John Galsworthy, St John Hankin, John Masefield* (London: Macmillan, 1986); Jean Chothia, *English Drama of the Early Modern Period 1890–1940* (London: Longman, 1996), ch. 3.

hotly contested, and what was too radical for some could be dismissed as tired and old-hat by others. Pinero's *The Second Mrs Tanqueray* (1893), in which a fallen woman commits suicide when her past resurfaces to wreck her marriage, provides a case in point. Listed by American critic Henry A. Beers in 1905 as part of an English theatrical renaissance, the play outraged the arch-conservative critic Clement Scott with its Ibsenic outspokenness and immorality, but was dismissed by Bernard Shaw as a 'conventional Adelphi piece' about a repentant sinner.[2] The traffic and movement of audiences, venues, and plays flowed easily from mainstream to fringe and back again, so that plays envisioned as minority fare could become wholesale hits, as was the case with Shaw's *Fanny's First Play*, which opened at Lillah McCarthy's Little Theatre in 1911 and went on to amass 623 performances—making it, as its author declared, 'the Charley's Aunt of the new drama'.[3] Playwrights were really making money from their plays and experiencing a greater degree of autonomy even while shifting the status of theatre as a more radical form.

New Drama has long been recognized as oppositional, questioning social and moral orthodoxies, and engaging directly in political debates. Shaw deliberately timed the premiere of *John Bull's Other Island* for November 1904 to coincide with the reopening of Parliament, and over subsequent months the play was seen by Prime Minister Arthur Balfour, by the leader of the opposition, Henry Campbell Bannerman, and by the future Liberal Prime Minister, H. H. Asquith. Beatrice Webb brought fellow members of the Royal Commission enquiry into the Poor Laws to see *Major Barbara*. Elizabeth Robins's *Votes for Women!* (1907) proclaimed its political affiliations and purpose in its title, and a host of suffrage plays from Evelyn Glover's *Mrs Appleyard's Awakening* (1912) to Beatrice Harraden's *Lady Geraldine's Speech* (1909) aimed explicitly at securing off-stage conversions of the kind enacted on stage.

Too often this emphasis on progressive thinking and material, economic, and legal conditions of contemporary life is critically associated with the more traditional dramatic style of 'social realism', thus omitting New Drama from histories of theatrical modernism which concentrate instead on the small European and Russian art-house theatres as the locus of stylistic innovation and experiment. This overlooks the bold stylistic experimentation that coexisted with active social engagement in plays by Shaw, Galsworthy, Robins, and Barker, and the Irish theatrical movement

---

[2] Henry A. Beers, 'The English Drama of To-Day', *North American Review* (May 1905), 74–6; *Illustrated London News* (22 July 1893); *Saturday Review* (16 March 1895). For a full discussion of the fallen woman motif in nineteenth-century theatre see Sos Eltis, *Acts of Desire* (Oxford: Oxford University Press, 2013).

[3] Shaw quoted in Dennis Kennedy, *Granville Barker and the Dream of Theatre* (Cambridge: Cambridge University Press, 1989), 118. Another playwright who easily straddled the supposed divide was J. M. Barrie: *The Admirable Crichton* opened at the Duke of York's Theatre and ran for an extraordinary 823 performances, and his one-act play *The Twelve-Pound Look* similarly opened at the Duke of York's and then went on to become a suffrage favourite, performed at a wealth of makeshift venues and meetings.

headed by Yeats, Synge, Martyn, and Lady Gregory.[4] The techniques and concerns long identified as central to modernism, from the self-conscious questioning of realist representation to the breakdown of language and the unknowable nature of the self, are all crucial to a wide range of 'new' dramas. Despite the need to negotiate censorship mechanisms and the pressures of the box office, 'New' playwrights consistently pushed at the bounds of acceptability, committed to exploring not just what the theatre of the time could do, but what theatre as an art form could be. New Drama thus challenges standard definitions of modernism that focus too exclusively on aesthetic innovation, showing that political engagement, artistic experimentation, and financial viability could and did coexist in the theatre.

Modernism and theatre

Theatre has hardly figured at all in the historiography of modernism, and a number of factors have contributed to its neglect.[5] One is that theatrical performance depends on successful collaboration, which requires consensus; this can signal a tendency towards conservativism rather than radicalism. Theatre often depends on audience support and approval in order to remain financially viable, which only adds to the perception of theatrical performance as capitulating to bourgeois tastes instead of challenging them, or alternatively of theatre 'preaching to the converted'. Then there is the tendency of theatre to draw on its own past, experimenting with existing forms and material rather than providing the complete break, or the 'shock of the new', which is so prized in the historiography of modernism. Theatrical modernism is not always sudden in its innovations but in many ways seamless, involving a redeployment of old methods. There is also a perception of theatre as lagging behind the other arts, reflecting what they were already doing rather than running alongside them and cross-influencing more prominent experiments in art, music, fiction, and poetry. And the ephemerality of theatrical performance—the lack of an object or an artefact to study—has proven a perennial stumbling block for this period as for every period; far easier for editors of modernism handbooks to refer to a Picasso painting or an Eliot poem than reconstruct an evening's theatre, especially if the evidence is scant and patchy. If drama does make it into discussions of modernism it is usually the text of a play rather than its performance, marginalizing

---

[4] A full consideration of the Irish theatre at the turn of the century lies beyond the scope of this chapter. See for example James W. Flannery, *W. B. Yeats and the Idea of a Theatre: The Early Abbey Theatre in Theory and Practice* (New Haven, CT: Yale University Press, 1989); Nicholas Grene, *The Politics of Irish Drama* (Cambridge: Cambridge University Press, 2000); Mary Luckhurst (ed.), *A Companion to Modern British and Irish Drama, 1880–2005* (Oxford: Blackwell, 2006); Shaun Richards (ed.), *The Cambridge Companion to Twentieth-Century Irish Drama* (Cambridge: Cambridge University Press, 2004).

[5] For a full discussion, see Kirsten Shepherd-Barr, 'Modernism and Theatrical Performance', *Modernist Cultures* 1/1 (May 2005), 59–68.

the very aspect of the genre that makes it unique. Theatre historians are used to this omission, but if one is approaching modernism as a phenomenon defined by its power to shock, its experimentation, and other features common to the movement, ignoring theatre leaves one with an incomplete picture, not seeing a vital element of cross-currents and exchanges across all the arts.

In addition to all these factors, there is the problem of theatrical realism. Not only have we forgotten how radical realism in the theatre was when it first emerged, but there lingers a common assumption that realism—the dominant mode of much New Drama—is antithetical to meta-theatricality and a self-conscious awareness of the medium itself, which are fundamental to modernism.[6] But as the following representative examples will show, these qualities coexist in the New Drama. Those elements associated with the seemingly bolder moves of Continental modernism can be found in New Drama from the 1890s to 1914, as theatre became a more active social tool, but not in the sense of the shock or the break, of disconcerting the audience. Indeed, far from lagging behind, theatre can be seen as a vital influence and inspiration for modernist experiments in other media, and many of the central elements of modernist theory and methodology are already present in Victorian theatre. The vibrant mixture of high and low art, juxtaposing different styles and genres in a host of modernist works from Eliot's *The Waste Land* (1922) to Joyce's *Ulysses* (1922), was fundamental to nineteenth-century theatre (as indeed it was to theatre through the centuries, from medieval mystery cycles and Shakespearean tragedy). A combination of generic styles and forms was common, appealing simultaneously to pit, gallery, and stalls, rooted in the evening's mixed bill of farce, burlesque, melodrama, and tragedy, and continuing even when Victorian theatre moved towards the single play (occasionally plus curtain-raiser). Oscar Wilde's *An Ideal Husband* (1895), for example, was described by one critic as offering 'high-class virtue and vice' to the gallery, paradoxes for the stalls, and Surrey-side melodrama for the rest.[7]

Similarly, direct acknowledgement of—and even appeal to—the audience remained a familiar and enduring ingredient in melodrama, and was part of the essential dynamic of music hall performance. It was hardly surprising, therefore, that when Marinetti drew up his 1913 manifesto for Futurist performance, 'The Variety Theatre', it was popular theatre's vibrancy, dynamism, exploitation of new technology, spectacular effects, audience collaboration, and riotous profusion of styles that provided the model.[8] Nor is it surprising that the high modernists

---

[6] Sheila Stowell, 'Rehabilitating Realism', *Journal of Dramatic Theory and Criticism* 6/2 (1992), 81–8.

[7] *Lika Joko*, 13 (12 January 1895), 244–5. For fuller discussion of Wilde's and Shaw's subversive use of Victorian theatre, see Martin Meisel, *Shaw and the Nineteenth Century Theatre* (Princeton, NJ: Princeton University Press, 1963); Eltis, *Revising Wilde* (Oxford: Oxford University Press, 1996).

[8] 'The Variety Theatre', 29 September 1913, reproduced in Vassiliki Kolocotroni, Jane Goldman, and Olga Taxidou (eds), *Modernism: An Anthology of Sources and Documents* (Chicago, IL: University of Chicago Press, 1998), 253–6. An edited version was published in the London *Daily Mail* on 29 November 1913, under the title 'The Meaning of Music Hall'.

generally were so engaged with theatre; one thinks of Joyce's *Exiles* (published 1918) and the Circe chapter of *Ulysses*, Woolf's *Between the Acts* and her play *Freshwater*, and Eliot, Isherwood, and Auden's various (and variously successful) attempts to revive verse drama for the modern stage.[9]

Early critics and audiences were alert to the vibrant generic mixture that characterized Shaw's plays, for example—though their connection to other modernist experiments in form were not necessarily grounds for praise. Beatrice Webb celebrated Shaw's discovery in *Man and Superman* of 'his *form*, a play which is not a play but only a combination of chapter, treatise, interlude, lyric – all the different forms illustrating the central idea, as a sonata manifests a scheme of melody and harmony'. Yet a critic writing in the *Nineteenth Century* deplored the modern failure to apprehend the discrete aims and limits of each form of art as manifested in the synaesthetic experimentation of Wagner's operas, Strauss's symphonic poems, and the 'disintegrated' theatre of Shaw, feeling that they inappropriately combined 'the pleasures of spectacle, lecture, and glorified pantomime'.[10]

Language and theatricality

The limitations and inadequacies of language are a central preoccupation of modernism. Language is revealed as an arbitrary sign system, inadequate to express reality or human experience, thus rendering realist representation inherently problematic. Furthermore, inherited meta-narratives of nation, race, gender, religion, duty, and justice are challenged, rewritten, and rejected as outdated and inadequate. From *Heart of Darkness* (1899) to *A Portrait of the Artist as a Young Man* (1916), the impossibility of articulating the unknown and unformed self is intrinsically linked to the failures and limitations of language itself. The insufficiency of language is a fundamental premise on which modernist literature is based; the impossibility of communication and expression form its subject matter. Theatre is certainly no exception. Shaw is in one sense the playwright of hyper-articulacy; every character from the cabinet minister to the chauffeur can explain his or her world view. Words have the power to disillusion, educate, and convert. Yet even in *Man and Superman*, in which characters exchange many thousands of words, discussing duty, marriage, idealism, realism, biology, civilization, and the destiny of mankind, the play ends with the revolutionary hero rendered speechless

---

[9] Indeed, there is an argument to be made about the parallel between the rise of dialogue in fiction and the rise of narrative in stage directions—a kind of bleeding or cross-fertilization of forms and techniques that also is typical of modernism. In the case of stage directions, this relates directly to the wider context of print culture, which lies beyond the scope of this discussion.

[10] Norman and Jeanne MacKenzie (eds), *The Diary of Beatrice Webb*, 4 vols (London: Virago, in association with the London School of Economics and Political Science, 1983), II, 267; Norman Bentwich, 'Euripides in London', *Nineteenth Century* (June 1906), 968–9.

by his fiancée's placid encouragement to 'Go on talking.'[11] Amid '*universal laughter*', the defeated hero splutters indignantly at the reduction of all his thought and ideas to mere noise, nothing but 'talking'.

The limitations of language have, of course, long been fundamental to the art of theatre; hence the crucial role of gesture, silence, and subtext, the banal words accompanying, masking, or revealing the unspeakable depth of feeling, as in the power of Lear's final request 'pray you, undo this button'.[12] Moments of heightened emotional and dramatic intensity are often silent, a familiar fact which renders it vital to read and think beyond the text, which is but one element in theatrical communication and expression. The failure of language, the inadequacy of inherited meta-narratives of justice and duty, and the inexpressibility of the inner self are vividly dramatized in Elizabeth Robins and Florence Bell's *Alan's Wife* (1893) and in John Galsworthy's *Justice* (1910), both plays which drew on the early Victorian melodramatic tradition of dumbshow, deploying the expressive potential of the body and illustrating how theatre redirected traditional techniques in order to explore modernist concerns.

Justice dramatizes the tragic fate of Falder, a weak-willed clerk who, on a desperate impulse, forges a cheque to enable the woman he loves to escape her murderously abusive husband. The second act is dominated by the long, heavy-handed speeches of defence, prosecution, and judgement in court, all of which unintentionally misrepresent and crudely simplify the inarticulate Falder's motives, which lie outside the accepted codes of marital and legal duties. Sentenced to three years in prison, Falder again falls victim to the fixed regulations and rigid language of the penal system. The scene that most forcefully brought home the cruel and dehumanizing effects of the British justice system, however, was entirely without speech. Locked alone in his cell—a thirteen foot by seven foot space whose claustrophobic dimensions were reproduced on the Duke of York Theatre's stage—Falder desperately strains to hear any sound of outside life through his door, listlessly stitches at the sewing work allotted him, and paces compulsively like a caged animal. As dusk thickens, the harsh cell light suddenly blinks on, leaving Falder '*gasping for breath*' at the sudden brightness—a discomfort the audience must have shared as their eyes too had to adjust. Then the sound of distant, dull beating on thick metal grows steadily, as prisoners across the jail hammer on their doors, and Falder loses his last shred of sanity: '*Panting violently, he flings himself at his door, and beats on it.*'[13]

This wordless scene is essentially one of internal not external action, a vivid articulation through body alone of psychological agony and collapse. Already in the

---

[11] Bernard Shaw, *Man and Superman*, in *The Bodley Head Bernard Shaw: Collected Plays with their Prefaces*, 7 vols (London: Max Reinhardt, 1971), II, 733.

[12] Shakespeare, *Lear*, V, 3.

[13] John Galsworthy, *Justice*, in *The Plays of John Galsworthy*, 3 vols (London: Duckworth, 1929), III, 261.

1890s the Italian actress Eleonora Duse had pioneered this kind of acting, particularly in her interpretations of Ibsen's heroines; critics repeatedly noted how she conveyed 'a physical though silent embodiment of inner anguish', which became her trademark.[14] The contrast between the essential mundaneness of Falder's actions and the intense mental anguish he is experiencing is as acute and painfully ironic as that of the suicidal Septimus Warren Smith in Virginia Woolf's *Mrs Dalloway* (1925). Galsworthy's innovative use of dumbshow had a palpable and unusually concrete impact: the Home Secretary, Winston Churchill, directly acknowledged the inspiration it provided for his reform of the penal system, alluding to it in parliamentary debates on the use of solitary confinement.[15]

Alan's Wife, anonymously written by Elizabeth Robins and Florence Bell, also deals with the problem of justice, and vividly depicts the central character's complex psychological state while refusing to parse the reasons for it. Jean Creyke has killed her infant son, but no one, including the audience, knows why, as she chooses to remain silent: she refuses to explain herself to her mother, the vicar, or the court, which is about to sentence her to death. Only at the very end of the play does she break her silence, and then only to say that she will soon meet her dead son in heaven. Her elective silence remains ambiguous and unexplained; the audience must interpret her motives, just as the reader of Joseph Conrad's *Heart of Darkness* and *Lord Jim* (1900) is confronted with similarly crucial narrative gaps and ellipses. Audiences and critics were and continue to be all too ready with their explanations: post-natal depression; eugenic euthanasia, since the baby suffers from some unnamed deformity; an extreme act of love.[16] One critic noted the play's importance in raising awareness of euthanasia and showing the need for a new critical vocabulary to address such issues. As Josephine McDonagh observes, this new kind of tragedy is 'a drama of impossible choice' that thus 'offers a heroic role for the woman, implicitly turning Medea into Agamemnon ... the play presents the [baby] killing as an act of bravery in the context of tragedy.'[17] Jean's actions and feelings simply do not fit with accepted behavioural norms. In the course of three short scenes, she changes utterly before our eyes, so we do not *know* her in the end—a

[14] Susan Bassnett, 'Eleonora Duse', in John Stokes, Michael R. Booth, and Susan Bassnett (eds), *Bernhardt, Terry, Duse: The Actress in her Time* (Cambridge: Cambridge University Press, 1988), 141. How far playwrights followed such developments in acting and incorporated those techniques into their texts is a key question, and one that challenges assumptions about the primacy of the dramatic script.

[15] See Manfred Weidhorn, *A Harmony of Interests: Explorations in the Mind of Sir Winston Churchill* (Cranbury, NJ and London: Associated University Presses, 1992), 23–5.

[16] For a succinct account of responses to the play, see for example Katherine E. Kelly, 'Alan's Wife: Mother Love and Theatrical Sociability in London of the 1890s', *Modernism/Modernity* 11/3 (2004), 550ff, also William Archer and J. T. Grein's prefatory comments to the published text of the play in *Alan's Wife: A Dramatic Study in Three Scenes* (London: Henry and Co., 1893).

[17] Josephine McDonagh, *Child Murder and British Culture 1720–1900* (Cambridge: Cambridge University Press, 2003), 179. See also Shepherd-Barr, *Theatre and Evolution from Ibsen to Beckett* (New York: Columbia University Press, 2015), 185–95.

reversal of the usual trajectory of dramatic character by which the audience gradually gets to know and empathize with him/her. The point that Robins and Bell enact is that there *is* no explanation; the motive for the killing must remain a mystery, and this relies on the actor's rendering of the inner psychological state; the audience must experience the muteness, denied the authority to fill it in. So the medium of performance is turned back on itself, withholding exactly what it has the potential to show, a modernist trait common to other genres such as painting and sculpture, poetry, and the novel.

The published text of the play, geared towards readers rather than spectators, gives explicit meanings to the silences, indicating parenthetically what Jean is thinking while she is silent. This is a technique that later playwrights like Eugene O'Neill (*Strange Interlude*, 1923), Brian Friel (*Philadelphia, Here I Come!*, 1964), and Tom Stoppard (*Night and Day*, 1978) would take one step further, having characters speak aloud their thoughts in a modern version of the theatrical aside. But even critics of the published version were divided over motivations and meanings. Archer's lengthy introduction attempted to resolve the ambivalence, stating that the play is 'not a tragedy of character' but of theme ('the clumsy and blundering cruelties of life' by Darwinian natural selection), and providing the kind of rational explanation that the play so carefully resists: Jean is not insane but simply 'a terribly afflicted woman . . . who acts as, somewhere or other in the world, some similarly tortured creature is doubtless acting at the very moment I write these words'.[18] Like Shaw's long prefaces it is an example of the para-text threatening to overwhelm the text—attempting to materialize what is unheard and unseen.

Realism and the New Drama

In *Henrik Ibsen and the Birth of Modernism* (2006), Toril Moi rightly observes that one reason for a widespread critical failure to give Ibsen his deserved place in the history of modernism is the tendency to regard realism as necessarily antithetical to the aesthetic and representational experiments of modernist poets, painters, and novelists. In fact, far from being opposed to meta-theatrical self-consciousness, realism in the theatre has often gone hand in hand with a heightened awareness of the mechanisms and conventions of dramatic representation and make-believe. This has been true for centuries, as seen for example in Falstaff's challenge to the myths of honour and heroic warfare in *Henry IV Part 1*, where his assertion of the reality and finality of death is accompanied by his play-acting of his own demise, his 'playing dead' inescapably emphasizing the parallel pretence of the actors 'really' dead on the stage's battlefield.

---

[18] William Archer, introduction to *Alan's Wife*, vi, xlii–xlvi.

T. W. Robertson brought a new level of naturalism to the Victorian theatre with his low-key intimacy of detail and staging. The tea-party scene in *Caste* (1867), his realist version of the Cinderella myth in which the lower-class heroine's rise to the aristocracy is complicated by the vulgarity of her relations, gave rise to the popular term 'cup-and-saucer drama' to describe his brand of carefully reproduced social manners. Yet the small but significant details of tea drunk from saucers and shared spoons sat alongside Robertson's teasing use of meta-theatrical self-reference. When the supposedly dead hero returns alive from the Crimea, his sister-in-law breaks the news gently to his wife by reminding her of a ballet in which she performed, where the hero miraculously returns from the dead, even playing the music which accompanied this theatrical miracle to herald the 'real' husband's entrance. The music that would normally have emanated from the orchestra in the pit is played on stage, crossing the proscenium arch and conflating theatrical convention and on-stage pretence. This playfully self-conscious mix of reality and theatricality was part and parcel of Robertson's new 'realism'; in *Birth* (1870) his cast includes a would-be playwright who wants to write a new form of drama 'from the life' and comments constantly on the dramatic potential of the romances and quarrels taking place around him.[19]

Shaw's realism was similarly complex and multi-textured. Anticipating Brecht's undermining of theatrical illusion through its deliberate exposure, Shaw emphasized the social realities of economic conditions, power structures, vested interests, and naturalistic causation. He located such material, scientific, and social analyses within overtly theatrical genres, from the seaside farce of *You Never Can Tell* (1897) to melodrama in *The Devil's Disciple* (1897), the mixture of toga-play and fable which constitutes *Androcles and the Lion* (1912), or the overt inter-theatrical allusion to Chekhov's *The Cherry Orchard* in his attack on the self-destructive aimlessness of the British upper classes in *Heartbreak House* (1919). Similarly, his 'Man of Destiny', Napoleon, talks of the harsh and mundane facts of warfare while having '*a keen dramatic faculty*' which makes him extremely clever at playing upon heroic ideals with all '*the arts of the actor and stage manager*'.[20] Shaw's characters deliver uncomfortable truths, explode conventional assumptions, and challenge tired dramatic expectations and stereotypes, while simultaneously displaying subtly nuanced degrees of theatricality, self-consciousness, and self-performance.[21]

Joyce was attempting to write for the theatre exactly when Shaw was developing some of his most powerful plays. Joyce's *Exiles* (written in 1915, published in 1918, and premiered in Germany in 1919) is usually ignored by critics or dismissed as

[19] *Birth* in T. W. Robertson, *Six Plays* (Ashover: Amber Lane Press, 1980), 294.

[20] *The Man of Destiny*, in *Bodley Head Bernard Shaw*, I, 608 (emphasis in original).

[21] For example, in a letter of March 1906 Shaw advised Harley Granville-Barker on directing the two actors playing Arab leaders in *Captain Brassbound's Conversion* in 1906 that he must not make Lewis Casson '*play out*' as 'It spoils the part completely & anticipates the Cadi, who plays out all the time'. Letter to Harley Granville-Barker, 14 March 1906, Bernard Shaw, *Collected Letters, 1898–1910*, ed. Dan H. Laurence, 4 vols (London: Max Reinhardt, 1972), II, 608.

youthful aberration; but the play instantly makes sense if it is understood in its the-atrical context—in terms of what else was going on in the theatre just before, dur-ing, and after its composition—rather than in relation to modernist prose. *Exiles* has more in common with theatre of the 1890s than with Edwardian drama. The dialogue shows the strong influence of late Ibsen (more symbolist than naturalist), of the Belgian symbolist playwright Maurice Maeterlinck, and of Oscar Wilde in his less humourous moments, while the stage directions rehearse the hackneyed con-ventions of nineteenth-century melodrama. Joyce's characters repeatedly 'pass their hands across their eyes' or brows to express anguish, and he puts Robert and Bertha in awkward, tableau-like poses during their most passionate scenes. Yet at the same time there are moments that seem straight out of Maeterlinck's proto-Absurdist plays *The Blind* or *The Intruder*: Joyce twice requires sudden gusts of wind and flick-ering lights to interrupt the action, gesturing vaguely towards some mysterious agency beyond the realm of everyday life.[22]

It is this interplay of different theatrical influences that makes the play both inter-esting and difficult to place. 'Joyce was struggling towards a new kind of theatre', writes John MacNicholas, a theatre defined by 'ambiguity and stylized silences . . . Wrapped in a method of pronounced pauses'.[23] *Exiles* thus hovers uncertainly between two distinct theatrical modes—one of the most striking examples of that transitional quality we defined in our Introduction to this volume, of 'late Victorian *into* Modern'.

The materiality of theatre

In a period when aesthetic innovation was closely allied not only to debates about the nature and limits of the artistic medium and the very possibility of representa-tion, but also to philosophical and psychological debates about identity, conscious-ness, and perception, the materiality of theatre was sometimes seen as an inescapable handicap. Theatre means buildings, bodies, costumes, scenery, the whole cumber-some paraphernalia of the external world and its literal embodiment on stage. In an article on *Exiles* in the journal *Drama* Ezra Pound castigated the entire genre, pro-nouncing it a 'gross', 'coarse' form of art, hardly saved by the playwriting itself since the 'whole tribe of playwrights' was just regurgitating 'diluted Ibsen'.[24] By the 1890s fashionable West End theatre was so in thrall to the luxurious display of *haute cou-ture* gowns and desirable furnishings, it prompted Shaw to dismiss the average play

[22] Shepherd-Barr, 'Reconsidering Joyce's *Exiles* in its Theatrical Context', *Theatre Research International* 28 (2003), 2: 176.
[23] John MacNicholas, 'The Stage History of Exiles', *James Joyce Quarterly* 19/1 (Fall 1981), 22.
[24] Forrest Read (ed.), *Pound/Joyce: The Letters of Ezra Pound to James Joyce, with Pound's Essays on Joyce* (New York: New Directions, 1967), 46.

as no more than 'a tailor's advertisement making sentimental remarks to a milliner's advertisement in the middle of an upholsterer's and decorator's advertisement'.[25] Despite theatre's potential for such commercial displays, to believe that theatre's engagement with modernist experimentation was limited by its inescapable presentation of the literal and the material is to misunderstand the intrinsic nature of theatre, its ability to be both literal and metaphorical, bodily and disembodied. So Yeats's famous question in 'Among School Children', 'How can we tell the dancer from the dance?' conjures the meta-theatrical complexities of Nora's tarantella dance in Ibsen's *A Doll's House* (1879), in which self-expression, seduction, hysteria, distraction, and display all troublingly and seamlessly mesh. The body on stage is never single but double: simultaneously the actor's body and the character's, with the relation between the two essentially metaphorical.[26] Theatre could play endlessly with this idea. In the first production of Shaw's *Man and Superman* in 1905, Jack Tanner's body was not just double but triple. Played by the actor Harley Granville-Barker and made up to look like Shaw himself, Tanner's presence became troublingly multiple and fluid, puzzling critics with questions of authority, identity, and autobiographical relevance similar to those prompted by the title and final double dates at the end of Joyce's *A Portrait of the Artist as a Young Man*.

The relation between the material, the spiritual, and the intellectual is constantly under debate in Shaw's drama, and lies at the heart of his early twentieth-century plays, from the final triumvirate in *Major Barbara* of Cusins, Barbara, and Undershaft—the Salvation Army evangelist, the intellectual professor of Greek, and the munitions manufacturing millionaire—to Father Keegan's concluding vision in *John Bull's Other Island* of an ideal Ireland 'where the State is the Church and the Church the people: three in one and one in three . . . It is a godhead in which all life is human and all humanity divine: three in one and one in three'.[27] In *Back to Methuselah* (1918-20) Shaw envisions a future where people will have shed their bodies, evolving to become pure energy, immortal and free to roam the stars. In *Man and Superman*, some fifty years before Samuel Beckett's dramatic experiments in fragmenting, entrapping, and multiplying the actor's bodily presence, Shaw used innovative stage techniques to problematize and interrogate the relation between body and identity, the actor's physical presence and the nature of human selfhood. Shaw's stage direction for the third-act transition from the desert of the Sierra Nevada to a Hell comfortably occupied not only by Don Juan and the Devil, but by the Commendatore turned statue and his seduced daughter Ana from Mozart's *Don*

---

[25] G. B. Shaw, *Saturday Review* (27 Feb 1897), 219. For more on theatre, fashion, and spectacle see Joel Kaplan and Sheila Stowell, *Theatre and Fashion, from Oscar Wilde to the Suffragettes* (Cambridge: Cambridge University Press, 1994) and Michael R. Booth, *Victorian Spectacular Theatre* (Boston, MA: Routledge & Kegan Paul, 1981).

[26] For an excellent discussion of this see Dan Rebellato, 'When We Talk of Horses: Or, What Do We See When We See a Play?', *Performance Research* 14/1 (March 2009), 17–28.

[27] *John Bull's Other Island*, in *Bodley Head Bernard Shaw* II, 1021.

Giovanni, calls for all the resources of lighting, music, costume, and above all the actors' bodies to conjure a mystical space where the relations between body, soul, and identity are revolutionized. The peaks of the Sierra vanish and the sky '*seems to steal away out of the universe*' leaving '*omnipresent nothing . . . no light, no sound, no time nor space, utter void*'.[28] Into this void is then conjured the presence of a body that is not a body:

> Then somewhere the beginning of a pallor, and with it a faint throbbing buzz as of a ghostly violoncello palpitating on the same note endlessly. A couple of ghostly violins presently take advantage of this bass [musical notation here] and therewith the pallor reveals a man in the void, an incorporeal but visible man, seated, absurdly enough, on nothing.[29]

Having required all the arts of theatre to depict the body incorporeal, Shaw then demands a further physical feat for the transformation of the actor who plays Ana, who must magically transform from an old crone:

> Whisk! The old woman becomes a young one, magnificently attired, and so handsome that in the radiance into which her dull yellow halo has suddenly lightened one might almost mistake her for Ann Whitefield.[30]

In Hell, as Juan explains, no one has a body, so everyone is free to choose their own age and appearance—a concept which is given life on stage through the arts of lighting, music, make-up, costume, gesture, voice, and bearing, plus the further complication of doubling the roles of Jack/Juan and Ann/Ana, whereby the actor's body signifies two different characters, enacting the potentially arbitrary connection between physical presence and inner mental or spiritual selfhood.

Shaw's detailed stage directions have often been explained as narrative devices, geared towards the reader rather than meant for literal enactment, but this robs them of their theatrical significance: they show him engaging closely with the possibilities of stagecraft, asking for the deployment of cutting-edge artistry to create innovative effects. Just as Wilde's symbolist *Salome* (1891) was influenced by the synaesthetic experiments of the French avant-garde and inspired modernist stage designs by Charles Ricketts, Nikolai Kalmakov, and Alexandra Exter, so Shaw's play inspired Ricketts to design for its Court Theatre premiere a stage set of black velvet, framed by electric lights which created the illusion of further darkening it, and filled with rich and brilliant costumes reminiscent of Velasquez.[31] Collaboration is key: the combination of the operatic musicality of the play's speeches with Ricketts's innovative design helped make the play a modernist

---

[28] *Man and Superman*, in *Bodley Head Bernard Shaw*, II, 631 (emphasis in the original).

[29] Ibid., II, 631–2.   [30] Ibid., II, 638.

[31] For further details of *Salome* in production, see William Tydeman and Stephen Price, *Wilde: Salome* (Cambridge: Cambridge University Press, 1996); for *Man and Superman*, see Kennedy, *Granville Barker*, 72–4.

Gesamtkunstwerk, which explored the borders between the physical and meta-physical worlds.

Just as the body on stage is simultaneously literal and metaphorical, so can material objects serve as the mundane props of everyday life as well as carrying suggestive symbolic resonance. Løvborg's manuscript in Ibsen's *Hedda Gabler*, for instance, is both a handwritten, easily mislaid and flammable package of papers, and a life's work, a love child born of his partnership with Thea Elvsted.[32] The realist three-walled box sets and crowd-filled street scenes of so many plays by Galsworthy, Robins, St John Hankin, and Barker do not connote plays whose dramatic methods are limited to strictly realist concerns and techniques. The Court Theatre production of Barker's *The Voysey Inheritance* (1905) involved emphatically material sets, in particular a vast din-ner table that dominated the Voyseys' dining room, forcing family members to manoeuvre awkwardly around its unwieldy bulk. Squeezed into the narrow space of the Court's proscenium arch, the table symbolized the family's wealth and social posi-tion and literalized the constricted choice and movement of family members forced to maintain this inherited status. As it is revealed that more than one generation of the family firm have embezzled investors' money, paying out the income while spending the capital, the family's wealth and status appear less as a material fact than as a care-fully constructed illusion. When Edward Voysey reproaches his father for using investors' money to maintain the family's lavish lifestyle, Mr Voysey retorts that it is precisely this expensive front which maintains the public's trust, thus securing the firm the liberty it requires to operate while appearing 'prosperous, respected and without a stain on its honour'.[33] In Barker's depiction of capitalist finance, business and theft become indistinguishable, just as the Voyseys' imposing table is both a solid and inconvenient fact and part of the illusion of respectability. The realist room is a stage set designed to support the family's social performance.

This shift in perspective—not just representing social realities but asking the audience to view them through new eyes and to alter their consciousness of them—characterizes many 'new' dramas. American playwright Susan Glaspell's seminal play *Trifles* (1916) offers a particularly striking example of this transformative gaze. Visiting the house of a murdered man, a male sheriff and country attorney find it bare of clues as they comb through the rooms; but their wives sitting in the kitchen begin to read in the trifling domestic details of discarded sewing, sloppy preserving, and a dead canary a tale of domestic abuse that explains the murderous actions of the dead man's wife. The conventional audience gaze, Glaspell implies, is male, and her play reveals a richer underlying narrative available only to the female gaze. Similarly, the British New Drama asked its audiences to re-envision the world from

---

[32] The mislaid manuscript/baby equivalent is one which Wilde comically reproduces in Miss Prism's three-volume novel 'of more than usually revolting sentimentality' in Wilde's *The Importance of Being Earnest.*

[33] Harley Granville-Barker, *The Voysey Inheritance,* in George Rowell (ed.), *Late Victorian Plays 1880–1914* (Oxford: Oxford University Press, 1972), 297.

a new perspective—most obviously that of women in plays by Githa Sowerby, Elizabeth Robins, Cicely Hamilton, and Clo Graves, as well as a host of suffrage plays, and in works by men such as Galsworthy, Masefield, St John Hankin, and Stanley Houghton—but also from the point of view of servants, miners, shop assistants, clerks, the unemployed, the criminal, and the work-shy.[34]

New Drama explored the theatricality of everyday life long before performance studies staked its claim to doing this. The second act of Elizabeth Robins's 1907 play *Votes for Women!* takes place in Trafalgar Square at a suffrage meeting at which a crowd is heckling the speakers trying to persuade them that women deserve the vote. This act was highly acclaimed for the way in which the on-stage audience and the actual audience blended seamlessly together. The audience was made aware of its status as an audience, even though not directly acknowledged as such, while watching scripted spontaneity, and the suspense came from wondering how the speakers would handle the hostile crowd. Ernestine Blunt takes the ridicule of the crowd and reroutes it; she handles their hostility expertly, and the play's central concern—that the private must become the public, that women must be willing to speak out publicly and to forge from their own lives political material and weapons—is enacted by performing the self in this very public, everyday space.

Far from being a straightforward and uncomplicated example of realism, clumsily indebted to the tradition of the well-made play, *Votes for Women!* can be considered a key moment in the historiography of modernism—using performance and the theatricality of the self to show the complexity of what public performance means. In many ways, it signifies the tendencies of the 'New' drama, which asked for a transformative gaze, recognizing the vitality and importance of the powerless and the marginalized and redefining the subject matter of theatrical art to encompass the mundane. New Drama required an altered consciousness, an ability to re-vision the ordinary, just as Marcel Duchamp asked viewers to recognize a urinal as a fountain, or Picasso revealed the bull's head in a bike saddle and handlebars.

The legacy of the New Drama

The wealth of innovative and experimental plays in the late Victorian and early Edwardian period notably did not translate into a revivifying transformation of

---

[34] For a focus on women and theatre of this period, see for example Julie Holledge, *Innocent Flowers: Women in the Edwardian Theatre* (London: Virago, 1981); Stowell, *A Stage of Their Own: Feminist Playwrights of the Suffrage Era* (Manchester: Manchester University Press, 1992); Penny Farfan, *Women, Modernism and Performance* (Cambridge: Cambridge University Press, 2004); Vivien Gardner and Susan Rutherford (eds), *The New Woman and Her Sisters: Feminism and Theatre, 1850–1914* (Ann Arbor, MI: University of Michigan Press, 1992); and Gay Gibson Cima, *Performing Women: Female Characters, Male Playwrights and the Modern Stage* (Ithaca, NY and London: Cornell University Press, 1993).

mainstream theatre in subsequent decades. Robins turned her attention from theatre to journalism, while the outbreak of the First World War redirected the energies
of many of those working in the theatrical avant-garde. Playwrights such as
Galsworthy, Masefield, and Barrie joined the government's propaganda unit, and,
with suffrage societies' agreement to suspend protests for the duration of the war,
many suffrage playwrights, actors, and producers concentrated their energies and
expertise on providing entertainment for the troops. Musical comedies and revues
providing light relief and escapist entertainment dominated the stage.

In the aftermath of the war, experimentation became financially riskier, as theatre ownership shifted from actor-managers to commercial investors in search of
profit, pushing up rents by as much as 1,000 per cent in the inter-war period, while
admission prices rarely rose by more than 50 per cent. The only way to balance this
equation was to secure large audiences and long runs in order to break even, thus
pushing the theatre towards the safe ground of guaranteed hits and crowd-pleasers.
Nonetheless, independent theatre societies and production companies continued
alongside the large commercial theatres, offering a lower budget theatrical scene in
which work by unknown or less mainstream writers could be presented, often providing a vital space for developing writers and works, which then progressed to the
larger West End venues.

Shaw continued to experiment with alternative theatrical forms, from the futurist comedy of *The Apple Cart* (1929) to visionary fantasy in *On the Rocks* (1933) and
puppet play in *Shakes versus Shav* (1949). The potential of verse drama was further
explored by writers such as Christopher Fry, T. S. Eliot, W. H. Auden, and
Christopher Isherwood, while innovations in theatrical form included hugely popular works such as *Hay Fever* (1925) and *Private Lives* (1930) by Noel Coward, one
of whose earliest plays, *The Young Idea* (1922), was strongly influenced by Shaw's
You Never Can Tell (1897). As Maggie Gale reveals in *West End Women* (1996),
female playwrights built on the pioneering work of their Edwardian predecessors,
establishing a visible and vital presence on the British stage, while the vibrancy and
direct political engagement of suffrage theatre could be seen in a wealth of dramatic
enterprises from Edith Craig's Pioneer Players to the pageants and sketches of the
Workers' Theatre Movement in the 1920s and 1930s. Similarly, the groundbreaking
repertory theatre of new dramas at the Court Theatre inspired the creation of sadly
short-lived repertory theatres in Manchester (1908) and Glasgow (1909), and more
sustained theatres in Liverpool (1911) and Birmingham (1913), as well as leading
many decades later to the eventual founding of the National Theatre in London. The
influence and inspiration of late Victorian and early Edwardian theatre reached far
forward, right up to the 'theatrical revolution' of the 1950s and 1960s when the
vitality, immediacy, and confrontational humour of Victorian music hall provided
forms and techniques to invigorate plays such as John Osborne's *The Entertainer*
(1957), Shelagh Delaney's *A Taste of Honey* (1958), and Theatre Workshop's *O What
a Lovely War* (1963). Once again drama's innovators brought a new engagement,

energy and edge to the theatre by reinventing, revising, and redeploying the techniques of the past.

FURTHER READING

Blackadder, Neil. *Performing Opposition: Modern Theater and the Scandalized Audience* (Westport, CT: Praeger, 2003).

Chothia, Jean. *English Drama of the Early Modern Period 1890–1940* (London: Longman, 1996).

Cima, Gay Gibson. *Performing Women: Female Characters, Male Playwrights and the Modern Stage* (Ithaca, NY and London: Cornell University Press, 1993).

Diamond, Elin (ed.). 'Modernity's Drama', *Modern Drama* 44/1 (Spring 2001).

Diamond, Elin (ed.). *Modern Drama* 43/4 and 44/1, double issue on redefining the field of modern drama (Winter 2000 and Spring 2001).

Eltis, Sos. *Revising Wilde: Society and Subversion in the Plays of Oscar Wilde* (Oxford: Oxford University Press, 1996).

Eltis, Sos. *Acts of Desire: Women and Sex on Stage. 1800–1930* (Oxford: Oxford University Press, 2013).

Farfan, Penny. *Women, Modernism and Performance* (Cambridge: Cambridge University Press, 2004).

Flannery, James W. *W. B. Yeats and the Idea of a Theatre: The Early Abbey Theatre in Theory and Practice* (New Haven, CT: Yale University Press, 1989).

Gardner, Vivien and Susan Rutherford (eds). *The New Woman and Her Sisters: Feminism and Theatre, 1850–1914* (Ann Arbor, MI: University of Michigan Press, 1992).

Grene, Nicholas. *The Politics of Irish Drama* (Cambridge: Cambridge University Press, 2000).

Holledge, Julie. *Innocent Flowers: Women in the Edwardian Theatre* (London: Virago, 1981).

Innes, Christopher. *Avant Garde Theatre, 1892–1992* (London: Routledge, 1993).

Innes, Christopher. 'Modernism in Drama', in Michael Levenson (ed.), *The Cambridge Companion to Modernism* (Cambridge: Cambridge University Press, 1999), 130-56.

Kelly, Katherine E. (ed.). *Modern Drama by Women, 1880s–1930s* (London: Routledge, 1996).

Kennedy, Dennis. *Granville Barker and the Dream of Theatre* (Cambridge: Cambridge University Press, 1989).

Kolocotroni, Vassiliki, Jane Goldman, and Olga Taxidou (eds). *Modernism: An Anthology of Sources and Documents* (Chicago, IL: University of Chicago Press, 1998).

Luckhurst, Mary. (ed.). *A Companion to Modern British and Irish Drama, 1880–2005* (Oxford: Blackwell, 2006).

McDonald, Jan. *The 'New Drama' 1900–1914: Harley Granville-Barker, John Galsworthy, St John Hankin, John Masefield* (London: Macmillan, 1986).

MacNicholas, John. 'The Stage History of Exiles', *James Joyce Quarterly* 19/1 (Fall 1981), 9–26.

Moi, Toril. *Henrik Ibsen and the Birth of Modernism* (Oxford: Oxford University Press, 2006).

Powell, Kerry (ed.). *The Cambridge Companion to Victorian and Edwardian Theatre* (Cambridge: Cambridge University Press, 2004).

Puchner, Martin. *Stage Fright: Modernism, Anti-Theatricality, and Drama* (Baltimore, MD: Johns Hopkins University Press, 2002).

Rebellato, Dan. 'When We Talk of Horses: Or, What Do We See When We See a Play?', *Performance Research* 14/1 (March 2009), 17–28.

Richards, Shaun (ed.). *The Cambridge Companion to Twentieth-Century Irish Drama* (Cambridge: Cambridge University Press, 2004).

Rowell, George (ed.). *Late Victorian Plays 1880–1914* (Oxford: Oxford University Press, 1972).

Shepherd-Barr, Kirsten. 'Reconsidering *Exiles* in its Theatrical Context', *Theatre Research International* 28/2 (2003), 169–80.

Shepherd-Barr, Kirsten. 'Modernism and Theatrical Performance', *Modernist Cultures* 1/1 (May 2005), 59–68.

Shepherd-Barr, Kirsten. 'Staging Modernism: A New Drama', in Peter Brooker, Andrzej Gasiorek, Deborah Longworth, and Andrew Thacker (eds), *The Oxford Handbook of Modernisms* (Oxford: Oxford University Press, 2011), 122–38.

Stowell, Sheila. 'Rehabilitating Realism', *Journal of Dramatic Theory and Criticism* 6/2 (Spring 1992), 81–8.

Stowell, Sheila. *A Stage of Their Own: Feminist Playwrights of the Suffrage Era* (Manchester: Manchester University Press, 1992).

Switzky, Lawrence. 'Shaw among the Modernists', *Shaw: The Annual of Bernard Shaw Studies* 31 (2011), 133–48.

Tydeman, William and Stephen Price. *Wilde: Salome* (Cambridge: Cambridge University Press, 1996).

Woodfield, James. *English Theatre in Transition, 1881–1914* (London: Croom Helm, 1984).

CHAPTER 9

WHO *WAS* THE 'NEW WOMAN'?

ANGELIQUE RICHARDSON

In the closing decades of the nineteenth century the New Woman, smoking, betrousered, Amazonian, and intellectual, strode—or bicycled—with a fanfare onto the pages of fiction and journalism, and even, though more quietly, into society. In both these modes she continued to be a subject of public attention through the Edwardian period. In the last two decades of the century, more than a hundred novels were written by or about her.[1] Denoting an early, self-conscious, and conspicuous expression of feminism that was satirized as much as it was celebrated, 'New Woman' was, however, a contentious term, seeking to bring together, and limit within a single definition, a number of social and political positions, as the voices of women themselves, or those sympathetic to the women's cause, vied with their opponents. In this chapter I examine some of its uses by the women who were described as New Women, as well as considering the fiction and plays of the men and women who were inspired to write about them.

From the outset, critics saw a distinction between the New Woman and her popular representations. For Mrs M. Eastwood, the author of 'The New Woman in Fiction and in Fact', the literary New Woman was 'a creation of the hyperbolically emancipated woman's riotous imagination'. Nonetheless, she concluded, the New Woman was 'a positive and tangible fact', one who campaigned not for social revolution but reform, refusing to marry the man 'whose morals are not as pure as her own'.[2] For others the New Woman was a term best consigned entirely to fiction. The social purity activist Elizabeth Chapman, author of *Marriage Questions in Modern Fiction, and Other Essays on Kindred Subjects* (1897), dismissed the New Woman as 'a journalistic myth' that had given rise to an 'interminable flood of gaseous chatter'. She argued 'it has become necessary sharply to emphasize the distinction between

---

[1] See Ann Ardis, *New Women, New Novels: Feminism and Early Modernism* (New Brunswick, NJ: Rutgers University Press, 1990), 4.

[2] M. Eastwood, 'The New Woman in Fiction and in Fact', *Humanitarian* 5 (1894), 376–9.

this phantom and the real reformer and friend of her sex and of humanity, whom I would call the "Best Woman".[3]

The women writers who were most commonly seen as New Women were the most hesitant about, and critical of, the term, considering it a reductive—and potentially controlling—homogenization of their often very different views. The term 'New Woman' was used first by Sarah Grand, albeit in lower case, in the *North American Review* in 1894, the year following the publication of her best-selling novel *The Heavenly Twins*:

> Both the cow-woman and the scum-woman are well within the range of the Bawling Brotherhood, but the new woman is a little above him, and he never even thought of looking up to where she has been sitting apart in silent contemplation all these years, thinking and thinking, until at last she solved the problem and proclaimed for herself what was wrong with Home-is-the-Woman's-Sphere, and prescribed the remedy.[4]

Grand later took responsibility for coining the term, showing a certain coolness about it, and emphasizing that she had envisaged 'a very different being from the caricature of femininity now presented to us under that name, and which the press so often gave me credit for creating'.[5] For Grand, the priority for women was to bring a new equality to marriage. Foregrounding questions of health and reproduction, she argued for and accentuated fixed gender differences. At the beginning of the new century, George Egerton, who had turned to the short story for her fleeting and experimental depictions of feminine subjectivity, publishing the iconic *Keynotes* (1893) and *Discords* (1894) for John Lane, also sought distance from the term New Woman. Often represented as the New Woman par excellence, and certainly the most satirized for her disruptive prose and sexually radical ideas, she remarked of the New Woman: 'I have never yet replied to myself in a satisfactory way – to the question what is she?'[6] She went on to declare 'I have never met one – never written about one. My women were all the eternally feminine – old as Eve – the term seemed to me to be one of those loose, cheap, journalistic catch words'. This was not a denial of her own significant contribution to *fin-de-siècle* debates on femininity so much as a determination to be seen to stand apart from the ideas of equality with which it

---

[3] Elizabeth Rachel Chapman, *Marriage Questions in Modern Fiction, and Other Essays on Kindred Subjects* (London and New York: John Lane, 1897), xiii.

[4] Sarah Grand, 'The New Aspect of the Woman Question', *North American Review* 158/448 (March 1894), 271.

[5] Athol Forbes, 'My Impressions of Sarah Grand', *Lady's World* (London), 21 (June 1900), 883. On the origin of the New Woman see, for example, Michelle Elizabeth Tusan, 'Inventing the New Woman: Print Culture and Identity Politics during the fin-de-siècle', *Victorian Periodicals Review* 31/2 (Summer 1998), 169–82, and Talia Schaffer, 'Nothing but Foolscap and Ink', in Angelique Richardson and Chris Willis (eds), *The New Woman in Fiction and in Fact* (Basingstoke: Palgrave Macmillan, 2001), 39–52.

[6] George Egerton to Ernst Foerster, London, 1 July 1900, in Ernst Foerster, *Die Frauenfrage in den Romanen Englischer Schriftstellerinnen der Gegenwart* (Marburg: N.G. Elwert'sche Verlagsbuchhandlung, 1907), 46–8, reproduced in Heilmann (ed.), *The Late-Victorian Marriage Question: A Collection of Key New Woman Texts*, 5 vols (London: Routledge/Thoemmes Press, 1998), V.

was associated: 'I never aim at any "equality" theory because I hold that there is no inequality. We are different animals that is all.'

Meanwhile for Olive Schreiner, author of the first New Woman novel, *The Story of an African Farm*, which appeared in 1883 under the pseudonym Ralph Iron, the term 'New Woman' was something of a misnomer. Taking care to emphasize the New Woman as a reality—'On every hand she is examined, praised, blamed, mistaken for her counterfeit, ridiculed, or deified—but nowhere can it be said, that the phenomenon of her existence is overlooked'[7]—it was to the notion of newness that she took objection. Engaging directly with the term in her pioneering treatise *Woman and Labour* (1911), on which she had been working from the 1880s, Schreiner argued that the women who were working towards social transformation formed part of a history of progress to which both sexes were party. Observing 'It is often said of those who lead in this attempt at the readaption of woman's relation to life, that they are "New Women"; and they are at times spoken of as though they were a something portentous and unheard-of in the order of human life', she declared 'the truth is, we are not new'. She repeated the point insistently, concerned to show that the aims and origins of the New Women were part of a wider, human struggle involving both sexes, rather than a possibly transient historical phenomenon:

> *We* are not new! If you would understand us, go back two thousand years, and study our descent; our breed is our explanation. We are the daughters of our fathers as well as of our mothers. In our dreams we still hear the clash of the shields of our forefathers as they struck them together before battle and raised the shout of 'Freedom!'[8]

New Women, for Schreiner, had 'the blood of a womanhood that was never bought and never sold; that wore no veil, and had no foot bound; whose realized ideal of marriage was sexual companionship and an equality in duty and labour'. They were the women who through the centuries had rejected codes of oppression and conformity, working alongside their male companions.[9] Anxious that, as a result of the very novelty of the New Woman, women did not become the sole focus of attention, leaving normative ideas of an essential, non-contingent masculinity unexamined, she observed that 'there exists at the present day another body of social phenomena, quite as important, as radical' as the New Woman, and that was the 'New Man'. As the modern woman objected to 'the companionship of a Tom Jones' so the modern man would object to 'an always fainting, weeping, and terrified Emilia or a Sophia of a bygone epoch'.[10]

With its colonial setting and complex experimental blending of realism with allegory, autobiography, polemic, and shifting perspectives, *The Story of an African Farm* had offered an early challenge both to gender boundaries and to the Victorian

---

[7] Olive Schreiner, *Woman and Labour* (London: Virago, 1978), 253.
[8] Ibid., 144, 147 (emphasis in original).   [9] Ibid., 145.   [10] Ibid., 257–8.

realist novel. As Schreiner herself saw, the disrupted narrative method turned away from what she described in the Preface as the 'stage method' of presenting characters in favour of 'a strange coming and going of feet'.[11] Schreiner went further in this novel than many of her female contemporaries in rethinking stereotypical roles. The young farmer, Gregory Rose, enthralled by Lyndall, is perhaps the first New Man of Victorian fiction. Described as a 'man-woman', one 'born for the sphere that some women have to fill without being born for it', he experiences 'womanhood', in the words of Lyndall 'the most experienced nurse I ever came in contact with'. In her conversations with Waldo Lyndall remarks, 'When I am with you I never know that I am a woman and you are a man; I only know that we are both things that think'.[12] Gender exists for her outside the strictures of determinism: 'we all enter the world little plastic things, with so much natural force, perhaps, but for the rest – blank; and the world tells us what we are to be, and shapes us by the ends it sets before us'; and she declares her recurrent hope that one day to be born a woman will not mean to be born 'branded'.[13] For the publisher and social reformer W. T. Stead, 'The whole woman movement of today may be summed up in Lyndall's startling and daring assertion'. He singled out *The Story of an African Farm* as striking 'the most distinctive note of the literature of the last decade of the nineteenth century'; it was a story whose influence 'can be seen or felt in all the literature of the Modern Woman'.[14] The success of the novel brought Schreiner into direct contact with *fin-de-siècle* London, and with Karl Pearson (with whom she had a brief and troubled relationship) and his radical Men and Women's Club. Running from 1885 to 1889 the club provided an important sounding board for early feminist ideas.

Another of the club's associates was Mona Caird, who would become the most polemical of the New Women. Her first novel, *Whom Nature Leadeth*, was published the same year as *The Story of an African Farm*, under the pseudonym G. Noel Hatton. In it she explored, through the artist Leonore Ravenhill, questions of female independence and the constraints of convention that Caird would foreground in her later writing. Other members included Emma Brooke, whose novel *A Superfluous Woman* (1894) took up the problem of syphilis; Dr Elizabeth Blackwell—who in 1859, with an MD from the United States, became the first woman to be included on the General Medical Council's register; Jane Hume Clapperton, the eugenist and author of *Scientific Meliorism and The Evolution Of Happiness* (1885) and *Margaret Dunmore: Or a Socialist Home* (1888); and Henrietta Müller, editor (under the name Helena B. Temple) of the progressive feminist *Women's Penny Paper* (from 1891 the *Woman's Herald*).

---

[11] Schreiner, *The Story of an African Farm*, ed. Joseph Bristow (Oxford: Oxford University Press, 1992), 27.

[12] Ibid., 164, 241, 205.   [13] Ibid., 223, 154.

[14] W. T. Stead, 'The Novel of the Modern Woman' (The Book of the Month), *Review of Reviews* 10 (July 1894), 65.

Schreiner's approach to the gender debate had most in common with Caird, who among the New Women was the most critical of biological determinism and its unquestioning acceptance. In 1888, still a relatively unknown novelist, Caird had published an article entitled 'Marriage' in the independent section of the *Westminster Review*, sparking the greatest newspaper controversy of the century. The *Daily Telegraph* immediately posed the question 'Is Marriage a Failure?'—'the Editor's table disappeared beneath the varieties of experience'[15]—and published three columns of letters daily during the months of July, August, and September, a selection from 27,000 from around the world. Like Caird, Schreiner stressed the historical rather than biological underpinning of social norms, emphasizing the extent to which they were subject to change: 'The continually changing material conditions of life, with their reaction on the intellectual, emotional, and moral aspects of human affairs, render our societies the most complex and probably the most mobile and unsettled which the world has ever seen.'[16]

Emerging at this time of unprecedented social transformation and heightened self-consciousness, the New Woman was a powerfully resonant term, for all its limitations and shoehornings, and marked a break with social and literary convention. For the *Humanitarian*, 'That very word "new", strikes as it were the dominant note in the trend of present-day thought, present-day effort and aspiration . . . The new art, the new literature, the new fiction, the new journalism, the new humour, the new criticism, the new hedonism, the new morality'.[17] The fictional New Woman coincided with an enhanced awareness of the extensive social influence of literature, in particular the novel. It was both a powerful means of expression for late-Victorian women—May Hartley described it as 'the sole recognized means at present for a woman to make her voice and power felt outside the narrow limits of her personal surrounding'[18]—and was also a significant vehicle for the articulation and dissemination of new ideas about sex and sexual relations. This was a debate to which the New Woman had much to contribute. Sarah Grand stressed that physiology should be taught in schools as a matter of course, and that a girl should 'certainly not, under any circumstances, be allowed to marry without full knowledge of all that is expected of her in marriage, and she should also be fully informed of the past life of the man whom she may be inclined to accept'.[19]

In 'The New Aspect of the Woman Question', which appeared in the *North American Review* the same year, Grand declared 'The Woman Question' is the Marriage Question.[20] This turning point is key to any consideration of the New

[15] Harry Quilter (ed.), *Is Marriage a Failure?* (London: Swan Sonnenschein, 1888), 2.

[16] Schreiner, *Woman and Labour*, 259.

[17] Mrs Morgan-Dockerell, 'Is the New Woman a Myth?', *Humanitarian* 8 (1896), 339.

[18] May Hartley, in opinions of literary advisers on *The Heavenly Twins*. Correspondence of Frances Elizabeth McFall, National Library of Scotland (emphasis in original).

[19] Grand, 'The Tree of Knowledge', *New Review* 10/61 (June 1894), 680.

[20] Grand, 'The New Aspect of the Woman Question', 276.

Woman. Whether she sought to reject or reform marriage, the subject not only allowed her to address seminal questions on the freedom, autonomy, and legal status of women, it also opened up matters of health, reproduction, and national efficiency as social purity and imperial discourses conjoined with these early and often maternalist expressions of feminism. W. T. Stead observed that the novels of the modern women were 'pre-occupied with questions of sex, questions of marriage, questions of maternity'.[21] Grand's lengthy novels provide case studies in marriages to degenerate men as she set about reforming the genre, rescripting the eighteenth-century romance plot so that instead of a wayward man marrying a 'spotless' heroine,[22] a physiologically aware woman subjected the character of any potential suitors to intense scrutiny, looking out also for physical signs of degeneration. Grand took Tobias Smollett's *The Adventures of Roderick Random* (1748) and Henry Fielding's *Tom Jones, A Foundling* (1749) as notable examples of precisely what the novel needed to distance itself from if it were to realize its scope as an agent of social change, and a vehicle of civic duty. Equally, she wrote against the Decadent aesthetic *fin de siècle* fictions that vied for attention with the purpose novel.

The Heavenly Twins opens with Evadne looking out inquiringly at an untried world: '[s]he wanted to know'. Its title resonant with Galton's nature–nurture studies, the novel tells the story of three women, engaging, from the outset, with questions of healthy and unhealthy reproduction and advocating a new, rational love working to eugenic ends while also addressing wider themes of autonomy and education. Evadne Frayling and Edith Beale make disastrous marriages to syphilitic degenerates, while Angelica Hamilton-Wells demands freedom in her marriage to an older man, which involves her leaving the house in Book IV, the novel's 'Interlude' dressed as a man to experience the world from a masculine, or at least less constrained, perspective. Evadne's censorious father finds that she has been reading 'histology, pathology, anatomy, physiology, prophylactics, therapeutics, botany, natural history, ancient and outspoken history, not to mention the modern writers and the various philosophies'.[23] An avid reader of Galton and Herbert Spencer from an early age, she refuses to enter into a sexual relationship with her new husband, Major George Colquhoun, an army surgeon, once she discovers his chequered past. Colquhoun tries to seduce her with the works of Zola, Daudet, and George Sand, but his project fails and he removes their fiction, of which Grand heavily disapproved, form her shelves. Unsurprisingly, the novel caused a sensation. Reprinted six times in its first year of publication, with Heinemann reporting a sale of 20,000 within a few weeks, more than five times as many copies were sold in the USA, where it made the overall bestsellers list for the 1890s, and it was translated into several languages.[24] Thirty years after the publication of *The Heavenly Twins*, in a foreword to a new

[21] W. T. Stead, 'The Novel of the Modern Woman', 65.
[22] Grand, *The Heavenly Twins* (Ann Arbor, MI: University of Michigan Press, 1992), 20.
[23] Ibid., 126.
[24] See Grand, 'Novelist of the Nineties', *The Times* (13 May 1943), 7; Frank Luther Mott, *Golden Multitudes: The Story of Best Sellers in the United States* (New York: R. R. Bowker, 1947), 181–2, 311.

edition (1923), Grand stated that she had achieved her purpose of outing the sexual double standard and the tabooed diseases it brought with it: '[D]inner tables resounded with the controversy, and, in their excitement, those who had most rigorously enjoined silence broke it themselves incontinently.'[25] This engagement with new scientific discourse marks all her novels. The eponymous heroine of her yellow-back novel, *Ideala: A Story from Life*, which she wrote in 1881 and published herself in 1888, acquires a copy of Huxley's *Elementary Physiology* (1866), the text of the lectures on elementary physiology he had given to a packed audience.[26]

But with her focus on the body, venereal disease, and sexual relations, Sarah Grand risked being conflated with the avant-garde; with late-century naturalists and decadents, the very writers from whom she sought to distance herself, or being dismissed as writing medical treatises in disguise. In his scathing article 'Tommyrotics', Hugh Stutfield declared that the new woman was a degenerate. Women, he declared, 'are chiefly responsible for the "booming" of books that are "close to life"—life, that is to say, as viewed through sex-maniacal glasses.'[27] 'When they are not talking of psychology, they are discussing physiology.' Referring to the New Woman's 'maddening faculty of dissecting and probing their "primary impulses"—especially the sexual ones', he declared that with 'her head full of all the 'ologies and 'isms, with sex problems and heredity, and other gleanings from the surgery and the lecture-room' her novels were practically treatises.[28] Other critics responded more positively. Stead observed that the 'phenomenal sale' of *The Heavenly Twins* was 'a small thing compared with the result she achieved in breaking up the conspiracy of silence in society on the serious side of marriage'. The book was 'a bomb of dynamite, which she exploded with wonderful results'. In the last twelve months, 'an astonished and somewhat bewildered society has been busily engaged in discussing the new demand of the new woman'.[29]

However, alongside this radical agenda was a more conservative one. Egerton would similarly conjoin radical ideas with a biologistic and maternalist agenda, arguing that women might stem the tide of degeneration through reproductive relations and the recognition of the maternal function outside of repressive codes of propriety and convention. In the context of late nineteenth-century British fears of racial decline and imperial loss, a feminism had developed that was both essentialist and eugenic.[30] Seeking political recognition for reproductive labour, it argued

---

[25] Quoted in Ann Heilmann, *Sex, Social Purity and Sarah Grand*, 4 vols (London: Routledge, 2001), I, 406.

[26] By 1885, *Elementary Physiology* was in its fourth, and numerously reprinted, edition, selling over 205,000 copies by 1915.

[27] Hugh E. M. Stutfield, 'Tommyrotics', *Blackwood's* 157/956 (June 1895), 844.

[28] Ibid., 836.

[29] W. T. Stead, 'The Novel of the Modern Woman', 65.

[30] See Richardson, *Love and Eugenics in the Late Nineteenth Century: Rational Reproduction and the New Woman* (Oxford: Oxford University Press, 2003).

that the contribution of women to nation and empire might be expanded if they assumed responsibility for the rational selection of reproductive partners. Essentialist feminism posed far less a threat to established gendered norms than feminisms that challenged biologistic arguments. Sarah Grand's was essentially a racial conservative feminism that developed from mid-Victorian social purity debates; Egerton adopted a more transgressive approach but also addressed questions of reproductive health, working towards similar maternalist goals.

Notwithstanding, one of the anxieties surrounding the New Woman was that she would lead women to reject their maternal role. This was a particular problem for the eugenist, science writer, and prolific novelist Grant Allen, who gave a distinctive voice to such concerns, arguing that if she chose to reject motherhood, the 'girl of the future' would soon be 'as flat as a pancake' and 'as dry as a broomstick'.[31] Writing in the *Nineteenth Century* in 1892 Mona Caird pointed to the fallacy inherent in biologistic arguments, remarking that if women 'are really insurgents against evolutionary human nature, instead of being the indications of a new social development, then their fatal error will assuredly prove itself in a very short time'.[32] Drawing from the outset on the liberal philosophy of John Stuart Mill and the evolutionary ideas of Charles Darwin,[33] Caird interrogated the discourses around heredity, speaking out against eugenists in her address to the Personal Rights Association in 1913, and offering a prescient and urgent denunciation of eugenics in her last two novels, *The Stones of Sacrifice* (1915) and *The Great Wave* (1931).

Much of the debate between the social purity New Women and anti-essentialists such as Caird and Olive Schreiner turned on the question of sexual difference and essentialism. Declaring in the *Nineteenth Century* that 'we shall never have really good mothers, until women cease to make motherhood the central idea of their existence',[34] Caird turned the language of degeneration on its head, arguing that a disease of civilization was not unhealthy reproduction or heredity, but a social emphasis on reproductive labour to the exclusion of all else. She wrote in *The Daughters of Danaus* 'the illegal mother is hounded by her fellows in one direction; the legal mother is urged and incited in another: free motherhood is unknown amongst us', denouncing 'the enormous pressure of law and opinion' that formed part of its conditions.[35] In her short stories, George Egerton developed an alternative vision: championing the cause of the 'illegal mother', she prioritized feminine

---

[31] Grant Allen, 'The Girl of the Future', *Universal Review* 7 (1890), 57.

[32] Mona Caird, 'A Defence of the So-called "Wild Women"', *Nineteenth Century* 31/183 (May 1892), 169.

[33] See Richardson, 'Against Finality: Darwin, Mill and the End of Essentialism', *Critical Quarterly* 53/4 (Dec 2011), 21–44. On Caird's engagement with Millian ideas see also Demelza Hookway, 'Liberating Conversations: John Stuart Mill and Mona Caird', *Literature Compass* 9/11 (Nov 2012), 873–83; and ' "The John Millennium": John Stuart Mill in Victorian Culture' (PhD thesis, University of Exeter, 2013).

[34] Caird, 'A Defence of the So-called "Wild Women"', 173.

[35] Caird, *The Daughters of Danaus* (London: Bliss, Sands & Foster, 1894), 342.

interiorities and, unlike Caird and Grand, she did not turn to periodicals to disseminate her ideas. As Egerton's fictions demonstrated, the short story, inconclusive
and experimental, was providing new ways of saying new things. Schreiner would
publish a collection of allegories, *Dreams,* in 1890, in part autobiographical, but
incorporating a number of perspectives and genres from parables to dreams, finding another means of breaking free from traditional narrative form, and in 1901
Egerton published her autobiographical epistolary novel *Rosa Amorosa: The Love
Letters of a Woman.* The New Woman of novels was regularly hemmed in, and often
defeated, by social circumstances, perhaps inevitably as the traditions of Victorian
realist fiction tended to suggest that social barriers were stronger than individual
will. But short stories and non-realist modes offered a release from these strictures
and also countered the rational narratives of the social purists. Analogous to the
female fiction writer's preference for the short story form was the female playwright's specialization in the one-act play form, exemplified by Emily Susan Ford's
Rejected Addresses (1892), Bessie Hatton's *Before Sunrise* (1909), Vera Wentworth's
An Allegory (1913), and the American playwright Susan Glaspell's *Trifles* (1916).
The short story proved especially suited to the exploration by women writers of
emerging concepts of femininity, and the most popular way of escaping the strictures of the realist form. The intriguing subject of Egerton's 'A Cross Line' is sketched
for a short, and only partially defined, period of her life, in a similarly unspecified
social context, in a form that is under no obligation to recount her possible difficulties and disappointments. The short story was also well suited to the circumstances
in which women wrote. In *A Room of One's Own* (1929), Virginia Woolf would
observe: 'The book has somehow to be adapted to the body, and at a venture one
would say that women's books should be shorter, more concentrated, than those of
men, and framed so that they do not need long hours of steady and uninterrupted
work. For interruptions there will always be.'[36]

Both Mona Caird and Schreiner wrote against contemporary essentialist agendas. In their different ways, they emphasized the nurturing rather than biologistic
nature of motherhood. Schreiner stressed that maternity needed to be integrated
with other forms of labouring production, looking towards 'a fuller and higher
attainment of motherhood', just as she insisted on the creative value of paternity—
this also formed part of her implicit questioning of the eugenic agenda.[37] Like
Caird, Schreiner subverted the discourse of degeneration, arguing that it was a
symptom of a lack of meaningful labour, and thus moving it from a biological to
a social framework. She described a woman who was not 'engaged in any social,
political, or intellectual or artistic labour' and 'could neither cook her own food
nor make her own clothes' as 'the most helpless case of female degeneration',

---

[36] Virginia Woolf, *A Room of One's Own; Three Guineas,* ed. Morag Shiach (Oxford: Oxford
University Press, 1992), 101.
[37] Schreiner, *Woman and Labour,* 127.

emphasizing that 'the danger of enervation through non-employment, and of degeneration through dependence on the sex function' existed 'among the wealthy, cultured, and brain-labouring classes'.[38]

Middle-class women were most likely to suffer the ill effects of a lack of labour, and invisibility outside the home, questions that were explored in New Woman fictions. Working-class women, however, who experienced a different set of deprivations and exploitations, were often excluded from the framework of the late-Victorian New Woman. George Gissing addressed these questions, for example noting the prohibitive cost of the bicycle, in his short story 'A Daughter of the Lodge', which first appeared in the *Illustrated London News* in 1901: 'May would have long ago bought a bicycle had she been able to afford it.[39] The middle-class Madden sisters, surplus to the marriage market in *The Odd Women* (1893), struggle to find fulfilling work: '[T]o serve behind a counter would not have been Monica's choice if any more liberal employment had seemed within her reach.'[40] By the novel's end Rhoda Nunn and Mary Barfoot run Great Portland Street School, an institution teaching women the skills needed to make them self-reliant. Rhoda explains to the dandified and somewhat misogynistic would-be feminist sympathizer, Everard Barfoot, that there needn't be 'a great number of unmarried women' claimed by domestic duties. She looks to a time when 'the whole course of female education is altered; when the girls are trained as a matter of course to some definite pursuit', declaring 'I would have no girl, however wealthy her parents, grow up without a profession.'[41]

The following year Caird alluded to the world outside the narrow enclaves of the New Woman when Algitha elects for useful employment among the poor in London, while downplaying the philanthropic element—which was something of a middle-class commonplace—in favour of a more transgressive pursuit of liberty. Even Sarah Grand, pushing a maternalist agenda, provides her heroines with out-lets and employment beyond, though not as alternatives to, marriage, with the pro-tagonist of *The Beth Book: Being a Study of the Life of Elizabeth Caldwell Maclure, a Woman of Genius,* becoming a successful public speaker. The following decade, in Elizabeth Robins's *Votes for Women!* Vida Levering cries: 'Some girls think it hardship to have to earn their living. The horror is not to be allowed to.'[42]

For the working class, though, labour could be a means of exploitation as much as fulfilment. This fell somewhat outside the New Woman's narrower sphere and might be seen as a limitation of this early expression of feminism. Nonetheless, the issues around working women were explored by several writers, including Hardy and Gissing, who also engaged with the New Woman. Labouring women punctuate

---

[38] Ibid., 120, 123.

[39] George Gissing, 'The Daughter of the Lodge', from *The House of Cobwebs and Other Stories* (London: Archibald Constable, 1906), republished in Angelique Richardson (ed.), *Women Who Did: Stories by Men and Women, 1890–1914* (Harmondsworth: Penguin, 2005), 270.

[40] Gissing, *The Odd Women*, ed. Patricia Ingham (Oxford: Oxford University Press, 2000), 15.

[41] Ibid., 112.   [42] Elizabeth Robins, *Votes for Women!* (London: Mills and Boon, 1907), 51.

Hardy's novels from the 1870s onwards, providing an early contribution to the debate on the role and nature of women. Several perform the work of men, from the suddenly wealthy Bathsheba, who decides to take on the work of farmer and steward, to the working-class Marty South who makes spars into the small hours to earn a subsistence wage. Hardy's New Woman, Sue Bridehead, expelled from teacher training, subsequently assists Jude in his work as a stonemason.

But perhaps one of the most disruptive of working women was the woman who wrote. Such women found themselves on masculine territory, especially in the case of poetry, seemingly threatening to abandon their allotted wifely and maternal roles. In *A Pair of Blue Eyes* (1873), Henry Knight warns Elfride 'that a young woman has taken to writing is not by any means the best thing to hear about her', warning her at least to confine herself to 'domestic scenes'. And the eponymous heroine of *The Hand of Ethelberta* (1876) is assumed to be rather a 'fast lady' when she takes to verse writing, taking on the masculine Anacreontic form. In the 1890s, New Woman poets deliberately moved outside of domestic scenes. Constance Naden took up new scientific discourse in 'The New Orthodoxy' (1894), as Amy addresses her conventional lover Fred, arguing for human–animal kinship: 'Things with fin, and claw, and hoof / Join to give us perfect proof / That our being's warp and woof / We from near and far win.'[43] Elsewhere she stresses the importance of female autonomy and subjectivity, with the speaker in her poem 'Love's Mirror' (1894) resisting her lover's idealism and challenging domestic ideals: 'Cast out the goddess! let me in; / Faulty I am, yet all your own.'[44] May Kendall's 'In the Toy Shop' (1894) dramatizes the passivity of the Victorian ideal of femininity through a doll who wishes to be human: 'You see on every wooden feature / My animation's nil. / How nice to be a human creature, / Get cross, and have a will!'[45] Others engaged directly with questions of literary expression, with A. Mary F. Robinson in 'The Sonnet' (1893) reclaiming the form as female—'the "wild instinctive song"' that women chanted for the Feast of May a thousand years ago. Speaking directly to the sonnet she implores kindness: 'be not rebellious in my hands / That ply the spindle oftener than the lute.'[46]

Although writing was still envisaged by some as a masculine pursuit, women were taking to the pen in such numbers that Schreiner felt it necessary, in *Woman and Labour*, to argue against any natural relation between women and writing: 'It is sometimes stated, that as several women of genius in modern times have sought to find expression for their creative powers in the art of fiction, there must be some inherent connection in the human brain between the ovarian sex function and the

---

[43]   Constance Naden, *The Complete Poetical Works* (1894), in R. K. R. Thornton and Marion Thain (eds), *Poetry of the 1890s* (Harmondsworth: Penguin, 1997), 44.

[44]   Naden, *Complete Poetical Works*, 27.

[45]   May Kendall, *Songs from Dreamland* (1894), in Thornton and Thain (eds), *Poetry of the 1890s*, 29.

[46]   A. Mary F. Robinson, *Retrospect and Other Poems* (1893), in Thornton and Thain (eds), *Poetry of the 1890s*, 58.

art of fiction.'[47] She pointed out that 'modern fiction' was the only art that could be exercised 'without special training or special appliances, and produced in the moments stolen from the multifarious, brain-destroying occupations which fill the average woman's life', and remarked that 'hidden within a third-rate novelist might well be a legislator, an able architect, an original scientific investigator, or a good judge'; professions then largely closed to women. As part of her critique of an essentialist position on gendered labour, and her desire to revalidate paternity no less than maternity, she turned to nature for examples of co-parenting, observing that songbirds 'build the nest together and rear the young with an equal devotion'.[48]

New Woman writing went to the heart of the male–female relation, and men made a significant contribution to the debates, a number, such as Hardy, George Gissing, Grant Allen, and H. G. Wells, producing New Woman novels. In the year that Hardy produced *Tess of the d'Urbervilles*, the century's most resounding attack on the sexual double standard, he declared, 'Ever since I began to write . . . I have felt that the doll of English fiction must be demolished, if England is to have a school of fiction at all'.[49] By this time he was friends with Mona Caird; he would shortly meet Sarah Grand when she turned up unexpectedly at Max Gate, and embark on a correspondence with George Egerton, whose short stories he read with interest. With *Jude the Obscure* (1895), which he considered turning into a play called 'The New Woman',[50] he came to intervene directly in the New Woman debates, offering through Sue Bridehead an exploration of a new autonomy and a powerful critique of female subordination. Sue declares: 'She, or he, "who lets the world, or his own portion of it, choose his plan of life for him, has no need of any other faculty than the ape-like one of imitation." J. S. Mill's words, those are. I have been reading it up. Why can't you act upon them? I wish to, always.'[51] Such moments of feminist consciousness erupt in the fiction, interrogating the basis of gendered inequality. *Jude the Obscure* appeared in the same year as Allen's notorious *The Woman Who Did* (1895): the two would be yoked together in Mrs Oliphant's incandescent 'The Anti-Marriage League'.[52] In his 'Plain Words on the Woman Question' Allen urged that women be educated along lines that best fitted them for reproduction and child rearing, lamenting that:

> instead of women being educated to suckle strong and intelligent children, and to order well a wholesome, beautiful, reasonable household—the mistake was made of educating them like men—giving a like training for totally unlike functions. The result

---

[47] Schreiner, *Woman and Labour*, 158.   [48] Ibid., 158, 186.

[49] Thomas Hardy to H. W. Massingham, 31 December 1891, in Richard Little Purdy and Michael Millgate (eds), *The Collected Letters of Thomas Hardy*, 8 vols (Oxford: Clarendon Press, 1978–88), I, 250.

[50] Millgate, *Thomas Hardy: His Career as a Novelist* (1971; Basingstoke: Macmillan, 1994), 312.

[51] Hardy, *Jude the Obscure*, ed. C. H. Sisson (Harmondsworth: Penguin, 1985), 286. The quotation is from ch. 3 of Mill's *On Liberty* (London: Longmans, 1859).

[52] Margaret Oliphant, 'The Anti-Marriage League', *Blackwood's* 159/963 (Jan 1896), 135–49.

was that many women became unsexed in the process, and many others acquired a distaste, an unnatural distaste, for the functions which Nature intended them to perform.[53]

He concluded: 'But what we must absolutely insist upon is full and free recognition of the fact that, in spite of everything, the race and the nation must go on reproducing themselves.' In *The Woman Who Did*, the Cambridge-educated Herminia Barton regards herself as 'living proof of the doctrine of heredity'. In contrast to 'a town-bred girl', she is a 'natural' woman who has devoted herself to 'this one great question of a woman's duty to herself and her sex and her unborn children'.[54] She declares that she can only love, and bear children, outside the constraints of marriage. Wells's New Woman novel, *Ann Veronica*, appearing in 1909, engaged with the eugenic aspects of the New Woman debates. Much of *Ann Veronica* takes place in biological laboratories. The heroine, a biology student at Tredgold Women's College, attains 'a state of unprecedented physical fitness'[55] with Capes, a married but separated demonstrator in the laboratory of Central Imperial College. The novel ends with her pregnant with Capes's child (this was the year that the first of the two children Wells fathered outside of his second marriage was born).

The New Woman in her myriad guises was to have at least as electrifying a presence on the stage. Henrik Ibsen's *A Doll's House* (1879) marked an early intervention in the portrayal of the relation between the sexes as Nora dramatically slams the door of the family home in an unprecedented bid for freedom at the play's close. It was performed in London a decade later as the experimental Free Theatre Movement brought Ibsen to the English stage. 'What can it mean?' asked an audience that contained such progressives as Eleanor Marx, Schreiner, George Bernard Shaw, Emma Brooke, Edith Ellis, and the poet Dolly Radford.[56] As playwrights and critics have noted, Ibsen was especially attractive to actresses, with Elizabeth Robins, who would become the New Woman of the New Drama, producing Ibsen plays through the 1890s.[57] It was a time when new life and new social ideas, notably feminism, were injected into the British stage.[58]

In *The Old Drama and the New* (1923) the journalist and theatre critic William Archer—married but in a relationship with Robins, with whom he had founded the New Century Theatre in 1897—would write 'the New Drama is quite literally a new

[53] Allen, 'Plain Words on the Woman Question', *Fortnightly Review* 36 (Dec 1889), 175.
[54] Allen, *The Woman Who Did* (Oxford: Oxford University Press, 1995), 30, 39, 41.
[55] H. G. Wells, *Ann Veronica* (Harmondsworth: Penguin, 2005), 278.
[56] Edith Lees Ellis, *Stories and Essays* (1914), quoted in Sally Ledger, *Henrik Ibsen* (Plymouth: Northcote House, 1999), 2.
[57] See Robins, *Ibsen and the Actress* (London: Hogarth Press, 1928); Tracy C. Davis, 'Acting in Ibsen', *Theatre Notebook* 39/3 (1985), 113–23; Vivien Gardner and Susan Rutherford, *The New Woman and Her Sisters: Feminism and Theatre, 1850–1914* (Ann Arbor, MI: University of Michigan Press, 1992), 11.
[58] On James A. Herne's *Margaret Fleming* (1890) and Robins and Bell's *Alan's Wife* as two quite distinct appraisals of maternity on the stage, see Kirsten E. Shepherd-Barr, ' "It Was Ugly": Maternal Instinct on Stage at the Fin de Siècle', *Women: A Cultural Review* 23/2 (Summer 2012), 216–34.

thing—a product of less than a generation'.[59] Bernard Shaw, a prominent player in the New Drama, staged the Woman Question through the 1890s, writing in his preface to Archer's *Theatrical 'World' of 1894*, 'the progress of a revolution in public opinion on what is called the Woman Question has begun to agitate the stage'.[60] He declared it was 'not possible to put the new woman seriously on the stage in her relation to modern society, without stirring up, both on the stage and in the auditorium, the struggle to keep her in her old place' (xxv–xxvi), something which can be seen in Shaw's own somewhat ambivalent portrayals of her.

In *Mrs Warren's Profession* (1893), which was refused a licence and not performed in London until 1902, and then only at a private club, Shaw combined his exploration with critique of capitalism and the economic underpinnings of prostitution. Mrs Warren, working as a prostitute, raises new questions about independence with her declaration: 'What is any respectable girl brought up to do but to catch some rich man's fancy and get the benefit of his money by marrying him?' Later she remarks: 'Women have to pretend to feel a great deal that they don't feel.'[61] Mrs Warren is strikingly autonomous, outlining a radical formula for independence based on self-respect rather than convention: 'Why am I independent and able to give my daughter a first-rate education, when other women that had just as good opportunities are in the gutter? Because I always knew how to respect myself and control myself.' Later in the play Praed remarks to Mrs Warren's daughter, Vivie Warren, ostensibly a New Woman: 'speaking as an artist, and believing that the most intimate human relationships are far beyond and above the scope of the law, that though I know that your mother is an unmarried woman, I do not respect her the less on that account. I respect her more.'[62]

However, Shaw shared with Wells and other Fabian socialists an affiliation with essentialist and eugenic ideas. The feminism of his plays is compromised to a degree by his ambiguity over the New Woman, especially in her social purity guise,[63] writing in 1897 that 'in order to realize what a terrible person the New Woman is it is necessary to have read that ruthlessly orthodox book, *The Heavenly Twins*'.[64] Thus, while the theatre was an important vehicle for radical new ideas, it was equally a site of caricature and opposition. Sydney Grundy's send-up, *The New Woman* (1894), which ran to 173 performances, lampooned social purity, and in Oscar Wilde's *An Ideal Husband* the following year, ideas of emancipation were given comedic

---

[59] William Archer, *The Old Drama and the New* (London: William Heinemann, 1923), 113.

[60] G. B. Shaw, Preface to William Archer, *Theatrical 'World' of 1894* (London: Walter Scott, 1895), xxiv–xxv.

[61] Shaw, *Mrs Warren's Profession*, in *Plays Unpleasant* (Harmondsworth: Penguin, 2000), 249, 251.

[62] Ibid., 250, 275.

[63] See Ian Clarke, *Edwardian Drama* (London: Faber, 1989), 108 on the lack of challenge to patriarchal attitudes in the play; see also Gardner and Rutherford, *The New Woman and her Sisters*, 23.

[64] Kerry Powell, 'New Women, New Plays, and Shaw in the 1890s', in Christopher Innes (ed.), *The Cambridge Companion to George Bernard Shaw* (Cambridge: Cambridge University Press, 1998), 87.

expression. The New Womanly Lady Chiltern declares herself to be a champion of the Higher Education of Women while Lady Markby remarks: 'In my time, of course, we were taught not to understand anything. That was the old system, and wonderfully interesting it was.'[65] Arthur Wing Pinero, one of the leading dramatists of the 1890s, gave the New Woman a much more sympathetic treatment in *The Notorious Mrs Ebbsmith* (1895), but his free-thinking, free-unioning heroine is ultimately limited by stereotype.

Notwithstanding the more ambivalent and satirical representations of the New Woman, the stage would provide an increasingly important space for the dissemination of radical and often distinctly unromantic ideas. In Shaw's view there was 'a struggle between the sexes for the dominion of the London theatres', a struggle in which the men's side was 'furthest behind the times'.[66] Women dramatists such as Robins, Florence Bell, and Cicely Hamilton would come to write more directly and earnestly of a wider range of women's experiences than the New Woman had allowed. In 1909 Hamilton, the campaigner and member of the Women Writers' Suffrage League, produced with Christopher St John (Christabel Marshall) the farcical and immensely popular one-act comedy *How the Vote was Won*, which promoted the suffrage through presenting the threat of a General Strike by women, underscoring women's labour as unrecognized. The *Pall Mall Gazette* responded that 'the fact that it is so acutely controversial is not at all against it—is, in fact, a virtue rather than a defect, for the Theatre of Ideas is upon us'.[67]

The questions of labour and the rights of women were increasingly taken up in Edwardian fiction and drama as the politicization of working-class women sharpened, and campaigners adopted new cultural forms for practical ends. By the 1890s more than a quarter of the female population was in paid employment and the number of women trade union members increased more than eightfold in the three decades from 1876, rising from 19,500 to 166,425.[68] Emerging pressure groups included the Women's Industrial Council (1894), the National Union of Women Workers (1895), the Women's Labour League (1906), and the Fabian Women's Group (1908), as well as numerous local and regional organizations. Feminist fiction was moving from the narrower concerns of the New Women to a focus on exploitative labour in shops, offices, or on the streets.

This politicization of women's labour found its way directly into the subject matter and tone of Edwardian and subsequent representations of the Woman Question. As supporters of the suffrage brought their cause to the theatre, it was also finding equally popular expression in short stories in political magazines such as *Votes for*

---

[65] Oscar Wilde, *The Major Works*, ed. Isobel Murray (Oxford: Oxford University Press, 1989), 433.

[66] Shaw, Preface to Archer, *Theatrical 'World' of 1894*, xxix, xxx.

[67] Dale Spender and Carole Hayman, *How the Vote was Won and Other Suffragette Plays* (London: Methuen, 1985), 20.

[68] Patricia Hollis, *Women in Public: The Women's Movement, 1850–1900* (London: George Allen & Unwin, 1979), 53.

Women, founded in 1907, and pro-suffrage collections such as Gertrude Colmore's *Mr Jones and the Governess and other stories* (1913), published by the Women's Freedom League. Hamilton sought to draw attention to the plight of shop girls and the economic politics of relationships in *Diana of Dobson's* (1908), set in Dobson's Drapery Emporium in Clapham. The impoverished shop girl in Katherine Mansfield's 'The Tiredness of Rosabel' escapes only through the fantasy of a romance with the upper-class Harry, in reality sexist and insolent, and the following year in Elizabeth Baker's *Chains* (1909) Maggie decides to stay on in the shop rather than choose a loveless marriage. That year, Hamilton published her extended meditation on the economic underpinning of marriage in *Marriage as a Trade*. Other plays drew attention to domestic mediocrity: in Florence Bell and Elizabeth Robins's *Alan's Wife* (1893), Jean's mother, Mrs Holroyd, sees her daughter's oppression captured in the dispirited remark 'I can't leave the saucepan'.[69]

While the New Woman was represented extensively on the stage, arguably the novel remained the most effective space for its in-depth treatment, just as the form lent itself to related questions of maternity and inheritance, with its almost inevitable exploration of relations between generations and between sexes. While Hardy would abandon the novel after 1895, returning to his first love, poetry, he remained convinced that the novel was the most effective place for social comment and debate, as his response to Harley Granville-Barker's *The Madras House* (1910), a conceptual play on the Woman Question, indicates. Barker, a polemicist, actor, and playwright, stood with Shaw in the vanguard of the New Drama. Performed to great acclaim in London, *The Madras House* depicts the oppression and capitalist exploitation of Edwardian women through the Huxtable family, with its six unmarried daughters, living off the profits of the Madras House—their Bond street drapery store which capitalizes hypocritically on the women's movement—with its live-in system of female employment and doll-like mannequins who speak no English. One of the employees, Marion Yates, pregnant from a liaison with a married store sales man, and determinedly independent, elects to raise her child by herself. Hardy wrote to Granville-Barker:

> I am almost sorry you did not write it as a novel. I have read it as one, anyhow. Its subtleties are to my mind largely wasted on the stage which, think what you will, addresses itself to people who are not very perceptive except the few who don't count among the mass. (That's why I always feel Shakespeare is largely wasted in acting.) I think it possible that you may ultimately drift into novel writing: I don't see how otherwise you can express all the complications that you discern in life.[70]

The New Woman's legacy in the twentieth century was twofold. Seeking to articulate a woman's point of view, turning from realist aesthetic to private female experience

---

[69] Florence Bell and Elizabeth Robins, *Alan's Wife*, in Linda Fitzsimmons and Vivien Gardner (eds), *New Woman Plays* (London: Methuen Drama, 1991), 10.

[70] Hardy to Harley Granville-Barker, 19 December 1925, in Purdy and Millgate (eds), *Letters of Thomas Hardy*, VI, 374.

and the exploration of states of consciousness, New Woman fiction would give birth to modernism, exploring fleeting subjectivities, most notably in the short story. As Egerton later wrote, 'if I did not know the technical jargon current today of Freud and the psychoanalysts, I did know something of complexes and inhibitions, repressions and the subconscious impulses that determine actions and reactions. I used them in my stories'.[71] In the following generation, Virginia Woolf, May Sinclair, and Dorothy Richardson would foreground fluid identities and varieties of divided consciousness. But, shaped by politics as much as aesthetics, the New Woman in the twentieth century merged with, and in some ways was eclipsed by the campaign for suffrage with its concomitant and pragmatic aesthetic.

Memory of the New Woman lingered long into the twentieth century. Looking backwards from the brink of war in 1939 to the last decades of the nineteenth century, Flora Thomson's *Lark Rise to Candleford* contains hints of an emergent New Woman. Mrs Spicer is a pioneer in the wearing of trousers, sporting a pair of her husband's corduroys, and Miss Lane in the Post Office stands out among her contemporaries as unwomanly—bicycling, reading *The Times,* keeping up with invention and scientific discovery, and not minding what people think about her. While the Victorian men and women who wrote about the New Woman differed in their motivations and approaches, they shared a commitment to social and individual freedom, and their writing provided a vital testing ground for the radical ideas of the *fin de siècle.* Through their dramatic representations, and through the challenge the New Woman herself posed to established conventions, she earned a remarkable place in literary and social history, giving rise to the modernist consciousness and setting a feminist agenda for the twentieth century.

ACKNOWLEDGEMENT

I would like to thank the Trustees of the National Library of Scotland for permission to quote from the papers of Sarah Grand (Frances Elizabeth McFall).

FURTHER READING

Ardis, Ann L. *New Women, New Novels: Feminism and Early Modernism* (New Brunswick, NJ: Rutgers University Press, 1990).

Bland, Lucy. *Banishing the Beast, English Feminism & Sexual Morality, 1885-1914* (Harmondsworth: Penguin, 1995).

Burdett, Carolyn. *Olive Schreiner and the Progress of Feminism: Evolution, Gender, Empire* (Basingstoke: Palgrave Macmillan, 2001).

---

[71] Egerton, 'A Keynote to *Keynotes*', in John Gawsworth (ed.), *Ten Contemporaries: Notes Toward Their Definitive Bibliography* (London: Ernest Benn, 1932), 58.

Burdett, Carolyn. *Olive Schreiner* (Plymouth: Northcote House, 2013).

Cunningham, Gail. *The New Woman and the Victorian Novel* (London: Macmillan, 1978).

Gardner, Vivien and Susan Rutherford. *The New Woman and Her Sisters: Feminism and Theatre, 1850–1914* (Ann Arbor, MI: University of Michigan Press, 1992).

Heilmann, Ann. *New Woman Fiction: Women Writing First-Wave Feminism* (Basingstoke: Palgrave, 2000).

Heilmann, Ann. *New Woman Strategies: Sarah Grand, Olive Schreiner, Mona Caird* (Manchester: Manchester University Press, 2004).

Heilmann, Ann and Margaret Beetham (eds). *New Woman Hybridities: Femininity, Feminism, and International Consumer Culture* (London: Routledge, 2004).

Ledger, Sally. *The New Woman: Fiction and Feminism at the Fin de Siècle* (Manchester: Manchester University Press, 1997).

Marks, Patricia. *Bicycles, Bangs, and Bloomers: The New Woman in the Popular Press* (Lexington, KY: University Press of Kentucky, 1990).

Richardson, Angelique. *Love and Eugenics in the Late Nineteenth Century: Rational Reproduction and the New Woman* (Oxford: Oxford University Press, 2003).

Richardson, Angelique and Chris Willis (eds). *The New Woman in Fiction and in Fact* (Basingstoke: Palgrave, 2001).

Rubenstein, David. *Before the Suffragettes: Women's Emancipation in the 1890s* (Brighton: Harvester, 1986).

CHAPTER 10

UTOPIAN THOUGHT AND THE WAY TO LIVE NOW

ANNE FERNIHOUGH

In 1907, the iconoclastic British socialist, A. R. Orage, took over the editorship of the *New Age*, a radical magazine that was to exert a profound influence on the development of modernist art and literature. In his editorial début, Orage outlined two versions of socialism, privileging one over the other: 'Socialism as a means to the intensification of man', he urged, 'is even more necessary than Socialism as a means to the abolition of economic poverty.'[1] This distinction between two social-isms was already a well-established one and would have been familiar to many of Orage's readers. In his socialist manifesto, *Merrie England* (1895), for example, Robert Blatchford had framed it as the difference between 'ideal socialism' and 'practical socialism'. Whereas practical socialism centred on governmental reforms such as the nationalization of the means of production and the eight-hour working day, ideal socialism was concerned more with personal liberty and spiritual growth than with economics and working conditions. Often seen as utopian, ideal social-ism was based on free cooperation rather than state control, and was in many respects a form of anarchism. Blatchford devotes most of his tract to elaborating the details of a practical socialism. Although he sees it to be no more than a step to the ultimate goal of ideal socialism, he has little to say about what the latter would entail other than the complete abolition of capitalism in any form: money would simply not exist in the socialist utopia of the future.[2]

Blatchford's reluctance to flesh out the detail of an ideal socialism, or even to delineate the skeleton of what it would be, is echoed in one of Orage's early *New Age* editorials where, as a champion of the more utopian, anarchistic brand of socialism, he confesses that: 'The very sketch of the complete building that is in

---

[1] 'The Future of the *New Age*', *New Age* (second ser.) 1/1:660 (2 May 1907), 8.
[2] Robert Blatchford (Nunquam), *Merrie England* (London: Clarion Newspaper Company, 1895), 100–3.

our mind we dare scarce talk about at present lest we be hounded from political society as utopians and ineffectual angels. Yet secretly we have our plans and are proud to be Utopians.'[3] Similarly, Dora Marsden, the controversial editor of the *Freewoman* magazine, founded in 1911, announces apocalyptically that 'Women will push open the door of the super-world' but has little to say about the nature of that super-world.[4] It is in the nature of apocalyptic writing, as Jacques Derrida has argued, that it promises and yet fails to bring to an end a process of deferral. With its constant opening of doors and breaking of seals, it promises revelation, a sight of the signified (super-world, perhaps), but leaves us instead with the shape of the signifier.[5] This is true of D. H. Lawrence's 1915 novel, *The Rainbow*, whose central character, Ursula Brangwen, is described on the book's original jacket as 'waiting at the advance post of our time to blaze a path into the future'. The novel ends with a classically apocalyptic vision: 'She saw in the rainbow the earth's new architecture, the old, brittle corruption of houses and factories swept away, the world built up in a living fabric of Truth, fitting to the over-arching heaven.'[6] This image of the rainbow arcing the sky over the industrial town of Beldover stays in the mind long after the book has closed, but ultimately we are left guessing about the reality ('the earth's new architecture') that the rainbow can only foreshadow.

It is unsurprising that architecture, on both a metaphorical and a literal level, should be a *leitmotif* of the utopian discourses of the late nineteenth and early twentieth centuries: the notion of place or space is, after all, germane to the very term 'utopia'. But so is the idea of an *absence* of place ('utopia', coined by Sir Thomas More and derived from the Greek, means 'no place' but is also a pun on the term 'eutopia', meaning 'good place'). *The Rainbow*'s conclusion encapsulates the double impulse within the term, gesturing towards a new architecture without revealing it. It also, ironically, expresses the desire for a completely new order of things by harking *back* to the rhetoric of 'a new heaven on earth' that had been a feature of early nineteenth-century millenarianism. Olive Schreiner's 1911 treatise, *Woman and Labour*, with its quasi-biblical cadences ('that strange new world that is arising alike upon the man and the woman'), is another clear example of this.[7] Socialists and feminists alike often envisaged the future in terms of the heavenly city or the New Jerusalem. But whilst many, like Orage, were reluctant to reveal what lay behind the doors or gates to the city, others were less so. In America, Edward Bellamy in his influential novel, *Looking Backward: 2000–1887* (1888), had given his readers the heavenly city in the form of Boston in the year 2000. At the centre of his vision, synecdochically

---

[3] 'Towards Socialism—IV', *New Age* (second ser.) 1/26:685 (24 October 1907), 407.

[4] 'The New Morality', *Freewoman* 1/4 (14 December 1911), 62.

[5] Jacques Derrida, *D'un ton apocalyptique adopté naguère en philosophie* (Paris: Galilee, 1983).

[6] D. H. Lawrence, *The Rainbow,* ed. Mark Kinkead-Weekes (London: Penguin, 1995), 459.

[7] Olive Schreiner, *Woman and Labour* (London: T. Fisher Unwin, 1911), 68.

representing utopia as a whole, is a vast shopping hall or department store. It is evoked by the novel's narrator, Julian West, as a kind of cathedral:

> I was in a vast hall full of light, received not alone from the windows on all sides, but from the dome, the point of which was a hundred feet above. Beneath it, in the centre of the hall, a magnificent fountain played, cooling the atmosphere to a delicious freshness with its spray. The walls and ceilings were frescoed in mellow tints, calculated to soften without absorbing the light which flooded the interior.[8]

Notwithstanding the sense of ineffability here, Bellamy's version of socialism was more practical than ideal. In place of a class-ridden society controlled by competing capitalist concerns, he advocated a democratic yet highly centralized nation state in which all aspects of consumption were carefully regulated. For some, his vision of a strictly regimented labour force was too militaristic. William Morris, for instance, felt that 'the *impression* he [Bellamy] produces is that of a huge standing army, tightly drilled, compelled by some mysterious fate to unceasing anxiety for the production of wares to satisfy every caprice, however wasteful and absurd'.[9] The last part of the quotation points to the consumer rather than the producer (Edith Leete, the novel's heroine is described as an 'indefatigable shopper'), and it is consumption rather than production that is at the heart of the novel's utopianism.[10] Moreover, *Looking Backward* renders largely invisible the acts of labour that produce the goods so rapturously consumed, putting Bellamy's commitment towards a meaningful socialism into question.

As these examples demonstrate, socialisms were so numerous and diverse during this period that the meaning of the term was stretched to breaking point. Samuel Hynes, in his classic study *The Edwardian Turn of Mind* (1968), goes some way towards explaining the contradictions inherent in the term: socialism at the turn of the century, he argues, was 'an open movement, an energy rather than a policy'. It assumed the progressive role in English life precisely because it was not a political party and could therefore accommodate a variety of groups and ideologies.[11] In light of this, it becomes easier to see how a magazine such as the *New Age* could be subtitled 'a socialist weekly' while embracing politically diverse positions. Orage himself advocates a version of Blatchford's ideal socialism but, crucially, he gives it a distinctly Nietzschean twist:

> Believing that the darling object and purpose of the universal will of life is the creation of a race of supremely and progressively intelligent beings, the *New Age* will devote itself to the serious endeavour to cooperate with the purposes of life.[12]

[8] Edward Bellamy, *Looking Backward: 2000–1887*, ed. Matthew Beaumont (Oxford: Oxford University Press, 2007), 60.
[9] William Morris, '"Looking Backward"', in *Political Writings: Contributions to Justice and Commonweal, 1883–1890*, ed. Nicholas Salmon (Bristol: Thoemmes, 1994), 422–3.
[10] Bellamy, *Looking Backward*, 59.
[11] Samuel Hynes, *The Edwardian Turn of Mind* (Princeton, NJ: Princeton University Press, 1968), 87.
[12] 'The Future of the *New Age*', 8.

To us, a century on, this Nietzschean version of socialism scarcely resembles socialism at all. But it was a version that was to impact dramatically on utopian thought in the period as well as on the development of modernist aesthetics. It is probably best understood by us today as a kind of hyper-individualism. Oscar Wilde, in 'The Soul of Man under Socialism' (1891), had argued that 'Socialism itself will be of value simply because it will lead to Individualism'.[13] For Wilde, as for Blatchford and Orage, this individualism has nothing to do with private property or with the competition of the marketplace; on the contrary, it refers to the individual creativity that is stifled in a capitalist society.

This hyper-individualistic socialism was in many ways at odds with Bellamy's vision of a state socialism in which all are equal in material terms, shop in the same centralized department store, and eat in the same centralized dining-house. David Parry's *The Scarlet Empire* (1906) was written partly as a riposte to *Looking Backward*, and envisages the lost continent of Atlantis as a dystopian 'Social Democracy'. Every citizen of Parry's Atlantis eats the same amount of fish gruel each day, lives in an identical, miserable hutch, is only allowed to utter a certain number of words per day, and so on. Atlantis is an anarchist's nightmare, a mega-bureaucracy in which anyone who expresses individuality is treated as a delinquent.[14] In Britain, this homogenization was frequently evoked in the terms of late-Victorian and Edwardian suburbia: Edward Carpenter, in his long poem *Towards Democracy* (1883–1902), described those who live in 'suburban runs and burrows' as 'machine made... thousands all alike'.[15] Slightly later, in *A Modern Utopia* (1909), H. G. Wells uses the inauspiciously named London suburb of Frognal as the antithesis of utopia.[16] As the feminist Beatrice Hastings wrily noted in a short story published in the same year, 'You can't get the Superman if you just marry in the ordinary, dull way and live in the suburbs'.[17] May Sinclair, a pioneer of the stream-of-consciousness technique in fiction, set her 1914 novel *The Combined Maze* in 'Acacia Avenue, with its tufted trees, with its rows of absurd and diminutive villas', a description that perfectly conveys the prejudices against suburbia at the time.[18]

Suburbia, then, was often the subtopia from which utopians in the period launched their flights of fancy, especially those who inclined towards anarchism. Marsden's 'super-world', it would seem, could not be accessed from the villas of Acacia Avenue any more than it could be accessed from Parry's Atlantis. More promising perhaps was Rudolf Steiner's double-domed 'Goetheanum', a performance

[13] Oscar Wilde, 'The Soul of Man', in *The Soul of Man and Prison Writings*, ed. Isobel Murray (Oxford: Oxford University Press, 1990), 2.

[14] David M. Parry, *The Scarlet Empire* (Carbondale and Edwardsville, IL: Southern Illinois University Press, 2001), 68, 9, 77.

[15] Edward Carpenter, *Towards Democracy* (1905; repr. London: GMP Publishers, 1985), 220.

[16] H. G. Wells, *A Modern Utopia*, ed. Krishan Kumar (London: J.M. Dent, 1994), 17.

[17] Beatrice Tina (pseudonym for Beatrice Hastings), 'Tête à Tête, à la Femme', *New Age* (second ser.) 4/22:759 (25 March 1909), 444.

[18] See the anonymous review of *The Combined Maze* in the *Egoist* 1/1 (1 January 1914), 49.

hall built on a hill in Dornach, Switzerland, in 1913. Steiner is best known today for his progressive views on education but was also a radically experimental architect, believing it impossible for the individual to grow and thrive in the wrong kind of building. Much as Steiner's educational policy opposed all kinds of uniformity and regulation, so the Goetheanum's fluidly organic form studiously avoided all right angles. It incorporated a principle of metamorphosis, derived from Goethe's interest in plants, whereby forms were repeated, but always in a metamorphosed state; the identical form never recurred. As Steiner himself explains in vitalist vein: 'Our building is not intended to cut one off [from the world]. Its walls should live...The forms of our building will be able to achieve what external institutions can never achieve.'[19] The Goetheanum was a far cry from the rational lineaments of Bellamy's Boston which, as Matthew Beaumont explains, was indebted to the tradition of city planning inherited from the utopian ideals of the Enlightenment.[20]

At around the same time that the Goetheanum was being built, Steiner developed an art of movement called 'eurythmy', another mode of entrance into the 'superworld'. As he explained in 1920, 'in eurythmy we present in the form and movement of the human organism a direct external proof of man's share in the life of the supersensible world'.[21] There were strong affinities with the dance philosophy of Isadora Duncan, who danced barefoot in Greek-style tunics that moulded themselves to her individual form. She promoted a Whitmanesque notion of 'the new nakedness' and of 'the highest intelligence in the freest body'.[22] Her attitude towards clothes and the body was similar to that of Carpenter, another Whitmanite, who dismissed conventionally dressed people as 'animated clothespegs' and was renowned for the open sandals he made and wore.[23] The *New Age* welcomed Duncan as the embodiment of the spiritual, anarchistically inclined socialism favoured by Orage. As one contributor asked, contrasting this kind of socialism with the statist variety, 'Is it Bellamy we mean, or this thing that Isadora Duncan shows us? Will you blue-book, or will you dance?'[24] There could hardly be a clearer expression of the divergent routes which socialism was taking at this time.

Importantly for the literary historian, these two alternatives were also infiltrating aesthetics, with many proto-modernists opting, metaphorically speaking, to dance, and to distance themselves from the 'blue-booking' of realist fiction. A great deal of the utopian fiction of the period, much of it inspired by Bellamy, fitted the blue-booking model and was not particularly experimental at a formal level. Often

---

[19] Rudolf Steiner, quoted in Hagen Biesantz and Arne Klingborg, *The Goetheanum: Rudolf Steiner's Architectural Impulse*, trans. Jean Schmid (London: Rudolf Steiner Press, 1979), 29, 33.

[20] Matthew Beaumont, 'Introduction', in Bellamy, *Looking Backward*, xx–xxi.

[21] Rudolf Steiner, *The Goetheanum*, 49.

[22] Isadora Duncan, 'The Dance of the Future' (1902 or 1903), in *The Art of the Dance*, ed. Sheldon Cheney (New York: Theatre Arts, 1928), 63.

[23] Carpenter, *Towards Democracy*, 30.

[24] W. R. Titterton, 'Isadora Duncan Preaching', *New Age* (second ser.) 3/12:723 (18 July 1908), 226.

it was a populist blend of romance, adventure story, and socio-political blueprint. This was true, for example, of Elizabeth Burgoyne Corbett's *New Amazonia: A Foretaste of the Future* (1889), a formally unadventurous novel in which Amazonia is a rationalistic, state-run utopia much like Bellamy's. But the more anarchistic strands of utopian thought were starting to impact on literature at a *formal* level. Modernist literary forms such as free verse and stream-of-consciousness prose, for example, were in some contexts the literary equivalents of the 'free body' championed by Carpenter and Duncan. 'Rational dress', the term that caught on for the loose and simple clothing favoured by late-Victorian and Edwardian radicals, was, in one sense, a misnomer: it didn't capture the sense of freedom involved, the emphasis on the untrammelled individual who could live independently of any externally imposed form.

Julian West, in *Looking Backward*, had alluded to the artificiality of women's fashions in 1887, to the way in which 'the almost incredible extension of the skirt behind by means of artificial contrivances more thoroughly dehumanized the form than any former device of dressmakers'.[25] Ezra Pound, in a 1913 poem, 'Salutation', fuses freedom of poetic form with a Carpenteresque vision of the wholly integrated, unencumbered self: '[T]he fish swim in the lake and do not even own clothing.'[26] Three years earlier, the Imagist poet F. S. Flint, in a clear example of Nietzschean individualism influencing modernist poetics, had described Pound's free verse as a literary 'superform': '[T]he form of the great, embracing and subtle rhythm, which, like a storm, creates itself as it goes along.'[27]

Flint's article predates by over a decade T. S. Eliot's well-known chapter, 'The Metaphysical Poets' (1921), in which Eliot propounds his theory of a 'dissociation of sensibility', yet his argument is similar to Eliot's in certain key respects. According to Eliot, a vital, robust, and fully integrated linguistic organism, exemplified in the metaphysical poetry of the Elizabethan age, devolved during the seventeenth century into a self-divided one, such that the poet could no longer express thought and feeling simultaneously.[28] More than ten years earlier, Flint posits a similar argument, relating a linguistic dissociation to the deracination brought about by industrial capitalism. The Elizabethan era and its language are evoked in prelapsarian terms:

> In Elizabeth's time the fields and flowers were always at hand, and there was a natural poetry on the lips of men; language had a racy flavour and vitality; but we who live in an age of bricks and mortar and machinery use a language which has no longer the life and freshness which were got from the proximity of town and country... And the language has become a set of newspaper counters.[29]

[25] Bellamy, *Looking Backward*, 9.
[26] 'The Contemporania of Ezra Pound', *New Age* (second ser.) 13/16:1092 (15 August 1913), 88.
[27] F. S. Flint, 'Verse', *New Age* (second ser.) 6/10:800 (6 January 1910), 234.
[28] T. S. Eliot, 'The Metaphysical Poets', in *Selected Essays* (London: Faber & Faber, 1932), 288, 287.
[29] Flint, 'Verse', 234.

Here Flint is drawing directly on Nietzsche's contempt for newspapers and the mass culture they represented: the rabble 'vomit their bile and call it a newspaper', he had ranted in *Thus Spoke Zarathustra* (1892). He saw journalists as the 'day-labourers of language', thereby linking journalism with capitalism and coinage (Flint's 'counters').[30] As opposed to the poetic 'superform', journalism is a kind of *Unterform*. So, by implication in Flint's article, is poetry which conforms to a regular rhythm (that of the metronome), compromising the integrity of individual poetic phrases. The novelist May Sinclair, who was herself interested in Nietzsche, has one of the characters in *The Tree of Heaven* (1917) translate the argument to prose, linking freedom from conventional syntax to 'the creative spirit itself'. The character in question, an avant-garde writer named Austen Mitchell, explains that '[b]y breaking up the rigid rules of syntax, you do more than create new forms of prose moving in perfect freedom, you deliver the creative spirit itself from the abominable contact with dead ideas'.[31] This sounds very much like a defence of the stream-of-consciousness prose that Sinclair would very shortly engage with herself, and it evinces a debt to the philosophical vitalism that played such a prominent role in utopian thought as well as modernist aesthetics, as will be shown shortly.

What is clear from both Flint's and Eliot's essays is the extent to which certain aspects of nineteenth-century utopian thought fed into modernist poetics, specifically those centring on the idea of an idyllic pre-industrial world in which, supposedly, human beings could live a fully individuated, uncompromised life. Morris's utopian fantasy, *News from Nowhere* (1890), for example, replaces Bellamy's urban vision with a more pastoral one, and his state socialism with a libertarian emphasis on individual creativity. Morris envisages a world in which the boundaries between work, art, and life have dissolved. Whereas in Bellamy's utopia, work and pleasure are dichotomized and the aim is to limit as far as possible the number of working hours each day, Morris's solution is to make work itself aesthetically pleasurable. This, for Morris, means keeping mechanization to a minimum and adopting a more 'organic' approach. In a tradition stretching back to Ruskin and beyond, Morris deplores the division of labour entailed in mechanized, factory production and the self-divided individual who results from this. He is indebted to Ruskin's famous polemic, 'The Nature of Gothic' (1853), where Ruskin observes that 'It is not... the labour that is divided; but the men: Divided into mere segments of men–broken into small fragments and crumbs of life'.[32] In line with this, anarchists such as Carpenter were to adopt a self-sufficient, rural lifestyle. From his cottage in

[30] Friedrich Nietzsche, *Thus Spoke Zarathustra: A Book for Everyone and No One*, trans. R. J. Hollingdale (London: Penguin, 1961), 77; Nietzsche, *Untimely Meditations*, trans. R. J. Hollingdale (Cambridge: Cambridge University Press, 1983), 50.

[31] May Sinclair, *The Tree of Heaven* (Teddington, Middlesex: Echo Library, 2006), 124.

[32] John Ruskin, 'The Nature of Gothic', in *The Stones of Venice, The Works of John Ruskin*, ed. E. T. Cook and Alexander Wedderburn, 39 vols (London: George Allen, 1903–12), X, 196.

Millthorpe, Derbyshire, which he eventually shared with his lover, George Merrill, Carpenter grew his own produce and sold it at the local market.

As already noted, this idealization of a pre-mechanized world in which individuals could be fully integrated and whole was to resurface at the level of form in modernist poetry and prose. Lawrence's idiosyncratic prose style, for example, with its pulsing, incantatory rhythms suggestive of breathing and the beating of the heart, could be seen, like Pound's poetic 'superform', to be the literary equivalent of the anarchistic, free body. Within the same cultural context, realism was being dismissed by proto-modernists as the equivalent of Carpenter's animated clothes peg or Bellamy's dehumanized woman, a self-divided form unnaturally encumbered by something supposedly extraneous to itself. In practice, this extraneous something was often a collectivist social or political agenda. When, in May 1911, H. G. Wells proclaimed in a lecture to *The Times* Book Club that the novel should be 'the parade of morals and the exchange of manners, the factory of customs, the criticism of law and institutions and of social dogmas and ideas', his view was starting to look old-fashioned, and was savagely attacked by J. M. Kennedy in the *New Age* a few weeks later.[33] Orage at the *New Age* was by now arguing that social issues were not the proper subject matter for literature, and that literature, if it was to avoid becoming propaganda, should deal with man's 'soul' and not with social conditions.

Robert Tressell's *The Ragged Trousered Philanthropists* (1914) resonates with the elegiac tones of Ruskin and Morris, and through the figure of the highly gifted artist, Owen, articulates the desire for a socialist utopia in which every individual can lead a full and creative life. Yet it is a classic example of the kind of realist work that modernists would come to disparage. Not only does it carry an explicit socialist agenda but, at a formal level, it is heavily reliant on 'outside' factors, on things it cannot fully assimilate, cannot fully transmute into the 'literary'. It imports, wholesale, letters, lists, political leaflets, newspaper clippings, all manner of songs, hymns, and ballads, bills, workers' time sheets and payslips. In other words, it is a novel which blue-books rather than dances, and it is arguably for this reason that it was largely neglected by literary scholars until comparatively recently.

One might have expected the First World War to have put paid to this idea that literature should avoid socio-political commentary; but in fact it was a view that persisted well beyond the war. Woolf, for instance, was one of its most vociferous exponents in the 1920s. In her famous essay of 1924, 'Character in Fiction', often referred to as 'Mr Bennett and Mrs Brown', she chastises those writers who make us feel we ought to 'join a society or, more desperately, to write a cheque'.[34] Specifically, she attacks Arnold Bennett, H. G. Wells, and John Galsworthy, branding them

---

[33] Quoted in Wallace Martin, *The New Age under Orage: Chapters in English Cultural History* (Manchester: Manchester University Press, 1967), 112.

[34] Virginia Woolf, 'Character in Fiction', in *The Essays of Virginia Woolf*, ed. Andrew McNeillie, 6 vols (London: Hogarth Press, 1986–2011), III, 427.

Edwardian 'materialists'. By now it was becoming a 'high modernist' orthodoxy to argue that any political agenda is somehow 'impure' or 'alien', a violation not just of the integrity of the individual but of the artwork itself.

Woolf's term for Bennett, Wells, and Galsworthy, 'materialists', resonates with a double meaning: not only do these writers, in her view, carry socio-political or economic agendas; they are also too reliant on the solid, material world, or rather they treat it in a prosaic way which misses what is vital and unique about human experience and human identity. Bennett, for example, has 'given us a house in the hope that we may be able to deduce the human beings who live there'.[35] Woolf cites a passage from *Hilda Lessways* (1911), in which Bennett describes a specific terrace of four houses, giving such mundane details as the rental incomes on the houses and the relative sizes of their gardens. The reference to Edwardian villadom brings us back to the idea of suburbia and its homogenizing impact. The implication is that Bennett's treatment of character is as homogenizing as Edwardian suburbia.

Woolf's approach draws on the philosophical vitalism that was so fashionable in the late nineteenth and early twentieth centuries. More specifically, it shows strong affinities with Bergson's work. Woolf, like many modernists, was almost certainly aware, albeit indirectly, of Bergson's distinction between intuition and intellect, and between real time (duration) and spatial time.[36] The linchpin of Bergson's philosophy was that each individual consciousness has its own uniqueness and its own *durée* (time) but that we have refused to recognize this by confusing time with space. Our understanding of time as a sequence of hours and minutes, of interchangeable units, is, Bergson argued, really a spatial notion. It is part of our misguided tendency to approach psychic experience, consciousness, in terms borrowed from the perception of *physical* objects. The faculty responsible for this deleterious confusion, according to Bergson, is the intellect, which can only deal with the mind in terms of physical, measurable entities. In *Creative Evolution* (1907), Bergson asserts that 'the human intellect feels at home among inanimate objects, more especially among solids', and that the abstract concepts on which the intellect depends are themselves, paradoxically, 'formed on the model of solids'.[37]

Bergson, then, helped establish the vitalist framework within which realism as a fictional mode could be disparaged as the literary embodiment of the intellect, breaking up the real time (*durée*) of individual consciousness into undifferentiated units. By the same token, it could be seen as the literary embodiment of suburbia. It was not simply that many realist fictions of the period were *about* life in the suburbs, conveying a suburban *content*; it was that the very *form* of realism could be seen as, in essence the form of suburbia, a form premised not just on homogeneity

---

[35] Woolf, *Essays*, III, 432.
[36] See Anne Fernihough, *Freewomen and Supermen: Edwardian Radicals and Literary Modernism* (Oxford: Oxford University Press, 2013), 91.
[37] Henri Bergson, *Creative Evolution*, trans. Arthur Mitchell (London: Macmillan, 1911), ix.

but on solidity (the red or yellow brick of late-Victorian and Edwardian villadom). In political rather than architectural terms, it could be seen to embody a democracy often presented as a dystopian system that stamped out individuality and even dragged humanity backwards in evolutionary terms. The philosopher William James, for example, whose work, like Bergson's, was to impact on stream-of-consciousness writing, argued the need for an educated elite to act as 'the yeast-cake for democracy's dough'.[38] The debate surrounding democracy was inseparable from eugenics and from fears that giving the vote to certain sections of the population (i.e. 'the mass') would devitalize the nation.

In vitalist terms, then, suffragism was often presented as a 'dead idea' involving the imposition of an 'artificial' intellect over a 'natural' intuition. In Wells's *Ann Veronica* (1909), the eponymous heroine rejects both suffragism and Fabianism, 'the comings and goings of audiences and supporters that were like the eddy-driven drift of paper in the street', in favour of becoming a student of the 'natural' world in the form of biology.[39] Cicely Hamilton, in her 1919 novel, *William—An Englishman*, has her two central characters, William and Griselda, abandon their socialist and suffragist ideals. The heady round of 'crowds, committees and grievances' in which their courtship has been conducted is contrasted with the mysterious reality of the natural world and 'the endless patience of the earth', encountered during their honeymoon in the Belgian Ardennes.[40] Both novels are governed by a rhetoric of the real and the unreal, the living and the dead. Democracy and its subsets (suffragism, Fabianism, etc.), are unreal 'abstractions', the hallucinatory product, like spatial time, of the Bergsonian intellect.

When Marsden founded the *Freewoman* magazine in 1911, she likewise set about defining the 'freewoman' as someone defiantly unconcerned with women's suffrage and with democracy more widely. In a fusion of Bergson, Nietzsche, and a third philosopher, Max Stirner, she distinguished between the anarchistic 'freewoman' and what she called 'bondwomen'. Stirner's 1844 anarchistic treatise, *The Ego and His Own* was undergoing a revival in certain radical circles at this time. Like Nietzsche, Stirner emphasized the individual's seemingly limitless capacities if only he could break out of the carapace of societal convention and belief. Like Nietzsche, too, he was opposed to intellectual abstractions of any kind, dismissing concepts such as 'equality', 'humanity', and 'law' as specious intellectual constructions premised on a notion of the collective rather than the unique, authentic self. He distinguished between *der Einzige* ('the single one') and *der Knecht* ('the bondman' in the first English translation of 1907) who was content to be shaped by social and political convention. In a feminized version of the bondman, Marsden argued that

---

[38] William James, 'The Social Value of the College-Bred', in *Writings 1902–1910* (New York, NY: Library of America, 1987), 1246–7.

[39] Wells, *Ann Veronica* (London: Virago, 1980), 130.

[40] Cicely Hamilton, *William—An Englishman* (London: Persephone Books, 1999), 35.

'Bondwomen are the women who are not separate spiritual entities—who are not individuals. They are complements, merely.'[41] For them, she believed, the vote might serve a limited purpose.

There are many literary equivalents in the period of Marsden's freewoman, and indeed of its opposite, the bondwoman. Sinclair's *The Tree of Heaven*, for example, presents suffragism as one of the various collectivist movements that threaten the integrity of the individual, making him or her answerable to the collective will of the state. Of one of the characters in the novel, Dorothy Harrison, Sinclair writes:

> She was afraid of the herded women... She loathed the gestures and movements of the collective soul, the swaying and heaving and rushing forward of the many as the one. She would not be carried away by it; she would keep the cleanness and hardness of her soul.[42]

Observing the frenzied welcome received by a group of suffragettes newly released from prison, Dorothy finds herself 'fascinated and horrified.'[43] The phrase 'fascinated and horrified' echoes the 'horrible fascination' that Lawrence's Ursula in *The Rainbow* had felt on witnessing a different kind of mass experience in the form of industrialized labour, 'human bodies and lives subjected in slavery to that symmetric monster of the colliery'. Like Dorothy, moreover, Ursula resists suffragism. For Ursula, we are told, '[t]he vote was never a reality. She had within her the strange, passionate knowledge of religion far transcending the limits of the automatic system that contained the vote... She was in revolt... she wanted to know big, free people'.[44] In effect, Ursula is pushing at the doors of Marsden's 'super-world'. For her this demands not just a rejection of suffragism but also a rejection of marriage. The same is true of the heroine of Sinclair's 1919 novel, *Mary Olivier*, where Mary terminates a love affair in order to protect what she calls her 'sacred, inviolable self'.[45]

This emphasis on 'singleness' of self inevitably impacted on discussions of gender and sexuality among radicals in the period. The relatively young discourse of sexology was one of the main channels through which the anarchistic desire for an unbounded, uninhibited self was expressed. Marsden enlisted the Viennese sexologist, Otto Weininger, in support of an essentially Stirnerian egoism. Weininger's controversial thesis, *Sex and Character* (1903), had been translated into English in 1906. In it he had made the notorious claim that '[w]omen... are nothing... Woman has no share in ontological reality'.[46] It is easy to see how, on encountering this claim, Marsden would have connected it in her own mind to Stirner's attack on the 'nothingness' of the type and the intellectual abstraction. In a creative misreading of Weininger, she took him to mean that individual women should not be reduced to an abstract category of 'woman', and she extended the argument to 'man' also. This

[41] 'Bondwomen', *Freewoman* 1/1 (23 November 1911), 1.
[42] Sinclair, *Tree of Heaven*, 63.   [43] Ibid., 114.   [44] Lawrence, *The Rainbow*, 324, 377.
[45] Sinclair, *Mary Olivier: A Life* (London: Virago, 1980), 290.
[46] Otto Weininger, *Sex and Character* (London: Heinemann, 1906), 174.

optimistic vision of a genderless society was shared by Thomas Baty, who in 1915 co-founded a journal entitled *Urania*. 'There are', Baty explained, 'no "men" or "women" in Urania.'[47] Miriam Henderson, the heroine of Dorothy Richardson's semi-autobiographical novel-sequence, *Pilgrimage*, manifests the same impulse to transcend the limitations of gender: 'I don't like men and loathe women', she declares in *Pointed Roofs* (1915), and in a later volume, she mentions Weininger by name. Her subversion of conventional syntax through stream-of-consciousness techniques can be seen in part as an attempt to evade the way in which, in Weininger's words, humanity is 'press[ed] by a vice into distinctive moulds'.[48]

Thomas Baty was far from alone in envisaging utopia as Urania. He had probably taken the term 'Uranian' from Carpenter, who in turn had imported it from the work of the German sexologist, Karl Ulrichs; it derived from the Greek *ouranios*, meaning 'heavenly'. Carpenter used the term with reference to what he called an 'intermediate sex', a sex comprising male and female elements. His idea of what he called the 'double temperament' of the Uranian was inspired in part by Shelley's 1821 treatise, 'A Defence of Poetry'. The poets in Shelley's chapter are 'the unacknowledged legislators of the world': all-seeing and all-knowing, they 'measure the circumference and sound the depths of human nature with a comprehensive and all-penetrating spirit'.[49] Transferring the argument from aesthetics to sexology, Carpenter argues in *The Intermediate Sex* that Uranians 'have a special work to do as reconcilers and interpreters of the two sexes to each other'.[50] They are in a privileged position, above partisanship and free of the limitation of gendered perspectives, 'free of all their lore' in the words of *Towards Democracy*:

> Thy Woman-soul within a Man's form dwelling,
> [Was Adam perchance like this, ere Eve from his side was drawn?] ...
> Strange twice-born, having entrance to both worlds –
> Loved, loved by either sex,
> And free of all their lore! ...
> Passing all partial loves, this one complete ...
> Dear Son of heaven – long suffering wanderer through the
> wilderness of civilisation –
> The day draws nigh when from these mists of ages
> Thy form in glory clad shall appear.[51]

[47] Quoted in Lucy Delap, *The Feminist Avant-Garde: Transatlantic Encounters of the Early Twentieth Century* (Cambridge: Cambridge University Press, 2007), 279.

[48] Dorothy Richardson, *Pilgrimage*, 4 vols (London: Virago, 1979), I, 31, III, 482; Weininger, *Sex and Character*, 36.

[49] Percy Bysshe Shelley, 'A Defence of Poetry', in *Political Writings, including 'A Defence of Poetry'*, ed. Roland A. Duerksen (New York: Meredith Corporation, 1970), 197.

[50] Carpenter, *The Intermediate Sex: A Study of Some Transitional Types of Men and Women*, 2nd edn, (London: S. Sonnenschein, 1909), 14.

[51] Carpenter, *Towards Democracy*, 331–2.

Sexual radicals in the period frequently deployed this kind of millenarian rhetoric but they did not all agree on the sex of the super-being they so eagerly awaited. Some, Weininger included, were predicting that the future of humanity would be a purer form of masculinity. However, in *Herland* (1915), Charlotte Perkins Gilman fantasized about a race of parthenogenetically created 'ultra-women, inheriting only from women'.[52] These differing views on sex in super-world impacted on the development of modernist aesthetics in diverse ways. The strident masculinism of the modernist poetics of T. E. Hulme and Ezra Pound has been well documented, while some aspects of modernist writing, specifically stream-of-consciousness prose, have often been construed as in some sense 'feminine'. But it was Carpenter's idea of a being 'free of all their lore' that came closest to the way in which modernism was understood and taught in universities well into the second half of the twentieth century. There was common ground between the idea that every individual should be free from the conventions governing sexual identity and the idea that the modernist artwork should not be in thrall to any given ideology. Woolf articulates this link when she argues, in *A Room of One's Own*, that the true artist is 'womanmanly or man-womanly'.[53] In a sense, Woolf's terminology traps her in the binary structure that she is seeking to avoid, as does, to a lesser extent, Carpenter's notion of an 'intermediate sex'. Baty's genderless world seems the more radical option, but what all these approaches have in common is the desire to privilege the individual over any form of identity politics.

If sexology was one of the channels through which the anarchistic desire to preserve an authentic, free self was articulated, so too was the diet-reform movement. Diet-reform was a key component of the utopian discourses of the period. Metaphors relating to health, hygiene, and diet feature prominently, for example, in Marsden's editorials. In a 1913 *New Freewoman* editorial devoted to the denunciation of 'alien causes' and 'abstract concepts', including suffragism, she invokes 'poison-diets', 'decaying sweetnesses', drug-taking, and drunkenness.[54] She can equate suffragism and drunkenness via a vitalist philosophical framework in which abstraction implies dissociation from the real, and the surrender to spurious 'alien causes', a surrender comparable to addiction. In Hamilton's *William—An Englishman*, William is introduced to socialism and alcohol on the same fateful evening and quickly becomes addicted to the former: the applause attendant upon his firebrand speeches '[goes] to his head like wine'.[55]

This preoccupation with the integrity of the self and the fear of contamination from outside influences extended, for many utopians within the period, to an obsession with the purity of food ('orthorexia') and a concomitant desire for literal

[52] Charlotte Perkins Gilman, *Herland* (London: The Women's Press, 1979), 57.
[53] Woolf, 'A Room of One's Own' in *A Room of One's Own and Three Guineas* (London: Chatto & Windus, 1984), 97.
[54] 'The Lean Kind', *New Freewoman* 1/1 (15 June 1913), 1.
[55] Hamilton, *William*, 15.

bodily purity. Magazines like the *New Age* were full of advertisements for 'non-flesh' restaurants, nature-cures, and nicotine-free cigarettes. James Joyce is an example of a writer who was fully immersed in this orthorexic cultural climate. *A Portrait of the Artist as a Young Man*, for example, was serialized in the *Egoist* in 1914 under Marsden's editorship. Earlier than this, however, as a student at University College, Dublin, Joyce had known Frances Sheehy-Skeffington, a passionate supporter of feminism, rational dress, and diet-reform. Sheehy-Skeffington appears in *Portrait* as Stephen Dedalus's fellow student, McCann. McCann is an Ibsen enthusiast, a champion of the individual in the face of all dogmas. He is also an advocate of fresh mountain air and summertime bathing, and a vegetarian tee-totaller, believing that 'a man should live without any kind of stimulant, that he had a moral obligation to transmit to posterity sound minds in sound bodies'.[56] Stephen pokes fun at this, remarking sardonically, 'You have connected Ibsen and Eno's fruit salt forever in my mind'. Yet, despite his sarcasm here, Stephen himself, as a fledgling young writer, fosters a utopian dream of 'forging anew in his workshop out of the sluggish matter of the earth a new soaring impalpable imperishable being'. Joyce, however, seems intent on puncturing this hubristic fantasy: it is directly followed by a scene in which Stephen eats a rather squalid breakfast of bread fried in dripping which reminds him of the muddy bathwater at boarding school.[57] It anticipates the more famous breakfast in *Ulysses* (1922), where Leopold Bloom relishes the grilled mutton kidneys 'which gave to his palate a fine tang of faintly scented urine'.[58]

Joyce was not alone in taking a mischievously insouciant approach to vegetarianism. In 1909, for example, the *New Age* features a series of 'Prophetic Paragraphs' in which 'Our Professional Sorceress' gives the reader a few choice glimpses into the socialist utopia of the future. One of them details a shocking lapse into 'carnivoracity' on the part of one hapless utopian: 'The prisoner was charged with the wilful and malicious killing, cooking, and eating of an animal, namely, a rabbit— (sensation)—a crime so horrible that it had practically disappeared from the purview of civilized jurisprudence.' The socialist David Eder, writing for the same magazine, adopts a similarly wry tone, pretending to pity those who, in their pursuit of 'the higher life', adopt an almost superhuman austerity: 'The poor mortal who has been harassed all day in the city…fights her or his way home through a raw London fog…and is offered a plateful of nuts and an apple and a cubic inch of Wallace Bread.'[59] In Katherine Mansfield's early story, 'The Luft Bad' (1910), set in a Bavarian health spa, one free-spirited woman abandons clothes and eats only nuts and raw vegetables, feeling herself grow 'stronger and purer' by the hour, and

---

[56] James Joyce, *A Portrait of the Artist as a Young Man*, ed. Seamus Deane (London: Penguin, 1992), 49.

[57] Ibid., 51, 183, 188.

[58] Joyce, *Ulysses*, ed. Hans Walter Gabler with Wolfhard Steppe and Claus Melchior (London: Bodley Head, 1986), 45.

[59] *New Age* (second ser.) 6/7:797 (16 December 1909), 154 and 6/3:793 (18 November 1909), 64.

regretting that 'The majority of us are walking about with pig corpuscles and oxen fragments in our brains'.[60]

Many vegetarians in the period were, of course, motivated by a hatred of cruelty to animals. Wells's narrator in *A Modern Utopia* 'cannot stand the thought of slaughter-houses', and in Gilman's *Herland* (1915), the vegan inhabitants of Herland are dismayed to hear of 'the process which robs the cow of her calf, and the calf of its true food' in order to supply human beings with cows' milk.[61] But as Mansfield insinuates in 'The Luft Bad', animal welfare was not always the prime motive: meat-eating could be seen to violate the sacredness of the individual, ignominiously embroiling her or him in the bodily substance of other creatures. This idea that the vegetarian was more autonomous and individuated than the meat-eater recurs in Lawrence's *The Rainbow* when Ursula goes to teach at a school which, unlike the Rudolf Steiner schools and other progressive schools fashionable in the period, is hell-bent on 'compelling many children into one disciplined mechanical set'. Only Ursula's fellow teacher, Maggie, manages to assert an untrammelled individuality in the face of what Lawrence calls 'this *unclean* system of authority'. She introduces Ursula to the wholesomeness of vegetarian hotpot, whereupon Ursula finds that her own, conventionally meaty fare 'seem[s] coarse and ugly beside this savoury, clean dish'. Lawrence continues, 'her soul rang in answer to a new refinement, a new liberty. If all vegetarian things were as nice as this, she would be glad to escape the slight uncleanness of meat'.[62] Whereas vegetarianism betokens refinement and liberty, meat, by implication, is as homogenizing and oppressive as the Brinsley Street school system.

Meat, however, was not seen as the only dietary threat to the integrity of the individual. The scale of industrial food production had been increasing from the late nineteenth century, creating anxieties about the origins and authenticity of food. This was an era in which all kinds of industrially produced convenience foods sprang into existence, often associated by radicals in the period with an irredeemable mass culture. In E. M. Forster's *Howards End* (1910), the food that the down-at-heel city clerk, Leonard Bast, and his lover, Jackie, eat in their run-down flat is, tellingly, all reducible to standardized, geometric shapes: 'They began with a soup square...dissolved in some hot water. It was followed by the tongue—a freckled cylinder of meat...—ending with another square dissolved in water (jelly: pineapple).'[63] In light of the fact that realism as a literary mode was often condemned as a form of convenience food or pap, too easily digested by the reader, it is tempting to see an autotelic dimension to Forster's novel here. He is perhaps aligning himself with other aspiring modernists who associated realism with the

---

[60] 'The Luft Bad', in Katherine Mansfield, *In a German Pension*, ed. Anne Fernihough (London: Penguin, 1999), 63.

[61] Wells, *A Modern Utopia*, 169; Gilman, *Herland*, 48.

[62] Lawrence, *The Rainbow*, 353–5 (emphasis added).

[63] E. M. Forster, *Howards End*, ed. Oliver Stallybrass (Harmondsworth: Penguin, 1986), 66.

masses and a lazy, mindless consumption. On the other hand, as we have seen, realism was often construed as a literary mode compromised by alien matter or, in dietary terms, undigested matter, *The Ragged Trousered Philanthropists* being a prime example of this. Both versions of realism evince a fear of the invasion of the self by something alien and contaminating. The modernist work, by implication, has fully digested and purified its subject matter: like the freewoman, it is fully integrated and individuated.

Unlike Leonard Bast's soup squares and jelly cubes with their supposedly homogenizing effects, there were many food bases and extracts on the market which attempted to conceal their industrial origins and to appeal to diet-reformers and simple-lifers as the key to bodily purity and longevity. Sometimes they were even presented as elixirs of life, proffering a transcendence of the flesh, an evolutionary fast track to a future from which bodily weakness had been banished. Usually they were vegetarian but not always. Bovril, for example, dating from 1889, took its name from the Latin *bos* (genitive, *bovis*), meaning 'ox' or 'cow', in combination with 'vril', the name of the energy fluid consumed by those supermen *avant la lettre*, the 'Vril-ya' of Edward Bulwer-Lytton's 1870 utopian novel, *The Coming Race*.

Wells's 1904 novel, *The Food of the Gods*, reads in many ways as a satirical commentary on the claims of such products. The two scientists at the centre of the novel devise a food-additive that accelerates growth. Envisaging it as 'the nutrition of a possible Hercules', they name it 'Herakleophorbia'.[64] It is initially tested on chickens who grow to enormous size but the careless managers of the chicken farm let it seep into the wider world where it wreaks chaos, creating hypertrophied rats and wasps, supersized vegetation, and, inevitably, giant human beings (one of the scientists willingly feeds Herakleophorbia to his own infant son without foreseeing the full consequences). Perhaps Wells is lampooning those hyper-individualistic utopians who were, in his view, too preoccupied with the notion of their own personal development at both a spiritual and physical level. The personal growth to which they aspire becomes, in *The Food of the Gods*, ludicrously literal. At the novel's conclusion, the young human giants find themselves under siege from the 'little people' who have brought them into being but who now wish to exterminate them. As one of the giants pleads, 'We fight not for ourselves but for growth – growth that goes on for ever. To-morrow, whether we live or die, growth will conquer through us. That is the law of the spirit for evermore.'[65] Once again Bergson springs to mind: according to one enthusiastic contemporary of Bergson, the philosopher's exhilarating message is that 'the future contains the possibility of... a real and cumulative enrichment of the sum of being'.[66] It is difficult to ascertain whether Wells in his novel is satirizing the

---

[64] Wells, *The Food of the Gods and How it Came to Earth* (London: Ernest Benn, 1926), 12. [All further page references are to this edition.]

[65] Ibid., 259–60.

[66] A. O. Lovejoy. *Bergson and Romantic Evolutionism: Two Lectures Delivered before the Union, September 5 and 12, 1913* (Berkeley, CA: University of California Press, 1914), 33–4.

optimism of Bergson and others like him or implicitly promoting the same optimism. What is clear is that Wells did not, either in this novel or in his work more widely, engage with the formal experimentation that utopian thought in the period often inspired. Wells serves as a useful reminder that utopian thought in the late nineteenth and early twentieth centuries brought realism and modernism together in unexpected ways. He also serves as a reminder that utopianism could, at one end of the spectrum, envisage new forms of humanity (or, in Lawrence's words in *Women in Love* [1920], 'utter new races and new species... new forms of consciousness, new forms of body'), and at the other, something as simple and homely as a new mode of transport offering unprecedented, low cost mobility to women and the working classes. As Wells prophesies in *A Modern Utopia*, 'cycle tracks will abound in Utopia'.[67]

FURTHER READING

Ardis, Ann L. *Modernism and Cultural Conflict, 1880–1922* (Cambridge: Cambridge University Press, 2002).

Baldick, Chris. *The Oxford English Literary History*, Vol. X: *1920–1940: The Modern Movement* (Oxford: Oxford University Press, 2004).

Caserio, Robert L. *The Novel in England, 1900–1950: History and Theory* (New York: Twayne Publishers, 1999).

Gillies, Mary Ann. *Henri Bergson and British Modernism* (Montreal, QC: McGill-Queen's University Press, 1996).

Kemp, Sandra, Charlotte Mitchell, and David Trotter (eds). *The Oxford Companion to Edwardian Fiction* (Oxford: Oxford University Press, 1997).

Levenson, Michael (ed.). *A Genealogy of Modernism: A Study of English Literary Doctrine 1908–1922* (Cambridge: Cambridge University Press, 1984).

Potter, Rachel. *Modernism and Democracy: Literary Culture 1900–1930* (Oxford: Oxford University Press, 1930).

Trotter, David. *The English Novel in History, 1895–1920* (London and New York: Routledge, 1993).

Weir, David. *Anarchy and Culture: The Aesthetic Politics of Anarchism* (Amherst, MA: University of Massachusetts Press, 1997).

[67] Lawrence. *Women in Love*, ed. David Farmer, Lindeth Vasey, and John Worthen (London: Penguin, 1995), 479; Wells, *A Modern Utopia*, 29.

PART III

MODES AND GENRES

CHAPTER 11

NATURALISM, REALISM, AND IMPRESSIONISM

ADAM PARKES

'After the Realists we have the Naturalists and the Impressionists. Such progress!'
Flaubert exploded in a letter to Turgenev in 1877.[1] The first exhibition of the impressionist painters in Paris had been held a mere three years earlier, and it would be
another two years before the first sustained attempt to define literary impressionism
appeared in print.[2] *Le Roman Expérimental*, Zola's best-known manifesto for literary naturalism, would not appear until 1880.[3] Already, Flaubert was consigning all
three of these modern movements to the grave. So much for all those literary efforts
to create an accurate representation of everyday life (realism), or incorporate scientific ideas about heredity and the environment (naturalism), or capture the encounter between external reality and consciousness (impressionism). Like the modern
myth of progress itself, these movements were passé. So soon? Such progress!

It is hard to overestimate Flaubert's significance for literary modernism, in
Britain and Ireland as in France, but was he right to dismiss realism and its most
significant early modernist developments in such summary fashion? Had aesthetic
modernism already lost the power to shock the audience that *Madame Bovary* had
demonstrated on its publication in 1857? One answer is that it had if Flaubert said
so. The pre-eminent writer associated with the term realism by nineteenth-century

---

[1] Francis Steegmuller (ed. and trans.), *The Letters of Gustave Flaubert*, 2 vols (London: Picador, 2001), 623.

[2] See Ferdinand Brunetière, 'L'Impressionisme dans le roman', *Revue de Deux Mondes* (15 November 1879), 446–59. The first time the term 'impressionists' was used in an aesthetic context was in April 1874. The occasion was an exhibition of thirty-one artists at the Paris studio of the photographer Nadar, which prompted Louis Leroy's feeble satire 'L'Exposition des impressionistes'. Although Leroy meant the name as an insult, Monet and his colleagues later adopted it as their collective title. See Linda Nochlin, *Impressionism and Post-Impressionism, 1874–1904: Sources and Documents* (Englewood Cliffs, NJ: Prentice-Hall, 1966), 10–14.

[3] Zola first used the term 'naturalism' in 1866, although he was pre-empted by a Russian critic in 1848. See F. W. J. Hemmings, *Emile Zola*, 2nd edn (Oxford: Clarendon Press, 1966), 154 n. 3.

French critics was tired of it. 'I execrate what is commonly called "realism", even though I'm regarded as one of its high priests,' Flaubert exclaimed in 1876. He declared himself a 'rabid old Romantic' instead. 'I value style first and above all, and then Truth,' he added, forging an opposition between style and realism that his own writings barely support.[4] Despite its strenuous attention to the details of ordinary middle-class life, and despite its claims (articulated by, among others, Flaubert) to describe this life from an impersonal point of view, realism scarcely gave an objective picture of the world. Even as it worked out various ways of trying to represent the world as it actually was, or as it seemed, realism (like any other literary mode) subjected reality to aesthetic stylization.

While Flaubert's dismissal of realism and its early modernist developments might be understood as an expression of impatience with the aesthetic debates of his time—debates that struck him as excessively concerned with artificial and, at best, partially useful labels—the impatience itself suggests tensions or paradoxes that proved endemic to realism, and that in some ways defined it. 'Realism, throughout the nineteenth century,' George Levine reminds us in a recent chapter, 'remained an ambivalent and often self-contradictory mode. It was most consistent in its determination to find strategies for describing the world as it was. It was inconsistent because every artist's conception of what the world was like differed and because the world changed from moment to moment, generation to generation.'[5] Paradoxically implicated in idealism, realism 'accommodates vague forms as well as concrete ones, and...it activates social visions as well as social facts', as Matthew Beaumont notes.[6] Liberating when viewed from one angle, because it bestows the 'freedom to feel and say' that Henry James called for in his essay 'The Art of Fiction' (1884), from another angle such elasticity could seem excessive, worryingly close to meaninglessness and formlessness, as James intimated elsewhere by describing nineteenth-century novels as 'large loose baggy monsters'.[7] If realism consisted of an ongoing effort to negotiate the 'broad notions of plausibility' to which it generally conformed,[8] sometimes those notions appeared to be stretched to the point of *im*plausibility. And if implausibility was an inevitable outcome, the so-called realist novelist might just as well describe himself as a romantic—Flaubert's point, precisely.

Another answer to our question is that Flaubert could not have been more wrong. Just as Claude Monet—in the sometimes overlapping, though not always parallel

---

[4] Steegmuller (ed.), *Letters of Gustave Flaubert*, 610, 315; George J. Becker (ed.), *Documents of Modern Literary Realism* (Princeton, NJ: Princeton University Press, 1963), 94.

[5] George Levine, 'Literary Realism Reconsidered', in Matthew Beaumont (ed.), *Adventures in Realism* (Oxford: Blackwell, 2007), 30.

[6] Beaumont, 'Introduction: Reclaiming Realism', in Beaumont, *Adventures*, 6.

[7] Henry James, *The Art of Criticism: Henry James on the Theory and Practice of Fiction*, ed. William Veeder and Susan M. Griffin (Chicago, IL: University of Chicago Press, 1986), 170; and James, *Literary Criticism*, ed. Leon Edel and Mark Wilson, 2 vols (New York: Library of America, 1984), II, 1107.

[8] Simon Dentith, 'Realist Synthesis in the Nineteenth-Century Novel: "That unity which lies in the selection of our keenest consciousness"', in Beaumont, *Adventures*, 40.

realm of painting—continued working the vivid colours and diffuse atmospheric effects of his impressionist style until his death in 1926, the aesthetics of realism, naturalism, and impressionism would imprint themselves in numerous ways on the literature of the long *fin de siècle* and beyond. The emergence of naturalism and impressionism helped to ensure literary realism's survival, if in newly complicated forms, through the modernist period. With its commitment to documenting social reality, naturalism did not differ significantly from realism in verbal style or narrative procedure. Rather, naturalism distinguished itself from realism by a theoretical narrowing of vision that emphasized logically incongruous ideas about the determinative influence on human personality both of the environment (which found the key to the self in external factors) and of heredity (which turned the search for that key inward and downward).[9] Linked less by logical compatibility than by a shared rhetoric of the extreme, naturalism's competing theories delivered tales of violence, degeneration, and downward social mobility.[10]

Unlike naturalism, literary impressionism tended to differentiate itself formally and stylistically from earlier models of realism, employing such techniques as achronological narration, multiple narrators, limited point of view, and intensely visual imagery to emphasize how the sense of reality depends on the perceptions and reflections of an individual human observer. Impressionism, too, offered tales of dissolution or breakdown, but its portraits of fragmentation typically occurred in the mind, not in society—or, if they did occur in society, they did so because they had happened in the mind first. In a seeming departure from George Eliot's canonical definition of realism as a 'faithful account of men and things as they have mirrored themselves in my mind', impressionism takes up Eliot's own quibbles—'The mirror is doubtless defective; the outlines will sometimes be disturbed; the reflection faint or confused'—and extends them to the point where defectiveness, disturbance, and confusion seem to be the rule, not the exception.[11] In this way, literary Impressionism, like naturalism, gravitates towards the extreme case. As it does so, however, its theoretical differences from naturalism break down, as the borders between internal and external worlds start to wobble and blur—as, indeed, they do in the theory and practice of naturalism.

The literary record affords ample evidence against Flaubert's claim about the fate of 'the Realists' and 'the Naturalists and the Impressionists'. The obvious examples are both French: the twenty novels of Zola's Rougon-Macquart cycle, the major monument of literary naturalism published between 1871 and 1893, and Proust's impressionist masterpiece, *À la recherche du temps perdu*, published in seven instalments from 1913 to 1927. But numerous examples might be summoned from other

---

[9] See Sally Ledger, 'Naturalism: "Dirt and Horror Pure and Simple"', in Beaumont, *Adventures*, 69–70.

[10] See Michael Levenson, *Modernism* (New Haven, CT: Yale University Press, 2011), 71.

[11] George Eliot, *Adam Bede*, ed. Valentine Cunningham (1859; Oxford: Oxford University Press, 1996), 175.

modern European literatures: the realism of the Scandinavian dramatists Ibsen and Strindberg, or the naturalist novels of Verga in Italy and Alas in Spain, or the impressionist fiction of the Russians Chekhov and Turgenev.[12] We might consider examples from North America: naturalism in Chopin, Dreiser, London, or Norris, Impressionism in Crane or James. Or we might turn to Britain, where realism, naturalism, and impressionism, far from dwindling into low-impact aesthetics, continued to assert their power to shock and surprise their readers, upsetting moral, social, and aesthetic expectations and provoking public controversies reminiscent of the *Madame Bovary* trial.

When Walter Pater published his *Studies in the History of the Renaissance* (1873), one of the founding texts of literary impressionism, some of his fellow Oxonians were affronted by its seemingly impious, hedonistic implications.[13] In 1888, after the House of Commons had debated the 'rapid spread of demoralizing literature in this country', legal proceedings were initiated against Zola's English publisher, Henry Vizetelly, and a second trial, in 1889, resulted in Vizetelly's imprisonment. Press accounts characterized Vizetelly as a purveyor of 'dirty fiction', while 'Zolaism' was called a 'disease', a 'literature of the sewer', insults that would be recycled by hostile reviewers of two of the twentieth century's most famous banned books, Lawrence's *The Rainbow* (1915) and Joyce's *Ulysses* (1922), both of which were explicitly compared with Zola.[14] Ibsen, too, incited strong reactions when his work appeared on the London stage. Championed as an implacable realist of the 'everyday' by George Bernard Shaw, Ibsen developed an interest in theories of heredity and sexuality that suggested strong parallels with Zola, and when his 1881 play *Ghosts* was performed in London in 1891, the torrent of critical abuse from scandalized reviewers closed it down after a single performance.[15]

Initially, however, it took some time for either naturalism or impressionism to make a significant mark on the British literary scene, or to distinguish itself from realism. Denying impressionism's relevance to literature, some writers and critics persisted in seeing Impressionism as an exclusively visual art. This was in spite of evidence—such as the influence of Baudelaire's art criticism on French impressionist

[12] On the realism and naturalism of Strindberg's 1880s dramas, see Becker, *Documents*, 394–406; and Claude Schumacher (ed.), *Naturalism and Symbolism in European Theatre, 1850–1918* (Cambridge: Cambridge University Press, 1996), 297–310. On Verga, see Jonathan Smith, 'Naturalism and Anti-Naturalism in Italy', in Brian Nelson (ed.), *Naturalism in the European Novel* (Oxford: Berg, 1992), 151–66. On Alas: Noël Valis, 'On Monstrous Birth: Leopoldo Alas's *La Regenta*', in Nelson, *Naturalism*, 191–209. On Chekhov: H. Peter Stowell, *Literary Impressionism: James and Chekhov* (Athens, GA: University of Georgia Press, 1980).

[13] See R. M. Seiler (ed.), *Walter Pater: The Critical Heritage* (London: Routledge and Kegan Paul, 1980), 53, 61–2, 95–6.

[14] See Becker, *Documents*, 352–82; R. P. Draper (ed.), *D. H. Lawrence: The Critical Heritage* (New York: Barnes and Noble, 1970), 96; and Robert H. Deming (ed.), *James Joyce: The Critical Heritage* (London: Routledge and Kegan Paul, 1970), 195.

[15] George Bernard Shaw, *Major Critical Essays: The Quintessence of Ibsenism. The Perfect Wagnerite. The Sanity of Art* (London: Constable, 1932), 139; Ledger, 'Naturalism', 76–7.

painters, or the influence of those same painters on James's prose—that literary and visual impressionism often animated each other. Ezra Pound reiterated the case against literary impressionism in 1912: 'Impressionism belongs in paint; it is of the eye.'[16] Thus Pound articulated a widespread resistance to work exploring affinities between different artistic media that ran counter to the interactions between literature, visual art, and music that characterized not only impressionism but also many other features of aesthetic modernism, and indeed some of Pound's own endeavours.

Meanwhile naturalism was often conflated with realism and with the 'novel of experiment' more generally. In 'The Limits of Realism in Fiction' (1890), an essay that essentially recapitulated Flaubert's claim that realism had already gone as far as it could go, Edmund Gosse equated naturalism with 'the most advanced realism'.[17] Thomas Hardy suggested that even if naturalism claimed to rest on modern scientific principles, as Zola had urged, it remained wedded to realism, 'an artificiality distilled from the fruits of closest observation'.[18] In the courtroom of public opinion, dramatized in the parliamentary debate on 'dirty fiction', realism simply meant Zola.[19] The formal distinction most commonly drawn in British literary circles of the 1880s was not between realism and naturalism, or between naturalism and impressionism, but between realism and romance, as illustrated in Andrew Lang's well-known article of 1886.[20] Hence James's effort in 'The Art of Fiction' to defend modern fiction against what he saw as two kinds of fantasists: moralizers such as Walter Besant, against whom James pressed the case for freedom of expression, and romancers such as Lang and Robert Louis Stevenson, whose 'clumsy' separation of realism from romance James simply refused.[21]

As well as defending modernist realism against moralizers and romancers, James's essay makes an early argument for literary impressionism. Revising realism and quietly pushing naturalism aside, James defines the novel as 'a personal, a direct impression of life'. Insisting that the novelist requires, above all, 'a capacity for receiving straight impressions' and adding that, 'if experience consists of impressions, it may be said that impressions *are* experience', James presses the case for a modern novel of consciousness.

> Experience...is an immense sensibility, a kind of huge spiderweb of the finest silken threads suspended in the chamber of consciousness, and catching every airborne

[16] Brita Lindberg-Seyersted, *Pound/Ford: The Story of a Literary Friendship* (New York: New Directions, 1982), 10.

[17] Edmund Gosse, 'The Limits of Realism in Fiction', in Becker, *Documents*, 387.

[18] Harold Orel (ed.), *Thomas Hardy's Personal Writings: Prefaces, Literary Opinions, Reminiscences* (New York: St Martin's, 1966), 134–8.

[19] Becker, *Documents*, 374, 354.

[20] Andrew Lang, 'Realism and Romance', in Sally Ledger and Roger Luckhurst (eds), *The Fin de Siècle: A Reader in Cultural History, c.1880–1900* (Oxford: Oxford University Press, 2000), 99–104.

[21] James, *Art of Criticism*, 175.

particle in its tissue. It is the very atmosphere of the mind; and when the mind is imaginative—much more when it happens to be that of a man of genius—it takes to itself the faintest hints of life, it converts the very pulses of the air into revelations.[22]

From this argument follows the full range of literary techniques, not all of them employed by James himself, which writers and critics have described as impressionist: not only achronological narration, multiple narrators, limited point of view, and intense visualization, but centres of consciousness, conjectural narration, narrative ellipses, and delayed decoding. James reinforces the case for Impressionism by appropriating metaphors previously claimed by British realism and French naturalism. When he characterizes experience as a 'huge spiderweb...suspended in the chamber of consciousness', he is remaking the web—one of George Eliot's favourite metaphors for social relations—in a new impressionist image that emphasizes how those relations are perceived.[23] In describing this 'spiderweb' as 'the very atmosphere of the mind', James establishes the impressionist's right to the metaphor of atmosphere over that of naturalist theory, in which the notion of an all-enveloping environment moulding every aspect of human existence is axiomatic. Thus James asserts impressionism's early independence from realism and endows it with an air of aesthetic sophistication and refinement— think of those 'finest silken threads'—that naturalism, with its reputation for 'sheer beastliness', would never have.[24]

Late-coming when read in light of Flaubert's aspersions, James's claims for an impressionist fiction reach back not only to French models in painting and literature but also to earlier British models, especially the impressionist art criticism of Pater and Ruskin. Paint the first impression that nature imprints on your eye, Ruskin had instructed the landscape painter, and you will 'reproduce that impression on the mind of the spectator', a translation of realism into impressionist terms that was clearly applicable to literary as well as to visual art.[25] 'In aesthetic criticism', Pater had written, 'the first step towards seeing one's object as it really is, is to know one's own impression as it really is, to discriminate it, to realize it distinctly'.[26] As well as reaching back, however, James's chapter points forwards to the critical and fictional practice of Conrad, Ford, and Woolf, who followed him in reinforcing the case for impressionism in part by downplaying naturalism.[27] When Conrad, for

---

[22] Ibid., 170, 178, 172.

[23] On Eliot's use of Darwin's metaphor of an 'inextricable web of affinities', see Gillian Beer, *Darwin's Plots: Evolutionary Narrative in Darwin, George Eliot, and Nineteenth-Century Fiction* (Cambridge: Cambridge University Press, 2009), 156–68.

[24] James, *Art of Criticism*, 172; Becker, *Documents*, 354.

[25] E. T. Cook and Alexander Wedderburn (eds), *The Works of John Ruskin*, 39 vols (London: George Allen, 1903–12), VI, 33.

[26] Walter Pater, *Studies in the History of the Renaissance*, ed. Matthew Beaumont (Oxford: Oxford University Press, 2010), 3.

[27] Some critics have claimed a strictly limited scope for literary impressionism in British writing. For Paul Armstrong, in *The Challenge of Bewilderment* (Ithaca, NY: Cornell University Press, 1987),

instance, wrote that he wanted to make the reader '*see*', he deprecated naturalism together with realism and romanticism as no more than 'temporary formulas' of the author's craft.[28] Woolf's famous call for a new kind of novel that records the 'myriad impressions' etched by experience on the human mind defines itself against 'materialist' fiction—against writing that, in its preoccupation with the external incident and detail of everyday life, descends from naturalism.[29]

As she advances the case for impressionism, Woolf increases the resistance to naturalism and other forms of so-called materialist fiction, by trespassing on the modern urban terrain that naturalism had claimed as its own. In the well-known sentences that urge the modern writer to 'record the atoms as they fall upon the mind', Woolf combines the language of impressionist aesthetics with a materialist theory of shock in a manner that may suggest not only traumatic wartime experience but also the everyday shocks and concussions of urban modernity.

> The mind, exposed to the ordinary course of life, receives upon its surface a myriad impressions—trivial, fantastic, evanescent, or engraved with the sharpness of steel. From all sides they come, an incessant shower of innumerable atoms, composing in their sum what we might venture to call life itself... Let us record the atoms as they fall upon the mind in the order in which they fall, let us trace the pattern, however disconnected and incoherent in appearance, which each sight or incident scores upon the consciousness.[30]

Just as Woolf's impressions 'engraved with the sharpness of steel' imply the thrusts of the bayonet, the image of a modern observer bombarded by an 'incessant shower of innumerable atoms' may also remind readers of the recently concluded First World War. At the same time, this second image perhaps evokes a wider contemporary phenomenon encountered in 'the ordinary course of life': repeated exposure to the sensations of modernity. Woolf seems to dramatize this double shock effect in the famous motor-car episode in *Mrs Dalloway* (1925). Rightly celebrated for its representation of a psyche fractured by wartime experience—the explosive sound of the car backfiring sends Septimus Smith's mind back to the trenches—this scene

---

the British impressionists were James, Conrad, and Ford. More recent work has expanded the range of British and Irish texts that might be read as impressionist to include works by Elizabeth Bowen, Thomas Hardy, Dorothy Richardson, Jean Rhys, John Ruskin, Arthur Symons, Oscar Wilde, H. G. Wells, and others. See Tamar Katz, *Impressionist Subjects: Gender, Interiority, and Modernist Fiction in England* (Urbana, IL: University of Illinois Press, 2000); Jesse Matz, *Literary Impressionism and Modernist Aesthetics* (Cambridge: Cambridge University Press, 2001); and Adam Parkes, *A Sense of Shock: The Impact of Impressionism on Modern British and Irish Writing* (New York: Oxford University Press, 2011).

[28] Joseph Conrad, *The Complete Works of Joseph Conrad*, 26 vols (New York: Doubleday, Page, 1925), XXIII, xi–xiv.

[29] Andrew McNeillie and Stuart N. Clarke (eds), *The Essays of Virginia Woolf*, 6 vols (London: Hogarth, 1986–2012), III, 33–4.

[30] Ibid., III, 33–4.

also models an everyday experience in what would soon be called the modern culture of distraction.[31]

> Every one looked at the motor car. Septimus looked. Boys on bicycles sprang off. Traffic accumulated. And there the motor car stood, with drawn blinds, and upon them a curious pattern like a tree, Septimus thought, and this gradual drawing together of everything to one centre before his eyes, as if some horror had come almost to the surface and was about to burst into flames, terrified him.[32]

The complex syntax of the last sentence draws the reader through the process by which Septimus's mind translates what it sees and hears into what, in his shell-shocked state, he remembers or imagines. The first four sentences—short, punchy, mono-clausal—capture the mind, or minds, in a state of distraction. Thus Woolf participates in a broader trend in impressionist writing, which often took up the urban subject matter associated with naturalism and employed such techniques as limited point of view and narrative ellipsis to convey the flickering variations of individual perception as it operated, not in James's finely aestheticized 'chamber of consciousness', but in the modern metropolitan arena of everyday collisions, concussions, and shocks.[33]

Impressionism itself sometimes shocked its early audiences, but eventually, as the examples of James and Woolf make plain, it established its place in British modernism. Naturalism, by contrast, was often cast as impressionism's uncouth ugly twin, or its badly behaved cousin from overseas. For naturalism was what happened in literature when realism combined with the Gothic, which manifested itself in various forms of violence and monstrosity including alcoholism, sexual degeneracy, murder, and suicide. The metaphor of monstrosity—employed by Zola, as in his description of the Voreux coal mine in *Germinal* (1885), to represent the capitalist system—signifies naturalism's chief debt to the Gothic. Indeed it may be the repressed Gothic element in realism that naturalism brings back to the surface.[34]

But in the eyes of many British writers and critics naturalism itself was a sign of the monstrous—especially when it was foreign, as it often seemed to be. Originating in Zola and a small cohort of French disciples that included (briefly) Huysmans and

---

[31]   Siegfried Kracauer's well-known essay, translated by Thomas Y. Levin as 'Cult of Distraction: On Berlin's Picture Palaces' in *New German Critique* 40 (1987), 91–6, first appeared in Germany in 1926. Some aspects of Kracauer's analysis were anticipated in Georg Simmel's classic account of the metropolitan psyche, 'The Metropolis and Mental Life' (1903). On Woolf and the culture of distraction, see Pamela L. Caughie (ed.), *Virginia Woolf in the Age of Mechanical Reproduction* (New York: Garland, 2000). For an excellent account of the interpenetration of Benjamin's theory of distraction and Freud's theory of trauma, with which Woolf's account of shock shares some affinities, see Tim Armstrong, 'Two Types of Shock in Modernity', *Critical Inquiry* 42/1 (2000), 60–73.

[32]   Virginia Woolf, *Mrs Dalloway*, ed. David Bradshaw (Oxford: Oxford University Press, 2008), 13.

[33]   James, *Art of Criticism*, 172.

[34]   'The evil beast crouching in its underground cave was sated with human flesh and its harsh wheezing had at last died away. The whole of Le Voreux had now fallen down into the abyss.' See Emile Zola, *Germinal*, trans. Peter Collier (Oxford and New York: Oxford University Press, 2008), 475.

(even more briefly) Maupassant, developed by German and Scandinavian dramatists, and inherited by American writers such as Norris and Dreiser, it appeared not to belong to a native British tradition. It was not just conservative reviewers or members of parliament who reviled naturalist fiction by foreign authors as 'bad reading for the masses' in Britain.[35] Writers themselves made the case against naturalism. James described the subject matter of Zola's *Nana* (1880) as a 'combination of the cesspool and the house of prostitution'. This material issued not from careful observation of reality but, James argued, from the distorted, distorting vision of the author himself.[36] In *Jacob's Room* (1922), Woolf emphasizes Mrs Norman's fear of her fellow train passenger Jacob Flanders by giving her a Frank Norris novel to read, one possible implication being that Jacob is no more civilized than the human beasts roaming the pages of naturalism. Foreign naturalism, that is, not British. Whether or not this was Woolf's intended meaning, critical tradition has tacitly confirmed the verdict—there have been few significant studies of naturalism in British literature.[37]

Even writers whose work showed strong naturalist tendencies, such as Arnold Bennett and George Moore, distanced themselves from naturalism. Bennett's *Clayhanger* (1910), for example, places a characteristically naturalist emphasis on the shaping power of the industrial environment, built up in painstaking detail, and on the hidden instincts and forces that impel characters often against their will. In his criticism, moreover, Bennett employs naturalist criteria to describe the novelist's selection of subject matter. 'Any logically conceived survey of existence must begin with geographical and climatic phenomena', he wrote in 'The Author's Craft' (1913). 'Geographical knowledge is the mother of discernment'. Further, 'every street is a mirror, an illustration, an exposition, an explanation, of the human beings who live in it'. A community, Bennett argues à la Zola, is 'the net result of the interplay of instincts and influences'. Yet Bennett did not count Zola as one of the novel's great pioneers. Unlike Balzac, Joyce, and Wells, Zola 'did nothing new', Bennett wrote in a later essay. 'He was merely a supercraftsman of unsurpassed industry and tenacity of purpose... who had hours of genius.'[38]

---

[35] Becker, *Documents*, 368.

[36] Henry James, '*Nana*', in Becker, *Documents*, 239.

[37] Thus Peter Keating's attempt to show how widely naturalism influenced late-Victorian fiction was swiftly followed by David Trotter's reiteration of the more common argument that British literature tried to avoid naturalism. See Keating, *The Haunted Study: A Social History of the English Novel, 1875–1914* (London: Secker & Warburg, 1989), 115–21, 285–329; and Trotter, *The English Novel in History, 1895–1920* (Abingdon and New York: Routledge, 1993), 118–21. See also David Bagulay, *Naturalist Fiction: The Entropic Vision* (Cambridge: Cambridge University Press, 1990), 29–39; and Lyn Pykett, 'Representing the Real: The English Debate about Naturalism, 1884–1900', in Nelson, *Naturalism*, 167–88. For a timely exception to this critical trend, see Simon Joyce, *Modernism and Naturalism in British and Irish Fiction, 1880–1930* (New York: Cambridge University Press, 2015).

[38] Samuel Hynes (ed.), *The Author's Craft and Other Critical Writings of Arnold Bennett* (Lincoln, NE: University of Nebraska Press, 1968), 9–11, 93.

The Anglo-Irish Moore has sometimes been cited as one of the rare exceptions to the anti-naturalist rule, but even he produced just one big naturalist novel, *A Mummer's Wife*, published by Vizetelly in 1885 and later acclaimed as a 'master-piece' by Bennett, before publicly renouncing naturalism and promoting Impressionism instead.[39] In Moore, as in Woolf, naturalism would now serve as a negative example against which to measure and define an impressionist aesthetic. When Moore, in *Confessions of a Young Man* (1888), characterized the self as 'like a smooth sheet of wax, bearing no impress, but capable of receiving any; of being moulded into all shapes', he was fashioning an impressionist model of subjectivity—fresh, malleable, fluctuating—in direct opposition to what he saw as Zola's scientific determinism. Moore's break with Zola was neither permanent nor complete: his best-known novel, *Esther Waters* (1894), would combine the impressionist's attention to narrative perspective and effects of immediacy with the naturalist's interest in degeneration plots and the pressures of environment. Before the 1880s were out, however, Moore was denigrating Zola's books as the 'simple crude statements of a man of powerful mind, but singularly narrow vision'.[40]

Rejected, disowned, naturalism dispersed. But it didn't dissolve entirely. It went underground, discovering various means of survival and influencing a wide range of modern writers including the early Joyce, in *Dubliners* (1914), and Lawrence, in *Sons and Lovers* (1913) and the snowbound Alpine finale of *Women in Love* (1920), a thrilling exploration of the natural environment's destructive power. Despite later disavowals, Moore too invites a naturalist reading of *A Mummer's Wife*, by quoting the French historian Victor Duruy in the epigraph: 'Change the surroundings in which man lives, and, in two or three generations, you will have changed his physical constitution, his habits of life, and a goodly number of his ideas.' The narrative itself debates this thesis, summoning tales of romantic disappointment to suggest that 'we change the surroundings, but a heart bleeds under all social variations'. Yet, with its frequent emphasis on the surrounding grimness, where all that changes in the 'sea of brick' is the name of the town, Moore's text insists on the visible supremacy of the industrial environment, tangible evidence of humankind's 'triumph over vanquished nature' and, more profoundly, of economic capitalism's triumph over pre-industrial notions of humanity. *A Mummer's Wife* begins in the sickroom of the heroine Kate Ede's husband and ends—after episodes of adultery, marital desertion, domestic violence, and alcoholism—with her own descent towards death, as her surroundings reduce her to the mixed metaphorical state of beast *and* machine: 'she gradually became like a worn-out machine, from which all rivets and screws had fallen, and miserable as a homeless dog, she rolled from one lodging to another;—after a few days driven forth from the lowest for dirt and dissoluteness.'[41]

---

[39] Ibid., 148.

[40] George Moore, *Confessions of a Young Man*, ed. Susan Dick (Montreal, QC: McGill-Queen's University Press, 1972), 49, 95.

[41] Moore, *A Mummer's Wife* (London: Vizetelly, 1885), 9, 300, 46, 73, 432.

Moore's novel was unusual among British or Irish works in declaring its allegiance to naturalism so openly, but naturalism's major ideas and metaphors—including its Gothic incidents and images of violence—featured in the work of authors who elsewhere registered explicit objections. Hardy, for example, contended that naturalism, with its emphasis on scientific documentation of external phenomena, failed to take account of 'what may be apprehended only by the mental tactility that comes from a sympathetic appreciativeness of life in all of its manifestations'.[42] Hardy expressed interest less in naturalism than in the literary possibilities suggested by impressionist painting, explaining in the Preface to *Jude the Obscure* (1895) that his novel was 'simply an endeavour to give shape and coherence to a series of seemings, or personal impressions, the question of their consistency or their discordance, of their permanence or their transitoriness, being regarded as not of the first moment'.[43] Yet in the novel itself Hardy, who acknowledged that Zola's own fiction was written by 'instinct',[44] sometimes moves closer to naturalist theory than such disclaimers allow for. Nowhere is this more apparent than in the episode when Jude discovers that his eldest son has slaughtered himself and his younger siblings. Abandoning his earlier scepticism of modern theories of heredity, Jude now expresses tragic recognition of 'Nature's law' of 'mutual butchery'. 'It was in his nature to do it', he tells Sue.[45] Thus naturalism has its say in Hardy's last novel.

James, too, went back on his disavowal of naturalism, and Conrad emulated him. As we have seen, James had complained bitterly about the 'foulness' of Zola's *Nana*. While working on *The Princess Casamassima* (1886), however, James declared himself 'quite the Naturalist'.[46] As well as consulting his own impressions of London, gleaned, he said, from 'walking the streets', James followed in Zola's documentary footsteps by visiting Millbank prison, in which the French mother of the hero, the diminutive bookbinder and terrorist conspirator Hyacinth Robinson, is incarcerated for killing his aristocratic English father. With its mixture of hereditary degeneracy and crime, this backstory itself clearly nods to Zola, if also to Dickens. Further, James echoes Zola's celebrated metaphor of a monstrous capitalist system by describing Britain's capital city as an 'immeasurable breathing monster'.[47] This metaphor—Zola's original together with James's rewriting—was then re-echoed by Conrad in his own tale of terrorism, suicide, and sacrifice, *The Secret Agent* (1907), whose figure of the Professor, an anarchistic explosives expert, is a major fictional descendant of Zola's Souvarine, the destroyer of the Voreux. Having deprecated

---

[42] Orel, *Thomas Hardy's Personal Writings*, 137.

[43] Thomas Hardy, *Jude the Obscure*, ed. Dennis Taylor (London: Penguin, 1998), 3–4. For Hardy's response to an exhibition of impressionist paintings that he saw in 1886, see Michael Millgate (ed.), *The Life and Work of Thomas Hardy* (Athens, GA: University of Georgia Press, 1985), 191.

[44] Orel, *Thomas Hardy's Personal Writings*, 135.

[45] Hardy, *Jude*, 308, 336.

[46] This in a letter of December 1884. See Henry James, *Letters*, ed. Leon Edel, 4 vols (Cambridge, MA: Belknap Press of Harvard University Press, 1974–84), III, 61.

[47] Henry James, *The Princess Casamassima*, ed. Derek Brewer (London: Penguin, 1987), 33, 480.

naturalism, as James had done, Conrad now depicts London as a monster slumbering at the bottom of an abyss like Zola's coal mine, devouring the city's inhabitants.[48]

Neither of these two last works presents an undiluted case of literary naturalism. James's naturalist visions in *The Princess Casamassima* are contained by a larger narrative structure that seems more closely aligned with Impressionism than with naturalism. For the most part, James limits the narrative to Hyacinth's point of view. The reader's perspective is mediated by the impressions of Hyacinth's sensitive consciousness: what the protagonist does not know the reader cannot know either. Similarly, Conrad's urban subject matter in *The Secret Agent* is filtered through a range of impressionist narrative techniques—achronological and elliptical narration, visualization, and delayed decoding—that allow him to capitalize on the new fictional possibilities presented by a new cultural phenomenon: the shocks and aftershocks of terrorist bombings in the age of global media and mediatization. In both James's *Princess* and Conrad's *Secret Agent*, naturalism and Impressionism combine forces, or, rather, a naturalist metaphor of a monstrous capitalist society is presented by means of impressionist narrative strategies that control the reader's perspective and response. In Hardy's *Jude*, too, the novel's naturalist content is delivered by an anonymous narrator who describes himself as the 'chronicler of these lives', on whose 'seemings' or 'personal impressions' the reader remains utterly dependent for information.[49]

Insofar as naturalist visions of society in James, Conrad, and Hardy are contained within the ironic, relativizing narrative structures of impressionism, naturalism seems to be relegated to a subordinate role in an emergent Anglo-American modernism. But naturalism infiltrated the metaphorical systems of impressionist texts and invaded their plots. Formally speaking, Galsworthy's *The Forsyte Saga* (1906–22) affiliates itself more closely with impressionism than with naturalism, as the limited third-person narrative is rotated among several different characters, relativizing narrative authority by suggesting how knowledge depends on each individual's perspective. But the saga's plot is in many ways driven by a naturalistic struggle for survival and dominance among the various members of the Forsyte family. Galsworthy indicates as much by writing of how the ageing patriarch Old Jolyon feels 'that secret hostility natural between brothers, the roots of which— little nursery rivalries—sometimes toughen and deepen as life goes on, and, all hidden, support a plant capable of producing in season the bitterest fruits'. As this example shows, Galsworthy employs metaphor to link the rivalry plot to natural processes that issue in both fruitfulness and decay, evolution and degeneration. Sometimes it seems that the upward thrust of social ambition, embodied by the Forsyte dynasty-in-the-making, may be thwarted by the counter-thrust of

---

[48] See Joseph Conrad, *The Secret Agent*, ed. Bruce Harkness and S. W. Reid (Cambridge: Cambridge University Press, 1990), 203, 224.

[49] Hardy, *Jude*, 401, 3–4.

naturalistic downward mobility, the fate that greets the majority of London's middle class, seen here emerging from their cabs into the fog: 'cabs loomed dim-shaped ever and again, and discharged citizens bolting like rabbits to their burrows... In the great warren, each rabbit for himself.' Galsworthy reinforces his naturalist survival plot at crucial moments by using the metaphor of the beast in humanity to picture characters in states of extreme emotion. When the estranged Irene returns to the house of her first husband, Soames Forsyte, she is 'like an animal wounded to death' as she re-enters the 'cage she had pined to be free of'; when Young Jolyon—Irene's future husband and Soames's cousin—appears at their house, Soames slams the door in his face with 'a sound like a snarl'.[50]

Naturalism invades the plots even of Impressionism's central achievements. Ford Madox Ford's *The Good Soldier*, first published in 1915, is widely regarded as a masterpiece of literary Impressionism, and the correspondences between the often self-referential narrative practices of the narrator, John Dowell, and the theoretical statements of his creator are impossible to deny. But those correspondences are sometimes taken to imply a sympathetic bond between author and narrator that hardly stands up to scrutiny. The two have obvious differences: Dowell is an American, a Quaker, and well-to-do; Ford was none of those things. But consider also what Dowell achieves under cover of relating the 'saddest story' he says he has ever heard: he rids himself of a wife he cannot bear, he inherits her money and then, after his friend Edward Ashburnham has cut his own throat, he gets the girl Edward could not have and acquires the Ashburnham family estate.[51]

Typically read as a moving tale of tortured desire narrated by a figure reflecting the author's own bewilderment in the face of personal and wider historical experience, *The Good Soldier* has at its core a naturalist tale of ruthless struggle for sex and money, a tale in which one character's upward mobility (Dowell gets richer and richer) occurs at the expense of another's downward slide (Edward gets poorer and poorer). One might argue that what really counts here is Dowell's Impressionism, the narrative techniques he employs—with his creator's backing—to convey his shock and confusion at the maelstrom of events that have torn apart what he had thought was a perfect, orderly social world. That is how *The Good Soldier* is usually approached: sympathetically, unsceptically, unironically. Dowell's notorious unreliability in matters of chronology is typically seen as epistemological, not moral, his confusion as inadvertent, not intentional. Yet there is nothing in Ford's text to reassure us of Dowell's sincerity. Nor is there any evidence, other than Dowell's own word, that his unreliability and confusion must be treated as symptoms of trauma, rather than as signs of a narratorial ruse, of a ploy to win the reader's sympathy and trust as he has

[50] John Galsworthy, *The Forstye Saga*, ed. Geoffrey Harvey (Oxford: Oxford University Press, 1995), 160, 252, 294, 297.

[51] Ford Madox Ford, *The Good Soldier: A Tale of Passion*, ed. Thomas C. Moser (Oxford: Oxford University Press, 1999), 7.

(he says) won Edward's. *The Good Soldier* may well be an impressionist tale of bewildered subjectivity, of a disorientated self suffering from symptoms of Impressionism while attempting to confront the disorder of the modern world. But it may also be read as a naturalist tale in impressionist camouflage. It may be read, in other words, as the story of what happens when a monster fakes impressionism and gets away with it: when he uses impressionist techniques as a rhetorical strategy in a struggle (with other characters) for sex and money or (with other characters and also the reader) for narrative authority.

Jean Rhys thought that Ford himself was faking it, and in her first novel, published as *Postures* in 1928 but later called *Quartet*, she took her revenge. Like Ford, with whom she had an affair, Rhys has been read as an impressionist, and her simple, lucid sentences certainly appear well suited to render the 'impression of the moment', as Ford had called for, and to illuminate the operations of a human consciousness tormented by what Rhys herself termed 'obsessions of love and hatred'.[52] But these same sentences also gesture outwards to suggest that what looks like inwardness may be a pose, a deliberate posture. Rhys redeploys *The Good Soldier*'s language of bewilderment and tortured desire as a style of self-presentation to show how in all their words and actions Heidler and his wife Lois—modelled on Ford and his companion Stella Bowen—are acting out a social and sexual strategy designed to control the autobiographical heroine, Marya Zelli. Thus, as he prepares to meet with Marya and her husband, Stephan, who has just completed a prison sentence for theft, Heidler 'carefully arranged his face to look perfectly expressionless', echoing the blank demeanour worn by Edward Ashburnam, but with this difference: expressionlessness comes naturally to Edward, Dowell implies, because he is a dumb blond, whereas in Heidler's case it has to be manufactured. Rhys frequently mimics Ford's language—Marya's relatives are described as 'quite good people' while the Heidlers are said to speak in a 'tone of puzzled bewilderment'—in order to satirize not only Ford's style but his intentions, intimating that his sentimentalism is the pose of a self-indulgent manipulator. '"I love you; I can't help it"', Heidler tells Marya. '"It's not your fault; it's not my fault. I love you; I'm burnt up with it. It's a fact. There it is, nobody's fault. Why can't you just accept it instead of straining against it all the time? You make things so difficult for me and for yourself."'[53] In reassigning the language of bewilderment and sentimentality used by Ford's narrator, Dowell, to Heidler, the character she based on Ford, Rhys suggests that those same qualities may amount to nothing less than a rhetoric of personality, of posture and imposture, which establishes Impressionism not merely as the innocent verbal record of intense emotional and psychological states but rather as a set of literary strategies that may be exploited for social as well as aesthetic

---

[52] Ford, 'On Impressionism', in Frank MacShane (ed.), *Critical Writings of Ford Madox Ford* (Lincoln, NE: University of Nebraska Press, 1964), 41; Jean Rhys, *Quartet* (New York: W. W. Norton, 1997), 97.

[53] Ibid., 138, 16, 98, 100.

purposes. Rhys collapses Dowell into Ford with a vengeance, indicting the author while providing indirect evidence for seeing his narrator, too, as a monster of manipulation.

Like *The Good Soldier*, *Postures* is built around a naturalist plot; unlike Ford's novel, Rhys's text is overt in exposing the naturalist foundations of its formally impressionist superstructure. Like all of Rhys's novels—most famously *Wide Sargasso Sea* (1966)—*Postures* tells a tale of downward mobility, or degeneration. Marya may come from 'quite good people', like Ford's well-to-do Edwardians, but she runs aground on the shoals of sex, alcohol, and poverty, and at the end of the novel is assaulted and left for dead by the duplicitous Stephan.[54] Rhys's arrangement of her characters mirrors the 'little four-square coterie' described in *The Good Soldier*, an explicit resemblance that may have motivated her decision in 1929 to retitle her novel *Quartet*. Evoking the formal order of musical composition, the new title also suggests formal restriction: not so much the solid construction of Dowell's 'four-square house' as the oppressive walls of a prison. 'It wasn't a minuet that we stepped', Dowell exclaims, 'it was a prison – a prison full of screaming hysterics'.[55] The prison—one of naturalism's central metaphors for the grinding mechanisms of an oppressive capitalist society—reappears in Rhys's text not only as Stephan's place of incarceration but also as a figure for wider forms of social oppression. Indeed Rhys combines the prison with the Gothic metaphor of the monster: when Marya goes to visit Stephan at Fresnes, 'a dark, dank corridor like the open mouth of a monster swallowed her up'. Rhys's monstrous devouring prison turns its inmates into animals; the prisoner's cell is a 'cage'. The prison is, however, a metaphor for a larger social condition, from which there may be no escape. ' "If anybody tried to catch me and lock me up I'd fight like a wild animal; I'd fight till they let me out or till I died," ' Marya tells Stephan. ' "Oh, no, you wouldn't, not for long, believe me," ' Stephan replies. ' "You'd do as the others do – you'd wait and be a wild animal when you came out ... When you come out – but you don't come out. Nobody ever comes out." ' Not content to let things rest so simply, Rhys indicates elsewhere that Marya's sense of entrapment may be the result of her entanglement with the Heidlers, or even of her own temperament. It is by sustaining both of these possibilities at once—this may be an impressionist tale of bewildered subjectivity, or it may be a naturalist tale of the individual ensnared by larger social forces like 'an animal caught in a trap'—that Rhys's first novel achieves its peculiar distinction.[56]

In Rhys's text, impressionism—especially Fordian impressionism—takes an ironic turn, as it becomes inseparable from the literary naturalism against which it had previously defined itself. Or rather, it took one of many ironic turns. In his later novels, Ford's impressionism turns back on itself and subverts its own premises, as impressions become mere impressions of impressions in a gesture that mimics the inflationary logic of the financial markets during the Great Depression: a surreptitiously realist

---

[54] Ibid., 16.   [55] Ford, *Good Soldier*, 9, 11.   [56] Rhys, *Quartet*, 55, 35, 136, 90.

gesture, in other words. In Woolf, too, impressionism proves unstable or double. It shifts in *To the Lighthouse* (1927) and *The Waves* (1931) towards the formal abstraction that is sometimes associated with 'post-impressionism', and yet returns in *The Years* (1937) to realism only to renew and reinforce it.[57] David Bradshaw's annotations to *Mrs Dalloway* make it very clear that this text, celebrated for its formal and stylistic experimentalism, remains thick with social and historical reference. If the novel exemplifies stream-of-consciousness writing, as is often claimed, the stream has banks and those banks are lined by actual buildings and historic monuments.[58] Woolf's London is, in this respect, a realist's London. Moreover, in merging literary impressionist technique with a materialist theory of shock, as we noted earlier, *Mrs Dalloway* illustrates on another level how experimental modernism remains implicated in realism: shock is shown to be a fact of modern life.

Indeed modernism's continued intimacy with realism is one of the crucial lessons, formally and aesthetically speaking, of the most famously experimental text of all: Joyce's *Ulysses* (1922). Setting out in the free-indirect mode of his 'initial style',[59] Joyce changed course in the middle of the book, shifting the balance from realism to mythic symbolism to such a degree that Ezra Pound—who had championed the early episodes as the apotheosis of Flaubertian realism—felt that something had gone wrong. 'Where in hell is Stephen Telemachus?' Pound asked.[60] Pound wanted Joyce's realism back. And that is what happened in the final episode. The classic case of modernist stream of consciousness and so, in a sense, of literary impressionism, Joyce's 'Penelope' episode represents a return to 'mimesis of mind', as modernism's supreme literary achievement, later hailed by Jean-François Lyotard as the first great postmodernist text, also reveals itself to be the last great Victorian realist novel.[61] Late Victorian into modern? Here, at least, modern shades into late Victorian.

FURTHER READING

Armstrong, Paul. *The Challenge of Bewilderment: Understanding and Representation in James, Conrad, and Ford* (Ithaca, NY: Cornell University Press, 1987).

---

[57] On Ford's late ironic turn, see Parkes, *A Sense of Shock*, 178–203. On Woolf's response to the 'post-impressionist' theory of her friend Roger Fry, who coined the term, see ibid., 146–77.

[58] David Bradshaw, 'Explanatory Notes', in Woolf, *Mrs Dalloway*, 166–85.

[59] Stuart Gilbert (ed.), *Letters of James Joyce*, 3 vols (New York: Viking, 1957), I, 129.

[60] Forrest Read (ed.), *Pound/Joyce: The Letters of Ezra Pound to James Joyce, with Pound's Essays on Joyce* (New York: New Directions, 1970), 158.

[61] The term 'mimesis of mind' is John Paul Riquelme's in *Teller and Tale in Joyce's Fiction: Oscillating Perspectives* (Baltimore, MD: Johns Hopkins University Press, 1983), 225. Jean-François Lyotard cites *Ulysses* as an exemplary instance of postmodernism, understood as 'not modernism at its end but in the nascent state', in *The Postmodern Condition: A Report on Knowledge*, trans. Geoff Bennington and Brian Massumi (Minneapolis, MN: University of Minnesota Press, 1984), 79–81.

Bagulay, David. *Naturalist Fiction: The Entropic Vision* (Cambridge: Cambridge University Press, 1990).

Beaumont, Matthew (ed.). *Adventures in Realism* (Oxford: Blackwell, 2007).

Jameson, Fredric. *The Political Unconscious: Narrative as a Socially Symbolic Act* (Ithaca, NY: Cornell University Press, 1981).

Joyce, Simon. *Modernism and Naturalism in British and Irish Fiction, 1880–1930* (New York: Cambridge University Press, 2015).

Katz, Tamar. *Impressionist Subjects: Gender, Interiority, and Modernist Fiction in England* (Urbana, IL: University of Illinois Press, 2000).

Keating, Peter. *The Haunted Study: A Social History of the English Novel, 1875–1914* (London: Secker & Warburg, 1989).

Levenson, Michael. *A Genealogy of Modernism: A Study of English Literary Doctrine, 1908–1922* (Cambridge: Cambridge University Press, 1984).

Levenson, Michael. *Modernism and the Fate of Individuality: Character and Novelistic Form from Conrad to Woolf* (Cambridge: Cambridge University Press, 1991).

Matz, Jesse. *Literary Impressionism and Modernist Aesthetics* (Cambridge: Cambridge University Press, 2001).

Nelson, Brian (ed.). *Naturalism in the European Novel* (Oxford and Providence, RI: Berg, 1992).

Parkes, Adam. *A Sense of Shock: The Impact of Impressionism on Modern British and Irish Writing* (New York: Oxford University Press, 2011).

Peters, John G. *Conrad and Impressionism* (Cambridge and New York: Cambridge University Press, 2001).

Saunders, Max. *Self Impression: Life-writing, Autobiografiction, and the Forms of Modern Literature* (Oxford: Oxford University Press, 2010).

Trotter, David. *The English Novel in History, 1895–1920* (Abingdon and New York: Routledge, 1993).

Watt, Ian. *Conrad in the Nineteenth Century* (Berkeley, CA: University of California Press, 1979).

CHAPTER 12

THE RISE OF SHORT FICTION

ADRIAN HUNTER

In accounting for the rise of the novel, Ian Watt had first to say what the novel was. The roster of defining characteristics he came up with—realism, particularism, individualism—performed the useful trick of describing both the formal properties of a genre and the world view of the people who consumed it. The short story has never had its Ian Watt, which is to say that the study of its narrative habits has tended to remain detached from an understanding of the circumstances that brought them about. This is not universally true—one thinks of exceptions such as Andrew Levy's *The Culture and Commerce of the American Short Story* (1993), for example, or Maggie Awadalla and Paul March-Russell's *The Postcolonial Short Story* (2012)—but it is true enough, and it helps to account for the time warp in which critical writing on short fiction often appears to be trapped. The contents page of a recent volume of essays typifies the presiding and enduring concerns of the field: the legacy of Poe, the relationship to the novel, cognitive approaches to storyness, closure, narrative framing, reader response theory, pragmatics, and discourse analysis.[1] Where history features at all in this work, it is as a series of period placeholders for critical concepts that are, to all intents, being applied *trans*historically.

The oddity of this situation is that short fiction studies, at least in English, is very obviously in thrall to a particular historical movement, modernism, and to modernist aesthetics as they were later incarnated in structuralist and post-structuralist critical theory. Even today, there is a strong inclination to treat the short story, *pace* Barthes, as an 'intransitive' body of writing—the 'distilled essence' of modernist narrative, as one critic puts it, long on aesthetic purposiveness and light on worldly purpose.[2] If anything, the mass professionalization of creative writing since the 1970s has only abetted this tendency to valorize a fragmentary, impressionistic,

---

[1] Viorica Patea (ed.), *Short Story Theories: A Twenty-First Century Perspective* (Amsterdam: Rodopi, 2012).

[2] Dominic Head, *The Modernist Short Story: A Study in Theory and Practice* (Cambridge: Cambridge University Press, 1992), 6.

minimalist aesthetic of the form derived ultimately from modernism. It may be that the 'workshop' environment of the creative writing classroom induces a dependency on readily 'teachable' forms such as minimalism; at any rate, the result has been to enshrine a version of the short story that, as James Wood points out, is 'essentially sub-Chekhovian': elliptical in its grammar, and 'monotonously fragmentary' in its effects.[3]

There are, though, signs that this situation is beginning to change. Paul March-Russell, for example, has recently taken issue with the 'reactionary ideological positions' concealed in many seminal accounts of the short story, and has suggested ways in which scholarship might break the 'deadlock' imposed by formalism.[4] In a different spirit, Ann-Marie Einhaus has brought to light a whole new corpus of primary materials through *The Short Story and the First World War* (2013). The advent of the 'new modernist studies', meanwhile, has not only transformed the study of canonical texts, but introduced an historical perspective at once more capacious and discriminating and self-reflexive than would have seemed likely during the heyday of 'Pound Era' criticism. For the student of short fiction, the possibilities opened up by the 'new modernist studies' are especially intriguing, not just because they extend the area of study chronologically and territorially, but because they allow for the recovery of work hitherto excluded by dint of its insusceptibility to modernist-formalist paradigms of reading. The 'new modernist studies' still talks about modernism, of course, using the term to refer to writing that is, in Rita Felski's words, 'formally self-conscious, experimental [and] antimimetic'.[5] What it rejects, however, is the assumption that modernism was '*the* aesthetic of modernity' at the turn of the twentieth century, and that modernism was (and is) coterminous with the period 1880–1920, rather than being a constituent of it, one discourse among many.[6] Furthermore, the 'new modernist studies' exposes the extent to which modernist self-fashioning was predicated on more than just the rejection of a phantasmagoric (and frequently feminized) mass cultural other, or the denigration of a particular group of Edwardian realists. Rather, it took the form of a widespread 'exiling' of rival genres, writers, and movements, including those associated with an earlier incarnation of avant-gardism, in the 1890s.[7]

All of this is of some moment to the study of short fiction, since the persistence of the modernist paradigm has had the effect of homogenizing the years 1880–1920, and

[3] James Wood, 'A Long Day at the Chocolate Bar Factory', *London Review of Books* 26/4 (2004), 26.

[4] Paul March-Russell, *The Short Story: An Introduction* (Edinburgh: Edinburgh University Press, 2009), 86.

[5] Rita Felski, *The Gender of Modernism* (Cambridge, MA and London: Harvard University Press, 1995), 25.

[6] Ann Ardis, *Modernism and Cultural Conflict, 1880–1922* (Cambridge: Cambridge University Press, 2008), 115.

[7] See Celeste M. Schenck, 'Exiled by Genre: Modernism, Canonicity, and the Politics of Exclusion', in Mary Lynn Broe and Angela Ingram (eds), *Women's Writing in Exile* (Chapel Hill, NC and London: University of North Carolina Press, 1989), 225–50.

of thereby masking the ideological conflicts and cross-currents that more precisely explain the short story's rise to prominence as a prestigious artistic form. In what follows, I return to the 1890s to examine some of the circumstances surrounding the remarkable elevation in the short story's fortunes in that decade. My aim in doing so is not merely to enlarge the historical record, but to demonstrate that it was in the 1890s, rather than in the 1910s, that the short story became aligned with values and practices of a literary avant-garde, and entered into its distinctively modernist phase.

Tales of the city

In her contribution to the volume *Outside Modernism*, Lynne Hapgood argues against taking the Men (and Women) of 1914 at their self-affirming word. She has in mind the modernist iconoclastic rejection of *fin-de-siècle* and Edwardian writers as so many unselfconscious realists, content to dwell in the familiar rooms of fiction inherited from their Victorian predecessors. On the contrary, Hapgood suggests, we should recognize that realism in this period was 'productively unstable and transformative', and that realist writers made a 'distinctive contribution' to the modernist struggle to define a new, great, age of literature. By reorienting our approach so as to detect the 'content-responsive innovativeness' of realist writing, Hapgood says, we can succeed both in bringing neglected work to attention, and in folding high modernism back into 'a democratic alliance of literary modes ... where difference and common heritage can be equally celebrated'.[8]

Revisiting modernism's complicated relationship to the prevailing modes of late-Victorian realism is particularly fruitful in the case of the short story in the 1890s, since it was in that decade that writers and critics began distinguishing between 'literary' and 'popular' varieties of the form, and a three-way alignment between realism, the short story, and various forms of cultural radicalism and avant-gardism came into being. We can trace the origins of that alignment to a sequence of chapters George Saintsbury published in the *Fortnightly Review*, in 1887-8, in which he contemplated the relative merits of the realist and romance modes in fiction. Saintsbury's preference was strongly for the latter, which he regarded as more intrinsically English. Tales of exoticism and adventure by the likes of Robert Louis Stevenson and H. Rider Haggard had about them, Saintsbury believed, a 'healthy beefiness and beeriness' that was much more to native tastes than the 'portraiture of manners' and 'dissection of character' favoured by the European realists.[9] Haggard, for his part, agreed with Saintsbury that realism was

---

[8] Lynne Hapgood, 'Transforming the Victorian', in Lynne Hapgood and Nancy L. Paxton (eds), *Outside Modernism: In Pursuit of the English Novel, 1900–30* (Basingstoke: Macmillan, 2000), 32, 22, 31.

[9] George Saintsbury, 'The Present State of the Novel: I', *Fortnightly Review* 42 (September 1887), 415.

not only superficial and modish but an affront to timeless universal principles of narrative and social justice. 'The love of romance', he wrote, 'is probably coeval with the existence of humanity'. The 'accursed' French naturalists, on the other hand, not only debased readers (especially women) but depressed them with their bloodless depictions of a 'dreary age'.[10]

The terms of debate that Saintsbury and Haggard established, and in particular the idea that romance had a wider and more essential appeal than realism, were rehearsed in chapters and reviews throughout the early 1890s by the likes of H. D. Traill, Maurice Thomson, James Sully, Mary D. Cutting, and Andrew Lang.[11] Defenders of the 'new realism', as it came to be called, were generally content to concede the point about popular taste; indeed, many were eager to underline the association of romance with lower and more populist forms of entertainment, because it implied that realism was more closely related to literariness. For Edmund Gosse, the special value of realism lay in its potential to completely revolutionize the forms of English fiction, first by divesting it of its perennial topic, 'amatory intrigue',[12] and then by finishing off, once and for all, 'the old "well-made" plot'.[13] Saintsbury would have agreed with that: realism was indeed anathema to the virtues of traditional storytelling. As he put it, quite the most deplorable thing about realism was its distinctly 'modern conception that a tale ought to tell nothing'.[14]

If 'plotlessness' was becoming a marker of 'literariness', it was also increasingly identified with a type of short story that was beginning to populate the pages of upmarket magazines. Henry James was among the first to spot the new species, seizing on the talent of younger writers, especially those associated with the *Yellow Book*, to render in a very few and fragmented words the 'impression...of a complexity or a continuity', and to transcend the generally facile purposes which the short story was called to serve in the popular journals of the day.[15] Many influential commentators echoed James's observations, singling out the 'plotless' short story— the story that 'begin[s] nowhere and end[s] nowhere'[16]—as a prestigious, rather than commercial, form. An 1897 *Bookman* symposium 'How to Write a Short Story', for example, made much of the way these new 'open' narratives, in which 'certain

---

[10] H. Rider Haggard, 'About Fiction', *Contemporary Review* 51 (February 1887), 172, 176.

[11] For a flavour of the debate see H. D. Traill, 'Romance Realisticised', *Contemporary Review* 59 (February 1891), 200–9; Unsigned, 'A New Novelist', *Westminster Review* 128/1 (April 1887), 841; Maurice Thomson, 'The Domain of Romance', *Forum* 8 (November 1889), 326–36; James Sully, 'The Future of Fiction', *Forum* 8 (August 1890), 644–57; Mary D. Cutting, 'Two Forces in Fiction', *Forum* 10 (October 1890), 216–25.

[12] Edmund Gosse, 'The Tyranny of the Novel', *National Review* 19/110 (April 1892), 170.

[13] Gosse, 'The Limits of Realism in Fiction', *Forum* 9 (June 1890), 399.

[14] George Saintsbury, 'The Present State of the Novel: II', *Fortnightly Review* 43/253 (January 1888), 118.

[15] Henry James, 'The Story-Teller at Large: Mr Henry Harland', *Fortnightly Review* 63/374 (April 1898), 653.

[16] Hall Caine, 'The New Watchwords of Fiction', *Contemporary Review* 57 (April 1890), 486.

points [were] hinted at rather than fully expressed', were premised on a rejection of more marketable forms of writing, and, by extension, of a docile reading public who didn't mind 'being fed with a spoon'.[17]

Among the contributors to the *Bookman* symposium was Arthur Morrison. Morrison is a fascinating writer to consider in the light of these debates, because he was able to write successfully for both the elite and popular sectors of the market. Widely known for the Martin Hewitt detective series published in George Newnes's *Strand Magazine* in 1893-4, Morrison was in the same years turning out stories of a quite different sort, and for a different form of 'capital', in W. E. Henley's highbrow *National Observer*. Simply by comparing the kinds of fiction Morrison wrote for these diverse venues, we can see more clearly how a particular version of the short story began to take on prestige as a literary form amenable to what we would now recognize as a distinctly modernist set of values.

Morrison's subject in almost all that he wrote was London and, like the Sherlock Holmes adventures they were commissioned to replace, his Martin Hewitt stories depicted a city that, for all its threatening social diversity, was yet susceptible to the superfine deductive faculties of the freelance detective.[18] Like Holmes, Hewitt was capable of navigating the whole urban precinct, putting faces and names to threateningly anonymous misdeeds and bringing the city 'back to human scale'.[19] Indeed, his modest middle-class demeanour and humble beginnings as a legal office clerk seemed designed to make him resemble the average *Strand* reader, and thus provided an even more reassuring presence to fearful Londoners than did the loftily aristocratic Holmes. Many of Hewitt's adventures were played out in squalid quarters of the city, where the sheer mass of diverse humanity was bound to overwhelm the resources of civil government and its agents. In 'The Case of the Dixon Torpedo', for example, Hewitt successfully pursues his quarry, a Russian forger trying to smuggle military secrets out of Britain, to Little Carton Street, Westminster,

> a seedy sort of place—one of those old streets that have seen much better days. A good many people seem to live in each house—they are fairly large houses, by the way—and there is quite a company of bell-handles on each doorpost—all down the side, like organ-stops.[20]

---

[17] Robert Barr, Harold Frederic, Arthur Morrison, and Jane Barlow, 'How to Write a Short Story: A Symposium', *Bookman* 5/1 (March 1897), 43.

[18] For an overview of Morrison's detective fiction see John Greenfield, 'Arthur Morrison's Sherlock Clone: Martin Hewitt, Victorian Values, and London Magazine Culture, 1894–1903', *Victorian Periodicals Review* 35/1 (2002), 18–36. On the cult of Holmes imitations and parodies more generally, see Peter Rigway Watt and Joseph Green, *The Alternative Sherlock Holmes: Pastiches, Parodies and Copies* (Aldershot and Burlington, VT: Ashgate, 2003).

[19] Richard Lehan, *The City in Literature: An Intellectual and Cultural History* (Berkeley, CA and London: University of California Press, 1998), 84.

[20] Arthur Morrison, 'The Case of the Dixon Torpedo', *Strand* 7 (January 1894), 569.

In 'The Affair of the Tortoise', another story in which a criminal holes up in the labyrinth of the East End, Hewitt remarks to the narrator (the stolid, Watson-like Brett) that ' "[t]here is nothing in this world that is at all possible... that has not happened or is not happening in London" ';[21] and yet, by combining the diligence of the clerk with an instinct for natural justice, he is able not only to uncover the *detectable* relations between things in the city, but also bring a moral intelligence to bear on its happenings. Modern London might play host to a whole 'criminal class' able to make an 'exclusive profession' of theft and violence, yet *Strand* readers could rest assured that by a combination of acute reasoning and sound principle, one could prepare, like Hewitt, for 'encountering this class when it became necessary'.[22]

The contrast with the stories Morrison wrote for Henley's *National Observer*, all of them set in the East End slum, could hardly be more stark. Where the Martin Hewitt stories deal in containment—both formally, and in the way they curb the feral elements of the city—the *Observer* stories stage their incompleteness, advancing towards some putative point of definition or disclosure only to swerve off into equivocation or lacunae. A sense of deficit and wilful curtailment pervades the narration, not least in the subdued and ironic third-person voice Morrison favours, which frequently alludes to the importance of motive and psychology, for example, only to forbid access to these determinants of character and action. 'To Bow Bridge' is a good example of what Morrison was able to achieve in these stories. It is a tale of fleeting travelling coincidence, centred on the observations of an unnamed passenger on a late-night tram mobbed with boisterous drinkers headed for Bow and last orders. From among the 'mass of people—howling, struggling and blaspheming',[23] three parties are singled out for observation: a quiet mechanic, a prostitute, and a woman who boards with three small children. The prostitute is brought into contact with the woman and children when the little girl stumbles and she helps her up. The well-dressed mother tries to overlook the proffered kindness but is powerless to resist the prostitute's subsequent intervention as they disembark from the tram. The story ends:

> The harlot, lingering, lifted the child again—lifted her rather high and set her on the path with the others. Then she walked away toward the Bombay Grab. A man in a blue serge suit was footing it down the turning between the public-house and the bridge with drunken swiftness and an intermittent stagger; and, tightening her shawl, she went in chase.
> The quiet mechanic stood and stretched himself, and took a corner seat near the door; and the tram-car, quiet and vacant, bumped on westward.[24]

---

[21] Morrison, 'The Affair of the Tortoise', *Strand* 8 (July 1894), 269.
[22] Morrison, 'The Quinton Jewel Affair', *Strand* 8 (July 1894), 60.
[23] Morrison, *Tales of Mean Streets* (London: Methuen, 1894), 87.
[24] Ibid., 93.

What is striking about 'To Bow Bridge' is the extent to which it is prepared to con-cede authority over its subject. There is nothing knowing in the narrator's encounter with the mechanic, the mother, or the prostitute; what pervades the narrative, rather, is a sense of what Elizabeth Bowen, describing her own short stories, would later call 'human unknowableness'.[25] Unlike the urban detective, or Dickens's Boz granting imaginary inner life to the 'little pantomimes' of Seven Dials and Monmouth Street, or even the narrator of Poe's 'The Man of the Crowd', confidently anatomizing the London tribes from the elevated repose of his coffee-house window, Morrison does not attempt to recuperate for some higher narrative purpose the arbitrariness and transitoriness of social character in the city. There is no more to say about the quiet mechanic with which the story ends because no more is known. To that extent, the narrative reflects the way in which cities 'promise plenitude, but deliver inaccessibil-ity', presenting to the observer a 'never-ending series of partial visibilities'.[26] Where a Holmes or a Hewitt might have made out the *detectable* relations between these glimpsed lives, the narrator of 'To Bow Bridge' is divested of any such power. He is in many ways more akin to the impersonal metropolitan dweller of Georg Simmel's classic 1903 chapter 'The Metropolis and Mental Life' who can pretend to knowledge and understanding of only a fraction of the many people he encounters daily. As Simmel describes, to register each contact in the modern city, to grant it emotional space, would be to fall into 'an unthinkable mental condition'[27]—hence the self-preserving disinterest, the blessed 'unknowableness', into which the urbanite retreats. In placing information of determining significance outside of the frame of the narrative, only then to allude to its unobtainability, Morrison offers a wholly different kind of encounter with the city from that dramatized in the detective story—an encounter in which the dissident elements, the enduring lawless drinkers and prostitutes, remain fugitive from order both civic and narrative.

In common with George Gissing, Richard Le Gallienne, Hubert Crackanthorpe, and others, Morrison found the 'plotless' short form peculiarly amenable to the rep-resentational demands of urban modernity. In many respects, a story like 'To Bow Bridge' answers to the vision Baudelaire (an important figure for many *fin-de-siècle* English writers) had presented some years earlier, of a literary form capable of ren-dering the experience of 'enormous cities' and their 'innumerable connections'—a form, as he foresaw in the dedicatory letter to his *Prose Poems* of 1862, that would eschew the fanciful fixtures of plot and closure, having 'neither head nor tail, since everything, on the contrary, is both head and tail, alternatively and reciprocally'.[28]

---

[25] Elizabeth Bowen, *After-Thought: Pieces about Writing* (London: Longman, 1962), 94.

[26] Hana Wirth-Nesher, *City Codes: Reading the Modern Urban Novel* (Cambridge: Cambridge University Press, 1996), 8.

[27] Donald N. Levine (ed.), *On Individuality and Social Forms: Selected Writings of Georg Simmel* (Chicago, IL and London: University of Chicago Press, 1971), 331.

[28] Charles Baudelaire, *The Prose Poems and La Fanfarlo*, trans. Rosemary Lloyd (Oxford: Oxford University Press, 1991), 30.

Of course, it is with high modernism that we generally associate the search for artistic media commensurate to the experience of urban modernity—a search that finds its apotheosis, at least for students of Anglo-American literature, in Eliot's *The Waste Land*. But as Georg Lukács reminds us, and the short story in the 1890s demonstrates, the origins of that quest lie further back, in the static descriptive mode of narration characteristic of late nineteenth-century naturalist writing. For Lukács, the naturalist text's tendency to present a 'superficial...fortuitous sequence of isolated static pictures', rather than to explore, or 'narrate', the inner 'vital relations' and 'transformational possibilities' of social life, marked the first stage in what, from an ideological point of view, was actually a retreat from the moral challenges that advanced capitalist culture posed.[29] Be that as it may, the point remains that the 'plotless' short story, in the way that it debunked any gesture towards narrative totality, substituting experience for explanation (or 'description' for 'narration', to use Lukács's terms), was evolving, well before Eliot or Woolf, a formally radical method of narrating the city and its multitudes.

Gendered genre

The forms and functions of 'plotlessness' would continue to dominate discussions of short fiction in the decades to come, as the magazine market fragmented further, and the scholarly literature surrounding the form began to develop in earnest. Studies such as Henry Seidel Canby's *The Short Story* (1902), Barry Pain's *The Short Story* (1916), Henry Albert Phillips's *Art in Short Story Narration* (1913), and Alfred C. Ward's *Aspects of the Modern Short Story: English and American* (1924), all follow James's lead in distinguishing not just between 'open' and 'closed' forms of story, but between the different categories of reader who patronized them. As Pain put it, 'those who want everything done for them by the author, and not to find their own imagination set to work...these are the readers whom the artist of the short story cannot please'.[30] These early assignments in critical definition are perhaps best understood as efforts to set the short story aside from its customary uses, detaching it once and for all from its reputation as a low-status popular genre and sometime fixture of the penny dreadful. In every case, the key to doing that was to insist that the radical, literary variant of the form should deal in social, urban, domestic, or psychological realism.

Nowhere was the connection between radicalism and realism more apparent than on the pages of the most widely read and influential avant-garde publication of the

---

[29] Georg Lukács, 'Narrate or Describe?', in *Writer and Critic*, trans. Arthur Kahn (London: Merlin Press, 1970), 144.

[30] Alfred C. Ward, *Aspects of the Modern Short Story: English and American* (London: University of London Press, 1924), 48.

day, John Lane's *Yellow Book*. In the short stories that dominated the literary content of Lane's journal, we find numerous studies of failed or failing marriages and restless New Womanhood, as well as portraits of contemporary masculinity that are wildly at odds with the resurgent male heroism of the romance. Under its editor, Henry Harland, the *Yellow Book* fashioned an ideological alliance between feminism, experimental realism, and avant-garde cultural politics that found its pre-eminent expression in the work of writers specializing in the short story, among them Ella D'Arcy, Evelyn Sharp, Frances E. Huntley (Ethel Colburn Mayne), Victoria Cross (Vivian Cory), George Egerton (Mary Chavelita Dunne), and Hubert Crackanthorpe, all of whom were alert to the ways in which the 'plotless' short story could be used to dramatize the ambivalent new reality of sexual and gender relationships and identity that feminism and the New Woman had brought into view. Indeed, as Teresa Mangum points out, the *Yellow Book*'s radical reputation was largely made by its willingness to run New Woman and bad marriage stories, works that were both formally experimental and prepared to explore and question the 'complex set of signs that demarcated masculinity and femininity'.[31] It was the sort of association that was crucial to the raising of the short story's status in this period, connecting the form to a radical social agenda and, by extension, to the cultural avant-garde.

Harland himself did much to direct debates about gender and femininity towards a consideration of the forms of literary fiction. In his 'Yellow Dwarf' column, he argued that mass-market popular fiction and the romance carried about them a taint of simplistic masculinism, whereas everything valuable and worthwhile in contemporary writing was 'feminine'—that is, 'fine, sensitive, distinguished...beautiful'.[32] Harland's sense of the 'feminine' perhaps carried more of a political charge than this vague invocation suggests, and extended to a genuine concern about the social and psychological predicament of the New Woman. To that end he was abetted by Ella D'Arcy, who had an editorial role on the *Yellow Book* and was instrumental in emboldening both Harland and Lane to steer the journal away from the Decadent sexual puerility of its sometime art editor Aubrey Beardsley, and towards a new, politicized public agenda. As her feisty correspondence with Lane makes clear, she had considerable influence over Harland and frequently acted independently of him, much to his irritation, describing herself as his 'Guardian Angel' and boasting of her power to 'completely revis[e] his Contents-list'.[33] More often than not, that meant installing female short story writers of her preference, George Egerton among them.

For many students of this period, Egerton's name has become synonymous with New Woman fiction, and with an ambivalent yet muscular brand of feminism. In

[31] Teresa Mangum, 'Style Wars of the 1890s: The New Woman and the Decadent', in Nikki Lee Manos and Meri-Jane Rochelson (eds), *Transforming Genres: New Approaches to British Fiction of the 1890s* (Basingstoke and London: Macmillan, 1994), 49–50.
[32] [Henry Harland], 'Dogs, Cats, Books, and the Average Man', *Yellow Book* 10 (July 1896), 12.
[33] Ella D'Arcy, *Some Letters to John Lane*, ed. Alan Anderson (Edinburgh: Tragara Press, 1990), 24.

respect of the short story, her importance lies in the way she tried to adapt the form to embody feminine experience, rather than merely to account for it. As her contemporary the German feminist Laura Marholm argued at the time, Egerton's determination to reject the precepts of masculine narrative was indicative of a 'new phase in literary production' that was also 'a new phase in woman's nature'.[34] A typical Egerton story (typical, that is, of her early work, before she turned to more overtly polemical writing) dramatizes a situation in which a man finds that the woman to whom he is married, or whom he pursues, exceeds the narratives and identity positions that once would have held her, and upon which he depends for a sense of his *own* identity. A favourite device of Egerton's is to debunk the impersonal myth-making adventurism and narrative determinations of the masculine romance tradition, just as her female characters debunk the fictions of containment that men would impose on them.

So, in 'A Little Grey Glove', for example, the male narrator who seeks primitivist liberation and the 'life of a free wanderer' in a country retreat, finds himself hooked (quite literally) by an adulterous woman whose physical capability and intellectual candour cause him to abandon his adventuring for the comforts of domesticity, contemplative solitude, and—because she forces a separation between them—waiting. Yet the story more than depicts the enthralment of one man to a scandalously liberated woman: in its very structure and form it stages the ruin of self-fashioning male adventurism and its narrative declarations. Just as the narrator finds himself setting aside the storytelling conventions by which he once would have asserted himself—'I felt the same sensation once before, when I got drawn into some rapids and had an awfully narrow shave, but of that another time'—so Egerton's text converts the interim suspensefulness of the quest story into a permanent interdiction against reconciliation, fulfilment, or closure.[35] It is not only male desire for possession and dominion that is indefinitely deferred at the end of the story but what Robert Louis Stevenson, writing to Sidney Colvin in 1891, termed the 'full close' that in the romance story provides for a particular sort of narrative satisfaction.[36]

Several recent critics have suggested that Egerton's work is ideologically incoherent, and even collusive with 'hierarchical notions of ethnic and cultural difference'.[37] Her feminism has also been questioned by those who see in her sexually candid women 'a tantalizing female figure' designed to 'tease and fascinate male taste'.[38]

[34] Laura Marholm, *Modern Women*, trans. Hermione Ramsden (London: Bodley Head, 1896), 81.

[35] George Egerton, *Keynotes* (London: Elkin Mathews and John Lane, 1893), 94, 108.

[36] Ernest Mehew (ed.), *The Selected Letters of Robert Louis Stevenson* (New Haven, CT and London: Yale University Press, 1997), 464.

[37] Laura Chrisman, 'Empire, "Race" and Feminism at the *fin de siècle*: The Work of George Egerton and Olive Schreiner', in Sally Ledger and Scott McCracken (eds), *Cultural Politics at the fin de siècle* (Cambridge: Cambridge University Press, 1995), 45.

[38] Gail Cunningham, ' "He-Notes": Reconstructing Masculinity', in Angelique Richardson and Chris Willis (eds), *The New Woman in Fiction and in Fact* (Basingstoke: Palgrave, 2002), 96.

I would argue that such apparent contradictions and tensions arise out of Egerton's equivocal, interrogative short story style and her attempt not simply to contest, but to find ways out of, patriarchy and its narrative determinations. Egerton described her own writing as an exploration of 'the *terra incognita* of [woman] as she knew herself to be, not as man liked to imagine her';[39] and that meant not simply dramatizing female rebelliousness, but challenging the masculine narrative imaginary itself. To that end she developed a highly elliptical and elusive short story technique that allowed her to circumvent the 'reserve-discourse' that, as Hélène Cixous describes, 'laughs at the very idea of pronouncing the word "silence" ',[40] and prematurely imposes points of closure on female discourse.

Typically, Egerton's stories are preoccupied with scenarios of postponement, deferral, and non-fulfilment, and with dramatizing the irremediable, unsolvable tensions and contradictions inherent in women's social, political, and sexual identity even as emancipation was under way. This might be another way of saying that her feminism was unsound, of course; but one might equally well argue that it is the result of Egerton's particular deployment of the short story to investigate the complex actuality of the female subject, as she does, for example, in 'An Empty Frame'. At the beginning of this story, the unnamed heroine is pictured restlessly stripping off her clothes in a boarding-house bedroom, releasing herself from 'ensheathing' garments until she stands 'almost free' as though in 'an intense nervous relief from a thrall'. It transpires that her state of emotional excitation is the result of her having discovered that a former lover of her husband's has been in contact with him. She is not so much distressed by the reappearance of this other woman as by thoughts of the intense and passionate lover whom she herself forsook—a 'great man' who might have made of her a 'great woman'—and of her decision to marry instead the man who 'seemed to need her most out of those who admired her'.[41]

The story presents, then, the familiar fictional scenario of confinement by male mediocrity reproduced in any number of New Woman stories and novels. But Egerton is more alert to the intrigues of motive and selfhood than that straightforward narrative of oppression and conflict can allow, and capitalizes on the interrogative qualities of the 'plotless' short story to sustain that ambivalence to the very limits of her text. At the moment when the woman reduces her husband to 'utter bewilderment' with her revelations about her former lover, she moves to reaffirm their intimacy, 'touch[ing] his cheek gently and lean[ing] her head against his arm' and explaining her anger towards him as an aspect of her 'complex nature'. She then places on the fire the empty picture frame that once held the image of her former lover. The final paragraph of the story dissolves into a dream sequence in which she

[39] Egerton, quoted in John Gawsworth, *Ten Contemporaries: Notes towards Their Definitive Bibliography* (London: E. Benn, 1932), 58.

[40] Hélène Cixous, 'Medusa', in Robyn. R Worhol and Diane Price Herndl (eds), *Feminisms: An Anthology of Literary Theory and Criticism* (Basingstoke and London: Macmillan, 1997), 355.

[41] Egerton, *Keynotes*, 116, 122, 119.

imagines her own head filling the frame and expanding in size until 'she seems to be sitting inside her own head, and the inside is one vast hollow'.[42] That final image is ambiguous, suggesting both the presence and the absence of self-knowledge; but it also functions as a figure of Egerton's narrative technique, for although the narration has been focalized through the female character, following the flow of her perception, it too is something of an 'empty frame' in the way it prevents access to her interior state and repeatedly protests its own impercipience: 'The eyes tell you little; they are keen and inquiring, and probe others' thoughts rather than reveal their own.'

The ambiguity surrounding the heroine's relationship to her husband arises directly from this studied impenetrability, for the story does not make clear why she rejected her former lover. Indeed, the scene where she recollects him is largely conducted through her memory of what *he* thought and declared, and it breaks off with an ellipsis, a series of dots on the page. That missing piece, that glaring aperture, becomes a kind of determining absence in the story, creating a blur around the heroine's motives and raising questions about the true nature of her relationship with her husband; in short, it unsettles the assumption that we are reading a story about a woman spiritually, intellectually, and emotionally contained by an unsatisfactory mate. The possibility emerges that her husband is precisely the sort of man she *does* need in order to assert her own identity. Her reducing him to bewilderment and then stroking his head until he falls asleep on her breast 'like a child' allows her to define herself in a way she could not with her former lover, who was, we are told, a 'grand confident compelling genius' with something of the 'untamed, natural man lurking about the mouth and powerful throat'. In other words, the inadequate and domesticated husband, the 'unlovely object in a sleeping suit' whom she blames for the failure of her life, becomes the necessary condition of her empowerment.[43]

But by not determining the reason for her rejection of the former lover, Egerton composes a far more nuanced and conflictual portrait of her heroine—and of female empowerment in general—than would otherwise be the case. Far from betraying a naive and idealistic 'optimism about feminist self-realizability',[44] her achievement here is to utilize the resources of the interrogative short story form to expose the paradox-strewn psychological reality of women's newly acquired selfhood.

The triumph of modernism

The aversion George Egerton's stories display to determinate utterances, completed actions, and ultimate meanings might well put the reader in mind of Virginia Woolf's argument that feminine writing ought to mean more than just writing by, or about, women. It must have a formal and representational quality to it, too:

---

[42] Ibid., 122–3.   [43] Ibid., 117, 123, 117–18, 120.   [44] Cixous, 'Medusa', 355.

'when we write of a woman, everything is out of place—culminations and perorations; the accent never falls where it does with a man.'[45] Those culminations and perorations and other gestures of narrative forcefulness are what Egerton, at least in her early work, consistently eschews.

How surprising, then, to discover that, with the notable exception of Katherine Mansfield, the later modernists scarcely make any acknowledgement of the work of Egerton or her contemporaries. Mansfield, the exception, read widely in 1890s fiction and poetry throughout her short career, developing a fascination with Oscar Wilde and with the sexual and artistic conflicts and excesses of the period, and her encounter with the cultural and gender politics of the 1890s and the figure of the New Woman is evident in such stories as 'The Tiredness of Rosabel', 'A Truthful Adventure', and throughout her collection *In a German Pension*. But more typically, the achievements of the earlier generation were either ignored, or exiled under the 'exclusionary moves and anxious territorialism' of the major modernists.[46]

Which observation takes us back to where we began, and the attempt to resituate high modernism as one among several competing or complementary discourses circulating in the period 1880-1920. Part of that attempt must involve the reconstruction of modernism's pre-histories, such as I have offered here, if for no other reason than to qualify the claims modernism would make about itself (and which institutional literary criticism is in the habit of reproducing). Where the 'rise' of the short story is concerned, this means assembling the evidence of a highly self-reflexive and experimental culture of writing, publication, and criticism extending from the early 1890s. But in addition, that work of historical recomposition needs to be complemented by an inquiry into the reasons why, and the mechanisms by which, the avant-garde literary cultures of 1890 and 1914 came to be disconnected from one another in the first place. Space permits me to venture two possible explanations that may pertain to the short story, and which I offer by way of conclusion.

The first has to do with venue of publication, which is something we need always to have in mind when addressing the short story. Though the magazine market in the 1890s was fairly fragmented, the lines of demarcation between different sectors were not so clear or rigid as they would become under modernism. This meant that short stories, even in radical guise, tended to appear in mainstream contexts that diminished or possibly even worked against their designs. Arthur Morrison's stories, for example, were published in W. E. Henley's ultra-conservative *National Observer*. Given the importance for later modernists of coterie identification, and the endeavours of Pound, Woolf, and others to control the means of production of their work, the dispersal of 1890s avant-garde and experimental writing across a large and sometimes unpropitious range of commercial publications may well have skewed (and continue to skew) an understanding and appreciation of its achievements.[47]

---

[45] Virginia Woolf, *Orlando: A Biography* (London: Granta, 1978), 195.
[46] Ardis, *Modernism and Cultural Conflict*, 4.
[47] It is worth adding here that the online *Modernist Magazine Project* is unlikely to make the task of

The second reason has to do with the success of what Gaye Tuchman has characterized as the process of 'edging women out' of positions of cultural authority in the modernist years—a process by which the institutionalization of men's control of the terms and definitions of high culture was enacted.[48] In fact this process began early on, and is evident on the pages of experimental magazines of the 1890s, as we can see in the case of the *Yellow Book*'s successor journal, the *Savoy*. By the end of the 1890s, the relationship that had developed between feminism and literary radicalism was rapidly being obscured as male writers and critics made a concerted effort to reinhabit and redefine the literary avant-garde. It was an act of appropriation that had a disproportionate effect on what was arguably the period's most explicitly 'feminized' literary form, the short story.

FURTHER READING

Ardis, Ann. *Modernism and Cultural Conflict, 1880–1922* (Cambridge: Cambridge University Press, 2002).

Armstrong, Tim. *Modernism: A Cultural History* (Cambridge: Polity, 2005).

Brake, Laurel. *Subjugated Knowledges: Journalism, Gender and Literature in the Nineteenth Century* (Basingstoke and London: Macmillan, 1994).

Felski, Rita. *The Gender of Modernism* (Cambridge, MA and London: Harvard University Press, 1995).

Hanson, Clare. *Short Stories and Short Fictions, 1880–1980* (Basingstoke: Macmillan, 1985).

Hanson, Clare (ed.). *Re-Reading the Short Story* (Basingstoke: Macmillan, 1989).

Head, Dominic. *The Modernist Short Story: A Study in Theory and Practice* (Cambridge: Cambridge University Press, 1992).

Hunter, Adrian. *The Cambridge Introduction to the Short Story in English* (Cambridge: Cambridge University Press, 2007).

Keating, Peter. *The Haunted Study: A Social History of the English Novel 1875–1914* (London: Secker, 1989).

Lehan, Richard. *The City in Literature: An Intellectual and Cultural History* (Berkeley, CA and London: University of California Press, 1998).

March-Russell, Paul. *The Short Story: An Introduction* (Edinburgh: Edinburgh University Press, 2009).

May, Charles E. (ed.). *The New Short Story Theories* (Athens, OH: Ohio University Press, 1994).

Shaw, Valerie. *The Short Story: A Critical Introduction* (London: Longmans, 1983).

Tuchman, Gaye. *Edging Women Out: Victorian Novelists, Publishers, and Social Change* (London: Routledge, 1989).

locating and identifying these (legitimately modernist) materials any easier for future scholars, since it largely excludes large-scale mainstream titles from its database. See http://modmags.dmu.ac.uk/home.html.

[48] Gaye Tuchman, *Edging Women Out: Victorian Novelists, Publishers, and Social Change* (London: Routledge, 1989).

CHAPTER 13

MOON VOYAGING, SELENOGRAPHY, AND THE SCIENTIFIC ROMANCE

MATTHEW TAUNTON

The rise to prominence of the scientific romance as a generic category in the 1880s and 1890s went along with wider changes in the market for fiction. The late-Victorian romance revival included scientific romances alongside gothic, adventure, and fantasy stories. These shared a young, largely male, lower-middle-class readership, and a cheap price.[1] Tracing the origins of 'science fiction'—a term coined in 1929—Roger Luckhurst reminds us of 'the permeability between these different kinds of writing, the hybrid and "impure" spaces from which the scientific romances appeared.'[2] Luckhurst argues that the opposition between the scientific romances and the emergent modernist aesthetic—as seen in the turn towards impressionism in the work of Conrad and James—has been overstated. Conrad and James admired H. G. Wells's scientific romances. It was only Wells's turn towards a politically didactic idiom in the Edwardian period that provoked James into the opening salvo of what was to become a longstanding disagreement, with profound consequences for literary history and taste.[3] It was, moreover, Wells's realist, Edwardian novels and not his scientific romances that later became the target of Woolf's influential polemics 'Modern Fiction' and 'Mr Bennett and Mrs Brown'.[4] Luckhurst concludes: 'Despite the early praise for his romances, these works have been buried under the subsequent objections to his turn to political futurology and

---

[1] See Anna Vaninskaya, 'The Late-Victorian Romance Revival: A Generic Excursus', *English Literature in Transition, 1880–1920* 51/1 (2008), 57–79.

[2] Roger Luckhurst, *Science Fiction* (Cambridge: Polity, 2005), 31.

[3] See also Simon J. James, *Maps of Utopia: H. G. Wells, Modernity, and the End of Culture* (Oxford: Oxford University Press, 2012), 19–29.

[4] Luckhurst, *Science Fiction*, 42; Virginia Woolf, *Selected Essays*, ed. David Bradshaw (Oxford: Oxford University Press, 2008), 6–12, 32–6.

the reduction of the novel to utilitarian vehicle for social policy.'[5] Literary history often works like this: the particular trajectory of Wells's career and 'the antagonistic nature of Wells's imagination' contributed to the idea that modernism and the scientific romance were fundamentally opposed.[6] This outcome was not inevitable, and other results could be observed elsewhere. As Anindita Banerjee has shown, in Russia modernism and science fiction frequently went hand in hand.[7]

Rather than attempting a top-down description of the 'scientific romance' as a genre, this chapter will take a specific object, the moon, as the starting point of its inquiry. This provides a licence to explore scientific romances in a wider intellectual context than generic taxonomy allows. The moon was a common destination in the interplanetary fiction of 1880–1920, although it was increasingly eclipsed by Mars as the destination of choice. Starting with an object rather than a literary–historical category also allows cutting across post-hoc generic categorizations that often obstruct rather than facilitate the understanding of literary texts and periods. The polarization between literary modernism and the scientific romance is particularly limiting. The reinvention of the moon was taking place in scientific romances, but also in modernist texts such as Joyce's *Ulysses*.

In our period the moon is caught between its ancient, poetic, mythological associations and newer scientific understandings. The moon is Diana (or Artemis) the huntress, feminine symbol of fertility and chastity. It is also, as telescopic observation, unmanned probes, and manned voyages have progressively confirmed, a barren lump of rock. A fascinating conversation between Simone de Beauvoir and Jean-Paul Sartre from 1974 shows succinctly what is at stake here. Sartre begins by recalling his youthful infatuation with the moon: 'I was very fond of it: it was poetic— it was pure poetry.' Turning to the Apollo moon landings, Sartre remarks:

> the moon means less to me since people go there…it changed the moon into a scientific object, and it lost the mythical character it had had up to then.

For Sartre, the moon was poetic and mythical until Neil Armstrong stepped onto its surface in 1969, at which point it became a scientific object. The landing is also clearly gendered for Sartre, representing the incursion of masculine science into a feminine realm of poetry and romance: chaste Diana violated.[8]

The year 1969 is a comparatively late date to begin mourning the moon's transformation from a mythological object to a scientific one. In fact, as Yasna Bozhkova has recently shown, the disenchantment of the moon became a stock image of French symbolist poetry of the nineteenth century. For Nerval, it was 'le desert des

---

[5] Luckhurst, *Science Fiction*, 46.   [6] James, *Maps of Utopia*, 19.

[7] Anindita Banerjee, *We Modern People: Science Fiction and the Making of Russian Modernity* (Middletown, CT: Wesleyan University Press, 2012).

[8] Simone de Beauvoir, *Adieux: A Farewell to Sartre*, trans. Patrick O'Brian (London: André Deutsch and Weidenfeld and Nicholson, 1984), 240–1.

cieux', and Bozhkova cites comparable examples from the poetry of Baudelaire and Rimbaud.[9]

Marjorie Hope Nicholson also situates the disenchantment of the moon in the nineteenth century, linking it to a scientific way of seeing.[10] Nicholson mourns the passing of tales like Francis Godwin's *The Man in the Moone* (1638), in which Domingo Gonsales travels to the moon in a chariot pulled by geese, part of a tradition that stretches back to ancient Rome and Lucian's satirical moon voyages. She complains that in more recent tales 'the kind of "science" that once liberated literary imagination has given way to "technology" that too often confines it within the limits of the plausible'. She pinpoints the date of the transition as 1835, the year of the Great Moon Hoax, in which readers of the *New York Sun* were duped by a series of articles detailing the discovery of a humanoid civilization on the moon.[11] It was also the year of Edgar Allan Poe's moon voyage story 'The Unparalleled Adventure of One Hans Pfaal', which he claimed was original in attempting '*verisimilitude* in the application of scientific principles'. Nicholson argues that:

> From this time on, writers of moon voyages will seek for *verisimilitude* and spend their efforts on attempts to make their planetary flights plausible. They will pride themselves on the application of scientific principles, weighing down their imaginations and ours with technical impedimenta.

For Nicholson, moon voyages after 1835 'gained verisimilitude, but…lost the excitement of breathless discovery'.[12]

The aim of this chapter is not to dispute with Sartre and Nicholson about the date of the moon's transformation from a mythological object into a scientific one, but to suggest that this paradigm is flawed. I claim instead that there are (at least) two moons: the scientific and the mythological, which orbit the earth simultaneously and exert their magnetic attractions on the scientific and literary imaginations.

George Locke's bibliography of interplanetary fiction shows that the numbers of titles classifiable as such increased throughout the nineteenth century, reaching a peak in the 1890s that coincided with the late-Victorian romance revival.[13] Early interplanetary fiction was dominated by the moon: seventeen out of the nineteen

---

[9] Gerard de Nerval, 'Artémis', in *Selected Writings* (London: Penguin, 1999), 368; Yasna Bozhkova, ' "Silver Lucifer": "Stellectric Signs" between Mina Loy and Roland Barthes', paper delivered at the Modernist Studies Association 15th Annual Conference, University of Sussex, 29 August–1 September 2013, Brighton.

[10] Marjorie Hope Nicholson, *Voyages to the Moon* (New York: Macmillan, 1948) is still the standard academic work on literary moon voyages. It focuses predominantly on pre-1800 material. The longer perspective, including nineteenth- and twentieth-century sources, has been more recently analyzed in Aaron Parrett, *The Translunar Narrative in the Western Tradition* (Aldershot: Ashgate, 2004).

[11] Nicholson, *Voyages to the Moon*, 237, 271; Parrett, *The Translunar Narrative*, 83–8.

[12] Nicholson, *Voyages to the Moon*, 239–40, 236.

[13] George Locke, *Voyages in Space: A Bibliography of Interplanetary Fiction* (London: Ferret Fantasy, 1975), 68.

pre-1800 titles Locke lists concerned travel to that satellite. Interplanetary fiction's interest in the moon seems to have reached its nineteenth-century peak around the time of the Great Moon Hoax of 1835, however. Jules Verne's *De la terre à la lune* (1865) and its sequel *Autour de la lune* (1870) were popular successes, and have been credited with 'turning an impossible dream into a believable technological adventure'.[14] Yet there was a downside to this plausibility: 'Verne was too exact in his science to posit any sort of life on the moon'.[15] While the mythical significance of the moon is repeatedly debated by Verne's characters, the novels replace 'the various influences which were attributed to her by the ignorance of former ages', with a modern, scientific understanding of the moon. Residues of the moon's mythos do persist, but in comic form: one of the dogs who accompanies the astronauts is named Diana—'who, launched into planetary spheres, wilt perhaps become the Eve of Selenite dogs!', as Michael Ardan, the most romantic (and therefore, we infer, deluded) of the astronauts, puts it.[16] Modern readers are likely to concur with China Miéville's judgement that Verne's extended technical descriptions are 'dull'.[17] Stripped of its mythological significance, and known by astronomers to be inert, in our period the moon might have seemed in certain respects a quaint or boring destination when set against a more distant Mars.

For in the course of the nineteenth century, Mars emerged as the destination of choice, the focus of eighty-eight novels and eighteen magazine stories, as against the moon's fifty-two novels and seven magazine stories, in the period 1801-1914. And while interest in the moon waned somewhat after 1835, Mars became increasingly prevalent in interplanetary fiction as the nineteenth century wore on, probably as a result of the 'immense amount of publicity Mars was receiving in the late nineteenth century as a possible abode for life'.[18] This stemmed from a public controversy about the existence of a network of Martian 'canals', first observed by Giovanni Schiapperelli in 1877. The Italian word 'canali' does not necessarily imply man-made channels, but the translation in the Anglophone newspapers as 'canals' led to widespread speculation that these confirmed the existence of a technologically advanced Martian civilization.

In 1892, as Mars passed closer to earth than it had done since Schiapperelli's first observations, the American astronomer Percival Lowell took up the canals as a cause, feeding a widespread Mars mania.[19] Martin Willis has shown how scientific

[14] R. G. A. Dolby, 'Introduction', in *From the Earth to the Moon & Around the Moon* (Ware, Hertfordshire: Wordsworth Editions, 2011), vii.

[15] Nicholson, *Voyages to the Moon*, 246.

[16] Jules Verne, *From the Earth to the Moon & Around the Moon*, trans. T. K. Linklater (Ware, Hertfordshire: Wordsworth Editions, 2011), 40, 237.

[17] China Miéville, 'Introduction', in H. G. Wells, *The First Men in the Moon* (London: Penguin, 2005), xvi.

[18] Locke, *Voyages in Space*, 67-8.

[19] Robert Crossley, 'Percival Lowell and the History of Mars', *Massachusetts Review* 41/3 (Autumn, 2000), 297–318.

romances such as Wells's *The War of the Worlds* (1898) and Garrett P. Serviss's *Edison's Conquest of Mars* (1898) engaged directly with the latest astronomical science, as 'contributions to an active set of discussions about visual authority and the role of the observer of, or witness to, Mars's planetary structures'. Willis goes on to argue that the conventional 'diffusionist hierarchy...in which science provides material for fiction' must be replaced by the notion of an 'unbroken continuum between astronomical practice and the literary text'.[20]

In the case of Mars, a lack of scientific consensus provided a ready-made controversy about the question of extraterrestrial life, providing novelists with ample material. But by the late-Victorian period the moon was generally deemed to be inhospitable for life. The comparison of these two celestial bodies is made explicit in Mark Wicks's scientific romance, *To Mars Via the Moon: An Astronomical Story* (1911). Wicks's narrator Wilfrid Poynders is clear about which interests him: '[T]he planet Mars has been an object of special interest to me, and I...have endeavored to make myself fully acquainted with all that has been discovered or surmised respecting it.'[21] The book is packed with astronomical knowledge and is dedicated to Percival Lowell, offering support to his theory of the canals by depicting an advanced Martian civilization. Poynders decides on a flyby over the surface of the moon as an afterthought: 'I thought we should all be glad to have a look at the moon from a close point of view now we have the chance.'[22] The trip to the moon is deadly dull: the features of the lunar surface are immediately explained away during a long lecture by Poynders about lunar astronomy, merely reconfirming established facts. Poynders says that 'my telescopic observations had prepared me for a great deal', and is adamant that the moon is uninhabited.[23] Wicks's preface makes it clear that the novel is intended to make the latest discoveries of astronomy accessible to a non-specialist young audience. Clearly aware on some level that the detailed confirmation that the moon is a lifeless lump of rock may bore this intended readership, Wicks has his humorous Scottish astronaut McAllister interrupt the lecture to complain of a 'considerable amount of information on a wee bit dry subject'.[24] Wicks is unambiguous on this point: if you want excitement, go to Mars.

Many writers of scientific romances seemed to agree and duly sent their protagonists there. However, a somewhat different picture of the genre begins to emerge if one pays attention to the hugely successful texts that resisted the trend for all things Martian and described voyages to the moon, where readers discovered strange other worlds that bypassed the prevailing scientific consensus about the moon's desertification. The most famous and widely read of the moon voyages of

---

[20] Martin Willis, *Vision, Science and Literature 1870–1920: Ocular Horizons* (London: Pickering and Chatto, 2011), 58, 60.

[21] Mark Wicks, *To Mars via the Moon: An Astronomical Story* (London: Seeley, 1911), 35.

[22] Ibid., 44–5.   [23] Ibid., 83–4, 90.   [24] Ibid., ix–xii, 63.

the period is H. G. Wells's *The First Men in the Moon* (1901). It was bracketed by Nicholson as a story of the modern ilk, and as such encumbered by 'overexact knowledge'.[25] But the same story was deplored by Verne for its *lack* of verisimilitude. Two men propel themselves to the moon using Cavorite, a fictional substance that blocks the action of gravity, of which Verne demanded 'show me this metal. Let [Wells] produce it'.[26] Verne's criticism missed the novel's commentary on the question—posed later by Sartre—of the relationship between scientific and romantic views of the moon.

At first glance, it is possible to see this dichotomy embodied in the novel's two central characters. In a 1941 chapter Orwell criticized Wells for seeing history as 'a series of victories won by the scientific man over the romantic man'.[27] In this novel, the eccentric scientist Cavor is opposed to Bedford, a bankrupted businessman turned playwright and the narrator of the story: the romantic, we presume.[28] Both men comment on the disenchantment of the moon, and the relationship between disenchantment and scientific knowledge is explored. Bedford questions why (from a financial perspective) they would want to travel to a 'dead world', and Cavor cites scientific evidence of the moon's desertification. As the pair approach the surface of the moon Bedford notes, anticipating Wicks's Poynders: 'I take it the reader has seen pictures or photographs of the moon, so that I need not describe the broader features of that landscape.'[29] Indeed, the novel's first readers were likely to have seen detailed pictures of the moon's surface. The moon was a difficult object to photograph, being both dimly lit and in constant motion relative to the earth. But the craters and the texture of the moon's surface were clearly captured in daguerreotypes by Whipple and Bond, displayed at the Great Exhibition in 1851.[30] In 1874, Nasmyth and Carpenter produced a popular book of lunar photography, *The Moon, Considered as a Planet, a World, and a Satellite*. The book was one of the first to make use of photo-mechanical printing, and went through several editions.[31]

How did the wide availability of such images affect the way the moon was seen and understood? In their book *Objectivity*, Lorraine Daston and Peter Galison set out a powerful argument that objectivity is not an inherent property of scientific discourse, but arose as recently as the mid-nineteenth century as a 'new way of

---

[25] Nicholson, *Voyages to the Moon*, 251.

[26] Quoted in Miéville, 'Introduction', xvi.

[27] George Orwell, 'Wells, Hitler and the World State', in *Essays* (London: Penguin, 1994), 188–93, 191.

[28] Parrett argues that Bedford and Cavor are 'the very embodiment of Snow's two cultures'. See Parrett, *The Translunar Narrative*, 96.

[29] Wells, *The First Men in the Moon*, 32, 41, 45.

[30] Marien Warner, *Photography: A Cultural History* (London: Laurence King, 2002), 25.

[31] The authors noted in a preface to the third edition that 'as enquiries for copies continue to be made we have been induced to bring out a new edition, in a more compact size and at a reduced price'. See Frances Robertson, 'Science and Fiction: James Nasmyth's Photographic Images of the Moon', *Victorian Studies* 48/4 (2006), 595–623.

studying nature', coinciding with the development of indexical recording media. They define objectivity as follows:

> To be objective is to aspire to knowledge that bears no trace of the knower—knowledge unmarked by prejudice or skill, fantasy or judgement, wishing or striving. Objectivity is blind sight, seeing without interference, interpretation or intelligence.[32]

Like Martin Willis (who draws on their arguments) Daston and Galison discuss Percival Lowell and the controversy over the Martian canals. Lowell could see the canals clearly through the lens of the telescope, but when photographs were taken for the purposes of publication, the images became blurry and ambiguous. Lowell toyed with the idea of retouching them, but concluded that this would be fatal: 'in the end accuracy, completeness, color, sharpness, and even reproducibility were sacrificed to mechanical objectivity.' Lowell was keen to stress that even his drawings of Mars constituted 'scientific data, not artistic delineations'. Daston and Galison thus describe an extraordinary shift among competing 'epistemic virtues', leading to our present situation where objectivity reigns supreme, rising above other virtues such as, say, accuracy (which might be better served by a bit of strategic retouching).[33]

For David Trotter, the literary modernism that was to emerge in the early decades of the twentieth century was itself indebted to a similar notion of objectivity, finding in the cinema an appealing 'image of the world made automatically'.[34] Perhaps the supposed disenchantment of the moon was an effect of an increasingly pervasive way of seeing attempts to remove any 'trace of the knower' from its purview?

As with interplanetary fiction, however, when we turn our attention from Mars to the moon, a different picture emerges. Nasmyth and Carpenter's book—the work of an amateur astronomer and a photographer, intended for a mass audience—did not follow Percival Lowell in the quest for astronomical objectivity. Their way of getting round the difficulty of photographing the moon itself was to make plaster models of it, based on their telescopic observations, and photograph those instead. While they did not seem to think of it in this way, by most standards their photographs were fakes. As Frances Robertson argues, 'Nasmyth does not appeal to the ideal of perceptual immediacy alone but also to a submerged ideal of embodied, craft-based production'.[35] The book included scientific data about the moon's surface, but it was also profoundly motivated by fantasy, complete with erupting lunar volcanoes simulated and photographed in the studio. Accounts of the cultural effects of early photography and cinema which, like Trotter's, follow André Bazin in stressing the indexicality of these new media as their most important feature risk

---

[32] Lorraine Daston and Peter Galison, *Objectivity* (Brooklyn, NY: Zone Books, 2010), 17.
[33] Ibid., 180, 33.
[34] David Trotter, *Cinema and Modernism* (Oxford: Blackwell, 2007), 4.
[35] Robertson, 'Science and Fiction', 599.

underplaying the parallel tendency towards pure fantasy embodied in trick photography and the kind of 'craft-based production' that Nasmyth and Carpenter engaged in.[36]

If the Lumière brothers inaugurated the tradition of cinema as realism, then Georges Méliès, above all in his own moon voyage *Le Voyage dans la lune* (1902), enabled another understanding of the possibilities of cinema. As this film shows, the indexicality of the medium—in Daston and Galison's terms, its 'objectivity'—in no way prevented it from dramatizing, and indeed visualizing, the most extraordinary adventures. Méliès's film follows Verne in terms of the means of transportation to the moon—a large projectile fired from an enormous gun—but after lift-off Méliès departs wilfully from the verisimilitude on which Verne had insisted. As the astronauts approach the moon, a grinning face appears in it, and the projectile lands in its eye. Their adventures on (and in) the moon then take much from Wells's fantastical descriptions, leaving behind the supposed objectivity of the indexical medium by deploying innovative photographic tricks.[37]

Wells's novel, instead of being constrained by scientific knowledge about the moon, adopts an analogous stance, profiting from its author's scientific understanding but choosing to suspend this wherever it risks getting in the way of the story. So while Bedford's initial description of the moon's surface defers to widely available lunar photography, when the pair land they experience a lunar dawn in which the desert is rapidly transformed by fast-growing plant life: '[A] bristling beard of spiky and fleshy vegetation was straining into view, hurrying tumultuously to take advantage of the brief day in which it must flower and then fruit and seed again and die.' This weird plantscape—which produces intoxicating, edible fungus—is aptly described as 'unreal', and is echoed by Méliès's giant, fast-growing lunar mushrooms.[38] By focalizing the story through Bedford, moreover, Wells uses his narrator's ignorance of science to allow the story to depart from verisimilitude. When Cavor describes his discovery of a gravity-resistant substance—the most obviously improbable aspect of the story—Bedford frankly glosses over 'technicalities entirely strange to me', and emerges from a 'haze of abstruse phrases' conceding: 'If only I had taken notes.'[39] The reader is thus denied any opportunity to test the plausibility of Cavor's research.

---

[36] See André Bazin, 'The Ontology of the Photographic Image', in *What Is Cinema* (Berkeley, CA and London: University of California Press, 2005), 9–16.

[37] Méliès describes his decision to eschew 'natural scenes' in order to 'specialize in subjects whose interest lies in their difficulty of execution', emphasizing the craft ('manual skills, manual labour of all kinds') that was involved in producing his fantastical scenes. See Georges Méliès, 'Kinematographic Views' (1907), trans. Stuart Leibman and Timothy Barnard, Appendix B in André Gaudreault (ed.), *Film and Attraction: From Kinematography to Cinema* (Urbana, IL: University of Illinois Press, 2011), 133–52.

[38] Wells, *The First Men in the Moon*, 57.   [39] Ibid., 12, 16.

Indeed, the putative disenchantment of the moon, for Wells, is a result not of scientific knowledge but of monopoly capitalism and imperialism, both associated with Bedford rather than Cavor. Bedford says of Cavor's suggestion that they fly to the moon that 'it's imperial' and, intoxicated after eating a lunar fungus, explicitly advocates that 'We must annex this moon... This is part of the White Man's Burden', alluding to Kipling's 1898 poem.[40] Bedford sees the moon as a land that is yet to be conquered and colonized. And when the Selenites are encountered—insectoid creatures of human dimensions who live inside the moon—it is the scientific man, Cavor, who urges Bedford to approach them with understanding, as intelligent beings, and Bedford who experiences 'not a little exultation' in smashing Selenites to pieces.[41]

Finding that gold is abundant on the moon—it is even used to make the chains in which the Selenites hold their terrestrial captives—Bedford travels back to earth a rich man. Cavor is left behind on the moon, where he comes to understand the ant-like structure of Selenite society, wherein 'every citizen knows his place' and indeed is biologically adapted, and subsequently reared, to fulfil a certain function. Selenites destined to become machine operatives are grown in jars with their fore-limbs protruding, leading Cavor to reflect that this is 'a far more humane proceeding than our earthly method of leaving children to grow into human beings, and then making machines of them'. Cavor, in his transmission from the moon, captures the odd experience of conversing with the Selenites by comparing it to 'the fable-hearing period of childhood... when the ant and the grasshopper talked together and the bee judged between them'.[42] As the story takes a dystopian turn, Cavor and Bedford have swapped places: the scientific man has become the romantic fantasist and the romantic is revealed as a base materialist. Both positions clearly have their dangers, but it is under the accumulative gaze of Bedford, and not the scientific one of Cavor, that the moon stands to lose its associations with fable.

In Garrett P. Serviss's *The Moon Metal* (1900), the moon's disenchantment is also linked to monopoly capitalism, although here advanced science and the new possibilities for accumulating wealth are conjoined rather than opposed. The story begins with the total paralysis of the global economy, following the discovery of vast reserves of gold in the South Pole. With gold now 'more common than iron', it rapidly loses its value and consequently the gold standard collapses.[43] Chaos prevails until a scientist, Dr Max Syx, comes forward with a new precious metal on which the world economy might be stabilized—the moon metal of the book's title. Syx has not visited the moon—nobody in this novella does—but has found a way of extracting this unique and beautiful element at long range, focusing 'a shaft of flying atoms' into a concave mirror. This is done in secret, under the pretext that the metal is mined and extracted from a terrestrial ore. By closely guarding the secret of the

---

[40] Ibid., 30, 78.   [41] Ibid., 123.   [42] Ibid., 184, 180.
[43] Garrett P. Serviss, *The Moon Metal* (New York and London: Harper Brothers, 1900), 7.

metal's extraction, Syx holds a global monopoly on money, and takes a commission of one per cent on it, becoming 'the financial dictator of the whole earth'. By calling Syx's metal 'artemisium', alluding to the Artemis of Greek myth, Serviss emphasizes the profanation of the mythical moon by its transformation into currency. When a rival scientist discovers Syx's technique and replicates it, he promises to extract the metal 'fresh from the veins of Artemis herself'.[44] And as Syx's secret gradually becomes common knowledge, 'ten thousand artemisium mills shot their etheric rays upon the moon, and our unfortunate satellite's ribs were stripped by atomic force', to the point where the moon loses its lustre, and the value of the new currency collapses. Both Wells and Serviss, then, concern themselves with a way of seeing the moon as an extension of the earth, as another territory ripe for exploitation, by which it loses its mythical meanings. The difference is that in *The Moon Metal* the 'looting of the moon' is begun and perpetuated by scientists, whereas in *The First Men in the Moon* Cavor's disinterested scientific outlook is opposed to Bedford's imperialist and acquisitive motivations.[45]

The romances of Wells and Serviss prompt us to modify significantly the Sartrean hypothesis that scientific objectivity led to the disenchantment of the moon; other romances seem even less amenable to such a reading. One would struggle, for instance, to accommodate Charles Hannan's *Thuka of the Moon* (1906) in Willis's 'unbroken continuum between astronomical practice and the literary text'.[46] It shares some features of the scientific romance, but testifies to the generic instability which Luckhurst describes, recalling the weird tales of Lord Dunsany and dabbling in weighty religious allegory. 'Imaginative but badly written', was Locke's pithy verdict.[47] The novel is set on the moon before there was life on earth—immediately posing a problem for its generic categorization as scientific romance. Yet the most canonical science fiction film of all time—George Lucas's 1977 *Star Wars*—began by announcing its setting 'A long time ago, in a galaxy far, far away'. Hannan's novel also deploys more familiar generic tropes of interplanetary fiction.

Thuka is born to a race of moonmen, who are rooted to the ground where they stand, but is distinguished from them as a thinker who can also move, and who aspires to join the highest gods Goata and Morata. To ascend to heaven, he must defeat the Craton, a quasi-allegorical monster that seems to represent evil itself, and manifests itself first as a 'crab-like form', then as a giant bird.[48] Thucka becomes a god and competes with the other gods in a game of chance to populate the valleys of the moon over which they respectively preside with the highest quality men they can create.[49] The arrival of women later stirs the moonmen into movement and action, but brings danger. They are drawn to the Pool of Orma (meaning 'the breath

[44] Ibid., 21, 140.   [45] Ibid., 155, 156.   [46] Willis, *Vision, Science and Literature*, 60.
[47] Locke, *Voyages in Space*, 33.
[48] Charles Hannan, *Thuka of the Moon* (London: Digby, Long & Co., 1906), 13.
[49] Ibid., 41.

of death') wherein they can see their reflections and as they stare, vanity is born. 'It was like a great eye placed in the centre of the plain', Hannan writes. 'Through this eye the Craton looked upon the doings of men.'[50] The pool swallows people up as they are drawn to it, and Thuka decides to give up being a god in order to return to the moon and fight the Craton, banishing evil from the face of the moon. He makes a deal with the other gods that if he should be defeated by the Craton, they will abandon the moon and seek another world where humanity might thrive. When Thuka sacrifices himself, the gods uphold their promise, and they divest the moon of its atmosphere, leaving it a barren rock.

This summary leaves out many details and hardly touches on the novel's bizarre but interesting take on the origins of the sexes—one that takes up and reconfigures the moon's mythical association with female fertility and chastity. In what sense does this interplanetary novel engage with contemporary science? One can imagine making the case that, even if it imagines a mythic past, the story's telos is the barren moon of contemporary selenography: Hannan refers to it as 'the first world of all— the world of the ancient moon, now twisted and dead and still'. But in so many other ways the tale deliberately discards scientific understandings of the moon, in favour of tapping what Hannan clearly feels is its continuing mythical potential—not the old myths of Diana or Artemis, but new ones. When Hannan's gods leave the moon behind, they place 'a silver light on the land', a 'reflection of heaven's silver sheen'.[51] It is this reflective quality of the moon that seems to attract Hannan, and in his hands the moon becomes a silver screen onto which earthly concerns—sexual, social, and religious—can be projected and reworked.

The proximity of the scientific romance to the tales of the supernatural that also circulated in the period is also evident in G. H. Ryan's *Fifteen Months in the Moon* (1880). Ryan's description of a futuristic, humanoid civilization on the moon engages with plausible scientific and technological advances and their social applications: the moon is equipped with high-speed monorails, and electricity is used for lighting as well as powering 'various contrivances in use for lifting, propelling and dragging of goods and carriages'.[52] Yet the story also touches the supernatural. The tale's protagonist, Mayfield, is able to travel to the moon after learning the secret of levitation, which he first encounters at a séance. The spiritualist in question, Mr Barton, describes his skill as achievable 'by purely natural means' and describes it in recognizably scientific (albeit incredible) terms: 'neutralizing the attraction of the earth towards that body by means of a purely physical effort… a simple exercise of volition'. Barton's séances operate by 'judiciously mingling a portion of spirit with the *aqua pura* of science', clothing science in spiritualist garb to attract a paying audience.[53] Still, Ryan was hardly striving for Poe's *verisimilitude* in the application

---

[50] Ibid., 121.   [51] Ibid., 1, 279–80.

[52] G. H. Ryan, *Fifteen Months in the Moon* (London: G. H. Ryan, 1880), 54.

[53] Ibid., 11–12.

of scientific principles'—the pretence that Barton's telekinesis is scientifically plausible is the thinnest of veneers. The examples of Ryan and Hannan show how new scientific ways of seeing the moon could coexist alongside the fantastic and the supernatural.

How far, then, can interplanetary fiction's rethinking of the literary and scientific potentials of the moon be sealed off from developments in literary modernism? From the point of view of contemporary readership, the separation seems absolute. Formally, as odd as the fiction I have been describing sometimes gets, it generally eschews recognizably modernist techniques. Yet the modernist moon was tied up with similar concerns. Marinetti's second futurist proclamation 'Let's Kill Off the Moonlight' is indicative of the futurist attitude to the moon, which tended to see it as a poetic symbol weighed down with romantic nostalgia, and one that needed to be killed off.[54] Mina Loy's 'Lunar Baedeker', as Bozhkova argues, counterbalances this desire to strip the moon of its sentimental trappings with an awareness of its lingering mythic power.[55] Such a balancing is also present in the 'Ithaca' episode of Joyce's *Ulysses* (1922), which is fundamentally concerned with the relationship between poetry and science. As such it shares some of the concerns of the interplanetary fiction I have been examining, if not its popular form. The passage in which Stephen and Bloom contemplate the stars and then the moon is pure scientific romance.

> What special affinities appeared to him to exist between the moon and woman?
>
> Her antiquity in preceding and surviving succeeding tellurian generations: her nocturnal predominance: her satellitic dependence: her luminary reflection: her constancy under all phases, rising and setting by her appointed times, waxing and waning: the forced invariability of her aspect: her indeterminate response to inaffirmative interrogation: her potency over effluent and refluent waters: her power to enamour, to mortify, to invest with beauty, to render insane, to incite and to aid delinquency: the tranquil inscrutability of her visage: the terribility of her isolated dominant resplendent propinquity: her omens of tempest and of calm: the stimulation of her light, her motion and her presence: the admonition of her craters, her arid seas, her silence: her splendour, when visible: her attraction, when invisible.[56]

In 'Ithaca', Joyce stages scientific examinations of questions that are frequently left to poetry—and here, the moon's affinity with woman is a sentimental romantic image ripe for deconstruction. But here is no futurist attempt to blot out the moon and its poetic meaning, or to strip the artemisium from its veins. For Andrew Gibson, Joyce's approach to science in 'Ithaca' is satirical: he 'parodies, perverts or defiles imperial science', rejecting objectivity while aligning it with British

---

[54] Filippo Marinetti, 'Second Futurist Proclamation: Let's Kill Off the Moonlight', trans. Doug Thompson, in *Critical Writings* (New York: Farar, Straus and Giroux, 2006), 22–31.

[55] Yasna Bozhkova, ' "Silver Lucifer" '.

[56] James Joyce, *Ulysses* (London: Penguin, 1992), 823–4.

imperialism, exploding a scientific discourse associated with colonial domination by injecting a dose of Gaelic 'fancy, inconsequence, random thinking, whimsy'.[57] There is not much of this anti-colonial, anti-scientific Joyce in Bloom's thoughts about the moon, it seems to me. Here scientific data about the moon support its mythical associations with femininity, rather than being at odds with them: the mythic moon coexists with the scientific one, and they illuminate each other. This is felt on the level of language, so that scientific discourse can be seen not always as a medium of disenchantment (or colonial domination for that matter), but as a vehicle for a new poetry. This insight Joyce shared with many writers of scientific romances, though he was unlikely to share a dinner table or a readership with them.

Joyce's play with the language of scientific objectivity was in various ways mirrored, albeit on a thematic rather than a formal level, in the scientific romances of the period. Those scientific romances, moreover, formed no consensus about the relationship between literary and scientific understandings of the moon. When we let our analyses of literature be driven by an object—here, the moon—rather than governed by questions of genre, conventional categories of literary history tend to break down. We are left instead with a range of ways of seeing. These interact at times with scientific ways of seeing but are not determined by these interactions, as Sartre and Nicholson implied. Willis's suggestion of a 'continuum' linking astronomy and literature is a welcome corrective to such deterministic thinking. In taking Mars as his example, Willis chose a site where the latest scientific debates actively fuelled the literary imagination, and vice versa. The science and the literature of Mars in this period lend themselves to being read as a continuum.

In turning our attention from Mars to the moon, however, we turn to a place where the possibilities of literature and the discoveries of science seemed to many to be at odds. Sartre's and Nicholson's complaints are symptomatic of a wider feeling that scientific knowledge must act as a dead weight on the poetic imagination. And yet, as we find in the work of writers as diverse as Joyce, Wells, Serviss, and Hannan, a mythical, fantastical, poetic moon continues to exist, not on a continuum with the scientific moon, nor necessarily in opposition to it, but in a parallel orbit.

FURTHER READING

Daston, Lorraine and Peter Galison. *Objectivity* (Brooklyn, NY: Zone Books, 2010).
James, Simon J. *Maps of Utopia: H.G. Wells, Modernity, and the End of Culture* (Oxford: Oxford University Press, 2012).
Lane, Maria. *Geographies of Mars: Seeing and Knowing the Red Planet* (Chicago, IL: University of Chicago Press, 2011).

---

[57] Andrew Gibson, '"An Aberration of the Light of Reason": Science and Cultural Politics in "Ithaca"', in Gibson (ed.), *Joyce's 'Ithaca'* (Amsterdam: Rodopi, 1996), 133–76, 171, 165.

Locke, George. *Voyages in Space: A Bibliography of Interplanetary Fiction* (London: Ferret Fantasy, 1975).

Luckhurst, Roger. *Science Fiction* (Cambridge: Polity, 2005).

Nasmyth, James and James Carpenter. *The Moon, Considered as a Planet, a World, and a Satellite* (London: John Murray, 1885).

Nicholson, Marjorie Hope. *Voyages to the Moon* (New York: Macmillan, 1948).

Parrett, Aaron. *The Translunar Narrative in the Western Tradition* (Aldershot: Ashgate, 2004).

Robertson, Frances. 'Science and Fiction: James Nasmyth's Photographic Images of the Moon', *Victorian Studies* 48/4 (2006), 595–623.

Trotter, David. *Cinema and Modernism* (Oxford: Blackwell, 2007).

Vaninskaya, Anna. 'The Late-Victorian Romance Revival: A Generic Excursus', *English Literature in Transition, 1880–1920* 51/1 (2008) 57–79.

Warner, Marien. *Photography: A Cultural History* (London: Laurence King Publishing, 2002).

Willis, Martin. *Vision, Science and Literature 1870–1920: Ocular Horizons* (London: Pickering and Chatto, 2011).

CHAPTER 14

SUPER-NICHES?

Detection, Adventure, Exploration, and Spy Stories

DAVID GLOVER

In most literary histories of the *fin de siècle* the passing of the Victorian era was the moment when the system of genre categories that is still in use today effectively came of age. Exact nomenclature may vary: 'adventure, romance, horror, crime, and sport', according to one historian; 'the detective novel, the adventure story, the sex novel, science fiction, even the spy novel', in the words of another.[1] But obvious differences aside, there is substantial agreement here. By the turn of the century, popular fiction was becoming increasingly specialized and the grammar of narrative types and subsets had begun to assume a recognizable structure.

Yet important questions remain. How distinct were the individual genres in practice? How far did they overlap? Why did some genres command a larger audience than others and what does this tell us about shifts in the nature of reading? In his 2005 book *Graphs, Models, Trees*, Franco Moretti put the cat among the pigeons by designating detective fiction and science fiction as 'super-niches', implying that these are genres that have somehow managed to transcend the limitations of the system as a whole. There is an immediate intuitive plausibility about this notion, although Moretti never offers a working definition of what constitutes a super-niche. Nevertheless, super-niches are integral to his ambitious and controversial research programme of mapping and quantifying the changing contours of the literary marketplace. In his exploratory analysis of genres between 1740 and 1900, Moretti identifies forty-four types of novel ranging from the 'picaresque' to 'imperial Gothic', which he sees as the result of 'six major bursts of creativity' or cycles of innovation when 'forms change once, rapidly, across the board, and then repeat

[1] Philip Waller, *Writers, Readers, and Reputations: Literary Life in Britain 1870–1918* (Oxford: Oxford University Press, 2006), 635; Nigel Cross, *The Common Writer: Life in Nineteenth-Century Grub Street* (Cambridge: Cambridge University Press, 1985), 221.

themselves' for twenty-five or thirty years before the process restarts.[2] In line with established thinking, Moretti's final surge of literary invention begins in the latter part of the 1880s. What distinguishes this conjuncture, however, is that the emergence of the super-niches throws the neat cyclical pattern into disarray. For these hyper-genres are no longer merely 'temporary structures' with a relatively short lifespan, but instead have attracted so large and diverse a readership as to reach beyond the confines of the normal cycle and become a permanent addition to the repertoire of popular fiction.

The super-niche is an intriguing concept, and in this chapter I will use it to rethink the history of popular genres between 1880 and 1920. But first I must make two critical points about Moretti's own approach, in order to avoid the over-concentration on literary form that is characteristic of his work. The first problem involves a tension within Moretti's definition of genre. As other critics have noted, the forty-four individual genres or subgenres that figure in his analysis often seem to be based on inconsistent principles of classification.[3] Yet elsewhere, in 'The Slaughterhouse of Literature', an earlier discussion of detective fiction, Moretti appears to make a virtue out of this arbitrariness by insisting that genres are not to be understood as a set of variations upon an archetypal or ideal structure, but instead consist of a loose collection of literary devices, branching off in a variety of directions, 'turning a genre into a wide field of diverging moves'—including chase sequences, locked rooms, or chains of deductive reasoning, to name but a few.[4] This is a capacious definition that already points towards the concept of the super-niche. But although that phrase does not occur in Moretti's essay, the same underlying contrast that is so important to *Graphs, Maps, Trees* is already prefigured here: a distinction between those genres or subgenres that follow the regular twenty-five year cycle and what Moretti refers to as 'large genres' that unfold over the *longue durée*. Interestingly, adventure stories are cited as the largest, most longstanding of large genres, the ultimate super-niche, while the detective story is described as 'a very simple genre'.[5]

Second, the meaning of the term 'niche' needs to be unpacked. The phrase 'niche market' is shorthand not just for a certain kind of text, but also includes a constellation of readers, interests, influences, and pleasures that define a particular sector of the fiction industry. And to speak of a niche in this context is to invoke the conditions that allow a genre to flourish since, as Moretti himself notes, the idea draws upon a biological metaphor. So, when the philosopher Ian Hacking refers to a niche, or more precisely 'an ecological niche', in *Mad Travellers* (1998), his fascinating

[2] Franco Moretti, *Graphs, Maps, Trees: Abstract Models for a Literary Theory* (London: Verso, 2005), 18–19.

[3] Tony Bennett, 'Counting and Seeing the Social Action of Literary Form: Franco Moretti and the Sociology of Literature', *Cultural Sociology* 3/2 (July 2009), 285.

[4] Moretti, 'The Slaughterhouse of Literature', *Modern Language Quarterly* 61/1 (March 2000), 217.

[5] Ibid., 212, 223.

book on the ephemeral nature of some types of mental illness, he is indicating the distinctive environment or habitat, a 'combination of circumstances', in which this or that particular species or phenomenon will thrive—or fade when conditions change.[6] If we link the notion of an ecological niche to Moretti's emphasis upon the internal diversity of genres, then the success of super-niches like detective fiction or adventure must be due to the historical conditions that encourage borrowing from other types of entertainment rather than to a formal process of literary influence. One factor that helps to explain the protean adaptability of the super-niche is the revolution in mass communications—ranging from the spread of new forms of visual culture like film to the growth of urban transport systems—which made some popular generic elements and devices less dependent on local contexts and local markets, enabling them to move between a variety of media and settings. For the first time a character like Sherlock Holmes could become a transnational success, eventually straddling both theatre and cinema, and appearing in American periodicals as diverse as the *Ladies' Home Journal*, *Munsey's Magazine*, and *McClure's*, publications that were as different from each other as they were from *The Strand*, the respectable, pro-imperial middle-class English monthly in which the great detective first rose to fame.

From the early 1880s popular narratives underwent a constant process of modernization. Nowhere was this more marked than in the case of the adventure story, which then occupied a dominant position in the genre system as a whole. While its deeply mannish preoccupation with risk, action, ordeal, and combat placed it among the oldest of literary genres, the adventure narrative diversified so radically that it began to fragment, losing much of its distinctiveness as it continued to take in new forms and new content.

Robert Louis Stevenson was a key figure in this transformation. When Stevenson championed the revival of romance at the beginning of the decade he helped to set in train three major developments. First, through the immense success of books like *Treasure Island* (1883) and *Kidnapped* (1886), initially serialized in the specialist periodical *Young Folks*, he added a new lustre to the boys' adventure story and bridged the gap between juvenile and adult fiction by putting a harsher, more demanding stress on the formation of masculinity. 'Oxen and wain-ropes would not bring me back to that accursed island', Jim Hawkins confesses ruefully at the close of *Treasure Island* and it is surely no accident that Stevenson's novel directly inspired H. Rider Haggard's African imperial romance *King Solomon's Mines* (1885).[7]

Second, Stevenson's crisp economical style was instrumental in making the single volume novel a highly attractive commodity and did much to undermine the

---

[6] Ian Hacking, *Mad Travelers: Reflections on the Reality of Transient Mental Illnesses* (Charlottesville, VA: University of Virginia Press, 1998), 55.

[7] Robert Louis Stevenson, *Treasure Island* (London: Penguin Books, 1999), 190.

prestige of the bulky, overwritten triple-decker than had been the mainstay of the commercial circulating libraries since the heyday of Sir Walter Scott. Significantly, Stevenson positioned himself *with* Scott's romantic passion, but *against* Scott's *longueurs* and undisciplined writing. And finally, Stevenson introduced a new spirit of urban adventure, not only by famously re-imagining the deserted nocturnal by-streets of London's busiest quarters as the haunt of a motiveless killer in his *Strange Case of Dr Jekyll and Mr Hyde* (1885), but also through the way in which he and his wife Fanny simultaneously recast London (or at least Soho) as 'the strategic centre of the universe' in *The Dynamiter* (1885), fuelled by 'the most continuous chink of money on the surface of the globe'—a phantasmagoric world that 'teems and bubbles with adventure'.[8] Here, three footloose young men down on their luck each pledge to turn detective, track down a mysterious wanted man, and claim the two hundred pounds reward advertised in the evening paper. Instead, they merely succeed in becoming transfixed by one extravagant story after another apparently told by a succession of itinerant Scheherazades who have come from Utah or Cuba to 'the Baghdad of the West'.[9] The novel ends with a railway bookstall inadvertently demolished by an Irish terrorist's bomb, as he eagerly seeks a copy of the evening paper which headlines the effects of one of his own infernal machines.

Stevenson's range and virtuosity reinforces the view that the adventure story is the original super-niche. Without qualification, however, it is a slightly misleading claim, for there are several specific and very important lines of development that deserve to be foregrounded. One has already been mentioned: the long-term tendency to identify tales of adventure with the mission of securing an empire, so that the stories themselves, in Martin Green's words, 'charged England's will with the energy to go out into the world and explore, conquer, and rule'.[10] Exploring, conquering, and ruling are surely the stuff of imperial romance, and there can be no question that these became the chief ingredients of H. Rider Haggard's considerable appeal. Stung by an intensely competitive desire to outdo Stevenson, Haggard's work underwent a remarkable sea change. Until 1885 he was the little-known author of disorganized and heavily melodramatic triple-deckers largely set in the Norfolk countryside. Then, once the irritant provided by *Treasure Island* had taken effect, Haggard was reborn as the author of extraordinarily successful single volume romances in which small bands of white men trek into the heart of Africa in search of the spoils of a lost civilization (maps, charts, and other illustrations are indispensable accoutrements in texts of this kind). *King Solomon's Mines* was snapped up by Stevenson's publisher Cassell and, on the back of an aggressive advertising campaign with posters appearing overnight throughout London, it became an immediate best-seller (unlike *Treasure Island*'s reputation, which grew relatively slowly). George du Maurier's *Trilby* (1894) is usually credited as the first nineteenth-century

---

[8] Stevenson, *The Dynamiter* (Stroud: Allan Sutton, 1984), 4, 6.   [9] Ibid., 1.
[10] Martin Green, *Dreams of Adventure, Deeds of Empire* (New York: Basic Books, 1979), 3.

best-seller, but one might think of it instead as the last of the great popular triple-deckers. Almost a decade earlier, the promotion of the shorter, utterly blood-curdling *King Solomon's Mines* and its enthusiastic reception among young and old—quickly followed by *She* and *Allan Quatermain* in 1887—had clearly pointed towards the publishing sensations of the future.

Readers turned to Haggard and his imitators for ferocious battle scenes, dreams of unimaginable wealth, and the frisson of racial and sexual otherness. It is not the theme of 'The Girl I Left Behind Me' whistled by Captain John Good as the three men begin their night journey across the desert, but 'the soft-eyed, shapely Kukuana beauty' whose pirouettes 'would have put most ballet girls to shame' that entrance and delight them and are a vital part of the quest.[11] At the same time, it is always a woman who will lead the men into danger—as the witch-like Gagool draws the heroes of *King Solomon's Mines* into the bowels of the earth in search of treasure, or as the cruelly regal 'She-who-must-be-obeyed' brings Horace Holly and Leo Vincey to an underground chamber where they will see the flaming pillar of eternal life.

Entrapment or confinement is the reverse side of the narrative of exploration, threatening to immobilize the protagonists in the face of forces that they will be unable to control. This trope is by no means limited to the bleaker moments of imperial romance. For in the form of the locked room, the 'Place of Death', as it is christened in *King Solomon's Mines*, is integral to the detective story. It is a set-up exemplary of the 'insoluble' mystery, either as a baffling location for the corpse or as a fortified position from which the potential victim awaits his or her fate, as does Julia Stoner in Arthur Conan Doyle's 'The Adventure of the Speckled Band' (1892) or the Foreign Secretary, Sir Philip Ramon, in Edgar Wallace's *The Four Just Men* (1905).

Yet the relay between the adventure tale and the detective story is more elaborate than the career of a single device. Again and again the detective narrative animates a disturbing causal chain that links the most distant reaches of empire to the seemingly mundane corners of the *patria*. Indeed, Caroline Reitz has insisted on the necessity of bringing 'the figures of the detective and the imperial explorer *together* in their proper global context', on the grounds that depictions of successful policing at the periphery of empire helped to legitimize the role of state power at home, disarming suspicion of the forces of law and order by creating the possibility of identification with the newly imagined detective.[12] In this argument, detectives are masters of local knowledge, making independent judgements in the field that will ultimately render the world a safer place. And local knowledge has its own peculiar pleasures and vicissitudes. Rudyard Kipling's maverick policeman Strickland is so

---

[11] H. Rider Haggard, *King Solomon's Mines*, ed. Robert Hampson (London: Penguin, 2007), 132, 180.

[12] Caroline Reitz, *Detecting the Nation: Fictions of Detection and the Imperial Venture* (Columbus, OH: Ohio State University Press), 80 (emphasis in original).

fascinated by native life in India that he thinks nothing of donning his favourite disguise and stepping 'down into the brown crowd' for a week or more, a predilection that allows him to pose 'as a *fakir* or priest' and solve 'the great Nasiban Murder Case'.[13] He has the complete confidence of his peers, yet despite his remarkable triumphs he is mistrusted not only by the Indians on whom he spies but by his departmental officials too. Strickland is not above intimidating native witnesses in a bogus divorce case, and enabling the falsely accused co-respondent to horsewhip the husband who has brought the court action against him. And in one particularly brutal tale, 'The Mark of the Beast', Strickland grimly resorts to torturing a leper to force him to remove the spell he has cast on an English friend who has desecrated an Indian temple.[14]

Perhaps unsurprisingly, there was some resistance when Kipling first tried to publish this story in England, suggesting that the politics of identification may sometimes have been more contradictory than Reitz suggests. More generally, the Strickland stories acknowledge and in a sense condone the dirty work of empire, representing the good of rough justice. But in valorizing the spirit rather than the letter of the law, Kipling controversially introduces a breach within legality itself that is not easily wished away. Officialdom cannot quite turn a blind eye here.

In fact, from a metropolitan perspective, the fallout from imperial adventures was often deeply problematic. The establishment of the partnership between Sherlock Holmes and Dr Watson was predicated upon the latter's melancholy return from the Second Anglo-Afghan War, an injured and disaffected man. As Zarena Aslami observes in her comparative study of G. A. Henty's militaristic boys' adventure story *For Name and Fame, or Through Afghan Passes* (1886) and the first Sherlock Holmes narrative *A Study in Scarlet* (1887), Conan Doyle begins where Henty's jingoism ends. 'The campaign brought honours and promotion to many', writes Watson, 'but for me it had nothing but misfortune and disaster'.[15] In Henty's fiction the resilience of the Afghan hill tribes serves as an object lesson to the British—indeed the Liberal politician William Gladstone once sought to evoke sympathy for this martial people by likening their travails to those of the Scottish Highlanders in the Jacobite Rebellion. By contrast, Aslami argues, *A Study in Scarlet* 'evokes, and then displaces anxieties about British aggression in imperialized sites' and in doing so allows for the recuperation of Watson's damaged self.[16] At the close

[13] Rudyard Kipling, 'Miss Youghal's *Sais*' (1887), in *Plain Tales from the Hills*, ed. David Trotter (London: Penguin, 1987), 52.

[14] Kipling, 'The Bronckhorst Divorce-Case' (1888), in *Plain Tales from the Hills*, 214–19, and 'The Mark of the Beast' (1890), in *Life's Handicap*, ed. A. O. J. Cockshut (Oxford: Oxford University Press, 1987), 178–91.

[15] Arthur Conan Doyle, *A Study in Scarlet*, in *The Penguin Complete Sherlock Holmes* (Harmondsworth: Penguin, 1986), 15.

[16] Zarena Aslami, *The Dream Life of Citizens: Late Victorian Novels and the Fantasy of the State* (New York: Fordham University Press, 2012), 81.

of the novel, when Watson offers to foster a wider public awareness of Holmes's extraordinary powers of analysis through his own writing, he is tacitly recognizing the latter's gift of candour and perceptiveness, the knowledge that Watson 'has undergone hardship and sickness' as his 'haggard face says clearly'.[17] This exchange is the cue for Holmes and Watson to embark on a series of 'adventures' (they are always 'adventures' and only secondarily 'cases') in which Watson is frequently advised to keep his old service revolver close at hand, and Holmes rapidly changes 'from the languid dreamer to the man of action'.[18]

The dual structure spelled out by Watson, with its alternation between intelligence and agency, mind and body, is firmly rooted in the imperial genealogy of the detective story which in turn can be extended back into earlier histories of conquest and military occupation. However, as the genre has developed there has been a tendency for these two components to become dissociated and identified with distinct subtypes. At the purely formal level the narratologist Tzvetan Todorov has claimed that the mystery and the adventure are the two basic structural variants of detective fiction.[19] But in historical terms the picture is far more complex than this analysis implies, with narrative elements being broken down and reassembled in untried combinations and settings as authors have sought to address new modes of contemporary experience that would maximize their readerships in a changing market. It is this fitful concern to update and reconfigure generic formulae that gives the super-niche its exceptional plasticity through the irregular production of unanticipated hybrid forms.

Consider the case of R. Austin Freeman, one of the earliest exponents of what would now be thought of as the classic English detective story. Freeman's turn to crime writing has an almost Watsonian ring to it, for he had been invalided out of his post as an assistant colonial surgeon in Accra after having contracted blackwater fever. His first book was a memoir—*Travels and Life in Ashanti and Jaman* (1898)— and he also tried his hand at an African imperial romance *à la* Rider Haggard, published as *The Golden Pool* in 1905. But Freeman's real success came with his creation of the lecturer in medical jurisprudence Dr John Thorndyke, whose obsessive concern to make the evidence speak, to subject it to the most rigorous technical scrutiny, brought the detective story into a closer alignment with a popular version of scientific methodology. In the stories he published in *Pearson's Magazine* from 1908-9, Freeman augmented the detailed illustrations routinely featured by this middle-class monthly with specially staged photographs of the most important clues. In 'The Anthropologist at Large', for example, readers were given 'three cross-sections of human hairs seen through the microscope', one of which was said

---

[17] Conan Doyle, *A Study in Scarlet*, 24.

[18] Conan Doyle, *The Hound of the Baskervilles: Another Adventure of Sherlock Holmes* (1902), in *The Complete Sherlock Holmes*, 689.

[19] Tzvetan Todorov, *Poétique de la prose: choix, suivi de nouvelles recherches sur le récit* (Paris: Éditions du Seuil, 1980), 73–4.

to have belonged to the burglar in the story, while the other two contrasting images help to identify its peculiar features. From the evidence of a hat that the criminal left behind at the scene of the robbery, Thorndyke identifies signs that its wearer has been exposed to mother-of-pearl dust at work and deduces from the stray hairs and the shape of the man's skull that the culprit was drawn from 'the yellow or Mongol races'.[20] From these traces he links the theft of Japanese artworks to a Japanese employee in a Limehouse mother-of-pearl factory.

Thorndyke is careful not to remove all the evidence from the art collector's home in order to give the police the same access to the clues that he has had. In embryonic form, this gesture expresses the substance of what was to become the dominant ideology of detective fiction in the 1920s, the notion that readers and their proxies within the text should have an equal, or at least a sporting chance of solving the mystery. At this stage, the notion of fair play remained largely implicit. Freeman, who did as much as anyone to champion this approach, did not set out the case for the intellectual integrity of the genre until May 1924 when he published an chapter on 'The Art of the Detective Story' in the serious-minded periodical *The Nineteenth Century and After*. There he argued that 'the plot of a detective novel is, in effect, an argument conducted under the guise of fiction' in which the investigator is pitted against a murderous adversary with everything to lose, 'a desperate player...who is playing for his life'.[21] Clues, evidence, and data serve as tokens in the game. Of course, Freeman's idealized model does not exactly fit the conditions that underpin the puzzle in 'The Anthropologist At Large', where only the reader who is in possession of the supposedly 'well-known anthropological facts' regarding the tripartite division of the human race on the basis of skin colour, dimensions of the skull, and hair type would be in a position to identify the criminals in the story.[22] Nevertheless, the idea that detective fiction was primarily a matter of what Dorothy L. Sayers was to call the 'quiet enjoyment of the logical' was slowly starting to take shape.[23]

Freeman's publishers undoubtedly hoped that Dr Thorndyke would do for *Pearson's* what Sherlock Holmes had done for *The Strand*, a considerable prize in the intensely competitive monthly fiction magazine trade, and the editors made much of the innovativeness of these stories and the light that they threw upon the role of the sciences in the investigation of crime. For all their unexpected twists and turns, however, Freeman's stories lacked incident (he always believed that there was an inevitable tension between drama and logical analysis) and his depiction of an attempt on Thorndyke's life in his 'detective romance' *The Red Thumb Mark* (1907)

[20] R. Austin Freeman, 'The Anthropologist At Large', *Pearson's Magazine* 27/158 (February 1909), 176–7.

[21] Freeman, 'The Art of the Detective Story', *The Nineteenth Century and After* 95/567 (May 1924), 718.

[22] Freeman, 'The Anthropologist at Large', 176.

[23] Dorothy L. Sayers, 'Introduction', in Sayers (ed.), *Great Short Stories of Detection, Mystery and Horror* (London: Gollancz, 1928), 15.

is curiously flat and understated. When *Pearson's* editor Percy Everett enthusiastically described Thorndyke as 'the first detective in fiction to appear without what is generally known as a "personality"', he inadvertently put his finger on Freeman's greatest weakness.[24]

Freeman's intellectualist credo represented a narrowing of focus, even compared to the Sherlock Holmes stories, though paradoxically it became the most influential rationale for detective fiction in the interwar period. But not all crime writers took this line. E. C. Bentley's innovative novel *Trent's Last Case* (1913) combined a sustained sense of mystery with a light, rather facetious touch that owed something to the social comedy of P. G. Wodehouse and was largely directed at debunking the Holmes mystique. 'I am Hawkshaw the detective', declares Philip Trent, the artist-cum-amateur detective, before launching into 'a short lecture on the subject of glass finger-bowls'.[25]

Although Bentley presents the reader with the baffling murder of an American plutocrat, an abundance of clues, and a cast of highly likely suspects, it is crucial that Trent's investigation ends in failure, a 'revelation of the impotence of human reason'. What particularly muddies Trent's vision is the love interest with which Bentley fleshes out the novel, an unshakeable fascination with the dead millionaire's wife. In an early chapter Trent secretly catches sight of Mabel Manderson looking out to sea, 'her face full of some dream', interrupted when she stretches her arms and body in a sudden 'gesture of freedom'.[26] This tableau is permanently imprinted on Trent's memory and he repeatedly returns to it in order to understand what this elusive and highly desirable woman wants. Recreated as a carefully composed canvas in Trent's artistic mind, this scene is reminiscent of the immensely popular Edwardian 'problem pictures', paintings by John Collier or Alfred Priest that provocatively resisted narrative closure while exposing the fraught moral economy of gender and sexuality.[27] Like detective fiction, problem pictures were concerned with the intelligibility of surfaces and the inscrutability of human motives and were often reproduced in newspapers and illustrated magazines.

Despite their difference in tone, Bentley's and Freeman's work spoke to the growing complexity of the urban environment, a multitudinous ensemble of signs and information including advertising hoardings, billboards, placards, newspaper headlines, photographic and film images, traffic signals, and street directions, all demanding new interpretive skills and forms of attention. In the issue immediately before the first Dr Thorndyke case appeared, for example, *Pearson's* published 'A Railway Dictionary' to help explain 'the meaning of many signs and

---

[24] 'Sparks from Our Anvil', *Pearson's Magazine* 26/155 (November 1908), 535.

[25] E. C. Bentley, *Trent's Last Case* (London: Thomas Nelson, 1913), 179.

[26] Ibid., 375, 144.

[27] See Pamela M. Fletcher, *Narrating Modernity: The British Problem Picture, 1895–1914* (Aldershot: Ashgate, 2003).

signals frequently seen but seldom understood' by suburban travellers.[28] In similar vein, Thorndyke's orderly process of scientific reasoning promised to cut a path through the welter of stimuli, separating what mattered from the transient and the inessential.

Yet despite Freeman's firm attachment to scientific modernity, he was dismayed by the ever-increasing pace of technological advance, particularly as reflected by other media in which he included 'the entertainments of the cinema' and 'the newspaper serial of the conventional type'. Here, and in the brasher and more unsavoury sorts of popular fiction, speed was intimately linked to suspense and the headlong rush of events was invariably accompanied by a para-military cornucopia of revolvers, automatic pistols, aeroplanes, and motor cars or motor boats, creating 'a crude and pungent sensationalism' (an increasingly vocal complaint among detective fiction writers in the interwar years).[29] If 'thrills' were the raison d'être of this kind of writing, in the hands of Erskine Childers, John Buchan, and even William Le Queux, they pointed towards a renewal of the militaristic adventure format that once again blurred the boundaries between established generic labels. Invasion scare stories and spy novels thrived upon the unstable political situation in Europe in the decades before the First World War, but they also encouraged the rise of the 'shocker' (later rechristened the 'thriller') which John Buchan's prefatory letter to *The Thirty-Nine Steps* (1915) neatly defined as a 'romance where the incidents defy probabilities, and march just inside the borders of the possible'.[30] This was to become the worst nightmare of authors like Freeman, with their imagined upper middle-class audience of 'theologians, scholars, lawyers, and to a less extent, perhaps, doctors and men of science'.[31]

Pearson's was very much a part of this trend. In its November 1908 issue it featured a story called 'The Air Battle Fleet. The Thrilling Narration of a Raid on England that was Grandly Repelled'. Walter Wood's predictable tale of a pre-emptive strike against the British Navy by an unnamed, but manifestly German, enemy ('Britain's most powerful and jealous rival') was designed to buttress political support for maintaining naval supremacy.[32] Here airships patently lacked the dependability of sea power since they were vulnerable to sudden shifts in wind currents, and collided with each other in mid-air when they were not being gunned down by British torpedo boats. Unlike *For Name and Fame* or *King Solomon's Mines*, invasion scare narratives like Wood's were directly concerned with the defence of the realm, showing that British interests *could* be protected once the nation recognized the dangers that it faced.

[28] G. A. Sekon, 'A Railway Dictionary', *Pearson's Magazine* 26/155 (November 1908), 543.
[29] Freeman, 'The Art of the Detective Story', 714–15.
[30] John Buchan, *The Thirty-Nine Steps* (London: Penguin, 2004), 3.
[31] Freeman, 'The Art of the Detective Story', 716.
[32] Walter Wood, 'The Air Battle Fleet', *Pearson's Magazine* 26/155 (November 1908), 492.

However, external threats were only half the story. In an image that harked back to tales of domestic terrorism from the 1880s such as *The Dynamiter*, Britain's downfall was already being prepared by a network of foreign spies who were searching out the country's weakest points and planning to sabotage its transport and communications infrastructure. As its title suggests, Wood's 1906 earlier novel *The Enemy in Our Midst* took the infiltration of the metropolis by dubious German immigrants as a sign of how blind the nation had become, a view that echoed the controversy around the passage of the restrictionist Aliens Act in 1905. Indeed, some novels pressed the warning still further by depicting Britain *after* the most feared scenarios were already a *fait accompli*, as in James Blyth's *Ichabod* (1910) or Saki's *When the Kaiser Came* (1913), both of whom depicted German invasion plans as a front for Jewish domination.

But it was the extraordinarily prolific William Le Queux who capitalized most effectively on anxieties about national security. In collaboration with Lord Roberts, Britain's most celebrated general and former Commander-in-Chief of the British Army, Le Queux spent months researching a convincing German invasion route for his 1906 novel, which Lord Northcliffe agreed to serialize in the *Daily Mail* on condition that the plan was altered to take in Britain's major cities, home to millions of potential *Mail* readers. When *The Invasion of 1910* first appeared in March 1906, it benefited not only from the *Mail*'s ample headlines, demotic prose, and short punchy paragraphs, but also from an eye-catching publicity campaign in which the paper was touted on the London streets by men dressed in pseudo-German uniforms and spiked helmets. The novel sold over a million copies and, when war finally broke out, Le Queux's taste for self-advertisement and media spectacle never deserted him. In October 1914 his film *If England Were Invaded* was released and he continued to support patriotic lobbies like the National Service League, while exposés with such titles as *The German Spy* (1914) or *German Spies in England* (1915) warned of the dangers represented by German nannies and waiters.

Le Queux prided himself on his command of the latest scientific developments, including radio, aerial warfare, and the 'dirty tricks' of modern espionage. As David Stafford has argued, his role was that of 'a mediator between his popular—or populist—audience, and the emerging international and technological order of the twentieth century'.[33] But his rival—and far more securely establishment figure— John Buchan took the diametrically opposite tack by stripping down the adventure narrative and returning to 'the old elemental fighting instincts of man'.[34] In *The Thirty-Nine Steps* (1916), Buchan's hero Richard Hannay has only his hard-won South African 'veldcraft' to rely on. Nothing is certain: the conspiracy of which he has been warned is a deliberate deception—disinformation designed to keep him in

---

[33] David Stafford, 'Conspiracy and Xenophobia: The Popular Spy Novels of William Le Queux, 1893–1914', *Europa* (Montréal) 3/3 (1982), 173.

[34] Buchan, *The Thirty-Nine Steps*, 11.

the dark—and for most of the novel he has no clear idea who is pursuing him or why. Fleeing for his life and desperate to outwit his pursuers, Hannay resembles the protagonist of an early one-reel chase film or the high-speed cinematic camera eye in a 'phantom ride' movie.[35] Although he boldly steals their car, Hannay is also being hunted by a monoplane and, to make matters worse, the police are trying to track him down, believing him to be the murderer of the man who had told him of the plot to destabilize Europe. When the outbreak of the First World War is announced in the novel's final paragraph and Hannay enlists, the reader is almost ready to accept that a kind of normality has returned.

This brief history reveals a contest between two large, overlapping genres as they jockey for dominance in the field of popular fiction, a contest in which super-niches dilate and contract when their boundaries are redefined. As the adventure story moved away from its military and imperial origins, two decisive changes occurred: on the one hand, a new preoccupation with narratives of national security and defence led to the rise of the spy thriller; and on the other, a steady focus upon domestic law and order, investigation, and surveillance brought about the consolidation of the detective novel. Super-niches are not monopolistic structures but should rather be viewed as amorphous zones of competition between contending subgenres that produce a variety of hybrid forms. The detective story borrowed some of its protective colouring from the adventure genre, only later seeking to differentiate itself from the unruly thriller, though some exceptionally successful writers like Edgar Wallace tended to ignore such distinctions altogether.

The long shadow cast by the First World War further complicated the instability of generic boundaries by giving a new emphasis to the importance of gender in popular narratives, as after 1918 more women writers successfully entered the field. Male heroes still followed the model provided by Richard Hannay or Le Queux's Duckworth Drew, with 'Sapper's' indomitable tough-guy Bulldog Drummond, a demobbed officer dedicated to tackling the unfinished business of the war, leading the fray against an interminable conspiracy of foreigners, revolutionaries, and turn-coats. Still it was a foreigner making his debut in 1920—the year that saw the publication of *Bulldog Drummond*—who would prove to be one of the twentieth century's most durable literary sleuths: the punctilious, almost effeminate Hercule Poirot in *The Mysterious Affair at Styles*. Christie's country house detective novel is set in wartime, though talk of distant suffering serves as a means of avoiding reference to shattering events that are closer to home. As the dense overgrowth of discrepancies, enigmas, and red herrings begins to accumulate, the entire household witnesses what turns out to be a murder in which the victim suffers a series of violent protracted convulsions, a scenario quite unlike the genteel trope of the body in the library that soon became a generic commonplace.

---

[35] See Cecil M. Hepworth, *Came the Dawn: Memories of a Film Pioneer* (London: Phoenix House, 1951), 44, 68.

But popular fictional conventions had not yet hardened as they were to do in the 1930s. Hercule Poirot's fussiness was a far cry from the wanton brutality mixed with bumptious repartee that formed Bulldog Drummond's stock in trade. Yet, as late as 1927, Christie was not averse to pitting Poirot against a ruthless international conspiracy in her thriller *The Big Four* (1927), when she thought she might kill the twin birds of mystery and adventure with one stone. Or consider developments in romance, confined to the merest subplot by 'Sapper' and Christie.

In her runaway best-seller *The Sheik* (1919), written while her husband was serving in the war, E. M. Hull blended violence and adventure into a love story which imagined a precociously boyish young Englishwoman being whisked off into a world of bellicose Arab tribes dominated by a sexually voracious Bedouin—in reality a white man—who repeatedly rapes her in a brutal, and brutally extended, prelude to their discovery of connubial bliss. Hull's novel shocked and titillated its readers, but its ripples spread out into a wider media complex that produced new versions of the transgressive figure of the white Bedouin, redefining the scope of the niche that a best-seller could inhabit for decades to come. As the image of Hull's Sheik Ahmed Ben Hassan blurred into that of the Hollywood matinée idol Rudolph Valentino in the film adaptation and simultaneously became confused with heavily romanticized recreations of the desert war hero Lawrence of Arabia (as publicized in *Strand Magazine* and the popular dailies), it was becoming increasingly apparent that even the largest of genres was not quite capacious enough to contain this tangle of cultural coincidences and contradictions.[36]

FURTHER READING

Bivona, Daniel. *British Imperial Literature, 1870–1940: Writing and the Administration of Empire* (Cambridge: Cambridge University Press, 2008).

Brantlinger, Patrick. *Rule of Darkness: British Literature and Imperialism, 1830–1914* (Ithaca, NY: Cornell University Press, 1988).

Bristow, Joseph. *Empire Boys: Adventures in a Man's World* (London: HarperCollinsAcademic, 1991).

Cawelti, John G. *Adventure, Mystery, and Romance: Formula Stories as Art and Popular Culture* (Chicago, IL: University of Chicago Press, 1976).

Denning, Michael. *Cover Stories: Narrative and Ideology in the British Spy Thriller* (London: Routledge and Kegan Paul, 1987).

Eisenzweig, Uri. *Le récit impossible: Forme et sens du roman policier* (Paris: Christian Bourgois Éditeur, 1986).

Green, Martin. *Dreams of Adventure, Deeds of Empire* (New York: Basic Books, 1979).

Knight, Stephen. *Form and Ideology in Crime Fiction* (London: Macmillan, 1980).

Moretti, Franco. *Graphs, Maps, Trees: Abstract Models for a Literary Theory* (London: Verso, 2005).

---

[36] See Steven C. Caton, 'The Sheik', in Holly Edwards (ed.), *Noble Dreams, Wicked Pleasures: Orientalism in America, 1870–1930* (Princeton, NJ: Princeton University Press, 2000), 99–117.

Mukherjee, Upamanyu Pablo. *Crime and Empire: The Colony in Nineteenth-Century Fictions of Crime* (Oxford: Oxford University Press, 2003).

Palmer, Jerry. *Thrillers: Genesis and Structure of a Popular Genre* (London: Edward Arnold, 1978).

Pittard, Christopher. *Purity and Contamination in Late Victorian Detective Fiction* (Aldershot: Ashgate, 2011).

Pratt, Mary Louise. *Imperial Eyes: Travel Writing and Transculturation* (London: Routledge, 1992).

Reitz, Caroline. *Detecting the Nation: Fictions of Detection and Imperial Venture* (Columbus, OH: Ohio State University Press, 2004).

Stafford, David. *The Silent Game: The Real World of Imaginary Spies* (Toronto, ON: Lester and Orpen Dennys, 1988).

PART IV

SITES AND SPACES
OF KNOWLEDGE

CHAPTER 15

SCIENTIFIC FORMATIONS
AND TRANSFORMATIONS

RACHEL CROSSLAND

In 1945, recalling his arrival in Cambridge in the early 1880s, the mathematician Alfred North Whitehead stated that at that time 'nearly everything was supposed to be known about physics that could be known' and that 'physics was supposed to be nearly a closed subject'. Yet in fact the years 1880–1920 would prove to be one of the most turbulent and revolutionary periods of scientific discovery to date, and for no science more than physics. 'By 1900', Whitehead recalled, everything had changed: 'the Newtonian physics were demolished, done for!'[1]

While there is certainly an element of exaggeration in his recollections, Whitehead is clear that bearing witness to this movement from a science apparently nearly completed to a science undergoing a series of radical revolutions had 'a profound effect' on him—forming, indeed, 'one of the supreme facts of my experience'.[2] Nor was Whitehead alone in such a reaction: the memoirs of the American historian Henry Adams repeatedly emphasize the movement into 'a new universe' provoked by science around the turn of the century, as well as the idea that '[n]othing so revolutionary had happened since the year 300'.[3]

A quick glance at a summary of the scientific discoveries made in the late nineteenth and early twentieth centuries serves to contextualize these responses:

> In all the history of physics, there has never been a period of transition as abrupt, as unanticipated, and over as wide a front as the decade 1895 to 1905. In rapid succession the experimental discoveries of X-rays (1895), the Zeeman effect (1896), radioactivity (1896), the electron (1897), and the extension of infrared spectroscopy into the 3 μm to 60 μm region opened new vistas. The birth of quantum theory (1900) and relativity

[1] Alfred North Whitehead, *Dialogues of Alfred North Whitehead*, ed. Lucien Price (London: Max Reinhardt, 1954), 341.

[2] Ibid., 341, 212.

[3] Henry Adams, *The Education of Henry Adams*, ed. Ira B. Nadel (Oxford: Oxford University Press, 1999), 319, 411, see also 320, 378, 382.

theory (1905) marked the beginning of an era in which the very foundations of physical theory were found to be in need of revision.[4]

The idea that such radical scientific developments should find their way into literary texts is by no means a new one, and modernist responses to Einsteinian relativity have received particularly critical attention over the years (see 'Further Reading'). Other critics, most notably Michael Whitworth, have emphasized the ongoing resonance of nineteenth-century scientific ideas with those of the early twentieth century.[5] Science, and in particular physics, was in a state of flux between the years 1880 and 1920. The old mechanical laws associated with Isaac Newton were increasingly found to be wanting, yet it took time for new theories to emerge, and even then the old laws could not be dismissed outright. As D. H. Lawrence wrote in *Fantasia of the Unconscious* (1922), just a few years after the experimental verification of Albert Einstein's general theory of relativity in 1919, 'Newton's Law of Gravitation... still remains a law, even if not quite so absolute as heretofore'.[6]

Perhaps unsurprisingly, the year 1900 has provided a useful dividing line for emphasizing the dramatic nature of the split in scientific ideas and approaches which occurred around the end of the nineteenth and start of the twentieth centuries. Both Whitehead and Adams privilege 1900 as a key marker in the developments they discuss, the latter suggesting that '[t]he child born in 1900 would, then, be born into a new world'.[7] However, as Pais's list indicates, the revolution in physics certainly began before the end of the twentieth century, and while it involved a radical transformation of many older scientific ideas, many of those ideas still survive in our twenty-first century understanding of the world around us. Nevertheless, the retrospective accounts of Whitehead and Adams suggest that such developments were perceived at the time as a radical break with the past—a theme repeatedly emphasized by contemporary press reports.

Scientific transformations

When it comes to immediate and dramatic reactions to scientific developments during this period, few can rival that which greeted Wilhelm Conrad Röntgen's discovery of X-rays on 8 November 1895. The first public notices announcing Röntgen's discovery appeared on the fifth and sixth of January 1896, while the first X-ray image

---

[4] Abraham Pais, *'Subtle is the Lord—': The Science and the Life of Albert Einstein* (Oxford: Oxford University Press, 1982), 26.

[5] Michael H. Whitworth, *Einstein's Wake: Relativity, Metaphor, and Modernist Literature* (Oxford: Oxford University Press, 2001).

[6] D. H. Lawrence, *Psychoanalysis and the Unconscious and Fantasia of the Unconscious*, ed. Bruce Steele (Cambridge: Cambridge University Press, 2004), 153.

[7] Adams, *Education*, 382. Adams does, however, acknowledge the 'convenience' of this date.

to be produced in the United Kingdom appeared as early as 8 January 1896. The newspaper and periodical press both encouraged and responded to widespread public interest in this strange new phenomenon, especially during the first half of 1896.[8] Some sense of the breadth of this interest can be gleaned from H. G. Wells's mention of 'Röntgen vibrations' in *The Invisible Man* (1897). The extent to which Wells could assume his readers' familiarity with this scientific concept is emphasized not only by his direct reference to X-rays, but by the fact that Griffin tells Kemp outright that these are not the 'sort of ethereal vibration' involved in his own experiments, suggesting that Wells expected his readers to make a similar assumption.[9]

When working at the crossover of literature and science, and considering the literary manifestations of scientific ideas, it is necessary to explore the ways in which specific writers may have come into contact with such ideas. While the extensive press response suggests that it may well have been difficult to avoid any knowledge of the discovery of X-rays, certain literary writers encountered them in a more direct, and thus, perhaps, more significant, manner. One such writer was Joseph Conrad who, on a trip to Glasgow in 1898, met the ear, nose, and throat specialist and X-ray pioneer John Macintyre.[10] Macintyre owned an early X-ray machine and, after dinner one night, entertained Conrad and the Scottish novelist Neil Munro by taking and printing X-ray photographs of their hands and, with Conrad, contemplating Munro's 'ribs and back-bone, the more opaque portions of my viscera, my Waterbury watch and what coins were in my pocket'.[11] On his return home Conrad excitedly recalled the evening in a letter to Edward Garnett, recounting his discussions with Macintyre 'about *the* secret of the universe and the nonexistence of, so called, matter'.[12]

C. T. Watts has suggested that Conrad's evening with Macintyre 'provided the "scientific" mechanism' for Conrad and Ford Madox Ford's *The Inheritors* (1901), and that Conrad discussed his experiences in Glasgow with Ford while negotiating the renting of Pent Farm.[13] Although there is nothing to confirm this suggestion in Conrad's letters to Ford from this period, Conrad stayed overnight with Ford one week after his return from Glasgow. In addition, Conrad's letter to Garnett shows

---

[8] See Linda Dalrymple Henderson, 'X Rays and the Quest for Invisible Reality in the Art of Kupka, Duchamp, and the Cubists', *Art Journal* 47/4 (Winter 1988), 324.

[9] H. G. Wells, *The Invisible Man*, ed. Patrick Parrinder (London: Penguin, 2005), 95.

[10] For Macintyre, who founded the first British radiological department in Glasgow in February 1896, see J. F. Calder, 'Radiology in Scotland', in A. M. K. Thomas (ed.), *The Invisible Light: 100 Years of Medical Radiology* (Oxford: Blackwell Science, 1995), 93. A series of Macintyre's pioneering X-ray cinematograph films are available online at http://ssa.nls.uk/film/0520.

[11] Neil Munro, *The Brave Days: A Chronicle from the North* (Edinburgh: Porpoise Press, 1931), 113.

[12] Joseph Conrad, *The Collected Letters of Joseph Conrad*, ed. Frederick R. Karl and Laurence Davies, 9 vols (Cambridge: Cambridge University Press, 1983–2007), II, 94. An X-ray photograph of Conrad's hand is reproduced as Plate 1 in vol. II of Conrad's *Collected Letters*.

[13] C. T. Watts, 'Joseph Conrad, Dr. Macintyre, and "The Inheritors"', *Notes and Queries* 14/7 (July 1967), 246.

Conrad linking his recent scientific experiences directly with 'the matter (there's no matter) of Pent Farm'.[14]

Watts sees Conrad's conclusions following his visit to Macintyre as 'anticipating' the explanation of the 'Fourth Dimensionists' in *The Inheritors*, and it is worth noting the appearance of certain images which suggest X-rays in this work.[15] The mysterious woman at the centre of the novel is described early on with reference to 'transparency' without 'frailness', an image which is reminiscent of Conrad's description of the appearance of Munro's body when X-rayed: 'too diaphanous to be visible'.[16] Meanwhile, Granger, seeing Gurnard's attention fixed on him, 'seemed to feel his glance bore through the irises of my eyes into the back of my skull', a feeling which is described as 'almost physical', 'as if some incredibly concentrant reflector had been turned upon me'. Similarly, Granger's final 'revelation', like his initial glimpse of the 'something beyond' of the Fourth Dimension, is experienced as a sort of seeing through of the world around him, a glimpse through the surface to the underlying 'falsehood'.[17] Likewise, Conrad's 1898 short story 'The Return' focuses on the penetration of hidden realities and on sudden revelatory visions, an idea that also appears in *Heart of Darkness* (1899) where it has been linked to 'the imaginative possibilities opened up by the discovery of X-rays'.[18]

While such images can be seen as somewhat commonplace for tales of this kind, which involve sudden realizations on the parts of their central characters, an awareness of the contemporary scientific context, and, more importantly, the 'imaginative possibilities' thereof, enables us to consider some of the connotations which may have been more readily present both to Conrad himself and to his contemporary audience. Developing a sense of the imaginative possibilities of a particular scientific development also allows us to follow Gillian Beer's lead in exploring 'transformation rather than translation' when working between and across disciplines. As Beer continues, '[s]cientific and literary discourses overlap, but unstably'.[19] Having said that, a number of critics have highlighted the fact that 'seeing into the brain was a major theme of x-ray literature from the beginning', thus demonstrating the relevance of X-ray-related terminology outside of a purely corporeal and skeletal focus, as well as emphasizing the instability of overlaps of this kind.[20]

---

[14]   Conrad, *Letters*, II, 95.

[15]   Cedric Watts, *Conrad and Cunninghame Graham* (Farnham: The Joseph Conrad Society, 1978), 13.

[16]   Joseph Conrad and Ford Madox Ford, *The Inheritors: An Extravagant Story* (Liverpool: Liverpool University Press, 1999), 5; Conrad, *Letters*, II, 95.

[17]   Conrad and Ford, *The Inheritors*, 61, 8, 136.

[18]   Conrad, *Tales of Unrest*, ed. Allan H. Simmons and J. H. Stape (Cambridge: Cambridge University Press, 2012); Martine Hennard Dutheil de la Rochère, 'Sounding the Hollow Heart of the West: X-Rays and the *technique de la mort*', in Nidesh Lawtoo (ed.), *Conrad's 'Heart of Darkness' and Contemporary Thought: Revisiting the Horror with Lacoue-Labarthe* (London: Bloomsbury Academic, 2012), 230.

[19]   Gillian Beer, *Open Fields: Science in Cultural Encounter* (Oxford: Oxford University Press, 1996), 173.

[20]   Henderson, 'X Rays', 332.

Of course, a writer's response to a specific scientific development is not necessarily registered immediately after they first become aware of that development. Robert Crawford has linked T. S. Eliot's image of 'a magic lantern [throwing] the nerves in patterns on a screen' from 'The Love Song of J. Alfred Prufrock' (1915) with an illustrated article on X-rays which appeared in the *St. Louis Daily Globe-Democrat* in 1897, when Eliot was eight years old.[21] Similarly, more than twenty years intervene between Virginia Woolf's direct encounter with X-ray technology and her first direct reference thereto in her professional writings. On 9 January 1897 the fourteen-year-old Virginia Stephen recorded at reasonable length in her diary the details of her accidental attendance at 'a lecture on the Rontgen [*sic*] Rays' at the Regent Street Polytechnic.[22] Although, as Whitworth has highlighted, '[t]he metaphorical themes of solidity and transparency run throughout Woolf's work, and are very often shaped through elements of a scientific discourse', Woolf's first explicit reference to X-rays does not appear until 1922, in her essay 'On Re-reading Novels'.[23] Here Woolf uses an X-ray metaphor in order to describe Percy Lubbock's approach in *The Craft of Fiction* (1921):

> But now – at last – Mr Lubbock applies his Röntgen rays. The voluminous lady [i.e. fiction] submits to examination. The flesh, the finery, even the smile and witchery, together with the umbrellas and brown paper parcels which she has collected on her long and toilsome journey, dissolve and disappear; the skeleton alone remains. It is surprising. It is even momentarily shocking. Our old familiar friend has vanished. But, after all, there is something satisfactory in bone—one can grasp it.[24]

In this passage Woolf seems to convey a sense of the shock and disorientation with which early X-ray images were received—after all, X-rays entailed not only a transformation of scientific ideas, but also a transformation of ideas and ways of viewing. Whitworth has emphasized that 'Woolf also sees the x-ray as a metaphor for reductiveness', yet something satisfactorily solid, definite, and lasting remains at the centre of this X-ray vision; what Woolf calls 'the solid and enduring thing'.[25]

Periodical formations

Woolf's and Conrad's engagements with X-rays highlight the role that chance can play in a literary writer's awareness of and interest in new scientific ideas, but other

[21] T. S. Eliot, *The Complete Poems and Plays* (London: Faber, 1969), 16; Robert Crawford, *The Savage and the City in the Work of T. S. Eliot* (Oxford: Clarendon Press, 1990), 8.

[22] Virginia Woolf, *A Passionate Apprentice: The Early Journals 1897–1909*, ed. Mitchell A. Leaska (London: Pimlico, 2004), 9–10.

[23] Whitworth, 'Porous Objects: Self, Community, and the Nature of Matter', in Jessica Berman and Jane Goldman (eds), *Virginia Woolf Out of Bounds. Selected Papers from the Tenth Annual Conference on Virginia Woolf* (New York: Pace University Press, 2001), 151.

[24] Virginia Woolf, *The Essays of Virginia Woolf*, ed. Andrew McNeillie and Stuart N. Clarke, 6 vols (London: Hogarth Press, 1986–2011), III, 341.

[25] Whitworth, 'Porous Objects', 153; Virginia Woolf, *Essays*, III, 341.

writers present us with examples of more direct and active engagements with science. Both Wells and Lawrence received a certain level of scientific training, the former under T. H. Huxley at the Normal School of Science, South Kensington, and the latter as part of his teacher training. Eliot, although not scientifically trained, was introduced to current scientific ideas during his graduate studies at Harvard through his attendance at Josiah Royce's philosophy seminars. Harry Costello's seminar notebooks demonstrate that Eliot was aware of relativity, quantum theory, and statistical mechanics at least as early as 1913–14, and also provide us with a tantalizing possible source for Eliot's 'suggestive analogy' of the catalyst in 'Tradition and the Individual Talent' (1919). In a paper on enzymes in May 1914 the physicist Leonard Troland referred to 'a piece of platinum block' as a catalyst, while in Eliot's analogy '[t]he mind of the poet is the shred of platinum'.[26]

Such examples are the exception rather than the rule, and it is important to consider the less formalized means by which the vast majority of writers gained awareness of contemporary scientific developments. One valuable, but still under-exploited, source in this regard is the generalist periodical.[27] While a significant amount of work has been done on disciplinary crossovers and popular science in nineteenth-century publications of this kind, there has been a tendency to impose a cut-off at 1900. Peter Bowler has highlighted this critical bias towards the Victorian period and sought to emphasize 'the continuing developments' in the early twentieth century.[28] Bowler's work thus helps to fill something of a gap that exists in studies of popular science between the artificially imposed divisions of 1900 on the one hand and 1919, the year in which Einstein, relativity, and popular expositions thereof burst onto the public scene, on the other. Bowler also highlights the fallacy of the traditional argument that once science became professionalized, scientists no longer engaged in science popularization.

Two periodicals may serve as examples supporting Bowler's arguments: the *Cornhill Magazine*, founded in 1859 and edited by Reginald John Smith between 1898 and 1916; and Desmond MacCarthy's short-lived *New Quarterly*, the ten issues of which appeared between 1907 and 1910. Both include reasonably accessible popular science articles by writers with a relatively high level of scientific training, and both place a particular emphasis on the newness of the scientific ideas they discuss. It is here that we see one of the benefits of periodical explorations of emergent scientific ideas: although writers of popular science books in this period were at times, in Whitworth's words, 'reluctant to write about the latest developments, in

---

[26] T. S. Eliot, *Selected Prose of T. S. Eliot*, ed. Frank Kermode (London: Faber and Faber, 1975), 40, 41; Harry T. Costello, *Josiah Royce's Seminar, 1913–1914: As Recorded in the Notebooks of Harry T. Costello*, ed. Grover Smith (New Brunswick, NJ: Rutgers University Press, 1963), 184. Note, however, that Troland's example is of hydrogen and oxygen, while Eliot's is of oxygen and sulphur dioxide.

[27] See Whitworth, *Einstein's Wake*, 19.

[28] Peter J. Bowler, *Science for All: The Popularization of Science in Early Twentieth-Century Britain* (Chicago, IL: University of Chicago Press, 2009), ix.

case their expositions became obsolete between submission and publication', periodical writers thrived on the transitory and ephemeral nature of both the form in which they were writing and the ideas which they were writing about.[29] Indeed, readers of the *Cornhill* were told that 'so actively is the study of this subject being pursued that it is not at all improbable our knowledge of the nature of the radium rays may be further advanced before this article reaches the readers of the *Cornhill Magazine*'.[30] Likewise, readers of the *New Quarterly* were assured that '[t]here is often more living interest in a survey of that border-land where the battle against our ignorance is actually being fought', while those of the *Cornhill* were frequently accompanied 'into the workshop' to be shown 'science in the making'.[31]

Despite similarities in their presentation of scientific ideas, however, there are some significant differences between the *Cornhill* and the *New Quarterly*. The science content of the former was by no means extensive, and during the years 1903–8 was provided more or less exclusively by W. A. Shenstone, FRS and senior science master at Clifton College, Bristol. In contrast, the *New Quarterly* sought, at least at first, to split its content more equally according to its subtitle: 'A Review of Science and Literature'. In addition, it employed a range of scientific contributors, including the President of the Royal Society, Lord Rayleigh. This inclusion of articles by different writers enabled an element of discussion and interaction between them, and no contributor was more prone to such responses than Norman Robert Campbell, an experimental physicist, Fellow of Trinity College, Cambridge, and member of the Cavendish Laboratory.

Campbell's most extreme response to another article in the *New Quarterly* is worth pausing over here, because it raises important questions about the reliability of popular science writing in general, as well as about MacCarthy's editorial policy in particular. Campbell's last two contributions to the *New Quarterly* were 'A Note on "Modern Views of Matter Criticized"' (October 1908) and 'The Physics of M. Gustave Le Bon' (April 1909). Both were written as direct replies to Norman Alliston's 'Modern Views of Matter Criticized' (June 1908). Unlike the majority of *New Quarterly* science contributors, Alliston does not appear to have been a practising scientist, and the aim of his article is to criticize, dismiss, and even deride recent scientific pronouncements on the nature of matter. Campbell's reply to this article in the very next issue is concise but delivered in no uncertain terms: 'The concept "matter" employed by Mr. Alliston is absolutely foreign to science'. Campbell offers two possible explanations for Alliston's mistaken approach, the most likely of which being, he asserts, that 'Mr. Alliston has been misled by some journalistic puff

[29] Whitworth, 'Physics: "A strange footprint"', in David Bradshaw (ed.), *A Concise Companion to Modernism* (Oxford: Blackwell, 2003), 206.

[30] W. A. Shenstone, 'Radium', *Cornhill Magazine* new ser. 14/84 (June 1903), 764.

[31] R. J. Strutt, 'Can We Detect Our Drift through Space?', *New Quarterly* 1/1 (November 1907), 92; Shenstone, 'The Electric Theory of Matter', *Cornhill Magazine* new ser. 23/134 (August 1907), 206.

into believing that the lucubrations of a remarkable Frenchman, M. Le Bon, are to be regarded as the works of a responsible man of science'.[32]

Two issues later, Campbell expanded on this view in an article on Gustave Le Bon in which he described Le Bon's writings as 'altogether worthless'. Although Campbell's attack on Le Bon seems rather personal at times, he goes on to make a bigger point about the necessity for scientists to engage in popularizing activities: 'While those who conduct research refuse to take any part in the popularization of the knowledge which they make, there can be no cure for the general ignorance and misunderstanding of all branches of science.'[33] Campbell's comment is somewhat ironic given that, with one exception, the publication in which he is writing seems to be committed to employing scientific researchers as popularizers, but it enables him to reinforce both his own programme in writing such popularizations and that of the *New Quarterly* as a whole.

Various questions remain regarding MacCarthy's editorial policy in relation to science, and we might also ask why the *New Quarterly* folded so quickly and why the scientific content was dropped altogether from its final two issues. But the *New Quarterly* does provide something like 'a survey of that border-land where the battle against our ignorance' was actually being fought in the early years of the twentieth century, as written by those who were actually fighting that battle. Moreover, considered together with the *Cornhill* and other similar publications, it gives an indication of the true extent to which 'science was deeply embedded in literary culture' at this time.[34]

Shared formations

So far the examples which we have considered have involved, in some form or other, the idea that scientific concepts and developments directly influence literary writers and their works. However, there is another form of crossover between the disciplines of literature and science with which studies in this field must also engage, variously known as the *zeitgeist*, cultural matrix, field of force, or other such term. This is the approach which states that 'ways of viewing the world are not constructed separately by scientists and poets; they share the moment's discourse'.[35] One example of such shared interest and language can be found in the approaches of three turn-of-the-century disciplines concerned with the movements of large masses and the place therein of the individual: molecular physics, crowd psychology, and literature.

---

[32] Norman Robert Campbell, 'A Note on "Modern Views of Matter Criticized"', *New Quarterly* 1/4 (October 1908), 634. See Norman Alliston, 'Modern Views of Matter Criticized', *New Quarterly* 1/3 (June 1908), 385–401.

[33] Campbell, 'The Physics of M. Gustave Le Bon', *New Quarterly* 2/6 (April 1909), 227, 240.

[34] Whitworth, *Einstein's Wake*, 45.

[35] Beer, *Open Fields*, 171.

Molecular physics emerged during the nineteenth century and is associated in particular with James Clerk Maxwell, who, in an address to the British Association in 1873, explored the difficulties inherent in studying large numbers of molecules:

> As long as we have to deal with only two molecules, and have all the data given us, we can calculate the result of their encounter, but when we have to deal with millions of molecules, each of which has millions of encounters in a second, the complexity of he [sic] problem seems to shut out all hope of a legitimate solution. The modern atomists have therefore adopted a method which is I believe new in the department of mathematical physics, though it has long been in use in the Section of Statistics.[36]

The recourse of physics to methods drawn from the field of social statistics has led Theodore Porter to describe these disciplines as parts of 'an interdisciplinary matrix'.[37] It is possible to extend such a matrix further by considering N. Katherine Hayles's idea that 'Different disciplines are drawn to similar problems because the concerns underlying them are highly charged within a prevailing cultural context'; and to carry out such an extension we need to consider the nature of the underlying concerns which encouraged, even necessitated, the emergence of social statistics as a discipline in its own right.[38] Chief among such concerns was a rapidly expanding population; the population of England and Wales alone more than doubled between 1841 and 1901, while the urban population in particular was growing at an unprecedented rate: 'Towns of over 100,000 inhabitants increased from six in 1841 to thirty in 1901—only London had been so large in 1801'.[39] Moreover, this was an increasingly organized, and thus potentially dangerous, labour force.

In addition to adopting the methods of social statistics, molecular physics also made frequent use of images and models of human crowds as a means of explaining molecular movements. Maxwell used such an image in his 1873 address in order to describe the difference between diffusion in a gas and in a liquid:

> in a liquid the diffusion of motion from one molecule to another takes place much more rapidly than the diffusion of the molecules themselves, for the same reason that it is more expeditious in a dense crowd to pass on a letter from hand to hand than to give it to a special messenger to work his way through the crowd.[40]

Shenstone explained the molecular make-up of a liquid in similar terms: 'close packing would cause molecules to jostle one another, like people in a panic-stricken

---

[36] James Clerk Maxwell, 'Molecules', *Nature* 8/204 (25 September 1873), 440.

[37] Theodore M. Porter, 'A Statistical Survey of Gases: Maxwell's Social Physics', *Historical Studies in the Physical Sciences* 12/1 (1981), 114.

[38] N. Katherine Hayles, *Chaos Bound: Orderly Disorder in Contemporary Literature and Science* (Ithaca, NY: Cornell University Press, 1990), xi.

[39] J. A. Banks, 'The Contagion of Numbers', in H. J. Dyos and Michael Wolff (eds), *The Victorian City: Images and Realities*, 2 vols (London: Routledge & Kegan Paul, 1973), I, 105.

[40] Maxwell, 'Molecules', 439.

crowd in the street who have ceased to observe the rules of the road.'[41] Recognizing the imaginative possibilities of such scenes, scientists used metaphors of this kind as a rhetorical device with which to help their readers to understand and visualize the scientific theories under discussion, as well as to legitimize those theories by relating them to everyday experiences.

Returning to the idea of an expanding interdisciplinary matrix, there is one further implication of this device: images of the crowd, familiar to both scientists and readers alike, suggest that such everyday experiences may themselves have influenced contemporary approaches to specific scientific questions. This is the argument which David Bodanis proposes in relation to Louis Pasteur's political ideas and work on bacteria; having highlighted the extreme population growth which we have already considered, Bodanis states that 'One would not need to have been M. Pasteur to be attuned to swarming masses with that going on.'[42] Indeed, the increasing organization and perceived danger of the crowd, emphasized in Shenstone's description above, led to the formation of a new discipline at the turn of the century: crowd psychology.

Perhaps the most significant figure in the field of crowd psychology, both then and now, is Gustave Le Bon, who seems to have had much greater success in this area than in his later foray into physics. Le Bon's 1895 work *La psychologie des foules* focused on the 'organized', or 'psychological', crowd, and the difference between this crowd and a mere 'mass of human beings' was described particularly clearly by William McDougall in 1920:

> There is a dense gathering of several hundred individuals at the Mansion House Crossing at noon of every week-day; but ordinarily each of them is bent upon his own task, pursues his own ends, paying little or no regard to those about him. But let a fire-engine come galloping through the throng of traffic, or the Lord Mayor's state coach arrive, and instantly the concourse assumes in some degree the character of a psychological crowd. All eyes are turned upon the fire-engine or coach; the attention of all is directed to the same object; all experience in some degree the same emotion, and the state of mind of each person is in some degree affected by the mental processes of all those about him. Those are the fundamental conditions of collective mental life.[43]

For any reader of Virginia Woolf the most striking thing about the passage above is its similarity to certain moments in *Mrs. Dalloway*, published just five years later. The early scenes involving the motor car and the aeroplane are particularly reminiscent of McDougall's description of a psychological crowd: in the former, 'Every one

---

[41] Shenstone, 'Matter, Motion, and Molecules', *Cornhill Magazine* new ser. 20/115 (January 1906), 71–2.

[42] David Bodanis, *Web of Words: The Ideas behind Politics* (Basingstoke: Macmillan, 1988), 21.

[43] Gustave Le Bon, *The Crowd: A Study of the Popular Mind* (London: T. Fisher Unwin, 1896), 2; William McDougall, *The Group Mind: A Sketch of the Principles of Collective Psychology with Some Attempt to Apply Them to the Interpretation of National Life and Character* (Cambridge: Cambridge University Press, 1920), 22–3.

looked at the motor car', just as 'the attention of all is directed to the same object' in McDougall.[44] Meanwhile, we are shown that 'all experience in some degree the same emotion', even if only for 'thirty seconds', when 'in all the hat shops and tailors' shops strangers looked at each other and thought of the dead; of the flag; of Empire'. This universally fixed attention on the motor car is preserved until the aeroplane appears, at which point 'Every one looked up'. Both incidents involve the formation of a psychological crowd as defined by McDougall and Le Bon, although it is worth noting that Mrs Dalloway herself only participates in the first.[45]

While *Mrs. Dalloway* presents us with a number of examples of the formation of a psychological crowd, *Night and Day*, published one year before McDougall's study in 1919, provides instead a repeated focus on what McDougall calls the 'mass of human beings'. Towards the end of this novel, Katharine seeks Ralph among the rush-hour commuters around Lincoln's Inn Fields, picturing the crowd as 'tend[ing] the enormous rush of the current—the great flow, the deep stream, the unquenchable tide'.[46] Despite the sense here that everyone is moving in the same direction, there is no indication that the individuals within this crowd are pursuing anything other than their own ends; indeed, it is Katharine's pursuit of *her* own ends that forces these other individuals to appear, both for her and for the reader, as 'two currents': 'More and more plainly did she see him [Ralph]; and more and more did he seem to her unlike any one else.'[47]

As the examples from Woolf's works indicate, crowds are represented in late nineteenth- and early twentieth-century literature in ways which seem to coincide with the emerging discipline of crowd psychology, but there are also parallels with scientific images of molecular movement. In particular, literary urban crowds are frequently described as jostling and colliding with each other, as in *The Inheritors*, *The Secret Agent* (1907), and *The War of the Worlds* (1898).[48] The idea of molecular collisions came to the fore in 1905 in Einstein's paper on Brownian motion—the movement exhibited by microscopic particles, like pollen grains or smoke particles, suspended in a medium made up of molecules of much smaller size and mass, such as water or air. Although Einstein was not the first to suggest that molecular collisions were the cause of this movement, he was the first to explain how it is that tiny molecules can cause such comparatively massive particles to move. Einstein did this through reference to random fluctuations among the tiny molecules, which

---

[44] Virginia Woolf, *Mrs. Dalloway*, ed. Stella McNichol (London: Penguin, 1992), 16.

[45] Ibid., 19, 22. Although I am not aware of any evidence that Woolf knew McDougall's work directly, Leonard Woolf's 1916 review of another popular crowd psychology text highlights the extent to which such ideas were familiar in Woolf's circle at this time. See L. S. Woolf, 'The Inhuman Herd', *New Statesman* 7/170 (8 July 1916), 327–8.

[46] Virginia Woolf, *Night and Day*, ed. Julia Briggs (London: Penguin, 1992), 374.

[47] Ibid., 374–5.

[48] Conrad and Ford, *The Inheritors*, 40; Conrad, *The Secret Agent: A Simple Tale*, ed. Bruce Harkness and S. W. Reid (Cambridge: Cambridge University Press, 1990), 131; Wells, *The War of the Worlds*, ed. Patrick Parrinder (London: Penguin, 2005), 98.

mean that a number of molecules suddenly collide with a specific particle at the same time and in the same direction, thus causing it to move in that direction, an explanation which relies on statistical measures.

Turning again to literary texts which describe individuals within urban crowds, it is interesting to note a curious emphasis on the respective sizes of particular characters in relation to that of the individuals making up the crowd. In *Night and Day*, Ralph sees the Lincoln crowd as 'only a dissolving and combining pattern of black particles' within which Katharine appears as 'a tall figure, upright, dark, and commanding, much detached from her surroundings'.[49] Likewise, the opening of *The Voyage Out* (1915) presents us with a couple, in comparison with which 'most people looked small', this majority being described as consisting of 'small, agitated figures'—an image which resonates particularly strongly with Brownian motion.[50] Of course, it is possible to think of this as a class issue, or as something of a cliché, or perhaps as a simple consequence of trying to combine the novel's traditional focus on one or more individuals with a new interest in urban mass living. Whatever the cause the respective sizes of individuals and their surroundings in the literature of this period are worth attending to, and perhaps nowhere more so than in *The Secret Agent*. As Stephen Arata has pointed out, 'Nearly without exception, characters in this novel are either overweight (Verloc, Michaelis, Winnie, Ossipon, Sir Ethelred), often repulsively so, or else so emaciated as to appear eaten away themselves (Yundt, the Assistant Commissioner, the Professor)'.[51] The strangely 'stunted' and 'undersized' nature of the Professor is particularly worthy of note, although the fact that he is both imagined and seen travelling on the tops of omnibuses is also significant.[52]

As the multiple strands of this extended interdisciplinary matrix suggest, the question of the relationship between the individual and the mass was an urgent one in the late nineteenth and early twentieth centuries, provoked at least in part by a rapidly expanding and organized population and increasing urbanization. The question manifested itself in a turn towards statistical measures and the development of crowd psychology, as well as an ongoing focus on distinct individuals in contrast to massed humanity in literary works. Practitioners working in each of these disciplines seem to have recognized both the underlying issue and some of the imaginative possibilities offered in answer to it by each of the other disciplines. But the intertwining and overlapping of the various elements of this matrix mean that it becomes difficult to isolate and highlight one specific influence upon a particular text or development—instead we see that different disciplines 'coalesce' in both the fact of approaching and the means of tackling a particular cultural

[49] Virginia Woolf, *Night and Day*, 193.
[50] Virginia Woolf, *The Voyage Out*, ed. Jane Wheare (London: Penguin, 1992), 3.
[51] Stephen Arata, '*The Secret Agent* (1907)', in Leonard Orr and Ted Billy (eds), *A Joseph Conrad Companion* (Westport, CT: Greenwood Press, 1999), 182.
[52] Conrad, *The Secret Agent*, 66, 67, 53, 227.

concern.[53] By exploring these disciplines together we are able to recover a sense of how the concerns underlying a specific problem were actually experienced at the time, within, between, and across traditional disciplinary divides.

Science was undergoing a series of radical transformations at the end of the nineteenth and start of the twentieth centuries. Scientific developments came to be known to literary writers of the period variously through formal scientific training and chance encounters through newspapers and generalist periodicals. But both science and literature were, and continue to be, part of wider contemporary culture, each using its own techniques, as well as techniques adopted from and shared with other disciplines, in order to explore and tackle the pressing questions of the time. In addition, both science and literature were undergoing revolutionary transformations while also maintaining elements of the older formations.

Stephen Brush's assertion that ' "Modernism" meant the collaboration of art and science to create the twentieth-century world' certainly seems valid.[54] As we have seen, physics was changing particularly rapidly and radically during this period. The periodical press provided multiple and varied means of dissemination for these new ideas, while writers like Woolf, Conrad, and Wells responded to these and other developments in diverse ways. However, even though science was changing rapidly, older scientific ideas continued to carry weight. As such, when looking at this period we need to consider the evolutionary developments of molecular physics and statistical methods as well as the revolutionary breaks of quanta and relativity. Beer argues that 'science and literature transform rather than simply transfer': she emphasizes 'transformation rather than translation'.[55] Such transformations become even more dramatic and significant when those disciplines are themselves, as both literature and science were at the turn of the twentieth century, undergoing radical metamorphoses.

FURTHER READING

Abbott, Edwin A. *Flatland: A Romance of Many Dimensions* (London: Penguin, 1998). Originally published in 1884, this text provides an example of the literary presentation of a scientific idea.

Broks, Peter. 'Science, Media and Culture: British Magazines, 1890–1914', *Public Understanding of Science* 2/2 (1993), 123–39. With Turner (below), one of a small number of critical texts to consider popular science across the 1900 divide.

---

[53] Beer, *Virginia Woolf: The Common Ground* (Edinburgh: Edinburgh University Press, 1996), 113.

[54] Stephen G. Brush, *The Temperature of History: Phases of Science and Culture in the Nineteenth Century* (New York: Burt Franklin, 1978), 129–30.

[55] Beer, 'Science and Literature', in R. C. Olby et al. (eds), *Companion to the History of Modern Science* (London: Routledge, 1990), 796; Beer, *Open Fields*, 173.

Cain, Sarah. 'The Metaphorical Field: Post-Newtonian Physics and Modernist Literature', *Cambridge Quarterly* 28/1 (1999), 46–64. Focuses in particular on T. S. Eliot.

Crossland, Rachel. 'Sharing the Moment's Discourse: Virginia Woolf, D. H. Lawrence and Albert Einstein in the Early Twentieth Century', DPhil thesis, University of Oxford, 2010. Explores the writings of Woolf and Lawrence in relation to the ideas presented in Einstein's 1905 papers.

Crossland, Rachel. '"[M]ultitudinous and minute": Early Twentieth-Century Scientific, Literary and Psychological Representations of the Mass', *Journal of Literature and Science* 6/2 (2013), 1–16. A more detailed analysis of the 'interdisciplinary matrix' of molecular physics, crowd psychology, and literature, with particular reference to Virginia Woolf.

Crossland, Rachel. 'Exposing the Bones of Desire: Virginia Woolf's X-ray Visions', *Virginia Woolf Miscellany* 85 (2014), 18–20. Explores Woolf's engagement with X-ray technology in more depth, including an analysis of her references thereto in *To the Lighthouse* (1927).

Friedman, Alan J. and Carol C. Donley. *Einstein as Myth and Muse* (Cambridge: Cambridge University Press, 1985). Provides a good overview of the changing responses to Einstein and his theories in literary works.

Mould, Richard F. *A Century of X-rays and Radioactivity in Medicine: With Emphasis on Photographic Records of the Early Years* (Bristol: Institute of Physics, 1993). A useful starting point for background on the emergence of and response to X-rays.

Noakes, Richard. 'The "world of the infinitely little": Connecting Physical and Psychical Realities Circa 1900', *Studies in History and Philosophy of Science* 39 (2008), 323–34. Highlights the overlap between scientific discoveries and spiritualist ideas.

Price, Katy. *Loving Faster than Light: Romance and Readers in Einstein's Universe* (Chicago, IL: University of Chicago Press, 2012). Provides analyses of press and literary responses to Einstein's theories of relativity during the 1920s.

Rigden, John S. *Einstein 1905: The Standard of Greatness* (Cambridge, MA: Harvard University Press, 2005). A useful introduction to Einstein's 1905 papers, including the special theory of relativity and Brownian motion.

Shenstone, W. A. *The New Physics and Chemistry: A Series of Popular Essays on Physical and Chemical Subjects* (London: Smith, Elder, 1906). This volume collects fourteen of Shenstone's seventeen articles for the *Cornhill Magazine*.

Turner, Frank M. 'Public Science in Britain, 1880–1919', *Isis* 71/4 (December 1980), 589–608. See also Broks (1993) in this list.

Whitworth, Michael H. 'Science in the Age of Modernism', in Peter Brooker et al. (eds), *The Oxford Handbook of Modernisms* (Oxford: Oxford University Press, 2010), 445–60. Includes analyses of popular science writing in generalist periodicals.

CHAPTER 16

SPIRIT WORLDS

TATIANA KONTOU

' "What we want", said Mr. Gradgrind, "is facts, facts, facts." '
Oxford Phantasmatological Society[1]

In 1881 the Oxford Phantasmatological Society published a pamphlet of its objectives to study 'so-called Supernatural Occurrences' bearing an epigraph from Charles Dickens's *Hard Times*. The utilitarian school master Mr Gradgrind compounds his life credo in his pedagogy by teaching his pupils to construct a rational, factual mode of thinking unsullied by imagination, reverie, and flights of fancy. Indeed fancy would threaten the accurate representation of the natural world, if his pupils were allowed to wallpaper a room with the images of horses or if they chose a flowery carpet. Horses do not trot about walls and one must not tread on flowers, let alone place hefty furniture upon them, so the fancifully decorated rooms would be a misleading misappropriation of reality.[2] Mr Gradgrind thunders that 'Facts alone are wanted in life',[3] and the Phantasmatological Society seemed to extend the motto to the afterlife or more accurately to 'so-called supernatural occurrences'.[4] In thinking about the appearance of ghosts or phantasms only facts would do, and if ghost stories were non-factual then they were just fanciful figments, not natural phenomena that could somehow be explained.

The society's pamphlet was distributed at its June meeting and the president of the Phantasmatologists, the gifted botanist H. N. Ridley, invited the society's members to first establish and then concentrate on the bare facts of ghost stories. Precision, cross-referencing, and contextualization were imperative in the

---

[1] Society for Psychical Research (SPR) Archives, Cambridge University Library, MS 208 B [Pamphlet of Oxford Phantasmatological Society, June 1881]. The quotation from *Hard Times* is inaccurate and should read: 'Now, what I want is Facts' declared by a visitor in Mr Gradgrind's school.

[2] Charles Dickens, *Hard Times* (1854; repr. London: Penguin, 2003), 12, 13.

[3] Ibid., 9.   [4] SPR Archives, MS 208 B.

discussion of any phenomenon under scrutiny, as the society's objectives illustrate. For each story told, members should ascertain:

> I. That it should be stated whether the occurrence came under the notice of more than one person: if so, as many independent accounts as possible should be given. II. That the place, time, and duration of the phenomenon should be accurately recorded. III. The information should be given of legends, tales, or rumours which existed prior to the occurrence.[5]

These guidelines for established and fledgling Phantasmatologists set the tone for the discursive style of Phantasmatological meetings. Accurate and factual ghost narratives would be the main pursuit of the society, but paradoxically the misquotation from *Hard Times*—by an author who was famous for his Christmas ghost stories, and who flirted with the supernatural even in his more realistic fiction—challenges the dynamics between factual narratives and ghost stories. Moreover, by the end of Dickens's novel, Mr Gradgrind comes to recognize the folly of his factual philosophy and allows feelings and emotions to exist alongside his reasoning faculties. Perhaps inadvertently, the epigraph to the Phantasmatological pamphlet had invited and made way for the imaginary and literary in the discussion of ghosts.

The Oxford Phantasmatological Society was not the first of its kind to find a home in institutions that brought together members of different disciplines with shared interests in discovering the veracity of ghostly accounts and rational explanations. In 1874, a select group of Cambridge scholars including the philosopher Henry Sidgwick, the classicist Frederic W. H. Myers, the humanist Edmund Gurney, and philosopher and eventual Prime Minister A. J. Balfour, as well as Balfour's sister, the mathematician (and later president of Newnham College and spouse of Sidgwick) Eleanor Balfour all came together to investigate spiritualist phenomena. In 1879 the old Oxford Phantasmatological Society (an earlier version of the Oxford Phantasmatological Society) was formed featuring among its members Sidgwick and the physicist William Fletcher Barrett. For the Oxford society, a largely elitist and exclusive group, the epithet 'Phantasmatological' (from Phantasm, an archaic word for ghost, derived from the Greek *fantazein*, to 'make something visible', 'to seemingly appear') was chosen to suggest the rigorously intellectual pursuits of the society. The name would also differentiate it from similar groups that had been established since the early 1850s, with the advent of modern spiritualism, to examine séance manifestations and related phenomena, such as the Ghost Society that was set up in Cambridge in 1851 and the Psychological Society of Great Britain that was founded in 1875 by Edward William 'Sarjent' Cox, who had exposed Mary Rosina Showers's fraudulent mediumship.[6]

---

[5] Ibid.

[6] For the history of spiritualism, see Janet Oppenheim, *The Other World, Spiritualism and Psychical Research in England, 1850–1914* (Cambridge: Cambridge University Press, 1985); Logie Barrow, *Spiritualism and English Plebeians, 1850–1910* (London: Routledge & Kegan Paul, 1986); for an account of its development by psychical researchers and spiritualists, see Frank Podmore, *Modern Spiritualism: A History and a Criticism*, 2 vols (London: Methuen, 1903) and Arthur Conan Doyle, *The History of Spiritualism* (London: Cassell, 1926).

The Oxford Phantasmatological Society was short-lived, but in February 1882 the group of Cambridge dons who were part of the Ghost Society met in London to officiate at the founding of the Society for Psychical Research (SPR), and a few months later the Oxford Phantasmatological Society pledged its allegiance to the SPR.[7] The SPR's membership list seems like a roll-call of eminent Victorians, among whom were chemist and physicist William Crookes, physicist Oliver Lodge, biologist Alfred Russel Wallace, Prime Minister William Gladstone, philosopher and psychologist William James, philosopher Henri Bergson, sensation author Rhoda Broughton, anthropologist Andrew Lang, Lewis Carroll, Arthur Conan Doyle, Sigmund Freud, and later Carl Jung.[8] The SPR's empirical approach to investigating spiritualist and related phenomena reflected the professional interests of its members who promised to engage in extensive and strictly scientific investigations.

Since 1848, when the two teenage sisters Margaret and Kate Fox introduced communication between the living and the dead at their home in Hydesville, New York, spiritualists and inquisitive scientists had engaged in investigations of the phenomena. The London Dialectical Society and the British National Association of Spiritualists would encourage their members to test the veracity of séance manifestations, but unlike these associations the SPR's membership did 'not imply the acceptance of any particular explanation of the phenomena investigated, nor any belief as to the operation, in the physical world, of forces other than those recognised by Physical Science'.[9] Michael Faraday, William Carpenter, and John Tyndall had examined the phenomena of table-tipping and spirit-rapping and were convinced that they were produced by the unconscious participation of séance goers. William Crookes had subjected the famous medium Daniel Dunglas Home to several tests but it was not until the formation of the SPR that such tests were conducted under the auspices of a formal society, whose findings were widely disseminated through publications such as the *Proceedings of the Society for Psychical Research (PSPR)* and the *Journal of the Society for Psychical Research*.

The SPR was a vibrant network of investigators who were educated, influential, and affluent. As Shane McCorristine has shown, 'the SPR connected itself to pioneering trends in the human sciences: from its base in the discipline of experimental psychology the Society reached out to the Nancy School of psychotherapy, adopted a statistical scope which pre-empted that of the mass-observation era, and proposed an advanced theory of hallucination which consummated a century of medical and psychiatric debate'.[10] Despite advances in psychology and studies of

---

[7] SPR Archives, MS 208 B [Letter 11/11/82].

[8] For histories of the SPR, see W. H. Salter, *The Society for Psychical Research: An Outline of its History* (London, 1948); Alan Gauld, *The Founders of Psychical Research* (London: Routledge & Kegan Paul, 1968).

[9] 'Objects of the Society', *Proceedings of the Society for Psychical Research (PSPR)* 1/1 (1882–3), 5.

[10] Shane McCorristine, *Spectres of the Self: Thinking about Ghosts and Ghost-Seeing in England, 1750–1920* (Cambridge: Cambridge University Press, 2010), 105.

hysteria, multiple personality, aphasia, hypnosis, catalepsy, and anaesthesia, the mind remained *terra incognita*, perhaps even a haunted space. Janet Oppenheim has argued that psychical researchers sought to reconcile advancements in new sciences with religious and spiritual beliefs of life after death, a stance that partially explains Psychical Research's impressive status quo in a *fin-de-siècle* culture that was still experiencing the after-effects of Darwin's theories. However, Roger Luckhurst persuasively suggests that 'part of the fascination of psychical research has been in coming to understand how it capitalized on the fissures of scientific naturalism, exploiting uncertainty and transition in knowledges and institutions of cultural authority'.[11] Although Psychical Research has been relegated today to an outré para-scientific departure, it was part of an authoritative epistemological nexus in the *fin de siècle*.

The SPR's objectives were more distinctive that those of its Oxford counterpart and extended beyond a discursive appraisal of the supernatural, its interests including a mixture of recognized and speculative phenomena:

1. An examination of the nature and extent of any influence which may be exerted by one mind upon another, apart from any generally recognised mode of perception.
2. The study of hypnotism, and the forms of so-called mesmeric trance, with its alleged insensibility to pain; clairvoyance and other allied phenomena.
3. A critical revision of Reichenbach's researches with certain organisations called 'sensitive', and an inquiry into whether such organisations possess any power of perception beyond highly exalted sensibility of the recognised sensory organs.
4. A careful investigation of any reports, resting on strong testimony, regarding apparitions at the moment of death, or otherwise, or regarding disturbances in houses reputed to be haunted.
5. An inquiry into the various psychical phenomena commonly called Spiritualistic; with an attempt to discover their causes and general laws.
6. The collection and collation of existing materials bearing on the history of these subjects.[12]

The intention of the SPR in studying mesmeric, spiritualistic, haunting phenomena and Carl von Reichenbach's Odylic force, a fluid uniting organic matter similar to Mesmer's magnetic fluid, was to 'approach these various problems without prejudice or prepossession of any kind, and in the same spirit of exact and unimpassioned enquiry which has enabled science to solve so many problems, once not less obscure nor less hotly debated'.[13] The *modus operandi* of psychical research would often create rifts between spiritualists who had joined the movement precisely

---

[11] Roger Luckhurst, *The Invention of Telepathy, 1870–1901* (Cambridge: Cambridge University Press, 2002), 2.

[12] 'Objects of the Society', 3–5.   [13] Ibid., 4.

because of evidence that manifestations were authentic and were willing to conduct séance experiments from the vantage point of the believer, and psychical researchers who questioned the reliability of evidence and adopted a sceptical or agnostic perspective in experiments. Rather frustratingly for spiritualists, psychical researchers who were at times unable to explain manifestations under scientifically recognized natural laws remained prudently inconclusive about the veracity of phenomena rather than insisting on their authenticity. Peter Lamont has called this tension 'a crisis of evidence' that exposed not so much the difficulty in assessing spiritualist accounts but rather orthodox science's shortcomings in verifiability and objectivity.[14]

What constitutes evidence and how far can we trust evidence when it comes to séances, haunted houses, and the existence of the Odylic force? Psychical researchers, similarly to phantasmatologists and inquisitive spiritualists, wished to distil evidence from misleading and sometimes outright fraudulent phenomena. However, talking and looking out for ghosts while framing these experiences in testimonials and scientific language were familiar tropes of literary genres such as the late Victorian gothic and the ghost story. In her seminal work on the ghost story, Julia Briggs uses the term ghost story loosely to 'denote not only stories about ghosts, but about possession and demonic bargains, spirits other than those of the dead, including ghouls, vampires, werewolves, the "swarths" of living men and the "ghost-soul" or *Doppelgänger*'.[15] Psychical researchers might not have been on the lookout for werewolves or ghouls, but the spirits of the dead, the phantasms of the living, possession, and the split or doubled self inadvertently forged an affinity with the Victorian ghost story. Chris Willis observes a remarkable coincidence when it comes to the collection and collation of spiritualist evidence that brings psychical research much closer to the literary realm than was intended by its propagators:

> It is interesting to note that the rise of the fictional detective coincided with the rise of spiritualism. Both began in the mid-nineteenth century and were widely popular in Britain from the turn of the century to the 1930s. Both attempt to explain mysteries. The medium's role can be seen as being similar to that of a detective in a murder case. Both are trying to make the dead speak in order to reveal a truth.[16]

Willis draws parallels between the medium, a conductor between the living and the spirits, and the figure of the detective who is an interpreter of material traces left on the dead body. The spiritual communications often rendered through materialized spirit bodies, ectoplasmic production, ghostly billets-doux, apported flowers, and the very material forensic clues demanded interpretation. Ronald R. Thomas traces the emergence of detective fiction alongside developments in criminology and

---

[14] Peter Lamont, 'Spiritualism and a Mid-Victorian Crisis of Evidence', *The Historical Journal* 47/4 (2004), 897–920.

[15] Julia Briggs, *Night Visitors: The Rise and Fall of the English Ghost Story* (London: Faber, 1977) 7.

[16] Chris Willis, 'Making the Dead Speak: Spiritualism and Detective Fiction', in Warren Chernaik, Martin Swales, and Robert Vilain (eds), *The Art of Detective Fiction* (Basingstoke: Palgrave, 2000), 60.

forensic science and posits the fictional detective as an astute reader of the body as a text.[17] I want to suggest that a closer link between the figure of the detective is that of the psychical researcher who garners evidence, assesses testimonies, and interprets clues drawing on rational thinking, acute powers of observation, and often cutting-edge technology and new scientific theories.

The quintessential detective Sherlock Holmes's scalpel-like rationality, crystalline observational powers, and acuity of interpretation might suggest an affinity with the medium who acquires knowledge through supernatural means, although Holmes's agency distinguishes him from the passive acceptance of the medium. However, as Sdrjan Smajic observes: 'detective fiction itself prompts us to regard rationalism's occulted supplements—or variants. Clairvoyance, telepathy and intuition … are not just uncannily reminiscent of the detective's mind-reading powers and miraculous feats of deductive reasoning, but are *versions* of these practices and vice versa.'[18] Clairvoyance and telepathy (a term coined by Myers to describe thought transference) were at the heart of the SPR's investigations and together with the rational detective story they seem to give rise to a *fin-de-siècle* and Edwardian literary phenomenon, the psychic detective or occult doctor. Among other critics such as Briggs, Smajic, and Luckhurst, Sarah Crofton traces the lineage of the occult doctor from Dr Martin Hesselius in Sheridan Le Fanu's *In a Glass Darkly* (1872), but has persuasively argued that 'authors of the *fin de siècle* drew upon the new tropes of detective fiction to create characters whose proofs of the occult both ape and undermine the detective's familiar explicative methods',[19] therefore plotting the occult detective or psychic doctor within the detective rather than the ghost story.

The Cinderella of the sciences

Trying to pre-empt the prejudice psychical research would encounter as a nascent interdisciplinary science, the philosopher Henry Sidgwick, in his first presidential address to the society, drew parallels between mesmerism, which had been demystified and renamed hypnosis, and the SPR's objectives:

> Thirty years ago it was thought that want of scientific culture was an adequate explanation of the vulgar belief in mesmerism and table-turning. Then, as one man of scientific repute after another came forward with the results of individual investigation, there was quite ludicrous ingenuity exercised in finding reasons for discrediting his scientific culture. He was said to be an amateur, not a professional; or a specialist with-

[17] Ronald R. Thomas, *Detective Fiction and the Rise of Forensic Science* (Cambridge: Cambridge University Press, 2004).

[18] Srdjan Smajic, *Ghost Seers, Detectives and Spiritualists* (Cambridge: Cambridge University Press, 2010), 181.

[19] Sarah Crofton, 'CSΨ: Occult Detectives of the fin de siècle and the Interpretation of Evidence', *Clues: A Journal of Detection* 30/2 (2012), 29–30.

out adequate generality of view and training; or a mere discoverer not acquainted with the strict methods of experimental research; or he was not a Fellow of the Royal Society, or if he was it was by an unfortunate accident.[20]

Sidgwick was alluding to the pioneers in hypnosis John Elliotson, James Braid, and William Carpenter, who had shown that mesmerism and table-turning were due to unconscious mental activities, or to the 'unconscious cerebration'[21] of participants. Spiritualists had used the language of mesmerism to explain séance phenomena, but had claimed that the movements of tables or automatic writing were caused by external, discarnate agencies rather than from parts of their own unconscious selves. Sidgwick had hoped that, just as mesmerism was scientifically explained, so would spiritualism be explicable irrespective of the investigators' professional affiliations. The question of amateur versus professional investigation, and the status quo of investigators, would play a formative part in any attack against psychical research. However, Sidgwick covertly urged perseverance. As one man after another investigated the 'vulgar' phenomena of mesmerism, so perhaps one psychical researcher after another might investigate phenomena that may be deemed 'vulgar' but would prove to be natural under the rubric of science.

In 1897, the occultist Professor van Helsing would make a similar speech to the rational Dr Seward in *Dracula*:

Do you not think that there are things which you cannot understand, and yet which are; that some people see things that others cannot?... Ah, it is the... fault of our science that it wants to explain all; and if it explain not, then it says there is nothing to explain. But yet we see around us every day the growth of new beliefs, which think themselves new; and are yet but the old, which pretend to be young – like the fine ladies at the opera. I suppose now you do not believe in corporeal transference? No? Nor in materialization. No? Nor in astral bodies. No? Nor in the reading of thought. No? Nor in hypnotism—[22]

Van Helsing's speech apes Sidgwick's presidential address by reversing the order of beliefs that have been proven explicable through science. He calls theories 'new beliefs' to illustrate the transience of scientific truths. Occult beliefs like the travelling of astral bodies and spirit materialization are paraded in front of the sceptical Dr Seward only to halt his disbelief and incredulity with the very tangible, explainable, scientifically proven 'hypnotism'.

The anthropologist and SPR member Andrew Lang employed an analogy derived from fairy tales to express the tensions between nascent sciences that were formulating their authority in this new cultural arena. Drawing on his own interests

---

[20] Henry Sidgwick, 'Address by the President at First General Meeting', *PSPR* 1/1 (1882–3), 8–9.

[21] Quoted in Richard Noakes, 'The Sciences of Spiritualism in Victorian Britain', in Tatiana Kontou and Sarah Willburn (eds), *The Ashgate Research Companion to Nineteenth-Century Spiritualism and the Occult* (Aldershot: Ashgate, 2012), 34.

[22] Bram Stoker, *Dracula* (1897; repr. London: Penguin, 1993), 246–7.

in anthropology, Lang employed figurative language to explain the status of psychical research in current scientific fora:

> Anthropology adopts the airs of her elder sisters among the sciences, and is as severe as they to the Cinderella of the family, Psychical Research. She must murmur of her fairies amongst the cinders of the hearth, while they go forth to the ball and dance with provincial mayors at the festivities of the British Association. This is ungenerous and unfortunate as the records of anthropology are rich in unexamined materials of psychical research.[23]

Here, a collector of fairy tales names psychical research the 'Cinderella' of sciences—an allusion that further propels psychical research towards the literary realm. Cinderella gets to go to the ball, enchant the prince, and finally establish her proper place in society because a fairy godmother, a kind spirit, has enabled her to evade her stepsisters' wiles through glamour. Perhaps, Lang seems to be intimating, in order for psychical research to attain its proper place amid her sister sciences, it needs similar magic: a real ghost has to make its appearance.

Ghost telling

What distinguished the real from the fictional in ghostly visitations fell within the SPR's 'Literary Committee', whose aim was to collect and collate stories that could be verified either by interviewing the percipient (the person who experienced the ghostly visitation or saw the apparition) or by a long correspondence between psychical researchers and percipients that would enable them to verify the account and also assess the credibility and objectivity of each testimony. Psychical researchers launched a prudently named Census of Hallucinations to determine the frequency of such experiences by sane persons. Myriads of letters detailing encounters with ghosts reached the SPR's offices in London and the onerous task of separating hoaxes from authentic accounts befell psychical researchers. The tension between testimony and anecdote was acknowledged in the committee's first report published in the *PSPR:*

> Further, we must warn future readers that the details of the evidence are in many cases not only dull, but of a trivial and even ludicrous kind; and that they will be presented for the most part in the narrator's simplest phraseology, quite unspiced for the literary palate. Our trials will resemble neither *The Mysteries of Udolpho* nor the dignified reports of a learned society. The romanticist may easily grow indignant over them; still more easily may the journalist grow facetious.... However caused, these phenomena are interwoven with the everyday tissue of human existence, and pay no more regard to what men call appalling than to what men call ridiculous.[24]

[23] Andrew Lang, *The Making of Religion* (London: Longmans, Green, 1898), 47.
[24] William Barrett, C. C. Massey, Rev. W. Stainton Moses, Frank Podmore, Edmund Gurney, F. W. H. Myers, 'Report of the Literary Committee', *PSPR* 1/1 (1882–3), 11.

The committee was eager to differentiate the reports in the *PSPR* from ordinary Christmas issues of periodicals that would feature ghost stories and warned readers that within the pages of the journal and *PSPR* an avid reader of fiction would find no pleasure. The report is uninviting. The cases are 'dull', 'trivial', bland for a palate used to ghost stories, sensation fiction, gothic novels. The gothic tradition of Ann Radcliffe is not a predecessor for the reports and those of a flighty mind or journalists seeking novelty will be disappointed. If anything, the reported ghost stories are not posited as extraordinary but have an organic connection: they are part of the 'tissue' of the quotidian human experience. Haunting, or the ghostly, thus becomes everyday: it is no longer extraordinary, no longer a storyteller's delight.

However, the allure of the ghostly narration and more specifically of the ghost story seems to infiltrate the offices of the SPR. Elsewhere in the report, Myers and his colleagues comment on the cliché of the ghostly apparition that comes complete with visual and aural effects at the stroke of midnight, as the howling dogs and the blue flames of candles raise ghosts. 'These are the ghosts of fiction, and we do not deny that now and then we receive apparently on good authority, accounts of apparitions which are stated to exhibit some features of the sensational type.'[25] Jacques Derrida comments on the hybridization of genres and writes of the impossibility of the unalloyed genre: 'And suppose for a moment that it were impossible not to mix genres. What if there were, lodged within the heart of the law itself, a law of impurity or a principle of contamination?'[26] Psychical researchers had chosen the impossible, creating a discourse on the ghostly that would remain pure, uncontaminated by the fictional and the folkloric—a new discourse in which ghosts had been renamed 'phantasms', haunted houses became 'phantasmogenetic centres', and thought transference was turned into the more intellectual-sounding 'telepathy'.

The SPR's discourse drew on established psychological terms (multiplex personality, aphasia, automatism) and developed new terms for thinking about the occult and the ghostly by applying Greek and Latin words to supernatural phenomena (telekinesis, metatheria, psychorrhagy). Indeed, Frederic Myers's magnus opus *Human Personality and its Survival of Bodily Death*, published posthumously in 1903, included a glossary of psychological and psychical terms that bore testament to the society's mission of establishing psychical research as an intellectually rigorous new science, immune to the lures of the fictional.

The phantasms of the living

The first *magnum opus* of the society would bring together the findings of the Census of Hallucinations that had been ongoing since the society's formation.

---

[25] Ibid., 139.
[26] Jacques Derrida, 'The Law of Genre', trans. Avital Ronell, *Critical Inquiry* 7/1 (Autumn, 1980), 55–81, esp. 57.

The co-investigators were Edmund Gurney (the principal author), Frederic Myers, and Frank Podmore. *Phantasms of the Living* was published in 1886 and collated over seven hundred testimonials of instances where a phantasm or an ideational apparition had been experienced by a percipient. Gurney felt that the book's title and subject matter needed explanation and stated in the introduction:

> the subject of this book is one which a brief title is hardly sufficient to explain. For under our heading of 'Phantasms of the Living' we propose in fact to deal with all classes of cases where there is reason to suppose, that the mind of another without speech uttered, or word written, or sign made;—has affected it, (that is to say by other means through the recognised channels of sense). I refer to apparitions; excluding indeed, the alleged apparitions of the dead, but including the apparitions of all persons who are still living.... And these apparitions, as will be seen, are themselves extremely various in character; including not visual phenomena alone but auditory, tactile or even, purely ideational and emotional impressions.[27]

Although the study attracted a great deal of criticism, it also brought together a community of people from all strata of society and geographical spaces of the empire that had experienced a form of apparition. The percipients would be cross-examined by Gurney, Myers, and Podmore and would attest to the veracity of their experience. Gurney endeavoured to explain the presence of phantasms under established and emerging theories on mourning and anxiety rather than bestow supernatural explanations. He concluded that there were three emotional states that would be responsible for the experience of phantasms: anxiety (about someone ill who might die), awe (a recent death being mourned), and expectancy (of someone's arrival).[28]

Gurney, Myers, and Podmore were keen to include testimonials that were to the best of their knowledge and critical assessment verifiable and objective. By shifting the focus to phantasms of the 'living' rather than the 'dead' and by referring to the phantasms perceived at the moment of death or danger as 'hallucinations' rather than disembodied spirits, psychical researchers launched a major study in their field that would stand up well under scrutiny. However, with the publication of *Phantasms of the Living* a major controversy surrounding the veridical nature of the hallucinations erupted from which Gurney never recovered.[29] Although Gurney's study was rigorous and engaged with psychological theories of anxiety, indeed pre-empting to an extent the diagnosis of post-traumatic stress disorder, it was not uncontaminated by genre writing. The epistolary novel, sensation fiction,

---

[27] Edmund Gurney, Frederick W. Myers, Frank Podmore, *Phantasms of the Living*, 2 vols (London: Trubner, 1886), I, 2.

[28] Ibid., I, 507.

[29] See A. Taylor Innes, 'Where Are the Letters? A Cross-Examination of Certain Phantasms', *Nineteenth Century* 22/126 (August 1887), 174–97; Luckhurst, *The Invention of Telepathy*.

life-writing, and the ghost story would inflect the two volumes of the study with literary tendencies.

Walter Benjamin lamented the end of storytelling in the nineteenth century, and blamed the rise of the novel and the fast exchange of information. Contemplating the importance of death in storytelling, he writes:

> It is however characteristic that only a man's knowledge or wisdom, but above all his real life—and this is the stuff that stories are made of—first assumes transmissible form at the moment of his death. Just as a sequence of images is set in motion inside a man as his life comes to an end—unfolding the views of himself under which he has encountered himself being aware of it—suddenly in his expressions and looks the unforgettable emerges and imparts to everything that concerned him that the authority which even the poorest wretch in dying possesses for the living around him. The authority is at the key source of the story. Death is the sanction of everything the storyteller can tell.[30]

Bearing in mind the transmitting possibilities of death, we may argue that Gurney's phantasms of the living paradoxically reified storytelling, and by appearing either as visual or aural hallucinations to the letter writers in *Phantasms* they mediated and participated in an act of telling their own life stories to whomever would care to listen.

For some literary figures, psychical research was a fertile environment for the emergence or invocation of the ghostly. Oscar Wilde's novella *The Canterville Ghost*, published in 1887 a year after the appearance of *Phantasms of the Living*, satirizes the SPR's language and methods of demystifying the occult. Having bought Canterville Chase, with its very own resident ghost, the Otis family are avowed disbelievers in the supernatural. The Canterville ghost is reduced to apply theatrical make-up and props to terrorize the imperturbable family. His pantomime ghostly effects have an unexpected result:

> The whole family were now quite interested; Mr. Otis began to suspect that he had been too dogmatic in his denial of the existence of ghosts, Mrs. Otis expressed her intention of joining the Psychical Society, and Washington prepared a long letter to Messrs. Myers and Podmore on the subject of the Permanence of Sanguineous Stains when connected with Crime. That night all doubts about the objective existence of phantasmata were removed for ever.[31]

Wilde's explicit references to the SPR and to Frederic Myers and Frank Podmore augment the veracity of his own story, and he has the fictional writers intending to open correspondence with two real-life figures of the SPR. Washington's intended letter on the permanence of blood-stains is placed to resonate with psychical research terminology. Although the removed stain has reappeared, the existence of

---

[30] Walter Benjamin, 'The Storyteller', in *Illuminations*, ed. Hannah Arendt (London: Pimlico, 1999), 93.
[31] Isobel Murray (ed.), *Oscar Wilde: Complete Shorter Fiction* (Oxford: Oxford University Press, 1998), 63.

'phantasmata' has been removed forever as has the allure of the ghostly. Perhaps, Wilde seems to be suggesting, the vocabulary of psychical research is as astringent as 'Pinkerton's Champion Stain Remover and Paragon Detergent'.[32]

If the SPR did not hold literary allure for Wilde, it fascinated the periodical press. The dazzling star of New Journalism, W. T. Stead, was an amateur spiritualist enquirer, a member of the SPR whose interests in the occult were channelled into his *Review of Reviews* and later in the short-lived journal *Borderland* (1893-7). He mimicked the SPR's intentions of collecting hallucinations in the 1891 Christmas issue of *Review of Reviews*. 'Real Ghost Stories: A Record of Authentic Apparitions' comes with a warning that echoes the report of the SPR's Literary Committee. Instead of cautioning the reader against the dryness of his collection, Stead warns 'that the narratives printed in these pages had better not be read by anyone of tender years, of morbid excitability or of excessively nervous temperament'.[33] In the first story, 'The Ghost that Dwells in Each of Us', Stead asks 'How can there be real ghost stories when there are no real ghosts?' He then introduces a story of multiple personality or 'submerged' consciousness. In another story in the collection, 'The Thought Body', Stead follows Gurney's example and describes a 'hallucination' seen by a young woman, whose testimony is corroborated by her family and by the theosophist Annie Besant, who also consulted on the experience of astral bodies.

To consolidate the verisimilitude of the ghost stories and forge links between the 'Real Ghost Stories' and the SPR, Stead asked for the support of the society and included in the issue a cut-out 'Census Paper for Taking Return of Hallucinations' that readers were invited to fill in and send to Henry Sidgwick at Cambridge. The cover illustration alluded to the reality of the stories within by depicting a female 'wraith' draped in antiquated Grecian attire descending a staircase while a male photographer was preparing to take her picture. The hefty photographic apparatus assembled and ready to capture the spirit implies that a manifestation is expected. Stead might also have been insinuating that the 'real ghost stories' were only posing as real just as a real woman might be posing as a 'wraith' on the cover.

The psychic detective

Pearson's magazine announced in its January 1898 issue the real ghost stories of Flaxman Low, written by E. and H. Heron, the pseudonym of the mother–son pair Kate and Hesketh Pritchard. The twelve stories were collected in a volume published under the title *Ghosts: Being the Experiences of Flaxman Low* in the following

---

[32] Ibid., 62.
[33] 'Real Ghost Stories: A Record of Authentic Apparitions' (Christmas 1891 issue of the *Review of Reviews*), 1.

year. Smajic contends that 'the Pritchards liberally borrow from Doyle and seek to establish Low's credentials by associating him with the Holmesian scientific method.'[34] However, the literary pair also traced Low over the popular figure of the psychical researcher and framed the stories as epistles posted to the authors similar to the letters received by Gurney, Myers, and Podmore. The 'Introduction' evokes both the epistolary form and the gothic tropes of authentic narratives that add credibility to the ghostly narrations:

> The following is an extract from a letter dated February 1896, and addressed to the authors—I think I may say that I am the first student in this field of inquiry who has had the boldness to break free from the old conventional methods, and to approach the elucidation of so-called supernatural problems on the lines of natural law.[35]

The letter's date problematizes Low's declaration of being the 'first student' who 'break[s] free from old conventional methods', since psychical research had been established for over a decade and was introducing statistics and psychology into its 'supernatural problems'. Low might have been suggesting that his methods were even more advanced than those of psychical research, and he is described in one story as 'Flaxman Low the psychologist'.[36] Elsewhere in the collection, Mr Flaxman Low attends an 'Anglo-American Society of Psychical Students',[37] and believes similarly to psychical researchers that 'there are no other laws in what we term the realm of the supernatural but those which are the projections or extensions of natural laws'.[38] The 'editors' of his experiences even pass remarks on Low's hybrid notes as they pore over his writings and catch 'through the steelblue harshness of facts the pink flush of romance, or more often the black corner of a horror unnameable'.[39] Flaxman Low, unlike psychical researchers, presents his stories under a pseudonym, implying that the secrecy of his identity enables those who truly suffer from the supernatural to seek his assistance while maintaining their anonymity, a privilege that could not be provided for spiritualists, participants in the Census of Hallucinations and psychical research. Although McCorristine shows how the 'second-world' of ghosts and ghost seeing could be investigated by the SPR with a generally liberated sensibility, attuned to both the popular concept of the ghost and the new psychical concepts surrounded by the emerging idea of telepathy,[40] I want to suggest that for the psychic detective and occult doctor detective story, it is precisely the secret and anonymity that enables authentic manifestations to occur.

---

[34] Smajic, *Ghost Seers*, 190.

[35] Kate and Hesketh Pritchard, *Ghosts: Being the Experiences of Flaxman Low* (London: C. Arthur Pearson, 1899), vii.

[36] 'The Story of No. 1 Karma Crescent', ibid., 206.

[37] 'The Story of Mr. Flaxman Low', ibid., 276.

[38] 'The Story of Konnor Old House', ibid., 223.

[39] 'The Story of Yard Manor House', ibid., 124.

[40] McCorristine, *Spectres of the Self*, 121.

Georg Simmel explains how the secret 'produces an enlargement of life: numerous contexts of life cannot even emerge in the presence of full publicity. The secret offers, so to speak, the possibility of a second world alongside the manifest world; and the latter is decisively influenced by the former'.[41] It seems that the psychic detectives of fiction operate within this 'second world' that is influenced by the stretched natural causes of the manifest world. Their authentic cases would greatly assist psychical research but the psychic doctor's chosen anonymity, as in the cases of Flaxman Low or of his 'silence' symbolically rendered in Algernon Blackwood's *John Silence: Physician Extraordinary* (1908), illustrates that the sources of these authentic stories will not be identified and therefore will remain hidden in the realm of the literary. Blackwood's John Silence is a man of means, a student of human and superhuman nature who 'has neither consulting-room, bookkeeper, nor professional manner'.[42]

In 'Case 1: A Psychical Invasion', John Silence is summoned to solve the mystery of a humorous writer's demise into writing weird tales. The shift in Felix Pender's genre from comedy to weirdness is something that has economic repercussions for him and his wife as well as psychical. John Silence will only take up the case if it does not prove to be a case of multiple personality, yet he abhors the word 'occultism' since for him there is nothing hidden under sun or moon and he prefers to be called 'wonderfully clairvoyant'.

> For the modern psychical researcher he felt the calm tolerance of the 'man who knows'. There was a trace of pity in his voice—contempt he never showed—when he spoke of their methods.
>
> 'This classification of results is uninspired work at best', he said once to me, when I had been his confidential assistant for some years. 'It leads nowhere, and after a hundred years will lead nowhere. It is playing with the wrong end of a rather dangerous toy. Far better, it would be to examine the causes, and then the results would easily slip into place and explain themselves.'[43]

John Silence's disapproval is not centred around the study of supernatural phenomena per se, but against the methods the SPR is using. Algernon Blackwood was not a member of the SPR yet his work is infused with the language and also methodology of SPR's members. John Silence accepts that there are vibrations that may lead to an understanding of other dimensions. The title of 'A Psychic Invasion' points towards psychical research, although this story is a story of spirit possession, the 'discarnate' spirit of an evil woman possessing the mind of the humorous author after he has used an excessive dose of 'cannabis indica'. The author is unable to conform to his chosen genre, his tales are warped, his stenographer abandons him as

---

[41] Quoted in ibid., 121.
[42] Algernon Blackwood, 'Case 1: A Psychical Invasion', *John Silence: Physician Extraordinary* (London: John Baker, 1908), 2.
[43] Ibid., 3.

she can no longer type the words of the author who is dictated to by the spirit of an evil woman.

William Hope Hodgson's *Carnacki the Ghost Finder* stories were originally published in *The Idler* in 1910 and appeared as a collection in 1913. Carnacki is a learned man and often consults a fourteenth-century manuscript. In dealing with haunted houses he uses photographic cameras and sixth-sense sensitive cats, but he does not disseminate his stories widely. Rather he invites friends to his dinner parties and acts as a Benjaminian storyteller. Although the *fin-de-siècle* and Edwardian psychic detectives are believers and investigators of supernatural phenomena that they deem explicable, they do not adhere to psychical research and are arguably critical of its methodology and dissemination of results. Similarly psychical research attempted to maintain an unalloyed method of collecting and understanding its findings that would not allow for fiction or genre writing to seep in.

FURTHER READING

Bown, Nicola, Carolyn Burdett, and Pamela Thurschwell (eds). *The Victorian Supernatural* (Cambridge: Cambridge University Press, 2004).

Cottom, Daniel. *Abyss of Reason: Cultural Movements, Revelations and Betrayals* (Oxford: Oxford University Press, 1991).

During, Simon. *Modern Enchantments: The Cultural Power of Secular Magic* (Cambridge, MA: Harvard University Press, 2002).

Grimes, Hilary. *The Late Victorian Gothic: Mental Science, the Uncanny and Scenes of Writing* (Aldershot: Ashgate, 2011).

James, William. *Essays in Psychical Research* (Cambridge, MA: Harvard University Press, 1986).

Owen, Alex. *The Darkened Room: Women, Power and Spiritualism in Late Victorian Britain* (Chicago, IL: University of Chicago Press, 1989).

Owen, Alex. *The Place of Enchantment: British Occultism and the Culture of the Modern* (Chicago, IL: University of Chicago Press, 2004).

Smith, Andrew. *The Ghost Story: 1840–1920* (Manchester: Manchester University Press, 2010).

Sword, Helen. *Ghostwriting Modernism* (Ithaca, NY: Cornell University Press, 2002).

Thurschwell, Pamela. *Literature, Technology and Magical Thinking, 1880–1920* (Cambridge: Cambridge University Press, 2001).

CHAPTER 17

CITYSCAPES

Urban Hyperspaces and the Failure of Matter in Late-Victorian and Edwardian Metropolitan Fictions

LAURENCE SCOTT

In his chapter entitled 'What is the Fourth Dimension?' (1884), the mathematician and philosopher Charles Howard Hinton considers the possibility of discovering geometric representations of algebraic expressions such as 2^4. That is, if 2^3 can be represented as a cube with sides of 2 units, then 2^4 designates a geometrical shape extending beyond the three standard spatial dimensions of height, width, and depth into a fourth spatial axis. Hinton was not alone in his fascination with higher dimensions of space. As the theoretical physicist Michio Kaku writes: 'The years 1890 to 1910 may be considered the Golden Years of the Fourth Dimension.'[1] Linda Henderson, in her extensive study on the cultural history of this idea, notes that Hinton was one of many prominent 'hyperspace philosophers' attempting to conceptualize a fourth dimension. The late-Victorian interest in a theoretically perceivable space beyond mundane three-dimensional reality generated a lively interdisciplinarity, such that writers and artists began to consider the implications of the transcendental inquiries being undertaken in both pure mathematics and physics.

A major literary popularizer of the fourth dimension was Edwin A. Abbott, whose novel *Flatland: A Romance of Many Dimensions* (1884) offers both a political allegory and a meditation on how beings from one dimension would interact with those from another. In the work's eponymous, two-dimensional plane world the narrator mocks his grandson for proposing spatial representations of algebraic expressions. 'The boy is a fool', the grandfather says, 'three-to-the-third can have no meaning in Geometry'.[2] Thereupon the disembodied voice of a 'Stranger' from

---

[1] Michio Kaku, *Hyperspace: A Scientific Odyssey through Parallel Universes, Time Warps, and the Tenth Dimension* (Oxford: Oxford University Press, 1994), 62.

[2] Edwin A. Abbott, *Flatland: A Romance of Many Dimensions* (Oxford: Oxford University Press, 2006), 82.

three-dimensional Spaceland interjects to defend the poor boy, but the grand-father's suggestion that certain analytical formulations become meaningless when applied geometrically was also the basis of a major rebuttal to the ideas of the hyper-space philosophers. Contemporary scholar Elizabeth Throesch traces these objec-tions, arguing that 'The concept of the fourth dimension grew out of a slippage between the languages of [algebraic and geometric] mathematics, a hypostatization of abstract symbols'.[3]

Hypostatization is the process by which immaterial concepts are given the weightiness of matter, a conversion of abstractions into physical objects. By consid-ering how hypostatization functions in literary works of the late nineteenth and early twentieth centuries, this chapter seeks to draw a connection between late-Victorian interest in the fourth dimension and contemporaneous literary representa-tions of the cityscape. In the London of this period, one can discern equivalent 'slippages' to that which Throesch describes. There is a trend in these texts to depict the metropolis as the result of incomplete hypostatization. It is as though London, for all its oppressive physicality and concreteness, has at the same time never fully materialized. Its sheer scale and complexity render it ontologically ineffable, and yet it is asked to carry an immense symbolic burden as a coherent totality. Victorian writers were long aware of the paradoxes generated from any plausible rendering of the capital, which G. W. M. Reynolds in the 1840s called 'The City of Fearful Contrasts'. While Victorian London officially represented the heart of imperialism in its triumphal architecture, statues, and monuments, there was inevitably an urban excess that defied the patency of this symbolization. As a result, by the end of the century, London began increasingly to be imagined as an ambiguous site, at once abstract and material.

The cityscapes in the texts I will examine here possess a precarious physicality. They are in various ways ruptured and permeable, and it is precisely this spatial disin-tegration that evokes notions of a transcendent world beyond the fragmented urban façade. At times these imagined Londons seem to be recorded from the perspective of a higher dimension. In *Flatland*, the three-dimensional visitor describes his percep-tion of two-dimensional space: 'From that position of advantage I discerned all that you speak of as *solid* (by which you mean "enclosed on four sides"), your houses, your churches, your very chests and safes, yes even your insides and stomachs, all lying open and exposed to my view.'[4] This dematerialization offers epiphanic moments in these late-Victorian visions of a London that shifts between encaging solidity and sublime ethereality, which, as I will suggest here, foregrounds the literary modernist notion of the city as a fragmented hybrid of the physical and the ideal.

---

[3] Elizabeth Throesch, 'Nonsense in the Fourth Dimension of Literature', in Cristopher Hollingsworth (ed.), *Alice beyond Wonderland: Essays for the Twenty-First Century* (Iowa City, IA: University of Iowa Press, 2009), 41.
[4] Abbott, *Flatland*, 86.

Experimentation with non-linear temporalities has become a defining feature of literary modernism. Robert T. Tally Jr, a scholar in the emerging fields of geo-criticism and the spatial humanities, notes that the modernist desire to represent the non-chronological movements of thought arguably results in a 'repression' of spatiality in modernist texts. However, he rightly raises the difficulty of cleanly separating the temporal from the spatial. 'In the modernists' apparent fascination with time', Tally writes, 'it is also possible to see a profound spatial anxiety, as the whirl of temporal flux represented in these texts is equally a bewildering reconfiguration of the problem of spatial location'.[5] Indeed, I contend that the perception of time is almost entirely dependent on spatiality; time manifests in alterations to material conditions. In H. G. Wells's *The Time Machine* (1895), which explicitly defines the fourth dimension temporally, the Traveller witnesses the passing of eons in the fluctuating ephemera of the spatial dimension. He recounts: 'I saw great and splendid architecture rising about me, more massive than any buildings of our own time, and yet, as it seemed, built of glimmer and mist.'[6] Moreover, the very notion of *simultaneity*, when used to describe the layering of temporal registers in modernist narratives, almost always evokes a coincidence between two spatialized moments.

The late-Victorian and Edwardian prelude to literary urban modernism involves the dematerialization of space. Before temporality could become non-linear, it seems, material reality had first to be fractured and fragmented. This spatial precursor to temporal fragmentation also mirrors the trajectory of intellectual engagement with the fourth dimension. The late-Victorian hyperspace philosophers such as Hinton developed theories of how a fourth dimension would intersect spatially with our own three-dimensional world. With the establishing of quantum mechanics in the early twentieth century, however, time became the widely accepted axis of four-dimensionality. It is therefore striking that in a text recognized as bridging late-Victorian and modernist writing, Joseph Conrad and Ford Madox Ford's *The Inheritors* (1901), we find a temporal fourth dimension (the 'future' of the Inheritors) made visibly apparent in the warping of physical space. Moreover, in this novel it is the cityscape that deforms to reveal an unknowable infinity. Here, the cityscape is the materialization of temporality. The past solidifies as Gothic architecture, and when a character meets ruin he is described metaphorically as a 'mediaeval city'.[7] Thus, when the city is transfigured, as in the novel's transcendent, fourth-dimensional visions, the inchoate future flows into the fissures.

In earlier urban literature, the city's solidity is often uncompromising and impermeable. A prime source of terror in Urban Gothic serials of the 1840s, such as G. W. M. Reynolds's *The Mysteries of London* (1844-6), inheres in the representation of

---

[5] Robert T. Tally Jr, *Spatiality* (Abingdon: Routledge, 2013), 37.

[6] H. G. Wells, *The Time Machine* (London: Penguin, 2005), 20.

[7] Joseph Conrad and Ford Madox Ford, *The Inheritors: An Extravagant Story* (Liverpool: Liverpool University Press, 1999), 120.

the city as a trap. Reynolds actively copied the earlier Parisian narratives of Eugène Sue, in which the corrupting effects of the city prohibit escape. Those characters terminally blighted by urban squalor, no matter how repentant, cannot transcend their metropolitan confines. Their dreams of flight seem possible to the last, but ultimately the city refuses to release them. Often, on the brink of happiness, these doomed urbanites are killed suddenly and pointlessly, sundered by the casual and callous violence of city life. The grip of the city, which re-emerges as a focus in the fatalistic tales of Arthur Morrison in the 1890s, produces in late-Victorian and Edwardian writing a dialectic of transcendence. A common idea in the literature of this period is that subjectivity is ineluctably entwined with a constrictive urban environment. As a result of this confinement, a preoccupation with escape is dialectically sharpened. Moreover, if the city cannot be fled from, if the moral purity of the pastoral cannot be regained, then perhaps transcendence can be found not outside the city's walls but *through* them. In this sense, the city comes to represent paradoxically both the prison and the portal. Here the city's inherent mysteriousness as an ineffable, incoherent topography lends itself to the idea that within the all-consuming metropolis there are strange rents and gaps through which alternative possibilities for subjectivity may be glimpsed.

The prison/portal dialectic arguably developed from a seam of nineteenth-century literary taste that had become fatigued with the fantastic. As English Gothic aged, a vogue emerged for what admiring French readers called *le surnaturel expliqué*. Ann Radcliffe's popularity was linked to her ability to suggest a fantastical situation that elegantly resolved itself without contravening any natural law. Similarly, the urban mysteries of the 1830s and 1840s, in both England and France, raided Gothic metaphor while staying faithful to reality, albeit a sensationalized one. Morrison's *A Child of the Jago* (1896) represents the next phase in this progression in its depictions of urban life that are almost entirely de-metaphorized and which also emphasize the closed, material system of the city. Whereas Reynolds describes the brutality of East End life by repeatedly imagining the women of the slums in bestial or satanic terms, Morrison rejects this figurative mode and instead offers wholly literal accounts of female street brawls.

In Morrison's *Tales of Mean Streets* (1895), the East End is encaging and ceaselessly watchful. There is 'no danger of losing yourself... the public houses are always with you'.[8] While the abstracted urban gaze forms a net of surveillance, the people themselves are described as ignorant: 'seeing nothing, reading nothing, and considering nothing'. The city's omniscience suppresses the vision of its citizens, and thus when a group of them travel from the familiar knot of alleys their own ability to see is activated. Morrison writes how, 'As the streets got broken and detached, with patches of field between, they began to look about them'.[9] This notion of failed

---

[8] Arthur Morrison, *Tales of Mean Streets* (London: Methuen, 1894), 34.
[9] Ibid., 25, 67.

vision returns in *A Child of the Jago*. Quoting from *Ezekiel*, Morrison's epigram invokes 'foolish prophets, that follow their own spirit, and have seen nothing!' The chokehold of the city dramatizes this inability to transcend one's depraved existence. As part of a modernization effort the Jago neighbourhood is being torn down, but this demolishing of the material city only reveals yet more sordid materiality. The wreckers '[lay] bare the secret dens of a century of infamy...letting light and air at last into the subterraneous basements where men and women had swarmed, and bred, and died like wolves in their lairs'.[10] Note that Morrison, in revealing not the *beyond* but the *below*, allows himself a rare metaphor, which rises from the rubble like the ghost of the Urban Gothic.

Morrison and other English writers of late-Victorian 'New Realism' tended to discourage comparison with contemporaneous European naturalists, and indeed Morrison even repudiated the term 'realist' when applied to his works. Nevertheless, such a comparison is productive here. Naturalism is structurally anti-transcendental because its narrative terminus inheres *within* the system of material conditions and dynamics of the fictional world it describes. Hence it is generically a tragedy of dashed dreams, embodied in *A Child of the Jago* by the young East Londoner Dicky Perrott's fatal career. As a boy, Dicky Perrott is accosted by the crazed Mister Beveridge, who shouts in Dicky's ear that 'It—never—does—to—see—too—much!'[11] He also implies that Dicky's ambitions to better himself are futile, since there is no escape from the destitution of the Jago besides routes that lead either to the gaol or the gallows. Beveridge is a taunting presence throughout the novel, shimmering between resigned containment and a manic urge to transcend. Although ostensibly a defeatist, Beveridge stalks the streets while 'stabbing the air with a carving knife, and incoherently defying "all the lot" to come near him'.[12] This symbolic renting of space suggests Beveridge's search for an impossible exit, somewhere beyond the oppressive encroachment of other people's physicalities, and indeed in Dicky's mind this lunatic is irrevocably associated with possibilities for transcendence. Years later, Dicky recalls the old man's warning, and in a naturalist declaration of defeat thinks how 'the Jago had got him. Why should he fight against the inevitable?' The city did indeed 'have him', since Dicky's dreams end when he is fatally wounded in a street fight. However, as he lies dying he thinks of the old man again, and asks the neighbourhood priest to tell the old man that 'there's 'nother way out—better'.[13]

While Morrison's unofficial naturalism dialectically produced a thwarted dimension of escape from urban misery, the late-century revival of the inexplicable supernatural in major texts such as *The Picture of Dorian Gray* (1891) and *Dracula* (1897) repopularized the possibility of beings and worlds beyond one's mortal ken. The hypostatizing turn engendered by multidisciplinary quests for the fourth dimension

---

[10] Morrison, *A Child of the Jago* (London: Methuen, 1896), 185.   [11] Ibid., 9.
[12] Ibid., 47.   [13] Ibid., 206, 345.

contributed to this return to the fantastic by calling into question the coherence of everyday matter and suggesting that reality was not confined within the limits of three-dimensional space. As the process of representing an abstraction as a realized object, hypostatization has implications for physical reality beyond this one-way materialization. Since the hypostatized object is a solidified intangibility, its very presence undermines the robustness of matter. That is to say, if the abstract can become concrete, then the reverse is also possible: the concreteness of perceivable reality can at any point be interpreted as the hypostatized embodiment of the metaphysical. Arguably it is this corollary to hypostatization that emerges memorably in canonical modernist representations of the city.

As Peter I. Barta argues of T. S. Eliot's urban poetry, 'every city object suggests an invisible force at work in the background'.[14] The cityscape's semiotic density, with its complex and ineffable system of signs that appears to stand for both extreme order and extreme chaos, is reflected in urban literature's preoccupation with deciphering and detective work. The consolation offered by the literary detective, who corrals the city's mysterious significations, is always tempered by the possibility that the city may one day offer a puzzle to which there is no earthly solution. While in modernism this anxiety appears in the undermining of absolute truths and the rise of a purely subjective articulation of experience, we also find in late-Victorian and Edwardian hypostatizing fiction an interest in the weakening of the correspondence between language and the reality it is meant to signify.

In the urban texts of the early twentieth century, the dematerialization of matter is reflected in a corresponding linguistic crisis. As matter and symbol become interchangeable, there arises at the level of language an intense ambivalence towards the robustness of signification itself. In H. G. Wells's fantastical fiction—for example *The Time Machine*, or stories such as 'The Door in the Wall' (1906) and 'The Remarkable Case of Davidson's Eyes' (1895)—the incredible adventures are presented to the reader by a more or less disinterested narrator. That is to say, for us they are always already a story, and the meta-narrator's rightful scepticism of what they have been told emphasizes the idea that these fantastic tales, while purporting to be true, may not be signifying any credible reality. In Arthur Machen's *The Great God Pan* (1894), a woman who is made to see into the reality 'beyond this glamour and this vision' of the mundane world physically disintegrates into a jelly-like substance.[15] The horrified onlooker records in this disintegration the emergence of what he calls simply 'a Form', but which he does not articulate in words. He does attest that 'the symbol of this form may be seen in ancient sculptures', which highlights art's liminal position as the concretization of a sign that does not necessarily

[14] Peter I. Barta, *Bely, Joyce, and Doblin: Peripatetics in the City Novel* (Gainesville, FL: University Press of Florida, 1996), 14.
[15] Arthur Machen, 'The Great God Pan', in Roger Luckhurst (ed.), *Late Victorian Gothic Tales* (Oxford: Oxford University Press, 2005), 184.

signify an aspect of our reality. Tellingly, we learn of the woman's transformation into jelly from a written account, and at the moment in the narrative when the strange Form appears there begin to be gaps in the writing. The manuscript becomes in places 'illegible'.[16]

The idea of an ambivalent, incomplete symbol provides the central drama of Wells's story, 'The Door in the Wall'. As a young boy Lionel Wallace discovers behind a green door in West London a wonderland of enchanting figures and creatures; the colours of its landscape are 'clean and perfect and subtly luminous'.[17] Its expansive dimensions—there are views of distant hills—transcend the network of dreary streets from which Wallace enters it. This pastoral utopia displaces the material city, and indeed the young boy experiences a serene inversion of urban stimuli: 'there were many things and many people ... [who] were beautiful and kind'. The crisis arrives when a 'sombre dark woman' shows him the pages of a book that contains 'not pictures, you understand, but realities' from his own life.[18] Wallace comes to the page displaying the 'reality' of him first contemplating the door in the wall. Suddenly the virtual city of the sombre woman's magical book slides into the realm of the actual, and Wallace finds himself back on the other side of the door, returned to West Kensington's miserable greyness.

Wells's story derives its power from destabilizing the boundary between the imagined and the real. Wallace's account of his adventure to a now middle-aged school friend is received with appropriate scepticism. Yet, for this friend who is also the story's meta-narrator, this fantastic tale contains 'a flavour of reality'. As Wallace describes the sudden reappearances of the door in the wall throughout his adult life, we are invited to interpret the story as an allegory of lost childhood imagination, whereby maturation bars re-entry into the dimension of juvenile make-believe. Most crucially, the door does not seem to be anchored in physical space. Wallace reports seeing it set in various walls in West London, always when he is on his way elsewhere, full of worldly concerns and distractions. As he recalls, 'Who wants to pat panthers on the way to dinner with pretty women and distinguished men?'[19] The symbolic aspect of the door, glimpsed sideways during key moments in Wallace's young adulthood, only intensifies when an ageing Wallace becomes an obsessed, nocturnal streetwalker, attempting to relocate the portal to a youthful paradise.

The story's climax highlights the ontological oscillation at the centre of Wells's tale. One night Wallace falls to his death through a door in some industrial hoarding at East Kensington Station, negligently left unsecured by two gangers and which screened a deep excavation. Tragedy results from Wallace's attempt to materialize

[16] Ibid., 229.
[17] Wells, 'The Door in the Wall', in *The Complete Short Stories of H. G. Wells* (London: J. M. Dent, 1998), 574.
[18] Ibid., 575.   [19] Ibid., 571, 580.

the symbolic, to search for a physical entryway into a purely epistemological realm. At the same time, his physical death follows the figurative logic of the door as metaphoric entrance to the lost world of childlike innocence. In other words, for Wallace to return to this world, his adult subjectivity must first be annihilated. The formal structure of this moral fable, with its grisly conclusion, in one sense confirms the veracity of his original experiences.

Thus, as with the virtual realities of the sombre woman's book, the story moves uneasily between the literal and the figurative. Indeed, the very pit into which Wallace fatally plunges functions as a mundane parody of a tunnel into the beyond. Rather than revealing a timeless wonderland, it exists to further the utterly modern and forward-thinking expansion of an urban railway network. The meta-narrator's concluding ambivalence extends the crisis of signification around which the story revolves. 'There are times', he claims, 'when I believe that Wallace was no more than the victim of the coincidence between a rare but not unprecedented type of hallucination and a careless trap.' But the theory he favours is that the door was the physical 'guise' of Wallace's ability to sense the transcendent. If we are to take Wallace's death literally, the door was asked to signify too much, a fatal hypostatization. Rather than offering a passage to the beyond it delivered Wallace into the mouth of materiality itself, with all the attendant and unambiguous dangers of a fall to earth. The narrator of Wells's tale leaves us with a final question: 'But did [Wallace] see it like that?'[20]

The erosion of the city's solidity in association with semantic destabilization, and the subsequent possibilities for transcendent vision also arise as themes in Conrad and Ford's *The Inheritors*. Here, too, we find another mysticized woman, this time a visitor from 'the Fourth Dimension' who enlists a solitary writer called Granger to assist in her political machinations on Earth. The book opens in a highly allegorical mode, with Granger and the Dimensionist passing through 'the old gateway'.[21] They are looking down upon Canterbury, when suddenly the mysterious woman makes an incomprehensible sound and thereupon the old Gothic city below undergoes a transcendental shift: 'One seemed to see something beyond, something vaster—vaster than cathedrals, vaster—than the conception of the gods to whom cathedrals were raised. The tower reeled out of the perpendicular. One saw beyond it, not roofs, or smoke, or hills, but an unrealized, unrealizable infinity of space.'[22]

This inclusion of a four-dimensional character punctures the novel's fictional space, producing a textual crossing of the fourth wall whereby Granger is able to interpret the supernatural events in which he is embroiled with a reader's knowingness. Repeatedly he thinks of the sublime Dimensionist in aestheticized terms, interpreting her allegorically. He tells us that 'she spoke like a book', that 'she wished me to regard her as a symbol, perhaps, of the future'. Later he misremembers that

---

[20] Ibid., 583, 584.   [21] Conrad and Ford, *The Inheritors*, 5.   [22] Ibid., 8.

she said 'she was a symbol of my own decay'.[23] This glimpse of the fourth dimension beyond the warped cityscape triggers in Granger a semiotic crisis that affects more than his comprehension of the beautiful Dimensionist. Indeed, everyday life begins to collapse into a series of representations. He notes how the Foreign Minister 'was only a symbol', and during his adventures people appear to him as proto-modernist abstractions: one man is a 'thin parallelogram of black with a mosaic of white about the throat'; another's face, albeit that of another Dimensionist, appears as 'a half-hidden, pallid oval'. In this world of signifiers he finds comfort in the solidity and reality of the crowds in Southampton Row, where there 'was safety in the contact with the crowd, in jostling, in being jostled'.[24]

Granger's association with the Dimensionist creates a phenomenological para-dox in which the typical experience of the concrete and the abstract are inverted. He observes that when he is in her company she is an idea, and it is only in absentia that she materializes into a person.[25] His sense of the Fourth Dimension is similarly inverted. Although he interprets her as wanting to symbolize the inevitable, earthly downfall of his Decadent civilization, she denounces the figurative, insisting that, 'You must take me literally if you want to understand'. Indeed, she tells him that her race has 'no feeling for art'. Her political schemes hinge on her materializing, and so she adopts the guise of his sister. 'I want to be placed', she tells him, and thus the empty signifier of 'Granger's sister' crystallizes into a tangible social position, such that even his own aunt treats them as siblings.[26] However, this disruption of signifi-cation further disorientates Granger. 'I never quite understood', he narrates, 'whether my aunt really knew that my sister was not my sister.' He also senses the cost of this ambivalence to his aunt, who herself most fully embodies the old order on the cusp of being swept away. He feels that the effect of epistemological oscilla-tion, in which a 'sister' simultaneously signifies both a real person and a void, has given his aunt 'the air of being disintegrated, like a mineral under an immense weight'.[27] The intrusion of this woman from beyond into the signifying chain meta-phorically dematerializes those most implicated in her false signification.

Granger's exposure to four-dimensionality impacts his perception of his urban surroundings. Following the initial encounter with the Dimensionist, in which Canterbury is contorted with revelation, Granger experiences London as 'an immense blackness' that 'had no interiors for me. There were house fronts, staring windows, closed doors, but nothing within; no rooms, no hollow places'.[28] This vision of an expansive, dark plane flattens the city into two dimensions. Just as the-ories of four-dimensional space were based on analogies from lower dimensional geometries, Granger's vision is also analogical. Since he has seen four dimensions, three-dimensional matter is, analogously, 'flattened', precisely as matter demoted from three to two dimensions would appear to him. But this city of closed doors is

[23] Ibid., 14, 9, 40.   [24] Ibid., 32, 55, 60, 40.   [25] Ibid., 127.   [26] Ibid., 47, 10, 23.
[27] Ibid., 97.   [28] Ibid., 35.

the only way he can articulate his transcendental perspective. Unlike in *Flatland*, where the three-dimensional visitor sees the landscape opened up before him, Granger's shifted perspective reveals nothing but a cityscape hollowed of depth and emptied of meaning.

As his involvement with the Dimensionists deepens, Granger's perception of the city becomes further evacuated of the material dimension, which also manifests linguistically. Even his sense of urban multitudes turns towards the virtual, such that his desert city is populated with immaterial throngs. 'They crowded upon me', he confesses. 'I saw Fox, Polehampton, de Mersch himself, crowds of figures without a name.'[29] This mob of nameless names comprises a vacated, sign-less reality. A moment later, the traumatic severing of matter from language reverses, and Granger hears those 'incomprehensible words' of his Dimensionist 'sister', this time as disembodied language severed from matter. The shock of those aural signifiers, which signify no knowable object, reverberates into the material city, such that the 'sheer faces of the enormous buildings near at hand seemed to topple forwards like cliffs in an earthquake, and for an instant I saw beyond them into unknown depths that I had seen into before'.[30]

In the novel's concluding scene, Granger and his 'sister' meet in his aunt's house, which now contains 'an immense white room'. The physical world's dematerialization culminates in a 'shadowless' realm of pure signification. The terrible Dimensionist has become 'like a white statue in a gallery', and she regards her mortal acquaintance, as Granger puts it, 'as if I were the picture of a man'. Immediately he advances this figuration from simile to metaphor, which mimics the progress from the metaphoric to the literal. 'Well, that was it; I was a picture, she a statue.'[31] That is to say, Granger can only experience this exchange in a transcendental space as the encounter between two aesthetic objects. The inhabitants of Abbott's *Flatland* can only perceive the two-dimensional cross section of three-dimensional matter and likewise the art object—the statue or the painting—is in this text the three-dimensional hypostatization of the transcendental.

Conrad returns to this vision of the city as a place of dislocated meaning in his later novel *The Secret Agent* (1907). However, unlike *The Inheritors*, this work does not portray a single transcendent universe of four-dimensionality but rather represents a solipsistic, individualized idea of a place beyond the cityscape. As in Morrison's *Jago*, London in *The Secret Agent* is an encroaching presence, thickly and claustrophobically materialized. Characters sense buildings and streets watching them; the novel is sinister with a disembodied, omniscient gaze. And yet, there is the possibility of escape. The story's anarchists and their associates are characterized by the dislocations and fissures in this material density that they inhabit or produce by their presence. We are repeatedly reminded of how an anarchist known simply as the Professor lives ascetically in a backroom 'far away' in Islington, in

---

[29] Ibid., 142.   [30] Ibid., 143.   [31] Ibid., 151.

which there is a large, padlocked cupboard. The anarchist Michaelis, an ex-prisoner, talks to himself as though still in 'the four white washed walls of his cell', unhearing of his companions and 'indeed indifferent' to them. When the protagonist Verloc visits his revolutionary superiors, he notices how an address, No. 1 Chesham Square, is written on a wall 'at least sixty yards' away from the building it designates.[32]

This London is spatially disorientated and perforated with seemingly unmappable zones. The Verlocs live above their shop of veiled goods in Brett Street, a narrow passage extending from 'an open triangular space of dark and mysterious houses'. Conrad describes this vicinity in consistently eerie terms: those who enter the blackness beyond the triangular clearing 'would never be heard of again'; a policeman whose beat crosses this neighbourhood 'seemed to be lost for ever to the force'; a passer-by of the Verlocs' shop seems 'to pace out all eternity... in a night without end'.[33] If Brett Street appears to disobey the normal laws of spatial orientation, Verloc himself is similarly disorientated in relation to the mundane world. Throughout the book he occupies a strange rift in spatio-temporal logic, such that he is neither in the world nor entirely out of it. Following a meeting with his anarchist superiors, Verloc's consciousness, Conrad tells us, reaches the door to his home instantaneously, while his 'mortal envelope' strolls through the streets. His subjectivity is organized around a total 'detachment from the material world'; he is separated from 'the phenomena of this world' by a 'Chinese Wall'. He begins, as his involvement in the terrorist plot deepens, to feel that 'he himself had become unplaced'.[34]

When Verloc convinces his brother-in-law Stevie to set off a bomb in Greenwich Park, the city attempts to assert its dominance over the Brett Street fissure. The single, legible remains from Stevie's disintegrated body is a triangular scrap of material from his coat, on the underside of which is the address that Mrs Verloc has sewn onto it, should her mentally handicapped brother ever be lost. From this remnant—a legible triangle to counter the triangular vortex bordering Brett Street—the mutilated body of the terrorist can thus be orientated and placed. Upon learning of her brother's involvement in the attack, and that her husband persuaded him to enact this horrific mission, Mrs Verloc herself is severed from materiality. The orientation of the Greenwich terrorist ironically displaces Mrs Verloc, since the traumatic knowledge of the explosion effectively propels Mrs Verloc into a transcendent fissure of her own.

Confronting the new reality of Stevie's death, her sense of the city surrounding the quiet channel of Brett Street is annihilated. Sitting in her kitchen, she contemplates, in an echo of the ascetic Michaelis, 'a whitewashed wall with no writing on it'. She stares at the wall's perfect blankness, but she is no longer able fully to perceive

[32] Conrad, *The Secret Agent: A Simple Tale* (Cambridge: Cambridge University Press, 1990), 53, 39, 17.
[33] Ibid., 116, 49.   [34] Ibid., 33, 120, 115.

such everyday realities. Indeed, the idea of her husband's involvement in her brother's hideous disintegration is spatialized in her mind: 'across that thought (not
across the kitchen) the form of Mr Verloc went to and fro'.[35] This phenomenological
layering of matter and idea resonates with Davidson's adventure in Wells's story, in
which the eponymous scientist involved in a laboratory explosion can suddenly see
both the London streets *and* tropical fish swimming off the shore of an island on the
other side of the world. Similarly, the grief-stricken Mrs Verloc occupies two planes
simultaneously, resulting in a petrifying double vision of both the physical world
of her domestic space and the horrific truth that lies behind it. Shortly after,
Mrs Verloc literalizes her metaphysical separation by changing into mourning wear,
donning a black veil that, for Verloc, turns his wife into 'a masked and mysterious
visitor of impenetrable intentions'.[36]

The bomb's impact upon the Verloc household renders the husband and wife
mutually unknowable. Inhabiting different transcendent solitudes and with no
communal semantic dimension between them, they become psychotic to each
other. While the notion of the urbanite's inherent secrecy is not particular to either
a late-Victorian or Edwardian sensibility, one can argue that in these later literary
periods we find it articulated in novel ways as a function of language. Rather than
the mid-Victorian trope of individuals possessing undisclosed stores of facts about
themselves, their souls like documents locked in private safes, we find in texts from
this period a move towards the paradox of a revealed unknowability. Through their
idiosyncratic relationships to a transcendent *beyond*, individuals are ultimately
illegible to those around them, displaced from communal discourse. This semantic
ambiguity amounts to a form of privacy that becomes a prominent theme of modernist subjectivity. When Clarissa Dalloway, in Virginia Woolf's most concerted
'London' novel, thinks that 'love and religion would destroy that, whatever it was,
the privacy of the soul', she is meditating on how traditional, institutionalized
attempts at transcendence, such as those related to faith or romantic attachment,
fail to account for the individual mind's intensely subjective relationship to language and meaning.[37] *Mrs. Dalloway* (1925) is a prose-paean to how the seemingly
random flow of urban stimuli prompts moments of transcendent being in the city
walker, little epiphanies that cannot adequately be communicated to others.

In Thomas Burke's *Limehouse Nights* (1916), the hardened young heroine Gina is
a London night club performer who offers her audiences a very late-Victorian,
Hellenophile escape from everyday life. Burke, whom Anne Veronica Witchard
reads as a liminal author positioned between traditionalism and modernism, writes
that Gina 'opened new doors to them, showing them the old country to which
to-day excursions are almost forbidden; the country of the dear brown earth and
the naked flesh, of the wine-cup and flowers and kisses and Homeric laughter'.

---

[35] Ibid., 182, 188.   [36] Ibid., 193.
[37] Virginia Woolf, *Mrs. Dalloway* (Oxford: Oxford University Press, 2008), 107.

However, the more striking opportunity for transcendence lies with Gina herself, for whom '[e]very street was a sharp-flavoured adventure, and at night each had a little untranslatable message for her'.[38] The ambiguity of 'untranslatable' here—could Gina 'read' the message at all, or was she the *only* person for whom it is legible?—foreshadows urban modernism's preoccupation with the mysterious, private modes of communication between the citizen and the street. In the 1920s, the surrealist founder André Breton described Paris as a 'cryptogram', a puzzle that staged through coincidences and chance encounters a series of shocks to awaken the perceptive urbanite to a higher reality.[39]

Ultimately the surrealist dilemma was how this personal transcendence could be broadened into a communal, politicized experience, a problem implicit within the earlier English texts explored here. Abbott's two-dimensional narrator is imprisoned for spreading his knowledge of three-dimensional space; Wells's Traveller is, at the story's close, exiled in time. An aspect of modernist existential crisis is the seemingly inevitable solipsism of transcendence, embodied in the incommunicability of the street walker's solitary epiphanies. In 1905, Madox Ford suggested the associated, illusory communality of public discourse, which attempts to elide this solipsism: 'We talk of the Londoner and we firmly believe there is a Londoner; but there is none.'[40] This idea evokes the great disappearing act of the modernist subject, who escapes, not through a magic door, but through the fissures of language itself, employing the decoy of a hypostatized public self to move among the crowds of similarly concretized ghosts.

FURTHER READING

Beaumont, Matthew. *The Spectre of Utopia: Utopian and Science Fictions at the fin de siècle* (Oxford: Peter Lang, 2011).
Bown, Nicola, Carolyn Burdett, and Pamela Thurschwell. *The Victorian Supernatural* (Cambridge: Cambridge University Press, 2004).
Goldhill, Simon. *Victorian Culture and Classical Antiquity* (Princeton, NJ: Princeton University Press, 2011).
Harding, Desmond. *Writing the City: Urban Visions and Literary Modernism* (London: Routledge, 2003).
Henderson, Linda. *The Fourth Dimension and Non-Euclidean Geometry* (Cambridge, MA: MIT Press, 2013).
Hinton, Charles Howard. *A New Era of Thought* (London: Swan, Sonnenschein & Co., 1888).
Randall, Bryony. *Modernism, Daily Time, and Everyday Life* (Cambridge: Cambridge University Press, 2007).

[38] Thomas Burke, *Limehouse Nights: Tales of Chinatown* (London: Brown, Watson, 1961), 219, 195.
[39] André Breton, *Nadja*, trans. Richard Howard (New York: Grove Press, 1960), 112.
[40] Ford, *The Soul of London* (London: Chiswick Press, 1905), 150.

Schleifer, Ronald. *Modernism and Time: The Logic of Abundance in Literature, Science, and Culture, 1880–1930* (Cambridge, Cambridge University Press, 2000).

Wells, H. G. 'The Remarkable Case of Davidson's Eyes', in *The Complete Short Stories of H. G. Wells* (London: J. M. Dent, 1998), 63–70.

Witchard, Anne Veronica. *Thomas Burke's Dark Chinoiserie: 'Limehouse Nights' and the Queer Spell of Chinatown* (Farnham: Ashgate, 2009).

CHAPTER 18

REGIONALISMS

PENNY FIELDING

'Region' is both a specific and an indeterminate concept. From the Latin *regere* (to direct), a region is a territory, and throughout its history the term has been used to mean a space determined by administration and regulation. In this sense, a region is something bounded and mappable. In another way, a region is more loosely defined, and has come to imply something quite different from, and often opposed to, the first sense. A region can be an area identified by any form of homogeneity—language, ethnicity, climate, or customs. Regionalism is a question of relations, but more specifically of different relational configurations that take on political and cultural contours that change according to historical demands. Are regions determined by a centre/periphery model ('London and the provinces')? Or is it something more like this definition from the philosopher of place, Edward Casey: 'any given place serves to hold together dispersed things, animate or inanimate; it *regionalizes* them, giving them a single shared space in which to be together'?[1]

In geographical terms an example might be 'the Lake District'—a more centripetal model in which the region is defined by something at its centre, for example the experiences of the people who live there. In this second sense, 'regionalism' has in the nineteenth century and onwards taken on the role of challenging what has been seen as the violence of imposed or authoritarian geographies such as urbanization, nationalism, or imperialism.[2] Regions are seen as organic outgrowths of the people who live there, each region being a distinct chronotope made recognizable by its inhabitants. Yet this same model of singularity can also turn back into a universalizing one when the way in which a region is imagined in literature becomes synecdochal for the nation itself as an essential expression of, for example, Englishness.

To complicate matters further, 'regional' sits in a nexus of terms that have been freighted with political and cultural values. It exists somewhere on a spectrum

---

[1] Edward S. Casey, *Remembering: A Phenomenological Study* (Bloomington, IN: Indiana University Press, 1987), 202.

[2] For a discussion of this use of 'regionalism', see Roberto M. Dainotto, *Place in Literature: Regions, Cultures, Communities* (Ithaca, NY: Cornell University Press, 2000), 1–33.

with 'parochial' and 'provincial', terms that themselves fluctuate with geographical and historical values. Ian Duncan points out that until the 1870s, regions were distinct localities, whereas the term 'provincial' carried an exemplary national role that began thereafter to pass into the realm of 'unpolished' or uncultivated: 'while "regional" implies a neutral or even positive set of multiple local differences, "provincial" connotes a negative difference...expressed as a generic or typical identity, within which any particular provincial setting may take the place of any other.'[3]

As a geographical term, then, a 'region' tends to expand or contract according to the political or social ideas that measure it and, as Victorian cultural geographies take on the contours of modernism, we can see how different concepts of the region both merge with and oppose each other in a series of encounters. Modernism does not mark a clear-cut break between older forms of local regionalism and a new international modernity. In fact, as a recent study of modernisms puts it, we should acknowledge in the period a 'tension between recognizing local movements and drawing connections across borders'.[4] Our period, tracing the move from Victorian to modern culture, recognizes that no territorial boundaries are fixed or impermeable. What we may think of as separate regions are crossed by movements of peoples, languages, texts, and modes of transport, and any given locality may be read in a wider geography. A poem by Robert Louis Stevenson, written in 1890, introduces this idea:

> [...]About, on seaward-drooping hills,
> New folds of city glitter. Last, the Forth
> Wheels ample waters set with sacred isles,
> And populous Fife smokes with a score of towns.[5]

This extract seems to define a region—south-east Scotland where Stevenson grew up—and the poem resonates with alliterative and assonant Scots place names that give a local, linguistic contiguity: Halkerside, Allermuir, Caerketton. But Stevenson's panoramic vista positions us above these local details, suggesting that places can only be known in their wider contexts or represented on a map. Furthermore, the poem's own wider geography is an international one. Stevenson is writing in the Gilbert Islands (now Kiribati) in the South Pacific and, as he thinks about his first home in Scotland, 'Continents / And continental oceans intervene' to remind him of this global, colonial perspective, where the sense of belonging to a locality is crossed with emigration and worldwide commerce.

---

[3] Ian Duncan, 'The Provincial or Regional Novel', in Patrick Brantlinger and William B. Thesing (eds), *A Companion to the Victorian Novel* (Oxford: Blackwell, 2005), 322.

[4] Douglas Mao and Judith R. Walkowitz, 'The New Modernist Studies', *Publications of the Modern Language Association of America (PMLA)* 123/3 (2008), 741.

[5] Robert Louis Stevenson, *Collected Poems*, ed. Janet Adam Smith (London: Rupert Hart-Davis, 1950), 270.

In terms of genre, the expansion and contraction of space in the period, and the differing conceptions of the region, are seen most clearly in novels. Earlier in the nineteenth century the dominant model for the geography of the novel had been the 'national tale' (and its variants) made popular by Walter Scott and Maria Edgeworth. These novels tend to follow a naive young hero from the national centre (usually London) to the Celtic peripheries of the Kingdom: rural Ireland or the Highlands of Scotland. In a genre closely related to the travel narrative, the protagonist acts as a kind of unconscious ethnographer—describing the stranger parts of Britain to a metropolitan readership—and underwrites national unity through a literal marriage with a woman from Scotland or Ireland. Later in this chapter we will see how these locations mutated and subdivided, and how by mid-century the national space of the novel was cleaving into new locations: the Brontës' Yorkshire, the Dorset of Anthony Trollope's *Barchester Towers*, and the Cheshire of Elizabeth Gaskell's *Cranford*. Amid this changing novelistic topography, an opposition emerges between a traditional, rural version of the nation and the encroaching modernity of the industrial city. The title of Gaskell's *North and South* (1855) introduces this idea as the Hale family moves from rural Hampshire to Milltown (a fictionalized Manchester). Gaskell expresses the transition from the felt, personalized local to the homogenized nation as a transition from experiential time, understood by individuals and communities, to the standardized national timetables of the railways: 'Railroad time inexorably wrenched them away from lovely, beloved Helstone, the next morning. They were gone.'[6]

North and South is a complex interrogation of how this opposition is produced by political ideas and their influence on the cultural imagination, but the acceleration of industrialization in nineteenth-century Britain gave rise to a defensive form of regionalism that identified traditional but distinctive forms of national identity pitted against the sameness of industrial modernity. For Alfred Austin, the much-derided successor to Tennyson as Poet Laureate, the idiosyncrasies of the English countryside were a last defence against the sameness of modernity. The region is here singular and local, but also synechdocal for something that can only be understood as a whole. The English landscape is individualistic and irregular, in opposition to the collectivism of modernity, but it is at the same time exemplary of *all* of England:

> One cannot well drive about England with one's eyes open, without observing indication after indication of the strong, independent individuality of the English character, which may yet prove our best safeguard against that exotic 'Collectivism' of which we hear so much. The very landscape, its shapeless fields, its irregular hedgerows, its winding and wayward roads, its accidental copses, its arbitrariness of form and feature, are a silent but living protest against uniformity and preconceived or mechanical views of life.[7]

---

[6] Elizabeth Gaskell, *North and South*, ed. Dorothy Collin and Martin Dodsworth (Harmondsworth: Penguin, 1970), 92.

[7] Alfred Austin, *Haunts of Ancient Peace* (London: Macmillan, 1902), 23.

Such views crystallized into a subgenre that become known as 'the regional novel', whose characteristics were later parodied in Stella Gibbons's *Cold Comfort Farm* (1932) as a mixture of primitive passions, archaic customs, and dialect language tied to a specific locality. The popularity of many regional novelists was intense, if sometimes brief. All of Constance Holme's Westmorland-set novels were published in the *Oxford World's Classics* series; they embody intense experience of rootedness to the land, filtered through both the consciousness of the educated landowner and the everyday life of dialect-speaking tenants and farmers, all expressed as a conservative bulwark of tradition and hierarchy in which the local stands for the national:

> Into a seething world of clashing interests and warring classes the tale of the Northern property, where the flower of ancestry still sprang purely as well from yeoman and peasant stock as from patrician, where law was less than loyalty, long service a matter of course, friendship and understanding things born of inbred knowledge – dropped like a mediaeval, blazoned shield into the arena of modern warfare.[8]

What we think of as the 'regional novel' is oddly poised between an exaggerated ruralism that embodies conservative values, and the attempt to establish a realist mode that could trace the relation of place to character as a general proposition about the relation of people to environment. Phyllis Bentley, herself a writer of regional fictions, sees these novels as the coming together of local description and naturalism, a movement that sought to reflect in fiction the determining effects of environment and heredity. Naturalism was a controversial mode associated particularly with French writing that emphasized the animalistic aspects of human beings, but in English fiction these qualities were diffused into a sense of local realism. Bentley describes this realism as 'a detailed faithfulness to reality, a conscientious presentation of phenomena as they really happen in ordinary life on a clearly defined spot of real earth, a firm rejection of the vague, the high flown and the sentimental, an equally firm contact with the real: these are the marks of the regional novel'.[9]

This emphasis on phenomena—how characters experience their locality in specific forms of consciousness—brings us to the most famous literary region in our period, Thomas Hardy's 'Wessex'. Hardy's sense of the local grows out of the complex exchange of different geographies and different sense of space that I outlined at the beginning of this chapter.

On the one hand, Wessex is a bounded, mappable space—Hardy included a map of Egdon Heath in the first edition of *The Return of the Native* (1878)—and it is marked by frequent references to its historical past. On the other hand, Hardy evokes a place that precedes all forms of cultural understanding, or even inscriptions of any kind. At the end of a chapter in which he tries various forms of

---

[8] Constance Holme, *The Lonely Plough* (London: Mills and Boon, 1914), 327.
[9] Phyllis Bentley, *The English Regional Novel* (London: Allen and Unwin, 1948), 45.

personification and association to describe Egdon Heath, Hardy moves back from these to suggest that the heath has a material singularity that cannot be known even through its own features:

> The sea changed, the fields changed, the rivers, the villages, and the people changed, yet Egdon remained... With the exception of an aged highway, and a still more aged barrow presently to be referred to—themselves almost crystallized to natural products by long continuance—even the trifling irregularities were not caused by pickaxe, plough, or spade, but remained as the very finger-touches of the last geological change.[10]

Elsewhere Hardy asks us to think about a place that is empirically knowable *only* to the people who live there. John Barrell describes the local geography of *Tess of the D'Urbervilles* (1891) as 'a way of knowing, so intense, so full, so detailed, that it cannot be acquired in more places than one, and cannot be exported from one place to another: it is not knowledge elsewhere'.[11] John Plotz takes this a step further, and argues that Hardy is not a regional novelist at all. Instead, his novels 'might be called "localist" by virtue of their obsession with registering how differently various individuals make sense of the world'.[12] Tess experiences her locality as a personal topography: 'Every contour of the surrounding hills was as personal to her as that of her relatives' faces.' The novel's effect is to oscillate between this hyper-local knowledge, available to Tess, and its positioning of her in a much larger perspective available to the reader. The image of the face is picked up later in the novel when Tess and her friend Marian are picking turnips, viewed in a wide angle between a featureless brown earth and white sky:

> So these two upper and nether visages confronted each other, all day long the white face looking down on the brown face, and the brown face looking up at the white face, without anything standing between them but the two girls crawling over the surface of the former like flies.[13]

The women remain in their rural 'region', but now it expresses the alienation and atomization associated with modernity. Tess and Marian have no human connection to the land on which they work and their individuality is lost in the huge, blank panorama.

Regionalism in the novel, then, is not always best served by thinking in the generic terms of the 'regional novel'.[14] Similarly, we should draw back from making a clear

---

[10] Thomas Hardy, *The Return of the Native*, ed. Simon Gatrell and Nancy Barrineau (Oxford: Oxford University Press, 1990), 6.

[11] John Barrell, 'Geographies of Hardy's Wessex', in K. D. M. Snell (ed.), *The Regional Novel in Britain and Ireland, 1800–1990* (Cambridge: Cambridge University Press, 1998), 101.

[12] John Plotz, *Portable Property: Victorian Culture on the Move* (Princeton, NJ: Princeton University Press, 2008), 92.

[13] Hardy, *Tess of the D'Urbervilles*, ed. Simon Gattrell, Juliet Grindle, and Penny Boumelha (Oxford: Oxford University Press, 2005), 42, 304.

[14] Raymond Williams points out the dangers of lumping all regional novels into the satirical orbit of *Cold Comfort Farm*, arguing that in making too sharp a distinction between romance and parody we miss what many rural novels of the nineteenth century have in common: 'the loss of a credible common

distinction between a rural regionalism and the global city. There has been a tendency to associate modernism with a wearied acknowledgement that the sameness of urban existence has enervated social life and alienated individuals from the possibly of experience itself. Most famous are T. S. Eliot's 'unreal cities' of *The Waste Land* (1922) where the former citadels of world empire, trade, or religion appear as ghostly versions of themselves reduced to a list that denies them spatial identity of any kind:

> Falling towers
> Jerusalem Athens Alexandria
> Vienna London
> Unreal[.][15]

But cities were equally depicted as distinct regions. George Gissing's *The Nether World* (1889), a picture of working-class life, is set almost entirely in the London district of Clerkenwell, a specificity that gives the novel the ethnographic boundedness that we associated with regionalism. Observing this, Raymond Williams's Marxian reading traces in Gissing's London-based novels of the 1880s and 1890s the tendency of the regional novel to focus on a specific group or class and to ignore the wider social and economic forces that produce that class: 'For one of the essential constituents of East End life was the existence—pressing and exploiting but of course by definition not locally and immediately visible—of the *West End*.'[16] Other novels put pressure on the regional model by showing the interconnectedness of places. The fragility of the defensive or recuperative model of literary regionalism is brilliantly exposed in H. G. Wells's *Tono-Bungay* (1909), which shows how the geography of England is torn between the imagined regionalism of aristocratic tradition and a new world of commercial progress. The son of a housekeeper, George Ponderevo grows up in Bladesover House subject to an ideology that naturalizes the social hierarchy of rural England as the whole nation, or what George calls 'a closed and complete social system':

> All about us were other villages and great estates, and from house to house, interlacing, correlated, the Gentry, the fine Olympians, came and went. The country towns seemed mere collections of shops, marketing places for the tenantry, centres for such education as they needed, as entirely dependent on the gentry as the village and scarcely less so. I thought this was the order of the whole world.[17]

When George grows up and leaves the patrician estate, he realizes that this is indeed a generalized order of privilege, not in the sense that this kind of rural location

---

world that we see in Hardy'. Williams, *The Country and the City* (Oxford: Oxford University Press, 1973), 253.

[15] T. S. Eliot, *Complete Poems and Plays* (London: Faber and Faber, 1969), 73.

[16] Williams, *Writing in Society* (London: Verso, 1983), 234 (emphasis in original).

[17] H. G. Wells, *Tono-Bungay*, ed. Patrick Parrinder and Edward Mendelson (London: Penguin, 2005), 15.

typifies Englishness, but in the demystification of such an assumption. Bladesover is everywhere not because it is a synecdoche for England but because national geographies are always structured according to social class:

> And as I have gone to and fro in London, in certain regions constantly the thought has recurred, this is Bladesover House, this answers to Bladesover House. The fine gentry may have gone; they have indeed largely gone, I think; rich merchants may have replaced them, financial adventurers or what not. That does not matter; the shape is still Bladesover.[18]

The London to which George Ponderevo moves to join his Uncle Edward is antithetical to the boundedness of the traditional regional space. It is part of a fantastically unstable global economy—the Ponderevos speculate on international stock and George turns from marketing the quack elixir Tono-Bungay to an equally useless product mined in West Africa—and marked in the novel by restless movement and the atomization of its inhabitants. E. M Forster's *Howards End*, published the following year in 1910, chronicles the city as a state of mutability, lacking any essential identity that can be derived from place: 'It was the kind of scene that may be observed all over London, whatever the locality—bricks and mortar rising and falling with the restlessness of the water in a fountain, as the city receives more and more men upon her soil.'[19] The distinction between rural and urban experience was itself rendered unstable by the growth of the suburb, which had the effect both of attempting a transformation of the city into a quasi-countryside by offering the assumed rural characteristics of fresh air and a quiet life, and of blurring the boundaries of place altogether by creating a liminal space in what should be a clear border between a city and its rural hinterland.

The publishing boom in genre fiction in the late nineteenth century took advantage of the increasing interactions between countryside and city to proliferate a Gothic motif, in which the rural regions are no longer havens of safety and familiarity. In Conan Doyle's detective fiction, the frequent train journeys taken by Holmes and Watson from London to the countryside are voyages into strange and uncanny territories. In the classic novel *The Hound of the Baskervilles* (1902), Watson's first sight of the Dartmoor in which secrets are buried is 'like some fantastic landscape in a dream'.[20] In *Dracula* (1897), the Count first lands at Whitby on the Yorkshire coast before making his way to London. The ghost stories of M. R. James, which appeared in collections between 1904 and 1925, frequently evoke the distinctive ghostly seascapes of the East Anglian coast, where unwary visitors are driven to

---

[18] Ibid., 100.

[19] E. M. Forster, *Howards End*, ed. Oliver Stallybrass (London: Penguin, 1983), 59. See Andrew Thacker, *Moving through Modernity: Space and Geography in Modernism* (Manchester: Manchester University Press, 2003), 46–79.

[20] Arthur Conan Doyle, *The Hound of the Baskervilles*, ed. Christopher Frayling (London: Penguin, 2001), 55.

death or distraction by supernatural forces. Arthur Machen's *The Three Imposters* (1895) moves between London and the Welsh Borders where traces remain of a strange primitive race.

At the end of the nineteenth century and into the twentieth, the city and the countryside were increasingly mirroring each other in aesthetic terms. One of the best-known literary regions of the early twentieth century comprises Arnold Bennett's 'Five Towns' of the industrial West Midlands. In the following scene, Bennett combines the 'romantic' aesthetic of the sublime, usually associated with spectacular natural sights, with the idea that regions produce and are produced by their inhabitants. After an extended description of the sublime, we are reminded that this aesthetic is contingent on the outside eye (a technique also used by Hardy to characterize the inhabitants of his Wessex):

> Still more distant were a thousand other lights crowning chimney and kiln, and nearer, on the waste lands west of Bleakridge, long fields of burning ironstone glowed with all the strange colours of decadence. The entire landscape was illuminated and trans-formed by these unique pyrotechnics of labour atoning for its grime, and dull, weird sounds, as of the breathings and sighings of gigantic nocturnal creatures, filled the enchanted air. It was a romantic scene, a romantic summer night, balmy, delicate, and wrapped in meditation. But Anna saw nothing there save the repulsive evidences of manufacture, had never seen anything else.[21]

At the same time, it was precisely in cities that the idea of regionalism became rec-ognized in the early twentieth century in the fields of environmental planning, architecture, and local government in town and city planning. Patrick Geddes, who redeveloped much of Edinburgh's Old Town, believed in a symbiotic relation between a district and its inhabitants, and argued that towns should be planned by reference to the occupations of their citizens and following an organic model of settlement.[22] Even the most industrial regions could be seen to develop in this way. In *Anna of the Five Towns*, Bennett uses another natural metaphor to describe the interconnectedness of the regional towns: 'Trafalgar Road is the long thoroughfare which...runs through the Five Towns from end to end, uniting them as a river might unite them' (29).

The literary map of Britain had become a fluid geography, in which the city and countryside moved between opposition, connection, and mirroring, and Victorian distinctions were breaking down. But the spaces of national geography could still take on their character from older cultural divisions. Scotland, Ireland, and Wales, national regions that had formerly constituted the settings of the national tale at the beginning of the nineteenth century, had altered geographically and politically. The Land Acts of the 1880s and 1890s began gradually to shift the ownership of property

---

[21] Arnold Bennett, *Anna of the Five Towns* (London: Penguin, 2001), 73.
[22] See Volker M. Welter, *Biopolis: Patrick Geddes and the City of Life* (Cambridge, MA: MIT Press, 2002).

away from the Protestant Anglo-Irish class in Ireland, and in all three nations extensive emigration throughout the nineteenth century had changed the distribution of population in ways that visibly altered the landscape.

The Real Charlotte (1894) by Somerville and Ross (nom de plume of Edith Somerville and Violet Florence Martin) echoes, in ironic mode, the earlier national tale model developed in Ireland by Maria Edgeworth. The young metropolitan hero is now a Dublin woman—Francie Fitzpatrick—who comes to stay with her cousin Charlotte in West Cork. Unlike the protagonist of the national tale, however, Francie is not a character through whom the reader explores an unfamiliar and romantic landscape. Rather we witness, through the machinations of Charlotte, a nation in which land ownership has become contested, and the Anglo-Irish aristocracy can no longer exert proprietary rights over the land. The novel reverses the national tale's optimistic belief in the improvement of the land under enlightened British control. Now 'ignorance, neglect and poverty'[23] is the destiny of the land, rather than a condition from which it may be redeemed.

The older associations of the Celtic areas of Britain with primitivism fragmented into different forms at the end of the century. The Welsh writer Caradoc Evans populated his short stories, starting with *My People* in 1915, with characters brutalized by their primal desires and material ambitions in a deliberate reversal of the trope of the Romantic 'peasant' who could bear national history. Evans was a controversial writer whose stories were seen as anti-Welsh, but his insistence on stripping the rural working class of any nostalgia and his often ironic narration associate him with a modernist voice.[24] Evans's Wales can be compared with a different form of regionalism in the form of what is sometimes called 'Celticism' (discussed in Chapter 4 of this volume). Celtic regions are layered spaces in which ethnographic specificity leads into locations of archetypal symbolism—sacred woods, holy wells, hollow hills. The imagery of water, fire, and woods recur in the poetry and plays of W. B. Yeats and his contemporaries, while at the same time new ideas in anthropology, notably in the work of J. G. Frazer, identified in the folk practices of Scotland, Ireland, and Wales the remnants of myths that had global uniformity. These supernatural places have a varying relation with the larger space of the nation. For Yeats, at least in the last decades of the nineteenth century, the revival of Celtic myth was an act of imaginative national renewal. For the Scottish writer William Sharp, who adopted the female writing persona Fiona Macleod, the Western Isles of Scotland were the last refuge of a dying spiritual culture. In his novella *Pharais* (1894), the Gaelic-speaking hero Alistair is seemingly reborn from the sea only to go mad and die.

In Scotland, a distinct form of the regional, rather than national, novel had become popular in the late nineteenth century. The 'Kailyard' school was parochial

---

[23] Somerville and Ross, *The Real Charlotte* (London: Capuchin Classics, 2011), 52.
[24] See Katie Gramich, 'Creating and Destroying "The Man Who Does Not Exist": The Peasantry and Modernity in Welsh and Irish Writing,' *Irish Studies Review* 17/1 (February 2009), 19–30.

in the literal sense in that its novels are generally set in country parishes in the Lowlands of Scotland. But it was held to be parochial in an evaluative sense, in that the Kailyard quickly became associated with a nostalgic and sentimental depiction of rural life that resisted both Scotland's demographic and industrial change and the experiments with naturalism that had entered into the wider stream of the novel. More recent critics have challenged this dismissal of the genre, pointing to the self-conscious narratives and generic diversity of 'Kailyard' novels,[25] but the most remarkable feat of the tradition was George Douglas Brown's powerful anti-Kailyard novel of 1901, *The House with the Green Shutters*. This novel explodes the centripetal model of regional fiction as, in the words of Cairns Craig, it 'constructs for us the model of a society in which the creative imagination and the community which it has to express are utterly sundered from one another'.[26]

The novel's antihero, John Gourlay, has made a small fortune as a carrier in the town of Barbie, but his business is now threatened by the coming of the railway, a development that most of the townsfolk and traders see as a way of increasing their profit. The novel is a culmination of the uneasy relation that the regional novel has with railways. In *Tess of the D'Urbervilles* this is made explicit: 'Modern life stretched out its steam feeler to this point three or four times a day, touched the native existences, and quickly withdrew its feeler again, as if what it touched had been uncongenial.'[27] Hardy's Wessex, as we have seen, is a negotiation between the sense of a single, bounded region and the place of all regions in larger social and economic networks. But in Brown's novel this delicate relationship is shattered. The community is merely a collection of interests seeking to maximize material gain. 'The Scot', the narrative voice remarks sardonically, has 'the forecasting leap of the mind which sees what to make of things—more, sees them made and in vivid operation. To him there is a railway through the desert where no railway exists, and mills along the quiet stream'. Amid this historical flux, Gourlay remains a fixed point but, unlike the characters in other regional novels, who are constructed by their environment in a naturalist mode, or who interact in a community, Gourlay acts and thinks out of 'brute force of character'[28] and is impervious to argument or feeling. Resistant both to change and to locality, the novel traces his ruin as he destroys his son and himself.

Elsewhere in Scottish fiction, John Buchan was exploiting the geographic freedoms afforded by genre fictions. Buchan's thrillers can be global, local, and regional all at the same time. Richard Hannay, the hero of *The Thirty-Nine Steps* (1915) and later novels, is geographically complex. Born in Scotland, he grows up in South Africa, and through his father's contacts he speaks fluent German. Wrongly

---

[25] See Andrew Nash, *The Kailyard and Scottish Literature* (Amsterdam: Rodopi, 2007).

[26] Cairns Craig, *The Modern Scottish Novel: Narrative and the National Imagination* (Edinburgh: Edinburgh University Press, 1999), 63.

[27] Hardy, *Tess*, 204.

[28] George Douglas Brown, *The House with the Green Shutters*, ed. Dorothy Porter (Harmondsworth: Penguin, 1985), 98, 44.

suspected of murder, Hannay escapes London by train to hide out in Scotland. *The Thirty-Nine Steps* gestures towards Scotland as a region of status, safety, and recuperation—the rural working people who take Hannay in have 'the kindly shyness of moorland places' and 'the perfect breeding of all dwellers in the wilds'.[29] But *The Thirty-Nine Steps* also acknowledges the provisional status of all such spaces. The novel repeatedly insists that identification with place can simply be a trick of the mind—Hannay disguises himself as a local road-mender by thinking himself into the role and the place, and the trick is given an imperial context when we learn that this is a technique Hannay picked up in Southern Africa:

> I remember an old scout in Rhodesia . . . once telling me that the secret of playing a part was to think yourself into it . . . So I shut off all other thoughts and switched them on to the road-mending. I thought of the little white cottage as my home, I recalled the years I had spent herding on Leithen Water, I made my mind dwell lovingly on sleep in a box-bed and a bottle of cheap whisky.[30]

The idea of the organic region characterized by the inherent nature of its habitants is challenged by the idea that all associations of people with place are performative—individuality is not given by a place, but rather subjects can take on the characteristics of any given place by conscious association rather than natural evolution, rendering all spaces provisional and fictional.

The Thirty-Nine Steps was published in 1915, but set a year earlier on the eve of the First World War. The novel ends with Hannay fighting off a German invasion, but the whole story falls under the shadow of coming war that gives Buchan's ideal landscapes a ghostly, haunted quality:

> I swung through little old thatched villages, and over peaceful lowland streams, and past gardens blazing with hawthorn and yellow laburnum. The land was so deep in peace that I could scarcely believe that. . . in a month's time, unless I had the almightiest of luck, these round country faces would be pinched and staring, and men would be lying dead in English fields.[31]

The war, as might be expected, fostered forms of nostalgia for the idealized rural regions that had grown up in opposition to industrial Britain and popular regional fiction continued to sell well. But the trauma of war and its consequent sense of spatial dislocation enters into literature, straining the sense of therapeutic or comforting regionalism. Rupert Brooke's apparently sentimental poem 'The Soldier' makes its idyllic vision of its speaker 'breathing English air, / Washed by the rivers, blest by suns of home' conditional on his death. This is a projection into the future: the poem starts 'If I should die, think only this of me' and details how he wants others to remember him rather than an actual memory.[32]

---

[29] John Buchan, *The Thirty-Nine Steps*, intro. John Keegan (London: Penguin, 2004), 28.
[30] Ibid., 53.   [31] Ibid., 40.
[32] *The Complete Poems of Rupert Brooke* (London: Sidgwick & Jackson, 1934), 148.

In the work of Edward Thomas, all of whose poetry was written during the First World War, this dislocated sense of a familiar but imaginary England is marked. Thomas is sometimes thought of as a regional poet, his poems capturing the landscapes particularly of the South Downs chalk-lands in Hampshire and Sussex. But as Stan Smith points out, these localities are often suspended from precise meaning or geographical certainty. It is not always possible to decide of what larger space they are a region: 'His landscapes repeatedly offer metonymies of a totality that cannot be grasped. At the heart of such metonymies is dispossession.'[33] Thomas's poem 'The Chalk-Pit' seems at first to reach out to a regional identity: the chalk pit could signify a spatial homogeneity based on work and the resources of the land. We could think back to Hardy's *Return of the Native* in which the 'Reddleman' Diggory Venn is dyed crimson by the red ochre he deals in. But Thomas's poem works to make its locality difficult to know. 'The Chalk-Pit' is a dialogue between two speakers, one of whom seems to be asking the way in a location he has previously either lived in or visited. The poem progresses through hesitant questions about people who may have lived and worked there, although the speaker is not sure if he really remembers the place or if 'another place / Real or painted, may have combined with it'. We are not given a precise location or history for the chalk pit although the poem seems always on the verge of admitting the stories it cannot trace or substantiate. The poem ends with the second speaker:

> You please yourself. I should prefer the truth
> Or nothing. Here, in fact, is nothing at all
> Except a silent place that once rang loud,
> And trees and us—imperfect friends, we men
> And trees since time began; and nevertheless
> Between us still we breed a mystery.[34]

The poem's last piece of dialogue starts by splitting the location into two possibilities for knowing it: the truth or nothing. But then Thomas acknowledges that these two may not be opposed, but may form a dialectic that indicates a modernist inclination to speculate on the metaphysics of nothings or the possibility that we exist only in our own consciousness. The location is empty and silent in that it cannot be the bearer of continuous history or even constitute a stable reality outside the thoughts of the speaker. The trees are intimately involved in human experience, but not in a rational or incremental way. Like the modernist invocation of primitive time to set against the linear history with which modernism breaks, the trees represent a 'mystery' with its sense of a sacred space not available to rational science.

---

[33] Stan Smith, '"Literally, for this": Metonymies of National Identity in Edward Thomas, Yeats and Auden', in Alex Davis and Lee M. Jenkins (eds), *Locations of Literary Modernism: Region and Nation in British and American Modernist Poetry* (Cambridge: Cambridge University Press, 2000), 115.
[34] Edward Thomas, *The Annotated Collected Poems*, ed. Edna Longley (Tarset, Northd: Bloodaxe Books, 2008), 89.

Thomas is a regional poet and a modernist poet. The characteristics of regional writing that we have seen throughout the period—the relations of human beings to the land, the division of the nation into homogeneous regions, the centripetal pull of associative places—are here transformed into something much less solid and much more questioning.

FURTHER READING

Bentley, Phyllis. *The English Regional Novel* (London: Allen and Unwin/PEN Books, 1948).

Dainotto, Roberto M. *Place in Literature: Regions, Cultures, Communities* (Ithaca, NY: Cornell University Press, 2000).

Davis, Alex and Jenkins, Lee M (eds). *Locations of Literary Modernism: Region and Nation in British and American Modernist Poetry* (Cambridge: Cambridge University Press, 2000).

Draper, Ronald P. (ed.). *The Literature of Region and Nation* (Basingstoke: Macmillan, 1989).

Entrickin, J. Nicholas. *The Betweenness of Place: Towards a Geography of Modernity* (Baltimore, MD: Johns Hopkins University Press, 1991).

Keith, W. J. *Regions of the Imagination: The Development of British Rural Fiction* (Toronto, ON: University of Toronto Press, 1988).

Pite, Ralph. *Hardy's Geography: Wessex and the Regional Novel* (Basingstoke: Palgrave Macmillan, 2002).

Plotz, John. *Portable Property: Victorian Culture on the Move* (Princeton, NJ: Princeton University Press, 2008).

Snell, K. D. M. (ed.). *The Regional Novel in Britain and Ireland, 1800–1990* (Cambridge: Cambridge University Press, 1998).

Stafford, Fiona J. *Local Attachments: The Province of Poetry* (Oxford: Oxford University Press, 2010).

Thacker, Andrew. *Moving Through Modernity: Space and Geography in Modernism* (Manchester: Manchester University Press, 2003).

Williams, Raymond. *The Country and the City* (Oxford: Oxford University Press, 1973).

CHAPTER 19

THE VIEW FROM EMPIRE

The Turn-of-the-Century Globalizing World

ELLEKE BOEHMER

The globalizing imperial world, *c.*1900

The accelerated transnational movement of capital, the outsourcing of labour, and the dissemination of information by internet that epitomizes the post-2000 world system appear on several levels to have been replicated—or at least anticipated—in the world of the 1890s. Few occasions could better illustrate the operation of this networked world than when, in 1897, the empire's ocean-spanning web of telegraph cables transmitted Queen Victoria's Diamond Jubilee message to her subjects around the world in about three minutes.[1]

The so-called 'global turn' in literary studies at the start of the third millennium has focused new attention on previous instances of globalization in history. This focus has fallen most centrally perhaps on the large-scale technological networking of the planet that accompanied the period of formal imperialism at the end of the nineteenth century, as this demonstrated particularly clear parallels with the present day. In a 2001 special issue of *PMLA* (Publications of the Modern Language Association of America) titled 'Globalizing Literary Studies', Edward Said drew attention to this changing focus. 'Political and economic globalization', he suggested, had 'since the end of the Cold War...been the enveloping context in which literary studies [were] undertaken.'[2] Yet, following his own previous scholarship, most notably in *Culture and Imperialism* (1993), Said might well have extended his 'enveloping context' back in time. In the globalizing present day, literary critical concerns have for the first time in decades embraced themes and issues that do not take the nation state as primary and

---

[1] Elleke Boehmer, 'Global Nets, Textual Webs; Or What Isn't New about Empire?', *Postcolonial Studies* 7/1 (2004), 11–26.

[2] Edward W. Said, 'Globalizing Literary Study', *Publications of the Modern Language Association of America (PMLA)* 116/1 (2001), 64–8.

normative—exploring, for example, experiences of migration and exile, and staging transnational and cross-regional collaborations.[3] This trend has been in part prompted, however, by an appreciation of how the late nineteenth century experienced a similar manifestation of economic influences culturally expressed.

The new globalizing of literary studies and the showcasing of 'world literature' it has brought about carries, therefore, a strong sense of recursiveness, given that similar formations were also registered in high imperial writing (that is, from around 1870 onwards), and even earlier. Indeed, global historians as well as literary critics have pointed to the remarkable depth and breadth of the manifold interconnections and transactions that characterized the British Empire at its world-embracing zenith forged between 1870 and 1914.

They examine, for example, the dense flow of raw materials, commodities, and information between countries and continents that this global network made possible, and consider how this traffic is pictured and refracted in the literary writing that bridged the century divide. They notice also how aspects of the realist novel's structure, such as its list-making devices, its compressions of space and time, and the genealogical connections it forges, capture something of the cross-border circulation of people and commodities through the empire's trade and transport networks. The 'transitive geopolitical business' of empire, as Elaine Freedgood writes, was reflected in the flow of commodities like mahogany furniture and Indian shawls through the pages of the mid-nineteenth-century novel.[4] As the century turned, this circulation of materials, merchandise, people, and messages between Britain and the empire became, if anything, more intensive and transcontinental—and also more prominently registered in literary expression. In this chapter, the circulation of expensive jewels sourced in colonial spaces in turn-of-the-century narratives, and the exchange (not to say theft) of land as property, will be taken as particularly vivid cultural markers of the intensive globalization of the period.

In his account of the accelerated formation of 'inter-national networks' at the end of the nineteenth century, the imperial historian C. A. Bayly further complicates the picture of an interconnected globalizing world both now and especially then. He proposes that the accelerated empire building of the 1800s was galvanized by and extended already existing global networks, such as had been laid down by patterns of migration, trade, and kinship-building in both the east and the west since at least the mid-eighteenth century.[5] By the nineteenth century's end therefore, there was

---

[3] '9/11'—that transformative, post-millennium development which was to become a concern for a host of novelists in the first decades of the new century—has itself been widely understood as the cataclysmic impact of transnational terrorism on homeland America.

[4] Elaine Freedgood, 'The Novel and Empire', *The Nineteenth-Century Novel 1820–1880*, in John Kucich and Jenny Bourne Taylor (eds), (Oxford: Oxford University Press, 2012), 379. See also Freedgood, *The Ideas in Things: Fugitive Meaning in the Victorian Novel* (Chicago, IL: Chicago University Press, 2006).

[5] C. A. Bayly, *The Birth of the Modern World 1780–1914: Global Connections and Comparisons* (Oxford: Blackwell, 2004).

little doubt that 'the British World economy', to borrow Andrew Thompson's phrase, itself animated by the ceaseless mass-migration of British peoples across the world, served as the engine of a vast intercontinental system of social, economic, and cultural flows and counter-flows—a great, chaotic, yet in parts also systematic, circulation both of ideas and of things. This system increasingly left its imprint not just on colonial literature as conventionally defined—that is, white writers of the so-called colonial periphery such as Rudyard Kipling, Joseph Conrad, or Olive Schreiner—but on mainstream or metropolitan cultural forms also. Thus the eastern motifs and sensual poses favoured by 1890s Decadent art unmistakeably register the impression on the metropolitan city of the ever-growing availability and accessibility (through trade and commerce) of Oriental *objets d'art* and commodities—Japanese prints, Chinese porcelain, and Indian silks. London in this period also played host to an increasing number of visitors and migrants from all parts of the empire. Their attire, habits, and sheer presence further developed and enhanced the inter-cultural textures of the city's already cosmopolitan life, and are registered in novels from Wilkie Collins's *The Moonstone* (1868) onwards.

In imperial historiography, the growing concern with global and inter-imperial developments across the modern world has raised questions about the degree to which current globalization in fact manifests in late imperial or 'empire' forms (as would appear to be implied in Michael Hardt and Antonio Negri's influential 2000 study, *Empire*). Does the high or formal imperialism of the late nineteenth century equate formally or experientially to what we now understand by globalization? There is certainly broad agreement that the global flows and formations of the nineteenth- into twentieth-century empire provide strong homologies or models for present-day developments, not least in the domain of the influential cultural and literary repercussions of these flows—that is, in how writing took the imprint of the ever more interconnected imperial world.

In or around 1900, as late Victorian society in Britain and its colonies became self-consciously modern, writers and artists began to seek radical new forms of language and expression through which to articulate their growing sense of global expansiveness. Literary texts and movements—novels, travel writing, poetry, poetry clubs, avant-garde circles, theatre, and performance, not least music hall—registered in multiple ways the moulding effects not only of the writers' widely shared sense of their own modernity, but also of the global reach of that modernity. We are relatively familiar with the relationship between speed and modernist writing; what this discussion contributes to the critical conversation is a particular attention to the planetary dimensions of that speeded-up circulation. The truncated or snap-shot instants captured in Imagist poetry, or the 'broken images' of T. S. Eliot's *The Waste Land*, for example, can be seen to reflect critically on the mere momentary glimpses of people and street scenes that were all that the traffic of goods and impressions in the ever-expanding metropolis afforded the passer-by.

To late Victorian but also early modernist poets, ever-faster global interconnection demanded sharply focused new symbols, epithets, and foreshortened generic forms such as these—forms through which to articulate the pace, rush, and bewilderment of the modern world. The relentlessly cross-border, hybridizing, and defamiliarizing energies of proto- and early modernist writing appeared especially responsive to the stimuli of late imperial globalization. All modernisms engage 'a common world of crisis, struggle, and possibility', as Laura Doyle observes.[6] It is a world that demands a relentless conceptual shuttling between the specific and the universal, the local and the planetary, and between networked space and cumulative time, to refer also to Mary Lou Emery's important work on peripheral Caribbean modernisms. Yet late Victorian literature, too, as we shall see, acknowledged the degree to which those dichotomies of here and far-away, and the local and the universal, were coming under what might be termed interconnective pressure from the forces of imperial globalization.

There are at least two possible analytic frameworks through which to understand late nineteenth-century imperial globalization, as it is expressed in literature and culture. The first follows the world-systems theory of Immanuel Wallerstein, which casts the world as 'one…but uneven', shaped by the unequal distribution of economic power across the globe. This view considers all societies—central, 'semi-peripheral', and peripheral—to share in a common matrix laid down by global capital and shaped by its requirements and demands, yet sees these societies as partaking in that matrix in prejudicial, inequitable terms. The approach places an overriding emphasis on powerful players on the international stage, not least nation states but also large world cities. By contrast, the second framework, which might be called postcolonial or transnational, and which bears the distinct mark of Homi Bhabha's thought, instead casts the world as a conglomeration of far smaller units and clusters (regions, islands, southern cities, small nations) that connect to each other on a variety of different levels. The accent here is on relationality and heterogeneity; and on diverse sources of contestation, both large and small. Therefore, whereas the first framework favoured a centre-margin model only partially mediated by the idea of the semi-periphery, the second privileges notions of ceaseless circulation and cultural traffic, as also put forward in the work of James Clifford, Arjun Appadurai, and Nicholas Thomas, among others.

Economies of value under empire from Trollope to Plaatje

The second and main section of this chapter sets out to draw these two analytical frameworks into conjunction (though not necessarily into synthesis), by looking at

---

[6] Laura Doyle, 'Modernist Studies and Inter-Imperiality in the Longue Durée', in Mark Wollaeger (ed.), *Global Modernisms* (Oxford: Oxford University Press, 2012), 669–96. See also Mary Lou Emery, *Modernism, the Visual and Caribbean Literature* (Cambridge: Cambridge University Press, 2007).

how an awareness of at-once-uneven *and* heterogeneous globalization marks a line of literary works running from the late nineteenth into the early twentieth century, or from late Victorian into early modernist times. In more concrete terms, the chapter turns to consider the emerging critical analysis of hierarchical imperial economics that distinguished a sub-strand of modernist writing particularly sensitive to the changing values brought by imperial globalization—here, the work of, most notably, Leonard Woolf and Solomon T. Plaatje, though in a more extensive analysis such writers as Joseph Conrad, Virginia Woolf, E. M. Forster, Jean Rhys, or Mulk Raj Anand might justly have been drawn into the discussion. The section explores what these authors had to say about exploitative and out-of-kilter migratory and commodity flows under empire—forces which to a considerable extent, it seems, escaped the notice of the preceding generation. It also begins to ask what forms and structures they deployed to express their critique.

The case I am making is that late nineteenth-century metropolitan writing tended to regard the wealth of empire that accumulated in the metropolis as detached from the peripheries whence it came, and hence from the labour that produced it. Later, in-part-modernist (or modernist-associated) writers exposed and explored the complicated, enmeshed, largely asymmetrical, and often exploitative channels of circulation through which that wealth flowed to Europe. Furthermore, they sometimes did so through their formal experimentation. That is to say, they shifted their critical and creative focus from the centre or semi-periphery relatively closer to the periphery. They were interested in the functioning of imperial trade networks not so much as a mode of transnational circulation that advanced the political and economic well-being of the metropolitan centres, and collaterally benefited the white settler colonies, but rather as operating in irregular ways to the disadvantage, in particular, of those on the non-settler periphery. To develop this case, the late-Victorian-early-modernist literary figuration of wealth, particularly the use of jewels as enigmatic tokens of the feverish harvest of raw materials, will be taken to offer a powerful gauge of imperial unevenness. As the named authors all to some extent considered the operation of imperial trade and commercial networks, the central question therefore is to what extent their work views empire as trammelling and even impeding (far from promoting) the production of national wealth and equitable exchange of commodities, as well as adversely affecting the moral health of nations.

To illustrate, the so-called 'diamond novel' of the second half of the nineteenth century provides an interesting counterpoint to engagements with global economics at the start of the twentieth. From around 1851, the year of that spectacle of manufactures, the Great Exhibition, the rapid commodification of Victorian culture at large was reflected in the increasing prominence of novel plotlines revolving around a quest for or the loss of a fortune, frequently in the shape of lustrous and exotic jewellery. In this commodity economy, the most precious gemstone of all, the diamond, became perhaps the most hypostatized luxury: durable, impenetrable, portable, and of foreign provenance, its glittering surfaces betraying no trace of its origins or the pains of conquest and labour that had gone into its extraction and refinement (so unlike that other established and fixed form of wealth, land). The case of the legendary Koh-i-Noor diamond is particularly indicative in this regard. In 1850 the young Maharajah Duleep Singh, deprived of his kingdom in Punjab, was coerced into presenting the Koh-i-Noor to Queen Victoria (the godmother of several of his children) as a gift. It was as emphatic and feudal a symbol as could be construed for the Sikh state's fealty to the British throne.[7]

Diamonds are pivotal in the plots of several Victorian novels, ranging from the more or less explicitly entitled *The Moonstone* (1868) by Wilkie Collins, and Anthony Trollope's *The Eustace Diamonds* (1871-3), to George Eliot's *Daniel Deronda* (1876). A subset of colonial novels set in southern Africa in which wealth is held in the form of diamonds, or the land claims which allow their extraction, further underlines what a complicated and important role the gemstone plays in the unfolding of late Victorian fictions such as Schreiner's *The Story of an African Farm* (1883) and *From Man to Man* (published in 1926, but mainly written during the 1880s), and H. Rider Haggard's *King Solomon's Mines* (1885). Indeed, in many of these novels, diamonds work tellingly in conjunction with the struggle to hold onto, traverse, and seek succour in landed property. The feisty—yet universally loathed—Lizzie Eustace in *The Eustace Diamonds*, for example, retreats to her Scottish estate as one way of keeping hold of the disputed legacy that is her diamond necklace, and loses the beautiful adornment only when she removes it from the estate. As the association of Lizzie and her necklace further suggests, diamonds figured in complex ways in relation to the value placed on women's bodies.

By the new century, however, and in particular after the calamitous Anglo-Boer War of 1899-1902, the connections between the raw materials that fuelled empire, the brutal 'uneven' methods of their extraction (from land and sea), and the fruits of that exploitation were increasingly held in suspicion, and subject to literary exposure. Certainly by the arrival of the one-time colonial officer Leonard Woolf's first novel, *The Village in the Jungle*, in 1913, and the African nationalist S. T. Plaatje's polemic *Native Life in South Africa* in 1916, followed by Woolf's *Stories of the East* in 1921, empire could no longer be simplistically seen as an invisible place of wealth extraction and commodity production dedicated solely to the enrichment and embellishment of the metropolis.

Several interlocking factors can be enumerated to account for this change—the shift from the smooth and untroubled surfaces of commodity production as represented in the diamond novel to spotlighting (as the jaded Assistant Government Agent Leonard Woolf does) the 'swaying, struggling forms' of the pearl fishers and the 'cold, civilized, corrupted cruelty' of empire to which they are in part subject (in

---

[7] Michael Alexander and Sushila Anand, *Queen Victoria's Maharajah: Duleep Singh, 1838–93* (London: Phoenix Press, 1980).

his story 'Pearls and Swine').[8] Among the more important of these factors were the divisive run-up to the Anglo-Boer War (1899-1902), shaped in particular by the anti-war campaigns in which figures such as Olive Schreiner had participated; and the way in which the unfolding of the war exposed the severe hardship and exploitation that accompanied and facilitated commodity production on the colonial periphery, in particular in respect of gold and diamond mines. The publication in 1902 of J. A. Hobson's influential *Imperialism*, his critique of empire as the instrument of private financiers, not the benefactor of nations or peoples, also played a key part—the book having stemmed in no small measure from the polemic of the anti-war campaign. A further important factor was the changing nature of industrial diamond mining from surface to depth (alluvial mining to Kimberley's 'big hole'). In Schreiner's *African Farm*, a strong contrast is set up between the diamond-like drops Lyndall squeezes (with effort) out of an ice plant or cactus, and the huge diamond ring she later reappears with at the farm. This jewel's origins and methods of extraction are never revealed to the reader.[9]

Importantly for this chapter's focus on form, the shift from surface to depth in the representation of colonial economic relations was accompanied by a growing movement from realism to more experimental novel forms. In his study of the divers and heterogeneous temporalities of the Bildungsroman, the cultural historian Jed Esty has traced how the classic developmental narrative, when set in colonial spaces, reflected in critical ways on the 'temporal paradox of empire'—its uncertainties, recursions, and contradictions. As Esty further elaborates, in dialogue with the work of Pheng Cheah, 'the genre-bending logic of uneven development...takes on a new and more intense form in modernism as it fixes its etiolated and broken allegories to the uncertain future of a colonial world system'.[10] Modernist narrative, in other words, registered the contortions and disruptions of the increasingly inequitable imperial world system more acutely, interrogatively, and disconcertedly than previous literary expression had done. Following on from Esty, it is my contention that the interiority and fragmentary continuities of modernist narrative, not excluding the short story, contributed in defamiliarizing ways to the new scrutiny to which imperial economics were now subject. Another important factor was that writers from the disrupted periphery, like Schreiner, Plaatje, and Anand, and writers with an experience of empire's asymmetrical upheavals, like Leonard Woolf, were now themselves contributing to and producing these more sceptical and analytic narratives.

In his moving and mordant story 'Pearls and Swine', Leonard Woolf is unambiguous about the taxing and often dangerous labour that goes into the extraction of

---

[8] Boehmer (ed.), *Empire Writing: An Anthology of Colonial Literature, 1870–1918* (Oxford: Oxford University Press, 1998), 427–8.

[9] Olive Schreiner, *The Story of an African Farm: A Novel* (London: Virago, 1989), 11, 153.

[10] Jed Esty, *Unseasonable Youth: Modernism, Colonialism, and the Fiction of Development* (Oxford: Oxford University Press, 2012), 36, 17, 25.

another adornment to which imperial possession contributed—pearls. He is also witheringly critical of the hypocrisy of empire's high-flown values when set against the dignity of this labour. Although, as he emphasizes, pearl fishing has proceeded off the coast of India and Ceylon since 'Solomon's time', and the technology of extraction remains primitive, under empire a situation pertains where the Imperial Government expropriates two-thirds of the pearls, and vigilantly polices the division of spoils.[11] 'Pearls and Swine' was drafted in around 1912, at the same time as *The Village in the Jungle*, not long after Woolf's return from colonial service, though it was published only in 1921, in pamphlet form by the Hogarth Press. R. L. Stevenson had already made use of a colonial pearl fishery as an arena for lurid, despotic avarice in *The Ebb-Tide* (1894). But it is the analytic thoroughness in its approach to economic, bureaucratic, and racial inequities—reaching forward to Steinbeck's *The Pearl* (1947)—that gives Woolf's story its prescience as a colonial narrative.

Guided in part by Hobson's insights, Woolf's acute dissective prose was by the early 1920s engaged in demonstrating how the extractive and exploitative patterns of empire were lodged 'deep within the logic of the capitalist practice of European countries'. Woolf had also, however, become disillusioned by inflated imperial values after his experience of working within inefficient and alienating bureaucracies as a colonial officer. Drawing from this experience, Woolf in *Empire and Commerce in Africa* (1919) and *Economic Imperialism* (1920) argued that the capitalist system linked together centre and periphery in a set of highly unequal relations.

> [J]ust as the holder of capital in Europe has been enabled to exploit the worker and consumer economically for his own profit, so the white man, armed with the power of the modern State, and the weapons of modern war, and the technical knowledge and machinery of modern industry and modern finance, can reduce to subjection, and then exploit economically for his own profit, the land and labour of the less developed Asiatic and African.[12]

Woolf's debt to Hobson here is clear, in particular to Hobson's work on imperial exploitation in his *War in South Africa* (1900), his collected articles on the Boer War for the *Manchester Guardian*, which were later expanded and more fully worked through in *Imperialism*. As Hobson wrote, imperialism 'implies the use of the machinery of government by private interests, mainly capitalists, to secure for them

---

[11] Boehmer, *Empire Writing*, 420–2.

[12] Leonard Woolf, *Economic Imperialism* (London: Swarthmore Press, Labour Publishing Co., 1920), 101–2. I am grateful to my DPhil students Dominic Davies and Priyasha Mukhopadhyay for their astute readings of Leonard Woolf's work. See Dominic Davies, 'Critiquing Global Capital and Colonial (In)justice: Structural Violence in Leonard Woolf's *The Village in the Jungle* (1913) and *Economic Imperialism* (1920)', *Journal of Commonwealth Literature* 50/1 (2015), 45–58; Priyasha Mukhopadhyay, 'Of Greasy Notebooks and Dirty Newspapers: Reading the Illegible in *The Village in the Jungle*', *Journal of Commonwealth Literature* 50/1 (2015), 59–74.

economic gains outside their country'.[13] In 'Pearls and Swine', however, Woolf was writing also from his own recent, visceral experience of empire's contradictions, its 'combined and uneven development' (as Trotsky might have put it), and this, too, informed his 1920s analysis.

Whereas the analysis in *Economic Imperialism* works at a cross-continental, global scale, that in 'Pearls and Swine' and *The Village in the Jungle* investigates the operations of global imperialism at a specifically local, experiential level, while also remaining aware of the chains of exploitation and commodity production that connect the labourer and the peasant in the colony, and the worker in the metropolis.[14] Or, as Woolf sees it in *Economic Imperialism*: 'Economic imperialism is only the logical application of capitalism and its principles to internationalism.'[15] As an Assistant Government Agent in Ceylon, in mostly provincial districts like Jaffna— which he drew on, in part, for 'Pearls and Swine'—and Hambantota, the area where the action of *The Village in the Jungle* unfolds, Woolf would have had a sense of being located at the interface between the colony's mining and agricultural sectors, plugged into both the metropolitan networks of capitalism that extended to the colonies, and the local communities on whom these international networks were increasingly encroaching and imposing.

In 'Pearls and Swine', Woolf adapts a characteristic Conradian frame narrative and the ironic juxtapositions it affords in order to investigate the interlocking hypocrisies of colonial possession—most notably that British rule was a benevolent force. As part of this investigation, the frame-within-a-frame structure also powerfully reflects the concentric circles of capitalist/colonial command and control—or structural violence, as Žižek terms it—that connect the respectable clubs of the metropolis with the stinking and chaotic pearl fisheries of the periphery.

In the smoking room of a Torquay hotel, in which retired colonial officers mingle with their British professional counterparts, a Commissioner tells the story of two deaths. There is the dignified death of an Arab pearl fisher off the Indian coast, due to complications resulting from deep-sea diving, which follows soon after the death from DTs (delirium tremens) of the dissolute colonial, White. Despite White's high-flown rhetoric, and his many plans to deal in India's 'hidden wealth', at first in the form of an Assamese tea plantation, but then also gold and 'radium', and of course pearls, his colonial exploits have been consistently destructive.[16] As this suggests, the pearls of the story, those metropolitan adornments-to-be, extracted with such difficulty and danger from the ocean bed, stand in for expropriated colonial wealth more generally. And White's horrible death agony, which erupts as it were from the

[13] J. A. Hobson, *Imperialism: A Study* (London: Unwin Hyman, 1988), 94.
[14] Woolf, *The Village in the Jungle* (London: Eland, 2008), and Woolf, 'Pearls and Swine', in Boehmer, *Empire Writing*, 415–30. See also my chapter on cross-national Woolf in Boehmer, *Empire, the National and the Postcolonial: Resistance in Interaction* (Oxford: Oxford University Press, 2002), which anticipates many of the points I make here about Woolf's insights into imperial exploitation.
[15] Woolf, *Economic Imperialism*, 101.   [16] Boehmer, *Empire Writing*, 423.

very centre of the concentric rings linking ocean periphery to metropolitan club, signifies the dehumanizing violence that, in Woolf's view, inevitably accompanies that extraction.

Jewels are not mentioned in *The Village in the Jungle*, but the possession and hire of land, and the uneven access to and use of land within the wider plantation economy then being developed in Ceylon, is crucial to the novel's action. As Douglas Kerr writes, Woolf gives us 'the point of view of people for whom a colonized space is not a possession but a native habitat', one often afflicted with drought.[17] By the period in which the novel is set, however, the poverty and suffering of the villagers (in the main the central character Silindu, his daughters, and Babun, his son-in-law) arise directly from the socio-economic formation within which they and their land are now bound, and into which they are tied by chain links of debt which benefit only middle-men. As in 'Pearls and Swine', though without its strong contrastive effects setting native against white man, their suffering becomes an expression of the deeply embedded, seemingly endemic structural violence through which capitalist (and hence also colonial) economies operate. Misfortune, we are told, is simply 'common in the life of a jungle village'.[18] An important passage early on in the novel points specifically to the wheels and cogs of uneven development and expropriation that drive this economic situation forwards:

> With the reaping of the chenas [plots for growing crops] came the settlement of debts. With their little greasy notebooks, full of unintelligible letters and figures, they descended upon the chenas; and after calculations, wranglings, and abuse, which lasted for hour after hour, the accounts were settled, and the strangers left the village, their carts loaded.[19]

Though characters like Silindu are most in need of the land's sustenance simply to stay alive, the lines of exploitation that connect their village to the colonial government in Colombo (and, beyond that, to the colonial capitalist system with its heart in London) serve merely to alienate them from their livelihood.

In ways interestingly related to Woolf, Sol Plaatje in his poignant *Native Life in South Africa* exposes the physical suffering, exploitation, and expropriation involved in the colonial conversion of land from an inhabited space to a material possession to be cleared and parcelled off. The 1913 South African Native Land Act against which his polemic was written sought to convert black landowners and tenants overnight into the servants of white diggers, or miners, and farmers.[20] Both the land and the fruits of the land, like precious stones, were being taken from those who originally inhabited the land. As with Woolf, but in even more graphic terms, Plaatje is aware of the fine calibrations of economic and political control linking the dispossessed, wandering peasant and the former cattle herder-turned-mine-labourer, with the lawmaker in Cape Town.

---

[17] Douglas Kerr, 'Colonial Habitats: Orwell and Woolf in the Jungle', *English Studies* 78/2 (August 2008), 158, 160.
[18] Woolf, *The Village in the Jungle*, 17.   [19] Ibid., 26.   [20] Boehmer, *Empire Writing*, 406.

After the Anglo-Boer War, Sol Plaatje, a former interpreter, turned his skills as an intermediary between African rights and British interests to good effect when he became the editor of the Cape's bilingual *Bechuana Gazette*, shifting to the editorship of the *Bechuana Friend* and of *Friend of the People* in 1912.[21] He also wrote for various other papers, including the *Diamond Fields Advertiser* and the *Pretoria News*, working together with other prominent African spokesmen to attempt to persuade the authorities through the force of irony, deference, and sentimentality, variously used, to recognize and extend African rights to self-representation. Importantly, his journalism was written in several languages, sometimes within the pages of one paper, and pitched at a variety of different levels, which allowed him very effectively to address various different audiences and tiers within Cape society.

In *Native Life*, Plaatje's castigating exposure of the peasants' expulsion from their land works as did his journalism through tessellated, layered, and collage-like methods. He uses inserted eye-witness narrative reports of black suffering and citations from official documents, along with the divergent angles of observation and commentary these afford, to evoke the breaks in historical and geographical continuity occasioned by this expropriation. Key points are quietly and sometimes caustically made through reiteration, and are addressed at one and the same time to two audiences, the British public first and foremost, and then his audience of middle-class Africans at home. This undermining of continuous form is pursued into his first and only novel *Mhudi* (1917/30), a tale of dispossession for which *Native Life* laid the conceptual groundwork. Here, once again, colonial power relations are defined by those who have, and not those who lack, land.

Plaatje's formal interrogation of the imperial exploitation that produced and permitted colonial commodity flows raises an interesting question that pertains also to Woolf. Were the critical perceptions of writers like Plaatje and Woolf a possible contributing factor to the structural experiments with which they were preoccupied—experiments that were, however, also associated more broadly with a response to the incursions of modernity? Certainly Woolf in *The Village in the Jungle* broke through to a new form—the ethnographic novel with its immersive focus on native bewilderment—in order to give expression to the 'bare life' of the jungle villagers. And Plaatje's multilayered, intentionally disruptive narrative effects are highly evocative of the dissonances that beset colonial subject formation.[22]

Conclusion

It is in the thoroughgoing yet subtle analyses of imperial depredation offered by the anti-colonial narratives and commentaries of Leonard Woolf and Solomon Plaatje (as well as Forster and Anand) that a counterweight might be found to the

---

[21] See Boehmer, *Empire, the National and the Postcolonial*, 131–9.   [22] Ibid., 179.

'orientalism' potentially entailed by the new worldliness of modernist studies. As Jed Esty warns in *Unseasonable Youth*, the global turn in modernism could carry the risk of turning the field into little more than a catalogue of exotic differences. Even in those cases where the new shapes of a globalized modernism move us beyond the east-west divisions of a more conventionally defined Anglophone modernism, we should take care lest our world picture remain nonetheless divided and unexamined—a world picture necessarily still split into the zones of centre, semi-periphery, and periphery, whose divisions are left uninvestigated.

As Mark Wollaeger writes in his account of this globalizing field, world modernism in its best or most productive sense should be seen as motivated by a radical cosmopolitanism, a movement beyond one's acknowledged position, an effort to work always in quest of transnational affinities and comparisons. Such globalizing analysis not only opens up a comparative space within Anglophone scholarship on modernism, but at the same time also changes the broader field picture, 'identifying charged nodal points' and drawing lines of connection between them in a way that throws established figures and knowledge into a changed light.[23] What is involved is far more than a simple add-on of previously ignored or marginalized modernist domains. Rather, the world picture that is developed, even if it is predicated on large-scale powers and broad sweeps of capitalist change, is at the same time vigorously mobile and provisional, moving constantly between local complexity and large-scale visions. 'Global', in other words, should here be taken to embrace 'worldly engagement', transnational and trans-regional forms of exchange, crossed planetary histories, and a provincializing of (Western) Europe.

In the formal yet also economically informed narrative experiments of Woolf and Plaatje lie critical routes around the concentric spatialization of early twentieth-century modernist writing that continues to take the Anglo-American world as the centre. Instead, this reading views the European or American modern as always already bound up in non-Europe and non-America, if in asymmetrical forms. It also attends carefully to the human and other costs involved in such uneven global expansion: to how, within ongoing colonial relations of exchange, things—like jewels— can come to stand in for people within ongoing colonial relations of exchange.

FURTHER READING

Appadurai, Arjun. *Modernity at Large: Cultural Dimensions of Globalization* (Minneapolis, MN: University of Minnesota Press, 1996).
Armstrong, Isobel. *Victorian Glassworlds* (Oxford: Oxford University Press, 2008).

---

[23] Wollaeger, 'Introduction', in Mark Wollaeger and Matt Eatough (eds), *The Oxford Handbook of Global Modernisms* (Oxford: Oxford University Press, 2012), 3–5.

Bayly, C. A. *The Birth of the Modern World 1780–1914: Global Connections and Comparisons* (Oxford: Blackwell, 2004).

Belich, James. *Replenishing the Earth: The Settler Revolution and the Rise of the Anglo-World 1783–1939* (Oxford: Oxford University Press, 2009).

Bell, Duncan. *The Idea of Greater Britain: Empire and the Future of World Order* (Princeton, NJ and Oxford: Princeton University Press, 2007).

Bhabha, Homi K. *The Location of Culture*, 2nd edn (London: Routledge, 2004).

Boehmer, Elleke. *Empire, the National and the Postcolonial 1870–1920* (Oxford: Oxford University Press, 2002).

Boehmer, Elleke. 'Global Nets, Textual Webs; Or What Isn't New about Empire?', *Postcolonial Studies* 7/1 (2004), 11–26.

Cheah, Pheng. *Spectral Nationality: Passages of Freedom from Kant to Postcolonial Literatures of Liberation* (New York: Columbia University Press, 2003).

Chrisman, Laura. *Rereading the Imperial Romance* (Oxford: Oxford University Press, 2000).

Clifford, James. *Routes: Travel and Translation in the Late Twentieth Century* (Cambridge, MA: Harvard University Press, 1997).

Darwin, John. *Unfinished Empire: The Global Expansion of Britain* (London: Penguin, 2013).

Davies, Dominic. 'Critiquing Global Capital and Colonial (In)justice: Structural Violence in Leonard Woolf's *The Village in the Jungle* (1913) and *Economic Imperialism* (1920)', *Journal of Commonwealth Literature* 50/1 (2015), 45–58.

Doyle, Laura and Laura Winkiel (eds). *Geomodernisms: Race, Modernism, Modernity.* (Bloomington, IN: Indiana University Press, 2004).

Doyle, Laura. 'Modernist Studies and Inter-Imperiality in the Longue Durée', in Mark Wollaeger and Matt Eatough (eds), *The Oxford Handbook of Global Modernisms* (Oxford: Oxford University Press, 2012), 669–96.

Emery, Mary Lou. *Modernism, the Visual and Caribbean Literature* (Cambridge: Cambridge University Press, 2007).

Esty, Jed. *Unseasonable Youth: Modernism, Colonialism and the Fiction of Development* (Oxford: Oxford University Press, 2012).

Freedgood, Elaine. *The Ideas in Things: Fugitive Meaning in the Victorian Novel* (Chicago, IL: Chicago University Press, 2006).

Freedgood, Elaine. 'The Novel and Empire', in John Kucich and Jenny Bourne Taylor (eds), *The Nineteenth-Century Novel 1820–1880* (Oxford: Oxford University Press, 2012), 377–91.

Hardt, Michael and Antonio Negri. *Empire* (Cambridge, MA: Harvard University Press, 2000).

Hobson, J. A. *Imperialism: A Study*, (1902; repr. 3rd edn London: Unwin Hyman, 1988).

Kerr, Douglas. 'Colonial Habitats: Orwell and Woolf in the Jungle', *English Studies* 78/2 (August 2008), 149–61.

Kriegal, Lara. 'Narrating the Subcontinent in 1851: India at the Crystal Palace', in Louise Purbrick (ed.), *The Great Exhibition of 1851: New Interdisciplinary Essays* (Manchester: Manchester University Press, 2001).

Kucich, John and Jenny Bourne Taylor. (eds) *The Nineteenth-Century Novel 1820–1880* (Oxford: Oxford University Press, 2012).

Mukhopadhyay, Priyasha. 'Of Greasy Notebooks and Dirty Newspapers: Reading the Illegible in *The Village in the Jungle*', *Journal of Commonwealth Literature* 50/1 (2015), 59–74.

Plotz, John. *Portable Property* (Princeton, NJ: Princeton University Press, 2008).

Richards, Thomas. *The Commodity Culture of Victorian England* (Stanford, CA: Stanford University Press, 1990).

Said, Edward W. *Culture and Imperialism* (London: Cape, 1993).

Thomas, Nicholas. *Islanders: The Pacific in the Age of Empire* (New Haven, CT: Yale University Press, 2012).

Wallerstein, Immanuel. *World Systems Analysis: An Introduction* (Durham, NC: Duke University Press, 2004).

Wollaeger, Mark and Matt Eatough (eds). *The Oxford Handbook of Global Modernisms* (New York and Oxford: Oxford University Press, 2012).

Woolf, Leonard. *Economic Imperialism* (London: Swarthmore Press, Labour Publishing Co., 1920).

Žižek, Slavoj. *Violence* (London: Profile, 2008).

PART V

MINDS AND BODIES

CHAPTER 20

RACE AND BIOLOGY

WILLIAM GREENSLADE

Introduction

The period 1880-1920 saw the emergence and then the qualified effacing of power-ful discourses of racial essentialism and biological determinism in a period which was profoundly influenced, even mesmerized, by the authority of Darwinian sci-ence. This chapter examines how these widely circulating discourses were integral to the development of eugenic ideas in this period, and explores how they gave writers typological resources both to voice such deterministic ideas and to offer points of resistance through the different subject positions that their texts could adopt.

Given the tenacious persistence of these ideas in Britain after the First World War, and on to the terror of the Holocaust, it is valuable to note examples of countervail-ing critical perspectives. In 1936 the Spanish philosopher Ortega y Gasset declared that '[m]an has no nature. What he has is history'.[1] Such a 'critique of the biologiza-tion of national identity', as Marius Turda puts it, is articulated by contrarians, such as the novelist Mona Caird, the philosopher William James, or the anthropologist Franz Boas, each of whom, for different reasons, contested the hegemony that forms of biological and racial determinism apparently commanded.[2]

But sceptics could coexist with believers. While in the Edwardian period Sidney Webb was exercised by the degenerative effects of 'interbreeding', for his fellow Fabian socialist, Sydney Olivier, this 'held the key to a strong, organic community'.[3] Indeed, recent scholarship has accentuated that the history and reception of the theory and practice of eugenics is not one of 'linear shift from unqualified support

---

[1] Quoted by Marius Turda, *Modernism and Eugenics* (Basingstoke: Palgrave Macmillan, 2010), 13.

[2] Turda, *Modernism and Eugenics*, 13.

[3] David Stack, *The First Darwinian Left: Socialism and Darwinism 1859–1914* (Cheltenham: New Clarion Press, 2003), 109.

to unqualified resistance', but is actually a more intriguing story of 'simultaneous enthusiasm and disquiet'.[4]

In a line drawn from the rationalist ideals of the eighteenth-century Enlightenment, late-Victorian scientists saw themselves in a struggle to wrest cultural and moral authority from the church. By cultivating forms of positivist knowledge, replacing tired theology with emancipatory investigation of the laws of nature, they hoped to usher in a more rational, orderly society. Here was a narrative fitting the aspirations of the rising middle classes, uncertainly poised between an established aristocracy legitimized by inherited privilege and the growing political presence of the increasingly organized masses. Founder of eugenics Francis Galton, harrier of Jewish immigrants Arnold White, and scientific writer and romancer H. G. Wells each saw their mission to inform in this light. Eugenics offered a science which would both reorder society to head off these sources of degeneracy, and legitimize the very technicist values by which they positioned themselves as upwardly mobile 'coming men' at the cutting edge of ideas of societal development, rooted in the 'Enlightenment myth of human perfectibility'.[5]

The growing prestige of science could be located in changing attitudes to race. '[T]he alliance of quantification and evolution, with its obsessive measuring and ranking of racially "other" bodies', as Lucy Bland suggests, was 'central to the development of "scientific" racism'.[6] By the mid-nineteenth century, the 'inequality of races' theory propounded by Gobineau and Knox was accompanied by a growth in comparative anthropometric techniques which, when allied to developments in ethnology and anthropology, placed the investigation of race on an ever more scientific footing. '[T]he central meaning of race had narrowed down to a differentiation of peoples based on physical difference and away from the looser usage linked to nation, language, genealogy or culture'.[7] '[A]ttitudes to race', Regenia Gagnier suggests, were changing from an 'older recognition of likeness or universalism' towards growing 'intolerance of difference'.[8]

---

[4] Philippa Levine and Alison Bashford, 'Introduction', in Bashford and Levine (eds), *The Oxford Handbook of the History of Eugenics* (Oxford: Oxford University Press, 2010), 19. Bashford and Levine's volume, together with Marius Turda's *Modernism and Eugenics* (2010), valuably open up the international dimension of eugenics, beyond Britain, America, and Europe. Over the past twenty years there has been considerable British and American scholarship on the theory and practice of eugenics. The relationship between the 'old' eugenics and the 'biotechnological revolution' of the twenty-first century is the subject of a special issue of *New Formations* (60 [Spring 2007]), edited by C. Burdett and A. Richardson under the title *Eugenics Old and New*.

[5] Turda, *Modernism and Eugenics*, 120.

[6] Lucy Bland, 'British Eugenics and "Race-Crossing": A Study of an Interwar Investigation', *New Formations* 60 (Spring 2007), 71.

[7] Ibid., 71.

[8] Regenia Gagnier, *The Insatiability of Human Wants* (Chicago, IL: University of Chicago Press, 2000), 106.

Determinism and essentialism: The uses of biology

The late nineteenth century saw an equivalent scientific turn in the new prestige accorded to literary naturalism and its leading exponent Émile Zola. While few novelists of this period 'stood dumb before the vastness of the conception and the towering height of the ambition', as did George Moore,[9] each, to a greater or lesser extent, entered protracted debates over the place of 'realism' and 'naturalism' in literature, prompted by cultural or ideological affiliation or by aesthetic resistance to Zola's injunction (in his 1880 essay 'Le Roman Expérimental') that novelists should 'operate with characters, passions, human and social data as the chemist and physicist work on inert bodies, as the physiologist works on living bodies.'[10]

Naturalist writers, if nothing else, privileged the processes of causation in their texts, stressing their complexity and multiplicity (as Strindberg does in his 1888 Preface to *Miss Julie*). However, few of them shared Zola's faith in the systematic representation of the core determinants of heredity and environment, embodied in his twenty novels tracing their reproductive consequences for a single family, *Les Rougon-Macquart*. Zola's extrapolation of evolutionary theory was Lamarckian in that characteristics (such as propensity to criminality, alcoholism, or prostitution) acquired through exposure to the environment were shown to pass to the next generation as inheritable qualities.[11]

Contemporary writers were creatively entangled in the deterministic languages of heredity, even if they were less than frank about acknowledging the influence of Zola himself. In Ibsen's *Ghosts* (1881), Oswald's tertiary syphilis is 'inherited' from his debauched father. However, subsequent research showed that '[t]here is no such thing as hereditary syphilis...if a new-born baby has syphilis it is because it has been handed over from mother to the foetus as an infectious disease.'[12] But the idea

---

[9] George Moore, *Confessions of a Young Man* (1886; repr, London: Heinemann, 1926), 75.

[10] Emile Zola, 'The Experimental Novel', in *The Experimental Novel and Other Essays* (New York: Haskell House, 1964), 18.

[11] Naturalism rose and fell in Britain at about the time that Lamarckian biology was itself becoming discredited by the 'germ-plasm' theory of August Weismann. The debate came to a head in the early 1890s when Herbert Spencer, the leading exponent of Lamarckian biology, debated with Weismann and others in the *Contemporary Review*. Weismann and later turn-of-the-century geneticists under the influence of the nineteenth-century botanist Mendel narrowed the range of characteristics which Lamarckians believed could be inherited. That the anti-Lamarckians, or neo-Darwinians, were on the ascendant in the 1900s only stiffened the resolve of the eugenically minded to look to negative eugenic panaceas for racial deterioration, since the environment could no longer offer a source for a racial improvement dividend. By 1926, Julian Huxley was quite clear that the '[o]ld Lamarckism is dead', arguing that 'numerous mutations occur which assuredly have no definite relation to use or to environment...to a great many apparently potent outer influences the germ-plasm is quite unresponsive'. See Julian Huxley, 'The Inheritance of Acquired Characters', in *Essays in Popular Science* (1926; repr. Harmondsworth: Penguin, 1937), 39.

[12] H. Kalmus and L. M. Crump, *Genetics* (London: Penguin, 1948), 149.

of inheritance is still crucial to the larger meaning of the play: the 'ghosts' which haunt Mrs Alving and her son are not only the 'invisible spirochetes of syphilis, but the internalized and virulent prohibitions of religion and bourgeois morality'.[13]

The apparently authoritative aetiology of inherited weakness promiscuously categorizes the 'other' as degenerate. Both Ibsen and Hardy understand this as a form of patriarchal control, perpetuating rigid, defensive, self-serving attitudes. In Ibsen's *A Doll's House* (1879), banker Torvald Helmer, afraid of losing his respectable position, invokes the idea of hereditary degeneracy to stigmatize his wife as the bearer of her 'father's irresponsible ways'.[14] Ibsen's ironic treatment here exposes both the doubtful authority of the speaker (unmasked as both self-interested and fearful), and the claims to scientific authority of the discourse itself. Hardy's Angel Clare, discovering that Tess is a fallen woman, condemns her in terms of familial degeneracy as 'an exhausted seedling of an effete aristocracy'. But Hardy voices Tess's counterposition addressing the loss of selfhood such an ascription implies: '[W]hat's the use of learning...that there is set down in some old book somebody just like me, and to know that I shall only act her part; making me sad, that's all.'[15]

In *Ghosts* Pastor Manders, spotting some volumes on her table, berates Mrs Alving for possessing what he suspects are advanced books, but which, she says, are 'the sort of thing' that make her 'feel, as it were, more confident'.[16] This 'sort of thing' could have included popular medical works such as the Malthusian *The Law of Population* (1877) by Annie Besant. British 1890s audiences for Ibsen's play might well have identified works like H. A. Allbut's *The Wife's Handbook* (1886) or J. M. Guyau's *Education and Heredity* (1891). Such handbooks, aimed at prospective parents, warned of the hereditary transmission of degeneracy. Sarah Grand, whose novel *The Heavenly Twins* (1893) features a marriage ruined by inherited syphilis, sounds like Mrs Alving when she writes that '[a]ll my little knowledge of the social questions I feel so strongly about I have collected from observation and medical books'.[17]

For the increasingly eugenically minded middle classes, a certificate of health for prospective married partners was deemed as important as the marriage certificate itself. As H. A. Allbutt suggested in *The Wife's Handbook* (1886), women or their parents should 'demand a recent certificate of freedom from syphilis from

[13] Elaine Showalter, 'Syphilis, Sexuality, and the Fiction of the fin de siècle', in R. B. Yeazell (ed.), *Sex, Politics, and Science in the Nineteenth-Century Novel* (Baltimore, MD: Johns Hopkins University Press, 1986), 105.

[14] Henrik Ibsen, *Four Major Plays*, ed. James Walter McFarlane (Oxford: Oxford University Press, 1998), 80.

[15] Thomas Hardy, *Tess of the d'Urbervilles*, ed. Christopher Venning and Eleanor Bron (1891; repr. London: Penguin, 2003), 126, 232.

[16] Ibsen, *Four Major Plays*, 101.

[17] Sarah Grand to F. H. Fisher, 22 March 1894, in Anne Heilmann and Stephanie Forward (eds), *Sex, Social Purity and Sarah Grand*, 4 vols (London: Routledge, 2000), II, 40–1.

all men proposing marriage'.[18] For Grant Allen in *The Woman Who Did* (1895), far better that a healthy baby be born outside wedlock than an unhealthy baby born in it. The inherited consequences of the contaminated marriage bed were no more starkly expressed than in Emma Frances Brooke's *A Superfluous Woman* (1894): 'on those frail, tiny forms lay heavily the heritage of the fathers. The beaten brows, the suffering eyes, expatiated in themselves the crimes and debauchery of generations'.[19]

Much New Woman fiction is written with pronounced eugenic urgency, as if anxious to escape the shadow cast by male 'vice'.[20] In M. M. Dowie's *Gallia* (1895) the eponymous heroine seeks positive eugenic, racial health: '[i]f I were to fall in love again it might be with someone... who would not be fine and strong and healthy, and of good stock. As it is... I shall marry solely with the view to the child I am going to live for.'[21] Gallia naturally chooses a healthy and virile male, but on strict eugenic principles, eschewing her romantic attraction to a man of lesser stock.

New Woman writers varied in their treatment of eugenics, ascribing differing importance to maternal influence. While novelists such as Brooke and Grand were implicitly essentialist, radical feminists, such as Mona Caird, believed that mothers made the mistake of 'privileging the future over the present... valuing life primarily as it signified race continuity'.[22] As Angelique Richardson notes, the preoccupation of New Woman fiction with eugenic themes contributes to its aesthetic limitations. In having 'to be entertaining as well as didactic... the novel required characters to change, or at least develop, in order to retain the reader's attention: eugenic ideology did not allow such flexibility'.[23] And Elaine Showalter has argued that '[w]hile male writers explored the multiplicity of the self... women were limited by the revived biological essentialism of post-Darwinian thought'.[24]

[18] Quoted in William Greenslade, *Degeneration, Culture and the Novel 1880–1940* (Cambridge: Cambridge University Press, 1994), 166. The family of the actress and novelist, Elizabeth Robins, was 'tormented by fears of hereditary mental instability brought about by intermarriage', and shared 'concern about [Elizabeth] becoming a mother'. See Angela V. John, *Elizabeth Robins: Staging A Life* (London: Routledge, 1995), 32, 33. In Robins's controversial play, *Alan's Wife* (1893), Jean Creyke murders the crippled child of a union with her racially desirable husband, Alan, who is killed in an industrial accident. Despite its ostensibly eugenic subject, the play is, in William Archer's words, a moving 'little tragedy' of 'fatality'. See Archer, 'Introduction' to *Alan's Wife* (London: Henry & Co., 1893), xlii, xlvi.

[19] Emma Frances Brooke, *A Superfluous Woman* (London: Heinemann, 1894), 275.

[20] For her innovative treatment of the eugenic plots of New Woman fiction, see Angelique Richardson's *Love and Eugenics in the Late Nineteenth Century: Rational Reproduction and the New Woman* (Oxford: Oxford University Press, 2003).

[21] M. M. Dowie, *Gallia* (London: Everyman, 1993), 129.

[22] Richardson, '"People Talk a Lot of Nonsense about Heredity": Mona Caird and Anti-Eugenic Feminism', in A. Richardson and C. Willis (eds), *The New Woman in Fiction and in Fact: fin-de-siècle Feminisms* (Basingstoke: Palgrave, 2001), 207.

[23] Richardson, *Love and Eugenics*, 215.   [24] Showalter, 'Syphilis, Sexuality, 110.

Yet writers on the New Woman did bring into focus a 'complex relationship between feminism, biology and biological essentialism',[25] from which a moderniz-ing sexual politics could be forged. In stories such as 'A Cross Line' and 'The Spell of the White Elf' (both from *Keynotes*, 1893), George Egerton made the question of biological essentialism problematic. Yet in a reviving of the 'reproductive body', fol-lowing concerns about physical and mental deterioration of the race from the turn of the century, ideological pressure, not least from civic-minded women them-selves, enjoins women to redefine maternity as a matter of duty to the imperial state.[26] They are urged on by positive eugenicists like C. W. Saleeby who in 1912, in response to the pressing claims of the suffragette movement, urged women not to desert the ranks of motherhood but to 'furnish an ever-increasing proportion of our wives and mothers, to the great gain...of the future'.[27] While the suffragettes were ambivalent about eugenic ideas, with the campaign for reproductive rights not yoked to eugenic solutions, for many middle-class women, as Wendy Kline notes in the American context, eugenic ideas held considerable appeal as a way to 'modern-ize morality by casting it as a racial and reproductive concept'.[28]

'Fatal fertility'

Ideas of eugenics proceeded by locating a 'dominant ethnic group as the repository of the nation's racial qualities' and 'pursuing biological, social and political means to assess and eliminate the factors seen as contributing to its degeneration'.[29] Such a bio-politics easily elided categorizations of the racially 'superior' and 'inferior' with the socially valuable and disposable. One such categorization centred on the urban 'residuum', a 'section of the urban population...both superfluous to the local labour requirements and biologically or morally incapable of productive labour'.[30] Here was 'one of a new set of social subjects' which, once identified and categorized, would become 'potential objects for state concern'.[31] The endlessly circulated idea of urban degeneration installed the idea that, in their dark recesses, cities harboured

[25] Richardson, 'The Birth of National Hygiene and Efficiency', in A. Heilmann and M. Beetham (eds), *New Woman Hybridities: Femininity, Feminism and International Consumer Culture, 1880–1930* (London: Routledge, 2004), 256.

[26] Gagnier, *The Insatiability*, 133.

[27] C. W. Saleeby, *Woman and Womanhood* (London: Heinemann, 1912), 14.

[28] Wendy Kline, *Building a Better Race: Gender, Sexuality and Eugenics from the Turn of the Century to the Baby Boom* (Berkeley, CA and London: University of California Press, 2001), 23.

[29] Turda, 'Race, Science and Eugenics in the Twentieth Century', in Bashford and Levine (eds), *Oxford Handbook of the History of Eugenics*, 67.

[30] Simon Szreter, *Fertility, Class and Gender in Britain 1860–1940* (Cambridge: Cambridge University Press, 1996), 113.

[31] Stuart Hall, *The Hard Road to Renewal: Thatcherism and the Crisis of the Left* (London: Verso, 1988), 108.

an uncontrollable, degenerative fecundity. This became an effective way of displacing onto biological categories middle-class anxieties about the growing prominence of the urban working class. George Gissing showed, in his early novels of the 1880s, that he was not immune from affiliating class with biologically lower forms of life. In *The Unclassed* (1884), the degraded environment of 'Litany Lane', in an East End slum, is captured in the figure of Slimy, his monstrous appearance calculated to induce a frisson of moral panic about the atavistic nature of 'residuum': 'a very tall creature, with bent shoulders, and head seeming to grow out of its chest... [h]e had laid on the counter, with palms downward as if concealing something, two huge hairy paws'.[32]

Concerns about the quantity and quality of the population grew through the nineteenth century. Thomas Malthus's key idea in his immensely influential *An Essay on the Principle of Population* (1798) was that population expanded exponentially, whereas the means of subsistence (including food production) increased only arithmetically, so leading to scarcity, poverty, and premature death. From Malthus's perspective, as Patrick Brantlinger puts it, 'mass starvation was just nature's—and Providence's—way of righting the balance in a society reeling from its own... lack of foresight and restraint'.[33] While the earnest members of the Malthusian League called for smaller families (which meant addressing the issue of contraception), eugenicists worried about the overall decline in fertility of the British race and wanted to discourage 'fatal fertility' among the eugenically undesirable. The statistician Francis Galton believed that Malthusian checks on population growth (war and disease as well as famine) had failed. Believing that the 'blind mechanism of natural selection could and should be brought under control',[34] he looked to hereditarian rather than environmental causes, proposing the science of eugenics in his landmark study, *Inquiries into the Human Faculty and its Development* (1883). For Galton the 'less eugenically desirable varieties' were outbreeding 'those whose race we especially want to have'.[35] The idea of differential fertility which was to gain such extraordinary prominence in biological and racial thinking over the next forty years, was now installed.

The differential birth rate between classes was of increasing concern, particularly given the overall decline in the national birth rate. Family size in late-Victorian Britain averaged 6, but fell to 3.4 in 1910 and to under 3 by 1914. To the alarm of commentators, the steep decline in the fertility of middle-class families was not matched in those of the working class. Charles Booth found a birth rate of 43 per thousand in London's poor districts, compared to 13.5 per thousand in the most affluent districts of the city.[36] Poverty was all too apparent in a society without

[32] George Gissing, *The Unclassed* (Brighton: Harvester, 1976), 66.
[33] Patrick Brantlinger, *Dark Vanishings* (New York: Cornell University Press, 2003), 106.
[34] Ibid., 193.
[35] Francis Galton, *Inquiries into the Human Faculty and its Development* (London: Macmillan, 1883), 21.
[36] R. A. Soloway, 'Counting the Degenerates', *Journal of Contemporary History* 17/1 (1982), 153.

universal welfare provision, experiencing fast-rising unemployment that reached over 10 per cent in the mid-1880s. By the turn of the century, as concern grew for the multiplication of the unfit in the wake of concern about fitness of military recruits for the Boer War, 28 per cent of the population of York, according to B. S. Rowntree's *Poverty: A Study of Town Life* (1901), were deemed to be living in poverty.[37]

At the intersection of these concerns—the fitness of the British race; concerns about imperial rivalry and competition; the existence of poverty at the 'heart' of Empire—were Jewish immigrants to Britain who from the 1880s sought refuge, mainly in London's East End, from the pogroms of Eastern Europe.[38] The fact that the East End of London came to be 'freighted with the most acute of contemporary anxieties' gave it a metonymic significance for 'discontents that were both more widespread and significant', and to which Jewish immigration had become central.[39] Of course, stereotypes of Jews as 'representatives of alien materialism' abounded in the last decades of the century: Du Maurier's manipulative Svengali, in *Trilby* (1894); Wilde's 'hideous' theatre manager with his 'greasy ringlets', in *The Picture of Dorian Gray* (1891);[40] and many popular melodramas, cartoons, and postcards.[41]

Opposition to Jewish immigration came from racist polemicists, such as Arnold White, W. H. Wilkins, and William Evans Gordon, but also from Ben Tillett, the dockworkers' leader. Their persistent campaigning led to a Royal Commission on Alien Immigration (1903), which paved the way for the controversial Aliens Act (1905) designed to exclude 'undesirable aliens', plausibly interpreted as Jewish immigrants, from entering the country. Anti-Semitic discourse of this period assimilated Jewish immigrants to the prevailing discourse of urban degeneration to account for both their fertility and their degraded state, in a fusion of biological and racial categories that turned on the paradox by which adaptation to lower conditions of life heralded a darkly Darwinian success story. For Lord Dunraven: '[t]hey can feed off the offal of the streets, and live in conditions in respect of indecency, dirt and overcrowding, incompatible with existence to an Englishman…It is the comparative indestructibility of the lower over the higher order of organism.'[42] In *The Time Machine* (1895), H. G. Wells pushed this idea to a dystopic extreme, when, drawing on Darwinian shock tactics channelled through 'scientific romance', he offered a vision of a devolutionary future in which a race of successfully adapted,

[37] See Peter Keating (ed.), *Into Unknown England 1866–1913* (London: Fontana, 1976), 196.

[38] Between 120,000 and 150,000 Jews settled in Britain between 1881 and 1914; see Eitan Bar-Yosef and Nadia Valman, 'Introduction', in Eitan Bar-Yosef and Nadia Valman (eds), *'The Jew' in Late-Victorian and Edwardian Culture* (Basingstoke: Palgrave, 2009), 12.

[39] Bar-Yosef and Valman, 'Introduction', 14.

[40] David Glover, *Literature, Immigration and Diaspora in fin-de-siècle England: A Cultural History of the 1905 Aliens Act* (Cambridge: Cambridge University Press, 2012), 94–6.

[41] Glover, *Literature, Immigration and Diaspora*, 88–93; Bar-Yosef and Valman, 'Introduction', 11.

[42] Earl of Dunraven, 'The Invasion of Destitute Aliens', *Nineteenth Century* 31/184 (June 1892), 988.

subterranean 'Morlocks' preys upon the race of Eloi—'decayed to a beautiful futility' as 'mere fatted cattle'.[43]

Surplus to requirements

Superfluity, as a matter of economics rather than biology, is directly addressed in Gissing's *The Nether World* (1889). John Hewitt, head of an ironically labelled 'Superfluous Family', bitterly recounts how he has failed to gain employment: '[w]ell I went...If there was one man standin' at Gorbutt's door, *there was five hundred*!...What was the use o' me standing there?'[44] In the same novel, Gissing captures a spectacle of humankind in the Clerkenwell slums: 'squalid houses, swarming with yet more squalid children. On all the doorsteps sat little girls...nursing or neglecting bald, red-eyed, doughy-limbed abortions in every stage of babyhood, hapless spawn of diseased humanity'.[45] 'Spawn' here yokes, naturalistically, nurture and nature, environmental and biological causation. The trope of degraded fecundity mixes with astute observation of how material pressures define the abject condition of the 'superfluous' poor. The plot of the more programmatically naturalist text, *Liza of Lambeth* (1897), Somerset Maugham's story of a working-class, South London street, describes the tragic consequences of unwanted procreation. Unaided by her incapable mother, Liza dies from a miscarriage, a consequence of an unsought pregnancy out of wedlock. The situation of the young and poor mothers that Liza embodies would soon be ripe for intervention by the British state through legislation as it navigated its eugenic turn out and beyond the First World War through to Marie Stopes's figure of 'Mrs Jones', who in the 'mean streets' of the city, in 1919, is, through her fertility, busy '*destroying the race*'.[46]

For Hardy, the overproduction of babies is assimilated to his examination of the disjuncture between 'natural' and 'social' law throughout his later fiction. When Tess discovers that her mother is pregnant again she feels 'Malthusian vexation with her mother for thoughtlessly giving her so many little sisters and brothers, when it was such a trouble to nurse those that had already come'. Her own baby, 'Sorrow the Undesired', dies a premature death, 'a bastard gift of shameless Nature who respects not the social law'.[47] The protagonist's son in *Jude the Obscure* (1895), Little Father Time, confronted by yet another mouth to feed, exacts his tragic, Malthusian retribution—'[d]one because we are too meny'.[48] Another preternaturally sensitive

[43] H. G. Wells, *The Time Machine* (London: Penguin, 2005), 58.
[44] Gissing, *The Nether World* (Brighton: Harvester, 1974), 22.   [45] Ibid., 129–30.
[46] Marie Stopes, 'How Mrs Jones Does Her Worst', *Daily Mail* (13 June 1919); see Greenslade, *Degeneration*, 209.
[47] Hardy, *Tess*, 37, 96.
[48] Hardy, *Jude the Obscure* (Oxford: Oxford University Press, 2002), 325.

boy, Stevie, in Conrad's *The Secret Agent* (1907) is made 'angry', by the habitual 'harrowing tales' of his sister Winnie's charwoman, Mrs Neale, 'oppressed by the needs of many infant children'.[49] Significantly, Stevie is allowed to compete for attention alongside his sister, and the narrator: the innocence of his anger is a form of answering back to the inexplicability of the persistence of scarcity, poverty, and deprivation—Malthusian and degenerationist diagnoses, both of which are exposed in the novel as bogus and self-serving.

Being 'surplus to requirements' is a persistent theme in texts of this period. Caught up in debates about national degeneration 'in the context of the Boer War debacle and mounting complaints about plummeting fertility'[50] is the questionable fitness, and so superfluity, of the adolescent or young male, represented in E. M. Forster's 'A Story of a Panic' (1904) or J. M. Synge's *The Playboy of the Western World* (1907). In *The Longest Journey* (1907), Forster pursues the idea of the male figure surplus to the requirements of the bourgeois social order in the neo-tragic victim Rickie Elliot, or in the unclassifiable Stephen Wonham. Stephen's creative eccentricity battles with the coercive power and patriarchal authority exercised by the petty headmaster Herbert Pembroke for whom men like Stephen need to be 'tidied up'. Pembroke's sister, Agnes, wishing that 'a man like that ought never been born', invests heavily in typecasting Stephen as 'other': he is 'illicit, abnormal, worse than a man diseased'.[51]

Eugenics and the state

Forster and Lawrence reach for more ambitious frames of reference in sharp, ideological confrontation with accepted social power founded on unquestioning patriarchy and moral censoriousness (underpinned by a Social Darwinian commitment to fitness), requiring a coercive marking out of the unacceptable 'other'. The Wilcoxes in Forster's *Howards End* (1910) live out these values in pursuit of Helen Schlegel who, late in the novel, is living in self-imposed exile from her family who are unaware that she carries an illegitimate baby by the (now unemployed) clerk, Leonard Bast. Increasingly an object of concern, she is lured back to England on a pretext, her condition thought to warrant mental treatment. The narrator ventriloquizes Henry Wilcox's damage-limitation strategy: '[t]he sick had no rights...one could lie to them remorselessly...the plan that he sketched out for her capture, clever and well-meaning as it was, drew its ethics from the wolf-pack.'[52]

[49] Joseph Conrad, *The Secret Agent* (London: Penguin, 2000), 175.
[50] Soloway, *Birth Control and the Population Question in England 1877–1930* (Chapel Hill, NC: University of North Carolina Press, 1982), 23.
[51] E. M. Forster, *The Longest Journey* (London: Penguin, 1989), 261.
[52] Forster, *Howards End* (London: Penguin, 2000), 241.

As the Edwardian state becomes involved in organizing private life, with 'the birth of healthy children...viewed less as an exclusively private matter',[53] the idea of the nation and the unthinking patriotism required to sustain it is also placed under greater scrutiny. Like Forster, D. H. Lawrence dissents from the psycho-military complex. In *The Rainbow* (1915) he anatomizes the project of imperial regeneration by challenging the viewpoint of the army officer, Anton Skrebensky, through his lover, Ursula Brangwen: ' "What do you fight for, really?" "I would fight for the nation". "For all that, you aren't the nation. What would you do for yourself?" '[54] Against Skrebensky's apparently common-sense assertion, Lawrence plays Ursula's persistent scepticism: these contrasting subject positions allow Ursula's terms of self-determination to expose Skrebensky's willingness to be read as sign and symptom of 'the nation'; for him, selfhood makes sense only in relation to the hegemony of the imperial state which now seeks an 'organic solution to the crisis of reproduction, from "above" '.[55]

One attempt at such a solution was a Royal Commission on the Care and Control of the Feeble-Minded which concluded that mental deficiency was an inherited condition, capable of being passed on, so installing 'a eugenic approach to higher grade mental defects, including so-called "feeblemindedness" '.[56] Following the first International Conference on Eugenics (University of London, 1912), a Mental Deficiency Bill, passed into law in July 1913, allowed local authorities to detain and segregate the 'feebleminded'. 'Defectives' subject to this legislation included 'not only paupers and habitual drunkards but women on poor relief at the time of giving birth to, or being found pregnant with, an illegitimate child'.[57] Kurtz's chilling call in Conrad's *Heart of Darkness* (1899) to 'exterminate all the brutes'[58] was a sentiment not confined to imperial adventurers in the African interior who had 'gone native', but was also circulated in the 'heart of Empire', its discursive double.

While the sterilization of the unfit failed to gain assent in Britain, the idea, and worse, was commonplace in talk among exasperated intellectuals who should have known better.[59] The 'lethal chamber', originally intended for the disposal of stray animals, is a menacing material presence in writing sympathetic to negative eugenic policies. While liberal-minded eugenicists like Saleeby distanced themselves from

---

[53] Turda, *Modernism and Eugenics*, 60.

[54] D. H. Lawrence, *The Rainbow* (London: Penguin, 2007), 289.

[55] Hall, *The Hard Road to Renewal*, 109.

[56] Edward Larson, 'The Rhetoric of Eugenics: Expert Authority and the Mental Deficiency Bill', *British Journal for the History of Science (BJHS)* 24/1 (1991), 48.

[57] Daniel Kevles, *In the Name of Eugenics: Genetics and the Uses of Human Heredity* (New York: Knopf, 1985), 99.

[58] Joseph Conrad, *Heart of Darkness* (London: Penguin, 2007), 62.

[59] Sterilization was introduced in certain US states from 1907. By the late 1920s, twenty-four states had passed sterilization proposals into law. See Richard Overy, *The Morbid Age: Britain between the Wars* (London: Penguin, 2009), 118; and Kevles, 'Eugenics in North America', in R. A. Peel (ed.), *Essays in the History of Eugenics* (London: Galton Institute, 1998), 216.

such prescriptions, the 'efficiency men' were less fastidious.[60] In 1910 Shaw advocated measures including 'killing a great many people whom we now leave living' through 'extensive use of the lethal chamber'.[61] Wells had set the tone in 1901 when he wrote that the 'ascendant' nation of the future will be the one which 'most resolutely picks over, educates, sterilizes, exports, or poisons its People of the Abyss'.[62] 'They should certainly be killed', Virginia Woolf wrote in her diary of a 'long line of imbeciles', while Lawrence envisaged a 'lethal chamber as big as Crystal Palace' for the disposal of 'the sick, the halt and the maimed'.[63]

War and after

Soon after the 'war machine' started to dispose of the fittest and finest, rather than types of the unfit, the eugenic establishment was quick to point out the dysgenic implications: 'the cream of the race will be taken and the skimmed milk will be left', predicted *Eugenics Review* in 1914.[64] But writers could see the war in a different light. In ridiculing the intrusive effects of the notorious Defence of the Realm Act, Rose Macaulay's brave *What Not: A Prophetic Comedy* (1918) satirized a eugenic state with its policies for 'the encouragement and discouragement of alliances in proportion as they seemed favourable or otherwise to the propagation of intelligence in the next generation'. Following the discovery that the minister in charge 'dares to dictate to the people of Britain who they may marry and what kids they may have . . . then goes and gets married himself . . . and hushes it up', the ministry is burnt to the ground in an act of public defiance.[65]

Yet the war actually seemed to galvanize racial and eugenic consciousness in the immediate post-war years.[66] In 1919 the settling in Britain of Indian and Caribbean sailors provoked race riots, prompting concerns about miscegenation, hybridity, and the dysgenic consequences of 'race-crossing' with 'distant' races.[67] The crossing of boundaries between races, which so disgusts Tom Buchanan in F. Scott Fitzgerald's *The Great Gatsby* (1925), disturbed high modernists too. The sensibility

[60] Dan Stone, *Breeding Superman: Nietzsche, Race and Eugenics in Edwardian and Interwar Britain* (Liverpool: Liverpool University Press, 2002), 126.

[61] Quoted in [Dan] Stone, *Breeding Superman*, 127.

[62] Wells, *Anticipations of the Reactions of Mechanical and Scientific Progress upon Human Life and Thought* (London: Chapman and Hall, 1901), 21.

[63] Quoted in Donald J. Childs, *Modernism and Eugenics: Woolf, Eliot, Yeats, and the Culture of Degeneration* (Cambridge: Cambridge University Press, 2007), 23; quoted in John Carey, *The Intellectuals and the Masses* (London: Faber, 1992), 12.

[64] *Eugenics Review* 6/3 (October 1914), 197–8, with the war promising a 'redemptive return to a biologically superior condition' (Turda, *Modernism and Eugenics*, 38).

[65] Rose Macaulay, *What Not: A Prophetic Comedy* (London: Constable, 1918), 12, 222.

[66] See Turda, *Modernism and Eugenics*, 71.   [67] Bland, 'British Eugenics', 68, 67.

and aesthetic practice of T. S. Eliot, for example, is freighted with the weight of racial and biological anxieties of the previous forty years. Whatever else there is to be said about Eliot's racism, in particular the offensive anti-Semitism of his *Poems* (1920), *The Waste Land*, and other writings,[68] the continuities between his deployment of racial and biological tropes and established eugenic discourse is certainly striking. The continuing belief in the inheritance of acquired characteristics, the differential birth rate, the trope of superfluity, the categorization and differentiation of groups defined by their identity as racial products—none of this is at the cutting edge of thinking by 1920. When Eliot speaks of contemporary cinema in 1922 as 'cheap and rapid-breeding',[69] his appalled sense of the degenerate vitality of the cultures of modernity is performed in thoroughly conventionalized bio-social terms.

And the war had a further consequence. New, effective forms of treatment for victims of shell shock, which relied less on the psychiatric Darwinism (so scathingly anatomized, in 1925, by Woolf in *Mrs Dalloway*) and more on techniques 'designed to get patients to re-live and re-experience painful "emotional memories"...buried from consciousness', helped prompt widespread interest in the talking cure and in Freudian analysis and its application more generally, in the post-war years.[70] In this new climate, Lawrence would come to characterize Clifford Chatterley in *Lady Chatterley's Lover* (1928) as a paralysed, rather than syphilitic, patriarch. The passage, then, from Sarah Grand's late-Victorian Evadne, beset by the dysgenic consequences of marital sex in *The Heavenly Twins*, to Connie Chatterley's ultra-modern enjoyment of non-marital sexual pleasure was just one indication of the lessening grip on literature of the discourses of racial and biological determinism, despite their all-too-evident cultural resilience.[71]

FURTHER READING

Bar-Yosef, Eitan and Nadia Valman (eds). *'The Jew' in Late-Victorian and Edwardian Culture* (Basingstoke: Palgrave Macmillan, 2009).
Bashford, Alison and Phillipa Levine (eds). *The Oxford Handbook of the History of Eugenics* (Oxford: Oxford University Press, 2010).

---

[68] Eliot's anti-Semitism is the subject of extensive critical attention by, among others, Juan Leon, 'Meeting Mr Eugenides: T. S. Eliot and Eugenic Anxiety', *Yeats-Eliot Review* 9/4 (1988), 169–77; Christopher Ricks, *T. S. Eliot and Prejudice* (Berkeley, CA: University of California Press, 1988); Bryan Cheyette, *Constructions of 'the Jew' in English Literature and Society* (Cambridge: Cambridge University Press, 1993); Anthony Julius, *T. S. Eliot, Anti-Semitism and Literary Form* (Cambridge: Cambridge University Press, 1995); Childs, *Modernism and Eugenics*, chs 4–6.

[69] T. S. Eliot, 'Marie Lloyd', in *T. S. Eliot: Selected Prose* (London: Faber, 1975), 174.

[70] Martin Stone, 'Shellshock and the Psychologists', in W. F. Bynum, Roy Porter, and Michael Shepherd (eds), *The Anatomy of Madness: Essays in the History of Psychiatry*, 2 vols (London: Tavistock, 1985), II, 255.

[71] This perspective is emphasized in Overy, *The Morbid Age*, ch. 3.

Brantlinger, Patrick. *Dark Vanishings: Discourse on the Extinction of Primitive Races, 1800–1930* (New York: Cornell University Press, 2003).

Burdett, Carolyn and Angelique Richardson (eds). 'Eugenics Old and New' (special issue), *New Formations* 60 (Spring 2007).

Childs, Donald J. *Modernism and Eugenics: Woolf, Eliot, Yeats, and the Culture of Degeneration* (Cambridge: Cambridge University Press, 2007).

Glover, David. *Literature, Immigration and Disapora in Fin-de-Siècle England: A Cultural History of the 1905 Aliens Act* (Cambridge: Cambridge University Press, 2012).

Greenslade, William. *Degeneration, Culture and the Novel 1880–1940* (Cambridge: Cambridge University Press, 1994 [2010]).

Kevles, Daniel. *In the Name of Eugenics: Genetics and the Uses of Human Heredity* (London: Pelican, 1986).

Larson, Edward. 'The Rhetoric of Eugenics: Expert Authority and the Mental Deficiency Bill', *British Journal of the History of Science* 24/1 (1991), 45–60.

Platt, Len (ed.). *Modernism and Race* (Cambridge: Cambridge University Press, 2011).

Richardson, Angelique. *Love and Eugenics in the Late Nineteenth Century: Rational Reproduction and the New Woman* (Oxford: Oxford University Press, 2003).

Showalter, Elaine. 'Syphilis, Sexuality and the Fiction of the fin de siècle', in R. B. Yeazell (ed.), *Sex, Politics, and Science in the Nineteenth-Century Novel* (Baltimore, MD: Johns Hopkins University Press, 1986), 88–115.

Soloway, R. A. 'Counting the Degenerates', *Journal of Contemporary History* 17/1 (1982), 137–64.

Szreter, Simon. *Fertility, Class and Gender in Britain 1860–1940* (Cambridge: Cambridge University Press, 1996).

Turda, Marius. *Modernism and Eugenics* (Basingstoke: Palgrave Macmillan, 2010).

CHAPTER 21

THE WILL TO FORGET

Amnesia, the Nation, and *Ulysses*

VINCENT J. CHENG

The discourses of Western culture are always enjoining us to *remember*, not to forget, warning us instead about the dangers of forgetting: those who don't remember the past are doomed to repeat it; Holocaust memorials enjoin Jews to 'never forget', just as the Hebrew Bible reminded them always to remember Zion, even by the rivers of Babylon; we are each urged to remember our roots, our identity; trauma victims are coaxed into recovering repressed memories so that they may heal and move on; and so on. Hardly anyone talks about the desirability or usefulness of forgetting. Indeed, amnesia—as a neurological condition—is always represented as a bad thing, a loss of a personal identity that one desperately needs to recover. After all, one's identity is basically constituted of one's memories: in its advanced stages, Alzheimer's disease arguably constitutes both the total loss of memory and the total loss of identity. Much scholarly and scientific work has been done, in recent decades, on issues having to do with memory, Alzheimer's, trauma, remembrance, memorials and monuments, truth and reconciliation (see Further Reading section for some of the more important recent studies).

Indeed, memory studies are a notable presence in current approaches to literature and culture, growing out of the ideas about memory developed by important thinkers in the period explored in this volume. The thinkers most influential and involved in issues of memory during this period were, arguably, Karl Marx, Ernest Renan, Friedrich Nietzsche, Henri Bergson, and Sigmund Freud. I will discuss the first three of these at length in this chapter.[1] It is, in large measure, precisely because

---

[1] Bergson's *Matter and Memory* (1896) argues the distinction between two types of memory: 'habit memory' involving certain automatic and repeated behaviours related to learned sensori-motor habits and mechanisms, and 'pure memory' in the form of personal memories surviving in the unconscious; most remembering, Bergson argues, combines these two types of memories. Bergson's ideas influenced, among others, Marcel Proust in his *Remembrance of Things Past* and the later theories of Maurice Halbwachs concerning collective memory (1950). See Henri Bergson, *Matter and Memory*, trans. Nancy

of these thinkers and theorists in the past two centuries—from Marx to the present—that memory studies has become such a vibrant and important field of study, in which we have been made repeatedly aware of the importance of remembering. But hardly anyone today—in medicine and neuroscience, in psychology and psychiatry, in studies of ethnicity and identity, in cultural and literary studies—ever talks about the desirability or usefulness of forgetting.

But I would suggest contemporary Western culture also has a collective fascination with amnesia. Actual amnesia, as a medical condition, is an extremely rare occurrence, yet in popular culture it is an extremely frequent occurrence. Stories of amnesiacs are the stuff of spy novels, mystery novels, popular films, television soap operas, science fiction, and sensational tabloid journalism. We can each think of numerous such examples of our collective cultural fascination with amnesia—in spite of the fact that almost no one has ever personally met or known an actual amnesiac. What is it about amnesia that is so fascinating—and even attractive—to the collective consciousness? Is it a trope for something deeper, something repressed? At the very least, what this phenomenon suggests to me is that we have, in fact, a cultural *will to forget*—a compulsive attraction/fascination for the idea of a clean slate. This notion, and the corollary ability to remake oneself, is a particularly long-standing tradition in American history from Benjamin Franklin's autobiography to the novels of Horatio Alger and Fitzgerald's *The Great Gatsby* (a tendency also seen in some of the upwardly mobile protagonists of the British Victorian novel). It is as if we have a need (even if in fantasy) to erase our past from our memory.

One of the most famous and defining examples of clinical amnesia was the case of a Second World War soldier who was shot in the head at the Battle of Smolensk. The Russian psychologist Alexander Romanovich Luria told this story in *The Man with a Shattered World: The History of a Brain Wound*. Luria also recorded a very different case history in a second book titled *The Mind of a Mnemonist: A Little Book about a Vast Memory*. The two cases are almost mirror images of each other as opposites: the story of the wounded, amnesiac soldier, and the story of a man who remembered virtually everything, the mnemonist. The first we understand as a tragic pathology. But, as the Jewish philosopher and historian Yosef Yerushalmi writes: 'the phenomenon of the mnemonist was no less pathological. If the brain-damaged man could not remember, the mnemonist could not forget. And so it was even difficult for him to read, not because, like the man of Smolensk, he had forgotten the meaning of words, but because each time he tried to read, other words and images surged up from the past and strangled the words and text he held in his hands.'[2] This is sensory and mnemonic overload:

Margaret Paul and W. Scott Palmer (New York: Zone Books, 1988); Maurice Halbwachs, *The Collective Memory*, trans. Francis J. Ditter Jr and Vida Yazdi Ditter (New York: Harper Colophon Books, 1980).

[2] Yosef Hayimi Yerushalmi, *Zakhor: Jewish History and Jewish Memory* (New York: Schocken Books, 1989), 106.

the world and the text are both too crammed with remembered meanings for the individual to function. As Luria himself notes: 'Many of us are anxious to find ways to improve our memories; none of us have to deal with the problem of how to forget. In [this man's] case, however, precisely the reverse was true. The big question for him, and the most troublesome, was how he could learn to forget.'[3]

The mnemonist's haunting dilemma, I would suggest, is not unlike that confronted by James Joyce's character Stephen Dedalus, and indeed by the Irish people, in the face of a traumatic colonial history: 'History,' says Stephen in *Ulysses*, 'is a nightmare from which I am trying to awake' (*U* 2.377).[4] To describe history as a nightmare from which one wants to awake implies a complex relationship between the past, trauma, suffering, sleep, waking, forgetting, memory, amnesia, and repression. As I have argued,

> for Stephen and his fellow Irishmen imperial history is very much an oppressive nightmare of the present from which it is hard to awake – if for no other reason than that its oppressive presence and hegemonic, discursive terminology is written all over the face of Ireland and of its cultural constructions, and thus forms the unavoidable hour-by-hour subtext and context of all their thought and experiences[5].

In the 'Hades' episode of *Ulysses*, for example, Dignam's funeral carriage conveys his mourners first past the statue of William Smith O'Brien, a patriotic hero of the failed rebellion of 1848; then past 'the hugecloaked Liberator's form', Daniel O'Connell's statue (*U* 6.249); then 'Nelson's pillar', the hated English imperial symbol (*U* 6.293); then the 'foundation stone for Parnell', now the Parnell Memorial in Parnell Square (*U* 6.320), and so on. The streets of Dublin become themselves a concrete text that one is never allowed to forget, a constant reminder of an oppressive colonial past and continued colonial subservience, denying the attractions of forgetting, denying the possibility of any relief from the nightmare of history. As with the mnemonist, the inability to forget and the sensory overload of too much memory produce an agonizing paralysis, a nightmare from which one cannot awaken.

In his chapter 'On the Uses and Disadvantages of History for Life' (first published in 1874), Nietzsche remarked that 'life in any true sense is absolutely impossible without forgetfulness':

> we must know the right time to forget as well as the right time to remember, and instinctively see when it is necessary to feel historically and when unhistorically. This is the point that the reader is asked to consider: that the unhistorical and the historical

[3] A. R. Luria, *The Mind of a Mnemonist: A Little Book about a Vast Memory* (New York: Basic Books, 1968), 67.

[4] James Joyce, *Ulysses*, ed. Hans Walter Gabler et al. (New York: Random House, 1986). As is the practice in Joyce scholarship, references to *Ulysses* will be cited in the text by chapter number and line number (e.g. *U* 13.385).

[5] Vincent J. Cheng, *Joyce, Race, and Empire* (Cambridge: Cambridge University Press, 1995), 169.

are equally necessary to the health of an individual, a community, and a system of culture.[6]

But, if health lies somewhere between total remembering and amnesia, between the mnemonist and the soldier in Smolensk, what is the right balance? As Yerushalmi asks: '[G]iven the need both to remember and to forget, where are the lines to be drawn?... How much history do we require? What kind of history? What should we remember, what can we afford to forget, what must we forget? These questions are as unresolved today as they were then; they have only become more pressing.'

What should we forget, and what should we remember? And *when* should we forget, and when remember? If both activities are important to the health of an individual, they are perhaps also both important to the health of a nation or a people. Which of the two is the more important, which is the greater danger? Yerushalmi himself is unequivocal on this issue. Asked to consider what might be the 'Uses of Forgetting,' he writes: 'In the Hebrew Bible they are not to be found. The Bible only knows the terror of forgetting. Forgetting, the obverse of memory, is always negative, the cardinal sin from which all others will flow.'[7] The key biblical text, Yerushalmi suggests, is to be found in the eighth chapter of Deuteronomy:

> Beware lest you *forget* the Lord your God so that you do not keep His commandments and judgments and ordinances... lest you lift up your hearts and *forget* the Lord your God who brought you out of the land of Egypt, out of the house of bondage... And it shall come to pass if you indeed *forget* the Lord your God... I bear witness against you this day that you shall utterly perish.   (Deut. 8:11, 14, 19)

On the other hand, Ernest Renan—as we shall see—has argued memorably that a nation's unity depends on the process of forgetting—and that for purposes of a nation's collective well-being, some things are better forgotten: 'It is good for everyone to know how to forget.'[8]

In defence of forgetting

William Faulkner wrote famously that in the American South '[t]he past is never dead. It's not even past.'[9] Indeed, for the modern world the past is a burden that one—whether an individual or a community—has to carry around. Many twentieth-century thinkers have been thus engaged in a 'memory crisis' arising out of this obsession with the power—and burden—of the past, what Milan Kundera calls 'the burden of memory.'[10] Freud of course (and psychoanalysis generally) was

[6] Cited in Yerushalmi, *Zakhor*, 107.   [7] Ibid., 107, 108.

[8] Ernest Renan, 'What is a Nation?', trans. Martin Thom, in Bhabha, *Nation and Narration*, 16.

[9] William Faulkner, *Requiem for a Nun* (New York: Random House, 1951), 92.

[10] Milan Kundera, *The Book of Laughter and Forgetting*, trans. Michael Henry Heim (New York: Penguin Books, 1981), 187.

fascinated with the power of the past over the present; but, as Anne Whitehead points out, Freud became increasingly aware that '[a]nalysis cannot remove the burden of the past, which we are fated to always carry within us... for we cannot simply "extinguish" the memory of the past; all of our attempts to do so are, indeed, paradoxically greeted by its more aggressive revival or return'.[11]

Friedrich Nietzsche and Ernest Renan, two late nineteenth-century thinkers, have been among the few advocates of forgetting, of the need to forget in the face of the burdens of history and memory. Karl Marx too, in his chapter on 'The Eighteenth Brumaire of Louis Napoleon' (1852), discusses how the burden of the past haunts and dictates the present, specifically how the French 'could not free themselves of the memory of Napoleon'. Marx thus advocates a turning against memory: 'The social revolution of the nineteenth century can only create its poetry from the future, not from the past.' For, as Marx famously writes in the opening of his chapter, '[t]he tradition of the dead generations weighs like a nightmare on the minds of the living'[12]—a line usually translated more directly as 'History weighs like a nightmare upon the brain of the living'.

Joyce's Stephen Dedalus echoes Marx's statement when, in the 'Nestor' episode of *Ulysses*, he complains that 'History... is a nightmare from which I am trying to awake' (*U* 2.377). Joyce's writings are threaded through obsessively by the nightmare and burden of history on turn-of-the-century Irish culture, at both the individual and the national levels. Indeed, Stephen's desire is for a form of what Milan Kundera, in *The Unbearable Lightness of Being*, calls 'lightness', specifically a form of amnesia that erases the nightmare of the past and the burdens of history, allowing for new and other imaginative possibilities.[13]

Nietzsche, like Renan, was himself an advocate of such forgetfulness. Like Stephen, Nietzsche regarded history as a burden we inevitably carry around and which weighs us down, and even expressed an envy of cattle for their ignorance of history and memory, and their consequent happiness which is based on continual forgetting: 'Consider the cattle, grazing as they pass you by: they do not know what is meant by yesterday or today, they leap about, eat, rest, digest, leap about again, and so from morn till night and from day to day, fettered to the moment and its pleasure or displeasure, and thus neither melancholy nor bored.' A human being, by contrast, is weighed down by the crushing and accumulated weight of the past. As a result, Nietzsche suggests, a human envies the cattle's obliviousness to history and memory, 'for though he thinks himself better than the animals because he is human, he cannot help envying them their happiness—what they have, a life neither bored nor painful, is precisely what he wants'. For 'the man says "I remember" and envies

---

[11] Anne Whitehead, *Memory* (New York: Routledge, 2009), 101.

[12] Karl Marx, *The Eighteenth Brumaire of Louis Napoleon*, excerpted in Michael Rossington and Anne Whitehead (eds), *Theories of Memory: A Reader* (Baltimore, MD: Johns Hopkins University Press, 2007), 99, 97.

[13] Kundera, *The Unbearable Lightness of Being*, trans. Michael Henry Heim (New York: Harper & Row, 1985).

the animal, who at once forgets and for whom every moment really dies, sinks back into night and fog and is extinguished forever. Thus the animal lives *unhistorically*: for it is contained in the present'.

For Nietzsche, as for Marx, happiness is to live in the present moment, unburdened by the nightmare which weighs on the brain of the living, and is defined by the 'ability to forget': 'In the case of the smallest or of the greatest happiness, however, it is always the same thing that makes happiness happiness: the ability to forget or, expressed in more scholarly fashion, the capacity to feel *unhistorically* during its duration'. Thus, memory is the enemy of inner peace, for the burden of a remembered history causes paralysis: 'He who cannot sink down on the threshold of the moment and forget all the past ... will never know what happiness is ... he would in the end hardly dare to raise his finger'. Thus, forgetting is necessary to happiness: 'Forgetting is essential to action of any kind, just as not only light but darkness too is essential for the life of everything organic'. Memory and 'the historical sense' are detrimental equally to a person or to a society, for 'it is altogether impossible to *live* at all without forgetting ... *whether this living thing be a man or a people or a culture*' (emphasis in the original).[14]

As a result, Nietzsche advocates a practice of 'active forgetfulness', a willed forgetting, for 'it is altogether impossible to *live* at all without forgetting'. Responding to the crushing burden of history, Nietzsche thus writes a defence of forgetting, in particular the forgetting of history. In the end, Nietzsche suggests, both remembering and willed/active forgetting—what Nietzsche calls the 'historical' and the 'unhistorical'—are necessary to the health and happiness of an individual, as well as of a nation:

> Cheerfulness, the good conscience, the joyful deed, confidence in the future—all of them depend, in the case of the individual as of a nation, ... on one's being just as able to forget at the right time as to remember at the right time; on the possession of a powerful instinct for sensing when it is necessary to feel historically and when unhistorically.[15]

Nation and forgetting

In approaching Joyce's *Ulysses*—as a literary case study of such dynamics—I want to turn first to Ernest Renan, a nineteenth-century French historian and philosopher, and (along with Nietzsche) one of the few staunch advocates of forgetting—or at least of the necessity of forgetting, perhaps even of the collective will and urge to forget. This takes place in Renan's important and influential 1882 lecture, 'Qu'est-ce

---

[14] Friedrich Nietzsche, 'On the Uses and Disadvantages of History for Life', excerpted in Rossington and Whitehead, *Theories of Memory*, 101–8.
[15] Ibid., 104.

qu'une nation?' (What is a Nation?). Joyce, we know, read and admired Renan's work: Stephen Daedalus cites Renan three separate times in *Stephen Hero*, the unpublished prototype for *A Portrait of the Artist as a Young Man*.[16] Renan is mentioned in the 'Scylla and Charybdis' episode of *Ulysses* (*U* 9.755-57) and Joyce, living in France, had visited Renan's birthplace (at Tréguier in Brittany).[17] Joyce was clearly familiar with a number of Renan's well-known works—including, I would suggest, 'What is a Nation?' Indeed, there are a number of passages in Joyce's own chapter 'Ireland, Isle of Saints and Sages' (1907) that seem almost direct echoes of passages and arguments in Renan's chapter.[18] And, of course, in the 'Cyclops' episode of *Ulysses* Leopold Bloom is asked to define a nation ('do you know what a nation means?' *U* 12.1419), echoing Renan's famous question and title.

'What is a Nation?' has been a foundational text for contemporary studies and understandings of nationalism and national identity.[19] Whereas previous scholars had tried to define the nation by criteria such as a race or an ethnic group having shared characteristics, Renan—in a revolutionary departure—defined it as the desire of a people to live together, which he articulated in his well-known phrase, *avoir fait de grandes choses ensemble, vouloir en faire encore* (to have performed great deeds together, to wish to perform still more). Renan writes:

> A nation is a soul, a spiritual principle. Two things, which in truth are but one, constitute this soul or spiritual principle. One lies in the past, one in the present. One is the possession in common of a rich legacy of memories; the other is present-day consent, the desire to live together, the will to perpetuate the value of the heritage that one has received in an undivided form... To have common glories in the past and to have a common will in the present; to have performed great deeds together, to wish to perform still more – these are the essential conditions for being a people.[20]

And what is required to solidify this desire to live together as a nation, Renan argues, is the process of forgetting. For purposes of a nation's collective well-being, some things are better forgotten:

> Forgetting, I would even go so far as to say historical error, is a crucial factor in the creation of a nation, which is why progress in historical studies often constitutes a danger for [the principle of] nationality. Indeed, historical enquiry brings to light

---

[16] Joyce, *Stephen Hero*, ed. John J. Slocum and Herbert Cahoon (New York: New Directions, 1959), 175, 189, 190.

[17] Richard Ellmann, *James Joyce* (Oxford: Oxford University Press, 1982), 567.

[18] Elsworth Mason and Richard Ellmann (eds), *The Critical Writings of James Joyce* (New York: Viking, 1959), 153–74.

[19] Renan is, however, a controversial figure in post-colonial studies—for, like many of his contemporaries, he defended colonialism as a laudable institution bringing civilization to the darker races, arguing that 'the regeneration of the inferior or degenerate races, by the superior races, is part of the providential order of things for humanity'. See, for example, Edward Said, *Reflections on Exile: And Other Literary and Cultural Essays* (London: Granta, 2001), 418–19; Robert Young, *Colonial Desire: Hybridity in Theory, Culture and Race* (London: Routledge, 1995), 69.

[20] Renan, 'What is a Nation?', 19.

deeds of violence which took place at the origin of all political formations, even those whose consequences have been altogether beneficial. Unity is always effected by means of brutality; the union of northern France with the Midi was the result of massacres and terror lasting for the best part of a century.

If unity is a forced condition, achieved through brutality, then the maintenance of that unity requires a shared willingness to forget the brutal past. Indeed, Renan notes that the ability of a nation's people to feel things in common depends on the erasing of memories of discord and violence against each other:

> Yet the essence of a nation is that all individuals have many things in common; and also that they have forgotten many things. No French citizen knows whether he is a Burgundian, an Alan, a Taifale, or a Visigoth, yet every French citizen has to have forgotten the massacre of Saint Bartholomew, or the massacres that took place in the Midi in the thirteenth century.[21]

(Many thousands of Huguenots were massacred in Paris on Saint Bartholomew's Day, 24 August 1572—an historical event Joyce also refers to twice in *Ulysses*, 8.622-4 and 15.2385.)

It is easy to think of examples in support of Renan's assertion—from the *Aeneid*'s suggestion of how forgetting past rancour allowed for the creation of the state of Rome—to the Troubles in Northern Ireland whose continuation were incited and facilitated for decades by the annual Orange marches by Protestants through Catholic neighbourhoods each July, constantly *reminding* Catholics of (that is to say, refusing to allow them to forget) their status as colonial subjects. It is only when both sides are willing to begin the process of forgetting past atrocities that a peace process becomes possible. As Renan puts it, 'it is good for everyone to know how to forget'.

Yet the question arises whether such collective amnesia can be permanent, or whether—as with repressed memories in trauma victims—there will at some point emerge a return of the repressed. Indeed, one could well think of the recent cycles of genocidal violence during the 1990s in what was formerly Yugoslavia as the result of a resurfacing (or active disinterment) of repressed collective memories of ethnic conflicts and hatreds between Serbs, Croats, and Bosniaks originating centuries earlier, all of which had been 'forgotten' for a few decades while the official narrative and national identity of the Yugoslav Federation prevailed. Renan himself was conscious of such a threat, and his warning now appears prescient in light of recent genocides in places like Serbia, Croatia, and Rwanda:

> Be on your guard, for this ethnographic politics is in no way a stable thing and, if today you use it against others, tomorrow you may see it turned against yourselves. Can you be sure that the Germans, who have raised the banner of ethnography so high, will not see the Slavs in their turn analyse the names of villages in Saxony and Lusatia, search

---

[21] Ibid., 11.

for any traces of the Wiltzes or of the Obotrites, and demand recompense for the massacres and the wholesale enslavements that the Othons inflicted upon their ancestors? It is good for everyone to know how to forget.[22]

National forgetting in *Ulysses*

Joyce's texts are frequently concerned with the dynamics of forgetting, as well as with the contrasting struggle to hold on to 'the memory of the past'. There are many interesting cases of psychological manoeuvres and self-deceptions by characters involved in the processes of remembering and forgetting. But these are cases of individual forgetfulness. In the rest of this chapter I want to focus briefly on two passages in *Ulysses* in which individual forgetting becomes symptomatic of, or connected to, collective forgetting—to national, cultural, and historical forgetting.

The second chapter of *Ulysses*, 'Nestor', an episode Joyce designated as concerning 'History', begins with a history lesson:

> – You, Cochrane, what city sent for him?
> – Tarentum, sir.
> – Very good. Well?
> – There was a battle, sir.
> – Very good. Where?
> The boy's blank face asked the blank window.   (*U* 2.1-6)

Stephen's young student Cochrane is only partially able to recall the history of Pyrrhus's war against the Romans on behalf of the Tarentines. Tarentum was a minor Greek colony, fighting against the powerful Romans; thus, the story/history Stephen is asking his class to remember is one of a battle against empire. But history, Stephen's interior thoughts suggest, is '[f]abled by the daughters of memory' (*U* 2.7)—for memory, like Cochrane, has a hard time remembering facts and details and instead imagines 'fables' or allegories:

> – I forget the place, sir. 279 BC.
> – Asculum, Stephen said, glancing at the name and date in the gorescarred book.
> – Yes, sir. And he said: *Another victory like that and we are done for.*
> That phrase the world had remembered. A dull ease of the mind. From a hill above a corpsestrewn plain a general speaking to his officers. (*U* 2.11-17)

What gets remembered, Stephen realizes, is discourse—in this case, the famous phrase attributed to Pyrrhus: *Another victory like that and we are done for.* What is forgotten and repressed (in the distillation of a battle into a single phrase the world

---

[22] Ibid., 15–16.

still remembers) are the actual and material circumstances at Asculum that led to Pyrrhus's comment in the first place, the facts behind the logic of a 'Pyrrhic victory': that is, the tremendous human slaughter and bloodshed that made another such victory unthinkable, even for the victors. Thus, Stephen's history book is 'gore-scarred' in more ways than one, as it tells the story of a general (Pyrrhus) speaking to his officers above a 'corpsestrewn' plain—while the world remembers only that catchy phrase, inducing 'a dull ease of the mind'. The discursive, collective memory whitewashes and simplifies painful or unpleasant historical details: what is forgotten (in favour of discourse) are gore and death.

Although Stephen's young Irish students might be expected to identify with a battle fought by a small colony against a powerful empire, 'For them, too', Stephen thinks, 'history was a tale like any other too often heard, their land a pawnshop' (*U* 2.46–7). It is perhaps easier to want to forget, to exercise the 'dull ease of the mind'. Stephen himself, however, like Luria's mnemonist, sees too much, and cannot forget. Even the game of hockey the students go on to play reminds Stephen of the ugly dynamics embodied in such play, which mimics (and sometimes enacts) actual violence:

> Again: a goal. I am among them, among their battling bodies in a medley, the joust of life…Jousts. Time shocked rebounds, shock by shock. Jousts, slush and uproar of battles, the frozen deathspew of the slain, a shot of spearspikes baited with men's bloodied guts.   (*U* 2.314–18)

The game itself is imaged by Stephen as training and preparation for battle and for killing (as in the Duke of Wellington's much-quoted but apocryphal remark about Waterloo being won on the 'playing fields of Eton'), as the sounds of sticks clashing and jousting for rebounds are but preludes to the 'gorescarred' and 'corpsestrewn' plains of war that await these young boys when they grow up. Again, what we forget and repress are blood and corpses; what we remember are stories and witty phrases ('another victory like that' and 'the playing fields of Eton'), the very discursive products that elide the 'gorescarred' and 'corpsestrewn' plains behind them.

Renan argues that national identity and unity depend on collective acts of forgetting. For a nation, such unity is obviously desirable. One might note that, for an empire, such unity is even more desirable (but perhaps harder to achieve), for—from the imperialist's standpoint—it is important for a colony and its colonial subjects to forget the history of bloody conquest (to bury the bloodstained hatchet, as it were) if they are to reimagine their own collective identity and future as a happy part of that empire. But for Stephen, a member of the conquered race, history is not so easily forgotten or repressed. In other words, it is the victors who would most want to forget past atrocities; it is the losers who most need to not forget. It is easier for Stephen's affluent and comfortable students—'Welloff people, proud that their eldest son was in the navy', living in villas off the 'Vico road, Dalkey' and sending their boys to an expensive school ('aware of the fees their papas pay') run by an

Ulsterman—it is easier for them to forget the troubled past of Ireland, 'a tale like any other too often heard', than for a poor Catholic like Stephen obsessed with the nightmare of history (*U* 2.24-47).

No one in *Ulysses* forgets more easily than Garrett Deasy, the headmaster under whom Stephen teaches. A Protestant and an Ulsterman, Deasy, ironically, accuses Stephen of forgetfulness:

> – You think me an old fogey and an old tory . . . I saw three generations since O'Connell's time. I remember the famine in '46. Do you know that the orange lodges agitated for repeal of the union twenty years before O'Connell did or before the prelates of your communion denounced him as a demagogue? You fenians forget some things.

> (*U* 2.268-72)

But it is Deasy himself who repeatedly forgets or misremembers or distorts historical facts—whether it is in quoting Shakespeare's 'put but money in thy purse' (Iago, Stephen reminds him); in claiming that a French Celt came up with the line 'that on [the British] empire the sun never sets'; or that Catholic prelates 'denounced' Daniel O'Connell (*U* 2.239-40, 248-9, 271-2). And he is certainly wrong in his self-satisfied announcement to Stephen that 'Ireland, they say, has the honour of being the only country which never persecuted the Jews . . . And do you know why? . . . Because she never let them in' (*U* 2.437-42).

Forgetting is a convenient luxury of the winners. It is clearly beneficial to the unity of a sovereign state or empire for its subjects to be able to forget the history of bloody conquest if they are to partake in a collective identity as members of such sovereignty. For the recalcitrant members of a subject colony resisting imperial rule, however, forgetting is precisely *not* desirable: it is the pre-conquest past, the traditional native culture, that one must hold on to, that one must try to reclaim, must try to still remember Zion by the rivers of Babylon, all the while not allowing oneself to be contaminated by the attractions of empire—by the 'fleshpots of Egypt', as it were.

Such remembering, however, can also be clouded by the discourse of nostalgia—and, as I have argued elsewhere,[23] by the discourses of purity and authenticity. It cannot incorporate present realities and hybridities into its logic, including the cultural hybridity and cosmopolitanism of many of its own citizens (such as Stephen Dedalus, Buck Mulligan, or Oscar Wilde)—for it would freeze Irishness in the nostalgic purity of a dead past, doomed to extinction in the face of modernity and history. How then can such a discourse deal with emigration—so important, after all, in Irish cultural history—unless it demand that (in Bruce Robbins's words) the eyes of the emigrant 'can only be trained on his lost home'?[24] It is the native 'soil' and

[23] Cheng, *Inauthentic: The Anxiety over Culture and Identity* (New Brunswick, NJ: Rutgers University Press), 46–61.

[24] Bruce Robbins, *Feeling Global: Internationalism in Distress* (New York: New York University Press, 1999), 95.

the homeland (so consecrated in Irish songs as 'the holy sod', 'the holy ground', 'the wee bit of green', and so on) that have to remain the only touchstones possible, the only images that can be allowed to be in one's memory continually, in order to maintain a nostalgic cultural identity that denies the existence of any other sorts of experience as genuine and acceptable.

This logic presents a dilemma for the turn-of-the-century Irish subject who, like Gabriel Conroy (in 'The Dead') or like Joyce himself, interacts with modern English or continental cultures, but especially so for the Irish exile—whether wild goose or emigrant—who is away from home but who wishes to maintain his or her 'Irishness'. 'The wild goose, Kevin Egan of Paris' in *Ulysses* (*U* 3.164) is a case in point: a portrait of the Fenian Joseph Casey who was imprisoned for his involvement in acts of Fenian violence in England,[25] Joyce's Kevin Egan is a Fenian espousing the discourse of Irish nationalism and authenticity, but ironically stranded in the centre of internationalism and cosmopolitanism, Paris. This is an irony not lost on his son Patrice, Stephen's friend, who tells Stephen: '*C'est tordant, vous savez. Moi, je suis socialiste. Je ne crois pas en l'existence de Dieu. Faut pas le dire à mon père*' (*U* 3.169–70); (my translation: It's hilarious, you know. Me, I'm a socialist. I don't believe in the existence of God. Don't tell my father that). Like Patrice, Stephen too is a freethinker living in Paris, eating *mou en civet* in his 'Latin quarter hat' 'when I was in Paris, *boul' Mich*' (*U* 3.174–9). The Boulevard Saint-Michel, a major street in the Latin Quarter on the Seine's Left Bank, was of course 'the cafe center of student and bohemian life at the turn of the century'.[26] In such an environment, the Fenian Kevin Egan tries to hold on to 'home' and to the memory of the past: at Rodot's patisserie (9 Boulevard Saint-Michel), he speaks to Stephen 'Of Ireland, the Dalcassians, of hopes, conspiracies, of Arthur Griffith' (*U* 3.226–7). And he complains about the degeneracy and sexual excess of Parisians:

> Licentious men. The froeken, *bonne à tout faire*, who rubs male nakedness in the bath at Upsala. *Moi faire*, she said, *tous les messieurs*. Not this *monsieur*, I said. Most licentious custom. Bath a most private thing. I wouldn't let my brother, not even my own brother, most lascivious thing…Lascivious people.   (*U* 3.234–8)

The repeated refrain of 'Lascivious people'—in the context of massages and baths—suggests a paranoid fear of the foreign and the degenerate ('the fleshpots of Egypt'), all embodied in the Parisian bohemianism and cosmopolitan freethinking indulged in by Stephen and indeed by Egan's own son Patrice. Rather, Egan tries to teach his son 'to sing *The boys of Kilkenny*' (*U* 3.257) and to keep his mind focused on 'home', as defined by a discourse identifying Irishness as the agrarian, Catholic, and republican west of Ireland, the nostalgic discourse glorified by the Fenianism through which he defines himself. As

---

[25] See Don Gifford and Robert J. Seidman, *Ulysses Annotated: Notes for James Joyce's* Ulysses (Berkeley, CA: University of California Press, 1988), 52.

[26] Gifford and Seidman, *Ulysses Annotated*, 53.

Stephen ruefully notes, 'In gay paree he hides, Egan of Paris, unsought by any save by me…They have forgotten Kevin Egan, not he them. Remembering thee, O Sion' (*U* 3.249–50, 263–4). Like the Israelites remembering Zion by the rivers of Babylon, Egan continues to train his eyes on the past and on the native soil of an authentic Ireland, trying not to forget, while he is stranded by the boulevards of a latter-day Babylon. Unable to admit or incorporate hybrid and foreign experiences as part of his own complex identity, he lives in an 'authentic' past already frozen in nostalgia.

So what the subject race, and the recalcitrant subject (like Kevin Egan) of a resistant colony, really hold on to, what they 'remember', Joyce shows us, is not actual memories, so much as rosy-tinted sentimentalism and nostalgia. Itself a 'forgetting' of sorts, often resulting in sentimentalized stereotypes of a 'national character' (as Seamus Deane points out[27]), usually bathed in a nostalgia for origins—what Homi Bhabha calls 'that attempt to hark back to a "true" national past'[28]—it perpetuates what David Lloyd calls 'the recurrent reproduction of Celtic material as a thematica of identity'.[29] This harking back to a nostalgia for national origins rewrites Irish history into one long, seamless tradition in which the endpoint is, of course, 'A Nation Once Again' (even though there never was, historically, an Irish 'nation' previous to 1922).[30]

Similarly, Benedict Anderson has made the point that nations tend to construct themselves as 'imagined communities' with a cohesive national character, sovereignties retrospectively endowed with a revisionist history of antiquity and racial purity: '[They] always loom out of an immemorial past, and, still more important, glide into a limitless future. It is the magic of nationalism to turn chance into destiny.'[31] As Anderson points out in his resonant discussion of Renan's use of 'memory' and 'forgetting', the favourite metaphor of emerging nations newly 're-discovering' their supposedly 'forgotten' ancient pasts (consider the Celtic 'Revival') is 'sleep' (or 'remembering'/reviving what had been forgotten). '[No other metaphor] seemed better than "sleep," for it permitted those intelligentsias and bourgeoisies who were becoming conscious of themselves as Czechs, Hungarians, or Finns [or, we might add, Celts] to figure their study of Czech, Magyar, or Finnish [or Celtic] languages, folklores, and musics as "rediscovering" something deep-down always known.'[32] But in order to *rediscover* something, you must have first *forgotten* it. In this discursive process, the newly 'reawakened' national

---

[27] Seamus Deane, 'National Character and National Audience: Races, Crowds, and Readers', in Michael Allen and Angela Wilcox (eds), *Critical Approaches to Anglo-Irish Literature* (Totowa, NJ: Barnes & Noble, 1989), 40–52.

[28] Bhabha, 'DissemiNation: Time, Narrative, and the Margins of the Modern Nation', in Bhabha, *Nation and Narration*, 303.

[29] David Lloyd, 'Writing in the Shit: Beckett, Nationalism, and the Colonial Subject', *Modern Fiction Studies* 35/1 (Spring 1989), 85.

[30] See also Cheng, *Joyce, Race, and Empire*, 215–17. The previous paragraph was partly adapted from various passages in *Joyce, Race, and Empire*, 198–200.

[31] Benedict Anderson, *Imagined Communities: Reflections on the Origin and Spread of Nationalism* (London: Verso, 1991), 11–12.

[32] Ibid., 196.

discourse 'remembers' what it had forgotten by constructing a nostalgic revisionism that (like Renan's national forgetting of brutal past massacres) glosses over the brutalities of the past as well as the existence of minority groups not fitting the imagined national identity—by imagining for the island a historically continuous community with a homogenous national character. Thus, national

> history rewrites itself as one long 'Irish' tradition (with mists of inevitability)—in which the differences between Milesians, Gaels, Celts, and even Danes and Spaniards get written out; in which the Anglo-Irish get bracketed; in which Jews get written out altogether (in spite of their material presence in one's midst); and in which the purity of an Irish 'race' is proclaimed in spite of the fact that there never was such a thing as an Irish 'nation' and in spite of the many racial/ethnic interminglings of the extended, pluralistic contact zone known as 'Ireland'.[33]

This sort of nativist nationalism is a nostalgic 'remembering' that Joyce decries as 'the old pap of racial hatred': 'What race, or what language,' Joyce wrote, 'can boast of being pure today? And no race has less right to utter such a boast than the race now living in Ireland.'[34]

Let me now, in conclusion, return to the topic of amnesia. Stephen Dedalus would like to slough off the nightmare of history which so weighs him down and from which he cannot awake. But, like Luria's mnemonist, he remembers too much, is much too keenly aware of the pawnshop of history that is Ireland. Indeed, Joyce shows us how the losers—the victims of colonialism—need desperately to remember, to hold on to the past, cannot afford to forget; but he also shows how such 'remembering' is itself a distortion and travesty of historical memory. Rather, at the level of nations and empires, the fascination with amnesia is a collective will to forget the unpleasantnesses of the past on the part of the *winners*, a Renanesque drive for national or imperial unity by forgetting the atrocities of the past. For Renan, this was a necessity for communal and national harmony. For Joyce, this is an elision of minority positions and groups that do not fit into the dominant view of national unity (as with Deasy's claim about the Jews not existing in Ireland).

I would like at this point to return to Nietzsche's and Yerushalmi's questions about how much we should remember and how much we should forget: 'Given the need both to remember and to forget, where are the lines to be drawn?...How much history do we require? What kind of history? What should we remember, what can we afford to forget, what must we forget?'[35] Joyce's *Ulysses*, indeed, points out the dangers of *both* forgetting and remembering, for in *Ulysses* even 'remembering', as we have seen, is a kind of forgetting, a Renanesque covering up of brutal realities and facts. Both Renanesque versions of national 'forgetting'/unity (as with

---

[33] Cheng, *Joyce, Race, and Empire*, 216–17.
[34] Mason and Ellmann, *Critical Writings of James Joyce*, 165–6.
[35] Yerushalmi, *Zakhor*, 107.

Deasy) and Irish nationalist 'remembering'/nostalgia (as with Kevin Egan and the Citizen) gloss over the complex realities of the diverse composition and frequently 'corpsestrewn' material realities of the Irish people and their history.

ACKNOWLEDGEMENTS

Several passages from this chapter were adapted, with permission, from Vincent J. Cheng, 'Amnesia, Forgetting, and the Nation in James Joyce's *Ulysses*', in Oona Frawley and Katherine O'Callaghan (eds), *James Joyce and Cultural Memory* (Syracuse, NY: Syracuse University Press, 2014), 10-26.

FURTHER READING

Anderson, Benedict. *Imagined Communities: Reflections on the Origin and Spread of Nationalism* (London: Verso, 1991).

Bhabha, Homi (ed.). *Nation and Narration* (London: Routledge, 1990).

Caruth, Cathy (ed.). *Trauma: Explorations in Memory* (Baltimore, MD: Johns Hopkins University Press, 1995).

Casey, Edward S. *Remembering: A Phenomenological Study* (Bloomington, IN: Indiana University Press, 1987).

Connerton, Paul. *How Modernity Forgets* (Cambridge: Cambridge University Press, 2009).

Langer, Lawrence L. *Admitting the Holocaust: Collected Essays* (New York: Oxford University Press, 1995).

Luria, A. R. *The Mind of a Mnemonist: A Little Book about a Vast Memory* (New York: Basic Books, 1968).

Luria, A. R. *The Man with a Shattered World: The History of a Brain Wound* (Cambridge, MA: Harvard University Press, 1972).

Nora, Pierre. *Les lieux de mémoire*, vol. I (Paris: Editions Gallimard, 1997).

Renan, Ernest. 'What is a Nation?', trans. Martin Thom, in Homi K. Bhabha (ed.), *Nation and Narration* London: Routledge, 1990), 8-22.

Ricoeur, Paul. *Memory, History, Forgetting* (Chicago, IL: University of Chicago Press, 2004).

Rossington, Michael and Anne Whitehead (eds). *Theories of Memory: A Reader* (Baltimore, MD: Johns Hopkins University Press, 2007).

Whitehead, Anne. *Memory* (New York: Routledge, 2009).

Yerushalmi, Yosef Hayim. *Zakhor: Jewish History and Jewish Memory* (New York: Schocken Books, 1989).

Young, James E. *The Texture of Memory: Holocaust Memorials and Meaning* (New Haven, CT: Yale University Press, 1993).

CHAPTER 22

THE POST-HUMAN SPIRIT OF THE NEOPAGAN MOVEMENT

DENNIS DENISOFF

In his poem 'Hymn to Pan' (1919), the occultist Aleister Crowley offers an image of Pan that, one suspects, few of his contemporaries eagerly embraced. Crowley presents the demigod as a transsexual, trans-species cyborg that is artificial and biological, mineral and vegetable, shepherd and sheep, sexual attacker and willing victim.

> I am thy mate, I am thy man,
> Goat of thy flock, I am gold, I am god,
> Flesh to thy bone, flower to thy rod.
> With hoofs of steel I race on the rocks
> Through solstice stubborn to equinox.
> And I rave; and I rape and I rip and I rent
> Everlasting, world without end.
> Mannikin, maiden, maenad, man,
> In the might of Pan.[1]

'Everlasting' and 'without end', Pan embodies a state of being where time and space lose any semblance of meaning, and identity becomes utterly unstable on the craggy rocks of the eternal. The narrator's repeated 'I' in the poem comes across less as an act of self-affirmation than as a desperate attempt at a sense of cohesion in an environment characterized by chaos. How, one is led to wonder, did such a rapacious, threatening persona leap forth from the pagan interests and aesthetics of the Victorian era?

During the nineteenth century, British attention to paganism arose through various historical events and cultural developments. These include fresh archaeological discoveries in Egypt and a growing interest in Egyptian history; the rise of spiritualism, theosophy, and new occult movements; the formation of the Folklore Society in 1878 and an increased investment in folkloric studies in general; and the late-Victorian

---

[1] Aleister Crowley, 'Hymn to Pan', *The Equinox* 3/1 (March 1919), 7.

Celtic Renaissance. Authors, artists, philosophers, scientists, and laypeople increasingly turned to Celtic, Eastern, Egyptian, Greco-Roman, and other forms of paganism for inspiration and values that were not driven by contemporary industrialism, materialism, and consumerism. From aesthetic motifs in Decadent art and literature to earnest engagements with nationalist and socialist politics, these interests and beliefs eventually cohered sufficiently to come to be known as the neopagan movement (which ran from roughly 1870 to 1920). During this period, the term 'neopaganism' was used to distinguish, from classical pagan mythology, the current set of spiritualities, cultures, and methodologies sustained by individuals who often felt a deep, personal investment in these ecological faiths and their seemingly uninhibiting philosophies and respect for diversity. Although the term has resurfaced recently to address forms of paganism from roughly the past fifty years, in this article I use 'neopaganism' to refer only to aspects of the later Victorian and Edwardian periods.

Crowley's 'Hymn to Pan', with its sadomasochistic revision of classical motifs, occult allusions, and articulations of heterodox identifications and desires, suggests the breadth of perspectives that the neopagan movement entertained. The demigod Pan himself rose to prominence in Western culture during the nineteenth century, his persona and relationship with British society altering as he fulfilled increasingly important spiritual, cultural, and philosophical roles. While the Romantic Pan had appeared predominantly as a pastoral spirit, the animistic version of Crowley's era was a force of nature depicted as horrifying in its utter implosion of conventional signifying systems and the notion of the human itself. This *fin-de-siècle* manifestation of Pan not only serves as a succinct formulation of the earth-based philosophies defined as neopaganism, but also foreshadows recent post-humanist and eco-spiritualist theorizations, or what Bron Taylor refers to as 'dark green religion'.[2] Like Crowley's hymn, both neopaganism and eco-theory have as a defining question the place of the humanist individual in a nature-centred belief system that stands in opposition not only to scientific materialism, but also to the industrialism and consumerism of the age. Adding writings by Edward Carpenter, E. F. Benson, and Michael Field to my consideration of Crowley's poem, I wish to offer a sense of the ways in which notably diverse works from turn-of-the-century Britain engaged a neopagan ecology that presaged recent post-humanist inquiry into the spiritual relationship of the self to nature.

The rise of eco-paganism

The acceptance of paganism in mainstream society has grown throughout the twentieth century, with an increasing number of legal, religious, and other institu-

[2] Bron Taylor, *Dark Green Religion: Nature, Spiritualty, and the Planetary Future* (Berkeley, CA: University of California Press, 2010).

tions acknowledging its validity, especially in Europe. This development has been buttressed by the attention paganism has continued to gain as part of a broad philosophical and environmental discussion regarding humans' function as a part of nature. Even thirty-five years ago, Margot Adler could propose that, if contemporary paganism were presented, as it accurately could be, as 'an intellectual and artistic movement whose adherents have new perceptions of the nature of reality, the place of sexuality, and the meaning of community, academics would flock to study it.'[3] Adler points out, however, that scholars in the 1970s, when she voiced this position, were uncomfortable with terms such as 'pagan' and 'witch', as well as with paganism's affiliation with the occult. That said, a number of scholars over the past forty years have published works that support outlooks and arguments also held by contemporary pagans. Some such as Gilles Deleuze and Félix Guattari, Jacques Derrida, and Timothy Morton have established key paradigms for our conceptions of species interrelations and the seeming anthropocentricism of contemporary notions of nature and environment.[4] Donna Haraway, Carey Wolfe, and others working from feminist, queer, and post-humanist perspectives have foregrounded de-individuation and inter-species communication while exploring the structural and imaginative limits of language.[5] And still others—such as Emma Restall Orr, and Chas Clifton and Graham Harvey—have theorized issues of ecology, diversity, and selfhood through discourses invested in paganism itself, giving rise to the field of eco-pagan studies.[6]

The richness and diversity of pagan perspectives over the centuries have resulted in a panoply of earth-based spiritualities that are not themselves in full accord. Indeed, recent scholarship often characterizes this very diversity and malleability as a key strength of paganism, responsible in part for its vitality and growth. This positive formulation of variety, changeability, and contradiction has found reinforcement from its kinship with scholarly approaches such as feminism, queer studies, and post-humanism. Similarly, pagan notions of the natural are neither fixed nor singular. Nature is recognized—to suggest some of the many perspectives—as a beautiful, threatening organic force; as one or more actual goddesses or gods; and as an organic environment that can exist, has existed, or does exist (at least in part) outside the anthropocene.

---

[3] Margot Adler, *Drawing down the Moon: Witches, Druids, Goddess-Worshippers, and Other Pagans in America Today* (Boston, MA: Beacon, 1986), 5.

[4] Gilles Deleuze and Félix Guattari, *A Thousand Plateaus* (Minneapolis, MN: University of Minnesota Press, 1987); Jacques Derrida, *The Animal that Therefore I Am* (New York: Fordham University Press, 2009); Timothy Morton, *Ecology without Nature: Rethinking Environmental Aesthetics* (Cambridge, MA: Harvard University Press, 2007).

[5] Donna Haraway, *Simians, Cyborgs, and Women: The Reinvention of Nature* (New York: Routledge, 1991) and *When Species Meet* (Minneapolis, MN: University of Minnesota Press, 2008); Carey Wolfe, *Animal Rites* (Chicago, IL: University of Chicago Press, 2003).

[6] Emma Restall Orr, *Living with Honour: A Pagan Ethics* (Ropley, Hants: John Hunt, 2007); Chas Clifton and Graham Harvey (eds), *The Paganism Reader* (London: Routledge, 2004).

Moreover, as Clifton and Harvey argue, the re-conceptions of nature that have arisen over the past two centuries due to industrialization and urbanization have fostered the reassessment and refashioning of paganism itself: 'Trends that underlay phenomena as diverse as the popularity of Romanticism and the creation of wilderness reserves also led to a re-evaluation of the meaning and associations of the word "pagan".'[7] Rather than say that paganism changed due to Romanticism and conservation, Clifton and Harvey astutely propose only that humans' assessments of earth-based spiritualities have changed. The possibility of an imperceptible, fundamental paganism remains unchallenged. Adler similarly notes that contemporary pagans 'sense an aliveness and "presence" in nature ... they tend to view humanity's "advancement" and separation from nature as the prime source of alienation'.[8]

Adler represents nature as a mysterious, living force, an agent operating beyond human control. But she also describes humans as distinct from this force and able to separate themselves from it—whether intentionally or through some sense of superiority. She notes, for example, that most pagan groups have 'grown up in cities, where the loss of enrichment from the natural world is most easily perceived'. Her claim is supported by the loudest voices of late-Victorian and Edwardian neopaganism, in which it was not the rural working class most invested in and engaged with nature that drove the movement, but a variety of urban, middle-class intellectuals and artists such as Crowley, Carpenter, Field, and Benson. As Adler implies, for the past two centuries, much of paganism has been locked into a Romanticist relationship between the individual human and a false ideal called nature, the latter being not a pre-existing earth-rooted force but the result of the bourgeois ego's sense of loss.

In making her point, Adler herself assumes that pagans develop their spiritual conception of reality on the foundational assumption of a coherent self that is rooted in the mind. This ego, then, creates a notion of nature as a separate player in the pagan experience—in fact, relies on such a gesture of alienation to establish its own selfhood. In *Ecology without Nature* (2007), Timothy Morton warns against just such a slippage. Approaching the subject from a nonpagan standpoint, Morton argues that the most effective way to ensure the welfare of all forms of sentient beings is to reject our popular idealization of nature because it assumes a humanist perspective that aestheticizes the ecological and thus offers a false view of reality. He proposes, instead, a model of ecology that is void of nature precisely because the latter has become a 'transcendental principle' tethered to a politics of truth and purity that is not innately inherent to the organic realm.[9] For Morton, if actual environmentalist change is to be achieved, the discussion must adopt a model that does not assume that humans and the environment exist as distinguishable phenomena.

---

[7] Clifton and Harvey, 'Introduction', in *The Paganism Reader*, 3.
[8] Adler, *Drawing down the Moon*, 4.   [9] Morton, *Ecology without Nature*, 12, 5.

While Morton himself works to avoid this, the risk with his model is that 'ecology' simply becomes a hollowed-out signifier that ultimately fulfils the same function as 'nature', with the Romanticist aesthetic replaced by a formulation that appears more objective because of its leaner, meaner design. Clifton and Harvey's sensitivity to the conceptual function of 'nature' in paganism, meanwhile, brings forward the importance of recognizing earth-based spiritualities as offering an ecological model, but one where 'ecology' refers to the mutating imbrications among all animist entities within the environment. In their post-humanist formulation, anthropocentrism is undermined while the ecological is enhanced and reinforced by the spiritual. Nevertheless, in eco-pagan scholarship there tends to remain a slip between the chalice and the lip; while the theorists have articulated the need for a post-Cartesian decentralization of the self within pagan ecology, practising pagans remain keenly sensitive to the difference between, on one hand, their individuated identities as responsible, engaged, and politicized members of modern society and, on the other, their transitory loss of selfhood during a spiritual act or experience.

Contributors to the neopagan movement of the previous century were well aware of this shifting mode of operation within the pagan identity. Humans in a de-individuated state would not be interested or able to theorize their position, it being one which itself questions the notion of the human, let alone the theorist. As Edward Carpenter's scholarly chapters demonstrate, late-Victorian and Edwardian concerns regarding Western society's health and prosperity (two traits often operating in conflict) were likewise recognized as fully enmeshed with neopaganism's attention to the issues of individuality that has proven a stumbling block in recent ecological and eco-pagan scholarship. Carpenter, Field, and Benson all propose variations on how a loss of selfhood might in fact enhance a collective intimacy and sense of mutual responsibility through the entire ecological context.

Edward Carpenter's quiet eye

Carpenter was vividly aware that the period during which he was writing was witnessing the culmination of a century marked by a growing interest in all things pagan. As he light-heartedly summarizes, the 'great boom in Sungods' in the earlier part of the nineteenth century was followed by 'the *phallic* explanation of everything', where 'deities were all polite names for the organs and powers of procreation'. Then came euhemerism, which proposes that deities were simply mythologized people, and finally, the neopagan movement, which 'thinks little of sungods, and pays more attention to Earth and Nature spirits, to gnomes and demons and vegetation-sprites'.[10]

---

[10] Edward Carpenter, *Pagan and Christian Creeds: Their Origin and Meaning* (New York: Harcourt, Brace, 1920), 10, 11.

One might sense flippancy in Carpenter's tone, but he took the subject of pagan spiritualities very seriously, bestowing a degree of validity on all of the approaches he mentions. At the same time, he did not define himself as a pagan, although his socialism, gay activism, rural lifestyle, and studies in theosophy and Eastern mysticism all reflect values found in neopaganism.

The rhetoric of Carpenter's best-known work, *Civilisation, Its Cause and Cure* (1889), explicitly reflects the influence of the home-grown socialism to which he was a key contributor, with its title chapter being first delivered in 1888 as a lecture to the Fabian Society. Carpenter envisions civilization as a disease curable only by having everyone develop a closer affinity with one's natural environment and 'inner nature', resulting in a network of mutual sympathy.[11] Citing John Ruskin, he describes society's sense of unrest as an unhealthy condition that permeates our moral nature, which he contrasts with 'the naive insouciance of the pagan and primitive world'.[12] Carpenter summarizes his position as follows:

> Thus three things, (1) the realization of a new order of Society, in closest touch with Nature, and in which the diseases of class-domination and Parasitism will have finally ceased; (2) the realization of a Science which will no longer be a mere thing of the brain, but a part of Actual Life; and (3) the realization of a Morality which will signalise and express the vital and organic unity of man with his fellows—these three things will become the heralds of a new era of humanity.[13]

It is, moreover, not an exclusively human society that Carpenter recognizes but one that would conceptually include other sentient beings. He commends animals, as well as 'early man', because 'an almost unerring instinct and selective power rules their actions and organization'. For Carpenter, the ideal is the development of humans through the process of civilization to a state free of self-consciousness akin to that experienced by certain animals and peoples, such as various African tribes, indigenous North Americans, and ancient Greeks who took part in 'Dionysiac festivals'. Civilized humans, conversely, can only allow themselves to exist in opposition to their environment; as Carpenter puts it, 'when Alderman Smith plants his villa [in nature], the gods pack up their trunks and depart'.[14]

It is in his chapter on 'Science of the Future' in the same work, however, that Carpenter articulates a neopagan ecology most eloquently. Much like Adler and Restall Orr, he envisions an age when science, 'by direct and the most living contact with Nature in every form, learning to enter into direct personal sense-relationship with every phenomenon and phase', will become 'fully conscious of a vast organization— absolutely perfect and intimately knit from its centre to its utmost circumference... existing inchoate or embryonic in every man, animal, plant, or other creature'. For Carpenter, this state will be characterized by 'patient listening and the quiet eye,

---

[11] Edward Carpenter, *Civilisation, Its Cause and Cure, and Other Essays* (London: George Allen, 1921), 257.
[12] Ibid., 18.   [13] Ibid., 11.   [14] Ibid., 40–1, 43, 44n., 63.

and love and faith', and the 'companionship of the animals and the trees and the stars', 'listening well what they themselves have to say'. In this passage the peculiar image of the eye that can but does not speak creates a conflation of the senses that fragments the traditional image of the coherent subject even as it posits an overarching trans-species universalism that seems calm and coherent.[15]

Published thirty-one years after *Civilisation*, Carpenter's *Pagan and Christian Creeds* (1920) more explicitly affirms the political implications of eco-paganism. Pagan scholar Thom van Dooren has recently argued that 'social, political, legal, and economic changes' are not sufficient to address ecological disparities; citing scholarship in deep ecology, ecofeminism, and Christian environmentalism as examples, he notes a growing awareness of the need for 'a worldview in which our deep kinship with others, both human and nonhuman, is acknowledged and honoured'.[16] The argument reiterates Carpenter's politics of the 'nature of the self' as an ecology of 'universal Equality' that is the 'mystic root-conception of Democracy'. For Carpenter, as for van Dooren, the boundlessness of the self does not mean one should ignore one's responsibility to others. 'The more vividly we feel our organic unity with the whole', he argues, 'the less shall we be able to separate off the local self and enclose it within any definition'.[17] Thus, after the book's exploration of various forms of belief, the final appendix of *Pagan and Christian Creeds* promotes human progress to an ideal, earth-based spirituality. He discourages the cult of individuality (as he had in *Civilisation*) and the self-consciousness that gave rise to religion itself, advocating instead a mental state akin to that of non-human animals, who cannot conceive of themselves as entities separate from their environment. Ultimately, Carpenter urges a creative mental engagement that would draw the individual into a non-humanist, all-inclusive perspective. E. F. Benson and Michael Field each offer distinct speculative renderings of the benefits and losses that such an experience could entail.

The post-human spirit of E. F. Benson's and Michael Field's pagan writing

There is no record of E. F. Benson having belonged to any occult societies,[18] but he would have been well versed in classical paganism from his studies at King's College, Cambridge, knowledge further developed by his participation in aesthetic circles

---

[15] Ibid., 132–3.

[16] Thom van Dooren, 'Dwelling in Sacred Community', in Ly de Angeles, Emma Restall Orr, and Thom van Dooren (eds), *Pagan Visions for a Sustainable Future* (Woodbury, MN: Llewellyn, 2005), 257.

[17] Ibid., 308.

[18] Nicholas Freeman, ' "Nothing of the Wild Wood"? Pan, Paganism and Spiritual Confusion in E.F. Benson's "The Man Who Went Too Far" ', *Literature and Theology* 19/1 (March 2005), 26.

that included individuals such as Oscar Wilde and Alfred Douglas.[19] His short story 'The Man Who Went Too Far' (1912) alone references a number of neopaganism's common tropes—including classical elements such as Pan, indigenous magical entities such as fays and fairies, and the romanticized spiritualization of a bourgeois rural lifestyle. The story also belies a stronger interest in paganism as a philosophical approach to life than records of this secretive author's life can confirm. The beginning of the work, for example, does more than assume a familiarity among his readers with aspects of contemporary paganism, engaging them in a serious ambivalence regarding its influence. 'The little village of St. Faith's', the narrator tells us,

> nestles in a hollow of wooded hill up on the north bank of the river Fawn in the county of Hampshire, huddling close round its grey Norman church as if for spiritual protection against the fays and fairies, the trolls and 'little people', who might be supposed still to linger in the vast empty spaces of the New Forest, and to come after dusk and do their doubtful businesses.[20]

Even in this very first sentence, one notes the narrator's anxious diminution of paganism seen as a threat to a traditional settlement literally defined by Christian faith. The image of an entire village structured, it would appear subconsciously or almost organically, against the influence of pagan forces is more than an effective conceit. At the time that Benson was writing his story, there existed in Britain a variety of pagan-inflected interests ranging from the idealization of a simple, rural lifestyle to a belief that earth-based spiritualities involved interaction with immoral (even satanic) forces beyond human control. Benson's story reflects this range of responses, from one character light-spiritedly mocking 'the smoking altar of vege-tarianism' to the narrator conflating paganism with the occult, and alluding to its immorality through adjectives such as 'monstrous' and 'devious'.[21] One concern regarding paganism's popularity was that a person could be drawn from the innoc-uous end of this range to the more threatening. In the opening image of 'The Man Who Went Too Far', the anxiety around this potential loss of self-control to a mon-strously all-consuming paganism initiates the philosophical conundrum that the story attempts to address.

Benson's hero is an artist named Frank Halton who has given up city life for a bucolic existence among the flowers, bees, and wild animals that exist on the edge of St Faith's. During a few years of living this lifestyle, he becomes—Dorian Gray-like—increasingly beautiful and youthful, much to the admiration of his older

[19] Edward Carpenter, Aleister Crowley, and Katherine Bradley all studied at Cambridge (like Benson), and engaged to varying degrees with same-sex desires. The pattern reflects the sympathetic continuities between gay and neopagan politics at Cambridge during the modernist era, although Benson's same-sex interests are less marked than others'.

[20] E. F. Benson, *Night Terrors: The Ghost Stories of E.F. Benson* (Ware, Herts: Wordsworth, 2012), 121.

[21] Ibid., 125, 122.

friend, Darcy, who comes for a visit from the city. If Dorian was plagued by what his society saw as a sexually inflected deviancy, Frank is depicted as going too far in the other direction, undermining the productivist ethos of modern British society by retiring to an isolated, rural, and idle life characterized by an excessively healthy diet and an intense intimacy with the local fauna. However, if the hero's need of a male servant does not forewarn the reader that Benson is fully aware of the naivety of this lifestyle ideal, Frank's egocentric description of his immersion into nature should make it apparent: 'I am one with it…the river and I, I and the river. The coolness and splash of it is I, and the water-herbs that wave in it are I also. And my strength and my limbs are not mine but the river's. It is all one, all one'. As with Carpenter, the 'paganism' depicted by Benson encourages the dissolution of ego accompanied by a 'great native instinct to be happy without any care at all for morality, or human law or divine law'.[22] This description, meant to celebrate a *loss* of selfhood in favour of a fluid notion of being, however, is ironically marked by the repeated resurfacing of an 'I' unwilling to drown. As with the narrator of Crowley's 'Hymn to Pan', Frank describes himself sometimes as subsumed by the pagan waters, and at other times as himself subsuming them. This vacillation suggests that Benson is not aiming simply to affirm the pagan, but to offer an earnest, somewhat sceptical engagement with the idealization of a universal harmony captured, for example, in Carpenter's 'quiet eye'.

Frank advocates a view of life and death as potential states of absorption into an ecosystem that would liberate one of responsibility, judgement, and grief. But as Darcy points out, his friend fails to recognize that suffering is also part of the ecological realm. Frank is, for example, utterly incapable of dealing with signs of sorrow or pain (when a child falls and begins to cry, the hero plugs his ears and flees in horror). Notably, when Darcy confronts Frank about his conflicted views, the latter proves open to the possibility that his final spiritual revelation at the moment of death may be that of the inevitability of suffering. Thus, when the demigod Pan who has been seducing Frank with his pipes throughout the story comes to him in the night and violently tramples him as he sleeps, the doubting Darcy only hears screams and registers terror on the victim's face. But as Frank gradually dies, his own visage, the narrator tells us, changes to one of blissful calm. The suggestion is that Darcy's cynicism closes him off from a pagan vision of the world and the release from social strictures that it offers; meanwhile, Frank's increasing sacrifice of his ego to the sensually alluring goat-god attains a mystical fulfilment beyond human comprehension and verbal articulation.

Thus, rather than moving to any particular resolution, the narrative builds a sense of panic while at the same time encouraging one to identify with Frank's climactic engagement with his own post-humanist self-dissolution. The story's homoeroticism, meanwhile, reflects the theoretical imbrication of the neopagan

---

[22] Ibid., 124, 133, 128.

movement with a queer vision of identity deconstruction that is also appearing in recent pagan scholarship.[23] The combination of the story's philosophical idealism and its hero's quest for happiness unhindered by 'morality, or human law or divine law' is, as Benson would have recognized, one that also characterized the sexual politics of the time.[24] Queer interests have been buoyed for over a century by paganism's conception of diversity and difference as spiritual sources of power and agency. However, as recent eco-pagan scholars have noted and as Michael Field's poetry demonstrates, one cannot assume that individuals who adapted pagan tropes and values to their queer interests consistently self-identified by gender and sexuality more forcefully than by spirituality.

In the past ten years, a considerable amount of scholarship has appeared on Michael Field (lovers Katherine Bradley and Edith Cooper) and their use of Greco-Roman paganism to celebrate lesbian desire, same-sex eroticism, and the fluidity of sexuality in general.[25] Their poetic engagement with classical motifs often spiritualizes the non-normative desires and affections to which they allude, thereby seemingly cleansing them of the perceived taint of carnal deviancy. As Yopie Prins, Marion Thain, and others have demonstrated, for those readers with the knowledge to translate the pagan references from a sexual standpoint, Field's poetry offers a reimagining of the age as one in which sensuality and sexuality need not be articulated through homophobic signifying structures. Likewise, reading the correlation in the other direction, the erotic explorations and queer affirmations of Field's verse support an understanding of their work as a sincere, spiritual engagement with the pagan politics of identity dissipation. Foreshadowing recent eco-pagan efforts to decentre the individual perspective in ecological engagements, the decision to represent themselves as a single force named Michael Field reflects a vision of identity as a shared, transmutational space.

The poets made a concerted effort to clarify that their 1892 collection, *Sight and Song*, is not merely a series of responses to famous paintings. Rather, it is an attempt, they explain in the preface, 'to express not so much what these pictures are to the poet, but rather what poetry they objectively incarnate'.[26] Like the hero of Benson's

---

[23] Recent discussions on the relationship of paganism to non-normative sexualities can be found in Adler's 'Radical Faeries and the Growth of Men's Spirituality', in *Drawing down the Moon*, 338–48. See also Haraway's discussion of 'a post-gender world' in *Simians, Cyborgs, and Women*, 150; and Marina Sala's 'Towards a Sacred Dance of the Sexes', in de Angeles, Orr, and van Dooren (eds), *Pagan Visions for a Sustainable Future*, 97–120.

[24] Benson, *Night Terrors*, 128. In Chapter 1 for this collection, Marcus Waithe notes that Edward Carpenter situated his homosexual vision primarily within classical and Renaissance paradigms.

[25] See, for example, the third chapter of Matthew Potolsky's *The Decadent Republic of Letters: Taste, Politics, and Cosmopolitan Community from Baudelaire to Beardsley* (Philadelphia, PA: University of Pennsylvania Press, 2012); Yopie Prins's *Victorian Sappho* (Princeton, NJ: Princeton University Press, 1999); Margaret D. Stetz and Cheryl A. Wilson's (eds), *Michael Field and Their World* (High Wycombe: Rivendale, 2007); and Marion Thain's *Michael Field: Poetry, Aestheticism and the Fin de Siècle* (Cambridge: Cambridge University Press, 2007).

[26] Michael Field, *Sight and Song* (London: Elkin Mathews and John Lane, 1892), p. v.

story, the women give themselves up to a form of other-worldly communication, an act of mediation that is also a participation in sympathetic conversations begun centuries earlier. Their artistic process, the poets explain, involves the erasure of human influence in an effort to attain 'sight as pure as the gazer can refine it', with the poets subordinating their own agency to 'what the lines and colours of certain chosen pictures sing in themselves'.

As the poetry suggests, this chain of correspondences extends beyond art forms to include the sensual discourse of pagan spirituality. Rather than create poetic renderings of visual renderings of a spiritual ecology, the poets give themselves up to the affective experience of the paintings' engagements with classical paganism. 'The effort to see things from their own centre', Field declares, 'by suppressing the habitual centralization of the visible in ourselves, is a process by which we eliminate our idiosyncrasies and obtain an impression clearer, less passive, more intimate'.[27] While the poets inevitably do leave their mark on their creative work, Field's emphasis is nevertheless on the act of decentring the self, giving up the ego to an immeasurable, transhistorical engagement which results in an enhanced intimacy.

The poems in *Sight and Song* emphasize pagan deities and Christian saints, particularly female ones, reflecting Field's interest in the relationship between women's power and their sensuality. The context for the vast majority of the poems' scenes, meanwhile, is the natural environment, which Field often portrays as a persona itself. The central characters in poems such as 'Correggio's *Saint Sebastian*', 'Giorgione's *Shepherd Boy*', and 'Piero di Cosimo's *Death of Procris*' are not simply positioned within a natural environment but portrayed as themselves part of the ecosystem. Most obviously, various poems include representations of fauns and angels in which the human and non-human are fused together. These hooved or winged inter-species figures generally function as symbolic reinforcements of the main subjects' own eco-pagan character. In poems such as 'Correggio's *Antiope*' and 'Botticelli's *Birth of Venus*' Field pushes the conflation further. Unlike Crowley's and Benson's depictions of pagan self-dissolution as violent and horrifying, Field's poems rewrite myth in order to foreground an erotic release of the self to an amorous pagan ecology.

In response to Correggio's painting *Antiope* (c.1528), Field sandwiches the glowing nude Amazon between a sleeping cupid and a satyr, offering a polytheistic rendering of Antiope's sensual spirituality. Following the traditional myth, 'Correggio's *Antiope*' notes that the satyr is actually Zeus (or Jupiter) in disguise who, enamoured by the hunter, is about to rape her. The god's deviousness imbues paganism with a note of cruel deception, but Field offers a unique contribution to the myth that undermines a correlation of paganism purely with characters who, like Zeus here, enact heteronormative power paradigms. The poem focuses almost entirely

---

[27] Ibid., v, vi.

on the figure of the sleeping Antiope, with Zeus appearing only towards the end and doing little more than allowing the reader a fresh vantage point to continue consuming the heroine's beauty. Throughout the piece, however, the Amazon is portrayed as entwined with the natural environment. As she 'cuddles on the lap of earth', next to her lies 'her woodland armory', a reference to the 'doe-skin' quiver of arrows in Correggio's painting, but also more subtly to the trees in which she is bowered; she lies

> curled beyond the rim
> of oaks that slide
> Their lowest branches, long and slim,
> Close to her side;
> Their foliage touches her with lobes
> half-gay, half-shadowed, green and brown.

'The supineness of her sleep', we are told, is 'Leaf-fringed and deep', the environment itself becoming an erotic agent, sliding its limbs along her body, caressing her with its leaves.[28] Thus, to Zeus's false and violent disguise, Field offers a pagan counter in the female warrior sensually engaged with the animate ecology itself.

A similar personification of the eco-pagan can be found in the poem 'Botticelli's Birth of Venus'. Botticelli's 1486 painting *The Birth of Venus* on which Field's piece is based has been interpreted as rendering the Neoplatonic notion that the admiration of physical beauty functions as an avenue to comprehending spiritual beauty. But Field opens the poem not with the tantalizing central figure but with a description of wavelets, a shell, roses, birds, then garments, a breeze, locks of hair on the wind, and only then, at the end of the first stanza, 'a girl' (13). Having just been born from the water's depths, Venus is portrayed less as a goddess than as an innocent, frail human with a 'chill, wan body' needing protection from the 'crisp air'. Botticelli's painting captures this moment of Venus's self-realization but, as Field describes, even as it is introduced the individual is already being enwrapped again within the ecosystem, as Flora's 'rose' cloak covered in flowers encompasses her cold flesh. Rather than confirming a Neoplatonic ideal, the poem dallies on the earthly elements in the artwork, eventually revealing the goddess in a fragile state of selfhood only to submerge her again, in the remaining three stanzas of the poem, among the natural elements and the pagan deities Flora, Zephyrus, and Boreas. Field ensures that the human figure is utterly, sensually human, rather than a deity controlling her surroundings. Or, more precisely, Venus is a sentient point of convergence among ecological elements that recognize no separation between the physical and the spiritual.

---

[28] Ibid., 16–18.

Conclusion

Timothy Morton has recently suggested that, to ensure the welfare of all sentient beings, we must first reject the idealization of the natural because this humanist aestheticization of the ecological creates a dysfunctional notion of reality. Meanwhile, eco-pagan theorists such as Chas Clifton and Graham Harvey have proposed that it is impossible to eradicate the spiritual from the ecological, but that an *awareness* of one's veneration of nature can help ensure a desired fluctuation between one's submergence into the eco-pagan, on the one hand, and one's responsible awareness of the mutual influences of all elements of the ecology in which humans exist, on the other.

Similarly, diverse contributors to the neopagan movement depicted a pagan spirituality capable of undermining anthropocentrism while enhancing a responsible contribution to the ecological network—what Edward Carpenter describes as an 'intimately knit' organization engaged to the core of all living entities (*Civilisation*, 132–3). While E. F. Benson acknowledges his own inability to be certain of the outcome of sacrificing one's selfhood to such an order, Aleister Crowley's 'Hymn to Pan' confidently celebrates submission to what he represents as a form of chaos. Field, meanwhile, depicts gods and martyrs as sentient entities characterized by their fragility, intimacy, and mutual reliance on the rest of the natural environment. Carpenter, Benson, Crowley, and Field are unified, however, in not using paganism to escape their society's anthropocentrism and hypocrisy, but to confront it. In *Pagan and Christian Creeds*, Carpenter proposes that one's comprehension of the ego as shaped by and part of a larger ecological network fosters a sense of anxiety, which spurs the imaginative conception of a state of consciousness that 'we here and there perceive in the rites and prophecies and mysteries of the early religions, and in the poetry and art and literature generally of the later civilizations' (16). As the creative engagements of Benson, Crowley, and Field suggest, the neopagan movement was not simply an engagement with ancient belief systems that seemed frighteningly overwhelming. Rather, presaging post-humanism, it was a response to the industrial, materialist, and homogenizing capitalism that was threatening to be all-consuming and de-individuating.

FURTHER READING

de Angeles, Ly, Emma Restall Orr, and Thom van Dooren (eds). *Pagan Visions for a Sustainable Future* (Woodbury, MN: Llewellyn, 2005).

Denisoff, Dennis. 'The Dissipating Nature of Decadent Paganism from Pater to Yeats', *Modernism/Modernity* 15/3 (2008), 431–46.

Harvey, Graham. *Contemporary Paganism: Religions of the Earth from Druids and Witches to Heathens and Ecofeminists,* 2nd edn. (New York: New York University Press, 2011).

Merivale, Patricia. *Pan the Goat-God: His Myth in Modern Times* (Cambridge, MA: Harvard University Press, 1969).

Morton, Timothy. *Ecology without Nature: Rethinking Environmental Aesthetics* (Cambridge, MA: Harvard University Press, 2007).

Orr, Emma Restall. *Living with Honour: A Pagan Ethics* (Ropley, Hants: John Hunt, 2007).

Taylor, Bron. *Dark Green Religion: Nature, Spirituality, and the Planetary Future* (Berkeley, CA: University of California Press, 2010).

CHAPTER 23

THEATRE AND THE SCIENCES OF MIND

TIFFANY WATT SMITH

As the nineteenth century slid into its twilight years, a clutch of writers—Max Nordau and H. G. Wells among them—expressed a fear that human culture was calcifying. The theory of degeneration held that the optimistic energy that had shaped the Victorian age was giving way to inertia and parasitism. Against this gloomy backdrop, it is perhaps a surprise to find the psychologists of the 1890s portraying themselves as energetic modernizers. Leaving behind the ad hoc experiments and self-observations of Victorian alienists and philosophers of mind, the new psychologists preached empiricism. 'In its strictest sense' wrote F. W. H. Myers in 1886, experimental psychology should 'attack the great problems of our mind not by metaphysical argument…but by a study, as detailed and exact as any other natural science'.[1] Professional societies were formed, such as the Psychological Society in 1901, and periodicals founded. Most significantly of all, between 1897 and 1903, the first laboratories—those emblems of scientific inquiry—were set up at the Universities of Cambridge and London, equipped with precision instruments for measuring the body's fleeting responses to sensory stimuli.[2]

If the *fin de siècle* may best be characterized as 'an epoch of endings and beginnings', this ambivalence is nowhere clearer than in the sciences of mind, preoccupied as they were with both a fear of entropy and the forward momentum required to consolidate and institutionalize a modern scientific discipline.[3] Nonetheless, it would be a mistake to conclude that the period's mental sciences broke entirely with the past or were bound by consensus. As Jenny Bourne Taylor reminds us, scientific

[1] W. H. Myers, 'Human Personality in the Light of Hypnotic Suggestion', *Proceedings of the Society of Psychical Research* 4 (1886–7), 1.

[2] See Alan Collins, 'England', in David B. Baker (ed.), *The Oxford Handbook of the History of Psychology: Global Perspectives* (Oxford: Oxford University Press, 2012), 188–91.

[3] Sally Ledger and Roger Luckhurst, 'Introduction', in Ledger and Luckhurst (eds), *The Fin de Siècle. A Reader in Cultural History, 1880–1900* (Oxford: Oxford University Press, 2000), xiii.

psychology remained 'a broad and flexible field' and, according to Roger Luckhurst, much of the 'expert knowledge' of the late nineteenth-century mental sciences had, in fact, an 'uncertain provenance'.[4] Certainly, new codified experimental procedures and technologies allowed certain categories of psychophysical knowledge such as attention or optics to prosper. But in the folds and fissures created as a new generation groped their way with recently invented machines, fell back on old approaches, and turned to amateurs and artists for insights, other ways of thinking about the human mind flourished.

One area of investigation that thrived in this messier context was that of motor mimicry—our compulsion to echo one another's gestures, sway in time with a crowd, and catch yawns. In the past twenty years, since the discovery of 'mirror neurons' in the early 1990s, involuntary imitation has again become important for psychologists, raising complex philosophical questions about the limits of individual agency and asking us to reconsider the nature of the self. However, such questions have a long and often unacknowledged history, their roots in the final decades of the nineteenth century. On the one hand, psychologists of the *fin de siècle* argued that compulsive imitation could explain the creation of societies, the acquisition of language, even the paradigmatic human virtue of sympathy. On the other hand, anxieties about degeneration were never far from talk of mimicry. Understood to burst forth from the deepest recesses of the primitive mind, the mimic instinct was deemed particularly forceful among non-Europeans, the uneducated, and the insane. It was blamed for fuelling virulent mob behaviour in the lower classes, and outbreaks of voguish opinions and fashionable attire among the effete. The coexistence of these conflicting attitudes towards the echoing body—it was both efficacious and dangerous—exemplify the ambivalence and doubled perspectives that cultural historians have found so distinctive of the *fin de siècle*.[5]

Attempts made by late nineteenth-century psychologists to understand and explain mimicry also reveal how indebted the new sciences of mind were to their wider cultural and artistic contexts. Theatre, one of the clearest cultural manifestations of the copying instinct, was also a vital experimental resource. Unlike a widened pupil or raised heartbeat, an outbreak of contagious giggling was not readily available for measurement in a laboratory. Instead, psychologists of the *fin de siècle* continued a tradition begun decades earlier, and enlisted the help of actors. Venturing forth from their new laboratories, scientists such as Theodore Ribot, Salomon Stricker, and James Sully visited music halls to conduct self-observations, monitored the behaviour of audiences at circuses, and drew on descriptions of

---

[4] Jenny Bourne Taylor, 'Psychology at the fin de siècle', in Gail Marshall (ed.), *The Cambridge Companion to the Fin de Siècle* (Cambridge: Cambridge University Press, 2007), 18; Roger Luckhurst, *The Invention of Telepathy, 1870–1901* (Oxford: Oxford University Press, 2002), 21.

[5] Ledger and Luckhurst, 'Introduction', xiii.

untrustworthy actors-turned-experimenters who pulled sorrowful faces at babies in nurseries to elicit imitative responses. Such experimental strategies may be approached, to draw on Gilles Deleuze and Félix Guattari's term, as 'assemblages', techniques through which discursive and material practices intersect.[6] While theatrical practices shaped scientific knowledge about involuntary imitation, theatrical examples and metaphors littered psychological writing on the topic, providing a conceptual framework within which psychologists could grapple with the unnerving implications of their theories. Theatre thus emerges in the *fin de siècle*'s sciences of mind as both a way of *doing*—an experimental resource—and a way of *thinking*—a conceptual one. Moreover, it was both a solution and a problem; for to imagine a world populated by mimics was to face the queasy prospect that we all might be unmasked as impostors and fakes.

Human 'copying machines'

In 1863 Charles Darwin, lamenting the pesky tendency of butterflies to look one moment like a predator, the next like a dead leaf, asked, 'Why to the perplexity of naturalists has nature condescended to the tricks of the stage?'.[7] But nature had stooped to theatrical tricks in humans too. By the 1860s, our compulsion to echo one another's gestures and facial expressions was becoming a key topic of psychological scrutiny, and cherished notions of authenticity, agency, and resilience began to falter.

The Victorians' interest in human mimicry can be traced back to phrenology, an early nineteenth-century science of mind which divined personality traits by feeling the ridges and lumps of a person's skull. According to its founder, Franz Joseph Gall, alongside faculties of mirthfulness and intuition, there resided in the anterior superior part of the brain an 'organ of imitation'. Gall confirmed its existence on examining the head of a thief in a Berlin prison. Announcing 'if this man had ever been near a theatre he would, in all probability, have turned actor', the astonished prisoner retorted that his crime was having 'personated a police officer to extort money'.[8] Leading German thespians Müler, Lange, and Brockmann were found to have the requisite lumps, as were Shakespeare, Garrick, and Molière whose heads Gall studied from portraits.[9] Yet, while actors were an invaluable resource for Gall, their talent for impersonation left him uneasy. On the one hand, imitation was

---

[6] Gilles Deleuze and Félix Guattari, *A Thousand Plateaus: Capitalism and Schizophrenia*, trans. Brian Massumi (London: Continuum, 2004), 504.

[7] Charles Darwin, '[Review of] Contributions to an insect fauna of the Amazon Valley by Henry Walter Bates', *Natural History Review* 3 (April 1863), 221.

[8] Recounted in Johann Caspar Spurzheim, *Phrenology: in connection with the study of physiognomy* (London: Treuttel, Wurtz and Richter, 1826), 27.

[9] Franz Josef Gall, *On the Functions of the Brain and of Each of its Parts*, trans. Winslow Lewis, 6 vols (Boston, MA: Marsh, 1835), V, 201–6.

deemed essential to the 'merry, witty or gay character' (the organ was conspicuously shrivelled among the gloomy or melancholic). On the other, those with an excessively engorged imitative organ were not to be trusted. As Gall's disciple Johann Caspar Spurzheim warned one schoolgirl, she should 'be guarded, or her imitation would be inconvenient to her'.[10]

By the 1830s phrenology had been discredited in scientific circles, but its ambivalence towards imitation lingered. In the following decades, alienists and mental philosophers such as William Carpenter and Herbert Spencer viewed imitation as an unruly, primitive instinct, which burst forth from the deepest recesses of the mind among those whose defences were congenitally or temporarily weakened. For this reason, it was assumed to be particularly pronounced among non-Europeans, the lower classes, and the insane, groups deemed least in control of their bodies. To mark them out as mimics was to taint them with theatricality, rendering their emotions mere burlesques. The theatricality of these compulsive copiers was underscored by the spectacular experiments in which men of science encountered them. For example, among the women diagnosed with hysteria and treated by the mesmerist John Elliotson at London's University College Hospital was the Irish domestic servant Elizabeth O'Key. In dramatic demonstrations, in which O'Key bore strong resemblance to a music hall comedienne with her call-and-response and sudden transformations in character, she astonished audiences of experts by impersonating—while in a trance and blindfolded—every movement Elliot made on stage (a phenomenon the mesmerists called 'traction').[11]

If asylum patients could be seized by fits of compulsive copying in dramatic asylum displays, primitive mimicry was frequently called forth in experiments on the 'lower races' too. Darwin reported that the 'savages', as he called them, of Tierra del Fuego were 'excellent mimics'. Already primed to associate non-Europeans with overt theatricality—not least because of the derogatory representations by blackface mimics in music halls—Darwin readily compared the tribesmen to actors: in their ceremonial dress, they 'resembled the representations of Devils on the Stage'.[12] An ad hoc experiment underscored their ludicrous theatricality: 'as often as we coughed or yawned, or made any odd motion [the indigenous people] immediately imitated us', wrote Darwin, confessing even that 'some of our party began to squint and look awry'.[13] By conflating them with theatricalized imitators, Victorian men of science emphasized the exotic alterity of non-Europeans, their inherent deviousness, and the apparently unstable nature of their minds.

---

[10] Spurzheim, *Phrenology*, 143, 116.

[11] See Alison Winter, *Mesmerized: Powers of Mind in Victorian Britain* (Chicago, IL: University of Chicago Press, 1998), 72–4.

[12] For the representation of race in Victorian theatre, see Hazel Water, *Racism on the Victorian Stage: Representation of Slavery and the Black Character* (Cambridge: Cambridge University Press, 2009).

[13] Darwin, *Narrative of the Surveying Voyages of his Majesty's Ships Adventure and Beagle between the years 1826 and 1836* (London: Henry Colburn, 1839), 228–9.

It has become a point of consensus among scholars of the Victorian period that the theatricality of such representations served to estrange mad, bad women and primitives even further. But what should we make of the fact that European men of science performed too? After all, Elliotson struck poses on stage; Darwin and the crew pulled faces. As had the phrenologists before them, mid-century scientists of mind enlisted theatrical resources to conduct their experiments on mimicry. This should come as no surprise, for the values and epistemologies of science and theatre in the Victorian period were not as distant as they may seem for us today. As Bernard Lightman, Jane Goodall, Iwan Morus, and others have argued, this was a period when the worlds of science and theatre were closely entwined: museums carried out anatomical investigations on dead circus attractions; experimenters devised ever-more elaborate technologies to astonish audiences in popular science shows.[14] However, it is important to recognize that, while they did condescend to theatrical tricks, these experimenters also staged a vital distinction between two types of performance. Contrasting the knowing imposture of the men of science and the mechanical imitations of those they studied, their experiments reminded onlookers that being able to switch the mimic impulse on and off was the mark of both a strong inhibitory reflex and iron self-control.[15] As James Paget warned in 1875, anyone might succumb to the submerged instinct to copy; only those with sufficient will to make a 'conscious effort' to resist it were immune.[16]

This view lingered for much of the century. As George Romanes put it in 1883, it was among the 'feeble-minded', the 'lower races', and children that a 'tendency to undue imitation is a very constant peculiarity'.[17] In Max Nordau's *Degeneration*, first translated into English in 1895, not only did degenerate aesthetes appear as if performing 'in a masked festival, where all are in disguises'; one of the symptoms of the illness was an 'irresistible passion for imitation... When he sees a picture, he wants to become like it in attitude and dress; when he reads a book, he adopts its views blindly'.[18] Yet, degeneration theory was not universally accepted, and by the 1870s there was a growing tendency to cast mimicry in a more positive light. While imitation was conventionally relegated to the 'lower races', Walter Bagehot put it at the centre of European experience, claiming that the 'innate tendency of the human mind to become like what is around it' generated national characteristics and in turn, the patriotic feelings on which the empire depended.[19] And though it was conventionally associated with a lack of genuine emotion, by the 1890s scientists of mind were turning to muscle mimicry to explain the virtue of sympathy. Recalling the theories of the

---

[14] See Jane Goodall, *Performance and Evolution in the Age of Darwin: Out of the Natural Order* (London: Routledge, 2002); Iwan Rhys Morus, 'Placing Performance', *Isis* 101 (2010); and Bernard Lightman, *Victorian Popularizers of Science* (Chicago, IL and London: University of Chicago Press, 2007).

[15] For the inhibitive reflex, see Roger Smith, *Inhibition* (London: Free Association Books, 1992).

[16] James Paget, 'Nervous Mimicry', in Paget, *Clinical Lectures and Essays* (London: Longman, 1875), 218.

[17] George John Romanes, *Mental Evolution in Animals* (London: Kegan, 1883), 225.

[18] Max Nordau, *Degeneration* (New York: Appleton, 1895), 9, 26.

[19] Walter Bagehot, *Physics and Politics* (London: King, 1872), 452.

eighteenth-century moralist Adam Smith, William Baldwin argued in 1895 that since 'the sight of the expression of emotion in another stimulates similar attitudes directly in us', imitation lies at the heart of our capacity for altruistic acts.[20]

By the 1890s, imitation was enjoying a new status, invoked to explain a range of cultivated behaviours, from aesthetic responses to the learning of manners. But this did not mean it was cleansed of its unnerving theatricality. When in 1893 T. H. Huxley announced humans to be 'the most consummate of all mimics in the animal world', he compared humans to 'emotional chameleons', recalling the primitivism of earlier debates.[21] Absorbing the emotions of others might generate altruistic feelings—the most human of virtues—but it also brought those who felt the pain of others close to the condition of exotic, shape-shifting lizards. And if mimicry allowed societies to flourish—according to Gabriel Tarde, society was in essence 'a group of beings who are apt to imitate each other'—it left its members vulnerable to the suggestions of malign influences, as if caught in a hypnotic reverie.[22] Whether an innate instinct or learned habit (psychologists remained divided on this issue), motor mimicry was both essential for 'civilized' life and a source of lingering suspicion. And it was through psychology's entanglements with theatre that this ambivalence continued to find its expression.

Thinking and experimenting with theatre at the *fin de siècle*

As Iwan Morus has argued, the proximity of scientific experiments and theatrical spectacles in the nineteenth century invites us to pay further attention to the role of performance in the 'process of constructing Victorian science'.[23] It is hard to miss the parts played by actors in the experiments that shaped changing understandings of the mimic body in this period. One might expect, however, that as psychology became increasingly empirical towards the end of the century, turning its attention to measurable physiological effects, its ties with theatre would loosen. In fact, the opposite seems to be true. Both Martin Willis and Roger Luckhurst have recently unearthed professional collaborations between *fin-de-siècle* psychologists and stage mediums, evidence that, at the turn of the century, the conduits between science and theatre, though not always obvious, remained open.[24]

[20] J. M. Baldwin, *Mental Development in the Child and the Race* (New York: Macmillan, 1895), 334.

[21] T. H. Huxley, *Evolution and Ethics*, ed. Michael Ruse (Princeton, NJ: Princeton University Press, 1989), 86.

[22] Gabriel Tarde, *The Laws of Imitation*, trans. Elsie Parsons (1890; repr. New York: Holt, 1903), 68.

[23] Morus, ' "More the Aspect of Magic than Anything Natural": The Philosophy of Demonstration', in Aileen Fyfe and Bernard Lightman (eds), *Science in the Marketplace: Nineteenth Century Sites and Experiences* (Chicago, IL and London: University of Chicago Press, 2007), 337.

[24] See Luckhurst, *The Invention of Telepathy*, and Martin Willis, *Vision, Science and Literature, 1870–1920: Ocular Horizons* (London: Pickering and Chatto, 2011).

In each of the four contexts in which the imitative instinct was investigated, theatre's presence lies in plain sight. According to Karl Groos, an early exponent of developmental psychology, children were 'small dramatist[s]', their ability to embody inanimate objects during their games comparable to the performances of 'the labourers in *Midsummer Night's Dream*, who were ready to take the part of the Wall or the Moon'.[25] In the asylum, 'echokinesia' was common among hysterical patients who mimicked the tics and contracted limbs of fellow patients. Thus, the neurologists Henry Meige and Eugene Feindel compared a patient—known as 'O'—to a circus performer: he had developed a 'veritable debauchery of absurd gesticulations, a wild muscular carnival'.[26]

Central to scientific debates on aesthetics in the 1890s was the idea of *innere Nachahmung* or 'inner mimicry'. In a series of experiments, the British novelist and psychologist Vernon Lee observed the 'mimetic acts and kinaesthetic disturbances' which arose as the artist Kit Anstruther-Thomson contemplated artworks, her weight shifting from side to side 'in order to follow [the] balance' of classical sculptures.[27] Lee used the verb 'to mime' to describe such visceral responses; among continental psychologists this phenomenon was dubbed *Einfühlung*, later rendered into English as 'empathy'.[28] Finally, imitation informed new theories of the group mind. According to the French psychologist Gustave Le Bon, theatres, already emotionally volatile spaces, enabled the virulent spread of dangerous passions through imitation. In one case, a stage doorman had to restrain a mob from attacking the actor who had portrayed the villain, so suggestible had it become.[29] By the end of the First World War, involuntary mimicry was regarded to be so widespread that the British psychologist Wilfred Trotter could compare society itself to a kind of theatrical performance. Anything drawing attention to one's difference from the group was felt in the tremors of 'shyness and stage fright'.[30]

What should we make of these references to tiny dramatists, clowns, and carnivals, to mimes, audiences, and stage fright? Since theatre may be the most conspicuous expression of the imitation instinct, it is unsurprising that psychologists were drawn to the stage for their examples and metaphors. It is certainly worth noting the way specific theatrical references shored up existing hierarchies of mental life. As Kirsten Shepherd-Barr and Sos Eltis remind us (Chapter 8 in this volume),

[25] Karl Groos, *The Play of Man*, trans. Elizabeth L. Baldwin (New York: Appleton, 1901), 301.

[26] Henry Meige and Eugene Clement Louis Feindel, *Tics and Their Treatment*, trans. S. A. K. Wilson (London, Sidney Appleton, 1907), 62.

[27] Vernon Lee and C. Anstruther-Thomson, 'Beauty and Ugliness' (1897), in Lee and Anstruther-Thomson (eds), *Beauty and Ugliness and Other Studies in Psychological Aesthetics* (London: John Lane, 1912), 119.

[28] For Lee's experiments and *Einfühlung*, see Carolyn Burdett, '"The subjective inside us can turn into the objective outside": Vernon Lee's Psychological Aesthetics', *19: Interdisciplinary Studies in the Long Nineteenth Century* 12 (Spring 2011).

[29] Gustave Le Bon, *The Crowd: A Study of the Popular Mind* (New York: Macmillan, 1896), 57.

[30] Wilfred Trotter, *Instincts of the Herd in Peace and War* (London: Fisher, 1919), 33.

theatrical culture in the last decades of the nineteenth century was diverse and versatile, though broadly speaking, melodramas, music halls, and circuses attracted working-class audiences, while the New Drama, influenced by European naturalism, held the educated middle classes in its sway. Thus, the comparison of mimicking children to Shakespeare's manual labourers-turned-amateur-actors reinforced the idea that the working classes lacked self-control. And by comparing 'O's tics to a carnival show, Meige and Feindel rendered his illness a caricature, unworthy of serious—or sympathetic—attention. By contrast, when Trotter suggested that those who did not automatically blend in with their surroundings experienced stage fright, he was invoking an anti-theatrical rhetoric familiar from the exponents of the New Drama. The apotheosis of the naturalistic style was an actress so absorbed in the depths of her genuine emotion that when the house lights came up and the audience applauded, she recoiled in horror at the realization that she was acting *for* anyone at all.[31] When compulsive imitation was yoked to theatricality, it was to the popular stage that psychologists most readily turned.

Yet we ought not to embrace these equations too firmly. It is certainly unsurprising that late nineteenth-century psychologists located compulsive imitation in the period's 'othered' bodies and minds. It is less expected that by the 1880s and 1890s, they also discovered it in themselves. The French psychologist Theodore Ribot, for example, joined audiences gathered in the street to watch a tightrope walker, describing 'imitating the movements of a rope-walker while watching him' and, ominously, of 'feeling a shock in one's legs when one sees a man falling'.[32] Vernon Lee regretted the fact that while Anstruther-Thomson enjoyed powerful 'mimetic acts and kinaesthetic disturbances', her own were rather milder.[33] One cannot help wondering whether, when British psychologist James Sully noticed the contagious giggles of 'yokels laughing at a clown', he also succumbed.[34] Or whether the German Hermann Lotze, who saw that crowds gathered around a pub billiards table moved their arms when a shot was taken, felt his own body will the ball forward too.[35]

In the early 1880s, the Austrian Salomon Stricker made the psychologist's immersion in these theatricalized encounters explicit by conducting a curious self-experiment in a music hall. Self-experimentation was a codified practice in German psychophysical laboratories of the second half of the nineteenth century, where psychologists received training to observe their own sensations and

---

[31] See Tiffany Watt Smith, 'Henry Head and the Theatre of Reverie', *19: Interdisciplinary Studies in the Long Nineteenth Century* 12 (2011).

[32] Théodule Armand Ribot, *The Psychology of the Emotions* (London: Scott, 1897), 232.

[33] Lee and Anstruther-Thomson, 'The Beauty Inside Us', 356.

[34] James Sully, *An Essay on Laughter* (London: Longman, 1902), 255.

[35] Lotze's example is quoted in James Sully, *The Human Mind, A Text-Book of Psychology*, 2 vols (London: Longman, 1892), II, 219.

responses (the practice was later adopted in Britain and America too).[36] 'I went to the theatre to see the gymnasts' wrote Stricker, 'and first watched one using a springboard'. Stricker described his visceral responses to the springing athlete as an 'inner mimicry': 'At the moment when he leaped...I had a distinct sensation in my chest, and the feeling, too, of motion in the muscles of my eyes.'[37] It was not simply that Stricker had entered a theatrical environment to observe its audiences: he deliberately, self-consciously monitored his own imitative responses as a participant in the event.

There are two conclusions to be drawn from these self-experiments. First, the psychologists' fascination with their own mimetic responses—even wishing, as did Vernon Lee, that they were stronger—marks an important transition in the fortunes of the imitative instinct: its migration, in the minds of those who studied it, from the margins of human experience to its centre. Second, it is clear that theatre was more than a casual metaphor used in psychological writing. Even as psychology was hardening into a modern scientific discipline, entering theatrical environments and staging theatrical encounters remained an important part of the experimental endeavour. Perhaps this fact is even more striking when we remember that among those who wrote and thought about theatre, the imposture and artifice of the stage were increasingly under attack. 'We are an age of method, of experimental science', wrote the playwright Émile Zola in his December 1878 manifesto 'Le Naturalisme au Théâtre', continuing that 'abstract characters' should be replaced by characters 'whose muscles and brain function as in nature'.[38] As dramatists turned to science, and scientists to theatre, the compulsion to imitate, newly framed as a universal compulsion, remained a source of nervousness for both, stained by its long association with fakes and frauds, counterfeits and concealments.

Theatre, failure, and suspicion in James Sully's *Studies of Childhood* (1895)

From chronoscopes to cine-cameras, the technologies of late nineteenth-century psychological laboratories were not only tools making hitherto unseen aspects of human experience available for scrutiny. They were also metaphors, ways of processing the period's changing conceptions of the human subject (in 1890, for

[36] See Kenton Kroker, 'The Progress of Introspection in America, 1896-1938', *Studies in History and Philosophy of Biomedical Sciences* 34 (2003).
[37] Salomen Stricker, *Studien über die Bewegungsvorstellungen* (Vienna: Braumüller, 1882), quoted and trans. in Groos, *The Play of Man*, 81.
[38] Zola reprinted it in *Le Roman expérimental* (Paris: G. Charpentier: 1880). For a full translation, see Eric Bentley, *The Theory of the Modern Stage: An Introduction to Modern Theatre and Drama* (Harmondsworth: Penguin, 1976), 363.

example, Tarde described the formation of the self as an 'inter-psychical photography').[39] For those who studied human mimicry, theatre was an important resource. Yet, in contrast to Tarde's confident metaphor, when the idiom of theatricality appeared in psychological writing, it was with some hesitation. This discomfort around theatre and its guilty charades is valuable for historians. It points up how theatre worked as both a resource and a problem for late nineteenth-century psychologists, both an experimental technique and the harbinger of profoundly uncomfortable questions about how a person compelled to imitate his or her surroundings might be capable of maintaining a stable, authentic self.

James Sully's pioneering work of developmental psychology, *Studies of Childhood* (1896), gives a striking example of this split perspective. As both Jenny Bourne Taylor and Sally Shuttleworth have described, Sully embodied many of the contradictions of the late nineteenth-century sciences of mind.[40] Having immersed himself in the techniques of German psychophysical laboratories, Sully played a key role in consolidating psychology as a university discipline in Britain in the 1890s, founding its first major laboratory at University College London in 1898. Yet he was also known for his contributions to the era's lively periodical culture, and his writing on music, literature, and drama. It was at the convergence of these artistic and scientific interests that Sully's work on child psychology took shape.

In 1893, Sully published an appeal in the journal *Mind* asking parents and teachers to supply him with information about the children in their care.[41] Under the heading 'sympathy and affectation', Sully received numerous anecdotes about children imitating their parents and siblings, acts that Sully described in *Studies of Childhood* as attempts at 'sympathetic apprehension'.[42] One child 'on finding that her mother's head ached... began imitatively to make-believe that her own head was hurt'. Another traced imaginary tears down her cheeks with her fingers upon seeing her sister weep. A further source was a 'curious document... a sort of diary kept by a father' chronicling 'the early doings and sayings of his boy'. Sully recognized the document did 'not always come up to the requirements of a rigidly scientific standard', but eagerly recounted a test performed by the boy's father.[43] The 'father pretended to cry', wrote Sully, thereupon the boy 'bent his head down so that his chin touched his breast and began to paw his father's face'. 'The experiment was repeated', wrote Sully, 'and always with a like result'. The language is surprising: what Sully quite plainly calls an 'experiment' also stages a theatrical relationship between

---

[39] Tarde, *Laws of Imitation*, 77.

[40] Taylor, 'Psychology at the fin de siècle', 24; Sally Shuttleworth, *The Mind of the Child: Child Development in Literature, Science and Medicine, 1840–1900* (Oxford: Oxford University Press, 2010), 288.

[41] For Sully's research, see Shuttleworth, *Mind of the Child*, 278.

[42] Sully, *Studies of Childhood* (London: Longman, 1896), 244.

[43] Ibid., 243, 399.

two people facing one another as actor and spectator, a fact not lost on the psychologist himself: 'A smile on the termination of the crying completed the curious little play.'[44] If, as Shuttleworth has argued, Sully's investigations transgressed boundaries between male and female, trained and amateur, laboratory and nursery, literature and science, they also traversed the emotional techniques of theatrical pretence (the 'curious little play') with those of an 'experiment'.[45] As Stricker's self-observation at the music hall had been elevated to the status of a formal experiment, so too were the amateur theatricals of weeping parents who glanced, like so many bad actors, from between their fingers to observe the effects of their histrionics upon their tiny experimental subjects.

Yet Sully was not naive as to the problems of the stage, or to what Jonas Barish calls theatre's 'ontological queasiness'.[46] In an chapter written in the 1870s, Sully revealed he was all too familiar with the discomfort that watching actors can produce—a theme which would become popular among those who wrote about theatre-going in the early twentieth century. Discussing how and why we sympathize with fictional characters, Sully argued that while live theatre might *seem* to make the 'belief in the reality … more instantaneous', in fact 'the distracting theatrical surroundings are very apt to check this delusion and to make our belief in the reality of a stage-action … fitful and evanescent'. While *reading* the great dramas of Lessing or Goethe (playwrights Sully admired) allowed for full immersion in the fictional world, the obtrusive 'spell-dissolving accompaniments of the stage'— which included not only clunky sets but also hammy acting—punctured the psychologist's absorption and pleasure.[47] By the early decades of the twentieth century, this critique was appearing regularly in novels in which theatre-goers, hoping to achieve some transcendent experience of emotional truth, report instead dissatisfaction at the shabby pretence of the stage, evidence of the period's anti-theatrical turn (Marcel's disappointment on seeing La Berma in the third volume of Proust's *À la recherche du temps perdu*, for example).[48] For Sully, theatrical encounters, as opposed to literary play-texts, were always characterized by failure, the audience's attempt to lose themselves in a fictional reality frustrated by insistent reminders that the onstage world was a mere simulation.

Such queasy feelings resurfaced almost thirty years later in *Studies of Childhood* and, in particular, in Sully's discussions of imitation. Sully repeatedly compares the play of children—an early expression of the imitative impulse—to professional theatre, admiring the infant's 'impulse to act a part' and the 'little play-scenes' which children create under tables and behind curtains, their imaginations propped up by

[44] Ibid., 408.

[45] Shuttleworth, *Mind of the Child*, 272.

[46] Jonas Barish, *The Antitheatrical Prejudice* (Berkeley, CA: University of California Press, 1981), 3.

[47] Sully 'The Representation of Character in Art', in Sully, *Sensation and Intuition: Studies in Psychology and Aesthetics* (London: King, 1874), 307.

[48] Marcel Proust, *The Guermantes Way* (1920; repr. London: Penguin, 2002), 47.

what Sully calls 'strong stage effects', as in 'the modern theatre'. Though such phrases elide children's play and the arts of the stage, elsewhere Sully argues this is not his intention at all. 'It is surely to misunderstand the essence of play to speak of it as a fully conscious process of imitative acting', he writes: the child 'truly at play' is simply absorbed in the experience, not in 'pleasing an audience'.[49] The fuzziness is intriguing, the gap between theatricality and motor mimicry expanding and contracting across the book's pages. Although children enact 'little play-scenes', with props and costumes, they are not *acting*, not really. The reason why becomes clear a page later, when Sully turns his attention to the topic of malicious misrepresentation. It is the *lying* children who are truly the 'little actors', writes Sully. It is 'little girls', he continues, displaying the familiar gendered anti-theatrical prejudice of the age, who deliberately flatter with 'acting and artfulness'.[50] Echoing an already entrenched suspicion towards actors, those ethically ambiguous creatures tainted by their association with spectacle and inauthenticity, for Sully it is in 'childish simulation' that the germs of the 'great moral evil, insincerity' can be found.[51] In her study of nineteenth-century childhood *The Mind of the Child*, Shuttleworth suggestively counterpoints Sully's work on child psychology with an analysis of Henry James's 1897 novel *What Maisie Knew*. The heroine of James's novel embarks on a 'career of deceit', writes Shuttleworth. 'James suggests that childhood itself becomes, for his heroine, a form of performance'.[52] In Sully's more ambivalent discussion, however, theatricality threatens to pervade the lives of all children, leaving the psychologist uncertain how to proceed; in turns, childish games are part of the same imitative impulse that produces theatrical creativity, and manifest a deceptive impulse that leaves infants teetering on the brink of moral decline.

Other theatrical problems rear their head in *Studies of Childhood*. In contrast to Sully's own 'fitful and evanescent' belief in theatrical worlds, certain groups—children and the working classes—have the opposite problem: highly impressionable, they are liable to confuse fiction with the facts. Sully describes seeing a ten-year-old boy watching a play in which troops prepare for battle. The boy, confusing fiction with reality, loudly protests that the cannon is not properly positioned. 'This reminds one', writes Sully, 'of the story of the sailors who on a visit to a theatre happened to see a representation of a mutiny on board ship, and were so excited that they rushed on the stage and took sides with the authorities in quelling the movement'.[53] Intended merely as a humorous aside, the anecdote locates one of the oldest theatrical problems—an actor's ability to befuddle an audience member, or at least *some* audience members— at the heart of a debate about motor mimicry. Such anecdotes about impressionable

---

[49] Sully, *Studies of Childhood*, 37, 41, 37.

[50] Ibid., 30. For disapproval of impersonation, see Barish, *Antitheatrical Prejudice*; for suspiciousness towards actresses, see Tracy C. Davis, *Actresses as Working Women: Their Social Identity in Victorian Culture* (Abingdon: Routledge, 1991).

[51] Sully, *Studies of Childhood*, 250.   [52] Shuttleworth, *Mind of the Child*, 332, 325.

[53] Sully, *Studies of Childhood*, 314.

audience members had been a feature of theatre-going for centuries: in 1660, Samuel Pepys recounts how 'a very pretty lady that sat by me, called out, to see Desdemona smothered'.[54] That similar stories, apocryphal or not, also caught the imagination of late nineteenth-century psychologists reminds us how important theatre had become for thinking about the group mind and its suggestibility. Theatrical performances, Sully seems to be hinting, not only risk the reliability of the individual subject; they also lure the impressionable into a condition of theatrical excess, turning some audience members into ludicrous performers too.

If Sully describes audiences identifying too much with theatrical representations, he also reminds us of the converse failure—when an audience member cannot believe an actor's performance enough. When Sully asks whether merely copying emotional facial expressions might lead the mimic to experience an echo of the feeling, he invokes the testimonies of actors. In 'all histrionic imitation', he writes, those who assume emotional facial expressions report experiencing a 'resonance of the feeling'.[55] That Sully should turn to actors, rather than his fellow psychologists, is somewhat strange: as Sully would have been well aware, William James had theorized a similar notion of emotional feedback loops ten years earlier.[56] But though Sully initially calls on actors for evidence, a footnote betrays a case of cold feet. How reliable a guide are actors really, he asks, to this notion that faking it leads to feeling it? How can they be sure, he wonders, that it's not their 'intense imaginative realization of the situation', rather than their bodies, which rouse the feelings?[57] Sully's earlier discussion of playing children as 'little actors' prefigures theatre's rather awkward landing in this argument. Though he turns to actors to illuminate the relationship between outward imitation and inner feeling, the reference unravels through doubts and self-contradictions.

How might we read these clumsy encounters with theatre in *Studies of Childhood*? Drawn to theatre as an explanatory device, Sully also recoils from it, as if alarmed by its unreliability. Though he laughs at those who experience a total absorption in the fiction, his own 'fitful and evanescent belief' fares little better, leaving him hesitating in the aisle, unable to quite swallow what theatre has to offer. One possibility is that these flashes of disquiet, while they reflect the creeping aversion to theatricality in modernist drama, may also alert us to a growing mistrust of theatre as an experimental resource, pointing up the period's wider transition from Victorian to modern experimental approaches.[58] Yet, in refusing to settle into a single meaning, the theatrical metaphors may also act, to invoke Gillian Beer's analysis of the role of

---

[54] *The Diary of Samuel Pepys*, Thursday 11 October, 1660, referred to in Julie Hankey (ed.), *Othello*, 2nd edn (Cambridge: Cambridge University Press, 2005), 17 n. 4. I am most grateful to Kirsten Shepherd-Barr for drawing my attention to this example.

[55] Sully, *Studies of Childhood*, 269.

[56] William James, 'What is an Emotion?', *Mind* 9 (1884), 190.

[57] Sully, *Studies of Childhood*, 269.

[58] Martin Puchner, *Stage Fright: Modernism, Anti-Theatricality, and Drama* (Baltimore, MD: Johns Hopkins University Press, 2002).

literary allusions in scientific writing, as 'repositories' for the wider philosophical problem at stake. As Beer argues, it was commonplace for nineteenth-century scientists to draw on literary examples for 'insights that tapped the further implications' of their theories.[59] While the stage metaphors in Sully's writing remind us of the period's alliance between theatre and science, they also point up discomfort around the prospect that acting—that maligned pastime of the Victorian moral world—might be fast becoming an inevitable part of the texture of modern life.

Modern organs of imitation

As dawn broke on the twentieth century, scientists of mind basked in a new cultural authority. Hailed for their ability to give scientific answers to age-old questions about the innermost workings of the mind, psychologists, with their laboratories, journals, and machines, belonged to a discipline highly conscious of its modernity. Yet, psychological practices and writing remained indebted to the wider artistic culture. While this chapter has focused specifically on the role of theatre in the new sciences of mind, similar arguments can be advanced for the entanglements of psychology with literature, music, and film, arguments that trace peripatetic routes across what today may appear to be secure epistemic boundaries.[60] Unable to apply the gaze of a microscope to the mimic body, or measure it with a precision instrument, those drawn to comprehend the human mimics could only do so by staging encounters between actors and audiences, ensuring that theatre remained a vital part of modern scientific practice. In turn, in scientific writing the unreliability of theatrical representation acted as a repository for all that was intensely concerning about the predicament of humans hopelessly compelled to replicate their surroundings. As involuntary muscle mimicry emerged as an inherent instinct common to all, so did the uncomfortable prospect that theatricality—with its slippages between faking it and feeling it, its mismatches between appearances and reality, and the queasy feelings of mistrust it elicited—might become constitutive of the twentieth-century self.

FURTHER READING

Clarke, Edwin and L. S. Jacyna. *Nineteenth-Century Origins of Neuroscientific Concepts* (Berkeley and Los Angeles, CA, and London: University of California Press, 1987).
Collins, Alan. 'England', in David B. Baker (ed.), *The Oxford Handbook of the History of Psychology: Global Perspectives* (Oxford: Oxford University Press, 2012), 182–210.

[59] Gillian Beer, 'Parable, Professionalization and Literary Allusion in Victorian Scientific Writing', in Beer, *Open Fields: Science in Cultural Encounter* (Oxford: Clarendon, 1996), 215.

[60] For example, see Laura Salisbury and Andrew Shail, *Neurology and Modernity: A Cultural History of Nervous Systems, 1800–1950* (Basingstoke: Palgrave Macmillan, 2010).

Ledger, Sally and Roger Luckhurst (eds). *The fin de siècle: A Reader in Cultural History, 1880–1900* (Oxford: Oxford University Press, 2000).

Luckhurst, Roger. *The Invention of Telepathy, 1870–1901* (Oxford: Oxford University Press, 2002).

Morus, Iwan Rhys. 'Placing Performance', *Isis* 101 (2010), 775–8.

Roach, Joseph R. *The Player's Passion: Studies in the Science of Acting* (Ann Arbor, MI: University of Michigan Press, 2001).

Salisbury, Laura and Andrew Shail. *Neurology and Modernity: A Cultural History of Nervous Systems, 1800–1950* (Basingstoke: Palgrave Macmillan, 2010).

Shuttleworth, Sally. *The Mind of the Child: Child Development in Literature, Science and Medicine, 1840–1900* (Oxford: Oxford University Press, 2010).

Shuttleworth, Sally and Jenny Bourne Taylor. *Embodied Selves: An Anthology of Psychological Texts, 1830–1890* (Oxford: Oxford University Press, 1998).

Stiles, Anne. *Popular Fiction and Brain Science in the Late Nineteenth Century* (Cambridge: Cambridge University Press, 2012).

Taylor, Jenny Bourne. 'Psychology at the fin de siècle', in Gail Marshall (ed.), *The Cambridge Companion to the fin de siècle* (Cambridge: Cambridge University Press, 2007), 13–30.

Watt Smith, Tiffany. *On Flinching: Theatricality and Scientific Looking from Darwin to Shell Shock* (Oxford: Oxford University Press, 2014).

Willis, Martin. *Vision, Science and Literature, 1870–1920: Ocular Horizons* (London: Pickering and Chatto, 2011).

CHAPTER 24

THE THEATRE OF HANDS

Writing the First World War

SANTANU DAS

In one of the most celebrated close-up shots in cinematic history, a palm—outstretched, exposed, prehensile—enters the frame against a grainy background as it reaches out towards a butterfly. In a thrilling sequence, the camera alternates between its caressing close-up of the hand and ominous focus on a sniper getting ready to take aim; a shot rings out, the hand judders and slowly drops down, limp and lifeless. This is the final shot from Lewis Milestone's classic film *All Quiet on the Western Front* (1930) as the protagonist Paul Bäumer gets killed. The lyricism of Remarque's novel with its message of the futility of war and the fragility of life is distilled by Milestone into this final gesture. If the First World War and cinema have a twinned history,[1] Milestone brilliantly aligns the sniper's with the cameraman's visual angle of the hand in another *double entendre* on 'shoot'. Cinematic history has it that it was Milestone's own hand in the final shot, as the actor playing Paul Bäumer had left the crew; anonymous, substitutable, it becomes everyone's, every hand. The slowing of time as the palm fills the screen and the fingers twitch and curl in death-agony introduces us not just to unconscious optics but to subcutaneous haptics: we wince, we tighten. The close-up, to return to Walter Benjamin's famous statement, does not just expand space and extend movement but reveals new structural formations. The closing shot highlights the film's and the novel's obsession with trope. Inside the film, it is a poetic counterpart to its most gruesome image—a pair of hands, severed from the body, clinging on to the barbed wire; beyond it, it pays tribute to novel's dramatization of touch and intimacy as it records Paul's discovery of his friend's death: 'Kat's hands are warm, I pass my hand under his

---

[1] See Laura Marcus, 'The Great War in Twentieth-Century Cinema', in Vincent Sherry (ed.), *The Cambridge Companion to the Literature of the First World War* (Cambridge: Cambridge University Press, 2005), 280.

shoulders in order to rub his temples with some tea. I feel my fingers becoming moist. As I draw them away from behind his head, they are bloody.'[2]

What is in a hand? Hands are the most conscious and at the same time the most intimate points of our contact with the surrounding world.[3] The long, gangly appendages that hang by our sides and end in the wondrous fingers do not just define us as primates but are the end-points of our evolution as human: they are fundamental to our 'making'—and subsequent mastery—of the world. No wonder it is the spark between fingers rather than the thrust of the male organ that informs that most famous depiction of Creation in the Sistine Chapel, as if life hovered on our fingertips. But is it a phenomenological adventure that the hand embarks on as it voyages through the world, or is it a history of feeling that it articulates? Or does its symbolic significance—as agency, aspiration, chance, or fragility—outweigh its constant dialogue with the self and the world? In his 'Letter on the Blind for the Use of Those Who See', Denis Diderot described a blind man who, when asked what he would ask for if he were granted a single wish, replied: 'I would just as soon have long arms: It seems to me that my hands would tell me more about what goes on in the moon that you can find out with your eyes and your telescope.'[4] On the other hand, in Martin Heidegger's famous account, it is the site of 'Dasein':

> The hand does not merely grasp and catch...but extends and receives, and not just things, but extends and receives in the other. The hand holds. The hand carries. The hand draws and signs, presumably because man is a sign...Every movement of the hand gestures within the element of thinking.[5]

An integral part of our thinking and being rather than mere tools for grasping, our hands also make us strangely vulnerable: our anxiety about their damage is proportional to our extraordinary investment in them. One of the most remarkable breakthroughs in medical science in recent years has been the creation for amputees of the 'bionic hand' that can 'feel' the shape, weight, and texture of what it handles. Our daily language is enmeshed in figures and metaphors of the hand—'Give me a hand', 'be at hand', 'at arm's length', 'hands-on', 'handover', 'handy', 'handle', 'the hand of chance', or just 'hands'. How does the hand, in the process of writing, remember its own self, touched by its inner history, marked by its gender and race, or shaped by questions of literary form? And conversely, how do we, as readers, feel the hand in the text as our eyes travel across the line and we turn or smooth the page?

---

[2] Eric Maria Remarque, *All Quiet on the Western Front*, trans. A. W. Wheen (1929; repr. Oxford: Heinemann, 1990), 245.

[3] See Gillian Beer, *Open Fields: Science in Cultural Encounter* (Oxford: Oxford University Press, 1996), 14.

[4] Quoted in Rod Michalko, *The Mystery of the Eye and the Shadow of Blindness* (Toronto, ON: University of Toronto Press, 1998), 82.

[5] Quoted in Will McNeill, 'Spirit's Living Hand', in David Wood (ed.), *Of Derrida, Heidegger, and Spirit* (Evanston, IL: Northwestern University Press, 1993), 112.

In the past couple of decades, there has been a swell of interest within both theoretical writing and literary criticism in emotion and the senses, in the 'affective' and the 'sensuous' as ways of opening up and understanding the textures of the past.[6] War writing, in particular, has been an area where the body has emerged as one of the most important sites of analysis. In his poem 'Recalling War', written some twenty years after the First World War, Robert Graves remembers it as a time when 'our youth became all-flesh and waived the mind'; singling out Isaac Rosenberg's 'Break of Day in the Trenches' for special praise, Siegfried Sassoon wrote: 'Sensuous frontline existence is there, hateful and repellent, unforgettable and inescapable.'[7] If combat is one area of human experience where the body as both agent and victim of violence is pushed to its limits, can a more intimate history of the war—as conflict rather than just as combat, involving both men and women, combatants, non-combatants, and civilians—be written through the trope of the hand?

The tension that Heidegger records between the hand as raw, prehensile antennae and the super-sophisticated think tank was pushed to an extreme in the trenches of the First World War. Previous conflicts—from the Napoleonic wars to Crimea and the Boer War—were all bloody and brutal, but the trench warfare on the Western Front pushed human experience to a new threshold of extremity, with its sustained shattering of the human sensorium on one hand and the intensity and intimacy of camaraderie on the other.[8] After three weeks at the front, Owen writes to his mother, 'I have not seen any dead. I have done worse. In the dank air, I have perceived it, and in the darkness, felt'.[9] In the original letter, the hand underlines the word 'felt', as it both remembers and represses the object. Touch here becomes the ground for both testimony and trauma. In Edmund Blunden's *Undertones of War* (1928), severed hands, like mushrooms, sprout from the 'ground' which is at once landscape and memory. As I have argued elsewhere, the visual world of everyday

[6] Two of the classic theoretical works about the poetics of the body and the senses remain Maurice Merleau-Ponty, *Phenomenology of Perception* (1945; repr. London: Routledge, 2002); and Gaston Bachelard, *Poetics of Space* (Boston, MA: Beacon, 1969). For more recent works, see Sara Danius, *The Senses of Modernism: Technology, Perception and Aesthetics* (Ithaca, NY: Cornell University Press, 2002); Susan Stewart, *Poetry and the Fate of the Senses* (Chicago, IL: Chicago University Press, 2002); Constance Classen (ed.), *The Book of Touch* (Oxford: Berg, 2005); Michael Serres, *The Five Senses: A Philosophy of Mingled Bodies* (London: Continuum, 2008); and Abbie Garrington, *Haptic Modernism: Touch and the Tactile in Modernist Writing* (Edinburgh: Edinburgh University Press, 2013).

[7] Robert Graves, 'Recalling War', in Beryl Graves and Dunstan Ward (eds), *The Complete Poems of Robert Graves*(London: Penguin, 2003), 359; Siegfried Sassoon, 'Foreword', reprinted in *The Collected Works of Isaac Rosenberg*, ed. Ian Parsons (London: Chatto, 1979), ix.

[8] The classic study in the area still remains Paul Fussell, *The Great War and Modern Memory* (Oxford: Oxford University Press, 1975); among recent works which provide a variety of perspectives, see Sherry (ed.), *Cambridge Companion*; Adam Piette and Mark Rawlinson (eds), *The Edinburgh Companion to Twentieth-Century British and American War Literature* (Edinburgh: Edinburgh University Press, 2012); and Santanu Das (ed.), *The Cambridge Companion to the Poetry of the First World War* (Cambridge: Cambridge University Press, 2014).

[9] Harold Owen and John Bell (eds), *Wilfred Owen: Collected Letters* (London: Oxford University Press, 1967), 429 (hereafter *CL*). The two words are underlined in the original letter.

life was replaced by the haptic geography of the trenches: in the dark, subterranean world of the Western Front, men navigated space not through the reassuring distance of their gaze but through the tactile immediacy of their bodies.[10] It was one thing to stand in the water-filled trenches, and quite another matter, Sassoon notes, to 'crawl along with mud-clogged fingers' like a rat or mole.[11] Creep, crawl, burrow, worm are recurrent verbs in trench narratives, suggesting the shift from the visual to the tactile. The earth could also be the ultimate refuge. In Remarque's *All Quiet*, the soldier, trying to escape shellfire, buries himself deep into the ground, ostrich-like, till 'our being, almost utterly carried away by the fury of the storm, streams back through our hands'.[12] If the hand claws, it also joins.

In the trenches, mutilation and mortality, loneliness, shelling, and the breakdown of language led to a new level of intimacy under which the tactile code of civilian society collapsed. Men nursed and fed their friends when ill; they held each other as they bathed together; and during the long winter months they wrapped blankets around each other. In his private diary, C. H. Cox remembers how his comrade 'died in my arms', while the French journal *Poil et Plume* (October 1916) records an incident where a severely wounded man fell on a stretcher bearer and said: 'Embrace me, I want to die with you'.[13] Here, touch fills in the gap left by language. In 2001, a French archaeological team digging around Arras discovered a row of twenty bodies buried arm-in-arm, identified as the Grimsby Chums. Insurgent under these linked arms are the hands of the comrades who had arranged these figures, turning the macabre into the poignant. Alain Jacques, the leader of the French archaeological team, noted: 'Can you imagine the friendship and dedication of those who went about laying down the remains in this way?'[14]

How are such moments and processes remembered and represented in the more self-conscious literature of the period? How do the soldier-poets draw upon their own experiences as well as on the 'literary' histories of the hand, with its own tics and habits? If male narratives tend to dominate war literature even today, an equally rich archive of experiences comes from women, particularly of those who volunteered as nurses. At the same time, some of the most delicate and tantalizing explorations of the hand come from the civilian writers of the time—both men and women—who seize upon the trope to examine the complex discourses of gender, sexuality, pacifism, damage, and agency surrounding the war. If hands and gestures pertain to every aspect of war, as to life, I shall here focus on the intensities of meanings the hand gathers in a few selected war texts in three significant contexts and genres: trench poetry by soldier-poets, nursing memoirs by women, and finally, two remarkable short stories by the civilian writers, D. H. Lawrence and Claire Goll.

---

[10]   Das, *Touch and Intimacy in First World War Literature* (Cambridge: Cambridge University Press, 2005), 35–72.

[11]   Sassoon, *The Complete Memoirs of George Sherston* (London: Faber, 1949), 305.

[12]   Remarque, *All Quiet on the Western Front*, 52.

[13]   C. H. Cox, 'A Few Experiences of the First World War', Imperial War Museum, 88/11/1; quoted in Stéphane Audoin-Rouzeau, *Men at War 1914–1918* trans. Helen McPhail (Oxford: Berg, 1992), 47.

[14]   *The Times*, 20 Jun 2001.

Wandering fingers: Victorian to First World War poetry

The literature of every period invests body parts with its own fears and fantasies, but hands have always retained their special grip on the imagination. From Lady Macbeth's 'Out, damn'd spot' or Lear's 'Let me wipe it first. It smells of mortality', to the dying Keats's 'This Living Hand', this trope has been used to produce some of literature's finest moments. But the nineteenth century was perhaps its belle époque. As early as 1833, Charles Bell's famous Bridgewater treatise on *The Hand, its Mechanism and Vital Endowments as Evincing Design* (1833) set the tone for the Victorian obsession with hands, finding some of its most complex expressions in the writing of the period. From Walter Pater's celebration of Winckelmann's 'unsinged hands'[15] to the hairy, bestial hands of Stevenson's Mr Hyde, from the long, lank, skeletal hand of Uriah Heep to the beautifully painted hands of Dorian Gray which start oozing blood, it is as if every Victorian emotion, anxiety, or idea—from degeneration, race, and disease through religion and science to gender and sexuality—wrote itself on and through the hand.[16] Tennyson's elegy *In Memoriam* (1849) for his beloved Arthur Hallam is, among other things, a ballet of fingers as it plays with Hallam's hand as sight, trace, metaphor, metonymy, or as 'dreamy touch', the focus of infinite desire and anxious deferral: from 'hands so often clasp'd in mine' to 'A hand that can be clasp'd no more' to the 'shining hand' of Christ.[17] But two moments are particularly important to our discussion here. The first is a tantalizing passage from John Addington Symonds in 1889 about hands as an expression of sexual conflict: 'For there is the soul in the fingers. They speak…I knew that my right hand was useless – firmly clenched in the grip of an unconquerable love, the love of comrades. But they [i.e. those who criticized me] stung me into using my left hand for work.'[18] The second is, as we shall see, eerily prescient, coming from D. H. Lawrence's 'The Prussian Officer', a short story written in 1914 about eros and authority in the military, where the older officer is tormented by the hand of his orderly: 'To see the soldier's young, brown, shapely peasant's hand grasp the loaf or the wine-bottle sent a flash of hate or of anger through the elder man's blood.'[19]

[15] Walter Pater, 'Winckelmann', in *The Renaissance: Studies in Art and Poetry* (Berkeley, CA: California University Press, 1980), 177.

[16] The fascinating interdisciplinary conference 'Victorian Tactile Imagination: Re-appraising Touch in Nineteenth-Century Culture', July 2013, Birkbeck, University of London, explored a range of approaches. The programme can be found at http://www.bbk.ac.uk/english/our-research/research_cncs/our-events/past-events/the-victorian-tactile-imagination/VTI_finalprogramme.pdf.

[17] Alfred Tennyson, 'In Memoriam', in *The Poems of Tennyson*, ed. Cristopher Ricks, Vol. II (Harlow: Longman, 1987), xx. Also see Christopher Craft, *Another Kind of Love: Male Homosexual Desire in English Discourse, 1850–1920* (Berkeley, CA: University of California Press, 1994); and Gillian Beer, 'Dream Touch', keynote address at 'Victorian Tactile Imagination' conference.

[18] Quoted in Craft, *Another Kind of Love*, 44–70.

[19] 'The Prussian Officer', in Brian Finney (ed.), *D. H. Lawrence: Selected Short Stories* (London: Penguin, 2000), 3.

In its combination of eros, loss, and conflict, the Victorians were writing the perfect trope for the war poets. If mourning for the dead comrade is the central rudder for trench poetry, the hand becomes the object of both memory and desire: 'I clasp his hand', 'your hands in my hands', 'That his fingers were stiff and cold / Which I clasped warm, last night—/ Encouraging'.[20] A day after the death of his beloved David, Sassoon wrote in his diary: 'For you were glad, and kind and brave; / With hands that clasped me, young and warm.'[21] In the ensuing elegy 'The Last Meeting', for the self-confessed homosexual poet–soldier, who had tried on Tennyson's robe during his time in Cambridge, the delicious drama of clasping and unclasping in *In Memoriam*'s 'dreamy touch' would acquire too much self-knowledge and erotic heat ('Who waits to feel my fingers touch his face') and had to be excised from the final published version.[22] Similarly charged, though in a different context, is its appearance in Isaac Rosenberg's 'Break of Day in the Trenches' where the 'droll rat' with 'cosmopolitan sympathies' touches 'This English hand. / You will do the same to a German'.[23] Irony and pathos, personal history and racial politics are held in taut balance as the word 'cosmopolitan' injects the rat with its creator's own transnational history. As the son of Jewish Lithuanian immigrants, Rosenberg would have been painfully aware of the fact that both the 'English' and the 'German' hand may be pulsing with common Jewish blood, making the war a horrible fratricide for the 'cosmopolitan' Jew.[24] Hidden histories, whether of sexuality or race, give way to a heavily stylized, class-based vision in Richard Aldington's extraordinary paean-cum-lament for 'Our Hands' where they become the very measure of loss:

I am grieved for our hands that have caressed roses and women's flesh, old lovely books and
  marbles of Carrara...
I am grieved for our hands that were so reverent in beauty's service, so glad of beauty of
  tressed hair and silken robe and gentle fingers, so glad of beauty of bronze and wood and
  stone and rustling parchment. So glad, so reverent, so white.
I am grieved for our hands.[25]

At an immediate level, the hands here epitomize all the strength and sweetness of Victorian aestheticism and the idea of progress irremediably tarred by the war;

---

[20] See Martin Taylor (ed.), *Lads: Love Poetry of the Trenches* (London: Duckworth, 1989), 95, 99, 96.

[21] Sassoon, *Diaries 1915–1918*, ed. Rupert Hart-Davies (London: Faber, 1983), 44–5.

[22] Sassoon, 'The Last Meeting'. The line, excised from the printed version, can be found in a rough draft of the poem in Cambridge University Library, E. J. Dent, MSS Add. 7973, S/75.

[23] 'Break of Day in the Trenches', in Vivien Noakes (ed.), *The Poetry and Plays of Isaac Rosenberg* (Oxford: Oxford University Press, 2004), 128.

[24] For further exploration of the poem, see Das, 'War Poetry and the Realm of the Senses', in Tim Kendall (ed.), *The Oxford Handbook of British and Irish Poetry* (Oxford: Oxford University Press, 2007), 73–100; and Neil Corcoran, 'Isaac Rosenberg', in *The Cambridge Companion to the Poetry of the First World War*, 105–6.

[25] Richard Aldington, 'Our Hands', in Michael Copp (ed.), *An Imagist at War: The Complete War Poems of Richard Aldington* (London: Associated University Press, 2002), 141.

memory and fantasy are fused and confused, as often in Aldington's *Images of War* (1917), in the last stance of beauty amid the horrors of the trenches. But class and anxieties around it, exacerbated by the war, remain central to this evocation and trope. In this class-bound vision, the difference between a pre-and post-war England can be summed up as the difference between Rupert Brooke's delicate pleasures in 'The Dead' ('Touched flowers and furs and cheeks') and T. S. Eliot's demotic vision in *The Waste Land*: 'On Margate sand / I can connect / Nothing with nothing. / The broken finger-nails of dirty hands'.[26]

But within the actual context of the war, no poet is as obsessed with the hand as Wilfred Owen. His brother Harold remembers Wilfred's hand as 'blue-veined, white and delicate'; on reading Rossetti's *Life and Writings of John Keats*, Owen wrote: 'Rossetti guided my groping hand right into the wound and I touched, for one moment, the Incandescent Heart of Keats'.[27] In Owen's early, pre-war poetry, the hand is a recurring trope, at once a *fin-de-siècle* literary inheritance and an archive of tortured, personal memory. In 'Maundy Thursday', as the narrator kisses the chalice, he is distracted by the server-boy: 'And yet I bowed, yea, kissed—my lips did cling. / (I kissed the warm live hand that held the thing)'.[28] In both England and France, Owen developed close friendships with young boys such as Vivian Rampton at Dunsden and Johnny de la Touche at Mergnac. Different impulses seem to be fused and confused in these friendships—a genuine affection, pastoral care, ease, and possibly a delicate eroticism—though it is neither possible to know how much Owen himself was aware of the heat of the moment, nor advisable to read them solely through an early twenty-first century lens:

> Now let me feel the feeling of thy hand
> For it is softer than the breasts of girls
>   ('Impromptu')
> Be better if I had not ~~touched my hand~~
>   ('We two had known each other')
> To my great friends I said 'Unhand ~~me~~
> For I has touched the god[ess] and touch me not
>   ('Perseus')[29]

[26] T. S. Eliot, 'The Waste Land', in *The Complete Poems and Plays of T. S. Eliot* (London: Faber, 1969), 70.
[27] *CL*, 161. For a more detailed investigation, see Das, 'Wilfred Owen and the Sense of Touch', in *Touch and Intimacy in First World War Literature*, 137–72. For three very different kinds of approaches to Owen's life, see Jon Stallworthy's classic *Wilfred Owen* (Oxford: Oxford University Press, 1974); Dominic Hibberd's *Wilfred Owen: A New Biography* (London: Weidenfeld & Nicolson, 2002); and Guy Cuthbertson's recent *Wilfred Owen* (New Haven, CT: Yale University Press, 2014).
[28] 'Maundy Thursday', in Stallworthy (ed.), *The Poems of Wilfred Owen* (London: Chatto and Windus, 1985), 86 (hereafter Owen, *Poems*).
[29] Stallworthy (ed.), *Wilfred Owen: Complete Poems and Fragments* (Oxford: Chatto and Windus, 1983), 76, 437, 467 (hereafter *CP&F*).

The last extract comes from the tantalizing 'Perseus' fragment, an interlinked series of five heavily revised and cancelled draft fragments which hint at some personal crisis. It was written shortly after Owen left—or was forced to leave—his job as the pastor's assistant at the vicarage at Dunsden: we do not know what exactly happened at the vicarage, for the relevant sections in the letter were scissored out by the Owen family. Owen scholar and biographer Dominic Hibberd speculates: 'Was he [Owen] remembering touching a boy's hand [Vivian Rampton at Dunsden] during spring idyll two years earlier? Had it really been Henriette who had excited him at Castelnau? Or had it been Raoul?'[30] Whatever be the case, the verb 'Unhand' betokens a rather extreme response: is it a classic example of the drama between the phobic and the erotic on the part of the homosexual but severely repressed poet? But from where does this anguished plea to 'Unhand' come? Blurring the boundaries between the experiential and the representational, the personal and the poetic, is the hand being used as the archive of intensely personal memory or a knowing literary trope, already injected with sexual dissidence by writers such as Symonds and Wilde?

Once in the trenches, Owen would return obsessively to the image of the hand— the site of guilty pleasure—but now the war adds a fresh dimension to its intensities of meaning. His war poetry may be described as one long process of 'unhanding' as this bearer of same-sex intimacy registers the full violence of both war and prohibition. As he begins to sing the hymn of sacrificial love, the warm hands of Vivian Rampton and de la Touche boys, the 'groping hand' and 'beautiful fingers' of 'To Eros' and 'Impromptu' get mutilated. Consider his poem 'Apologia Pro Poemate Meo':

> For love is not the binding of fair lips
> With the soft silk of eyes that look and long.
> By joy, whose ribbon slips,–
>
> But wound with war's hard wire whose stakes are strong;
> Bound with the bandage of the arm that drips;
> Knit in the webbing of the rifle-thong.[31]

At one level, this is a convincing piece of trench realism. And yet, for one familiar with his juvenilia, it is also a moment of homosexual panic. To begin with, one might ask, what is the connection between innocent, though admittedly heterosexual, love and 'the bandage of the arm that drips'—with blood? with pus?—except in a context of misogyny on one hand and sadomasochistic violence on the other? For 'joy's ribbon' resurfaces with a macabre twist as torn and reddened flesh in the metaphor of the 'webbing of the rifle-thong'. On the other hand, the hand that cannot be touched, legally or morally, is cut off as same-sex intimacy is redefined as the 'greater love' of comrades. For a person as obsessed with beautiful hands as Owen,

---

[30] Hibberd, *Wilfred Owen*, 122.

[31] 'Apologia Pro Poemate Meo', *CP&F*, 124. The poem has elicited different responses. It evokes for Simon Featherstone 'the terrible and absurd world of war', in *War Poetry: An Introductory Reader* (London, Routledge, 1995), 104; while Adrian Caesar, who underlines the celebration of suffering in Owen's verse, has called it a 'sado-masochistic hymn', in *Taking it Like a Man: Suffering, Sexuality and the War Poets* (Manchester: Manchester University Press, 1995), 150.

his war poetry throws up just stumps; when it does appear, it is the site of pain and horror, as in the opening of his famous 'Disabled':

> He sat in a wheeled chair, waiting for dark,
> And shivered in his ghastly suit of grey,
> Legless, sewn short at elbow.[32]

In the above lines, the sibilance insidiously draws us into the moment: we wince and tighten. In spite of the comma after 'legless', the alliteration ('sewn short') drives us forward and we stop only after 'short'. The word 'sewn' is pulled in different directions, aurally and visually. But as we complete reading the whole line, we realize that it is not only at the knees, as the sibilance and caesura after 'short' have deluded us to believe, but at the elbows that the soldier has been cut short. Owen's finest verse trades on such frisson between the eye, the hand, and the ear. Real-life violence jousts with aesthetic surprise as the relation between art and violence is pushed to its insidious climax.

The hand surfaces again—unsurprisingly—in his most explicit engagement with his beloved poet John Keats in 'Exposure', as he refigures the Keatsian bower within the trench landscape. A partly cancelled line from a related poem—'~~Fastening of feeling~~ fingers on my wrist'—connects the unknown hands that had been laid on Owen's arms 'in the night, along the Bordeaux streets' with the sensuous threat of the snow in this poem: 'Pale flakes with fingering stealth come feeling for our faces.'[33] The draft manuscript dwells tantalizingly on the moment of phantasmatic handshake or handgrip as the fingers of the snow are now 'feeling' the hands of young soldier:

> the ~~this~~   fasten on
> ~~Before~~ ᵀt onight, frost will ~~have fixed~~ this mud and us,
>   puckering
> Shrivelling many hands, ~~and wrinkling~~ foreheads crisp.
>   dead   ~~their hands~~
> ~~The~~   ~~Fingers~~ will ~~stretch and hang upon a strange vain~~
>   these
> And Ww e ~~must that can wield a pick or shovel~~
> ~~And~~ We, ~~rest we that~~ can, take pick or shovel in ~~weak~~ grasp.[34]
>   ~~stark~~

In a piece of textual 'unhanding', the 'vain grasp' is deleted from the final version which simply states: 'Shrivelling many hands'. This poem, like 'Greater Love' or 'Disabled', raises disturbing questions about the relation between the political and the aesthetic, particularly between the responsibility of a war poet and a private masochistic imagination. Repressed homoeroticism and a Decadent poetic inheritance, combined with the loathing of war, contribute to such tortured images.

---

[32] 'Disabled', *CP&F*, 175.
[33] *CP&F*, 460; *CL*, 234; *CP&F*, 185. For a detailed discussion of the poem, see Hibberd, *Owen the Poet* (Basingstoke: Macmillan, 1986), 78.
[34] *CP&F*, 366–7, 370

The favourite trope appears for one last time in 'Strange Meeting', veering between the fantasized moment of hand-combat with the linguistic thrust of 'jabbed and killed' and the infinite pity of the live hand becoming 'loath and cold':

> I knew you in this dark; for so you frowned
> Yesterday through me as you jabbed and killed.
> I parried; but my hands were loath and cold.
> Let us sleep now...[35]

Owen is regarded as the patron saint of the 'pity of war', and with abundant reason. But of all the trench poets, he is also the one who draws us, Caravaggio-like, into moments of extreme sense experience, weaving linguistic–tactile fantasies around processes we would otherwise flinch from: moments when limbs are sliced off ('limbs knife-skewed'; 'shaved us with his scythe'); the flesh is ripped apart ('shatter of flying muscles'; 'Ripped from my own back / In scarlet shreds'; 'limped on, blood-shod'); or the mouth starts bleeding ('I saw his round mouth's crimson deepen as it fell').[36] A visceral thrill as well as an acute physical empathy constitutes the body in pain in Owen's poetry, hovering around moments when we no longer know where the *is* ends and the *was* begins. If the hand was already an established trope in the pre-war years, Wilfred Owen pushes it towards its obsessive and tortured climax in the 'trenchscape' of the First World War. Veering between too, too solid flesh, a signifier and a symbol, it emerges as a complex palimpsest where pre-war erotic history, *fin-de-siècle* inheritance, the violence of war, and a certain masochistic imagination are combined. This is very different from the sanitized image of Owen as the quintessential war poet and cultural icon we are usually given.

The nurse's hand: Reaching out, falling short

If hand becomes a recurring image in trench poetry, there is another genre equally obsessed with the hand: nursing memoirs by women. Indeed, the profession of nursing can be said to be the translation of medical knowledge into the hand of care. The American writer Mary Borden, who volunteered as a nurse and set up her mobile hospital unit just behind the lines on the Western Front, notes in her remarkable modernist memoir *The Forbidden Zone* (1929): 'You are continually doing things with your hands': soothing the patient, giving injections, irrigating wounds, changing bandages, sterilizing equipment, tidying the bed, assisting in operations.[37]

---

[35] Owen, *Poems*, 126.   [36] *CP&F*, 166, 165, 169, 178, 140, 123.
[37] Mary Borden, *The Forbidden Zone: A Nurse's Impressions of the First World War* (London: Heinemann, 1929), 124.

Or consider the following journal entry written on 4 February 1917 aboard a hospital ship by Mary Ann Brown, a private nurse, who served wounded Turkish soldiers:

> Very busy. Amp. of rt arm (Turk died a few hrs later) Amp left leg. Spinal Anaesthetic. Amp.rt leg. Spinal Anaesthetic. Turk quite happy, smoked a cig. all the time they were sawing off his leg. One amp. of fingers. one amp. of thumb one secondary haemorrhage. one incision of leg 7 altogether, no off duty, finished 6:30.[38]

Here, the body parts are compressed into disjointed syntax and abbreviated time. Written under the pressure of the moment, with the hand perhaps still raw from the operations, the tone is flat, factual, and emotionless, as if efficient nursing service—the amputation of limbs in this case—had necessitated the amputation of one's own sensitive nerves. Brown's more celebrated colleague Vera Brittain writes about the 'self-protective callousness' required to 'dress unaided and without emotion, the quivering stump of a newly amputated limb'.[39] The language may quiver with emotion, but not the hand.

From the early years of the war, hundreds of thousands of women—often middle-class Edwardian ladies—volunteered in thousands to work as Voluntary Aid Detachment (VAD) nurses and thus serve the wounded. The VAD organization was created on 16 August 1909 but it was the First World War that changed its role.[40] On 1 August 1914, there were 47,196 female VAD nurses and by 1 April 1920 their numbers had swelled to 82,857.[41] Unlike professional nurses, they did not have a long period of training nor the 'self-protective callousness' developed through years of experience. Many, like Brittain, were just out of school; and for most, it was their first encounter with the male body. During the war years, nursing was considered the woman's best chance of 'doing their bit' in a war which contemporary ideology, like Freud's Little Hans, believed happened only at the 'fwont'. Vera Brittain writes about the terrible sense of marginalization and alienation felt by women during the war years, the sense of being cut off from her beloved Roland serving in the trenches by a ring of secret, almost bodily, knowledge shared supposedly only by combatants—something that James Campbell has called 'combat gnosticism'.[42] Read in this light, Owen's injunction to women at the end of 'Greater Love'—'Weep, you may weep, for you may touch them not'[43]—reveals its bitter misogynistic force. The work of feminist

---

[38] M. A. Brown, 'Diary', Department of Documents, Imperial War Museum, 88/7/1.

[39] Vera Brittain, *Testament of Youth: An Autobiographical Study of the Years 1900–1925* (1933; repr. London: Virago, 1978), 176, 216.

[40] See Sharon Ouditt, *Fighting Forces, Writing Women: Identity and Ideology in the First World War* (London: Routledge, 1994), 7–46, for an excellent account of First World War women's nursing.

[41] Arthur Marwick, *Women at War 1914–1918* (London: Fontana, 1977), 168.

[42] James Campbell, 'Combat Gnosticism: The Ideology of First World War Poetry Criticism', *New Literary History* 30/1 (1999), 203–15.

[43] 'Greater Love', in Owen, *Poems*, 143.

critics such as Jane Marcus, Margaret Higonnet, and Claire Tylee has done much to challenge this ideology, and highlight women's war experience.[44]

Hands are the actual points of contact between the nurses and the wounded body of the soldier. In the nursing memoirs, it is indeed over these hands that some of the most intimate conflicts are endlessly negotiated. In the preface to *The Forbidden Zone*, Borden writes: 'I have dared to dedicate these pages to the Poilus *who passed through our hands* during the war.'[45] At the very beginning of her text, hands—at once metaphoric and literal—are used to announce her special status as nurse-narrator and stake her claim on the body of the combatant and by extension on the domain of 'combat gnosticism' from which they have been excluded: what comes across is a sense of the precarious ownership of experience. Midway through the text, she muses: 'How many men had passed through my hands during the last thirty-six hours?'[46] Sixty years after the war, the historian Lyn MacDonald, while interviewing a group of octogenarians who served as nurses in the war, writes: 'What comes through most strongly is their remarkable resilience... "Oh dear, I'm sorry to be so clumsy. It's these stupid stiff fingers of mine." It was an apology I heard literally scores of times as a photograph slipped to the floor, or two drops of tea into a saucer.' MacDonald continues, 'The "stupid stiff fingers" were most scarred when they were lanced to release the pus from a septic hand.'[47] Gladys Stanford, a First World War nurse, remembers how she got 'a very bad septic hand doing that [dressing], because VADs didn't wear rubber gloves. Only the Sister wore gloves, and if you got the slightest prick it always went septic.'[48] Indeed, in a grim moment in Irene Rathbone's autobiographical novel *We That Were Young* (1932), the nurse-narrator Joan falls ill from a septic infection in the hand: in her fevered consciousness, she sees her hand, 'crimson and tight-skinned on the counterpane', 'swollen to the dimensions of a nightmare German sausage'. The infection happens after a grim round of dressing and cleaning wounds in course of which the patient has to shut his eyes and clutch Joan's arm as a little bodkin-shaped instrument was 'probing' into his lacerated muscles: 'to *feel* it [was] almost unendurable' Joan writes.[49] In her

---

[44] See Jane Marcus, 'Corpus/Corps/Corpse: Writing the Body in/at War', in Helen Zenna Smith (eds), *Not So Quiet... Stepdaughters of War* (New York: The Feminist Press, 1989), 241–300; Claire M. Tylee, *The Great War and Women's Consciousness: Images of Militarism and Womanhood in Women's Writings, 1914–64* (Basingstoke: Macmillan, 1990), 55; Margaret Higonnet et al. (eds), *Behind the Lines: Gender and the Two World Wars* (New Haven, CT: Yale University Press, 1987); Higonnet, 'Authenticity and Art in Trauma Narratives of World War I', *Modernism/Modernity* 9/1 (January 2002), 91–107; and *Nurses at the Front: Writing the Wounds of the Great War* (Boston, MA: Northeastern University Press, 2001).

[45] Borden, *Forbidden Zone*, 1.   [46] Ibid., 168.

[47] Lyn MacDonald, *Roses on No Man's Land* (Basingstoke: Papermac, 1980), 12.

[48] Ibid., 169.

[49] Irene Rathbone, *We That Were Young* (1932; repr. New York: Feminist Press at the City University of New York, 1989), 197.

nightmare, acts such as probing, plunging, and digging into men's bodies, that one regularly comes across in nurses' memoirs, are not just shameful reversals of gender roles: they are figured as unambiguously hostile, phallic, and predatory ('German sausage'). Is the sense of guilt due to the inadvertent pain she has inflicted while dressing the wounds, or is it an internalization of the 'guilt male writers also projected on the disturbing figures of the nurse',[50] as Jane Marcus has argued, or are such feelings endemic to situations of traumatic witnessing?

While recent criticism has fruitfully employed the category of gender to understand women's war and particularly nursing experiences, the pain and conflict in women's nursing memoirs often lie not just in the sense of being a woman and thus barred from specific kinds of male experience, but rather—and cutting across the gender divide—in certain deeper ethical and epistemological problems inherent in bearing testimony to situations of extreme bodily agony. As I have argued elsewhere, much of the trauma in nursing memoirs lies in their agonizing awareness of the incommensurability and absoluteness of physical pain—a condition that cannot be shared—resulting in the 'impotence of empathy' on the part of the witnessing subject.[51] Consider the following passage from one of the earliest nursing memoirs—Enid Bagnold's *A Diary without Dates* (1915)—where touch is deliberately avoided, as a mark of both respect and distance:

> But the anaesthetist could not be found.
>
> It was all very fine for the theatre people to fill his shoulder chockfull of plugging while he lay unconscious on the table; they had packed it as you might stuff linen into a bag: it was another matter to get it out.
>
> I did not dare touch his hand with that too-easy compassion which I have noticed here, or whisper to him, 'It's nearly over...' as the forceps pulled at the stiffened gauze. It wasn't nearly over.
>
> Six inches deep, the gauze stuck, crackling under the pull of forceps, blood and pus leaping forward from the cavities as the steady hand of the doctor pulled inch after inch of the gauze into light. And when one hole was emptied there was another, five in all.
>
> Sometimes, when your mind has a grip like iron, your stomach will undo you; sometimes, when you could say 'Today is Tuesday, the fifth of August', you faint. There are so many parts of the body to look after, one of the flock may slip your control while you are holding the other by the neck. But Waker had his whole being in his hands, without so much as clenching them.
>
> When we had finished and Sister told me to wipe the sweat on his forehead, I did so reluctantly, as one were being too exacting in drawing attention to so small a sign.[52]

[50] Jane Marcus, 'Afterword', in Irene Rathbone, *We That Were Young* (New York: Feminist Press at the City University of New York, 1932), 492.

[51] Das, *Touch and Intimacy*, 175–203.

[52] Enid Bagnold, *A Diary without Dates* (1918; repr. London: Virago, 1979), 122–3.

What makes the passage so very difficult to read is the level of precision and detail without any emotional outlet. The hand of the nurse, the point of our identification in the text, is held back, only to be replaced by the hands of the doctor pulling out the stiffened gauze: the tactile is supplanted by the haptic—close-up vision as touch. If physical pain, as Elaine Scarry has noted, cannot be shared,[53] Bagnold draws upon a structure of bodily damage and detail to break through a representational crisis: the verb 'crackling' combines sound, touch, and texture ('stiffened gauze'), especially when produced 'six-inches deep'. The precise detail about surgical pene-tration into Waker's body becomes a penetration into the readers' consciousness, creating an emotional vertigo in the act of reading: we lurch between the twin acts of reaching out and holding back. The five gaping wounds create a gap in the nurse's—and our—comprehension. What is remarkable is the way we are guided through the trope of the hand, from 'I dare not touch' to the 'steady hand of the doctor' to the extraordinary metaphoric eruption—human resilience itself as a hand holding the different parts of the body together as a 'flock' while it is actually being penetrated by the hand—till, at the end of the paragraph, the body is reclaimed by Waker, his open fists eluding our grasp. We are made to realize, once more, the incommensurability of the body in pain. Yet, for that moment in the text, four hands—that of the nurse–narrator, the doctor, Waker, and the reader—are com-pacted through an act of visceral tightening. The much sought-after release comes in the final sentence with its echoes of Saint Veronica wiping the face of Christ.

Civilian contact: Touching, feeling, flinching

But what happens when these war-ravaged bodies and minds come back home? How does wartime violence affect civilian domestic spaces in a post-war society? In his novel *Back to Life* (1920), Philip Gibbs noted how men came back from the war 'restless, morbid, neurotic' and there was an 'epidemic of violence'.[54] In recent years, research into domesticity in the interwar period has revealed how cases of domestic violence went up, conjugal relations often broke down, and women found their husbands 'changed'.[55] Literary texts have long indicated that all was not quiet on the family-front in post-war Britain. From the shell-shocked Chris Baldry in *The Return of the Soldier* (1918) to Sir Clifford, who was shipped back to England 'in pieces' in *Lady Chatterley's Lover* (1928), to the gassed, aggressive, and oversexed Rafe in Hilda Doolittle's *Bid Me to Live* (begun in 1939, published in 1960), the returned soldiers who populate post-war fiction are not just studies in damaged masculinity but represent the way the

---

[53] Elaine Scarry, *The Body in Pain: The Making and Unmaking of the World* (Oxford: Oxford University Press, 1985), 5.

[54] Philip Gibbs, *Back to Life* (London: Heinemann, 1920), 221.

[55] Ibid., 221. Also see George Simmers, 'A Strange Mood', in Kate Kennedy and Trudi Tate (eds), *The Silent Morning* (Manchester: Manchester University Press, 2014), 60–76.

violence and ooze of the trenches had seeped into the innermost core of domestic life. Here, I would focus on two short stories by two civilian writers—D. H. Lawrence and Claire Goll—that dramatize these conflicts with remarkable power. Unsurprisingly for this chapter, the hand becomes a central motif in each.

Lawrence had a very fraught relation with the First World War. He was twice declared unfit for military service by the army medical board: during the examination, he was stripped naked and physically humiliated and was later accused of being a spy because of his German wife. The war becomes for him a traumatic experience, powerfully evoked in novels such as *Women in Love* and *Aaron's Rod*.[56] But his short story 'The Blind Man' takes us in a very different direction. The hero is Maurice Pervin, a war veteran blinded in the war. But the loss of vision has strangely empowered him as Maurice, and with him the readers, move from the visual world into a rich, seductive world of darkness and of touch, the 'sheer immediacy of blood-contact'. Maurice lives with his wife Isabel in 'unspeakable intimacy', interrupted however by fits of 'black misery'.[57] The story begins as the couple is visited by Isabel's friend, Bertie Reid, 'a barrister and a man of letters, a Scotchman of the intellectual type'—the antithesis of the 'passionate, sensitive' Maurice. War blindness here becomes a historical anchor to plumb some of Lawrence's favourite themes—masculinity, intimacy, sexuality, blood-consciousness—and explore the submerged world of emotion and affect around everyday objects and movements and gestures. Lawrence here displays some of his most evocative prose. Domestic space is uncannily evoked through isolated sounds—Maurice's heavy footsteps, or his low voice muffled with the rain-washed darkness of the barn—but more often, almost obsessively, through the hand, as seen and as felt: 'He seemed to know the presence of objects before he touched them…It was a pleasure to stretch forth the hand and meet the object, clasp it, and possess it in pure contact.' The narrative draws us eerily close to the scene so that we observe 'the delicate, tactile discernment of the large, ruddy hands' negotiating knife, fork, and napkin, or the 'delicate touches of the knife-point' on the food, or the 'warm-looking fingers' smelling the violets.[58]

The hand is the site of a peculiar erotic charge: like a healed wound, it both fascinates and disturbs Isabel and Bertie. Midway through the story, Bertie goes into the dark, damp barn to look for Maurice feeding the animals. Amid the intimacy of the barn, Maurice suddenly asks Bertie how disfigured his face is, and as the lawyer feels a 'quiver of horror', the blind man continues 'Do you mind if I touch you?':

> But he suffered as the blind man stretched out a strong, naked hand to him. Maurice accidentally knocked off Bertie's hat.
>
> 'I thought you were taller', he said, starting. Then he laid his hand on

---

[56] D. H. Lawrence's *Women in Love* and *Aaron's Rod* were published in 1920 and 1922, respectively, but they were both written during the war. Also see Hugh Stevens, 'Sex and the Nation: "The Prussian Officer" and Women in Love', in Anne Fernihough (ed.), *The Cambridge Companion to D. H. Lawrence* (Cambridge: Cambridge University Press, 2001), 49–65.

[57] 'The Blind Man', in Finney, *D. H. Lawrence*, 301.   [58] Ibid., 308, 311.

> Bertie Reid's head, closing the dome of the skull in a soft, firm grasp,
> gathering it, as it were; then, shifting his grasp and softly closing
> again, with a fine, close pressure, till he had covered the skull and the
> face of the smaller man, tracing the brows, and touching the full, closed
> eyes, touching the small nose and the nostrils, the rough, short
> moustache, the mouth, the rather strong chin. The hand of the blind man
> grasped the shoulder, the arm, the hand of the other man. He seemed to
> take him, in the soft, travelling grasp.[59]

Lawrence's handling of language here is almost uncanny, as the sentences ebb and flow with the accretive intensity of the clauses. Blindness becomes a brilliant device: is this repressed eroticism masquerading as phenomenological exploration and all the more erotic for it, as the incantatory prose—with the rhythmic repetition, the gentle hiss of sibilants, and the 'delicate hesitancy'[60] of commas—mimics the scene with so fine a pressure, as the hand gropes, pauses, recognizes, and feels the nose, the moustache, the chin? But 'naked', that redundant adjective vital to Lawrentian affect, hints at the senses of exposure and violation on which this drama of arousal and assault turns. Maurice finally asks: 'Touch my eyes, will you? – touch my scar'. As Bertie, quivering with revulsion but hypnotized, lays his fingers on the scarred eyes, Maurice covers them with his own hand and presses Bertie's fingers upon his disfigured eye-sockets, 'trembling in every fibre and rocking slightly'.[61] As the fingers interlock, we as readers—even as we flinch—are drawn into that closed space without knowing what exactly is happening or into whose fingertips—Bertie's or Maurice's—our sympathies flow. Trudi Tate has observed that the scene is full of 'static, suppressed violence', with hints of anal penetration.[62] However, the linguistic intimacy or contagion between the Bertie's 'quiver' and Maurice 'trembling' makes the scene palpitate perilously between seduction and violation, the phobic and the erotic. Intimate, violent, tender, with each running into the other, the scene touches us on that fragile spot where categories collapse—not just the homo/hetero threshold, endlessly attractive for the sexually conflicted Lawrence—but a more fundamental fusion and confusion between horror and pleasure, tenderness and abuse, phenomenology and eroticism, voyeurism and tactility.

In historical terms, if life in the trenches led to the breakdown of civilian tactile norms among men, the above passage is one of the most powerful imaginings of male touch and intimacy within the civilian context in post-war British fiction. What challenged heterosexuality in post-war British society was not sexual

---

[59] Ibid., 316.
[60] John Bayley, *The Short Story: Henry James to Elizabeth Bowen* (London: Palgrave, 1988), 126–7. Also see Abbie Garrington, *Haptic Modernism: Touch and the Tactile in Modernist Writing* (Edinburgh: Edinburgh University Press, 2013), 164–5.
[61] 'The Blind Man', 316.
[62] Tate, *Modernism, History and the First World War* (Manchester: Manchester University Press, 1998), 107.

dissidence per se but the veterans' powerful memories of same-sex intimacy and intensity which went beyond the conventional categories of gender and sexuality. In formal terms, the above scene almost stages the strange linguistic power of Owen's poetry, in the way Owen, Maurice-like, half-seduces, half-forces the reluctant yet curious reader through word and sound to 'feel' the wounds, as in the above-quoted passages from 'Disabled' or 'Exposure'. At the end of the story, Bertie is like a 'mollusc' whose shell has been broken. But what about Isabel, one may ask?

Claire Goll's 'The Hand of Wax' imagines the return of the soldier and his interruption of post-war civilian society from the perspective of the wife. But the situation here is fundamentally different from that in Rebecca West's more celebrated novel. The returned soldier is not shell-shocked like Chris Baldry, or blinded like Lawrence's Maurice; instead, he has lost his right arm. Claire Goll (née Clarisse Liliane Aischmann) was a German poet and novelist who was born in Nuremberg to wealthy Jewish parents and, during the war years, went to Geneva to study philosophy.[63] She moved in pacifist and expressionist circles, collaborated on pacifist papers in Switzerland such as the *National-Zeitung*, had an affair with Rainer Maria Rilke, and married the Jewish poet Ivan Goll. In 1918, she published a pacifist collection of stories *Die Frauen erwachen* (*Women Awake*, 1918) in which 'The Hand of Wax' appeared. The collection was dedicated 'to all sisters', and as Margaret Higonnet notes in her insightful introduction to the story, contemporary reviewers turned her into a sort of 'female Barbusse'. Later, the couple moved to Paris, where they knew writers and artists such as Joyce, Colette, Gide, and Picasso.

Like Lawrence's, Goll's story also begins with the act of waiting: a young woman stands 'searching, anxious' at the railway station for her wounded husband returning from the war.

> When their eyes met fear shot through her like an electric shock. Her glance fell to the level of the hand and remained there as if glued to it, so that he began to move it uncomfortably to and fro. Like a white animal, pale and ghostlike, the hand seemed to creep out of his sleeve. A hand made of wax.

And more: 'The woman trembled as she imagined being accidentally touched by it'.[64] Published in 1918, when the returned soldier has acquired an almost saintly status and his wounds sacralized, the tremor of revulsion, even if inadvertent, is a sharply dissident response. As the story unravels, we realize that Ines is a committed pacifist who is haunted by the violence he has inflicted on the enemy side. She accosts him directly, noting that 'every one of our victories' merely proves that 'we are better at killing':

[63] For information on Claire Goll, see Margaret Higonnet (ed.), *Lines of Fire: Women Writers of World War I* (New York: Penguin, 1999), 88–9. The biographical details about Goll are taken from Higonnet's Introduction.

[64] Claire Goll, 'The Hand of Wax', in Agnes Cardinal, Dorothy Goldman, and Judith Hattaway (eds), *Women's Writing on the First World War* (Oxford: Oxford University Press, 2002), 245.

He too became harsh and played his trump card: 'Is this the thanks we get for sacrificing our hand on the altar of the fatherland?'

Thus confronted she remained silent. How often in future would the hand and his
heroism be used against her?[65]

As he recounts his exploits—particularly about killing a young, married soldier who
had asked for mercy—she cries out: 'You are no better than a murderer'. Later in the
night, as she lies beside her husband, she is haunted by this unknown soldier her husband had killed. Suddenly, 'her hand came into contact with something smooth and
soft': it is the hand of wax her husband had taken off and its 'protruding fingers' seem
to point at her. Bodily disgust is compacted with political critique and expressionist
fantasy: the 'hand of wax' begins to grow bigger and bigger till it 'filled the entire
room, every one of its fingers pointing at her with an accusing: You!' It begins to
'creep' upon her, any moment it is going to 'touch' her, it is going to 'lie on top of her
for the rest of the night, every night'. Traumatized, she gets up, unwraps a poisonous
pill and 'her face grew composed as she drank it down slowly and to the last drop'.[66]

What is remarkable about the story is the way the hand is at once metaphorical
and visceral: it becomes the battleground for the fight between nationalism and
pacifism while being a daily object of trauma and shrinking. The two come together
in the terrifying night vision, joining the accusatory force of the war propaganda
posters ('YOU') with sexual disgust, as it articulates the untold story of thousands
of women who had to sleep with severely wounded men, and yet could never give
voice to their feelings in face of the 'greater' sacrifice. If Connie in *Lady Chatterley's
Lover* moves from Sir Clifford to the undamaged and virile war veteran Mellors, her
more politically aware literary cousin Ines in Goll's story cannot accept either. The
'hand of wax' ultimately becomes a symbol of her own seared conscience, of the
indirect 'hand' of women in the 'murder'. Goll's story remains one of the most
haunting and coruscating explorations of the ownership of and responses to indirect responsibility.

Writing about modern subjectivity in 1977, Roland Barthes notes:

> for us the 'subject' (since Christianity) *is the one who suffers*: where there is a wound,
> there is a subject: *die Wunde! Die Wunde!* says Parsifal, thereby becoming 'himself'; and
> the deeper the wound, at the body's centre (at the 'heart'), the more the subject becomes
> a subject: for the subject is *intimacy* ('The wound…is of a frightful intimacy').[67]

In the experiences of the First World War, the hand emerges as both the subject and
the bearer of a similar 'frightful intimacy'. The war brutalized the male body to an
unprecedented degree, but also created moments of unique intensity—in the battlefields, the war hospitals, or in post-war civilian life—which were mediated and

---

[65] Ibid., 246.   [66] Ibid., 249–50.

[67] Roland Barthes, *A Lover's Discourse: Fragments*, trans. Richard Howard (London: Vintage,
2002), 189.

understood through or projected on our most expressive and intimate body parts. Symonds's *fin-de-siècle* observation that 'there is soul in the fingers—they speak' would acquire a fresh lease of life in the trenches of the First World War. The hand that had touched the 'wound' of another—whether that of a dying comrade or of an injured patient-soldier or a combatant-husband—now probes into its own 'wound' and *writes*.

FURTHER READING

Buck, Claire. *Conceiving Strangeness in British First World War Writing* (London: Palgrave, 2015).

Cole, Sarah. *Modernism, Male Friendship and the First World War* (Cambridge: Cambridge University Press, 2003).

Das, Santanu. *Touch and Intimacy in First World War Literature* (Cambridge: Cambridge University Press, 2005).

Das, Santanu. (ed.) *The Cambridge Companion to the Poetry of the First World War* (Cambridge: CambridgeUniversity Press, 2014).

Einhaus, Ann-Marie. *The Short Story and the First World War* (Cambridge: Cambridge University Press, 2013).

Fussell, Paul. *The Great War and Modern Memory* (Oxford: Oxford University Press, 1975).

Garrington, Abbie. *Haptic Modernism: Touch and the Tactile in Modernist Writing* (Edinburgh: Edinburgh University Press, 2013).

Higonnet, Margaret (ed.) *Nurses at the Front: Writing the Wounds of the Great War* (Boston, MA: Northeastern University Press, 2001).

Kendall, Tim. (ed.) *The Oxford Handbook of Twentieth-Century British and Irish Poetry* (Oxford: Oxford University Press, 2007).

McLoughlin, Kate. *Authoring War: The Literary Representation of the War from the Iliad to Iraq* (Cambridge: Cambridge University Press, 2011).

Sherry, Vincent. *The Great War and the Language of Modernism* (New York: Oxford University Press, 2003).

Sherry, Vincent. (ed.) *The Cambridge Companion to the Literature of the First World War* (Cambridge: Cambridge University Press, 2004).

Stewart, Susan. *Poetry and the Fate of the Senses* (Chicago, IL: Chicago University Press, 2002).

Tate, Trudi. *Modernism, History and the First World War* (Manchester: Manchester University Press, 1998).

CHAPTER 25

THE CULT OF THE CHILD REVISITED

Making Fun of Fauntleroy

MARAH GUBAR

' "We want to be left alone!" ' So say a delegation of child citizens who march into the office of a city mayor in 'The Children That Lead Us' (1908), a brief comic fantasy by Jewish-American journalist Simeon Strunsky. This piece skewers the excesses and hypocrisies of the phenomenon that English poet Ernest Dowson had celebrated in his 1889 essay 'The Cult of the Child'. In the process, it reveals how integral child-centred art was to transatlantic mass culture in the period from 1880–1920.

One by one, Strunsky's young protesters step forward as representatives of various aggrieved 'unions' who object to young people being 'overworked' by Anglo-American adults both symbolically and literally.[1] For example, whereas Dowson views the trend of small children playing starring roles on the turn-of-the-century stage as 'an enormous boon', Strunsky has a delegate from 'Local No. 16 Children of Weak and Tempted Stage Mothers' complain that playwrights too frequently deploy heartstring-tugging child characters as the saviours of their parents' disintegrating marriages.[2] In so doing, he highlights how young people were simultaneously being exalted for their capacity to resolve adult conflicts and exploited as labourers both onstage and elsewhere.

To reinforce this point, Strunsky juxtaposes a jaunty representative of the 'Union of Precocious Magazine Children'—who wants the mayor to pledge that 'no magazine fiction child under the age of twelve shall be represented as possessing an amount of intelligence greater than the combined wisdom of its parents'—with a

---

[1] Simeon Strunsky, 'The Children that Lead Us', *Bookman* 35/207 (February 1908), 589–93.
[2] Ernest Dowson, 'The Cult of the Child', repr. in Desmond Flower and Henry Maas (eds), *The Letters of Ernest Dowson* (London: Cassell, 1967), 433–5.

painfully abashed delegate from the 'Amalgamated Union of Cash Girls and Juvenile Cotton Mill and Glass Factory Operatives' (590–2). The mayor finds it 'impossible to decide' whether this working-class child is thirteen or twenty-five because she seems both stunted and prematurely aged by poverty and labour. Nor does Strunsky ignore the effects of racial divisions on young people. A white child protests against the genetic purification policies advocated by British eugenics enthusiasts such as 'Mr. Sidney Webb, Mr. Francis Galton [and] Mr. George Bernard Shaw', while a black child describes how overwhelmed African-American children feel about Booker T. Washington's injunction that they are 'charged with th' future of the negro race'.[3]

Long-forgotten send-ups such as this one, I contend, should prompt us to revise our critical story about the cult of the child. To begin with, rather than limiting our focus to English authors and making gender and sexuality the central terms of our analysis, we should follow in Strunsky's footsteps and regard the cult as a transatlantic phenomenon that coincided with the rise of consumer capitalism and registered a wide array of contemporary anxieties, including concerns about class stratification and racial tension. Too often, we assume that childhood's allure for adults during this era stemmed from its perceived remoteness from adulthood; on this account, adult authors portray childhood as 'a world apart' in order to stage imaginary retreats from the pressures of modern life.[4] Such peaceful detachment forms no part of Strunsky's picture of how his contemporaries treat young people. On the contrary, his child protesters complain that they are so often enlisted to intervene in adult affairs that they feel compelled to go on strike. They are not innocent 'others' so much as precocious intermediaries charged with 'the task of solving the gravest problems' of modern existence, from the rocky state of turn-of-the-century gender and race relations to widespread worries about class conflict and rising materialism.[5]

Following Strunsky's lead, I contend that the authors most closely associated with the cult do not deny or ignore social concerns. They acknowledge and attempt to resolve them, albeit in a way that badly backfired. Since the cult is often referred to but rarely defined, let me pause to observe that if there is one trait that all cult-related cultural artefacts share, it is the habit of setting up the child as the epitome of attractiveness, a figure whose power to charm can literally and figuratively stop traffic, transfixing—and often, humanizing—everyone they meet. As the wide range of cultural references in Strunsky's piece suggests, the cult's origins were both transatlantic and trans-generic, comprising short prose by Charles Lamb and Nathaniel Hawthorne, novels by Charles Dickens and Harriet Beecher Stowe, and

---

[3] Strunsky, 'The Children that Lead Us', 592.

[4] Adrienne E. Gavin and Andrew F. Humphries, *Childhood in Edwardian Fiction: Worlds Enough and Time* (New York: Palgrave Macmillan, 2009), 65, 1–13; Dieter Petzold, 'A Race Apart: Children in Late Victorian and Edwardian Children's Books', *Children's Literature Association Quarterly* 17/3 (Fall 1992), 33–6.

[5] Strunsky, 'The Children that Lead Us', 590.

poetry by Algernon Charles Swinburne and Eugene Field. In the closely interlinked realms of literature, drama, and visual art, male as well as female children were exalted by female as well as male artists. For all the attention that Charles Dodgson and John Ruskin focused on little girls, for instance, their contribution to the cult pales in comparison to that of Frances Hodgson Burnett, an Anglo-American novelist and playwright whose most popular child protagonist during her lifetime was the half-English, half-American boy who inherits the title of 'Little Lord Fauntleroy'. This boundary-blurring figure exerted a profound influence on American children's writers such as Annie Fellows Johnston and anticipated the equally spectacular success of J. M. Barrie's *Peter Pan*.

Sometimes, artists associated with the cult attribute the irresistible child's appeal to their unsullied innocence. More often, however, the allure of crowd-pleasing child protagonists derives not from their perfect purity, but from their ability to oscillate back and forth between categories such as child and adult, male and female, rich and poor, even black and white—and, in so doing, help others around them to follow suit, thus destabilizing the notion that human beings can be neatly sorted into opposed identity categories. Burnett's Little Lord Fauntleroy, Johnston's Little Colonel, Barrie's Peter Pan: these exemplars of the cult, I contend, function as go-betweens who bridge the gap between radically different worlds, even as they embody conventionally opposed qualities in their own persons.

In the more sentimental of these narratives, the child's ability to make social divisions seem non-binding leads members of conflicting groups to treat one another with more tolerance, respect, and kindness. As a means of solving the world's problems, this strategy has drawbacks, as contemporary satirists such as Strunsky were all too happy to point out. Once you posit the existence of a child exemplar who remains unmarked by poverty or prejudice—and who helps other characters act as if they, too, are unaffected by their social location—you have come dangerously close to suggesting that privation and bigotry are not serious problems. They can be easily overcome by individuals, and thus no systemic solutions need be pursued.

And yet we should resist the temptation to heap praise on the satirists and skewer the sentimentalists for indulging in nostalgic escapism. For as we will see, the cult narratives and the parodies they inspired alike expressed concern about the excesses and inhumanities engendered by capitalism, even as both cashed in on the popular appeal of the figure of the child. We often denounce the sentimentalists for not doing enough to alleviate class or racial prejudice, pointing out that they do not treat black children exactly the same as white ones, nor poor ones precisely like their higher-born peers.[6] True enough. But surely Johnston and Burnett should get

---

[6] Christopher Parkes, *Children's Literature and Capitalism: Fictions of Social Mobility in Britain, 1850–1914* (Basingstoke: Palgrave Macmillan, 2012), 101–29, 130–59; Ara Osterweil, 'Reconstructing Shirley: Pedophilia and Interracial Romance in Hollywood's Age of Innocence', *Camera Obscura* 24/3 (2009), 9–10.

some credit for insisting that children of different classes and races can be good friends, a progressive move during this era. We miss this point partly because later versions of these stories downplay or eliminate their ethical underpinnings, and partly because we too often presume that children's authors adopt a more 'conservative' or 'unquestioning' stance towards the culture they inhabit than other kinds of writers.[7] In fact, many of the most ingenious contemporary send-ups of *Little Lord Fauntleroy* and his ilk appeared in child-oriented texts by E. Nesbit, F. Anstey, and various dramatists who catered to family audiences. Critics and bookmen such as Strunsky, Max Beerbohm, and Henry James were not alone in exposing the excesses and hypocrisies of the cult; children's writers, too, made fun of Fauntleroy.

Little Lord Fauntleroy, The Little Colonel, Peter Pan: these cult narratives were not singular texts so much as multipart commercial phenomena, stories about crowd-pleasing children that were themselves huge crowd-pleasers, appealing to a diverse audience of children and adults, men and women, Americans and Brits, readers and playgoers and filmgoers. Serialized in a children's magazine in 1885, Burnett's *Little Lord Fauntleroy* became an international bestseller the following year, thanks in part to the spectacular popularity of various stage productions on both sides of the Atlantic. Multiple film versions of *Fauntleroy* appeared, including a 1921 silent version starring Mary Pickford and a 1936 talkie featuring Freddie Bartholomew. Johnston's *The Little Colonel*, published in 1895 in both America and England, was the first instalment in a series that sold 'between one and two million copies' during the author's own lifetime, and inspired a Shirley Temple film of the same title in 1935.[8] Many of Johnston's sequels likewise came out in British editions, garnering praise from English, Scottish, and Irish reviewers who noted that she was 'speedily securing for herself an extended circle of readers in England'.[9] The character of Peter Pan first appeared in *The Little White Bird* (1902), a novel J. M. Barrie wrote for adults, before starring in the blockbuster drama *Peter Pan*, which debuted in London in 1904 and New York in 1905. Next came a variety of prose retellings, most notably *Peter and Wendy* (1911)—Barrie's novelized rendition of the play—as well as multiple films including the silent version directed by Herbert Brenon in 1924.

By the time Barrie introduced Peter to the public, the terms of the cult were so well established that he could simultaneously exploit and make fun of them. No one can resist Peter's charm, which is linked to his status as an intermediary figure or 'Betwixt-and-Between'.[10] Rather than remaining ensconced in the remote realm of

---

[7] Elizabeth Parsons, 'Ideology', in Philip Nel and Lissa Paul (eds), *Keywords for Children's Literature* (New York: New York University Press, 2011), 114; Jackie Wullschläger, *Inventing Wonderland* (New York: Free Press, 1995), 8.

[8] John T. Dizer, 'The Little Colonel and the World She Lived in: The Fiction of Annie Fellows Johnston', *Dime Novel Round-Up* 68/2 (April 1999), 52.

[9] 'Novels and Stories', *Glasgow Herald*, 8 March 1900, 9.

[10] J. M. Barrie, *The Little White Bird*, in *The Works of J. M. Barrie* (London: Hodder and Stoughton, 1928), 129.

Neverland, Peter shuttles endlessly back and forth between the domestic and the fantastic realm and enables other characters (and readers, and playgoers) to do the same. Despite the fact that he himself declares, 'I want always to be a little boy and to have fun' (I.i.398–9), Peter is a boundary-blurring figure rather than a static, stable one: male, but typically played by a female; an eternal child, often embodied by an adult; human, but able to fly like a bird; living, yet strongly associated with the dead.[11] By existing in a state of constant fluctuation between identity categories, Peter serves as a role model both for adults wishing to reclaim their childhood and for ordinary bourgeois children such as Wendy and John Darling, who have already internalized the strict age, gender, and class norms that govern their culture, and who therefore have to learn from Peter how amusing it is to ceaselessly switch sides—a game they never fully master.

Thus, the opening scene of *Peter Pan* sets up the Darling children as foils to Peter in that they have been deeply shaped by the particular gender and class positions they inhabit. Taking after his father, who loudly asserts his own authority as 'master in this house' (I.i.287), John 'despises' girls and spouts sexist comments about the profound 'difference between gentlemen and ladies' (I.i.454; 93–7).[12] Similarly, we soon learn that Wendy takes after her mother in that both of them 'always liked to do the correct thing,' as when Mrs Darling chooses to employ servants even though the family cannot afford it, or Wendy plays the part of gracious 'hostess' and house-wife to Peter when he first enters the nursery.[13] 'Children know such a lot now', says Peter (I.i.410), and one of the things the little Darlings know is that their middle-class status is precarious, because Mr Darling blusters through the nursery bellow-ing that if he does not make a good impression at the work-related dinner party he and his wife are about to attend, he will lose his job and the 'children will be thrown into the streets' (I.i.133).[14] Parental class anxiety triggers all the action that follows: Peter can steal away the children because their parents are off trying to solidify the breadwinner's standing at the office and the servants they have engaged in order to keep up with the Joneses—a dog nursemaid and a child maid-of-all-work—prove unable to protect them.

By planting a precocious child labourer in the midst of this domestic scene, Barrie anticipates Strunsky's point that Edwardian cosseting of middle-class 'dar-lings' went hand-in-hand with the economic exploitation of their working-class peers, who were sometimes treated like dogsbodies. In other words, at a time when the notion of the 'economically useless but emotionally priceless child' still had not gained complete acceptance, Barrie draws attention—albeit in a comic way—to

---

[11] Sarah Gilead, 'Magic Abjured: Closure in Children's Fantasy Fiction', *Publications of the Modern Language Association of America (PMLA)* 106/2 (March 1991), 286.

[12] Barrie, *Peter Pan and Other Plays* (Oxford: Oxford University Press, 1995).

[13] Barrie, *Peter and Wendy*, in *Peter Pan* (Peterborough, ON: Broadview, 2011), 73, 71.

[14] Ann Wilson, 'Hauntings: Anxiety, Technology, and Gender in *Peter Pan*', *Modern Drama* 43/4 (Winter 2000), 595–610.

how unevenly adopted this ideal was, and to the extra financial pressure it placed on male breadwinners.[15] The opening pages of *Peter and Wendy* are full of anxious jokes about money, as when the narrator observes that Mr Darling 'was one of those deep ones who know about stocks and shares. Of course no one really knows, but he quite seemed to know'. Whereas Mrs Darling dotes on each new baby as a priceless treasure, her husband tries to tot up exactly how much they will cost before agreeing to keep them: raising economically useless middle-class children proves so expensive that Wendy only 'just got through... and Michael had even a narrower squeak'.[16]

Although Peter can take the child out of the bourgeois nursery, he cannot take the bourgeois nursery out of the child. Once transplanted to Peter's underground home in Neverland, Wendy instantly reconstitutes the domestic set-up she has left behind, infantilizing Michael by making him sleep in a makeshift cradle and throwing so much energy into cooking and sewing that 'really there were whole weeks when... she was never above ground'.[17] Peter sometimes plays the patriarch to Wendy's housewife, but unlike her he prefers to oscillate between different identity categories rather than fully committing himself to any particular one. 'It is only pretend, isn't it, that I am their father?', he asks Wendy, who 'droops' with despair at his refusal to cleave to her and the lost boys (IV.i.113–14). Rather than decisively accepting or declining this role, Peter flips back and forth between revelling in the respect accorded to him as an adventure-seeking 'Great White Father' and throwing himself into 'a new game' that 'consisted in pretending *not* to have adventures, in doing the sort of thing John and Michael had been doing all their lives, sitting on stools flinging balls in the air, pushing each other, going out for walks and coming back without having killed so much as a grizzly' (emphasis added).[18] Once again, Barrie invites his audience to view the useless middle-class child as an odd, if not unnatural, phenomenon: 'To see Peter doing nothing on a stool was a great sight... [it] seemed to him such a comic thing to do.'[19]

In a passage that encapsulates the dynamic I am singling out as a dominant characteristic in many cult narratives, we learn in *Peter and Wendy* that our hero regards 'white' and 'redskin' as similarly non-binding categories and charms everyone around him—including both lost boys and 'Indian[s]'—into following suit:

> One of Peter's peculiarities... was that in the middle of a fight he would suddenly change sides. At the Gulch, when victory was still in the balance... he called out, 'I'm redskin to-day; what are you, Tootles?' And Tootles answered, 'Redskin; what are you, Nibs?' and Nibs said, 'Redskin; what are you, Twin?' and so on; and they were all redskin; and of course this would have ended the fight had not the real redskins, fascinated by Peter's methods, agreed to be lost boys for that once, and so at it they all went again, more fiercely than ever.[20]

---

[15] Viviana A. Zelizer, *Pricing the Priceless Child* (Princton, NJ: Princeton University Press, 1994), 209.
[16] Barrie, *Peter and Wendy*, 55–6.   [17] Ibid., 107–8.   [18] Ibid., 124, 109.
[19] Ibid., 109.   [20] Ibid., 137, 140, 110.

As he does elsewhere with age and gender categories, Barrie here represents racial identities as performative and exchangeable. Yet this choice does not seem motivated by any serious ethical convictions regarding the evils of bigotry. Instead, it seems of a piece with Barrie's comic impulse to 'pastiche' prior ways of writing for children.[21] Indeed, just a few chapters later, he spends several paragraphs poking fun at the representation of 'paleface' versus 'redskin' battle tactics in adventure stories by showing what would happen if Native Americans actually adhered to the so-called 'traditions of their race'. When the pirates attack them, Barrie's Indians stand frozen in place—and thus, get slaughtered—because 'it is written that the noble savage must never express surprise in the presence of the white'.[22] Unlike the makers of Walt Disney's animated *Peter Pan* (1953), whose offensive 'What Made the Red Man Red?' scene purports to provide 'the real true story of the red man, / No matter what's been written or said',[23] Barrie exposes the absurdity of this literary stereotype, but with such a light touch that he can easily be misunderstood as endorsing it.

But to return to the Gulch switcheroo, that episode takes aim at a different literary target: sentimental cult narratives starring child exemplars who so attractively embody both sides of various binaries that they persuade everyone around them— even those who seem irredeemably 'set in their ways'—to follow suit and become less committed to the norms and prejudices belonging to their sociocultural position. Annie Fellows Johnston's *The Little Colonel* (1895) provides a perfect example of this sort of story. Set in the post-Civil War South, this critically neglected children's novel introduced Anglo-American readers to five-year-old Lloyd Sherman, nicknamed 'the Little Colonel' because she resembles her imperious grandfather, a dyed-in-the-wool Southerner and former colonel in the Confederate army, who before Lloyd's birth disowned her mother for daring to marry a Yankee. When the Sherman family is forced for financial reasons to move back to Kentucky, little Lloyd wins her way into her grandfather's home and heart and then brokers a truce between the warring sides of her family. In so doing, she symbolically reconciles North and South, a task for which she is especially suited because of her mixed parentage. Her very name attests to this ability to facilitate the peaceful coexistence of opposing forces, since it yokes together the Old South (as personified by her grandfather Lloyd, a proud plantation owner) with the man who helped mastermind its destruction (General William Tecumseh Sherman, loathed by Southerners for razing such homes).

Like Peter Pan, the Little Colonel hovers in between such categories as male and female, child and adult, animal and human. Although she is adorably cute in a

[21] Jacqueline Rose, *The Case of Peter Pan* (Philadelphia, PA: University of Pennsylvania Press, 1992), 78.
[22] Barrie, *Peter and Wendy*, 137–8.
[23] Sammy Fain (music) and Sammy Cahn (lyrics), 'What Made the Red Man Red?', in *Peter Pan* (Disney, 1953), dir. Clyde Geronimi, Wilfrid Jackson, and Hamilton Lusky.

girlish way, Lloyd's name, short hair, and hoydenish behaviour make her a gender-bending figure. 'I de'pise to be a little lady', she declares. She talks with a childish lisp, yet Johnston emphasizes that little Lloyd 'had lived among older people so entirely that her thoughts were much deeper than her baby speeches would lead one to suppose'.[24] In fact, Lloyd often behaves in more 'brave and womanly' ways than her own mother, hiding her anxieties so as not to trouble Mrs Sherman, a flighty, 'girlish' person.[25] By turns knowing and naive, this 'little woman' also straddles the line between animal and human, since Johnston repeatedly links Lloyd to her equally cute and curious dog, Fritz, as when the old colonel first observes these 'stray guests' pressing their collective noses against the entrance gate to his estate.[26]

This opening scene is one of many moments when Lloyd appears poised on some kind of 'threshold'. Like Peter Pan, who first appears as a face at the window of the Darlings' nursery, the Little Colonel is closely associated with liminal space, including fences, hallways, doors, and steps. Tellingly, the conclusion of Johnston's story finds Lloyd declaring her intention not to move in to the grand estate she will someday inherit from her grandfather, nor to remain in her parents' cottage, but instead to continue moving back and forth between them: 'I'm to live in both places at once.'[27] She is, indeed, a stray. Director David Butler brilliantly enlarged on this theme by incorporating into the 1935 film version of *The Little Colonel* a staircase dance modelled on the ones that Shirley Temple's African–American co-star Bill 'Bojangles' Robinson had made famous in his vaudeville routine. Noting that she and Robinson held hands while moving up and down the steps, Temple later recalled, 'We were the first interracial dancing couple in movie history'.[28]

This edgy dance faithfully reflects Lloyd's status in Johnston's text as a character who troubles the colour line. Despite being raised in the North by parents who speak unaccented English, the Little Colonel pronounces words such as 'howevah', 'yo'ah' and 'suh' exactly as African-American characters in the novel do and prides herself on behaving in other ways 'just like a little niggah'.[29] As Johnston's use of this offensive word attests, she never manages to distance herself completely from the racial prejudices of her time. Nevertheless, she deploys the figure of the boundary-blurring child as part of an ethically motivated effort to help combat bigotry. In her role as go-between, Lloyd not only persuades a stubborn old Southerner to embrace his Northern son-in-law, she also convinces him to behave more respectfully towards the former slaves whom he still treats as despised inferiors. In what Dennis Duffy rightly characterizes as the primal scene of the series, Lloyd's grandfather

---

[24] Annie Fellows Johnston, *The Little Colonel* (Gretna, LA: Firebird Press, 1998), 38, 31.
[25] Ibid., 108, 78.   [26] Ibid., 83, 14.   [27] Ibid., 93, 161.
[28] Shirley Temple Black, *Child Star: An Autobiography* (New York: Warner Books, 1988), 98.
[29] Johnston, *The Little Colonel*, 39.

catches her making mud pies with May Lilly and Henry Clay, the children of his African-American cook.[30] He angrily tries to reassert a strict line of division between the races by rudely ordering 'you little pickaninnies' off 'my premises'. But Lloyd successfully defies him, continuing to mix freely with her friends and forcing him to become more tolerant. In a later scene, for example, the old colonel over-hears Lloyd and May Lilly trading stories about goats, including one obnoxious animal that Lloyd compares to her gruff grandfather. Though sorely tempted to 'order May Lilly back to [her] cabin', the colonel restrains himself and allows the children to continue chatting and playing together.[31] Too charmed by Lloyd to remain fully committed to his old prejudices, he eventually welcomes into his home everyone he has formerly banished, including her parents, his former slaves, and even little Fritz.

Because *The Little Colonel* is set on a beautiful Kentucky plantation, it is tempting to assume that Johnston romanticizes the Old South as Joel Chandler Harris does in his notoriously racist *Uncle Remus: His Songs and His Sayings* (1880). Through his characterization of a cheerful, avuncular male servant, Harris promotes the self-serving white fantasy that African-Americans enjoyed being slaves so much that they were loath to leave the dear old plantation. Proponents of this 'plantation myth' pretended that slaves had been treated like treasured relatives and therefore accepted the white family as their own, as Remus does when he dotes on the little white boy who calls him 'Uncle'.[32] But Johnston adopts a more ambivalent stance towards the past than Harris, as indicated by her decision to dub the old colonel's plantation 'Locust'.[33] This name refers to the type of tree that graces the long avenue that leads to the colonel's stately home. But it also brings to mind a plague the Bible describes God visiting on the Egyptians as punishment for their refusal to free the Jews from slavery: the locusts that 'eat every tree which groweth...out of the field' (Exodus 10:5). The double valence of 'Locust' reminds us that one family's protec-tive shelter can be another's blight. A home that serves as a blessed haven for white people can be a hellish place for their black servants.

Pressing this point, Johnston paints an unflattering picture of the old colonel as a tyrant who makes life miserable for those around him. His former slaves—including the Little Colonel's nursemaid Becky—fear and 'hate' him, because 'they had learned from experience that Old Marse Lloyd had a tigah of a tempah in him'. Unfortunately, the film version of *The Little Colonel* downplays the intensity of their resentment in the process of transforming the African-American characters into more one-dimensional racist stereotypes. Butler's Becky, for example—played by Hattie McDaniel—comes across as a conventional 'Mammy' figure.

---

[30] Dennis Duffy, 'Four Colonels, Two of them Small, With Six Arms Among Them', *Canadian Review of American Studies* 24/2 (Spring 1994), 2.

[31] Johnston, *The Little Colonel*, 42, 126.

[32] Joel Chandler Harris, *Uncle Remus: His Songs and his Sayings* (New York: Penguin, 1982), 47.

[33] Johnston, *The Little Colonel*, 9.

In Johnston's narrative, however, Becky is a more complex character. To be sure, Mrs Sherman perceives Becky as the perfect servant, and little Lloyd regards her as a beloved mother figure. But Becky herself expresses an underlying unhappiness that raises the question of whether she enjoys serving the Little Colonel any more than she did the big one. While taking Lloyd for a walk, Becky begins to sing a 'crooning chant...as mournful as a funeral dirge':

> The clouds hang heavy, an' it's gwine to rain.
> Fa'well, my dyin' friends.
> I'm gwine to lie in the silent tomb.
> Fa'well, my dyin' friends.
>
> It's a world of trouble we're travellin' through.
> Fa'well, my dyin' friends.[34]

Nothing could be further in tone from the cheerful songs that Harris attributes to Uncle Remus, which feature lyrics such as 'Nigger mighty happy w'en he layin' by c'on'.[35] The effect of Becky's 'sorrow song'—to borrow a term from W. E. B. Du Bois's *The Souls of Black Folk* (1903)—is to undercut 'happy darky' discourse by suggesting that she has serious thoughts and relationships that the Shermans do not know about.[36] Unlike many Mammy figures from this era, she is not wholly defined by her relationship to the white family she serves. The Little Colonel intuitively recognizes that this revelation problematizes the intimacy she shares with Becky: ' "Oh, don't, Mom Beck," sobbed the child... "it makes me so lonesome when you sing that way" '.[37] By hinting that social divisions exist that even the most adorable child cannot dissipate, this scene serves as a check on the fantasy that drives the rest of the novel: namely, that an adorable, boundary-blurring child can resolve America's racial and geographic tensions, bringing together groups who used to be bitterly opposed to one another.

Johnston's story owes an obvious debt to Burnett's tales of irresistibly precocious problem solvers, who manage, as Beverly Lyon Clark notes, to 'bridge gaps in age, class, gender, [and] nationality'.[38] The parallels with *Little Lord Fauntleroy* are especially striking. Raised in poverty by his American mother in New York City, young Cedric Errol suddenly inherits great wealth along with an English title from his dead father's side of the family. After arriving at the grand estate he will someday own, Cedric melts the heart of his snobby old grandfather, the Earl of Dorincourt, who years before 'raged like a tiger' and disinherited the boy's father for daring to marry an impoverished American girl. Just as little Lloyd reconciles North and South, little Fauntleroy brings together America and

---

[34] Ibid., 23, 16, 33.   [35] Harris, *Uncle Remus*, 166.

[36] W. E. Burghardt Du Bois, *The Souls of Black Folk: Essays and Sketches* (Chicago, IL: A. C. McClurg & Co., 1903), viii.

[37] Johnston, *The Little Colonel*, 34.

[38] Beverly Lyon Clark, *Kiddie Lit* (Baltimore, MD: Johns Hopkins University Press, 2003), 47.

England, democrats and aristocrats. By story's end, the earl—whose prejudice against 'America and Americans' is originally 'very strong'—welcomes into his home Cedric's old friend Mr Hobbs, a New York City grocer who has similarly been persuaded by Cedric to renounce his 'very bad opinion of "the British"'' in general and the aristocracy in particular.[39]

Indeed, everyone Cedric meets—whether English or American, rich or poor, old or young, male or female, animal or human—quickly succumbs to his 'irresistible' charm, which derives from his uncanny ability to inhabit all these categories simultaneously. Like Peter Pan and Lloyd Sherman, Cedric is a gender-bending figure who enjoys a special kinship with animals. When he meets his grandfather for the first time, he 'stray[s] forward together' with a large dog who—though usually distrustful of strangers—has taken an instant liking to him. In the course of this scene, Burnett stresses how 'brave' and 'manly' Cedric is while also rhapsodizing about his long hair and frilly lace-and-velvet garment, soon to be marketed as the 'Fauntleroy suit'.[40] Burnett anticipates Johnston's explanation for the Little Colonel's precocity by noting that Cedric exhibits 'a mixture of maturity and childishness' because 'he has lived more with older people than with children'. Just like Johnston's 'little woman', Burnett's 'little man' seems knowing one moment and naive the next, leading the adults around him to wonder just how much he understands about the world and the inner lives of adults around him.[41]

That said, the plot of Little Lord Fauntleroy hinges on Cedric's apparent cluelessness about money and class status. Failing to recognize that his grandfather is a mercenary snob, Cedric treats him as if he were a kind and liberal man, thus prompting the earl to begin acting in accordance with this idealized vision of himself. Similarly, because Cedric regards everyone he meets as a friend, regardless of their socio-economic status, they return the favour. During his first trip down the grand, tree-lined avenue that leads to his grandfather's estate—shades of Locust!— Cedric expresses a naive intention to make playmates of the gatekeeper's children. His friendly manner prompts the children's mother and all the other servants at Dorincourt to welcome him like a long lost son, as when the housekeeper tears up and murmurs, 'It's a great day, this'. Any resentment that might have accrued from years of labouring under the thumb of the 'savage' earl instantly evaporates. Servants do not mind being servants, Burnett suggests, when the person they serve seems not to 'realize' his own exalted status.[42] The rigours and hardships of working-class life apparently leave no scars.

Indeed, Cedric himself grows up in poverty yet appears untouched by economic deprivation. When told that he has inherited a fortune, for example, his only desire is to give away his grandfather's money to needier neighbours. Influenced by his example, his old friends Mr Hobbs and Dick the bootblack operate as if they, too,

---

[39] Frances Hodgson Burnett, Little Lord Fauntleroy (Mineola, NY: Dover, 2002), 4, 18, 8.
[40] Ibid., 42–3, 56–7.   [41] Ibid., 49, 6.   [42] Ibid., 55, 76, 55.

were unconstrained by their socio-economic status. Late in the novel, these working-class New Yorkers travel to England to unmask an impostor who pretends that *her* son is the earl's rightful heir, as if the expense and bother of such a trip constituted no obstacle. Moreover, Mr Hobbs then decides to remain in England permanently so as 'to be near [Cedric], an' sort o' look after him'. Apparently, no ties—whether social or familial, patriotic or economic—tether him to his old life. Indeed, the same Mr Hobbs who called for the violent overthrow of the aristocracy at the beginning of the story now identifies himself so closely with the upper crust that he acts 'more aristocratic than his lordship himself', reading the Court news every morning and following 'all the doings of the House of Lords'.[43] Class identity emerges here as a performative choice, entirely unconnected to such crassly material facts as how much money you have or who your parents are.

An obvious irony of the *Fauntleroy* phenomenon is that Burnett made a fortune from a narrative that seems to assert so insistently that money does not matter. Burnett's contemporaries were not blind to this point. Anticipating Strunsky, the creative team behind David Henderson's fairy-tale extravaganza *Bluebeard, Jr.* (Chicago Opera House, 11 June 1889) sent onstage a troupe of child performers, all dressed in Fauntleroy suits, to sing a parodic song that laid bare how Burnett was cashing in on the figure of the priceless child. Not only does the very first line of Fred Eustis and Clay Greene's song 'Little Lord Fauntleroy' (1889) focus on the merchandise—'We are dress'd out in the latest thing for boys'—the third and fourth ones point out that 'Mrs. Frances H. Burnet [*sic*] / Will a mighty fortune get, / From her little Lord Fauntleroys'.[44] Thus, by the time the company of Fauntleroys describe themselves as 'delectable in very many ways', we should not expect that they will follow up this observation by listing various moral virtues that Burnett ascribes to her hero. Still, it comes as something of a shock that the boys are bragging about their marketability:

> We are read by men and women, girls and boys,
> Capital a lot of Companies employs,
> We are played upon the stage,
> Of all novels we're the rage,
> We are little Lord Fauntleroy's [*sic*].[45]

Whereas Burnett repeatedly insisted on Cedric's singularity and specialness, this song prodded playgoers to notice that consumer demand had created a sort of assembly line that was cranking out one Cedric after another. 'Countless' productions of *Little Lord Fauntleroy* were touring the US in 1889 and, as a contemporary journalist noted, 'each has to carry two of his little lordships; for the Society for the Prevention of Cruelty to Children will not let one youngster carry the weight of the

---

[43] Ibid., 172.

[44] Fred J. Eustis and Clay M. Greene, 'Little Lord Fauntleroy', in *Gems from the Latest Spectacular Extravaganza Bluebeard, Jr.* (New York: Richard A. Saalfield, 1889), 11.

[45] Ibid., 12–13.

seven performances per week. These precocious children make a great deal of money, and are worth much in dollars and cents to their parents'.[46]

Because it is so tempting to side with the parodists against Burnett, it is worth noting that the creators of *Bluebeard, Jr.* were themselves cashing in on the commercial appeal of child performers, not only in this number but in a lengthy scene in which young actors played various nursery-rhyme characters in a transparent attempt to draw in the lucrative 'children of all ages' demographic.[47] By the same token, we can read *Little Lord Fauntleroy* as registering Burnett's anxieties about a capitalist system that produced many losers for every winner. In keeping with his general slipperiness as a character, Cedric is not, in fact, completely untouched by poverty, but rather both untouched and touched by it; one of his 'very mature' characteristics is his intimate knowledge of how difficult and unpleasant the lives of poor people are, whether he is worrying over the old apple-woman whose bones ache from standing outside in the rain or informing his grandfather that the unhygienic living conditions of his tenants breeds sickness 'and the children die; and it makes [people] wicked to live like that, and be so poor and miserable'.[48]

Burnett also includes in her narrative a pair of dark doubles for Cedric and his mother in the form of the 'rival claimants' to the earl's fortune, whose disruptive presence reinforces the point that not all poor households are as happy as Cedric and his mother seem to be.[49] Unlike the improbably uncalculating Mrs Errol—who disliked her job when she was single yet 'never once thought it an advantage that [her lover] was an earl's son'—the working-class mother who pretends that her little boy deserves to inherit the lordship instead of Cedric is 'openly mercenary'. Gentle, loving Mrs Errol dotes on her son and remains patient, kind, and generous no matter what her material circumstances are. Meanwhile, her dark counterpart indulges in violent domestic rages, including one in which she throws a plate that leaves a visible, permanent scar on her son's face. In this way, Burnett raises the possibility that some victims of reduced circumstances will 'carry the mark' of that experience for the rest of their lives.[50]

Similarly, Burnett never suggests that the selfish old earl has been totally transformed by interacting with Cedric, only that he begins to behave better so as not to upset his kind-hearted grandson. He and Mr Hobbs never become intimate friends, for example, nor does the earl ever seem truly touched by the plight of his impoverished tenants. Similarly, Johnston does not suggest that the old colonel will himself befriend African-Americans, only that he will tolerate his granddaughter's decision

[46] 'The Lounger', *Critic* (New York) 11/262 (5 Jan. 1889), 7.

[47] Marah Gubar, 'Entertaining Children of All Ages: Nineteenth-Century Popular Theater as Children's Theater', *American Quarterly* 66/1 (March 2014), 1–34.

[48] Burnett, *Little Lord Fauntleroy*, 22, 114.

[49] Ibid., 146; Ariko Kawabata, 'Rereading *Little Lord Fauntleroy*: Deconstructing the Innocent Child', in Angelica Shirley Carpenter (ed.), *In the Garden* (Lanham, MD: Scarecrow, 2006), 33–49.

[50] Burnett, *Little Lord Fauntleroy*, 17–18, 133, 142.

to do so. These children's stories are thus less sentimental than similar adult-oriented narratives by Dickens and George Eliot in which confirmed old misers are completely cured of their miserliness as a result of interacting with young people. Eliot's cultural capital is such that she rarely gets made fun of, yet how fully *Silas Marner* (1861) indulges in the fantasy that an adorable child can trump commercial concerns! When old miser Marner's gold sovereigns get stolen, he mistakes the golden curls of a child who has toddled into his house for his lost treasure. After he adopts her, this 'precious' little one 'link[s] him once more with the whole world' because everyone around him—young and old, rich and poor, male and female—cares so passionately for her well-being.[51] In a baldly literal substitution, yellow curls replace yellow coins and everyone profits. *Silas Marner* should be regarded as an urtext of the cult of the child.

Rather than assuming that late-Victorian and Edwardian children's authors created more nostalgic and escapist texts than their peers writing for adults, we should recognize that they produced interestingly ambivalent iterations of the priceless child plot. By the end of *The Story of the Treasure Seekers* (1899), for example, E. Nesbit has so thoroughly ironized the notion that family members are worth their weight in gold that readers are invited to recognize such sentiments as 'rot'.[52] She and her understudied contemporary F. Anstey often make fun of Burnett's child exemplars, producing comic reincarnations of characters like Fauntleroy to press home the point that idealizing adult rhetoric about children corresponds neither with what young people are actually like, nor with how grown-ups treat them. Whereas Burnett and other adherents to the cult depict children as irresistible autocrats who wrap adults around their little fingers, Nesbit and Anstey lay comic and sometimes poignant emphasis on how frequently young people fail to influence the world around them as they hope to do. Such ineffectuality, they suggest, is linked to children's lack of money and other material resources, but also to their physical smallness and the fact that older people often disregard the opinions and desires of younger ones, however much they may claim to treasure them.

For readers today, this satirical stance seems more appealing than Burnett's sentimentality, particularly when we consider how her clumsy and sometimes self-contradictory efforts to engender cross-class empathy have backfired. We can blame stories such as *Little Lord Fauntleroy* for popularizing what I call the 'Meet the Servants' scene, in which working-class labourers line up to express to an adorable young person the thrill they take in serving them, as they do in more recent cult narratives such as *Annie* (Alvin Theatre, 21 April 1977). 'Life is so unnerving / For a servant who's not serving / He's not whole without a soul to wait upon', sings one such re-energized worker in Disney's *Beauty and the Beast* (1991), keeping the plantation myth alive by exulting in the return of 'those good old days when we were useful'.[53]

---

[51] George Eliot, *Silas Marner: The Weaver of Raveloe* (New York: Penguin, 1985), 226, 190.

[52] E. Nesbit, *The Story of the Treasure Seekers* (New York: Palgrave Macmillan, 2013), 133.

[53] Alan Menken (music) and Howard Ashman (lyrics), 'Be Our Guest', in *Beauty and the Beast* (Disney, 1991), dir. Gary Trousdale, Kirk Wise.

To my mind, such contemporary iterations are more politically retrograde than their late nineteenth-century source texts, since the ethical concerns about poverty and prejudice that informed earlier blockbusters such as *Fauntleroy* and *The Little Colonel* have disappeared from view. Burnett and Johnston were writing at a time when class and racial prejudice were still so deeply entrenched that many authors failed to represent working-class or African-American people at all, or portrayed them in viciously dehumanizing ways. Though they did not entirely succeed, they were trying to promote the 'progressive and democratic' notion that children from different classes shared a common humanity.[54] The critical commonplace that late nineteenth- and early twentieth-century children's literature depicts childhood nostalgically as 'a world apart' starts to seem woefully inadequate when we consider the socially engaged child protagonists created by Burnett, L. T. Meade, Kate Douglas Wiggin, and L. M. Montgomery, not to mention the richly disruptive streak of irony that runs through the work of Barrie, Nesbit, Rudyard Kipling, Beatrix Potter, and L. Frank Baum. Anglophone children's literature from this era is far more stimulating, heterogeneous, and integral to mainstream mass culture than we generally allow.

ACKNOWLEDGEMENTS

I am grateful to Beverly Lyon Clark, who gently encouraged me to resist my own propensity merely to make fun of Fauntleroy. Many thanks, as well, to Troy Boone, Carey Mickalites, and Christopher Parkes for their inspiring and important work on capitalism, class, and turn-of-the-century representations of childhood; to Courtney Weikle-Mills, Pamela Robertson Wojcik, and Kieran Setiya for their perceptive feedback; and to the organizers of this volume for their patience and open-mindedness.

FURTHER READING

Birkin, Andrew. *J. M. Barrie and the Lost Boys: The Love Story That Gave Birth to Peter Pan* (New York: Clarkson N. Potter, 1979).
Freeman, Elizabeth. 'Honeymoon with a Stranger: Pedophiliac Picaresques from Poe to Nabokov', *American Literature* 70/4 (1998), 863–97.
Gubar, Marah. *Artful Dodgers: Reconceiving the Golden Age of Children's Literature* (Oxford: Oxford University Press, 2009).
Kincaid, James. *Child-Loving: The Erotic Child and Victorian Culture* (New York: Routledge, 1992).
Lebailly, Hugues. 'C. L. Dodgson and the Victorian Cult of the Child', *The Carrollian* 4 (Autumn 1999), 3–31.
McGavock, Karen L. 'Cult or Cull? *Peter Pan* and Childhood in the Edwardian Age', in A. Gavin and A. Humphries (eds), *Childhood in Edwardian Fiction: Worlds Enough and Time* (Basingstoke: Palgrave Macmillan, 2009), 37–52.

[54] Parkes, *Children's Literature and Capitalism*, 135.

MacLeod, Kirsten. 'M. P. Shiel and the Love of Pubescent Girls: The Other "Love That Dare Not Speak Its Name"', *English Literature in Transition 1880–1920* 51/4 (2008), 355–80.

Mendelssohn, Michèle. '"I'm not a bit expensive": Henry James and the Sexualization of the Victorian Girl', in Dennis Denisoff (ed.), *The Nineteenth-Century Child and Consumer Culture* (Burlington, VT: Ashgate, 2008), 81–93.

Mickalites, Carey. 'Fairies and a Flâneur: J. M. Barrie's Commercial Figure of the Child', *Criticism* 54/1 (Winter 2012), 1–27.

Nelson, Claudia. *Boys Will Be Girls: The Feminine Ethic and British Children's Fiction, 1857–1917* (New Brunswick, NJ: Rutgers University Press, 1991).

Parkes, Christopher. *Children's Literature and Capitalism: Fictions of Social Mobility in Britain, 1850–1914* (Basingstoke: Palgrave Macmillan, 2012).

Polhemus, Robert M. 'John Millais's Children: Faith, Erotics, and *The Woodman's Daughter*', *Victorian Studies* 37/3 (Spring 1994), 433–50.

Robson, Catherine. *Men in Wonderland: The Lost Girlhood of the Victorian Gentleman* (Princeton, NJ: Princeton University Press, 2001).

Roth, Christine. 'Ernest Dowson and the Duality of Late Victorian Girlhood: "Her Double Perversity"', *English Literature in Transition 1880–1920* 45/2 (2002), 158–75.

Roth, Christine. 'Babes in Boy-Land: J. M. Barrie and the Edwardian Girl', in Donna R. White and C. Anita Tarr (eds), *J. M. Barrie's 'Peter Pan' In and Out of Time: A Children's Classic at 100* (Lanham, MD: Scarecrow Press, 2006), 47–67.

Sardella-Ayres, Dawn. '"Some of Your Father's Miserable Yankee Notions": Annie Fellows Johnston's *The Little Colonel*', MPhil thesis, University of Cambridge, 2013.

Saville, Julie F. 'The Romance of Boys Bathing: Poetic Precedents and Respondents to the Paintings of Henry Scott Tuke', in Richard Dellamora (ed.), *Victorian Sexual Dissidence* (Chicago, IL: University of Chicago Press, 1999), 253–77.

Sorby, Angela. *Schoolroom Poets: Childhood, Performance, and the Place of American Poetry, 1865–1917* (Durham, NC: University of New Hampshire Press, 2005).

Taylor, Jenny Bourne. 'Between Atavism and Altruism: The Child on the Threshold in Victorian Psychology and Edwardian Children's Fiction', in Karín Lesnik-Oberstein (ed.), *Children and Culture: Approaches to Childhood* (New York: Palgrave Macmillan, 1998), 89–121.

Vicinus, Martha. 'The Adolescent Boy: Fin-de-Siècle Femme Fatale?', in Richard Dellamora (ed.), *Victorian Sexual Dissidence* (Chicago, IL: University of Chicago Press, 1999), 83–106.

Wood, Naomi. 'Creating the Sensual Child: Paterian Aesthetics, Pederasty, and Oscar Wilde's Fairy Tales', *Marvels & Tales* 16/2 (2002), 156–70.

CHAPTER 26

INTERSEXIONS

Dandyism, Cross-Dressing, Transgender

JANA FUNKE

Late nineteenth- and early twentieth-century literature and culture were characterized by a fascination with ambiguously gendered or cross-gendered figures, such as the New Woman and the New Man, the male and female dandy, the crossdresser and transvestite, and the sexual invert. Rather than stand alone as discrete phenomena, these figures indicate a wider and specifically modern interest in a spectrum of gendered and sexual as well as aesthetic, social, and political possibilities that were explored in different ways at the turn of the twentieth century. The three terms mentioned in the title of this chapter—'dandyism', 'cross-dressing', and 'transgender'—indicate the exceptional richness and openness characterizing debates about gender and sexuality at this particular historical moment. Overdetermined and unstable, such terms refer to various forms of desire, identification, and embodiment that are closely related and similar in the challenges they pose to fixed gender binaries and sexual codes. There are also, however, important differences that become apparent when historicizing 'dandyism', 'cross-dressing', and 'transgender' and placing them in the context of a period that witnessed the emergence of new terms like 'transvestism' or 'intersex', which were understood and defined in relation to other neologisms, such as 'homosexuality' or 'sexual inversion'.

Despite the fact that the late nineteenth and early twentieth centuries saw the development of such new vocabularies, this historical moment has also been viewed as a period in which possibilities concerning the representation of the sexed body, gender, and sexuality, especially in literary writing, diminished. This alleged shift has often been tied to the emergence and popularization of scientific and medicalized understandings of gender and sexuality in the period from 1880 to 1920 and beyond. It has been argued, for instance, that the turn of the twentieth century witnessed the rise of a 'surgical modernism' that brought to an end more open-ended engagements with the body, selfhood, and sexuality at the *fin de siècle*.[1] Here, the transition from the *fin de siècle* to the modernist period is understood as a shift from appearance to essence, from ambiguity to singularity, and from aesthetic possibility to scientific reductivism. Similarly, some feminist scholars have suggested that the growing authority of sexual science at the turn of the century narrowed down possible ways of understanding the female body and female desire.[2] This has led to a tendency to understand the development of what is called Sapphic or lesbian modernism over the course of the early twentieth century as a form of opposition to sexual science, with key texts like Virginia Woolf's *Orlando* (1928) or Djuna Barnes's *Nightwood* (1936) being credited with debunking or challenging a masculinist scientific and medical discourse.

In keeping with such broad narratives, the New Woman and the dandy have been grouped together as belonging to a discursive moment at the *fin de siècle* that predated the rise of sexual science towards the end of the nineteenth and beginning of the twentieth century in Europe. In particular, the year of 1895 has been seen as a turning point witnessing not only the Wilde trials, but also the publication of a series of *Punch* cartoons hailing the demise of the New Woman.[3] The dandy and the New Woman fell victim to a moral panic concerning allegedly 'decadent' and 'deviant' genders and sexualities, but it has also been argued that these figures were increasingly affected by views of gender and sexuality derived from or linked to sexual science. In particular, dandyism and New Woman writing have been presented as more open-ended in their understanding of cross-gendering, figuring gender crossing in terms of masquerade or appearance instead of insisting on an essential and fixed inner gender and sexual identity, an idea that has come to be associated with sexual science.

In particular, it has been suggested that the effeminate dandy and the masculine New Woman began to be read in terms of same-sex desire, and, more specifically, in terms of identity-based models of homosexuality. With regard to dandyism, many scholars have suggested that it became more difficult after the Wilde trials to tease apart effeminacy and homosexual desire, and to view cross-gendering purely in terms of masquerade rather than as an expression of an essential homosexual self, with Wilde coming to represent the prototype of the effeminate homosexual.[4]

---

[1] Tim Armstrong, *Modernism, Technology and the Body: A Cultural Study* (Cambridge: Cambridge University Press, 1998).

[2] See, among other works, Sheila Jeffreys, 'Women and Sexuality', in June Purvis (ed.), *Women's History: Britain, 1850–1945: An Introduction* (Abingdon: Routledge, 1995).

[3] See Nicholas Freeman, *Drama, Disaster and Disgrace in Late Victorian Britain* (Edinburgh: Edinburgh University Press, 2011), 178 and Sally Ledger, *The New Woman: Fiction and Feminism at the Fin de Siècle* (Manchester: Manchester University Press, 1997), 96.

[4] See, for instance, Ed Cohen, *Talk on the Wilde Side: Towards a Genealogy of a Discourse on Male Sexualities* (London: Routledge, 1993); Moe Meyer, 'Under the Sign of Wilde: An Archaeology of Posing', in Moe Meyer (ed.), *The Politics and Poetics of Camp* (London: Routledge, 1994), and Alan

With regard to the New Woman, sexual science has been both credited with and blamed for making it possible to read cross-dressing as expressive of lesbian desire. Few critics have pointed out that this 'sexualization' of the New Woman opened up new ways of articulating sexual possibilities.[5] More frequently, however, it has been argued that cross-dressing was increasingly viewed as a clinical (and often pathological) symptom of female homosexuality, which further stigmatized as sexual deviants women who did not conform to social models of femininity.[6] It has also been suggested that, in reading cross-dressing as an expression of an inner self, sexual science made it more difficult to discern the pragmatic or political motivations behind cross-dressing that were central to New Woman writing.

While not unfounded, the assumption of such broad changes obscures important continuities between the *fin de siècle* and the early twentieth century. Indeed, the modernist period did not witness any straightforward or easily discernible shift towards a more rigid scientific or medical framing of the gendered and sexual self. For a start, sexual scientific publications were not widely accessible to non-professional readers, particularly in Britain, where such texts were heavily regulated and even censored in the opening decades of the twentieth century. Moreover, literary writers who did have access to such materials engaged with these in unorthodox ways to negotiate creatively ideas about gender, sexuality, and the self. Most importantly, however, sexual science itself must not be misconstrued as a monolithic and reductive field of debate. Quite the contrary, sexual science existed in productive dialogue with literary negotiations of the gendered and sexual self. Leading British sex psychologist Havelock Ellis, for instance, read, edited, and reviewed literary fiction throughout his life. Like other continental sexual scientists, including Austro-German psychiatrist Richard von Krafft-Ebing and German-Jewish physician Magnus Hirschfeld, Ellis drew widely on literary sources in his sexual scientific studies.[7] As such, sexual science cannot be neatly separated from literary production.

Moreover, sexual science offered new and flexible ways of thinking and conceptualizing gender and sexuality. Indeed, the familiar and influential Foucauldian

---

Sinfield, *The Wilde Century: Oscar Wilde: Effeminacy and the Queer Moment* (New York: Columbia University Press, 1994). For important critical perspectives on Wilde as the 'first homosexual' see, for instance, H. G. Cocks, *Nameless Offences: Homosexual Desire in the Nineteenth Century* (London: Tauris, 2003), Matt Cook, *London and the Culture of Homosexuality, 1885–1914* (Cambridge: Cambridge University Press, 2003), and Kerry Powell, *Acting Wilde: Victorian Sexuality, Theatre, and Oscar Wilde* (Cambridge: Cambridge University Press, 2009).

[5] See Esther Newton, 'The Mythic Mannish Lesbian: Radclyffe Hall and the New Woman', *Signs* 9/4 (Summer 1984); Ledger, *New Woman*, 144–5.

[6] See, for instance, Ann Heilmann, *New Woman Fiction: Women Writing First-Wave Feminism* (Basingstoke: Palgrave, 2000), 128.

[7] See Heike Bauer, *English Literary Sexology: Translations of Inversion, 1860–1930* (Basingstoke: Palgrave Macmillan, 2009); Anna-Katharina Schaffner, *Modernism and Perversion: Deviance in Sexology and Literature, 1850–1930* (Basingstoke: Palgrave Macmillan, 2011).

account of the rise of Western *scientia sexualis* flattens out crucial complexities in the ways in which sexual scientists came to understand the body–mind relation and notions of selfhood. In particular, Foucault's narrative suggests that the concept of a 'hermaphroditism of the soul' (a male brain in a female body or vice versa) produced a modern understanding of the homosexual as a clearly defined 'type' marked by physical and psychological difference.[8] However, sexual science did not collapse the physical and the psychological; nor did it conflate cross-gender identification and same-sex desire to produce homosexual identity. Quite the contrary, sexual scientists sought to develop nuanced frameworks to understand the gendered and sexual self. For instance, socialist reformer and poet Edward Carpenter drew on sexual scientific rhetoric to introduce the notion of an 'intermediate sex' in *The Intermediate Sex: A Study of Some Transitional Types of Men* (written in the 1880s, but first published in England in 1908). While Carpenter did pursue a taxonomic project in producing 'sexual types', the concept of 'sexual intermediacy' and 'transitionality' also captures the flexible ways in which physical sex, gender, and sexuality were understood in the early twentieth century.

Similarly, Hirschfeld developed a model of '*Sexuelle Zwischenstufen*' (literally: intermediate sexual steps) to demonstrate that '[t]he number of actual and imaginable sexual varieties is almost unending'.[9] Thus, the 'intermediate type' constructed within sexual science could take on a bewildering variety of meanings: physically and psychologically, the individual could display masculine and feminine traits, but such cross-gendering did not necessarily have a sexual dimension; conversely, same-sex desire was not always tied either to cross-gender identification or to physical traits associated with the opposite sex.

This definitional openness has led to much scholarly debate over how to read and make sense of the different forms of desire and embodiment represented in early twentieth-century scientific and literary writings. Jay Prosser, for instance, has argued that Foucault's privileging of homosexuality led to an oversight with regard to what would later be described as 'transsexual' subjectivity: in reading cross-gender desire as symptomatic of homosexuality, such accounts effectively erased the histories and voices of subjects for whom cross-gender embodiment was not, or at least not primarily, an expression of same-sex desire.[10] Historically, Prosser's argument is directed primarily against a Freudian psychoanalytic tradition, emerging at the beginning of the twentieth century and circulating in England in the 1910s and, increasingly, the 1920s and 1930s, which viewed cross-gender desire as symptomatic of homosexual desires. Freud did not understand cross-gender desire as anything other than the expression of unacknowledged homosexuality, thus subsuming

---

[8] Michel Foucault, *The History of Sexuality*, 3 vols (New York: Vintage, 1990), I, 43.

[9] Magnus Hirschfeld, *Transvestites and the Erotic Drive to Cross-Dress* (New York: Prometheus Books, 1991), 228.

[10] Jay Prosser, *Second Skins: The Body Narratives of Transsexuality* (New York: Columbia University Press, 1998).

gender expression under sexual object choice.[11] While it is crucial to draw attention
to the often overlooked significance of cross-gender identification in these debates,
privileging cross-gender desire over same-sex desire also misses the point that late
nineteenth- and early twentieth-century sexual science tended to view physical sex
traits, gender identification, and sexual desire as related, and that it offered a number of different models to map these relations.

In England, Ellis and John Addington Symonds, a Renaissance and classical scholar,
jointly authored *Sexual Inversion* (first published and promptly banned as obscene in
England in 1897). They drew loosely on the aetiological model of same-sex desire
offered by German jurist and homophile campaigner Karl Heinrich Ulrichs, who had
introduced the idea that male homosexuality was the result of an individual being
born with a female brain in a male body. However, Ellis and Symonds did not identify
any specific markers of physical difference; nor did they insist on reading homosexuality as necessarily tied to cross-gender identification. Indeed, in their discussion of
male sexual inversion, they were keen to emphasize that the male sexual invert was
psychologically and physically 'masculine'.[12] This was part of a strategic move on
behalf of both authors to assert the health of the sexual invert and challenge pejorative
understandings of male homosexuality as linked to effeminacy and, therefore,
pathology, degeneration, and Decadence, especially after the Wilde trials.

Sexual inversion in women was more strongly tied to masculinity, but, again,
Ellis and Symonds did not mention specific markers of physical difference that
would unmistakably identify the female sexual invert. They maintained that the
female sexual invert often 'feels more at home' in male clothing, but also stated
explicitly that cross-dressing could serve 'practical' purposes and must not be conflated with same-sex desire, since 'a woman who is inclined to adopt the ways and
garments of men is by no means necessarily inverted'.[13] Thus, cross-dressing was
highly overdetermined in *Sexual Inversion*, a text that acknowledges that women
might cross-dress for pragmatic and practical purposes, but also suggests that they
might do so to express same-sex desire or to signal an inner sense of masculinity.

Over the course of the 1910s, some sexual scientists began to distinguish
explicitly between cross-gender identification and same-sex desire. In 1910,
Hirschfeld, for example, coined the term '*Transvestismus*' (translated into English
as 'transvestism' or 'cross-dressing') to set apart the desire to cross-dress from
homosexual desire. Ellis followed suit in a 1913 article published in the medical
journal *The Alienist and Neurologist*, a 1920 article in the *Medical Review of
Reviews*, and a longer chapter in his final 1928 volume of the *Studies in the
Psychology of Sex*. Ellis was 'puzzled by occasional cases . . . of people who took

[11] Ibid., 51.
[12] See Ivan Crozier, 'Introduction: Havelock Ellis, John Addington Symonds and the Construction
of *Sexual Inversion*', in Havelock Ellis and John Addington Symonds (eds), *Sexual Inversion*, ed. Ivan
Crozier (Basingstoke: Palgrave Macmillan, 2008), 54–5.
[13] Ibid., 173–4.

pleasure in behaving and dressing like the opposite sex and yet were not sexually inverted', and coined the terms 'sexo-aesthetic inversion' and 'Eonism' (after the historical Chevalier d'Éon) to describe cross-gender desire as distinct from same-sex desire.[14] He figured cross-gender desire primarily as a psychological and aesthetic phenomenon in which actual cross-dressing is only a minor and comparatively insignificant symptom. Instead, cross-gender desire is played out in the realm of fantasy and dreams—Ellis, for instance, discussed at length the 'dream-system'[15] developed by one of the individuals whose case he records—and finds expression in the eonists' (implicitly heterosexual) 'impulse to project themselves by sympathetic feeling into the object to which they are attracted, or the impulse of inner imitation'.[16] Here, eonism is understood as an organic condition with far-reaching psychological implications; it is not yet, at this historical moment, linked to the desire to physically change sex or alter the body using those medical technologies (mainly hormonal treatments and early surgical interventions) that had started to be developed over the course of the 1910s and 1920s. Instead of a 'surgical modernism' that rigidly constructs a physical body to secure gender binaries and a stable sense of self, then, sexual science could also offer more nuanced psychological readings of cross-gender desire.

As such, the first decades of the twentieth century, like the final decades of the nineteenth century, were marked by considerable definitional openness: within sexual science, cross-gendering and cross-dressing could be indicative of same-sex desire, but this was not necessarily the case; cross-gender desire was increasingly understood to express a deeper sense of self and embodiment, but this psychological dimension was not yet framed within a rigid medical framework of surgical or hormonal intervention. In this sense, drawing on terminologies developed later in the twentieth century, it can be helpful to distinguish between 'transsexuality' and 'transgender': 'transsexuality' often describes the desire to change sex physically with the help of medical technologies, whereas 'transgender' serves as an umbrella term comprising different forms of cross-gender desire and practice, only some of which might be linked to the desire to change aspects of the physical body.[17] 'Transgender' is particularly helpful when thinking about the early twentieth century in that it signals emphasis on an inner self that finds expression not only through the practice of cross-dressing, but also through various imaginative forms of cross-gendering. As such, transgender is not limited to the wish to change sex physically nor is it necessarily tied to the desire to claim a stable and static gender identity.

---

[14] Havelock Ellis, *Studies in the Psychology of Sex: Eonism and Other Studies* (Philadelphia, PA: F. A. Davis, 1928), VII, 7.

[15] Ibid., VII, 40.   [16] Ibid., VII, 27.

[17] Cf. Susan Stryker, *Transgender History* (Berkeley, CA: Seal Press, 2008), 1–29. Stryker points out that 'transsexual' is often used to refer to 'people who feel a strong desire to change their sexual morphology' (18). However, uses of terminology are still unstable and, as such, 'transsexual' can also be claimed by individuals who choose 'neither hormones nor surgery' (21).

Given that sexual science did not simply produce reductive labels and identity categories, it is necessary to develop a more nuanced understanding of the ways in which sex, gender, and sexuality were negotiated within and across literary and sexual scientific writings between 1880 and 1920. While this period was characterized by crucial shifts in the understanding of the self and its relation to the sexed body, gender, and sexual desire, important continuities persisted. These become apparent when examining the intersections between *fin-de-siècle* dandyism, New Woman cross-dressing, and early twentieth-century literary accounts of cross-gender identification and same-sex desire.

The *fin de siècle* witnessed not only the reinvention of the dandy as dandy–aesthete, but also the rise of the New Woman. While ideologically distinct (if not opposed in crucial ways), in the popular imagination the New Woman and the male dandy were often linked as figures of Decadence, in particular because of their perceived attack on established gender roles and sexual codes.[18] Cross-gendering offers one means of thinking about this uneasy alliance between two very different products of *fin-de-siècle* culture. For a start, the dandy and the New Woman were identified in terms of their respective 'effeminate' or 'masculine' sartorial self-presentation; in public criticisms of the New Woman and the dandy–aesthete, their sense of style and dress was a pivotal marker of their deviance.[19] More importantly, dandyism and New Woman writing itself employed cross-gendering to carve out new understandings of the self that defied social conventions and expectations. For the dandy and, in particular, the New Woman, cross-gendering also served to articulate political forms of protest and revolt.

The dandiacal rejection of nature, essence, or substance in favour of artifice, appearance, and style has often been read in terms of gender transgression. Jessica Feldman, for example, has influentially conceptualized the dandy as 'neither wholly man nor wholly woman, but as the figure who blurs these distinctions'.[20] As such, the figure of the dandy challenges the idea that the individual can ever be defined within gender binaries and contests essentialist claims according to which gender dualisms are grounded in nature or the body.[21] In this sense, dandyism approaches a performative understanding of gender as an effect or product of stylized acts and utterances. This view has aesthetic implications in that gender is seen as a textual construct, but it also holds out the promise of developing alternative and potentially subversive modes of selfhood and self-presentation. Dandyism, for instance, was often tied to self-conscious political opposition, particularly to traditional bourgeois models of masculinity.

[18]   See, for instance, Ledger, *New Woman*, 94–100.
[19]   Heilmann, *New Woman Fiction*, 124.
[20]   Jessica Feldman, *Gender on the Divide: The Dandy in Modernist Literature* (Ithaca, NY: Cornell University Press, 1993), 11.
[21]   Ibid., 12–13. See also Marjorie Garber, *Vested Interests: Cross-Dressing and Cultural Anxiety* (New York: Routledge, 1992).

The alleged triumph of style over substance and appearance over essence that allowed the male *fin-de-siècle* dandy-aesthete to imagine himself by assuming gender attributes of the opposite sex, however, did not lead to a collapse of gender binaries or an effacement of the physical body. Dandyism was often criticized as 'feminine' in its defiance of social codes of middle-class masculinity and tied to an assumed feminization of modern culture, but the male dandy's cross-gendering was itself ironically predicated on a rejection of the female body. In Oscar Wilde's *The Picture of Dorian Gray* (1891), for example, Dorian's assumption of 'feminine' traits is valorized within the novel's aestheticist framework while 'woman' continues to be, in Sally Ledger's words, represented as 'hopelessly corporeal, physical and leadenly material'.[22] As such, the promise of a self unburdened by the limitations of the natural and material body is shown to be a decidedly male privilege, predicated on the assumption of an essential difference of the female body. Despite the performative potential of this particular mode of cross-gendering, then, dandyism also insisted on reading the female body as 'natural', thus securing binary and hierarchical understandings of gender.

Such divisions between mind and body, and appearances and essences tended to remain unresolved. Indeed, as Elisa Glick suggests, what is queer about the *fin-de-siècle* dandy is not the performative undoing of essence in favour of appearance, but the staging of the 'queer split between appearance and essence'.[23] In Wilde's novel, Dorian seems to unite soul and body in accordance with Greek ideals of masculinity and beauty, but this illusion is itself predicated on the split between the painting (essence) and the self (appearance). As such, the text troubles but does not ultimately transcend the trope of a divided self caught between the desires of the body and the demands of the mind. In fact, *fin-de-siècle* dandyism (and aestheticism more generally) shared with sexual science an interest in mapping the relation between 'soul and body, body and soul', to borrow Lord Henry's words in *The Picture of Dorian Grey*.[24] Lord Henry rejects as reductive 'the arbitrary definitions of ordinary psychologists', who would impose a rigid Cartesian opposition between the rational mind and the desiring body. Instead, he takes on the role of a scientific observer and sets out to conduct his own 'scientific analysis of the passions', using Dorian as the case study of his elaborate psychological experiment.[25] The specific British brand of sexual science or, to use Ellis's own preferred term, 'sex psychology' which emerged in the 1890s would also set out to challenge the views of 'ordinary

[22] Ledger, *New Woman*, 108. See also Rita Felski, 'The Counterdiscourse of the Feminine in Three Texts by Huysmans, Wilde and Sacher-Masoch', *Publications of the Modern Language Association of America (PMLA)* 106/5 (1991).

[23] Elisa Glick, *Materializing Queer Desire: Oscar Wilde to Andy Warhol* (Albany, NY: State University of New York Press), 20.

[24] Oscar Wilde, *The Picture of Dorian Gray*, ed. Joseph Bristow (Oxford: Oxford University Press, 2006), 51.

[25] Ibid., 52.

psychologists', situating (often unacknowledged or forbidden) sexual desires at the very heart of a new understanding of the sexual self. Sexual science was markedly different from dandyism and aestheticism in viewing such desires and sensations as firmly rooted in nature. Nevertheless, there was a shared fascination with transgressive desires and behaviours that called for the development of new psychological understandings of selfhood that would account for the demands of the physical body and its potentially unruly desires.

New Woman writing of the *fin de siècle* would take up similar questions around the split between appearance and essence, the gendered self and its relation to the body, and develop them in different directions to open up new forms of autonomous selfhood for women. In particular, New Woman authors drew on the trope of female-to-male cross-dressing to explore these issues.[26] Cross-dressing as a man or boy could fulfil a number of different purposes for the New Woman heroine. For a start, it could serve as a pragmatic means to lay claim to forms of power otherwise reserved for men. The eponymous heroine of Lady Florence Dixie's utopian New Woman novel *Gloriana, or the Revolution of 1900* (1890), for instance, cross-dresses as a man, becomes Britain's first female prime minister, and passes legislation that will transform the country into a socialist feminist utopia. More frequently, cross-dressing offered female characters access to a more personal experience of mobility and freedom. In Sarah Grand's *The Beth Book* (1897), for instance, Beth cross-dresses as a boy to explore the space of the city with her male friends. Similarly, in Grand's *The Heavenly Twins* (1893), Angelica exchanges identities with her identical twin, Diavolo, and cross-dresses as a boy, which enables her to move and interact more freely with other male characters; it also makes it possible for her to attend her brother's tutorials and prove herself capable of excelling intellectually.

In addition to fulfilling political goals or opening up personal freedoms, cross-dressing in New Woman fiction also raised complicated questions about selfhood by exploring the relation between mind, body, self-presentation, and social role. It allowed writers to interrogate to what extent masculinity and femininity were fixed psychological traits or fundamentally shaped by social interaction and experience. For instance, Angelica discusses with the Tenor how adopting male clothing affected not only her outward behaviour, but also her inner self:

[H]aving once assumed the character, I began to love it; it came naturally; and the freedom from restraint, I mean the restraint of our tight uncomfortable clothing, was delicious. I tell you I was a genuine boy. I moved like a boy, I felt like a boy; I was my own brother in very truth. Mentally and morally, I was exactly what you thought me.[27]

---

[26] For a more general discussion of cross-dressing and the New Woman, see Heilmann, *New Woman Fiction,* 118–41.

[27] Sarah Grand, *The Heavenly Twins* (Ann Arbor, MI: University of Michigan Press, 1992), 456.

Angelica acknowledges that she began to cross-dress for pragmatic reasons, initially experiencing a sense of liberation. Cross-dressing is also shown to alter her very sense of self, however. Angelica is not only defined socially by the clothes she wears, but she is also shaped psychologically by this experience. Angelica's desire for boyhood is presented as an outcome of social conditions that force women to adopt male roles to lay claim to the freedom they should rightfully be able to experience as women. But the meaning of cross-dressing also exceeds this pragmatic dimension, since it allows Angelica to express a 'natural' part of herself in the process of becoming and being recognized as a boy.

Similarly, Katherine Cecil Thurston's later New Woman novel *Max* (1910) explores the psychological complexities of cross-dressing in a dream-like mirror scene that depicts a female character stepping out of the cross-gendered role she has assumed. The novel tells the story of a Russian Princess called Maxine, who cross-dresses as a boy, Max, to escape from the prospect of a loveless marriage. Maxine passes successfully, and it is only when Max tries on a female wig in private that his gender identity becomes blurred:

> Max leaned forward, quivering to a new impulse, and raising the heavy coils, twisted them swiftly about his head . . .
>
> There are moments when a retrospective impression is overwhelming – when a scent, a sight, a sound can quicken things dead – things buried out of mind.
>
> Max looked and, looking, lost himself. The boy . . . was effaced as might be the writing from a slate, and in his place was a sexless creature, rarely beautiful, with parted tremulous lips and wide eyes in which subtle, crowding thoughts struggled for expression.[28]

Max's performance of femininity triggers memories of his former life as a woman, effacing the boy like 'writing from a slate'. Yet, the narrative does not, at this moment, affirm his 'true' sex (as female) nor does it imply that his inner sense of self is defined by an essential femininity. As Max's outer self-presentation shifts from masculine to feminine, his inner thoughts and feelings reflect the merging and blending of the different gender roles he has assumed and experienced over the course of his life: Max does not step back into his former female role, but 'loses himself', becoming a beautiful 'sexless creature' with indeterminate thoughts that cannot find 'expression'.

If Grand and Thurston seem to favour appearance over essence, clothing over the actuality of the physical body, this is not to suggest that New Woman writing dematerialized the female body. Quite the contrary, cross-dressing narratives in New Woman fiction tend to be episodic—Grand called the chapter on Angelica's cross-dressing 'an Interlude'—concluding with the return to a female self and an arrival in heterosexual marriage. Rather than viewing this as an affirmation of simple biologistic understandings of the female body, however, cross-dressing

---

[28] Katherine Cecil Thurston, *Max* (New York: Harper & Brothers, 1910), 178.

could also serve as a means to negotiate precisely how the body and sexual relations were read and experienced, as is evident in the relation between the Tenor and the Boy in *The Heavenly Twins*—'two disguised and self-inventing characters . . . [debating] the malleability of sexual difference and sexual relationship'.[29] That these personal transformations with their sexual and political implications could only be experienced in an 'interlude', set apart from the rest of the realist narrative in the case of Grand's *The Heavenly Twins*, or marked generically as fantasy in the case of Dixie's utopian novel *Gloriana*, can be read as a strategy of containment; it also, however, serves to draw attention to the difference between a less than satisfying present and an imagined future, opening up a space in which political goals and new forms of selfhood and female embodiment could be articulated.

The development of alternative forms of subjectivity and relationship models between men and women also led to an interest in the figure of the New Man. Some New Woman writers viewed the assumption of feminine attributes by men as dangerously 'decadent'. This makes Olive Schreiner's depiction of the New Man via the trope of male-to-female cross-dressing in *The Story of an African Farm* (1883) all the more striking. Like Angelica/Diavolo or Maxine/Max, Gregory Rose assumes the female role of Rose for pragmatic reasons—to nurse Lyndall. However, this act of cross-dressing is, from the start, presented as having a more personal and also pleasurable dimension, since the female role corresponds so exactly with Gregory's 'feminine' emotional and physical traits, such as his gentleness, empathy, and physical 'softness', which can all be read as characteristic of the ideal of the New Man. Cross-dressing is more than a form of disguise for Gregory Rose. Indeed, Ann Heilmann goes so far as to argue that Gregory experiences 'an emotional, psychological and even, almost, physical sex change . . . [and] becomes in effect a "woman"'.[30] It is by adopting the guise of Rose that Gregory seems to affirm his 'real' self.

The process of cross-dressing, which enables Rose to 'become' a woman, is presented as a fantasy or dream; it is also viewed as an experience that confirms an emotional and physical 'truth' of Gregory Rose's self, who, the novel suggests, has on some level been female all along. More than any other of the New Woman novels discussed in this chapter, then, *The Story of an African Farm* blurs the political and personal dimensions of cross-dressing. In shifting emphasis away from the purely pragmatic and primarily public uses of cross-dressing and towards its employment as a mode of self-presentation that can transform, but also express an inner self, the novel strongly anticipates later conceptualizations of transgender desire.

Such understandings of cross-gendering were shaped increasingly by sexual science over the course of the early twentieth century. Some sexual scientific models

---

[29] John Kucich, 'Curious Dualities: *The Heavenly Twins* (1893) and Sarah Grand's Belated Modernist Aesthetics', in Barbara L. Harman and Susan Meyer (eds), *The Nineteenth Century: Feminist Readings of Underread Victorian Fiction* (New York: Garland, 1996), 198–9.

[30] Heilmann, *New Woman Strategies: Sarah Grand, Olive Schreiner, and Mona Caird* (Manchester: Manchester University Press, 1988), 142.

began to view cross-gender practices and desires as forms of identification that were understood in biologistic terms and could also be tied to the wish to change sex physically. Personal narratives like the *Autobiography of an Androgyne* (1918), published under the pseudonym 'Earl Lind' and introduced by Austro-American medical doctor Alfred W. Herzog, for example, indicate the development in the 1910s of proto-transsexual sensibilities. American author Lind (also known as 'Ralph Werther' and 'Jennie June') embraced the diagnostic categories of 'androgynism' and 'passive sexual inversion' and underwent a voluntary castration at the age of 27.[31] The *Autobiography of an Androgyne* charts the emotional and psychological dimensions of cross-gendering, but ultimately situates these within a medicalized framework that insists on biologically grounded identity categories such as the 'androgyne' or the 'sexual invert'.

Other autobiographical narratives that were also articulated in dialogue with sexual science continued to explore the political, psychological, and creative dimensions of cross-gendering without affirming such rigid typologies. Bryher (Annie Winifred Ellerman), for instance, began to write a series of autobiographical novels in the late 1910s after meeting and befriending Ellis and studying his work. Her first novel, *Development*, which Ellis read and on which he commented in draft form, was published in 1920. Throughout *Development* and *Two Selves* (1923), her second autobiographical novel, Bryher's alter ego, Nancy, expresses her desire to be a boy while also charting her growing awareness of same-sex desires. According to Joanne Winning, Bryher 'conflates some kind of transsexuality with lesbian sexuality, seeing the two perhaps as a seamless continuum'.[32] While cross-gendering is linked to lesbian erotics in Bryher's novels, cross-gender identification is highly overdetermined and, as such, cannot be understood in terms of 'transsexuality'. Nancy's wish to be a boy needs to be situated within a longer literary tradition of female cross-dressing in which cross-gendering serves to express women's 'frustrated desire for action', mobility, and freedom.[33] Bryher, like earlier New Woman writers, appropriated the trope of cross-dressing to highlight social restrictions and educational inequalities experienced by women and, particularly, girls. In this sense, Nancy's longing for boyhood is not simply due to a congenital or inborn condition, nor is it primarily linked to the desire to be a man; instead, Bryher continued to present cross-gendering as a pragmatic response to the social disadvantages suffered by women.

At the same time, Nancy's wish to be a boy is also expressive of a deeper sense of self and has a crucial somatic dimension, which cannot, however, be collapsed with the transsexual desire to alter the body and change sex, and can be understood

---

[31] Earl Lind, *Autobiography of an Androgyne* (Amsterdam: Fredonia Books, 2005), 2.

[32] Joanne Winning, 'Introduction', in Bryher, *Two Novels: Development and Two Selves*, ed. Joanne Winning (Madison, WI: University of Wisconsin Press, 2000), xxxiv.

[33] Martha Vicinus, 'The Adolescent Boy: Fin-de-Siècle Femme Fatale?', in Richard Dellamora (ed.), *Victorian Sexual Dissidence* (Chicago, IL: University of Chicago Press, 1999), 83.

more productively in terms of transgender desire. Indeed, arguably the most inter-esting link between Bryher's use of cross-gendering and sexual scientific debates about cross-gender desire has very little to do with the (at this historical moment still remote) possibility to change physical sex characteristics. Instead, the narrative centres on the imaginative, aesthetic, and creative impulses that both Bryher and Ellis associated with cross-gender identification or, to use Ellis's evocative term 'sexo-aesthetic inversion'. Like Ellis, Carpenter, and Radclyffe Hall, who all main-tained that 'intermediate types' were often born with special imaginative and crea-tive talents, Bryher valorized cross-gender desire as indicative of inborn and organic aesthetic abilities, including synaesthesia.[34] As such, Nancy's cross-gendering is tied to the ability to express herself in writing, to create a self that is both essentially grounded in the body and yet textually constructed. Crucially, Bryher figured development as an ongoing and open-ended process of self-construction without final aim or goal, thus once again resisting the finality of 'changing sex' and inhab-iting stable and static identity categories.

Bryher's autobiographical fiction was produced during a period of transition in which cross-gendering continued to hold different meanings: it could be read as a practical and political response to social restraints, as the expression of an inner longing for masculinity, as a signal of physical difference, and as a means to articu-late same-sex desire. It is possible to argue that this representational openness began to narrow down over the course of the 1920s. The widely publicized obscenity trials of Hall's *The Well of Loneliness* in 1928, for instance, have been understood as a watershed moment as a result of which masculine or cross-dressing women became legible in terms of lesbian identity as 'sexual inverts'.[35] Unlike Bryher, Hall's work of the late 1920s and early 1930s drew explicitly on sexual scientific models of sexual inversion and embraced a biologistic framework to affirm the sexual invert's inborn difference and to naturalize female same-sex desire. However, Hall's fiction also continued to reflect and exploit the definitional instabilities of sexual science. The masculinity claimed by Hall's protagonist, Stephen Gordon, for instance, is shown to be a sartorial effect and crucially dependent on elaborate processes of self-presentation. In this sense, Hall drew on and appropriated earlier understandings of dandyism to negotiate the relation between natural essence and appearance in dialogue with sexual science.[36]

---

[34] Laura Doan, *Fashioning Sapphism: The Origins of a Modern English Lesbian Culture* (New York: Columbia University Press, 2001), 149.

[35] For nuanced readings of this historical moment, see in particular, Doan, *Fashioning Sapphism* and Alison Oram, *Her Husband Was a Woman! Women's Gender-Crossing in Modern British Popular Culture* (London: Routledge, 2007).

[36] For a discussion of Radclyffe Hall's female dandyism, see Glick, *Materializing Queer Desire*, 63–82. See also, for instance, Joe Luchesi, ' "The Dandy in Me": Romaine Brooks's 1923 Portraits', in Susan Fillin-Yeh (ed.), *Dandies: Fashion and Finesse in Art and Culture* (New York: New York University Press, 2001) on American expatriate painter Romaine Brooks.

Hall's short story 'Miss Ogilvy Finds Herself', written in the mid-1920s, but first published after *The Well of Loneliness* in 1934, complicates further any chronological narratives that insist on the decline of representational possibilities over the course of the modernist period.[37] In a fantastical dream sequence that interrupts the otherwise realist narrative, the masculine female protagonist of the short story finds herself reincarnated in the body of a Stone Age man. As such, the text seems to signal an emerging proto-transsexual sensibility. Yet Hall also relied on an earlier tradition of New Woman writing in which cross-gendering was frequently framed within fantastic or dream-like episodes and presented as a means to open up new opportunities for women. Indeed, Miss Ogilvy's longing for masculinity is initially inspired by her desire to serve at the front in the First World War, a possibility that is painfully foreclosed to her due to the fact that she is a woman. In this sense, Hall's work of the late 1920s and early 1930s demonstrates that earlier uses of cross-gendering including those explored within *fin-de-siècle* dandyism or New Woman fiction continued to be employed over the course of the early twentieth century, often in direct dialogue with ideas derived from sexual science.

As such, early twentieth-century understandings of cross-gendering cannot be set apart neatly from *fin-de-siècle* dandyism or New Woman writing and cannot be understood by pitting literary experimentation against sexual scientific taxonomies. If cross-gender and sexual desire became more important in marking and defining the self, there was no straightforward shift towards a more rigid medicalized framework that insisted on stable identity categories and privileged narrow biological explanations. Instead, conceptualizations of gender and sexuality shifted slowly and unevenly over the period from 1880 to 1920: cross-gendering did not always signal same-sex desire and continued to be understood in its practical and political as well as its psychological and somatic dimensions. Indeed, it is the profound fascination with the multifaceted driving forces behind and the manifold expressions of the gendered and sexual self that holds together the very different literary and scientific articulations of gender and sexuality produced in this historical moment.

FURTHER READING

Ardis, Ann L. *New Women, New Novels: Feminism and Early Modernism* (New Brunswick, NJ: Rutgers University Press, 1990).

Bland, Lucy and Laura Doan (eds). *Sexology in Culture: Labelling Bodies and Desires* (Chicago, IL: University of Chicago Press, 1998).

Caughie, Pamela. 'The Temporality of Modernist Life Writing in the Era of Transsexualism: Virginia Woolf's *Orlando* and Einar Wegener's *Man Into Woman*', *Modern Fiction Studies* 59/3 (2013), 501–25.

---

[37] For further discussion of an unpublished draft of 'Miss Ogilvy Finds Herself' in relation to New Woman writing, see Jana Funke, *The World and Other Unpublished Works by Radclyffe Hall* (Manchester: Manchester University Press, 2016).

Dellamora, Richard. *Radclyffe Hall: A Life in the Writing* (Philadelphia, PA: University of Pennsylvania Press, 2011).

Doan, Laura. *Disturbing Practices: History, Sexuality, and Women's Experience of Modern War* (Chicago, IL: Chicago University Press, 2013).

Doan, Laura and Jane Garrity (eds). *Sapphic Modernities: Sexuality, Women and National Culture* (Basingstoke: Palgrave, 2006).

Garelick, Rhonda K. *Rising Star: Dandyism, Gender, and Performance in the Siècle* (Princeton, NJ: Princeton University Press, 1998).

Halberstam, Judith. *Female Masculinity* (Durham, NC: Duke University Press, 1998).

Hausman, Bernice L. *Changing Sex: Transsexualism, Technology, and the Idea of Gender* (Durham, NC: Duke University Press, 2006).

Miller, Monica. *Slaves to Fashion: Black Dandyism and the Styling of Black Diasporic Identity* (Durham, NC: Duke University Press, 2009).

Richardson, Angelique and Chris Willis (eds). *The New Woman in Fiction and in Fact* (Basingstoke: Palgrave, 2001).

Richardson, Angelique. (ed.) *Love and Eugenics in the Late Nineteenth Century: Rational Reproduction and the New Woman* (Oxford: Oxford University Press, 2003).

Rosario, Vernon A. *Science and Homosexualities* (New York: Routledge, 1997).

Showalter, Elaine. *Sexual Anarchy: Gender and Culture at the fin de siècle* (London: Virago, 1992).

Stevens, Hugh and Caroline Howlett (eds). *Modernist Sexualities* (Manchester: Manchester University Press, 2000).

Taylor, Clare L. *Women, Writing, and Fetishism, 1890–1950* (Oxford: Oxford University Press, 2003).

Vicinus, Martha. *Intimate Friends: Women Who Loved Women, 1778–1928* (Chicago, IL: University of Chicago Press, 2004).

PART VI

POLITICAL AND SOCIAL SELVES

CHAPTER 27

POLITICAL FORMATIONS

Socialism, Feminism, Anarchism

RUTH LIVESEY

The period 1880–1920 witnessed the emergence of a socialist movement and the Labour Party in Britain, anarchist attacks on the state, and fresh impetus in the women's suffrage campaign. These three, fairly distinct, political formations were shaped by a host of radical groups that flourished during this period, from clubs that sought to revolutionize sex relations through frank discussion in the drawing room, to movements aiming to establish a new international socialist world order by mass campaigning.[1] The climate that gave rise to these political formations at the end of the nineteenth century was to exercise an extraordinary degree of influence on the modern British state. Whether we look to the provision of social welfare and the National Health Service that grew out of the 1942 Beveridge Report, or to the power of mass trades unionism and the long struggle for equal pay of the later twentieth century, the legacy of the political formations of the period 1880–1920 shaped much of what it was—and still just about is—to be a citizen of modern Britain.[2] But one distinctive characteristic of these early radical formations—one that fell away during the twentieth century—was the way in which literature and the arts were knitted into the texture of politics. Although by 1920 it was common for left-wing thinkers to distance themselves

---

[1] See Stephen Yeo, 'A New Life: The Religion of Socialism in Britain, 1883–1896', *History Workshop Journal* 4 (1977), 5–56; Lucy Bland, *Banishing the Beast: English Feminism and Sexual Morality* (1995; repr. London: IB Tauris, 2001), 3–47; Deborah Nord, *Walking the Victorian Streets: Women, Representation and the City* (Ithaca, NY: Cornell University Press), 198–205; Ruth Livesey, *Socialism, Sex, and the Culture of Aestheticism in Britain, 1880–1914* (Oxford: Oxford University Press, 2007), 44–85; Thomas Linehan, *Modernism and British Socialism* (Basingstoke: Palgrave, 2011).

[2] William Beveridge (1879–1963) was in 1903 a resident of Toynbee Hall, the university settlement house in the East End, and undertook research for the Fabian socialist Beatrice and Sidney Webb during the Royal Commission on the Poor Laws in 1905–9. Radical recommendations in the Minority Report of that commission resurfaced in Beveridge's own 'Social Insurance and Allied Services' (1942), best known as the Beveridge Report.

from the utopian hopes of the *fin de siècle*, late nineteenth-century literature was a forcing ground for the exploration of possible alternative futures for sexual relations, for social equality, and for the individual's rejection of capitalist modernity.

Some of the more explicitly polemical short fiction published in socialist periodicals at the time give a fascinating insight into the intense wave of hope that a new life and social order was imminent at the *fin de siècle*.[3] In the theatre, meanwhile, George Bernard Shaw's works began to provoke and tease distinctions between political platform and stage.[4] But this chapter focuses chiefly on the novel; works by Olive Schreiner, William Morris, and others are testament to how the radical political energies of the 1880s and 1890s pushed against the conventional limits of literary form in pursuit of social transformation. As recent critics have pointed out, for all that self-consciously modernist twentieth-century writers like Virginia Woolf and Roger Fry and the editor Alfred Orage sought to distance their work from such early experimenters in the politics of art and art in politics, an intellectual debt—even in the shape of studied rejection—is evident between the generations.[5] In crossing the conventional boundaries of periodization between the literature of the *fin de siècle* and that of early modernism, such complex two-way traffic between radical politics and literary aesthetics becomes visible. The brief study of the uses of anarchism in Henry James's *The Princess Casamassima* (1886) and Joseph Conrad's *The Secret Agent* (1907) that closes this chapter gives some sense of how the radical politics of the period fuelled the aesthetic interests even of those writers most careful to distance themselves from political clubs and coteries. The figure of the anarchist in particular, I suggest, is a means to dramatize some of the pressing questions raised by high art in this period.[6] Futile and self-destructive as these fictional anarchists are, they play out the implications of standing outside the mass culture of modern city life and the limited effect of any one individual's creative acts. The anarchist, in these aesthetic visions, is the dark double of Matthew Arnold's description of the cultural critic and artist in the modern age: an alien striving against the sheer weight of the crowd.[7]

[3] For some excellent examples, see the first two volumes of Deborah Mutch, *British Socialist Fiction, 1884–1914*, 5 vols (London: Pickering and Chatto, 2013).

[4] For a full study of this crucial aspect of politics and art in the period, see Tracy C. Davis, *George Bernard Shaw and the Socialist Theatre* (London: Praeger, 1994).

[5] Ann Ardis, *Modernism and Cultural Conflict, 1880–1922* (Cambridge: Cambridge University Press, 2002), 143–72; Livesey, 'Socialism in Bloomsbury: Virginia Woolf and the Political Aesthetics of the 1880s', *Yearbook of English Studies* 37 (2007), 126–44.

[6] For an extended argument relating to this see David Weir, *Anarchy and Culture: The Aesthetic Politics of Modernism* (Amherst, MA: University of Massachusetts Press, 1999).

[7] Matthew Arnold, *Culture and Anarchy* (1869), in R. H. Super (ed.), *The Complete Prose Works of Matthew Arnold*, 11 vols (Ann Arbor, MI: University of Michigan Press, 1960–1977), V, 110.

Writing a socialist future

Historical accounts of the emergence of socialism and its struggle with anarchism in Britain tend to place a particular emphasis on the 1880s and early 1890s as an epoch of utopian hopes that shaped a more pragmatic labour movement in the early twentieth century.[8] At the *fin de siècle* a rising generation of educated working men and women in Britain was possessed by a sense that an epoch of social transformation was just around the corner. Industrial capitalism was at its height and urban poverty increasingly visible in an era of investigative journalism and social exploration, but an older order of aristocratic government apparently was drawing to a close. Thanks to successive extensions of the voting rights of men in 1867 and 1884, a new era of democracy seemed inevitable. A wave of mass trades union action, including the match-girls' strike of 1888 and the London Dock strike of 1889, made visible the strength of an organized working class. Repressive acts by government, on the other hand, such as the use of the military to end a demonstration in Trafalgar Square in November 1887, gave protesters a sense that a final confrontation was imminent.

By the time the Parliamentary Labour Party took shape as an affiliation of left groupings in 1900, however, the prospect of revolution in Britain seemed more distant and attention had shifted to parliamentary politics and legislative reform.[9] Writers who had been involved in radical politics in the 1880s—particularly those associated with the influential Fabian Society—distanced themselves from the lively mix of political, ethical, and artistic ideals that had fired them in their youth. The labour activist Isabella Ford gently satirized the initial optimism of her art-student heroines in an era 'when we were all socialists more or less' in her novel of middle-class London radicals in the 1880s, *On the Threshold* (1895).[10] Gertrude Dix's novel *The Image Breakers* (1900) provides a rather darker retrospect on the emotional consequences of doctrines of free love and self-determination for women radicals, while in *Attainment* (1909) Edith Ellis reflected on the practical difficulties that resulted from experiments in communal life by 1880s socialists.[11] In his preface to *Major Barbara* (1907) the leading Fabian propagandist, George Bernard Shaw,

---

[8]   See, for example, Stanley Pierson, *British Socialists: The Journey from Fantasy to Politics* (Cambridge, MA: Harvard University Press, 1979); and Mark Bevir, *The Making of British Socialism* (Princeton, NJ: Princeton University Press, 2011).

[9]   The forerunner of the Parliamentary Labour Party, the Labour Representation Committee, had its founding conference in 1900.

[10]   Isabella Ford, *On the Threshold* (London: Arnold), 29.

[11]   See Sally Ledger, *The New Woman: Fiction and Feminism at the fin de siècle* (Manchester: Manchester University Press, 1997), 52–60; Diana Maltz, 'Ardent Service: Female Eroticism and New Life Ethics in Gertrude Dix's *The Image Breakers* (1900)', *Journal of Victorian Culture* 17/2 (2012), 147–63; and Jo-Ann Wallace, 'Edith Ellis, Sapphic Idealism and The Lover's Calendar', in Laura Doan and Jane Garrity (eds), *Sapphic Modernities: Sexuality, Women, and National Culture* (Basingstoke: Palgrave, 2006), 183–201.

argued that this 1880s radicalism and its idealistic lifestyle experiments had limited appeal for the 'common man': ' "Cease to be slaves, in order that you may become cranks" is not a very inspiring call to arms.'[12] What really mattered for a socialist future, according to Shaw and the Fabians, was the redistribution of money.

For much of the twentieth century, the version of history left by Fabians like Shaw—especially within the British Parliamentary Labour Party—was fairly widely accepted. British radical politics, that is, experimented with some far-out, cranky ideas in the 1880s and early 1890s which entertained anarchism, feminism, and sexual dissidence together with socialism: communes, back-to-the-land smallholdings, rational dress, sexual abstinence, same-sex relationships. But by the late 1890s socialists had knuckled down to more scientific programmes of social reform and booted out the anarchists, while feminist members found a fresh outlet in the renewed energies of the women's suffrage movement. The image of the ineffectual, outdated, homespun-and-sandal-wearing, free-loving leftie of the Edward Carpenter type is skewered perfectly in the Fabian E. Nesbit's sketch of Eustace Sandal in *The New Treasure Seekers* (1904): 'a vegetarian and a Primitive Social Something', according to her child narrator, Oswald Bastable, who spends his time giving 'glimpses of the Life Beautiful' to 'the sort of people who live in Model Workmen's Dwellings'.[13] More recently though, these sorts of attempts to fuse ethical and social revolutions—to transform the individual as much as the mass—have begun to draw attention in their own right, rather than as an embarrassing awkward phase in the growth of socialism. One of the features of radical politics in these decades was that a growing sense of need for collective intervention, whether in the shape of an increased role for the state in alleviating poverty, an uprising of workers, or mass suffrage protests, went hand in hand with a belief that change was also needed within individuals. Literature, many activists believed, played a crucial role in helping stir up such inward revolution. The genres of literature that became important within the movement help us, in turn, to understand something of the complex history of ideas that fuelled radical politics in this era. For much of the twentieth century socialism was to be associated with realism in art and literature. Yet looking back to the period examined here reveals how frequently radical fiction subverted realist conventions in pursuit of a political, and artistic, avant-garde.

Although an important instance of the rise of explicitly socialist politics is the founding of the first Marxist socialist group in Britain—the Democratic Federation—in 1881, the intellectual roots of the resurgence of radical politics during this decade are complex.[14] British socialism and anarchism owed much to early nineteenth-century radicalism and romantic Tory protests against a capitalist 'cash nexus' epitomized by Thomas Carlyle and John Ruskin. During the late nineteenth century,

---

[12] George Bernard Shaw, 'Preface', *Major Barbara* (1905; repr. London: Penguin, 1945), xii.

[13] See Maltz, 'The Newer New Life: A. S. Byatt, E. Nesbit and Socialist Subculture', *Journal of Victorian Culture* 17/1 (2012), 79–84.

[14] Founded by H. M. Hyndman, the first meeting took place in 1881. From 1884, it was known best under its later title, the Social Democratic Federation.

these long-standing critiques of the industrial era, grounded in debates about beauty and ugliness, individual flourishing and a mechanistic society, were revitalized by several newer influences, including the works of Marx and Engels. Perhaps more surprisingly, an ethos of self-cultivation drawn from the work of American Transcendentalists, most notably Ralph Waldo Emerson, and aesthetic writers such as Walter Pater, also played a significant part in the era's radical political formations.[15] Partly thanks to these literary and aesthetic roots, writers and artists were prominent in the socialist revival of the 1880s. Writing in 1889, Oscar Wilde noted how well-equipped the movement was in terms of the fine arts, reaching expression through the work of 'poets and . . . painters . . . art-lecturers and . . . cunning designers . . . powerful orators and . . . clever writers'.[16] Socialism promised a new life of beauty as well as economic justice for what Wilde dubbed such 'poetical socialists'; a prospect of flourishing individuality when old conventions were swept away along with the current arrangements of capital and labour.

For this generation of aesthetic radicals, 'social reformatory zeal' as Alfred Orage termed it 'was not allowed to interfere with our pursuit of personal "moments"' of self-expression.[17] Early socialist organizations such as the Fellowship of the New Life (founded 1883), the nationally significant Independent Labour Party (founded 1893), and even the supposedly more pragmatic and policy-oriented Fabian Society (founded 1884) give ample evidence of these mixed influences of economic critique and the pursuit of new ethics. In their founding missions and in the memoirs of early members a commitment to examining and reshaping the self goes hand in hand with broader political aims. Although this fusion of introspection and revolution was not sustained, it created a common space in which sexuality, sexual difference, ethical living, and experimental communes were subjects of serious exploration alongside the broader questioning of capitalism.

The spread of Marxist thinking during the 1880s, however, gave a sharper analytical edge and keen expectation of revolution even to Wilde's 'poetical socialists'. Karl Marx and Friedrich Engels were, of course, resident in Britain from the late 1840s and wrote many of their most significant works in response to the example of British capitalism. The circle of radical émigrés that formed around Marx and Engels in London during the 1880s—and the work of Marx's daughter Eleanor—emphasized a distinctly internationalist, 'scientific' analysis of capitalism and its seemingly inevitable demise in a proletarian uprising.[18] The poet and designer, William Morris, who had caused controversy by announcing his commitment to socialism in a public lecture in 1883, claimed reading Marx's *Capital* (1867) was central to his conversion (even though the economic sections gave him 'agonies of confusion of

[15] See also Terry Eagleton, 'The Flight to the Real', in Sally Ledger and Scott McCracken (eds), *Cultural Politics at the Fin de Siècle* (Cambridge: Cambridge University Press, 1995), 11–22.
[16] Oscar Wilde, 'Poetical Socialists', *Pall Mall Gazette*, 13 February 1889, 3.
[17] 'R.H.C.' [Alfred Orage], 'Readers and Writers', *New Age* 14 (13 November 1913), 50.
[18] See John Stokes (ed.), *Eleanor Marx: Life, Work, Contacts* (London: Ashgate, 2000).

the brain').[19] Yet thanks in part to the development of Marxist politics over the ensuing decades, this intertwining of 'scientific' socialism and the more 'utopian' hopes and dreams of writers and artists like Morris has remained, until recently, relatively obscure.[20] The sorts of artistic forms that sustained and energized radical political formations in Britain during this period have, for a long period of critical history, simply been of the wrong sort of genre to garner much attention from Marxist literary criticism.

A letter written by Friedrich Engels in 1888 to Eleanor Marx's friend Margaret Harkness explains something of this oversight. In 1886 Harkness had moved into a block of workers' dwellings in East London to research her first novel, *A City Girl* (1887). Like many educated, middle-class women in search of work and independent existence during this period, she had found an interest in the condition of urban slum residents and went to live alongside her cousin, Beatrice Potter (later Webb), who was embarking on her own political education as a philanthropic rent collector near the docks. Harkness sent a copy of the resulting novel to Engels, keen to hear his opinion. Engels was generous about her narrative of the seduction and abandonment of a working-class girl, but equally clear how it fell short of what he believed was needed in socialist art. Despite her research, Engels was convinced Harkness's novel was not 'realistic enough': 'Realism, to my mind, implies, besides truth of detail, the truthful reproduction of typical characters under typical circumstances.'[21] *A City Girl*, Engels believed, lacked such realism because the working class featured as a passive mass, moved only by the actions of outsiders. This, Engels argued, was simply not the truth of the matter, the true tendency of historical materialism, the reality of his own experience of struggle alongside the militant proletariat. Harkness's ambivalent depiction of middle-class socialists and philanthropists exploring working-class neighbourhoods plays with some of the radical potential of early nineteenth-century British melodramas. Its tale of a seamstress, Nelly Ambrose, seduced and abandoned by a bourgeois radical could have been drawn from plots of the 1830s; but the bubbling anger of class resentment that fuels the political spirit of such earlier dramas is absent in a deeply pessimistic plot. Nelly's desires for the good things in life—the surface glamour of the theatre, a trip on a river boat, a gentlemanly lover—are shown to be part of the self-defeating nature of a degraded working class.[22]

Engels's letter to Harkness has become a staple item in collections of early source material on Marxist literary criticism. It brings into focus, as Elizabeth Miller has

[19] Bevir, *Making of British Socialism*, 92. William Morris, 'The Aims of Art', in May Morris (ed.), *The Collected Works of William Morris*, 25 vols (London: Longman, 1912–15), XXIII, 91.

[20] A recent corrective is Anna Vaninskaya, *William Morris and the Idea of Community: Romance, History, and Propaganda, 1880–1914* (Edinburgh: Edinburgh University Press, 2010).

[21] Engels to Margaret Harkness, April 1888. Repr. Marxist Internet Archive https://www.marxists.org/archive/marx/works/1888/letters/88_04_15.htm.

[22] On Harkness and the wider question of genres of the socialist novel, see Elizabeth Miller, *Slow Print: Literary Radicalism and Late Victorian Print Culture* (Stanford, CA: Stanford University Press, 2013), 82–121.

recently pointed out, a critique of late nineteenth-century literary naturalism that runs from Engels to Georg Lukács and Frederic Jameson: that the pessimism and hereditary determinism epitomized in descriptions of the working class by Émile Zola or George Gissing or Harkness reflect only a middle-class view of 'reality'.[23] When Engels's letter is placed in its late nineteenth-century British context, however, it becomes clear just how out of step his demand for an art of the typical and real was with the literary culture of that time and place. The vogue for literary naturalism during the 1880s and 1890s has left us with some memorable narratives of slum life such as Gissing's *The Nether World* (1889) or Arthur Morrison's *A Child of the Jago* (1896). Such fictions are invaluable in understanding middle-class anxiety about the poor—and in particular the nature of London's East End—in the late nineteenth and early twentieth centuries and the political journeys of thinkers like Beatrice Webb and William Beveridge. But these are far from what Engels believed to be the most useful and truthful sort of art: social realism of a sort most closely associated with the historical novels of Balzac or Walter Scott, narratives in which characters are moved by the forces of history and yet can play their part in shaping it—unlike the foredoomed slum residents of these later naturalist fictions who are destined from birth to repeat the failures of their forebears and never move.

From the 1880s into the twentieth century, social and historical realism of the sort praised by Engels smacked of the deeply old-fashioned in a world striving to be modern. Literary naturalism, by contrast, characterized one important tendency of that world of the modern, but it also embodied a structural pessimism about the possibility of social transformation at odds with socialism itself. Naturalism, however, was only one strand of the avant-garde in the arts during this period—and one soon to find itself on the wane. It was quite another aspect of contemporary art that dominated the so-called 'religion of socialism' in Britain during this period: that of deliberate anti-realism and the world of possibility beyond the everyday. Forms of romance, dream, and allegory charting a voyage inwards to the self flourished in the radical moment of the *fin de siècle*. These genres are closer kin to the artistic legacy of the aesthetic movement and have a palpable influence on some of the later experiments of literary modernism.[24]

Modern fiction and the woman radical

At the end of 1883, the journalist Henry Norman published a critical survey of recent novels under the title 'The Theories and Practice of Modern Fiction'. He was

---

[23] Miller, *Slow Print*, 97.

[24] See Caroline Sumpter, *The Victorian Press and the Fairy Tale* (Basingstoke: Palgrave, 2008), 88–230.

not impressed by what had passed over his desk during the previous year. Only the French had any sort of theory of contemporary fiction—and that was limited to debates around literary naturalism sparked off by Zola. In Britain the practice of fiction was dominated by escapist adventure stories. In the midst of shocking journalistic exposés of the poverty of London's East End, the novelist Walter Besant, for example, had published what the author himself termed 'an impossible story'—a romance of the slums, entitled *All Sorts and Conditions of Men* (1882). 'In these days when the most serious questions of our social life are those of the relation of the rich to the poor and of the future of the poor in our civilisation,' Norman warned, 'it is not a pleasant sight to see Mr Besant frisking about in the solemn fields of political economy', proposing a workers' cooperative and sociable dancing in a 'Palace of Delight' as a solution to the problems of free-market capitalism and sweated labour.[25] Even grim naturalism, Norman suggested, might be preferable to such froth. Much more to Norman's taste was *The Story of an African Farm* (1883), published under the pseudonym 'Ralph Iron' but, Norman guessed correctly, the work of a young female author from South Africa. This sort of work held out hope for the future of fiction: a new sort of instruction for readers interested in modern life, its problems, and new ethical solutions.[26]

The work of the South African author in question, Olive Schreiner, came to be a touchstone for many men and women seeking a new life of freer sexual and social relations in the decades to come. Contemporary readers interpreted *The Story of an African Farm* as a novel about the emergence of secular ethics in an era of doubt, an avatar of the 'great socialistic revolution', and the grounds of fresh energy in the feminist movement that fed in to the later 'New Woman' debates of the 1890s.[27] Schreiner's narrative of three children growing to maturity on a South African farm seemed to prove that the same radical currents of thought were stirring the whole globe. The orphaned young boy Waldo (the name, like Schreiner's pseudonym, a hint of the influence of Emerson) discovers an old copy of John Stuart Mill's *Political Economy*, reads the chapter on Saint-Simonian communism, and has an ecstatic response in which his 'heavy body quivered with excitement'. Waldo discovers he is 'not alone, not alone' in his questioning the inequity of 'old, old relations between man and man'. For all that the book is seized and burned and he is beaten and imprisoned by the grotesque Boer woman

---

[25] Henry Norman, 'Theories and Practice of Modern Fiction', *Fortnightly Review* 34 (1883), 880–1.
[26] A good example of the odd relations between politics, practice, and literature is that by 1889 a campaign inspired by Besant's novel had raised enough money to build a People's Palace of amusement and instruction for the poor on East London's Mile End Road. Schreiner, meanwhile, threw herself into the socialist movement and tried to live out radical new relations between the sexes in London, at high personal cost, and struggled to complete further works.
[27] Edward Aveling, 'A Notable Book', *Progress* 2/3 (1883), 162; Olive Schreiner, *The Story of an African Farm*, ed. Joseph Bristow (Oxford: Oxford University Press, 1992); Carolyn Burdett, *Olive Schreiner and the Progress of Feminism: Evolution, Gender, Empire* (Basingstoke: Palgrave, 2001); Livesey, *Socialism*, 73–101.

farmer Tant' Sannie and her vicious sidekick, Bonaparte Blenkins, in the next chapter.[28] Waldo's loss of faith, charted in an extraordinary vision of the child's fear of eternal damnation that opens the novel, is replaced by a secular allegory in which creative labour gives purpose to existence. Otherwise, in a phrase which haunts the novel, modern life risks being a great blank in which 'it was all play, and no one could tell what it had lived and worked for. A striving, and a striving, and an ending in nothing'.[29]

The first half of the novel is dominated by rage against the power of the stupid and cunning over talented idealists, and a search for a meaning in individual lives in a world without God. But there is a shift in emphasis from Waldo's refusal of traditional religious submission to authority in the second part of the novel which takes place when the children reach adulthood. The preternaturally intellectual Lyndall returns from her quest for an education frustrated at the expectation that she should spend time at finishing school arranging flowers and embroidering foot-stools. Waldo's new ethical vision of a life made meaningful by labour is simply no good to her, Lyndall points out. For to men the world says:

> *Work*; and to us [women] it says—*Seem*! To you it says—As you approximate to man's highest ideal of God, as your arm is strong and your knowledge great, and the power to labour is with you, so you shall gain all that human heart desires. To us it says—Strength shall not help you, nor knowledge, nor labour.

And, in a phrase that resonated within the feminist movement for decades to come, Lyndall's hope is for a future in which 'to be born a woman will not be to be born branded'.[30]

Although Lyndall's death after bearing an illegitimate child suggests a pessimistic vision, her articulate anger—and her refusal of self-abnegation—was a watershed in the nineteenth-century history of women's protest and the female bildungsroman. Unlike George Eliot's Maggie Tulliver or Dorothea Brooke, or Elizabeth Barrett Browning's Aurora Leigh, Lyndall does not sacrifice individuality in the service of others. On her deathbed she stares at her own 'white face in the glass', which had so often told her ' "We are not afraid . . . we will fight, you and I" '; she refuses to give up her self, even in death. Schreiner's radical assertion of individualism works against the veneration of female altruism within nineteenth-century liberalism.[31] This rage against a loss of self, and against postponing the particular claims of wom-anhood for the greater good of mankind, was all the more significant in terms of the novel's reception, because the woman's movement in Britain was relatively subdued during the 1880s and 1890s.

---

[28] Schreiner, *African Farm*, 76.   [29] Ibid., 74, 101.

[30] Ibid., 154–5, 152; For Schreiner's enduring influence, see Vera Brittain, *Testament of Youth* (1933; repr. London: Virago, 1978), 41.

[31] Schreiner, *African Farm*, 252. Thomas Dixon, *The Invention of Altruism: Making Moral Meanings in Victorian Britain* (Oxford: Oxford University Press, 2008), ch. 7.

Even though discussions of sexual equality, marriage, and reproduction were common in radical and liberal circles, organized campaigns and petitions on the legal standing of women and the vote were less visible than in the previous two decades. It was not until the early years of the twentieth century that the former members of the Independent Labour Party, Emmeline and Christabel Pankhurst, formed the Women's Social and Political Union and launched the militant suffrage campaign. At the same time, the increased prominence of the question of women's suffrage created fresh conflict and divisions within the socialist movement that challenged some of its long-term supporters like Isabella Ford.

The great pleasure of Schreiner's novel, however, is that it eludes and exceeds these political and intellectual contexts. It remains a fascinatingly odd book and—like Schreiner's later *Dreams* (1890)—its refusal to sit comfortably within contemporary categories of literary genre is undoubtedly part of that fascination. For example, although Lyndall and Waldo die at the end of the novel, apparently having strived and ended with nothing, the narrative reliance on fractured temporalities and dream allegories takes this far beyond the determinist pessimism of naturalist fiction. The second part of the novel opens with an extended caesura on the passing of time, 'Times and Seasons', that envelops the experience of Waldo and Lyndall in an idea of universal development—and which presages Woolf's later breaks in conventional fictional temporalities in *To the Lighthouse* (1927). Again and again the narrative aspect of the bildungsroman is interrupted by allegories and tableaux that in the very density of their prose form demand a universal application beyond the limited lives of the protagonists on the farm. Out of Africa, in a future life made up of the seemingly pointless struggles of countless individuals, a new life of hope and freedom can be born out of the strivings of desire. The plot itself gives form to such possibilities in the shape of Lyndall's would-be lover, Gregory Rose. Towards the end of the novel Gregory embraces the strongly marked feminization of his character to disguise himself as a woman. Leaving his own clothes behind in the 'red bed' of a 'deep gully' or 'sloot' in the veld, Gregory chooses to be reborn from this primal maternal landscape as a woman. He experiences the pleasures of willing self-abnegation to nurse an unknowing Lyndall on her deathbed.[32] A life beyond the everyday 'branding' of men and women; a world in which the genius of all can flourish wherever they find themselves; a hope for greater good even with the death of God: the chinks and fractures that interrupt realism in Schreiner's bildungsroman offer a vision of a future life, but one shaped in human art rather than spiritual transcendence.

Steeped as she was in the scriptural fabric of her upbringing in a missionary family, Schreiner's very prose style offered a radical secular substitute for those emerging from traditional religious belief into a new life of socialism and feminism. In a similar fashion, poems and ballads by William Morris, Edward Carpenter, and

---

[32] Schreiner, *African Farm*, 238.

many others took the place of hymnals in meetings of so-called Labour Churches and at the opening of political meetings. The very title of Morris's extended ballad, *The Pilgrims of Hope* (1885–6), like Carpenter's even longer evolving prose-verse experiment, *Towards Democracy* (1883–1902), bears witness to the consciousness of becoming within radical politics in these decades. The new life—whether of sexual equality, radical democracy, or anarcho-syndicalism—was in process and its followers were pilgrims to a destination that, by its very nature, demanded realization right here, if not right now. Communally chanting the urgent rhythms of Morris's opening to *Pilgrims*, 'The Message of the March Wind', or Carpenter's 'England Arise' inscribed that sense of collective journey, making socialists through rituals of prose, verse, and song.

But the idea that the socialist future was one in which the needs of the collective would outweigh that of any particular individual or group presented an aesthetic and political problem for many followers. Feminist socialists worried that women had scarcely yet gained the status of individuals in British legislature and that emphasizing progress for all would mean the deferral of rights for women; while for many artists and writers involved with the movement, a loss of individuality meant the end of all meaningful high art.[33] Perhaps the best-known example of socialist anti-realism from this period, William Morris's *News from Nowhere* (1890), is preoccupied by this question of individualism, socialism, and art. Characters in Morris's future utopia speak out against the form of the novel as emblematic of all the wrongs of nineteenth-century bourgeois individualism. Even those novels seemingly interested in the plight of the poor, Ellen argues, demand that ' "towards the end of the story we must be contented to see the hero and heroine happily living in an island of bliss on other people's troubles . . . drearily illustrated by introspective nonsense about their feelings and aspirations" '.[34] As Patrick Brantlinger has pointed out, Morris's text is paradoxically, therefore, an anti-novel, repudiating the most respected genres and forms of high art of the late nineteenth century as a necessary loss for the sort of socialist future he envisaged.[35]

Morris's *News from Nowhere* was written as a riposte to Edward Bellamy's *Looking Backwards* (1888)—the latter a vision of a future state-socialist America in which the means of production and distribution are nationalized. In contrast to Bellamy's techno-utopia, Morris's dream-visitor to the future, William Guest, travels forwards to a medievalized London in which the state as an entity no longer exists and the Houses of Parliament have been repurposed as a dung market. At the time Morris

---

[33] June Hannam and Karen Hunt, *Socialist Women: Britain, 1880–1920s* (London: Routledge, 2001), 105–33; Regenia Gagnier, *Idylls of the Marketplace: Oscar Wilde and the Victorian Public* (Stanford, CA: Stanford University Press, 1986), 29–34.

[34] Morris, *New from Nowhere and Other Writings*, ed. Clive Wilmer (Harmondsworth: Penguin, 1993), 175–6.

[35] Patrick Brantlinger, '*News from Nowhere*: Morris's Socialist Anti-Novel', *Victorian Studies* 19 (1975), 35–49.

wrote *News from Nowhere*, he was embroiled in struggles between anarchists and other factions of the Socialist League, a group which had itself splintered from the Social Democratic Federation in 1884. Read in this context, *News from Nowhere* writes a future in which centrally planned state socialism has given way in due course to the life of the commune; a world in which individual choice and self-expression has come into natural harmony with the common good. Its stateless nation, determined by local folk-motes, has much in common with the anarcho-communism preached by the Russian émigré, Prince Peter Kropotkin, a frequent visitor to London who settled there from 1886. But it is an anarchism held together by an ideal of common culture and a universal desire for the beautiful that emerges afresh once all the falsehoods of capitalist society have been stripped away.

In works by Henry James and Joseph Conrad from this period, however, Morris's utopian fusion of culture and anarchism in pursuit of common good comes into collision with a determinedly modern present. Both writers, whose experiments with the novel form kept that genre at the heart of high art in the twentieth century, had a complex relation to debates on culture and democracy in Britain, due in part to their own standing as foreign-born nationals.[36] In James's *The Princess Casamassima* and Conrad's *The Secret Agent*, culture no longer provides a bulwark against violent anarchy and individualism in the way imagined by Matthew Arnold in the 1860s and refigured in Morris's socialist aesthetics. Amid the spectacle of a modern London, the lone figure of the anarchist wandering the streets, prepared to destroy in order to create, becomes a disturbing avatar for the critic as artist. Arnold argued that high culture was nothing less than the pursuit of perfection by the individual. In these darkly satiric fictions, however, the pursuit of perfection paves the way for an attack on the mass culture of modernity.

Culture and the anarchist

In the middle of Henry Norman's review of the direction of fiction in 1883 he reflected on the likely fortunes of Henry James. James had achieved early success with tales of Americans abroad such as *Roderick Hudson* (1875), *Daisy Miller* (1879), and *The Portrait of a Lady* (1881) but, Norman wondered, what kind of material could he find for his 'clever books' when the 'international episode has become a bore, when an English Lord is no longer an object of curiosity at Newport

---

[36] See Jonathan Freedman, *Professions of Taste: Henry James, British Aestheticism, and Commodity Culture* (Stanford, CA: Stanford University Press, 1990); Livesey, 'Democracy, Culture, and Criticism: Henry James Revisits America', in Ella Dzelzainis and Ruth Livesey (eds), *The American Experiment and the Idea of Democracy in British Culture, 1776–1914* (Farnham: Ashgate, 2013), 179–86; Robert Hampson, *Conrad's Secrets* (Basingstoke: Palgrave, 2012), 79–99.

and an American no longer *ipso facto* welcome in Mayfair'.[37] What followed from James, in fact, were two novels that explored current political formations and identities: *The Bostonians* (1886), which revolves around the feminist movement and women's freedom in New England, and *The Princess Casamassima* (1886), a story of anarchism in London. The latter novel follows the fortunes of a refined young bookbinder, Hyacinth Robinson, who presumes himself the illegitimate son of an aristocrat. Raised in an unlovely London courtyard by his adoptive mother, a dressmaker, the novel imagines Hyacinth almost accidently promising to sacrifice himself for the anarchist movement in an impassioned moment. He finds himself pulled between opposing emotional forces that lead to his eventual suicide: anger at exclusion from the leisured old world of culture and beauty, desire to possess that world represented by the Princess Casamassima, repulsion from the low pleasures of modern popularism, and attraction to its frank, vigorous energy (personified in the luscious figure and appetites of his shop-girl friend, Millicent Henning). James himself seemed almost surprised by the turn in his interests from the clash of aristocratic old and moneyed new worlds to a study of contemporary London. 'You see I am quite the naturalist', he wrote to a friend in December 1884, after relating that he had been to Millbank prison to research the setting of the opening scene in the latter novel.[38]

Few critics these days go as far as Lionel Trilling's assertion that every aspect of *The Princess Casamassima*'s plot of secret oaths and mysterious European networks of would-be assassins 'is confirmed by multitudinous historical records'.[39] But James was certainly responsive to the cosmopolitan—and sometimes rather glamorous— texture of anarchism and revolutionaries in London during this period. After the fall of the revolutionary Paris Commune in 1871 (itself commemorated in Morris's *Pilgrims of Hope*), London was a place of political asylum for many who, like the radical bookbinder Eustache Poupin and his wife in James's novel, had thought to see their political dreams realized. The journalist and Proudhonist anarchist, Charles Longuet, for example, fled France for London, where he married Karl Marx's eldest daughter Jenny the following year. The former bookbinder, Johann Most—seen by many as the source for several of James's characters in the novel— settled in London in 1878 where he launched his radical newspaper *Freiheit* (Freedom). Most's headline celebrating the assassination of Tsar Alexander II in 1881 led to his arrest and imprisonment in Britain. During these same years, Sergey Kravchinsky—best known by his pseudonym Stepniak—came to settle in Britain

---

[37] Norman, 'Theories and Practice', 875.

[38] Leon Edel (ed.), *The Letters of Henry James*, 4 vols (Cambridge, MA: Harvard University Press, 1974–1984), III, 61.

[39] Lionel Trilling, '*The Princess Casamassima*' (1948), in Leon Wieseltier (ed.), *The Moral Obligation to be Intelligent: Selected Essays* (Chicago, IL: Northwestern University Press, 2008), 157; Weir, *Anarchy and Culture*, 69–74; Deaglán Ó Donghaile, *Blasted Literature: Victorian Political Fiction and the Shock of the Modern* (Edinburgh: Edinburgh University Press, 2011), 39–55.

and became an intimate part of the radical circles of artists and writers in London. The realization that Stepniak had been responsible for the assassination of the chief of the Russian secret police in 1878 did little to cool his relations with Constance Garnett. Garnett's enthusiasm for Russian literature was fuelled by the friendship and her translations were later crucial in bringing the works of Turgenev and Chekhov to a younger generation of novelists including Woolf and D. H. Lawrence.

James's introduction to *The Princess Casamassima* is unapologetic about the vague sketch he provides of anarchism, only wanting to tantalize with dim glances of 'what "goes on" irreconcilably, subversively, beneath the vast smug surface' of contemporary society.[40] Hyacinth is conceived as a would-be cosmopolitan man of books 'capable of profiting' from 'civilisation' and culture 'yet condemned to see these things only from the outside—in mere quickened consideration, mere wistfulness and envy and despair'.[41] In this manner, James's novel reframes some familiar aesthetic preoccupations in his works through the media of radical politics and literary naturalism. James was always fascinated by what he called '*penetralia*': the alluring appearance of an inner sanctum of refinement, truth, and culture cordoned off by a velvet rope. As Tony Tanner points out, in narrative content and form alike, James's works take characters and readers right to the doorway of these inmost spaces and relish hovering just outside. In James's later fiction, this process of wanting 'to penetrate; but also . . . to be prevented *from* penetrating' attaches to the only ever partial glimpses given of characters' interiority and motives in those novels.[42] But in this fiction of James's problematic middle phase, the *penetralium* is realized as sociopolitical content, rather than as narrative technique. The barrier between Hyacinth and the inner sanctum he desires is down to his class position, not a psychological limitation. He is only an alien held at the border of high culture because his sort of labour in the world of books is alienated, limited to hand-tooling leather covers for a fixed price. Even the self-declared anarchist Princess Casamassima is surprised—and a little disappointed—that this specimen of the people she adds to her collection dares go beyond crafting the outside of books and reads Schopenhauer.[43]

Hyacinth, in a clear echo of James himself, trembles on the verge of aesthetic potential with his 'exquisite specimens' of books, full of 'finer touches'. '"You have a manner, like a master"', his old friend Vetch, the musician, assures him. '"With such talent and such a taste, your future leaves nothing to be desired. You will make a fortune and become a great celebrity."'[44] The Princess herself, by contrast, puts her beautiful things into storage so she can experience the aesthetic deprivation of the common people; all in pursuit of something that feels, to her, like urgently modern experience. She collects anarchists and causes instead of books and bibelots with a

---

[40] Henry James, *The Princess Casamassima*, ed. Derek Brewer (Harmondsworth: Penguin, 1987), 48.
[41] Ibid., 34.
[42] Tony Tanner, *Henry James and the Art of Non-Fiction* (Athens, GA: University of Georgia Press, 1995), 19–20.
[43] James, *The Princess Casamassima*, 329.   [44] Ibid., 561.

ruthless appetite for fresh impressions. In James's aesthetic version of a political novel, the future of art itself—personified by Robinson—is in a state of self-destructive paralysis, torn between old aristocratic culture and the inevitable dawn of mass populism. This critical artist simply cannot decide which world to destroy and which world to preserve and thus makes an end to himself. Meanwhile the traditional connoisseur and patron of the arts, the Princess, abandons her aristocratic husband, and even Hyacinth with his aesthetic leanings, in her pursuit of something that '*is* real . . . *is* solid'.[45] Turning her back on cosmopolitan high culture and the pursuit of beauty she echoes James's satirical experiment with naturalist fiction, embracing the utterly unidealistic, phlegmatic anarchist, Paul Muniment, who approaches revolution in a manner akin to his profession: a wholesale chemist.

Although Fenian attacks for the cause of Ireland occurred throughout the 1880s, the only direct anarchist action in Britain during this era took place in 1894. In the early 1890s, Constance Garnett's young sister-in-law Olive was drawn into the anarchist enterprise of the teenaged Rossetti children who printed the radical newspaper the *Torch* in their father William Michael's basement.[46] In their own way, Olivia and Helen Rossetti were continuing a long family tradition of avant-garde aesthetic ideals and cosmopolitan politics that could be traced back through a commitment to Italian nationalism and the cause of the oppressed within the Pre-Raphaelite Brotherhood. The Rossettis' cousin, Ford Madox Hueffer (later Ford Madox Ford), witnessed how their involvement came to an end in the wake of Martial Bourdin's apparent attempt to bomb the Greenwich Observatory in 1894. Ford, in turn, related the events to his friend and collaborator, Conrad; and although *The Secret Agent* is set in 1886, it is a clear reflection of events surrounding that later attack.[47]

Yet in Conrad's satiric vision the idealistic enthusiasm of these youthful anarchist-aesthetes is inverted. The London representatives of the anarchist 'FP' movement in *The Secret Agent* are extraordinarily lazy, corpulent, ageing men, eager to pursue indolence and live off women where possible. Despite the novel's retrospective setting, its milieu is also far from the cosmopolitan aesthetic avant-garde of the mid-1880s. Conrad's London is a starkly modern world in which all are bound together as cogs in a social mechanism and nothing, it seems, including beauty, can escape or stand above its automated, material processes. The anarchist apostle Michaelis intones, '"All idealization makes life poorer. To beautify it is to take away its character of complexity—is to destroy it"'.[48] Even music—up until the late nineteenth century the most transcendent, evanescent art form—has become subject to mechanical reproduction in the world of this novel. In a central scene in the novel

---

[45] Ibid., 330.

[46] Barry C. Johnson (ed.), *Olive and Stepniak: The Bloomsbury Diary of Olive Garnett, 1893–1895* (Birmingham: Barletts Press, 1997).

[47] For the significance of the chronologies of the novel see Hampson, *Conrad's Secrets*, 79–90.

[48] Joseph Conrad, *The Secret Agent* (Harmondsworth: Penguin, 1994), 42.

an automated player piano bashes out the 'painfully detached notes' of various 'national airs' in the background.[49] Art is no resource for collective social renewal; culture has been broken up into reproducible fragments, bound to loop around, endlessly the same, much like the perpetual game of cat and mouse between the Metropolitan Police and the London underworld. Meanwhile, Stevie, the mentally impaired young man who blows himself up accidently in Greenwich Park, spends all his time drawing circles with a pair of compasses.

Only the single-minded figure of the bomb-making chemist, the Professor, stands outside this resolutely inaesthetic world. In his pursuit of a perfect detonator and his singular vision of creating a blasted world beyond the present, he provides the nearest thing the novel has to an idealist committed to his art. In this violent refiguring of the artist as terrorist, Conrad's novel reflects something of the Nietzschean tendencies of avant-garde movements in both politics and the arts by the early twentieth century. By 1911 Ernest Radford, a poet and former member of Morris's Socialist League, wrote to Alfred Orage to complain that the leading social-ist arts magazine, the *New Age*, had become a mere 'hotch-potch of Nietzsche' and 'megalomaniac's notions': the editor swiftly dismissed Radford's idealism and senti-mentality as an outdated hangover from the 1880s.[50] Writing on the verge of war a few years later, Orage himself hoped for a 'cleansing elemental bath' for the nation that would allow a return to 'simple truths' in the world of politics and of art.[51] The violent overthrow of the current order and a period of anarchy was the only way to rid the modern era of a high art wrapped up in self-regarding Decadence and the cheap emptiness of life for the masses under capitalism. Just a few years later, the Russian Revolution and its aftermath was to prove a testing ground for this genera-tion who had twined together radicalism in politics and in the arts.

FURTHER READING

Ardis, Ann. *Modernism and Cultural Conflict, 1880–1922* (Cambridge: Cambridge University Press, 2002).

Beaumont, Matthew. *Utopia Ltd: Ideologies of Social Dreaming in England 1870–1900* (Leiden: Brill, 2005).

Beaumont, Matthew. *The Spectre of Utopia: Utopian and Science Fictions at the fin de siècle* (Oxford: Lang, 2012).

Britain, Ian. *Fabianism and Culture: A Study in British Socialism and the Arts* (Cambridge: Cambridge University Press, 1982).

Burdett, Carolyn. *Olive Schreiner and the Progress of Feminism: Evolution, Gender, Empire* (Basingstoke: Palgrave, 2001).

---

[49] Ibid., 72; see Tim Armstrong, 'Player Piano: Poetry and Sonic Modernity', *Modernism/modernity* 14/1 (2007), 1–19.

[50] Ernest Radford, 'A Friendly Letter', *New Age* 9 (13 July 1911), 259.

[51] 'Readers and Writers', *New Age* 4 (13 Nov. 1913), 50.

Livesey, Ruth. *Socialism, Sex, and the Culture of Aestheticism in Britain, 1880–1914* (Oxford: Oxford University Press, 2007).

Miller, Elizabeth. *Slow Print: Literary Radicalism and Late Victorian Print Culture* (Stanford, CA: Stanford University Press, 2013).

Mutch, Deborah. *British Socialist Fiction, 1884–1914*, 5 vols (London: Pickering and Chatto, 2013).

Ó Donghaile, Deaglán. *Blasted Literature: Victorian Political Fiction and the Shock of the Modern* (Edinburgh: Edinburgh University Press, 2011).

Oliver, Hermia. *The International Anarchist Movement in Late-Victorian London* (London: Croom Helm, 1983).

Rowbotham, Sheila. *Edward Carpenter: A Life of Liberty and Love* (London: Verso, 2008).

Vaninskaya, Anna. *William Morris and the Idea of Community: Romance, History, and Propaganda, 1880–1914* (Edinburgh: Edinburgh University Press, 2010).

Waters, Chris. *British Socialism and the Politics of Popular Culture, 1884–1914* (Manchester: Manchester University Press, 1990).

Weir, David. *Anarchy and Culture: The Aesthetic Politics of Modernism* (Amherst, MA: University of Massachusetts Press, 1999).

CHAPTER 28

'THE END OF LAISSEZ-FAIRE'

Literature, Economics, and the Idea of the Welfare State

BENJAMIN KOHLMANN

In 1926 Leonard and Virginia Woolf's Hogarth Press published a short treatise by John Maynard Keynes entitled *The End of Laissez-Faire*. Keynes, a member of the Woolfs' Bloomsbury circle, argued that economic individualism—enshrined in the libertarian ideology of laissez-faire—had approached its demise. While observing that the aftershocks of the First World War were dealing a death blow to the old economic system, Keynes also insisted that the roots of its legitimation crisis lay in the preceding decades when new economic, legal, and philosophical arguments had prepared the groundwork for the modern welfare state. Keynes is now widely recognized as a key critic of economic libertarianism, but debates by cultural historians often fail to acknowledge that his works self-consciously built on a line of economic thinkers who had redefined cultural understandings of collective welfare, self-interest, and the potential of market failure from the 1880s onwards. For example, literary scholars writing in the wake of current financial crises tend to associate economic discourse with an uncritical promulgation of (neo)liberal ideology—a tendency which can produce myopic assessments of the role which turn-of-the-century economists played in early critiques of laissez-faire. Paying attention to early critiques which emerged within the discipline of economics can also prompt a rethinking of the dominant literary–historical account according to which the theorization of consumerism in marginal-utility economics was the single most significant intellectual contribution by economists to the development of turn-of-the-century writing. According to this still-influential narrative, the subjectivist calculus of marginal utility economics, introduced by W. S. Jevons's *Theory of Political Economy* (1871), entailed a mathematization of economic inquiry that eventually led to the isolation of economics from other cultural discourses.[1]

---

[1] See, for example, Regenia Gagnier, *The Insatiability of Human Wants: Economics and Aesthetics in Market Society* (Chicago, IL: University of Chicago Press, 2000) and Michael Tratner, *Deficits and Desires* (Stanford, CA: Stanford University Press, 2001).

Refocusing critical debates about the relationship between literature and economics around questions of welfare and the common good makes it possible to recuperate the wider significance of economic discourse in the cultural contexts of the period 1880–1920.

As Keynes noted in *The End of Laissez-Faire*, proponents of classical laissez-faire—from the French Physiocrats and Adam Smith in the eighteenth century to David Ricardo and Harriet Martineau in the early nineteenth—had maintained that individuals pursuing their private economic interests were also maximizing collective welfare measured in terms of aggregate wealth. It was only towards the end of the nineteenth century, Keynes submitted, that economists had begun to explore cases in which individual gain and the realization of collective welfare diverged. Keynes's own work exhibits particular continuities with the tradition of welfare economics which was ushered in by the economist and moral philosopher Henry Sidgwick in the 1880s and 1890s. As was common, Sidgwick taught political economy as part of the Moral Sciences tripos at the University of Cambridge. At Cambridge Sidgwick was the mentor of Alfred Marshall and through Marshall, who would move on to teach economics at the same university, his influence extended to the next generation of welfare economists, including Arthur Cecil Pigou and Keynes himself. In *The Principles of Political Economy* (1883) Sidgwick analyzed cases—most notably financial speculation and the formation of monopolies—in which there existed a 'marked divergence between private interest and public interest'. As a consequence of the mid-century speculation boom, reckless imperial trading, and the high unemployment levels during the so-called great depression of 1873–9, Sidgwick concluded, the 'old belief' in the 'harmony' of self-interest and 'the interest of the whole community' had 'lost its hold on the mind of our age'.[2]

Earlier economists had claimed that a natural equilibrium of wealth existed within any given economic system, but the recent crises had exposed a slippage between the descriptive and normative valences of the term 'natural' itself: 'for by the term "natural" as commonly used, the notion of "what generally is," or "what would be apart from human interference," is suggested in vague combination with that of "what ought to be" or "what is intended by a benevolent Providence"'.[3] Economists, Sidgwick pointed out, had blurred the distinction between hard economic facts and a metaphysical belief in the covert workings of a benign 'Providence'.[4] Sidgwick's examination of this ambiguity revealed the quasi-religious content out of which earlier economic arguments had been constructed. As a result of this slippage, he argued, the belief in domestic and global laissez-faire and in the invisible hand of the market had never been a purely economic ideology; instead 'it was a

---

[2] Henry Sidgwick, *The Principles of Political Economy*, 3rd edn (London: Macmillan, 1901), 408, 486. For further discussion of Sidgwick in the context of late-Victorian literary culture, see Benjamin Kohlmann, 'Self-Interest versus Social Interest? George Eliot, Political Economy, and the Common Good', *History of Political Economy* (forthcoming).

[3] Sidgwick, Principles, 19.

[4] Sidgwick cites Adam Smith's 'invisible hand' of the market as a prominent example of this tendency.

prophecy' predicting a future of peace, happiness, and plenty for all.[5] The analysis in *Principles* also helps to explain why the breakdown of the harmony between individual and collective welfare struck Sidgwick quite literally with the force of a religious crisis.[6] The task Sidgwick set himself was to establish a new principle which would fix the broken link between the individual pursuit of gain and the well-being of the social body. The Preface to *Principles* associated the 'pass[ing]' of 'the halcyon days of political economy' with economists' narrowing focus on the measurement of individual happiness, and Sidgwick tried to assemble a new 'social point of view', a new totalizing social vision, out of Jevons's emphasis on subjective desires. If it was possible to quantify individual happiness, he contended, combining these distinct figures would yield a measurement of aggregate welfare.[7] Sidgwick's search for a 'social point of view' acknowledged that economic systems were subject to cyclical crises, and it led him to the insight that 'governmental interference' was no longer to be seen as merely 'a temporary resource' but as 'a normal element of the organization' of the economy.[8]

Principles forms part of a strand of economic thinking about welfare whose wider discursive presence has been all but invisible in literary–historical accounts of the period. Historians of economic thought, by contrast, have recently begun to reassess the influence which economic thinking about welfare had after 1880 on the rise of the welfare state in Britain.[9] These new accounts of the field's early disciplinary history indicate that economic ideas about social welfare continued to make reference to a shared ground of cultural assumptions about the relationship between individual desire and the common good. Paying attention to these debates within economics in turn illuminates the ways in which literary writers sought to comprehend the passage from mid-Victorian liberalism and its notion of a minimal, localized state towards the more active state that was codified through the new social legislation of the early 1900s. This chapter will begin by exploring instances from a range of novels in which the pursuit of personal financial gain runs counter to collective welfare; it will then, in a second step, consider some of the discursive affinities between literary works and economic arguments for state-organized welfare in the early 1900s.

---

[5] Frank Trentmann, 'The Strange Death of Free Trade: The Erosion of "Liberal Consensus" in Great Britain, *c.*1903–1932', in Eugenio Biagini (ed.), *Citizenship and Community* (Cambridge: Cambridge University Press, 1996), 224.

[6] See Steven Medema, '"Losing My Religion": Sidgwick, Theism, and the Struggle for Utilitarian Ethics in Economic Analysis', *History of Political Economy* 40 (2008), 189–211.

[7] For references to Jevons, see Sidgwick, *Principles*, p. v, 4–5; for the 'social point of view', see 133–4.

[8] Sidgwick, *Principles*, 414.

[9] See esp. Roger Backhouse and Tamotsu Nishizawa (eds), *No Wealth but Life: Welfare Economics and the Welfare State in Britain, 1880–1945* (Cambridge: Cambridge University Press, 2010).

Speculative Fictions

A particularly glaring example of the divergence between self-interest and collective well-being was the economic havoc wreaked by financial speculators on various occasions during the late nineteenth century. As John Stuart Mill warned in *Chapters on Socialism* (published posthumously in 1879), speculating, unlike investing, encouraged a 'gambling spirit in commerce'.[10] Speculators, Mill and others argued, desired to pocket money without having to work for it, and the lack of regulations in the trade and finance sector helped to trigger the international economic recession which started in the 1870s and lasted well into the 1890s. Fictional characters who are (or act like) speculators figure in several mid-Victorian novels such as Charles Dickens's *Nicholas Nickleby* (1838–9) and *Little Dorrit* (1857), but they proliferate in the decades around 1900. They include major and minor characters, from Augustus Melmotte in Trollope's *The Way We Live Now* (1875) through Mrs Cheveley in Oscar Wilde's *An Ideal Husband* (1895) and Bennet Frothingham in George Gissing's *The Whirlpool* (1897) to Frank Cowperwood in Theodore Dreiser's *The Financier* (1912) and the banker–investor Smith de Barral in Joseph Conrad's *Chance* (1913).

The most famous case of a renegade speculator is certainly Trollope's Melmotte who arrives in London to woo new investors for the construction of a railway line in North America. Yet even though Melmotte's speculations lead to the ruin of many other characters, the figure of Melmotte eludes the melodramatic moralization that often attaches to speculators in earlier Victorian novels. As Regenia Gagnier has observed, 'Melmotte himself is silent, inarticulate among Trollope's brilliant dialogues, almost without content'.[11] There is a sense in which Melmotte's absence from the text's key scenes mirrors the fluidity and immateriality that characterizes the speculator's wealth. Even before Melmotte's physical appearance is described ('a large man, with bushy whiskers and rough thick hair, with heavy eyebrows, and a wonderful look of power about his mouth and chin'), his elusive place in the narrative is explained by reference to the immaterial nature of his wealth: Melmotte's fortune, the narrator observes, was 'generally supposed to be fathomless, bottomless, endless'.[12] Melmotte may be spectacularly rich and his fall spectacularly disastrous, yet the success of his financial schemes paradoxically lies in the fact that the bulk of his wealth never takes on material form, that it is in constant flux, being permanently invested and reinvested into new enterprises and stocks. Melmotte's curious

---

[10] J. S. Mill, *Principles of Political Economy and Chapters on Socialism* (Oxford: Oxford University Press, 2008), 406.

[11] Gagnier, 'Money, the Economy, and Social Class', in Patrick Brantlinger (ed.), *A Companion to the Victorian Novel* (London: Blackwell, 2005).

[12] Anthony Trollope, *The Way We Live Now* (Oxford: Oxford University Press, 1999), 31, 19.

lack of substance in the narrative, all the more striking when contrasted with his monumental physical appearance, thus points to his peculiar place in the economic system the novel depicts. Like de Barral, the financier in Conrad's *Chance* who dies before the action starts but whose past deeds drive the novel's plot, Melmotte represents capital-in-circulation: he 'was a mere sign, a portent. There was nothing in him'.[13] The economic system of unregulated trade tilts in favour of monopolists like Melmotte and de Barral who already possess money, making it easy for them to trick others out of theirs. These asymmetries of commerce and trade—and the market collapses which they were likely to produce—constitute a central criticism of the Victorian economic system in Trollope's novel, much as they do in Sidgwick's *Principles* and other classic economic studies such as Marshall's *Principles of Economics* (1890) and Pigou's *Wealth and Welfare* (1912).

Many novels of the period 1880–1920 turn to speculators in order to portray the hazards which arose from self-interest once it was allowed to run rampant in unregulated markets. While some authors share Trollope's worries about fluid value which is grounded in intangibles, others weave the rhetoric of self-interest into the language of their novels and use it to drive their plots. As one might expect, the latter tendency is especially marked in naturalistic novels, a genre known for its trademark fatalism about the destructiveness of human desires. Gissing's *The Whirlpool* is a case in point. The novel's plot reads in some respects like a sequel to *The Way We Live Now*: like Melmotte at the end of Trollope's narrative, the rich financier Bennet Frothingham commits suicide in the early chapters of Gissing's novel when he learns that his speculations have imploded; and while the ending of Trollope's narrative sees Melmotte's daughter leave for San Francisco, *The Whirlpool* describes the life of Alma Frothingham following her father's ruin and death. But Gissing's novel also shows that the failure of a single speculator does not put an end to the hegemonic model of economic laissez-faire with its emphasis on self-interested motives as the driving force of human action. Indeed, in Gissing's novel Frothingham senior's death is the occasion for a much broader exploration of the pervasiveness of acquisitive desire across all fields of human life. The novel's plot is propelled by an unrelenting logic of self-interest, when one of the male protagonists is drawn into financial speculation (he 'wanted money, money, and saw no other way of obtaining it'), while the other, Harvey Rolfe, starts to court the beautiful orphaned Alma.[14] When Rolfe sits down to pen a letter to Alma, he reminds himself that 'assuredly it must not read like a commercial overture. He had great difficulty in writing anything that seemed tolerable. Yet done it must be, and done it was; and before going to bed he had dropped his letter into the post. He durst not leave it for reperusal in the morning light'. 'It must not read like a commercial overture'—but, Gissing implies, that is precisely what Rolfe's letter amounts to: it is a speculative

---

[13] Joseph Conrad, *Chance* (Oxford: Oxford University Press, 2008), 58.
[14] George Gissing, *The Whirlpool* (London: Lawrence and Bullen, 1897), 4.

wager, a commercial proposition driven in part by Rolfe's expectation that the impecunious Alma cannot afford to turn him down. Unbeknownst to Rolfe, however, Alma is very much her father's daughter. She hopes that by marrying Rolfe she will improve her social position and erase the stigma associated with her maiden name. Having accepted Rolfe's proposal, Alma decides to pursue a musical career despite her mediocre talents. Discussing her decision with a friend, she asks: 'You know my old revolt against the bonds of the amateur. I'm going to break out—or try to. What would you give for my chances?' 'My dear,' her female friend replies, 'I am no capitalist . . . For such a bargain as that you must go among the great speculators.'[15] Alma's choice of a musical career, although seemingly far removed from her father's line of work, is pursued with an eye to fame and money, and her friend's response signals that she instinctively grasps the implications of the commercial language in which Alma's proposal is couched ('bonds . . . what would you give').

If Gissing's novel illustrates how even the most intimate, domestic spheres of social interaction are permeated by the logic of speculative commerce, Conrad's *Nostromo* (1904) projects the critique of unchecked self-interest onto a global scale. Ayşe Çelikkol has recently identified a nineteenth-century literary genre which championed the alleged beneficent effects of unregulated markets. Extending from Walter Scott and Harriet Martineau to Charlotte Brontë, these 'romances of free trade' idealize the figure of *homo economicus*, painting him as a subject who 'thrived in commercial networks'. In these works *homo economicus* is presented as resolutely anti-authoritarian and independent, but he also serves as a 'celebration' of the spirit of transnational 'interdependence' enabled by free trade.[16] Conrad's earliest novels, in particular *Almayer's Folly* (1895) and *An Outcast of the Islands* (1896), commonly start as free-trade romances before shifting stylistic registers, but *Nostromo* arguably constitutes Conrad's most sustained effort to remould the genre's formulaic structures into a more adequate representation of the later stages of European imperialism. It makes sense, then, following E. M. Forster, to see *Nostromo* as a failed 'Romance about Capital' which begins by presenting an idealized view of unregulated trade, but which ends by undermining this romanticized vision as the free play of self-interest gives way to a searching critique of global laissez-faire.[17]

Charles Gould, one of the protagonists of Conrad's novel, inherits a silver mine in the fictional South American republic of Costaguana. Unlike other mine owners, however, he refuses to take a purely exploitative commercial interest in his new property.

[I]ts safety, its continued existence as an enterprise, giving a return to men—to strangers, comparative strangers—who invest money in it, is left altogether in my

---

[15] Ibid., 114, 235.

[16] Ayşe Çelikkol, *Romances of Free Trade: British Literature, Laissez-Faire, and the Global Nineteenth Century* (Oxford: Oxford University Press, 2011), 63, 66.

[17] Philip Gardner (ed.), *The Journals and Diaries of E.M. Forster*, 3 vols (London: Pickering and Chatto, 2011), I, 165.

hands. I have inspired confidence in a man [the American financier Holroyd] of wealth and position . . . I would never have disposed of the Concession as a speculator disposes of a valuable right to a company—for cash and shares, to grow rich eventually if possible, but at any rate to put some money at once in his pocket. No.[18]

Gould, who has studied mining in England, takes a proprietary pride in his inheritance. He believes that it is his sacred duty to keep the mine 'safe' so as to ensure that it keeps 'giving a return to men—to strangers', thus invoking the spirit of responsibility and mutual trust which Çelikkol identifies as a key feature of romances of free trade. Conrad's attempt to describe the *homo economicus* of imperial commerce as a multi-sided character, rather than as a mere vector of material desires, resonates with the insistence by economists like Sidgwick, Marshall, and Keynes that 'economic man'—the abstract, hyper-rational, male model of rational agency—failed to do justice to the complexity of economic decision making. As Alfred Marshall noted in his influential *Principles of Economics*, economists ought to 'deal with man as he is: not with an abstract "economic" man; but a man of flesh and blood'.[19] As Conrad's plot unfolds, however, the novel suggests that Gould's idealism is an anachronism in this age of rapacious late-imperial commerce. As one protagonist claims towards the end of the novel, markets eviscerate character: 'There is no peace and rest in the development of material interests. They have their law and their justice. But it is founded on expediency, and is inhuman'.[20] The novel, like Gissing's *The Whirlpool*, presents an historical situation in which human motives are increasingly amenable to Jevonsian computation and quantification in terms of 'material interests'.

However, Conrad's text also participates in another set of economic discourses about the origins of imperialism and globalized speculation. As the economist J. A. Hobson argued in several of his works (most prominently his 1902 book *Imperialism*), the root causes of imperialism lay in the domestic economies of the imperialist powers. It was the chronic shortfall of domestic consumption (what Hobson labelled 'underconsumption') which had driven speculators, financiers, and traders to find new capital markets in the colonial 'periphery'. Hobson's argument exposed the flaws of the classical equilibrium theory of laissez-faire articulated by Say's Law (according to which production created its own demand), and it had a great influence on later economic writers, including Leonard Woolf (*Empire and Commerce in Africa*, 1920) and Keynes. The narrative trajectory of *Nostromo* reflects the interaction between domestic and global economic spheres sketched out by Hobson, as the Republic of Costaguana descends into a civil war which is backed by foreign financiers like Holroyd and driven in part by the desire for

---

[18] Conrad, *Nostromo* (Oxford: Oxford University Press, 2007), 55.
[19] Alfred Marshall, *Principles of Economics*, 8th edn (London: Macmillan, 1920), 26–7. The first edition, from 1890, expresses similar ideas.
[20] Conrad, *Nostromo*, 366.

possession of Gould's mine. By drawing attention to the complex networked effects of the economic world-system, *Nostromo* can thus be seen to scramble the more straightforward adventure plots of earlier free-trade romances like H. Rider Haggard's *King Solomon's Mines* (1885) which celebrated (and lavishly rewarded) the resilience of individuals embracing the hazards of colonial adventure.[21]

Hobson's idea that the causes of imperialist expansion were to be found in the domestic economy, a realm in which the state could meaningfully intervene, formed part of a larger group of arguments which proposed that the imbalance between individual gain and collective well-being had to be remedied first of all at the national level. These debates about the reorganization of the national economy were characterized, as the third book of Sidgwick's *Principles* correctly suggested, by a gradual shift from the earlier political-economic focus on production towards questions of wealth distribution. 'Between 1900 and 1920', a recent commentator notes, 'the semantics of "welfare" subtly changed', as what had been 'a strictly individualist concept' came to be redefined in collectivist terms.[22] At the heart of discussions about the distribution of national wealth and the reorganization of collective welfare were questions about the state's ability to compensate for the impact of economic crises on individuals' lives and about the provisions the state might offer against unemployment. These reforms at the national level, some hoped, would help to stabilize the international order by stimulating domestic demand and thus defusing conflict between the imperial powers. But these debates also inevitably involved discussion of how the state should pay for these expenses: how were different types of wealth to be distinguished and how should they be taxed? And was a large-scale redistribution of wealth, which many socialists pushed for, at all desirable?

Towards the Welfare State: Literature and Reform

Few of these questions were entirely new, but as the result of various developments at home—including political factors such as organized working-class pressure, the emergence of the Independent Labour Party in 1893, and the break-up of the two-party system of liberals and conservatives—they were now coming more pressingly to the fore. Some on the left aired the notion that a 'stronger' interventionist state would be able to bend the economic laws which earlier political economists had described as immutable. H. G. Wells, a sometime member of the socialist Fabian Society (founded

---

[21] On Haggard and (financial) risk-taking, see Francis O'Gorman, 'Speculative Fictions and the Fortunes of H. Rider Haggard', in O'Gorman (ed.), *Victorian Literature and Finance*, 157–72. For Victorian fictions about risk, including Harriet Martineau's, see Elaine Freedgood, *Victorian Writing about Risk* (Cambridge: Cambridge University Press, 2000).

[22] José Harris, 'Economic Knowledge and British Social Policy', in Mary O. Funer and Barry Supple (eds), *The State and Economic Knowledge* (Cambridge: Cambridge University Press, 2003), 397.

in 1884), insisted in his essay collection *The Making of Mankind* (1904) that '[t]he days of mystic individualism have passed; few people nowadays will agree to that strange creed that we must deal with economic conditions as though they were inflexible laws'.[23] Governments, Sidgwick might add, were tasked with prising apart the descriptive and normative meanings conflated in the idea of 'natural' economic laws and with remodelling the economy according to principles of distributive justice.

Economic arguments that fed into early twentieth-century welfare legislation and which found an echo in literary works included the extension of the concept of 'rent' by Hobson, Marshall, and others to signify different types of 'unearned income'; the recognition that there was bound to be an 'irreducible minimum' of unemployment in capitalist societies; and the substantial development of Mill's idea of 'externalities' (costs of economic transactions which accrue to otherwise uninvolved third parties) by Sidgwick, Marshall, Pigou, and others.[24] These economic arguments reconfigured the relationship between individual and collective welfare, and they provided material from which fiction writers could construct the new 'social point of view' that Sidgwick had called for in place of the metaphysical certainties of classical political economy.

Wells was a member of the Fabian Society between 1903 and 1906 (one of his sponsors being George Bernard Shaw), and Wells's novels of the early 1900s frequently address issues debated by the society, including questions of socially generated wealth and of earned and unearned incomes. In *Kipps* (1905), for example, the novel's lower-middle-class protagonist Artie Kipps unexpectedly discovers that he has inherited his grandfather's large fortune. While the novel's first draft, entitled *The Wealth of Mr Waddy* (written in the late 1890s, prior to Wells's involvement with the Fabians), focused on the character of Artie's grandfather, an egomaniacal rich man of Melmottian proportions, the published version abandons this satirical stock figure to explore the effects which the legacy has on Kipps's life. By inheriting his grandfather's money Kipps becomes a rentier, that bête noire of turn-of-the-century socialists. The extension of the term 'rent' to signify not just returns on landed property but any kind of unearned income had gained currency among English socialists with the posthumous publication of Mill's *Chapters on Socialism*, and it had been seized on eagerly by Sidney and Beatrice Webb and others. The term also entered the academic discourse of economics. As Marshall observed in a famous aside in *Principles of Economics*, landed rent was in reality only 'the leading species of a large genus' which also prominently included inherited wealth.[25] Artie

---

[23] H. G. Wells, *Mankind in the Making* (London: Chapman and Hall, 1904), 176.

[24] On rent, see Peter Groenewegen, 'Marshall on Welfare Economics and the Welfare State', in Backhouse and Nishizawa, *No Wealth but Life*, 25–41; on externalities, see Medema, *The Hesitant Hand: Taming Self-Interest in the History of Economic Ideas* (Princeton, NJ: Princeton University Press, 2009); on the 'irreducible minimum', see William Beveridge, *Unemployment: A Problem of Industry* (London: Longmans, 1909).

[25] Marshall, *Principles of Economics*, 412.

initially embraces the opportunity for social rise, and he becomes engaged to the beautiful but calculating Helen Walshingham who aims to establish herself and her brother in London's high society. Artie is saved from marrying Helen when he meets his former childhood friend Sid, who shocks Artie by pointing out to him that he holds no right to his wealth, because he has not 'earned' it. ' "I'm a Socialist, you see," said Sid, "I don't 'old with Wealth. What *is* Wealth? Labour robbed out of the poor. At most it's only yours in trust." ' In a later scene Artie meets Sid's socialist mentor Masterman (modelled on the politician of radical views, C. F. G. Masterman) who explains Sid's principled rejection of personal wealth. Money is no longer 'what it ought to be, the token given for service': it has ceased to be significant as an embodiment of social relations and, by becoming untethered from the social realm it has become the symbol of the increasingly self-referential sphere of global speculative commerce.[26] Unlike Sid, Masterman does not suggest that it would be best to do away with money as such; instead he proposes that money can be reinvested with social value if its distribution is reorganized on fairer principles.

The two collections of politico-economic chapters, *Anticipations* (1901) and *The Making of Mankind*, which Wells published around the time he wrote *Kipps*, suggest that a more meaningful distribution of money can be attained by way of new forms of taxation. Echoing Fabian arguments and anticipating C. F. G. Masterman's influential *The Condition of England* (1909), Wells argues that the overhauled tax system will feature new 'laws of inheritance' and death duties, a graduated and progressive income tax, as well as direct taxes on 'ground-rents' and financial speculation.[27] Private wealth will be subject to special taxes, Wells submits, insofar as it is socially created or insofar as no personal effort went into obtaining it—categories broad enough to subsume capital gains through inheritance, speculation, landed property, and other sources. The tax system will thus offer a reasonably accurate image of the kinds of wealth created at particular points in the social system; and the money so generated will be redistributed among the needier members of the community or spent on public works. *Kipps* nods towards these debates. As Artie leaves Masterman's house, he looks at the world around him afresh—with the eyes, as it were, of a tax collector:

His soul looked out upon life in general as a very small nestling might peep out of its nest. What an extraordinary thing life was to be sure, and what a remarkable variety of people there were in it.

He lit a cigarette, and speculated upon that receding group of three, and blew smoke and watched them. They seemed to do it all right. Probably they all had incomes of very much over twelve hundred a year.[28]

[26] Wells, *Kipps* (London: Penguin Books, 2005), 180, 228. Fittingly, Artie's money is later gambled away by Helen's brother who is a financial speculator, leaving Artie free to marry his childhood sweetheart Ann.

[27] Wells, *Anticipations of the Reactions of Mechanical and Scientific Progress upon Human Life and Thought* (Mineola, NY: Dover, 1999), 41–5.

[28] Wells, *Kipps*, 237.

The 'variety of people' whom Artie observes in this passage corresponds to a wide variety of 'incomes', which in their turn correspond to a scale of graduated income tax levels.

The debate among economists about the widening of the fiscal base in order to fund new welfare measures culminated in the early 1900s. As the economic historian Martin Daunton notes, following the Budget of 1894 'attention turned from the equity of the tax system to issues of equality and the use of the fiscal system to alter the structure of society'.[29] The utopian dimension of Wells's fiction and chapters in this period is closely related to this search for state institutions which more accurately reflect transformations in society and which are more responsive to human needs. For example, Wells notes in *Anticipations* that

> in dealing with speculation, the New Republic will have the power of an assured faith and purpose, and the resources of an economic science that is as yet only in its infancy. In such matters the New Republic will entertain no superstition of *laissez faire*. Money and credit are as much human contrivances as bicycles, and as liable to expansion and modification as any other sort of prevalent but imperfect machine.[30]

'Superstition' is a key word here as it helps to recall the religious connotations which invested the idea of a system of natural economic laws governed by 'benevolent Providence'. 'It was pleasant to believe,' Shaw submitted in his contribution to *Fabian Essays in Socialism* (1889) apropos of Adam Smith's economic theories, 'that a benevolent hand was guiding the steps of society; overruling all evil appearances for good.'[31] But it is possible to wonder if the emerging contours of the welfare state, as envisioned in Shaw's contributions to the 1889 *Fabian Essays* and in Wells's more explicitly utopian novels of the early 1900s, were not designed to effect a very similar re-enchantment of an alienated social world which Jevons's subjectivist theory of pleasure had described as radically atomized.[32] The 'economic science as yet only in its infancy' foreseen in Wells's *Anticipations* and the applied 'Art' of economics anticipated in the third book of Sidgwick's *Principles* were to be the means by which this new social world was brought into being.[33]

It has been easy for literary scholars to overstate the role which socialism played in the extension of statal mandates in the early 1900s, owing in part to the illustrious literary names associated with the movement during this period. However,

---

[29] Martin Daunton, *Just Taxes: The Politics of Taxation in Britain, 1914–1979* (Cambridge: Cambridge University Press, 2002), 52.

[30] Wells, *Anticipations*, 177.

[31] G. B. Shaw, 'Economic', in Shaw (ed.), *Fabian Essays in Socialism* (London: Fabian Society, 1889), 27.

[32] Jevons's arguments in favour of subjectivism fit seamlessly into the popular narrative of modernization which stresses the alienation and fragmentation of the social sphere. See, for example, Jevons's observation that 'Every mind is . . . inscrutable to every other mind, and no common denomination of feeling is possible', in his *Theory of Political Economy* (London: Macmillan, 1871), 21.

[33] See also the chapter on 'Utopian Economics' in *A Modern Utopia* (1905), which calls for a new and 'real criterion of well-being'. Wells, *A Modern Utopia* (London: Penguin, 2005), 60.

notwithstanding Wells's resounding dismissal of the Liberal Party's reformism in *The New Machiavelli* (1911), authors more commonly associated with liberalism also offered sustained reflections on the rise of the welfare state in their fictions. As Lauren Goodlad observes, the so-called New Liberal reformers of the early 1900s struggled to reconcile Gladstonian liberalism, which insisted that social and economic reform had to start with the moral reformation of character, and socialism, which typically pushed for changes in the extraneous, environmental circumstances which shaped character.[34] It is possible to locate a writer such as E. M. Forster, who famously claimed in 1946 that he belonged to the 'fag-end of liberalism', in this hybrid tradition.[35] Forster's modernist novel *Howards End* (1910), for example, responded to the intense public debates which preceded the introduction of unemployment insurance as part of the National Insurance Act in 1911. In doing so, it explored how the social rights codified by the 1911 Act affected individual lives, instead of concentrating on the large-scale institutional reforms that were central to Wells's fictions.

The economist Steven Medema has shown that the emergence of new ideas about collective welfare in economics was closely related to the analysis of cases (now known as 'externalities') in which unregulated market behaviour inflicted losses on uninvolved third parties. Unemployment, generally recognized by the 1910s as an inherent feature of capitalist markets, could also be seen to fall into this category. The term 'unemployment' had only been coined in the 1880s when it began to replace an older moralistic vocabulary which attributed joblessness to personal shortcomings, such as idleness, or to lack of moral probity. Testifying before a royal commission, Alfred Marshall observed that since the causes of unemployment tended to be systemic, it made no sense to use the old term 'pauperism' to signal moral condemnation; instead, Marshall argued, it was necessary to recognize the ineradicability of a certain level of 'poverty' in mass commercial societies.[36] With the introduction of unemployment insurance in 1911, the Liberal government acknowledged the general validity of these arguments. Compulsory unemployment insurance no longer distributed specific goods in the spirit of charity; instead it provided the unemployed with regular sums of money.

Chapter 15 of *Howards End* begins by alluding to the language of the 1911 welfare reforms. The well-to-do Schlegel sisters, Helen and Margaret, have decided to make the downtrodden Leonard Bast, a member of the lower-middle class, the object of their charity and to exert a cultural influence on him. While attending an

---

[34] Lauren Goodlad, *Victorian Literature and the Victorian State* (Baltimore, MD: Johns Hopkins University Press, 2003), 192–237.

[35] E. M. Forster, *Two Cheers for Democracy* (New York: Harcourt, 1951), 56.

[36] Quoted in Goodlad, 'Character and Pastorship in Two British "Sociological" Traditions: Organized Charity, Fabian Socialism, and the Invention of New Liberalism', in Amanda Anderson and Joseph Valente (eds), *Disciplinarity at the fin de siècle* (Princeton, NJ: Princeton University Press, 2002), 251.

informal political discussion club organized by some friends, Margaret advocates giving money, rather than specific goods, to people like Leonard. 'Give them a chance', she implores. 'Give them money. Don't dole them out poetry-books and railway-tickets like babies. Give them the wherewithal to buy these things.'[37] When Helen and Margaret walk home after the dinner party, they meet their friend, the wealthy capitalist Henry Wilcox. The sisters tell Henry about their plans to support Leonard, and Margaret mentions that Leonard is a clerk at the Porphyrion Fire Insurance Company. 'My dear Miss Schlegel,' Henry interrupts, 'I will not rush in where your sex has been unable to tread. My only contribution is this: let your young friend clear out of the Porphyrion with all possible speed'. The Porphyrion, Henry explains, 'will smash' because it lacks reinsurance. The sisters pass on Henry's advice, and Leonard, eager to satisfy his benefactresses, abandons his job. He takes on a minor position as a bank clerk at a significantly reduced salary, and when the bank encounters financial difficulties, Leonard is one of the first to be laid off. In the absence of a safety net, Leonard, the former insurance clerk, falls into the abyss of unemployment. When Henry is confronted by the Schlegel sisters, he refuses to accept responsibility for Leonard's fate. If anyone is to blame, he notes, it is the cap-italist 'system':

> Don't take up that sentimental attitude over the poor. The poor are poor, and one's sorry for them, but there it is. As society moves forward, the shoe is bound to pinch in places, and it's absurd to pretend that anyone is responsible personally. Neither you, nor I, nor my informant, nor the man who informed him, nor the directors of the Porphyrion, are to blame for this clerk's loss of salary. It's just the shoe pinching.[38]

Henry's self-serving comment is a reminder that blaming the system is a way to dispel personal guilt and to avoid taking responsibility for the lives of others. When it is read along these lines, the passage presents Forster's indictment of that abstract figure of economic rationality, 'economic man', who fails to see beyond the reach of his own interests. On Henry's account, complex economic systems render the moral categories of compassion and responsibility obsolete.

The debates which preceded the National Insurance Act did not rely primarily on appeals to charitable empathy, but on an acuter sense of who were the most vulner-able members of the British economic system and of who were its profiteers. Forster's exploration of these questions recalls this emphasis on the economy's systemic logic, on the ways in which self-interested behaviour at one point in the system can pro-duce misery at another. Among the Schlegel siblings, only Margaret catches a glimpse of the foundations on which her comfortable existence rests. She tells her aunt:

> You and I and the Wilcoxes stand upon money as upon islands. It is so firm beneath our feet that we forget its very existence. It's only when we see someone near us tottering

---

[37] Forster, *Howards End* (Boston, MA: Bedford, 1997), 121.
[38] Ibid., 126, 171.

that we realize all that an independent income means . . . I begin to think that the very soul of the world is economic, and that the lowest abyss is not the absence of love, but the absence of coin.[39]

The economic 'soul of the world', as Sidgwick had noted in *Principles*, was not a quasi-spiritual or self-perfecting entity, directed towards salvation by a benign Providence, but a body of historically contingent laws governing the social distribution of wealth. Their privileged rentier lifestyle, Margaret realizes, has profoundly shaped her family's politics and their cosmopolitan tastes. Leonard aspires towards a similar ideal of upper-middle-class cultivation, but the novel hints that his lack of education will forever bar him from it. While Forster's novel acknowledges the systemic pressures at work in the economy, it also indicates that Britain's entrenched class system will not simply melt into air with the Edwardian welfare reforms. Indeed, as socialists and other political radicals recognized, the Liberal Party's reforms were not designed to effect a complete reordering of the Victorian politico-economic system. The same can be said of Forster's novel, in which the working classes are out of sight, if not completely out of mind. 'We are not concerned with the very poor', the narrator notes early on, 'They are unthinkable, and only to be approached by the statistician or the poet'.[40] It is not clear who is speaking here and to whom, who precisely the pronoun 'we' includes or excludes. Even so, the sentence articulates a class bias that folds Forster's authorial voice back into the cultural and economic limitations of Helen and Margaret's point of view.

The yearning epigraph of *Howards End*—'Only connect'—famously gives expression to Forster's hope that a shared culture will be able to defuse the tensions created by economic injustice and class bias. But then, by the 1910s, such Arnoldian hopes had begun to wear thin. The Bloomsbury artist Roger Fry, writing on 'Art and the Great State' in 1912, noted that the idea of culture as a 'spiritual' link between classes was an illusion fabricated by artistic rentiers (including members of the Bloomsbury circle) who, 'while working their life long for the plutocracy, have been vehement Socialists'. When regarded exclusively 'from the point of view of the community as a whole' it was indeed hard to discern whose needs (modernist) high art was intended to satisfy.[41] Fry's imagined perspective of the 'community as a whole' recalls Sidgwick's search for a new 'social point of view' as well as Forster's nostalgic epigraph ('Only connect'). Yet while Sidgwick continued to believe in the life-sustaining value of an art whose guardians were the well-heeled few, Fry's chapter implies that the only meaningful definition of the common good is in terms of an improved distribution of *economic* wealth.[42] Keynes, Fry's Bloomsbury *confrère*, agreed in his momentous post-war book *The Economic*

---

[39]   Ibid., 67.   [40]   Ibid., 55.

[41]   Roger Fry, 'Art and the Great State', in Wells (ed.), *Socialism and the Great State* (London: Harper, 1912), 252, 268.

[42]   Sidgwick, *Principles*, 522.

Consequences of the Peace (1919). The war had destroyed once and for all the Victorian 'economic Eldorado, this economic Utopia' which ran on the comforting myth that in the future there would be plenty for all. However, it was possible that, 'as we must pray they will, the souls of the European peoples [will] turn away this winter from the false idols which have survived the war'.[43] Writing in the winter of 1919, Keynes was looking ahead with a mixture of apprehension and hope to a more austere future in which collective welfare was no longer the natural outcome of laissez-faire but in which it would have to be won in the face of constant adversity and the looming threat of economic depression.

FURTHER READING

Backhouse, Roger E. 'Sidgwick, Marshall, and the Cambridge School of Economics', *History of Political Economy* 38/1 (2006), 15–44.

Backhouse, Roger E. and Tamotsu Nishizawa (eds). *No Wealth But Life: Welfare Economics and the Welfare State in Britain, 1880–1945* (Cambridge: Cambridge University Press, 2010).

Floud, Roderick and Paul Johnson (eds). *The Cambridge Economic History of Modern Britain*, vol. 2: *Economic Maturity, 1860–1939* (Cambridge: Cambridge University Press, 2004).

Gagnier, Regenia. *The Insatiability of Human Wants: Economics and Aesthetics in Market Society* (Chicago, IL: University of Chicago Press, 2000).

Gagnier, Regenia. *Individuality, Decadence and Globalization: On the Relationship of Part to Whole* (London: Palgrave Macmillan, 2010).

Goodlad, Lauren. *Victorian Literature and the Victorian State: Character and Governance in a Liberal Society* (Baltimore, MD: Johns Hopkins University Press, 2003).

Medema, Steven. *The Hesitant Hand: Taming Self-Interest in the History of Ideas* (Princeton, NJ: Princeton University Press, 2009).

O'Gorman, Francis (ed.). *Victorian Literature and Finance* (Oxford: Oxford University Press, 2007).

Robbins, Bruce. *Upward Mobility and the Common Good: Toward a Literary History of the Welfare State* (Princeton, NJ: Princeton University Press, 2009).

Thane, Pat. *The Foundations of the Welfare State* (London: Longmans, 1982).

---

[43] J. M. Keynes, *The Economic Consequences of the Peace* (New York: Harcourt, 1920), 10, 285.

CHAPTER 29

REPRESENTING WORK

SOS ELTIS

In his vision of a future socialist utopia, *Looking Backward, 2000–1887* (1887), Edward Bellamy likened society at the end of the nineteenth century to a huge coach, on top of which the favoured few sat, admiring the scenery, while the starving many dragged the tremendous weight through mud and over stones, driven on by desperate hunger.[1] This representation of work for the vast majority of the population as inhuman drudgery within a system of absurd and obscene inequality indicated a radical shift in views from only a few decades earlier. Samuel Smiles's mid-century best-seller *Self-Help* (1859) prescribed self-control, discipline, determination, application, and, above all, hard graft as the means to advancement in a socially mobile world, while Thomas Carlyle celebrated work as not only the key to self-realization but itself a form of divine worship, no matter how humble or arduous: 'All work,' he declared, 'even cotton spinning, is noble; work alone is noble.'[2] These values were fictionally validated in the mid-century bildungsroman, such as Charlotte Brontë's *Jane Eyre* (1847), Charles Dickens's *David Copperfield* (1850), and Dinah Craik's *John Halifax, Gentleman* (1856), just as the failure to submit to the necessary discipline of daily toil proved the undoing of Hetty Sorrel in *Adam Bede* (1859) and Richard Carstairs in *Bleak House* (1852–3).

The *fin de siècle* saw the culmination and consolidation of a century-long transition from a predominantly agrarian workforce, combining a range of different occupations and skills with considerable seasonal variation, to a predominantly urban population, reliant on large employers of relatively unskilled labour.[3] This shift in working conditions is perhaps most clearly reflected in the coining of the term 'unemployment' in the 1880s, a term that had not previously been easily applicable to diverse and mutable patterns of employment. Instead, workers were

---

[1] Edward Bellamy, *Looking Backward, 2000–1887* (Oxford: Oxford University Press, 2007), 8.

[2] Thomas Carlyle, *Past and Present* (London: Chapman and Hall, 1843), 192.

[3] See Krishan Kumar, 'From Work to Employment and Unemployment: The English Experience', in R. E. Pahl (ed.), *On Work: Historical, Comparative and Theoretical Approaches* (Oxford: Blackwell, 1988), 138–66.

employed in increasingly large organizations where the division of labour was the ruling principle; as Adam Smith had famously observed of pin-makers, dividing each process into component parts, and allotting each motion to an increasingly specialized individual was seen as the secret of efficient manufacture. Modern workers tended not to sell the products of their labour but the labour itself in the form of repetitive tasks measured in regularized hours, overseen and ordered by managers, whether as factory workers and shop assistants or increasingly within new white-collar jobs as clerks and typists.

This growth of larger diversified systems was greeted by Herbert Spencer in his *Principles of Sociology* (1876–83) as evidence of social progress, complex commercial organizations being likened to the 'higher' echelons of evolution, where increasingly sophisticated organisms developed organs to perform each particular biological function. This model found its apotheosis in the management theories of Frederick Winslow Taylor, who advocated the reduction of the worker to a precisely directed cog in a machine, as he put it: 'In the past the man has been first; in the future the system must be first.'[4] The obstacles to individual mobility for the increasingly disempowered and specialized worker were clear—a pancreas can hardly be promoted to become a brain—nor is transplantation from one system to another easily achieved, as Forster's Leonard Bast discovers in *Howards End* (1910), when, having given up his clerkship at an insurance company, he realizes that once out of his 'groove' he is unemployable: 'I could do one particular branch of insurance in one particular office well enough to command a salary, but that's all.'[5]

Literary expressions of concern about the plight of the workers were hardly a *fin-de-siècle* innovation. Mid-century novels by Elizabeth Gaskell, Dickens, and Benjamin Disraeli, among others, had expressed anxiety about the reduction of individuals to 'hands', and called for greater communication and understanding between the classes to avoid the looming threat of social violence. John Ruskin, the most prominent and influential mid-century critic of contemporary labour conditions, condemned the demand for precision rather than individual creativity in production which reduced men to mere tools, dividing not just their labour but the workers themselves, who are 'broken into small fragments and crumbs of men; so that all the little piece of intelligence that is left in a man is not enough to make a pin, or a nail, but exhausts itself in making the point of a pin or the head of a nail'. The modern worker must polish the points of pins with 'sand of human soul', in contrast to the medieval craftsman whose freedom of thought and creativity

---

[4] Frederick Winslow Taylor, *The Principles of Scientific Management* (New York and London: Harper, 1911), 8.

[5] E. M. Forster, *Howards End* (Harmondsworth: Penguin, 1983), 225. For a study of modernist writers' responses to and reproduction of the language of scientific management, see James F. Knapp, *Literary Modernism and the Transformation of Work* (Evanston, IL: Northwestern University Press, 1988).

produced flawed, vivid, and individualized Gothic art and architecture, and whose conditions of production it was the nineteenth century's duty to recapture.[6]

Fin-de-siècle and early twentieth-century representations of work tended to mirror Ruskin's concern with the impoverished spiritual and psychological state of the worker, as against earlier novelists' concentration on wider apprehensions about social cohesion.[7] Denied a sense of individual agency, identity, or fulfilment, and reduced to an insignificant constituent part of a vast machine, many contemporary writers saw modern workers as being alienated not only—in a Marxist sense—from the products of their labour, but from themselves.

Representing work not as a problem to be solved but as an experience, a crucial element of life in a mechanized industrial society, was a concern across the arts from the 1880s to the 1920s. The angular muscle blocks and lines of aerodynamic distortion in Umberto Boccioni's sculptures *Unique Forms of Continuity in Space* (1913) and *Spiral Expansion of Muscles in Action* (1914) gave perfect physical expression to the Futurists' fascination with dynamic motion and the human body as machine, expressing in three dimensions the pervading theoretical and literary concern with the interchanges between scientifically systematized bodies and animated machines.[8]

But such representations risked re-enacting the very distortions and diminutions they portrayed as against the worker's own experience of such processes. Early film was similarly entranced by the spectacle of work, but until expressionist techniques were developed to render the camera's eye subjective, the spectacle remained external (as in Louis Lumière's early footage of workers leaving his factory) and potentially superficial: so Lumière's 'Demolition of a Wall' (1896) shows workers destroying a wall with heavy pick-axe blows, only for the footage to be reversed and the wall magically resurrected, the blows transformed into weightless ballet. Many of the narratives of early cinema performed a similar resurrection, bringing to the screen early Victorian melodramas about the value of hard work as the key to happiness and social inclusion—as in R. W. Paul's *Buy Your Own Cherries* (1904), a temperance film in which the worker abandons idleness and liquor for honest graft and the loving embrace of his family.

It was the naturalist novel that offered the most effective means of representing both the material and environmental conditions of working life and the inner

---

[6] John Ruskin, 'The Nature of Gothic', in *The Stones of Venice*, vol. II (1853). See Dinah Birch (ed.), *John Ruskin: Selected Writings* (Oxford: Oxford University Press, 2004), 43–4.

[7] See Carolyn Lesjak, *Working Fictions: A Genealogy of the Victorian Novel* (Durham, NC and London: Duke University Press, 2006) for analysis of the mid-Victorian novel's elision of the actual experience of work.

[8] For further discussion, see John C. Welchman, 'Colour, Light and Labour: Futurism and the Dissolution of Work', in Valerie Mainz and Griselda Pollock (eds), *Work and the Image*, 2 vols (Aldershot: Ashgate, 2000), II, 61–90, and Mark Seltzer, *Bodies and Machines* (Routledge: New York, 1992).

experience of those doing the work. The period 1880 to 1920 saw a proliferation of fiction centred on the lives of working people, from clerks and typists, to painters, sailors, builders, journalists, and photographers.[9] The shopworker was, however, a particular favourite, serving to exemplify a range of issues surrounding the changing conditions of modern employment. The last decades of the nineteenth century heralded the growth of the department store, the systematizing of retail into huge organizations, subsuming what had previously been the business of individualized and diverse shops into one vast building, within which also dwelt an army of workers, part of whose payment commonly included board and lodging in the company's dormitories. One strikingly optimistic fictional representation was Émile Zola's *Au Bonheur des Dames* (1883), which offered a Spencerian evolutionary vision of the department store as 'la réalisation moderne d'un palais du rêve' (the modern realization of a dream-palace), transformed under the joint guidance of its manager Mouret and Denise, an assistant who has endured its workers' Darwinian struggle for survival, into an ideal employer. Its workers are no longer 'un grain de mil sous une meule puissante' (a grain under a powerful millstone), but are instead recognized as the enduring metal of the machine itself, kept strong by every benefit from maternity leave and long-term contracts, to medical care, a library, grammar lessons, and fencing.[10] But this sophisticated machine is, of course, ultimately designed simply to stimulate an irresistible desire, regardless of need or utility, leaving the female customer 'dépouillée, violée . . . avec la volupté assouvie et la sourde honte d'un désir contenté au fond d'un hôtel louche' (stripped, violated . . . with the sated senses and the dull shame of a desire satisfied in a shady hotel).[11]

No such optimism characterized British writers' depiction of the modern shop or the workers' position in it. In Wells's *Kipps: The Story of a Simple Soul* (1905), for example, Mr Shalford, the proprietor of the Folkestone Drapery Bazaar, fancies himself a provincial Mouret. With his constant cry of 'System! System everywhere. Fishency', he remains complacently unaware of the errand boys fighting in the cellars or an assistant dozing at his counter. Shalford's arrival prompts the assistant to fold damask 'exactly like an automaton that is suddenly set going'.[12] Indentured as

---

[9] Critical analyses of such fiction have, therefore, necessarily tended to focus either on the work of individual authors or on a particular segment of the workforce. See for example Emma Liggins, *George Gissing, the Working Woman, and Urban Culture* (Aldershot: Ashgate, 2006); Jonathan Wilde, *The Rise of the Office Clerk in Literary Culture, 1880–1939* (Basingstoke: Palgrave Macmillan, 2006); Christopher Keep, 'The Cultural Work of the Type-Writer Girl', *Victorian Studies* 40/3 (Spring 1997), 401–26; see also Mary Wilson, *The Labors of Modernism: Domesticity, Servants, and Authorship in Modernist Fiction* (Farnham: Ashgate, 2013).

[10] Émile Zola, *Au Bonheur des Dames* (Paris: Gallimard, 2011), 297, 196. For a detailed analysis, see Rachel Bowlby, *Just Looking: Consumer Culture in Dreiser, Gissing and Zola* (New York and London: Methuen, 1985), ch. 5. Bowlby's characterization of Denise as the 'eternal feminine', however, humanizing Mouret's system, tends to establish rather too stark a gender divide between female shoppers and male managers, minimizing the role of Denise's ability to analyze and redesign the business.

[11] Ibid., 489.

[12] H. G. Wells, *Kipps: The Story of a Simple Soul* (London: Penguin, 2005), 32, 33.

an apprentice at fourteen, Kipps's life is one of tedium, exhaustion, and futile absurdity. Shalford has 'set himself assiduously to get as much out of Kipps and to put as little into him as he could', while the assistant has learnt how to measure and fold material, repeat phrases, and 'practise a servile obedience to a large number of people'. Despite Shalford's vaunted efficiency, Kipps endures endless, unnecessary hours of rolling, folding, and measuring of goods 'because of the cheapness of the genteeler sorts of labour and the dearness of forethought in the world'. Earning salaries too meagre to permit of saving, the workers are, as one puts it, 'in a blessed drainpipe, and we've got to crawl along it till we die'.[13] Nor is there any space for Mouret's creative artistry in arranging and selling goods; in Wells's *The History of Mr Polly* (1910), an ebullient shop assistant is inspired to dress a window with a tumbled profusion of fluffy towels and eye-catching labels, and is swiftly fired for a mad attempt to wrest control of '*my* window' from his outraged manager.[14]

Au Bonheur des Dames is a bildungsroman, not of Mouret or Denise, but of the store itself, whose formation and rise give the novel its central structure. Wells's shop-assistant tales have no such coherent form; there is no central agency driving them, whether human or evolutionary. As modern workers, Kipps and Polly cannot control their destinies and do not aspire to do so, but rather are buffeted by accident and whim, producing the fractured, episodic narrative of the naturalist novel. Kipps rises to fortune, falls, and recovers through no agency of his own, inheriting and losing wealth by chance, himself subject to the conditioning forces of class etiquette, which demand he purchase unwanted goods to establish his social position. The perspective, however, is resolutely that of the worker who sells the goods and the servant behind the scenes, not the aspiring bourgeois customer. In *Mr Polly*, for example, the narrative notes one shop worker's 'superhuman' generosity in staying to help his colleagues when he might have gone home, which 'No one who has not worked for endless days of interminable hours, with scarce a gleam of rest or liberty between the toil and the sleep, can understand how superhuman'.[15] The double negative leaves the reader who has not experienced such labour doubly excluded from claiming knowledge of either the suffering or the heroism of such workers. Kipps and his sweetheart Ann find their newfound wealth obliges them to purchase a mansion rather than the modest home they would prefer, but Ann does redesign the plans so no servant need carry water up endless stairs as she once did.

Though Wells's novels do not allow the middle-class reader a complacent sense of vicariously knowing the exhaustion and tedium of those who service them, at least such a reader is allowed an equal distance from the customer whose self-indulgent dawdling prolongs the heavy hours of the shop workers, or from the mistress who pries into her maid's private life. In the theatre, however, the audience's

---

[13] Ibid., 35, 37, 41.
[14] H. G. Wells, *The History of Mr Polly* (London: Weidenfeld and Nicolson, 2010), 23.
[15] Ibid., 13.

perspective is inescapably that of the external viewer, its gaze falling equally upon the
shop worker and the other goods on display. The late Victorian stage was dominated
by dramas of upper-class life, set in luxurious drawing rooms and ballrooms, offering
the manufacturers of high-class goods and fashion a valuable opportunity to advertise
their wares through set and costumes.[16] The new genre of musical comedy made even
more explicit the stage's role as shop window for the audience as consumer of both the
shop girl and her wares. J. W. Dam's *The Shop Girl* (1894) set the fashion, opening with
a joyous chorus of male and female assistants in the Royal Stores:

> This noble institution of financial evolution
> Is the glory of our British trade.
> It's the wonder of our nation as a mighty aggregation
> Of all objects grown or made.
> Every product of the planet since geology began it
> In our mile on mile of floors
> From a cat to a cucumber if you only have a number
> We will sell you at the Royal Stores.[17]

In the exuberantly unreal world of musical comedy, the department store is, like
Zola's *Bonheur*, a triumph of commercial and natural evolution and an ideal
employer. The eponymous shop girl, Bessie Brent, happily evades all the store's
rules, running rings round her floor manager and finally securing marriage to a
rich aristocrat, while her equally nubile colleagues entertain customers on stage and
in the auditorium, their good looks supposedly attesting to the benign working
conditions of both shop and theatre.

As the 'shop-girl musical' became a genre in itself, with titles such as *The Girl
from Kays* (1902) and *The Girl Behind the Counter* (1906), a number of playwrights
challenged their idealized representation of shop workers by offering a more realistic view of life behind the counter. Harley Granville-Barker's *The Madras House*
(1910) and Elizabeth Baker's *Miss Tassey* (1910), for example, show the cribbed and
confined lives of assistants for whom the living-in system was a form of indentured
slavery, every aspect of their lives controlled and exploited to produce the glamour
and abundance of the shop floor. The most successful of such corrective dramas was
Cicely Hamilton's *Diana of Dobson's* (1908), a rewrite of Cinderella in which a shop
assistant marries an aristocrat, but only once he has tried and failed to earn an independent living, as a result of which he realizes that he need not find a wealthy spouse
as his annual income of £600 is ample for both himself and Diana. The play opens
in the living-in dormitory in Dobson's, where exhausted shop girls struggle to bed

---

[16] For further details, see Joel Kaplan and Sheila Stowell, *Theatre and Fashion from Oscar Wilde to
the Suffragettes* (Cambridge: Cambridge University Press, 1995), and Michael R. Booth, *Victorian
Spectacular Theatre, 1850–1910* (Boston, MA: Routledge and Kegan Paul, 1981).

[17] H. J. W. Dam, *The Shop Girl*, British Library, Lord Chamberlain's Plays Collection, Add MS
53562B, Act I, p. 4. 'objects' is mistyped as 'aobjects', but corrected here.

while discussing the circumscribed and joyless lives they lead working fourteen hours a day for £13 per annum plus board and lodging.

Hamilton did not, however, allow the audience a complacent sense of intimacy with the overworked employees. Instead the play uneasily reminded them of their position as privileged voyeurs of the intimate rituals of those who were usually arrayed for their benefit. As the women took off the false hair, ribbons, and collars which constituted their professionally attractive uniforms, the conventionally erotic revelation of the striptease was inverted as the assistants listlessly removed their costumes to reveal the underfed and overworked women beneath. Reviewers reflected the discomfort of this display: a critic in the *Stage* condemned the scene as 'wanting in taste' while noting, with an inescapable suspicion of disappointment, that 'these different stages of undress do not happen to be made pretty'. The *Pall Mall Gazette*'s reviewer pruriently warned that nothing more was revealed than 'a gleaming shoulder – a pink vest – a peering foot'.[18] When Diana receives a windfall inheritance of £300 and buys herself a glorious month in which she can experience all the luxury and attention that her position as a worker denies her, the play moves to the more conventional theatrical milieu of upper-class opulence, but the audience is not allowed to forget the first-act vision of the labour on which such affluence is based. Diana, in the guise of a rich widow, refuses a proposal of marriage from Sir Jabez Grinley—not, as he supposes, because he worked his way up from the lowly position of office boy to become the owner-proprietor of Dobson's, but because she refuses to join him in 'grind[ing] a fortune out of underpaid work-girls'.[19] It is Diana's awareness of the labour value rather than the market value of Sir Jabez's goods which makes them too costly in human terms for her to buy them.

The contrast between the commercialized glamour of the counters and the deprivation of the living-in shop worker effectively challenged employers' claims that their control over workers' lives was rooted in a paternalist concern for their welfare and morals. There was a blurred line between exploiting the sexual allure of young women to attract customers—with the concomitant sacking of those past their sexual prime, like the ageing shop assistant who commits suicide rather than face the inevitable poverty which awaits her in Baker's *Miss Tassey*—and actual prostitution, a line which became particularly blurred when workers' wages were often set so low that many women were forced into casual prostitution to supplement them. It is this ambiguity that George Gissing ironically exploits in his account of the long hours, poor diet, and pitiful wages of female shop workers in his 1893 novel *The Odd Women*, when he comments caustically of Monica Madden's employers that 'so generous and confiding were they, that to each young person they allowed a latchkey. The air of Walworth Road is pure and invigorating about midnight; why should the

---

[18] *Stage*, 13 Feb 1908, *Pall Mall Gazette*, 13 Feb 1908, reproduced in Cicely Hamilton, *Diana of Dobson's*, ed. Diane F. Gillespie and Doryjane Birrer (Peterborough, ON: Broadview, 2003), 171, 173.

[19] Hamilton, *Diana of Dobson's*, 119.

reposeful ramble be hurried by consideration for weary domestics?' The emptiness of any pretence at benevolence is clear, whether or not Monica's employers are knowingly complicit in the sale of sexual services to supplement meagre wages.[20]

The driving force was, of course, not paternalism but capitalism, as employers competed to extract maximum work for minimum wages, while selling the product as profitably as possible—the margin of profit being greatly increased by the surplus value added to the goods by the glamour of their commercial setting and by their symbolic power as markers of class and status. This was the essential logic conditioning the full panoply of occupations and professions, from highest to lowest, which, in the view of a host of writers, sidelined all concerns with quality, art, social benefit, or individual fulfilment in the name of profit alone. The most polemical critique of this equation was probably offered by Robert Tressell's seminal socialist novel *The Ragged Trousered Philanthropists*, which was completed in 1910 and first published in severely abridged form in 1914. Depicting in detail the arduous, precarious, and poverty-haunted lives of a group of house painters, Tressell highlights the injustices and absurdities of a system where managers and employers—with pantomime-villain names like Sweater, Grinder, Didlum, Starvem, and Slyme— compete to undercut other firms, reducing their prices by forcing the painters to cut corners, adulterate paint, and hide flaws to secure the highest payment for the shoddiest and cheapest product. The capitalist marketplace is not an engine for improvement in Tressell's analysis, but rather an absurd and self-perpetuating system which drives ever downwards both the quality of goods and the conditions of the workers.

Even criminality runs on the same essential capitalist principles, producing a similarly self-perpetuating and degraded system, as envisioned by Arthur Morrison in *A Child of the Jago* (1896), a novel which was greeted as the height of fictional naturalism. The skilled workers of the impoverished East End parish of the Jago practise a range of criminal trades from burglary to 'cosh-carrying'—the latter being 'the major industry of the Jago', involving a 'craftsman' armed with a foot-length rod of iron who stuns and robs any stranger lured by his female accomplice, 'whose duty it was to keep the other artist going in subjects'.[21] Morrison ironizes the conventional distinction between honest industry and idle and easy criminality. The criminals of the Jago are a rare exception to the general rule of fictional workers, taking pride in their craft, honed through observation and experience. Their work is skilled and arduous, whereas young Dicky Perrott's fleeting experience of honest employment as a shopkeeper's assistant and a rushbag maker proves a 'fascinating pastime' and a 'fresh delight'.[22] But Dicky's fence, Aaron Weech, is the profit-making employer unwilling to lose such an industrious and promising worker, and so he gets Dicky fired from the shop for supposedly plotting robbery, and thus

---

[20] George Gissing, *The Odd Women* (London: Virago, 1980), 25.
[21] Arthur Morrison, *A Child of the Jago* (Oxford: Oxford University Press, 2012), 13.
[22] Ibid., 92, 95.

retains the boy's valuable services as a prolific and skilled pickpocket. The Jago is but the mirror image of the mainstream economy, where women are paid such pitiful rates for matchbox-making that their children must turn to criminality or starve.

The debasing pressure of the marketplace on the individual worker and the products of his/her labour extended to literature itself. As new theatres were built, fed by growing transport networks, and the publishing industry expanded rapidly, encouraged by cheaper paper prices, new printing technologies, and increased literacy rates, many writers fought to secure fairer wages for their labour, campaigning for tighter copyright laws and improved royalty payments. The foundation at the *fin de siècle* of professional bodies such as the Society of Authors and the Dramatists' Club, designed to support authors in their negotiation with employers and consumers, ran side-by-side with a series of literary movements rooted in a resistance to the ideology and dominance of the marketplace, from aestheticism and high modernism to early socialism. The writer and artist, according to all these doctrines, was quite specifically not figured as a hard-working wage earner. He/she was instead more likely to take the form of the criminal–artist celebrated in Wilde's 'The Soul of Man under Socialism' (1891) for pursuing self-realization with no regard for either law or public opinion—a figure realized on stage in George Bernard Shaw's *The Doctor's Dilemma* (1906) as Louis Dubedat, an idle, dishonest, scrounging, lying wastrel who commits bigamy, never pays his debts, and paints pictures of enduring beauty.[23]

The most comprehensive anatomizing of the professional writer's position in relation to these changing conditions of labour was offered by George Gissing, in bitterly comic and ironic detail, in his 1891 novel *New Grub Street*. Jasper Milvain, a self-styled 'literary man of 1882' epitomizes the new breed of jobbing writers, whose 'Honest journey-work' consists of a day starting at 7.30 a.m. and ending around 10 p.m., in the course of which he reads and reviews a volume, writes a gossip column, an essay, and a long opinion piece, earning him approximately ten to twelve guineas for prose which by his own calculation has the literary value 'of the contents of a mouldy nut'.[24] His colleague Whelpdale invents for himself the new occupation of 'literary adviser', reading and correcting manuscripts and recommending them to publishers, for like Milvain he recognizes that literature is now a trade and writers must tailor their product to prevailing tastes. Idealists—or those wedded to artistic standards—fall by the wayside: Edwin Reardon's talent cannot

---

[23] For further discussion of aestheticism and the literary marketplace, see Philip Waller, *Writers, Readers and Reputations: Literary Life in Britain, 1870–1918* (Oxford: Oxford University Press, 2006); Jonathan Freedman, *Professions of Taste: Henry James, British Aestheticism, and Commodity Culture* (Stanford, CA: Stanford University Press, 1990); Michael Anesko, *'Friction with the Market': Henry James and the Profession of Authorship* (Oxford: Oxford University Press, 1986); and Josephine Guy and Ian Small, *Oscar Wilde's Profession* (Oxford: Oxford University Press, 2001).

[24] Gissing, *New Grub Street* (Oxford: Oxford University Press, 1993), 8, 180–1.

support himself and his ambitious wife as he is unable to churn out multiple volumes of fiction to order; and Harold Biffen spends years of penury crafting a realist novel of real literary merit, but '*Mr Bailey, Grocer*' is too repulsive and tedious in its accuracy, precision, and subject matter to have any appeal to the general public. Reardon and Biffen both die in despairing poverty, unable to survive in an explicitly Darwinian environment where books and writers must compete not on merit but through their ability to reduce literature to an easily consumed commodity—or in other words to 'Chit-Chat', Gissing's mocking reference to the magazine *Tit-Bits* which had recently been launched in 1882.[25]

At a time when women were fighting for access to the professions, and not only for the right to work but to be recognized as workers, the self-respect, economic independence, and sexual freedom which came with earning one's own living were not to be taken lightly, no matter what hardships were involved in their acquisition. If self-made men were hard to find, self-made women abounded. St John Hankin's *The Last of the De Mullins* (1908) and Elizabeth Baker's *Edith* (1912), for example, are comic dramas in which resourceful businesswomen blow slower-witted men off their complacent feet in a whirlwind of energy and common sense. Arnold Bennett's novel *The Old Wives' Tale* (1908) similarly charts Sophia Baines's recovery from penniless isolation in a Paris brothel to become owner-manager of a luxurious hotel, courtesy of hard graft and a fine eye for a bargain, both honed through her youthful employment in the family drapery shop. A host of plays, from Shaw's *Mrs Warren's Profession* (1893) to Inez Bensusan's *The Apple* (1909) and H. M. Harwood's *Honour Thy Father* (1912), offered angry testimony to the exploitation and sexual vulnerability of women denied training or access to decently paid professions and trades, and forced to endure sexual harassment, sweated labour, and wages so low as to leave women no choices but prostitution or destitution.[26]

When sufficiently well paid to provide economic independence, however, the pleasures of female employment were to be celebrated—so, in Amy Levy's *The Romance of a Shop* (1888), the titular 'romance' does not denote the sisters' emotional adventures, but rather their successful establishment of a photographic business. Indeed, women's greatest hardship in the view of both male and female writers was to be denied the right to work, held hostage to the middle-class family's social status, and kept in hours of enforced idleness, as in Githa Sowerby's *Rutherford and Son* (1912), where it is not only the family business but the family itself which is identified as the 'Moloch' to whose social status the daughter's life is

---

[25] Ibid., 459. The novel's readers could congratulate themselves on more discerning taste for Biffen-esque realism; as the one reviewer noted, 'the ordinary reader of the circulating library fiction will probably not care to read Mr Gissing's three volumes', *Court Journal*, 25 April 1891, 710.

[26] For further discussion of the theatrical depiction of women's work in relation to prostitution, see Sos Eltis, *Acts of Desire: Women and Sex on Stage, 1800–1930* (Oxford: Oxford University Press, 2013).

sacrificed, cut off from the meaningful productivity and fulfilment of the working women around her.[27]

Dorothy Richardson's thirteen-volume (or chapters, as she preferred to call them) autobiographical novel, *Pilgrimage* (1915–38), perfectly exemplifies the complexity and ambivalence of many literary representations of women's work, while being one of the first works to use experimental modernist techniques to depict the heroine's direct experience of work and how it impacts upon her ever-shifting and developing sense of identity. Miriam Henderson is, like the sisters in Gissing's *The Odd Women* or Harwood's *Honour Thy Father*, a middle-class girl thrown unprepared into the job market by family misfortune. Miriam moves through a range of posts, from schoolteacher in Germany and North London, to private governess and then secretary to a dental surgery, the disruptions and transitions of her life portrayed through the myriad flickering impressions of her mind—each 'waking incongruously other thoughts, and plaiting incessantly the many-coloured and innumerable threads of life', as Virginia Woolf noted admiringly of the novel.[28] Free from the naturalist novel's anthropologically observant eye and voice, *Pilgrimage*'s series of abrupt shifts, meditations, and immediate sensations matches Miriam's own preference for liminality. Admired by a novice for her professionalism, Miriam finds herself 'pondering uneasily over her own dislike of appearing as a successful teacher', and later finds freedom instead in the 'borderland' of London north of the Euston Road.[29]

Just as Richardson's novel deliberately eschewed both romance and 'the current masculine realism', so Miriam's employment in a dental surgery, where she also takes lunch with the family of one of the surgeons, both bridges and evades the supposedly separate spheres of domesticity and professional employment. So Miriam contrasts herself with her friends Mag and Jan, office workers who humorously report their insistence that the city workers do not spit or swear in return for being granted the honour in their dingy warehouse of a 'bright petunia-clad feminine presence'. Miriam, by contrast, 'was somehow between two worlds, neither quite sheltered, nor quite free'.[30] In one chapter of fractured, fluctuating narrative Richardson reproduces the rushed, overlapping tasks which fill Miriam's day as secretary, from cleaning instruments to adding accounts—work which can shift in an instant from 'quiet continuous companionship' to 'a prison claiming

[27] Githa Sowerby, *Rutherford and Son*, in Linda Fitzsimmons and Viv Gardner (eds), *New Woman Plays* (London: Methuen, 1991), 150. For further discussion, see Stowell, *A Stage of Their Own: Feminist Playwrights of the Suffrage Era* (Manchester: Manchester University Press, 1992), and Sally Ledger, *The New Woman: Fiction and Feminism at the fin de siècle* (Manchester: Manchester University Press, 1997).
[28] Virginia Woolf, review of Dorothy Richardson's *The Tunnel*, *Times Literary Supplement* 13 Feb 1919.
[29] Richardson, *Backwater* (1916), in *Pilgrimage*, 4 vols (London: Virago, 1979), I, 274; Dorothy Richardson, *The Tunnel* (1919), ibid., II, 29.
[30] Ibid., II, 162–3.

her by the bonds of the loathsome duties she had learned', when a dentist addresses her in the 'brusque casual tone' he sometimes used to 'the boys downstairs, or to cabmen'.[31] Similarly crucial are the material conditions of Miriam's employment: it is the vital five shillings added to her wage of £1 a week which enable her to add bicycle hire for a holiday and to supplement her essential diet of an egg and a roll in an ABC cafe.[32]

By contrast, it was not the internal impressions of the working woman but the concrete externals which were realized in the journalism and literature of the suffragists' campaign for the vote, where women's status as wage earners and taxpayers became a central plank, and the staging of women's work formed the core of a series of suffrage dramas. The most popular of these was Evelyn Glover's *A Chat with Mrs Chicky* (1912), in which Mrs Houlbrook tries to persuade her brother's charwoman to sign her anti-suffragist petition. Mrs Chicky, however, continues to work around the seated lady, sweeping the floor, washing and scouring the hearth, and folding dust sheets, while humorously undermining the anti-suffragist's arguments with her apparently innocent comments. When Mrs Houlbrook declares that men's and women's work belongs to separate spheres and neither should interfere with the other, Mrs Chicky observes that male MPs are constantly legislating on the 'women's sphere' of domestic and childcare issues, while rights to legitimate children are assigned exclusively to the father. But it is Mrs Chicky's ceaseless work that most effectively renders absurd the middle-class woman's unthinking platitudes:

> MRS HOULBROOK: Can't you see that the right to vote really depends on physical force—strength, you know—and that women haven't got that? (MRS CHICKY *finding* MRS HOULBROOK *in her way gets up and pushes her, chair and all, a foot or so centre with perfect ease.*)[33]

The very mundanity of Mrs Chicky's occupations, everyday actions never usually put on stage but now comically made the focus of the audience's but not the anti-suffragist's attentions, makes humorous and political capital of the labour that is so easily overlooked.

For all the heightened literary awareness of the position of the modern worker, there was widespread scepticism at the notion of turning back the clock to recapture some lost idyll of creative labour. The repeated figuring of the industrial machine as Moloch, the primitive god of Tophet to whom human sacrifice was made—a vision given its most vivid expression in Fritz Lang's 1927 film *Metropolis*—reverses the evolutionary narrative of social progress by reducing the processes of

---

[31]   Ibid., II, 73, 182, 207.

[32]   For Miriam's further dual role as both worker and consumer, see Scott McCracken, 'Embodying the New Woman: Dorothy Richardson, Work and the London Cafe', in Avril Horner and Angela Keane (eds), *Body Matters: Feminism, Textuality, Corporeality* (Manchester: Manchester University Press, 2000).

[33]   Fitzsimmons and Gardner, *New Woman Plays*, 110.

new technology to an atavistic throwback, while its pessimistic looping back undermines any faith in the notion of a Ruskinian pre-industrial past.

Thomas Hardy, a writer deeply embedded in the rhythms and textures of agricultural labour, undermined the premises behind any such nostalgic visions: there is little to choose between the 'joyless monotony' and 'automatic regularity' of Tess's manual labour, digging up frozen swedes or slicing turnips to feed them into a hand-turned masher, and her ceaseless feeding of the new steam-driven thresher, the 'creature from Tophet'.[34] Similarly, Jude Fawley's ambitions to become a bishop may be a symptom of 'the modern vice of unrest', as he loses sight of the equal dignity and worth of stonemasonry in his obsessive aspiration to study at Christminster. But Hardy specifically rejects Ruskin's idealizing of the Gothic as a site of self-expressive vision and craft: as the narrator of *Jude the Obscure* (1895) notes, the 'old poetry' of the colleges' ancient buildings was simply the 'modern prose' of 'precision, mathematical straightness, smoothness, exactitude' worn down by time to produce the 'jagged curves, disdain of precision, irregularity'—the medieval worker was equally subject to a dehumanizing demand for perfection.[35]

D. H. Lawrence, the novelist of this period perhaps most deeply and urgently concerned with the problems of work and selfhood, similarly combined an increasing disgust with modern industry and a scepticism for nostalgic remedies. Lawrence's mature novels are saturated by the textures, rhythms, and experiences of working life, and chart a transition in his attitudes to systematized labour. In *Sons and Lovers* (1913), the blue coal-dust scars on Walter Morel's body mark the history of his dangerous and difficult occupation as a miner, work which brings him dignity, community, and status, while the mine itself blends with the landscape, in his son Paul's eyes, as 'something alive almost—a big creature', with its trucks 'standing waiting, like a string of beasts to be fed'.[36]

In *The Rainbow*, however, published just two years later in 1915, the pit and the towns that serve it are likened by Ursula Brangwen to 'some gruesome dream, some ugly, dead, amorphous mood become concrete', the colliers themselves 'like spectres'.[37] Submission to working in the mines means complete subservience, reducing home life to a 'little side-show' where a man is nothing but 'a meaningless lump—a standing machine, a machine out of work'.[38] Where earlier generations of the Brangwen family seamlessly wove together the rhythms of work and emotion, of outer and inner life, whether calming a hysterical child while feeding cattle or courting a lover while stacking sheaves of corn, Ursula finds that, in order to work as a teacher in a modern school, she must abandon her individual identity and any personal relationship with her pupils, to fulfil 'the graceless task of compelling

[34] Thomas Hardy, *Tess of the D'Urbervilles* (1891; repr. London: Penguin, 1985), 392, 394, 404, 405.
[35] Hardy, *Jude the Obscure* (London: Penguin, 1985), 131.
[36] D. H. Lawrence, *Sons and Lovers* (London: Penguin, 1987), 242, 154.
[37] Lawrence, *The Rainbow* (Oxford: Oxford University Press, 1997), 343–4.
[38] Ibid., 346–7.

many children into one disciplined, mechanical set, reducing the whole set to an automatic state of obedience and attention, and then of commanding their acceptance of various pieces of knowledge'.

This is the universal condition of modern employment, equally damaging for the highest and the lowest: in caning a child into submission, Ursula too 'burnt her sensitive tissue'.[39] There is no way back from the heightened consciousness that characterizes Ursula's educated independence—Ruskinian craftsmanship offers a distraction, not a solution, for her equally baffled father. The root of the corruption lies within, in the self-destructive impulse towards annihilation of individuality in the systems of the state: the colliery-manager Tom Brangwen and his fiancée Winifred Inger find their 'consummation' in the colliery where 'the impure abstraction, the mechanisms of matter' free them from 'the clog and degradation of human feeling' (348). The essential difference is between those who resist, like Ursula who ends the novel with a vision of the colliers casting off their 'horny covering of disintegration' and issuing forth in 'new clean bodies' to a new way of living, and those like Gerald Crich who takes over his father's mining business in *Women in Love* (1920).[40] Gerald imposes a Taylorist management system which erases his own agency and will as profoundly as it does the men's, and leaves him with nothing beyond the slide towards death—and this essential difference, as the later novel insists, is rooted in human relations and sexual identities, of which the larger systems of finance, technology, and class are merely a result.[41]

The solution lay in the future not the past, whether in Lawrence's revolution of the spirit, or in the more material revolutions envisaged by a number of socialist writers, who imagined a range of utopias from the agrarian localism of William Morris's *News from Nowhere* (1890) to the state-controlled technologies of Bellamy's *Looking Backwards* and Wells's *A Modern Utopia* (1905), where both labour and its fruits were to be evenly distributed. For most the answer was less visionary and more practical, a choice between individual compromise and escape. Emigration remained a perennial solution to British industrial malaise—just as Elizabeth Gaskell's factory workers sailed for Canada at the end of *Mary Barton* (1848), so a clerk escapes the drudgery of long hours and low pay to the frontier life of a farmer in Australia in Elizabeth Baker's play *Chains* (1909); a flight not from labour to idleness but rather into more demanding and life-enhancing employment.

Wells's Mr Polly escapes his imprisonment in the retail trade and finds his ideal employment not in a division but a diversity of labour, as handyman at a riverside pub, responsible for a multifarious list of jobs, Dickensian in its length, ranging from tarring fences and digging potatoes to swabbing out boats and chasing hens.[42]

---

[39] Ibid., 381, 403.   [40] Ibid., 348, 493–4.

[41] For a discussion of Lawrence's theories on and representation of labour after *Women in Love*, see Morag Shiach, *Modernism, Labour and Selfhood in British Literature and Culture, 1890–1930* (Cambridge: Cambridge University Press, 2004).

[42] Wells, *Mr Polly*, 150.

Appropriately, perhaps the most optimistic depiction of work as personal fulfilment in this period is by a woman. Elizabeth Baker's play *Partnership* (1917) ends with her driven businesswoman Kate engaged to the artistic and relatively lackadaisical Fawcett, from whom she has learnt to temper work with pleasure, retaining her private emotional identity alongside her professional status. The partnership of the title is an ideal marriage of romance and work, artistic creativity and financial acumen. For all the sunny optimism of Baker's resolution, it is grounded, as are all the works mentioned here, in a recognition of the fundamental human necessities so often denied to workers under modern industrial capitalism: controlled hours, a living wage, gender equality, self-respect, an outlet for creativity, and a balance between life and work.

FURTHER READING

Anesko, Michael. *'Friction with the Market': Henry James and the Profession of Authorship* (Oxford: Oxford University Press, 1986).

Bowlby, Rachel. *Just Looking: Consumer Culture in Dreiser, Gissing and Zola* (New York and London: Methuen, 1985).

Eltis, Sos. *Acts of Desire: Women and Sex on Stage, 1800–1930* (Oxford: Oxford University Press, 2013).

Freedman, Jonathan. *Professions of Taste: Henry James, British Aestheticism, and Commodity Culture* (Stanford, CA: Stanford University Press, 1990).

Guy, Josephine and Ian Small. *Oscar Wilde's Profession* (Oxford: Oxford University Press, 2001).

Horner, Avril and Angela Keane (eds). *Body Matters: Feminism, Textuality, Corporeality* (Manchester: Manchester University Press, 2000).

Keep, Christopher. 'The Cultural Work of the Type-Writer Girl', *Victorian Studies* 40/3 (Spring 1997), 401–26.

Knapp, James F. *Literary Modernism and the Transformation of Work* (Evanston, IL: Northwestern University Press, 1988).

Ledger, Sally. *The New Woman: Fiction and Feminism at the fin de siècle* (Manchester: Manchester University Press, 1997).

Lesjak, Carolyn. *Working Fictions: A Genealogy of the Victorian Novel* (Durham, NC and London: Duke University Press, 2006).

Liggins, Emma. *George Gissing, the Working Woman, and Urban Culture* (Aldershot: Ashgate, 2006).

Mainz, Valerie and Griselda Pollock (eds). *Work and the Image*, 2 vols (Aldershot: Ashgate, 2000), II: *Work in Modern Times: Visual Mediations and Social Processes*.

Pahl, R. E. (ed.). *On Work: Historical, Comparative and Theoretical Approaches* (Oxford: Blackwell, 1988).

Seltzer, Mark. *Bodies and Machines* (New York: Routledge, 1992).

Shiach, Morag. *Modernism, Labour and Selfhood in British Literature and Culture, 1890–1930* (Cambridge: Cambridge University Press, 2004).

Stowell, Sheila. *A Stage of Their Own: Feminist Playwrights of the Suffrage Era* (Manchester: Manchester University Press, 1992).

Waller, Philip. *Writers, Readers and Reputations: Literary Life in Britain, 1870–1918* (Oxford: Oxford University Press, 2006).

Wilde, Jonathan. *The Rise of the Office Clerk in Literary Culture, 1880–1939* (Basingstoke: Palgrave Macmillan, 2006).

Wilson, Mary. *The Labors of Modernism: Domesticity, Servants, and Authorship in Modernist Fiction* (Farnham: Ashgate, 2013).

PART VII

AUTHORSHIP, AESTHETICS, AND PRINT CULTURES

CHAPTER 30

READING AESTHETICISM, DECADENCE, AND COSMOPOLITANISM

MICHÈLE MENDELSSOHN

One of the uncanny things about reading is that it can feel a lot like travelling. And so, just like that, we get carried away. To read is to be transported somewhere else. How we go and where we go depends on a sacred contract between strangers, an intimate pact between an author and a reader who consents to be carried away. Being kidnapped by a book is perhaps one of the greatest pleasures there is. For many readers, travelling in place is a strange but familiar sensation. Reading is a rapture that ultimately leaves us physically unmoved even though a book may move us intellectually or emotionally. So the act of reading hinges on a paradox: we can be cosmopolitans without ever leaving the library. When we look up from the page, we are still where we were when we started. Though nothing has changed, everything seems different. We have visited another time and place. That's why we talk about the uncanny feeling of being carried away by a book or 'enraptured by reading', as J. Hillis Miller puts it.[1]

Late nineteenth- and early twentieth-century aesthetes and decadents were especially attuned to this paradoxical feeling, and sought out its peculiar forms of transport. Take Oscar Wilde, for instance. A French contemporary of Wilde's remembered him as someone who 'believed he was living in Italy during the Renaissance, or in Greece at the time of Socrates', not in England under Queen Victoria.[2] One reason for this was that Wilde had been thoroughly trained in classics at Trinity College Dublin before he arrived to take his second undergraduate degree at Oxford. There he fell under the spell of the classicist Walter Pater whose 1873 *Studies in the History*

---

[1] J. Hillis Miller, *On Literature* (London: Routledge, 2002), 29.
[2] E. H. Mikhail (ed.), *Oscar Wilde: Interviews and Recollections*, 2 vols (London: Macmillan, 1979), I, 191.

of the Renaissance invites and even encourages literary rapture. Here is Pater describing reading the Italian Renaissance philosopher Pico della Mirandola:

> To read a page of one of Pico's forgotten books is like a glance into one of those ancient sepulchres, upon which the wanderer in classical lands has sometimes stumbled, with the old disused ornaments and furniture of a world wholly unlike ours still fresh in them.[3]

This quotation encapsulates a way of reading and of seeing the world that was formative for Wilde's generation as well as later aesthetes and decadents. When we encounter beauty in any form, the key questions we need to ask, according to Pater, are these:

> What is this song or picture, this engaging personality presented in life or in a book, to *me*? What effect does it really produce on me? Does it give me pleasure? and if so, what sort or degree of pleasure? How is my nature modified by its presence, and under its influence?[4]

With these questions, Pater laid down some of the central principles of aesthetic criticism—which is to say critical appreciation of any beautiful object. But he also gives us a way of thinking about ourselves in relation to art, literature, and culture that is immensely valuable because it acknowledges and sanctions the vital importance these experiences have on us. In other words, it invites us to feel, meditate, and reflect on where we go when we are enraptured or carried away.

Like us, characters in later nineteenth- and early twentieth-century fiction were prone to get carried away by their reading. Like Wilde, they became time-travelling cosmopolitans because of it. In Henry James's 1890 novel *The Tragic Muse*, Gabriel Nash (another Oxford-trained aesthete and reader of Pater) denies that he lives in London and in the nineteenth century. 'I drift, I float,' he says.[5] I am only in London, Nash concedes, 'when I'm not at Samarcand!'[6]—the fabled city now in Uzbekistan. And James himself was susceptible to such literary transports. In the early 1900s, while preparing the Preface to the New York edition of his novel, he drifted back to late 1880s Paris, where he had written part of it. 'Re-reading the last chapters of *The Tragic Muse*, I catch again the very odour of Paris, which comes up in the rich rumble of the Rue de la Paix—with which my room itself, for that matter, seems impregnated.'[7] What did it mean to read this way in the late nineteenth and early twentieth century? And why did aesthetes and decadents seek out the pleasures this sort of reading offers? What did it do to them? In what follows, I will explore the importance of this phenomenon

---

[3] Walter Pater, *The Renaissance: Studies in Art and Poetry*, ed. Adam Phillips (Oxford: Oxford University Press, 1986), 27.

[4] Ibid., xxix.

[5] Henry James, *Novels, 1886–1890: The Princess Casamassima, The Reverberator, The Tragic Muse*, ed. Daniel Mark Fogel (New York: Library of America, 1989), 720.

[6] Ibid., 718.

[7] Henry James, *The Tragic Muse*, ed. Philip Horne (London: Penguin, 1995), 6.

and consider the cultural and political significance of these historically contingent forms of reading. My subject, then, is the feeling that certain kinds of reading provoked around the turn of the century. The main question I want to let hover over what follows is this one: Why did these feelings become so significant at a historical moment punctuated by debates over race, ethnicity, and nationhood; rising anti-Semitism; ethnic cleansing and the Dreyfus Affair; international conflicts including the Anglo-Zulu War (1879), the Second Afghan War (1878–80), the Anglo-Egyptian War (1882), the Boer War (1899–1902), the First World War (1914–18), and the Anglo-Irish War (1919–21)?

A solidarity of the senses

Charles Baudelaire's seminal 1863 essay collection, *Le peintre de la vie moderne*, articulates many of the principles that have come to define modernity. Baudelaire's sketches form a *catalogue raisonné* ranging from modern manners to the man of the world. On the question of cosmopolitanism—of what it is, what it does, what it feels like—he tells us this:

> To be away from home and yet to feel oneself everywhere at home; to see the world, to be at the centre of the world, and yet to remain hidden from the world—such are a few of the slightest pleasures of those independent, passionate, impartial natures which the tongue can but clumsily define.[8]

The hero of Baudelaire's reflections is the person who survives the onslaught of urban modernity. He does this, Baudelaire says, by becoming 'a kaleidoscope gifted with consciousness'.[9] In every interaction, he melts into the flickering life around him and explains it, Baudelaire says, 'in pictures more living than life itself'. Aesthetic cosmopolitanism often articulates itself through the senses. It is no surprise, then, to find that aesthetes and decadents sought out the pleasures this sort of reading offers.

For the sound of cosmopolitanism, we turn to poetry. So, for instance, the English aunt and niece collectively known under the pen-name Michael Field tell us that their 1892 poetry collection, *Sight and Song*, aims to 'translate into verse what the lines and colours of certain chosen pictures sing in themselves'.[10] Their poems achieved this through jewel-like descriptions of Italian paintings ranging from Tintoretto to Bellini. The collection does something more, however: it is a travel guide for English readers and, as such, acts as a Baedeker to beauty. This is because the location of every painting that inspired these ekphrastic poems is given as part

---

[8] Charles Baudelaire, *The Painter of Modern Life, and Other Essays*, ed. Jonathan Mayne, 2nd edn (London: Phaidon, 1995), 9.
[9] Ibid., 10.   [10] Michael Field, *Sight and Song* (London: Bodley Head, 1892), p.v.

of their title. So via their verse-pictures, these poems take readers from the Louvre to the Accademia of Venice and beyond.

Of the *fin-de-siècle* novelists, perhaps Joseph Conrad comes closest to what Pater had in mind when he wrote that 'all art constantly aspires towards the condition of music'.[11] Conrad's aesthetic manifesto, his 1897 Preface to *The Nigger of the 'Narcissus'*, is imbued with his experience of foreignness and indebted to Paterian literary impressionism. The artist, Conrad writes, speaks to our shared sense of beauty, as well as 'to the latent feeling of fellowship with all creation; and to the subtle but invincible conviction of solidarity that knits together the loneliness of innumerable hearts: to that solidarity . . . which binds men to each other, which binds together all humanity'.[12]

Cosmopolitans, too, were bound each to each by their lonely hearts. And even when alone decadent cosmopolitans found fulfilment by seeking out experiences that would stimulate their senses. More often than not, this meant multi-sensory experiences recorded in a style that privileged a jewelled diction and lavish syntactical pile-ups. The first paragraph of *The Picture of Dorian Gray* (1890) exemplifies this mode. The decadent Lord Henry watches as 'the fantastic shadows of birds in flight flitted across the long tussore-silk curtains that were stretched in front of the huge window, producing a kind of momentary Japanese effect, and making him think of those pallid jade-faced painters of Tokio who, through the medium of an art that is necessarily immobile, seek to convey the sense of swiftness and motion'.[13] Here Lord Henry's multi-sensory impressions are mirrored in Wilde's style and his combination of artistic forms. In this staging of Lord Henry's impressions, the curtained window 'is at once a picture frame and a stage set for the action'.[14] Part of that action is Lord Henry's cerebral voyage from London to Tokyo and back, a flight of fancy prompted by the birds fluttering across the imported silk curtains. Lord Henry's intellectual pilgrimage pays homage to another signal moment of synaesthetic decadent cosmopolitanism: the aborted voyage to London undertaken in the golden book of decadence, Joris-Karl Huysmans's 1884 novel *À rebours*. This is the poisonous book that Dorian Gray buys nine copies of in Paris. While reading one of them, Dorian feels that Huysmans's decadent hero embodies all the 'moods through which the world-spirit had ever passed'.[15] Here again, Wilde's own

---

[11] Pater, *The Renaissance*, 124.

[12] Joseph Conrad, *The Nigger of The 'Narcissus': An Authoritative Text, Backgrounds and Sources, Reviews and Criticism*, ed. Robert Kimbrough (New York: Norton, 1979), 145–6.

Rebecca Walkowitz notes how the intertwined strands of cosmopolitanism operate in Conrad: on the one hand, he is preoccupied by 'the geographic cosmopolitanism of immigration, international travel, and colonialism', and, on the other, 'the aesthetic cosmopolitanism of literary impressionism and Decadence, whose values the novels reproduce and whose urban meanderings and ambiguous poses are crucial to his later texts'. Rebecca L. Walkowitz, *Cosmopolitan Style: Modernism beyond the Nation* (New York: Columbia University Press, 2006), 36.

[13] Oscar Wilde, *Collins Complete Works of Oscar Wilde* (Glasgow: HarperCollins, 1999), 18.

[14] Victoria Rosner, *Modernism and the Architecture of Private Life* (New York: Columbia University Press, 2005), 32.

[15] Wilde, *Works*, 96.

book mirrors his character's impression of another book. Indeed, Chapter 11 of *The Picture of Dorian Gray* offers an admiring, abbreviated pastiche of Huysmans's novel.

In *À rebours*, Des Esseintes, the reclusive hero, contemplates leaving France to escape the corrosive ennui from which he suffers. Reading Dickens has given him exciting 'visions of English life' so he plans to travel to England to find fresh sensations.[16] He forces himself out of his suburban refuge and, en route to England, stops in a Parisian tavern, where he feels as if he is already in London. Around him, people are talking about the weather and eating rumpsteak pie, just like in England. To Des Esseintes, the people have become Dickensian characters. Living fictions seem to step from the page: *Bleak House*'s Mr Tulkinghorn and *David Copperfield*'s Mr Wickfield seem to appear before him in the flesh. 'Wasn't he in London now, surrounded by London's smells, atmosphere, inhabitants, food, utensils?' Huysmans asks. Going to England would only be a disappointment. 'I've seen what I wanted to experience and see', our armchair cosmopolitan reasons, 'I've been steeped in English life, I would be insane to risk losing, by an ill-advised journey, these unforgettable impressions'.[17] So Des Esseintes goes home. By living through English literature, his English voyage has reached its terminus *ad quem* while still in Paris.

Late nineteenth-century French and English decadent writings often make the eyes gateways to the other senses. These texts privilege sight even when working synaesthetically on characters and readers. More often than not, what we talk about when we talk about aesthetic cosmopolitanism is the way it *looks*. The priorities of today's critics map neatly onto the *fin-de-siècle's* obsession with visual culture. This suggests the dominance of 'surface reading'—the descriptive mode described by its proponents as 'immersion in texts (without paranoia or suspicion about their merit or value)'.[18] Yet alongside this critical approach, we need to preserve modes of 'suspicious' and 'symptomatic' reading, as well as theoretical interventions that pride themselves on lip-reading and listening to stifled voices.[19] To completely abandon these kinds of 'symptomatic reading' would be to discard the salutary and redemptive socio-political capacities of our discipline, and of the humanities.

---

[16] J. K. Huysmans, *Against Nature*, ed. Nicholas White, trans. Margaret Mauldon (Oxford: Oxford University Press, 2009), 105.

[17] Ibid., 114.

[18] Stephen Best and Sharon Marcus, 'Surface Reading: An Introduction,' *Representations* 108/1 (Fall 2009), 16.

[19] As Felski and Kucich note, suspicious reading is, in part, an 'intellectual exercise in demystification' and a testament to 'the specific skill humanists bring to data: interpretation' (Rita Felski, 'Suspicious Minds', *Poetics Today* 32/2 (2011), 216; John Kucich, 'The Unfinished Historicist Project: In Praise of Suspicion', *Victoriographies* 1/1 (2011), 65. I am thinking of the work of Eve Kosofsky Sedgwick and of those who have followed in her wake in privileging queer analytical models. Eve Kosofsky Sedgwick, *Between Men: English Literature and Male Homosocial Desire* (New York: Columbia University Press, 1985), 7.

This form of reading enables us to give a different quality of attention to the letters of the young Henry James, for example. In his fiction James was almost as closeted as could be, but he carefully used his cosmopolitanism to signal his allegiances. So on his first visit to Italy, the twenty-six-year old marvelled at the good looks of the sunlit Italian men he saw 'screaming—bare-chested, bare-legged, magnificently tanned and muscular'.[20] These Italian men, the young Henry told his older brother, the psychologist William James, 'are a very effective lot'. James was not often this unguarded about what turned him on, though he remained a champion gossip and flirt.[21] He had a horror of blackmail, and took steps to protect himself, steps that included building backyard bonfires where letters served as tinder and burned with a hard, gem-like flame.

Though James lived most of his life in Europe, his cosmopolitan credentials are engraved on his tombstone at Cambridge, Massachusetts: he was a 'citizen of two countries and interpreter of his generation on both sides of the sea'. The critic for *The Yellow Book* described James's cosmopolitanism as a cold affair, and accused him of being undemonstrative of 'love, both for his own countrymen and for England'.[22] This description owes more to perceptions of James's attitude to love and sex—which he called 'zoological sociability'[23]—than to the warmth of his feeling for internationalism. To be a cosmopolitan, James explains in his 1886 novel, *The Princess Casamassima*, is to be 'exempt from every prejudice'.[24] It doesn't spare one from the disappointment of not finding the real world as satisfying as its fictional representations, as a young aesthete discovers in one of James's early comic tales. In Paris, this American complains, 'I never meet those opportunities that we hear about and read about—the things that happen to people in novels and biographies'.[25]

James used cosmopolitanism as a shorthand for a sensual solidarity he could hardly speak of. It became symbolic of sympathies that were, in the nineteenth century, unutterable. In 1877, he met the reformer and historian of homosexuality John Addington Symonds. James bragged about the encounter in a letter to his brother and also mentioned he had visited London's Cosmopolitan Club. But it would be seven years before James wrote to Symonds himself. In this letter, we listen to James's niceties about Symonds's writings on Italy, and hear him

[20] Henry James, *Letters*, ed. Leon Edel, 4 vols (Cambridge, MA: Harvard University Press, 1974–84), I, 142.
[21] For examples of James's flirtatiousness, see Henry James, *Dearly Beloved Friends: Henry James's Letters to Younger Men*, ed. Susan E. Gunter and Steven H. Jobe (Ann Arbor, MI: University of Michigan Press, 2001).
[22] Lena Milman, 'A Few Notes Upon Mr. James', *The Yellow Book* (October 1895), 73.
[23] Henry James, *Literary Criticism: French Writers, Other European Writers, the Prefaces to the New York Edition*, ed. Leon Edel and Mark Wilson (New York: Library of America, 1984), 939.
[24] James, *Novels, 1886–1890*, 311.
[25] Henry James, *Complete Stories, 1874–1884*, ed. William Vance (New York: Library of America, 1999), 495.

confess his 'unspeakably tender passion' for the place.[26] 'I wanted to recognize this', James explains, emphasizing the point. What does James really want to recognize? That they both care about Italy? Certainly. But Italy is also a symbol that demands recognition. Within a few years of James's letter, Symonds's 1883 pamphlet, *A Problem in Greek Ethics: Being an Inquiry into the Phenomenon of Sexual Inversion*, was being passed from hand to hand among a circle of sexually curious, mostly homosexual, men.[27] James's library contained almost all of Symonds's works. 'It seemed to me', James wrote to Symonds, 'that the victims of a common passion should sometimes exchange a look.'[28] Perhaps they looked to Italy together because they could not speak— homosexuality was not decriminalized in Britain until 1967. What James doesn't give voice to, what he doesn't say, could be encoded in the language of cosmopolitanism.

Fear and desire

Cosmopolitans in this period read in unusual ways that affected their relationship to the real world. Aesthetic and decadent cosmopolitanism differs from the usual models of national belonging which often defined international affiliations in the period.[29] By purchasing Victorian periodicals, like *The Cosmopolitan*, *The Yellow Book*, or *Cosmopolis*, readers gained a purchase on something that defined their way of being in the world.[30] Decadent print cultures challenged national models of identity and replaced them with new forms of community: 'a republic of nothing but letters' composed from a 'cosmopolitan constellation of books and readers.'[31]

But as desirable as this might have been to some, it struck fear in others. How was the aesthetic cosmopolitan perceived by those who were not members of his tribe? Two fin-de-siècle novels published within a few years of each other give us a clear sense of his ambivalent reception. As such they capture the structure of feeling cosmopolitans generated. George Du Maurier's 1894 bestseller, *Trilby*, gives us a British opera diva and her mesmeric Jewish mentor. Conversely, Henry James's 1890 novel *The Tragic Muse* tells the story of a Jewish opera diva and her English mentors.

Du Maurier made cosmopolitanism the signature of *Trilby*'s most sinister character. 'He went by the name of Svengali, and spoke fluent French with a German

---

[26] James, *Letters*, III, 30.
[27] Wendy Graham, *Henry James's Thwarted Love* (Stanford, CA: Stanford University Press, 1999), 32.
[28] James, *Letters*, III, 30.
[29] See Amanda Anderson, *The Powers of Distance: Cosmopolitanism and the Cultivation of Detachment* (Princeton, NJ: Princeton University Press, 2001), 147–76; Matthew Potolsky, *The Decadent Republic of Letters: Taste, Politics, and Cosmopolitan Community from Baudelaire to Beardsley* (Philadelphia, PA: University of Pennsylvania Press, 2013), 135–53.
[30] Tanya Agathocleous, *Urban Realism and the Cosmopolitan Imagination in the Nineteenth Century: Visible City, Invisible World* (New York: Cambridge University Press, 2011), 53.
[31] Potolsky, *The Decadent Republic of Letters*, 150, 163.

accent.'[32] Svengali is 'so offensive to the normal Englishman', Du Maurier writes, that he compels his narrator to become the provincial reader's friend. 'I will translate him into English,' he promises, reassuring the English reader that he will omit Svengali's accent because it transforms 'a pretty language into an ugly one.'[33] Du Maurier's anti-cosmopolitanism was well-judged and contributed to the novel's success. By comforting the provincial English reader, Du Maurier also performed an intellectual and emotional lowering that spoke to rising anti-Semitic sentiment in Britain. From the 1880s onwards, the frequency and severity of anti-Jewish massacres in Eastern Europe led to an unprecedented influx of Jewish immigrants to Britain. Negative feelings towards these fifty thousand new arrivals led to the restrictions of the 1905 Aliens Act. Still, the pogroms continued unrestricted into the 1920s.

In *Howards End* (1910), E. M. Forster gives us this protective foreign policy in miniature by turning it into a domestic one. The novel's cosmopolitan heroines—the Anglo-German Schlegel sisters—open their doors to foreigners of all sorts, from bearded musicians to German cousins and *louche* 'acquaintances picked up at Continental hotels.'[34] This alarms their parochial English aunt, and her response captures the flutter of fear over alien invasion that Du Maurier successfully exploits. In Forster's novel, the individual English home becomes a synecdoche for the nation at large in the early twentieth century.

While in *Trilby* cosmopolitanism could stand for a repugnant foreignness, in *The Tragic Muse* it represented something certain middle-class English people strived for. In the opening chapter, the parochial Biddy Dormer meets the enigmatic aesthete Gabriel Nash. She would have taken him for 'very foreign', James writes, except for the fact that he speaks English. Biddy wonders how Nash 'seemed to draw rich effects and wandering airs from [his English]—to modulate and manipulate it as he would have done a musical instrument.'[35] James plays on the cosmopolitan's 'wandering airs' to insinuate his kinship to wandering Jews. Like Du Maurier with his mesmerizing Svengali, James wants us to notice the musical quality of the cosmopolitan's voice. And he wants us to detect that, like music, this voice can transport us in ways that are apt to thrill and terrify. There is another reason Biddy, the simple English girl, responds in this way: Gabriel Nash is loosely based on Oscar Wilde, James's Irish frenemy, and Wilde's cultivated English accent was known to wander. How does Biddy feel when she meets Nash? She fears that 'she should pass with this easy cosmopolite for a stiff, scared, English girl, which was not the type she aimed at'. That may not be what Biddy wants to be, but it is who she is. 'He won't hurt us,' her brother reassures her. 'On the contrary he'll do us good.'[36] Several hundred

---

[32] George Du Maurier, *Trilby*, ed. Elaine Showalter (Oxford: Oxford University Press, 1998), 11.
[33] Ibid., 23.
[34] E. M. Forster, *Howards End*, ed. Paul B. Armstrong (New York: Norton, 1998), 13.
[35] James, *Novels, 1886–1890*, 717.   [36] Ibid., 719, 721.

pages later, the cultural tonic has worked and the provincial Biddy marries a cosmopolitan English diplomat.

The examples of Du Maurier's Svengali and James's Nash illustrate how cosmopolitanism functions as a crucible of late nineteenth- and early twentieth-century fear and desire. They combine a fear-inducing foreign element with an aspirational programme of higher culture and sophistication. So what I'm suggesting is this: in this period, cosmopolitanism is a paradox that pulls in two different directions (one about phobia, the other about fetishizing). This is surprising because cosmopolitanism, at its root, is not beset by such divergent tensions. The word cosmopolitanism combines the word *cosmos* (from the Greek for the universe, an ordered and harmonious system) and the *polis* (the ideal city state). Literally and metaphorically, cosmopolitanism contains a kind of harmony of the spheres.

The voice of cosmopolitanism

Part of the paradox of cosmopolitanism is that it speaks in multiple accents and voices. *Salome*, the play Oscar Wilde wrote in 1891, is one of the best instances of this kind of performed and performative aesthetic cosmopolitanism. Its content and history are closely intertwined. *Salome* is important, as Julia Prewitt Brown notes, because 'Wilde was the first of the extraordinary line of Irish-European playwrights who helped fashion modernist European drama'.[37] As Katherine Worth observes, in this play 'written by an Irishman living out of Dublin and writing in French,' it is as if Wilde 'were holding out his hand across fifty years to Beckett'.[38]

Wilde reimagined the New Testament stories of the seductive daughter of Herodias dancing before her stepfather, Herod, and demanding the head of John the Baptist. When Jokannan (John the Baptist) first sees Salome he cautions her, 'speak not to me. I will not listen to thee, I listen but to the voice of the Lord God'.[39] Jokanaan's provocation spurs her on and Salome's mission becomes nothing less than redeeming the experience of being a female in a society that does not listen to its women. So she speaks the only language in which she knows she will be acknowledged, using her sexuality and her body to make herself heard. In the end, she removes her mask in triumph. It was all a ruse, she tells Jokannan's severed head. 'Thou didst treat me as a harlot, as a wanton, me, Salome,' she crows in her penultimate speech.[40]

To make Salome interesting as more than a sex object, Wilde needed to endow her with an inner life that would be progressively revealed to the audience through her words and actions. By setting up the drama in this fashion, he succeeded in

---

[37] Julia Prewitt Brown, *Cosmopolitan Criticism: Oscar Wilde's Philosophy of Art* (Charlottesville, VA: University Press of Virginia, 1997), 25.

[38] Quoted in ibid., 25.   [39] Wilde, *Works*, 590.   [40] Ibid., 604.

making Salome's psychology actual and relevant to late nineteenth-century ideas about women's relationships to gender ideology and their increasingly vocal demands for equality. In 1890, a year before he began composing *Salome*, Wilde extolled the harmonizing powers of cosmopolitanism. To be cosmopolitan was to view the world critically, to read it deeply, and to question it. He explained his position thus:

> It is Criticism that makes us cosmopolitan . . . It is only by the cultivation of the habit of intellectual criticism that we shall be able to rise superior to race-prejudices . . . Criticism will annihilate race-prejudices, by insisting upon the unity of the human mind in the variety of its forms . . . The change will of course be slow, and people will not be conscious of it. They will not say 'We will not war against France because her prose is perfect,' but because the prose of France is perfect, they will not hate the land. Intellectual criticism will bind Europe together in bonds far closer than those that can be forged by shopman or sentimentalist . . . How little we have of this [cosmopolitan] temper in England, and how much we need it! [41]

Across the Channel, in the pages of *Le Figaro*, even the French nationalist Maurice Barrès admitted 'we are certainly moving towards a culture that will be more cosmopolitan than national'.[42] But he soon turned chauvinist again: he claimed one could find in French literature all of the nuances that readers thought they discovered in foreigners. 'In fact, even the anxious quasi-epileptic compassion that we love in Dostoyevsky (and in Dickens)' already exists in French literature, Barrès argued.[43]

By the summer of 1892, the French actress Sarah Bernhardt had come to England to play *Salome* in French. Rehearsals were underway. Suddenly, the play was denied a licence by the censor. With *Salome* hanging in the balance, Wilde also suspended his nationality. 'I am not at present an Englishman', Wilde told to the Parisian reporter for *Le Gaulois*, while awaiting the censor's final verdict.[44] 'I am an Irishman, which is by no means the same thing', Wilde explained. Though it was an awkward position, it was entirely consistent with his theory of cosmopolitanism. 'If the Censure refuses *Salome*', Wilde said, 'I shall leave England and settle in France, where I will take out letters of naturalization. I will not consent to call myself a citizen of a country that shows such narrowness in its artistic judgment.'[45]

In the late nineteenth century, cosmopolitanism meant freedom. It liberated the artist from 'the service of religion, conventional morality, party politics, diplomacy, patriotism, the state or any of the other forces which try to reduce art to a means to

---

[41] Ibid., 1152–3.

[42] 'Cela est certain, nous allons vers une culture qui sera plus cosmopolite que nationale'. Maurice Barrès, 'La Querelle Des Nationalistes Et Des Cosmopolites', *Le Figaro*, 4 July 1892, 1.

[43] 'Et en effet, cette angoisse, cette compassion poussée jusqu'à l'épilepsie que nous adorons dans Dostoïewski (et dans Dickens), elle est dans notre Michelet', ibid.

[44] Mikhail (ed.), *Interviews*, I, 190.   [45] Ibid., I, 188.

their ends'.[46] Art for art's sake did not mean that art should necessarily be divorced from these ideals. But it emancipated art from the forced marriage it had often had to endure with them. Wilde's position gives us a sense of the reasons why cosmopolitanism began to be resented, feared even, despite its attractions. Rooted in art rather than in the nation, Wilde's cosmopolitanism demonstrates the advantages and the disadvantages of the mode: art flowers in rooted cosmopolitanism, but these roots can easily be transplanted elsewhere. The province of the mind is eminently transportable. This was more than a pose. It was a politics. This legacy resonates in twentieth-century literature as well.

Seeing the universe: Prose, politics and passion

In one of her most important chapters on the state of early modernist writing, 'Mr. Bennett and Mrs. Brown', Virginia Woolf observes that 'the men and women who began writing novels in 1910 or thereabouts had this great difficulty to face—that there was no *English* novelist living from whom they could learn their business'.[47] This was less of a problem for the writer who published *Howards End* in 1910—a novel conspicuously absent from Woolf's chapter. Though E. M. Forster was a cosmopolitan aesthete, he nevertheless remained a deeply English novelist even when he criticized his countrymen. His cosmopolitanism proposes itself as an alternative to knee-jerk nationalism and offers independence from petty patriotism. 'No national character is complete', Forster writes in his 'Notes on the English Character'.[48] 'We have to look for some qualities in one part of the world and others in another.' Here, Forster sounds like Wilde a few decades earlier, arguing that the major benefit of cosmopolitanism is its insistence on 'the unity of the human mind in the variety of its forms'.[49]

Howards End shows us how nineteenth-century aesthetic cosmopolitanism carried over into the twentieth century. The novel pits the liberal, cultured, imaginative Anglo-German Schlegel sisters, Margaret and Helen, against the imperialist, business-minded Wilcoxes. Wedged between these two factions is Leonard Bast, a weak-hearted autodidact. The Schlegels' objective is to help in humanity's 'building of the rainbow bridge that will connect the prose in us with the passion'.[50] Why? Because the bridge spans life with beauty. Without this bridge, Forster warns, 'we are meaningless fragments, half monks, half beasts, unconnected arches that have never joined into a man'.[51]

---

[46] T. S. Champlin, 'Doing Something for Its Own Sake', *Philosophy* 62/239 (1987), 47. Quoted in Helen Small, *The Value of the Humanities* (Oxford: Oxford University Press, 2013), 66.

[47] Virginia Woolf, *Mr. Bennett and Mrs. Brown* (London: Hogarth, 1924), 11 (emphasis added).

[48] Forster, *Howards End*, 310.   [49] Wilde, *Works*, 1152–3.

[50] Forster, *Howards End*, 134.   [51] Ibid., 135, 134.

Before 1914, the growing British hostility towards Germany due to trade rivalry and the mounting possibility of military conflict gave rise to nervousness and antagonism. We can count as a bridge-building effort the very fact that Forster decided to make the novel's well-intentioned heroines, the Schlegel sisters, Anglo-German, but not 'Germans of the dreadful sort'. Still, they are viewed with suspicion by the English Wilcoxes. Margaret's chrysanthemums are sniffed at for being too exotic to be suitable flowers for a funeral. 'She isn't really English', the youngest Wilcox explains. 'She's a cosmopolitan', the eldest Wilcox, Charles, adds.[52] 'I cannot stand them, and a German cosmopolitan is the limit.' Charles Wilcox represents the imperial type expanding England's reach to encompass the world but annihilating everything he touches. 'He is a destroyer', Forster explains. 'He prepares the way for cosmopolitanism, and though his ambitions may be fulfilled, the earth that he inherits will be grey.'[53]

Cosmopolitanism is not innocuous, Forster reminds us when he sends Margaret Schlegel to visit her husband to be, Henry Wilcox, at the London offices of the Imperial and West African Rubber Company. On his company's map, the world appears quartered and hung. On closer inspection of it, Margaret notices that Africa looks 'like a whale marked out for blubber'.[54] She shrinks back. 'Imperialism always had been one of her difficulties', the narrator tells us. It's worth pausing to worry with Margaret Schlegel for two reasons. First, because imperialism is also one of the difficulties that besets Forster's oeuvre, as post-colonial critics of *A Passage to India* (1924) have underscored. And second, because imperialism also haunts cosmopolitanism. Karl Marx and Friedrich Engels pointed this out in *The Communist Manifesto*'s discussion of the 'cosmopolitan character' of modern consumption (about which there will be more to say momentarily).[55] Margaret knows that cosmopolitanism can be mistaken for imperialism—a lesson that should not be lost on us in this great age of global and multinational trade.

So what makes Schlegel cosmopolitanism better than Wilcox imperialism? For Forster, it is the fact that it is activated by the binding force of love.[56] What is heroic in the Anglo-German Schlegels is that, even though their bridge-building fails, they are *trying* to build a link between themselves and the world around them. Forster gently mocks their idealism though he shares much of it, like a parent teasing a beloved child whose imperfections he shares. Forster gives us a rooted cosmopolitanism that carefully negotiates art, politics, and ethics. The literary critic and political theorist Frederic Jameson put it nicely when he described Forster as 'both moral and aesthetic all at once' because he offers 'an aesthetic pattern of relationships that

[52] Ibid., 22, 75.   [53] Ibid., 229.   [54] Ibid., 141.

[55] Karl Marx and Friedrich Engels, *The Communist Manifesto*, ed. David Harvey (London: Pluto Press, 2012), 38.

[56] Forster, *Howards End*, 186.

confirms it as a social reality.'[57] And there have been other important ways of thinking about what such feelings can do. The political scientist Benedict Anderson has given us the expression 'imagined community', to describe the feeling of shared values and aims, while the anthropologist Arjun Appadurai has given us the phrase 'community of sentiment' to describe how imagining and feeling things together enables a group to take collective action.[58]

In the last part of this chapter, I want to suggest that Forster's aesthetic cosmopolitanism enables a politically engaged take on modernity of the kind enacted by James and Wilde and more recently theorized by Anderson and Appadurai. What I mean by this is that, in *Howards End*, cosmopolitanism is both an aesthetic and a political proposition. Read this way, the novel's well-known epigraph—'Only connect . . . '—sounds in tune with the upheavals of the twentieth century. By 1936, Forster's injunction became urgent. That year, the Spanish Civil War broke out. Nazi Germany violated the Treaty of Versailles and occupied the Rhineland. Stalin initiated the Great Purge in the Soviet Union. Forster didn't mince his words. 'The nations must understand one another, and quickly; and without the interposition of their governments,' he said, underlining the conciliatory power of art.[59]

How, then, do we take up Forster's directive to 'only connect'? One of the ways in which his cosmopolitans connect is through conversations about art. Here is Margaret trying to do it with Leonard when they meet, for the first time, at a Beethoven concert: 'Do you think music is so different to pictures? . . . What is the good of the Arts if they're interchangeable? What is the good of the ear that tells you the same as the eye?' Forster emphasizes what Leonard feels in this moment. 'Oh, to acquire culture! Oh, to pronounce foreign names correctly!' he sighs. Margaret's incomprehensibility arouses profound cravings in him. Leonard is envious of the Schlegels for being cultivated, for having the leisure 'to see life steadily and to see it whole'.[60]

Margaret has probably read Marx and Engels and the art critic John Ruskin and much more besides. Forster owned at least three of Ruskin's books, including a fine morocco-bound edition of *The Stones of Venice*, a mid-Victorian manual of public taste that aligns architecture and morality, and was republished in the early 1880s in a travellers' edition targeted at tourists. The art historian Kenneth Clark said it was impossible to read *The Stones of Venice* 'without a thrill, without a sudden resolution to reform the world'.[61] And so it is with Ruskin's great book that Leonard sets out to capture a bit of the cosmopolitanism he longs for. In Chapter 6 of *Howards*

[57] Frederic Jameson, 'Modernism and Imperialism', in T. Eagleton, F. Jameson, and E. W. Said (eds), *Nationalism, Colonialism, and Literature* (Minneapolis, MN: University of Minnesota Press, 1990), 59.

[58] Arjun Appadurai, *Modernity at Large: Cultural Dimensions of Globalization* (Minneapolis, MN: University of Minnesota Press, 1996), 8.

[59] Forster, *Howards End*, 310.

[60] Ibid., 30, 31, 42 (the quotation is from Arnold's 'To a Friend').

[61] Kenneth Clark, *The Gothic Revival* (London: Pelican, 1964), 1881.

End, we sit with Leonard as he reads *The Stones of Venice*. As he reads the chapter on Torcello, a Venetian island he will never visit, Leonard reflects reverently, 'the rich man is speaking to us from his gondola'.[62] But Leonard cannot connect with *The Stones of Venice*, though he admires Ruskin's 'voice in the gondola . . . piping melodiously . . . full of beauty, full even of sympathy and the love of men'.[63] Leonard cannot travel to Venice literally or intellectually. He is no armchair cosmopolitan. He is no Des Esseintes reading Dickens in *À rebours*, no Dorian Gray reading Huysmans, no Henry James reading John Addington Symonds. Leonard does not clamber into Ruskin's gondola. He has missed the boat, and Forster makes sure that we see this. We may say that this smacks of elitism, and it does. That is Forster's point—and it is Ruskin's too, as we shall see.

'We are not concerned with the very poor. They are unthinkable, and only to be approached by the statistician or the poet', Forster's comic magisterial narrator intones at the beginning of the scene in which we witness Leonard reading. There are good reasons to hear this sneering, ham-Dickensian voice as ironic; first, because Chapter 6 actually does 'the unthinkable' by constraining us to think about poverty. Forster made sure of that. This is why he bothers to take us into Leonard's mind and to endow him with intelligent reveries. So he makes us see through Leonard's eyes and think through Leonard's mind about his material and intellectual conditions. The second reason the narrator's irony matters is that it announces a Marxist commentary on the scene of Leonard reading. The furniture of Leonard's mind matches the furnishings of his subterranean London flat. These shabby material conditions inform his mental conditions: he cannot follow Ruskin because his makeshift flat is dark and stuffy, his stomach is rumbling, he is tired, the family in the flat above is singing hymns, and his fiancée is calling him to bed. Leonard believes in effort, and so he tries to shut his ears to the plangent world around him. But he still fails.

Leonard is modern economic man: he wants to be cosmopolitan, but he can't afford to be. To see Leonard reading Ruskin is to witness him being culturally tantalized and, in Forster's words, 'craving better [intellectual] food'. To see him with the cosmopolitan Schlegels is to hear his 'empty stomach assert[ing] itself'.[64] Here Forster enacts a form of gruesome connoisseurship by inviting his educated readers—those who have read their Ruskin—to see this allusion to Ruskin as darkly comic. Forster's grim inside joke is that *The Stones of Venice* predicts Leonard's condition and foretells exactly this state of affairs in its explanation of modern labour's stultifying effects. Labour's chief flaw, Ruskin explains, is that it exhausts individual intelligence and leaves hard-working men with nothing but the 'crumbs of life'.[65] No wonder then, that Leonard is condemned to crave.

---

[62] Forster, *Howards End*, 31.   [63] Ibid., 38.   [64] Ibid., 36.
[65] John Ruskin, 'The Nature of Gothic', in E. T. Cook and Alexander Wedderburn (eds), *The Stones of Venice, The Works of John Ruskin*, 39 vols (London: George Allen, 1903–12), X, 196.

A few years before Ruskin's observations about the dehumanizing nature of modern labour, Marx and Engels's *The Communist Manifesto* was already worrying about the 'cosmopolitan character'[66] of modern consumption in similar terms. Leonard has had a taste of culture and he wants more. What was once threatening is now desirable, the exclusive seems to be democratized as the global becomes local. Forster shows us how Leonard is subject to the mechanisms of international consumption and cosmopolitan desire. He inhabits the same cultural moment that Marx and Engels point to when they observe how modern man hungers for foreign flavours. 'In place of the old wants', Marx and Engels write,

> satisfied by the productions of the country, we find new wants, requiring for their satisfaction the products of distant lands and climes. In place of the old local and national seclusion and self-sufficiency, we have intercourse in every direction, universal interdependence of nations. And as in material, so also in intellectual production. The intellectual creations of individual nations become common property. National one-sidedness and narrow-mindedness become more and more impossible, and from the numerous national and local literatures, there arises a world literature.[67]

Leonard knows, Forster writes, that 'his mind and his body had been alike underfed, because he was poor, and because he was modern they were always craving better food'.[68] He is the twentieth-century counterpart to Oliver Twist, the little rebel who dared to ask for more. Leonard is doomed through no fault of his own. His farcical murder, partly attributed to a shower of books, takes us back to Hardy's *Jude the Obscure* (1895), the tragedy of another working man destroyed by the culture he so admired. But that is another story.

No one who reads *Howards End* can fail to notice the price the characters pay for their beliefs. Still, Forster does not surrender his cosmopolitanism, though by the novel's end he has shown what it costs. Neither cosmopolitanism nor imperialism is without flaw. Even though Leonard doesn't manage to 'push his head out of the grey waters and see the universe',[69] others will. Forster's exclusion of Leonard is a troubling form of gatekeeping. But to dwell only on the fact that Leonard has missed the boat is to miss another vital truth that Forster is setting before us. Culture endures.

In 1927, Forster delivered a series of lectures at Cambridge that he later published as *Aspects of the Novel*. 'We are not concerned with' Dostoyevsky's message, Forster told his privileged audience, repeating the haunting formulation he had used to begin Chapter 6 of *Howards End*. 'What matters', Forster continued, 'is the accent of his voice, his song',[70] and what Dostoyevsky does to us. To press this point, Forster returned to an image very similar to Leonard's encounter with Ruskin. Reading Dostoyevsky, Forster said, gives us 'the sensation of sinking into

[66] Marx and Engels, *The Communist Manifesto*, 38.
[67] Ibid., 39.   [68] Forster, *Howards End*, 35.   [69] Ibid., 38.
[70] Forster, *Aspects of the Novel*, ed. Oliver Stallybrass (London: Penguin, 2000), 123.

a translucent globe and seeing our experience floating far above us on its surface, tiny, remote, yet ours'. In other words, cosmopolitan reading allows us to connect with the universe that Leonard longed for, to achieve what he could not. What cosmopolitan reading can do, Forster implies, is enable us to push ourselves beyond the limits of our own minds. When we do that, we can go beyond the limits of our own watery grey matter: we can travel outwards into the *cosmos* and the *polis* without even leaving home.

FURTHER READING

Agathocleous, Tanya. *Urban Realism and the Cosmopolitan Imagination in the Nineteenth Century: Visible City, Invisible World* (New York: Cambridge University Press, 2011).

Anderson, Amanda. *The Powers of Distance: Cosmopolitanism and the Cultivation of Detachment* (Princeton, NJ: Princeton University Press, 2001).

Casanova, Pascale. *The World Republic of Letters* (Cambridge, MA: Harvard University Press, 2004).

Freedman, Jonathan. *Professions of Taste: Henry James, British Aestheticism, and Commodity Culture* (Stanford, CA: Stanford University Press, 1990).

Freedman, Jonathan. *The Temple of Culture: Assimilation and Anti-Semitism in Literary Anglo-America* (Oxford: Oxford University Press, 2000).

Keirstead, Christopher M. *Victorian Poetry, Europe, and the Challenge of Cosmopolitanism* (Columbus, OH: Ohio State University Press, 2011).

Stiegler, Bernd. *Traveling in Place: A History of Armchair Travel* (Chicago, IL: University of Chicago Press, 2013).

Walkowitz, Rebecca L. *Cosmopolitan Style: Modernism beyond the Nation* (New York: Columbia University Press, 2006).

CHAPTER 31

PARODIES, SPOOFS, AND SATIRES

JAMES WILLIAMS

Theft and restitution

In the library of Merton College, Oxford is a pair of self-portraits by alumnus Max Beerbohm. 'The Theft, 1894' shows the young Beerbohm, then twenty-two and in his fourth year at the college, making off with a library book along a dark corridor, glancing nervously over his shoulder. His high white collar and slicked hair make him look exaggeratedly schoolboyish; he wears a mustard yellow suit with a wide check that Wodehouse's sartorial censor Jeeves might have politely put down to youthful high spirits. In the second, 'The Restitution, 1920', an older, wiser Beerbohm walks back along the same corridor with the same book. He was forty-eight in 1920 (and would live thirty-six more years) but he draws himself as a geriatric caricature, bent-backed with a cane, bespectacled, his long white beard and moustaches giving him a look of Blake's Urizen. The drawings parody Beerbohm himself, youth and age, responsibility and irresponsibility, and in a broader way the gap between the *fin de siècle* and the brink of the 1920s. These twenty-six years are presented as a lifetime's span, and at the same time as contained within the simple narrative arc of borrowing and returning a library book: we are reminded of how much separates the year 1920 from the nineteenth century, and of the scores of mundane continuities and human lives that bring them together.

Between those years, Beerbohm had made himself the gadfly on the wall of the English literary world, capturing his contemporaries, and prominent figures of the recent past, in irresistibly witty pen-and-ink drawings of spare and elegant accuracy. They marked him out as the sharpest-eyed caricaturist of the times, and made him famous by the age of twenty-four. Beerbohm's writing career began as an essayist for 1890s publications including *The Yellow Book* (1894–7), and later his celebrity was secured by twelve years as drama critic for the *Saturday Review* (1898), and by his novel *Zuleika Dobson* (1911). The peak of his career as a literary parodist came in 1912 with his collection of spoofs of *fin-de-siècle* authors, *A Christmas Garland* (though, like the 'Theft/Restitution' diptych, this work too reached across the years: he had published versions of five of the pieces as early as 1896).[1] Contemporaries were quick to acclaim the work as a landmark. 'It is too early to say with confidence', wrote the critic Christopher Stone in 1915, 'that Mr. Max Beerbohm's *Christmas Garland* constitutes the finest set of parodies that have ever emanated from one brain; but there are not a few critics who would endorse such an estimate'.[2]

The best of Beerbohm's parodies is probably that of Henry James, 'The Mote in the Middle Distance', not least because it understands so intuitively parody's double agency as mockery and homage:

> It was with the sense of a, for him, very memorable something that he peered now into the immediate future, and tried, not without compunction, to take that period up where he had, prospectively, left it. But just where the deuce *had* he left it? The consciousness of dubiety was, for our friend, not, this morning, quite yet clean-cut enough to outline the figures on what she had called his "horizon," between which and himself the twilight was indeed of a quality somewhat intimidating.[3]

Beerbohm, looking back to the great men of the 1890s, might be seen as nostalgic, as trying 'to take that period up where he had … left it'. But Christmases are moments for looking backwards and forwards, and parody is nothing if not double-edged: Beerbohm's grappling with the unlocatable periods of James's late prose stages for us, in a revealing way, the difficulty of grappling with extreme modernity, with an art which seems to be 'peering…into the immediate future'. James himself was delighted by Beerbohm's *A Christmas Garland*, reading it with 'wonder and delight', and declaring himself henceforth incapable of writing without feeling that he was 'parodying himself'.[4] The weird doubling effect of parody could, for James, be something like the weird doubling of self-consciousness: the feeling that he had become a spectator of his own creative processes. What was once heard in the inner ear of private composition was now also overheard, as if in a public space.

A common thread in Beerbohm's parodies of Henry James was, to adapt that phrase of Christopher Stone's, 'the emanation of the brain': the epistemic fogginess of James's prose in which the mind's privacy and the outside world are not sharply demarcated. Beerbohm's caricature 'London in November and Mr Henry James in London' depicts the portly novelist straining to see, through the London smog, his hand in front of his face. The caption reads: '…It was, therefore, not without something of a shock that he, in this to him so very congenial atmosphere, now perceived

---

[1] See David Cecil, *Max: A Biography* (London: Constable, 1964), 145.

[2] Christopher Stone, *Parody* (London: Martin Secker, 1915), 50.

[3] Max Beerbohm, *A Christmas Garland*, ed. N. John Hall (New Haven, CT and London: Yale University Press, 1993), 3.

[4] Henry James, quoted in Beerbohm, *A Christmas Garland*, x–xi.

that a vision of the hand which he had, at a venture, held up within an inch or so of his eyes was, with an almost awful clarity being adumbrated…'.[5] Beerbohm's title here plays off two senses of 'in': time ('in November') and location ('in London'), and getting our bearings in this picture, and in the caption, requires a moment of orientation. The slight squint we must make to resolve this semantic opaqueness brings us into sympathy with the James of the cartoon: searching, straining, peering at something supremely obvious. It is the same note we have just heard struck in 'The Mote in the Middle Distance': 'he peered now into the immediate future…'.

True caricature, Beerbohm later wrote, was 'the exaggeration of the whole creature, from top to toe…The whole man must be melted down, as in a crucible, and then, as from the solution, be fashioned anew. He must emerge with not one particle of himself lost, yet with not a particle of himself as it was before.'[6] Everything is lost and everything preserved: parody is its own kind of theft and restitution, an appropriation of identity and a powerfully sympathetic act of identification. The levels of sympathy in Beerbohm's spoofing of James are complex, and worth dwelling on. There is Beerbohm's identification with his subject, the sympathetic enterprise of writing like James; and there is the sympathy between us and Beerbohm's caricature of James, between our peering at the syntax of the writing and James's struggling to make out his hand. But then there is a sympathy, too, between the features of James's prose that Beerbohm mocks and the kind of mockery that that prose is already engaged in. Consider a passage of *The Turn of the Screw* (1898) similarly taxed with the problems of seeing clearly:

> I began to take in with certitude and yet without direct vision the presence, a good way off, of a third person. The old trees, the thick shrubbery, made a great and pleasant shade, but it was all suffused with the brightness of the hot still hour. There was no ambiguity in anything; none whatever in the conviction I from one moment to another found myself forming as to what I should see straight before me and across the lake as a consequence of raising my eyes.[7]

The parodic is not limited to parodies of particular texts: what James is up to in *The Turn of the Screw* is a complex satirizing of the epistemological doubt at the heart of the gothic enterprise. One respect in which Beerbohm and James are in sympathy, then, is in their feeling for the *Zeitgeist*, their sense that the referential and the parodic are elements in the modern air, like the swirling smog 'in November…in London'. When we recognize those elements at work in Beerbohm, we are drawn into a game that Beerbohm and his target already share. What starts off looking like a private insult comes to look very quickly like a shared joke, and a shared joke is a tiny microcosm of literary sociability.

---

[5] Ibid., plate 1.   [6] Beerbohm, *A Variety of Things* (New York: Knopf, 1928), 127–8.
[7] James, *The Turn of the Screw and Other Stories*, ed. T. J. Lustig (Oxford: Oxford University Press, 1992), 154.

Cultures of parody

If parody involves its own forms of theft and restitution, then for the literary world of the turn of the century, *pace* Proudhon, theft is property. The parodies, spoofs, and satires of the periodicals (an iceberg of which Beerbohm's genius is only the tip) can be read as evidence of a shared sense of ownership, a shared investment in a common literary currency and cultural stock. The period fostered a culture of parody, or more accurately cultures of parody, since the literary press was everywhere plural, a web of overlapping factions and readerships (as Patrick Leary has written, even the editorial community behind a periodical like *Punch* represented a collaboration of multiple 'interconnected social, professional, and financial interests'[8]). Parody was among the varieties of sociable intercourse which made these 'interconnections' possible, one of the forms of companionship underwriting the 'very congenial atmosphere' of literary community in which writers like James or Beerbohm moved.

The genre of literary parody around the turn of the century was occasionally rude, and generally in rude health.[9] Critics of the time might compare the efforts of their contemporaries unfavourably with the romantic heyday of Horace and James Smith's *Rejected Addresses* (1812) and the mid-century wit C. S. Calverley (who died in 1888), but there was no shortage of parodic writing in the popular press. Humorous magazines such as *Fun, Judy, Tit-Bits, Sketchy Bits*, and, most influential of all, *Punch* remained the most plentiful source, and successful parodists in major magazines could emerge as literary names in their own right. Most spoofs in the period, however, appear anonymously and without fanfare, part of the glue holding

---

[8] Patrick Leary, *The Punch Brotherhood: Table Talk and Print Culture in Mid-Victorian London* (London: British Library, 2010), 1.

[9] In addition to the examples this chapter will discuss, evidence for this view can be found in various strands of culture between 1880 and 1920. For example the popularity of stage burlesques, such as G. R. Sims and Henry Pettit's *Faust up to Date* (1888) and W. S. Gilbert's *Rosencrantz and Guildenstern* (1891), kept spoof alive in London theatres until the mid-1890s. Shakespearean spoof (well treated by Stanley Wells, 'Shakespearean Burlesques', *Shakespeare Quarterly* 16/1 (Winter 1965), 44–61) lived on after the demise of burlesque in other forms, such as Gene Buck and Herman Ruby's 1912 hit song 'That Shakespearean Rag', incorporated into *The Waste Land*. Polemics around gender frequently turned on satires and spoofs, such as the parodic sequels to Ibsen's *A Doll's House* written from 1890 onwards by Walter Besant ('The Doll's House and after'), Bernard Shaw ('Still after the Doll's House'), and others (on this see Bernard F. Dukore, 'Karl Marx's Youngest Daughter and *A Doll's House*', *Theatre Journal* 42/3 (October 1990), 308–21; and more generally a satiric spirit animates the various anti-feminist 'New Woman' lampoons such as Sidney Grundy's *The New Woman* of 1894—see Jean Chothia (ed.), *'The New Woman' and Other Emancipated Woman Plays* (Oxford: Oxford University Press, 1998). The suffragette Alice Duer Miller showed that feminists could spoof just as well as their opponents in her parodies of anti-suffrage petitions 'Why We Oppose Pockets For Women' and 'Why We Oppose Votes for Men', in *Are Women People?: A Collection of Rhymes for Suffrage Times* (New York: George H. Doran, 1915).

magazine issues together. A characteristic example from *Punch* in 1882 accompanies a cartoon of an ageing, foppish gentleman, leaning into a mirror and attempting a tricky comb-over:

> One more try at a parting! Not many
> Locks circle my head, I regret;
> But a few, the most hardy of any,
> Are left on the crown of it yet.[10]

The poem is entitled 'Moore Modernized', or 'Song for a Thin-Thatched Dandy', and its joke hangs on common recognition of the song 'One Bumper at Parting', from the fifth number of Moore's *Irish Melodies* (1815):

> One bumper at parting!–though many
> Have circled the board since we met,
> The fullest, the saddest of any,
> Remains to be crown'd by us yet.[11]

The title of *Punch*, alongside its other allusions, suggests the sharing of a convivial drink, and Moore's song moves in this society, a melancholy celebration of 'the tears of the cup'. It may be odd to call the parody sympathetic, with its comic purchase achieved by transposing Moore's heartfelt verses into a perversely banal context; yet the magpie-like appropriation of turns of phrase ('crown'd' to 'the crown' is verbally light-fingered) is not without its restitution. Its concern with the trivial losses of male ageing, especially among a middle-aged male readership, is closer to the *carpe diem* of Moore's drinking song than first appears.

Moore's *Irish Melodies* were parlour songs, already strongly associated with shared pleasure, but parody could lampoon, in its companionable way, more solitary modes of literary expression. In an 1884 article on parody in *Chambers's Magazine* the anonymous author offered a spoof of Wordsworth's 'She dwelt among the untrodden ways' which turns the poem's fascination with isolation back on the poet in an unflattering light:

> He lived among the untrodden ways,
> To Rydal Mount that lead;
> A bard whom there were none to praise,
> And very few to read.
>
> Unread his words – his *Milk-white Doe*
> With dust is dark and dim;
> It's still in Longman's shop; and oh!
> The difference to him![12]

---

[10] *Punch's Almanack for 1883* (7 December 1882), in *Punch* 84 (1883), v.

[11] A. D. Goodley (ed.), *The Poetical Works of Thomas Moore* (Oxford: Oxford University Press, 1910), 225.

[12] 'The Muse of Parody', *Chambers's Journal*, 2 February 1884, 72.

Parody, in an influential account by Linda Hutcheon, is 'repetition with difference. A critical distance is implied between the backgrounded text being parodied and the new incorporating work, a distance usually signalled by irony'.[13] One of the tricks that this repetition can perform is to imagine alternative ways things might have turned out, other lives for texts, parallel universes like the one where Wordsworth languishes unread. The knowing—even smug—joke being that for the parody to work, Wordsworth cannot be 'unread', either by the poet or the reader. It's a poem about forgetting that trades on a shared memory, and it raises profound questions—about the literary canon, and what might lead to one poem being widely learnt by heart while another sits 'in Longman's shop'—while remaining gloriously uninterested in the answers.

Like other forms of literary marginalia, parodies, spoofs, and satires have a disconcerting knack of refocusing our attention onto questions that are far from marginal. One of the stars of *Punch*, Sir Owen Seaman, published a selection of his parodies in 1902 as *Borrowed Plumes*. Like the Beerbohm of *A Christmas Garland*, Seaman specialized in sharply drawn pastiche of the prose style of contemporary novelists. His selection of 'Choice sayings' of Marie Corelli are miniature case studies in intellectual overreach, pearls of banality which all the same can't quite shake off the big questions they exquisitely fail to ask:

> *Oggì! Oggì!* cry the ice-cream wayfarers from far Campanian hills. To-day! To-day! How true! There is no time precisely like the present. The past is over; the future yet to be.
>
> …
>
> What is the Good? And what is the Beautiful? Who can say? All we know is that both terms are synonymous, the one quite as much as the other.[14]

The bathetic collapse of 'all we know is that both terms are synonymous' is a beautifully staged pratfall, but the range of the joke is wide: if Marie Corelli takes a dive here, the whole system of nineteenth-century aesthetic idealism which is garbled suddenly looks wobbly too ('Beauty is truth, truth beauty, the one quite as much as the other').

Parody becomes, like the Wildean quip, or the deductive inferences of Sherlock Holmes, one of the characteristic ways in which *fin-de-siècle* culture collapses the gap between the significant and the trivial, the large- and small-scale—and this very tendency is the target of much good parody:

> I found Hemlock Jones in the old Brook Street lodgings, musing before the fire. With the freedom of an old friend I at once threw myself in my usual familiar attitude at his feet, and gently caressed his boot…

---

[13] Linda Hutcheon, *A Theory of Parody: The Teachings of Twentieth-Century Art Forms* (London and New York: Methuen, 1985), 32.

[14] Owen Seaman, *Borrowed Plumes* (London: Constable, 1902), 73.

'It is raining,' he said, without lifting his head.

'You have been out, then?' I said quickly.

'No. But I see that your umbrella is wet, and that your overcoat has drops of water on it.'

I sat aghast at his penetration.[15]

This is from the second series of *Condensed Novels* by American parodist Bret Harte, published in 1902 (the original *Condensed Novels*, models for Seaman and Beerbohm, appeared in 1867 and were variously reprinted during the 1870s and 1880s). What Harte satirizes is not so much Holmes as Watson, the imbecile hero-worshipper. There is a shared joke between readers of Conan Doyle, then (haven't we too, just occasionally, had such uncharitable thoughts about Watson?). But again, the joke has a wide reach: Harte's 'Hemlock Jones' calls to mind Plato's *Phaedo*, and so the note of adulation suggests Watson's overhyping of Holmes as a kind of modern Socrates, and playfully exploits the dynamics of Conan Doyle's narration in which, as in Plato, we always hear one admiring voice above all others.

Sherlock Holmes was an immediate target for parody and, as with *The Turn of the Screw*, was already a form of spoof insofar as Holmes's methods echo, in ironized form, those of Doyle's tutor Joseph Bell, MD. As *The Adventures of Sherlock Holmes* (1892) bore a dedication to Bell, E. W. Hornung's *Raffles: The Amateur Cracksman* (1899) bears the telling dedication 'TO/A.C.D./THIS FORM OF FLATTERY'. Raffles, a gentleman thief, is Holmes's criminal equivalent, and the Watson-like narrator, Bunny, has something of the hero worship that Harte sent up (Hornung makes him Raffles's former school fag). Richard Lancelyn Green, editor of both Conan Doyle and Hornung, disagrees: 'Hornung did not "imitate" Sherlock Holmes. Had he done so, Raffles would have been a "Napoleon of crime" similar to Professor Moriarty and he would have matched wits with a great detective.'[16] But while Green is right to resist simplistic identifications, his argument confuses imitation of Sherlock Holmes with schematic correspondence to the world of *Sherlock Holmes*. As the art critic Tom Lubbock has acutely written, 'a work of art...should be more than the sum of its parts...But it is also the sum of its parts'.[17] Raffles is more than a parody of Holmes, but he is also a parody of Holmes: and it is an altogether more lasting parody for not being too obvious:

'Cricket,' said Raffles, 'like everything else, is good enough sport until you discover a better. As a source of excitement it isn't in it with other things you wot of, Bunny, and the involuntary comparison becomes a bore. What's the satisfaction of taking a man's wicket when you want his spoons?'[18]

---

[15] Bret Harte, 'The Stolen Cigar Case', in *Condensed Novels: Second Series* (Boston, MA and New York: Houghton Mifflin Company, 1902), 39–40.

[16] E. W. Hornung, *Raffles: The Amateur Cracksman*, ed. Richard Lancelyn Green (London: Penguin, 2003), xxxvi.

[17] Tom Lubbock, *Great Works: 50 Paintings Explored* (London: Frances Lincoln, 2011), 37.

[18] Hornung, *Raffles*, 39.

What Raffles takes from Holmes is not his profession or his ethics: rather, he sends up Holmes's world-weariness, his refined sense that even pleasurable things are, from a higher point of view, 'a bore', at best enjoyable distractions: ' "It saved me from ennui," [Holmes] answered, yawning. "Alas, I already feel it closing in upon me! My life is spent in one long effort to escape from the commonplaces of existence. These little problems help me to do so." '[19] Hornung took from Conan Doyle, but like Raffles swiping a man's spoons he was careful to cover his tracks.

The cricketer and 'amateur cracksman' is a supreme example of parody as theft and restitution. Raffles is a parody par excellence, because in him Hornung identifies parody's sociable pleasure and its implicit wickedness. Parody is a kind of gentlemanly theft, and as such it has its glamour and its moral unease. Just as literary parodies abound in magazines of the period, so too do (largely anonymous) chapters and articles about parody, tending to agonize, or make a show of agonizing, over its naughtiness or impiety. But the fun was keenly recognized, and the commonplace solution to this dilemma was a sense of fair play. 'Parody may be as clever, laughable, and amusing as you can make it', wrote *Chambers's Journal* in 1884, 'but it should always be good-natured, fair, and gentlemanly'.[20] Parody, like cricket, was a man's game whose potential roughness necessitated a kind of masculine integrity. It was for the fairer sex, at least anecdotally, to voice objections: 'A lady-friend of the writer's lately said, in regard to one of the best-known poems of a distinguished poet: "I admired and liked it once; but I can hardly read it now, since I saw that dreadful parody of it that appeared in *Punch*." '[21]

Moral judgements were best left oblique. A piece entitled 'The Ethics of Parody' in *The Academy and Literature* for May 1903 ended on a rhetorical note both emphatic and inconclusive:

> It is easy enough to turn Wagner on the piano organ, to hurl Raphael through a magic lantern, and to take Omar for a round of golf. But by so doing we are depreciating an intellectual security. These are things that help, console, inspire. Is it worth while to barter them for a laugh at three and sixpence (net)?[22]

Well, is it? At this pitch of stylized outrage, the writer prefers to raise questions than to make pronouncements. The question is kept hanging in the air, no matter how strongly the nudge to answer 'no'.

[19] Arthur Conan Doyle, *The Adventures of Sherlock Holmes*, ed. Richard Lancelyn Green (Oxford: Oxford University Press, 1993), 74.
[20] 'The Muse of Parody', 73.   [21] Ibid., 71.
[22] 'The Ethics of Parody', *The Academy and Literature*, 23 May 1903, 514. The reference to Omar Khayyám is from Henry Boynton, *The Golfer's Rubáiyát* (London: Grant Richards, 1903).

Parodies of culture

'Now, the first thing to be said about Parody', wrote Sir Arthur Quiller-Couch, 'is that it plays with the gods: its fun is taken with Poetry, which all good men admit to be a beautiful and adorable thing, and some would have to be a holy thing.' The true parodist is a reverent man, wrote 'Q', because the reverent man 'knows unerringly "how far to go", as they say'.[23] By the time Quiller-Couch sang this gentlemanly tune in 1912 it was already a familiar ditty. The more repetitiously this note is struck by English men of letters, the more irresistible it is to speculate what kinds of anxieties run beneath the insistence on decorous restraint. Impiety is only one of the concerns that mimicry has provoked across the centuries, as Steven Connor has argued.[24] Beneath cautions like that of Quiller-Couch runs, faint but persistent, the fear that the mischievous energy of spoofing might tend to the anarchic or the revolutionary: that quipping at Wordsworth could be the first step on a Rake's Progress that might call more fundamental forms of authority and prestige into question. This chapter has argued that cultures of parody were important social forces in the life of English letters, but insofar as parody is social, it is political too. It makes sense to ask whether the politics of parody tended towards the radical, as both detractors and defenders seemed to fear, and what its relation might be to the critical, revolutionary (and reactionary) energies of modernism.

On the face of it, Quiller-Couch's concern seems misplaced. Parody, far from being revolutionary, is naturally conservative insofar as it affords an acceptable and tame outlet for non-deferential sentiment. Like Bakhtin's 'carnivalesque', the anarchic character of parody can be read as superficial, a pressure valve allowing the continued survival of the (political or aesthetic) status quo. The stronger version of this claim would be that parody simply laughs at the new and the different. G. K. Chesterton's 'To a Modern Poet' is representative of a powerful and immediately recognizable conservative streak in early twentieth-century parody:

> Well,
> What
> about it?...
>
> Now you mention it,
> Of course, the sky
> is like a large mouth
> shown to a dentist.

---

[23] Arthur Quiller-Couch, foreword to Stanley Adam and Bernard White (eds), *Parodies and Imitations Old and New* (London: Hutchinson, 1912), vi.

[24] Stephen Connor, *Dumbstruck: A Cultural History of Ventriloquism* (Oxford: Oxford University Press, 2000), 223–5.

and I never noticed
a little thing
like that.[25]

Chesterton's 'like a large mouth / shown to a dentist' cocks a snook at the medical inertia which opens 'The Love Song of J. Alfred Prufrock' (1917): '... the evening is spread out against the sky / Like a patient etherized upon a table.'[26] The poem was published in 1925, but mentally it is stuck in the world of the mid-1910s, fighting a rearguard action against a poetic modernism already a decade old. The literature of 1900–20 is often dramatized in popular memory as a conflict between forces of artistic conservatism (the Edwardian, the Georgian) and artistic revolution (modernism in its various forms), and Chesterton's trenchant spoof of Eliot plays obligingly into this narrative of *kulturkampf*. Its lack of concern for detail (the versification of 'To a Modern Poet' is far from Eliot's practice) reads like a demonstration of the lack of art which Chesterton thought characterized all *vers libre* without distinction: a battle line is drawn. In 1904, Carolyn Wells had distinguished different forms of parody: *word-rendering*, *form-rendering*, and 'by far the most meritorious', *sense-rendering*, which 'follows a train of thought precisely along the lines that [the author parodied] would have pursued from the given premises'.[27] Chesterton attempts this final kind of parody but lacks the sympathy for Eliot that Beerbohm had for Henry James. This is not a product of a sociable culture of parody but a satire against the new literary culture, mocking from the outside a new sensibility which had itself mocked what had gone before.

Parody is a form of literary self-consciousness, a knowing relationship between texts, and much modernism of the early century is peopled by narrators tortured by the awareness that they live parodic lives, lives that repeat with ironic distance and difference the stories of the past:

> I am no prophet—and here's no great matter...
> No, I am not Prince Hamlet, nor was meant to be...[28]

J. Alfred Prufrock's is a life of ironized diminution, a life lived in painful awareness of the gap between a Somebody and a Nobody. In this respect, like much else in modernism, Eliot's poem has deep affinities with the popular parody and satire of the *fin de siècle*. Mr Prufrock is close kin to Mr Pooter, from George and Weedon Grossmith's satire of petit-bourgeois suburbia *The Diary of a Nobody* (1892), another narrator prone to characterize himself by what he is not. 'I fail to see,' writes Mr Pooter in the 'Introduction' to his diary, 'because I do not happen to be a "Somebody"— why my diary should not be interesting', instead insisting that: 'You must take us as

---

[25] G. K. Chesterton, *Collected Poems* (New York: Dodd, Mead, & Company, 1932), 40, 41.

[26] T. S. Eliot, *The Complete Poems and Plays* (London: Faber, 1969), 13.

[27] Carolyn Wells, *A Parody Anthology* (New York: Charles Scribner's Sons, 1904), xxv.

[28] Eliot, *Complete Poems and Plays*, 15, 16.

we are: we're homely folk.'[29] Pooter resolutely and irrepressibly refuses to experience being a 'Nobody' as tragic, where Prufrock embodies Arthur Symons's conception of the Laforguean poet as 'metaphysical Pierrot',[30] the melancholy fool. But the white-faced Pierrot is also the close relative of the mime, the physical parodist of movement.

There are points where Prufrock and Pooter read like participants in the same satirical joke, where their worlds overlap with striking exactness and the boundaries of the tragic and comic become difficult to ascertain:

> February 18.– Carrie has several times recently called attention to the thinness of my hair at the top of my head, and recommended me to get it seen to...[31]

The Diary of a Nobody, like Seaman's *Borrowed Plumes*, had its first appearance in *Punch*, but it is not only Pooter who is a literary descendant of the magazine's 'Thin-Thatched Dandy', the ageing man worried about 'the thinness of my hair':

> ...indeed there will be time
> To wonder, 'Do I dare?' and, 'Do I dare?'
> Time to turn back and descend the stair,
> With a bald spot in the middle of my hair
> (They will say: 'How his hair is growing thin!)[32]

Both texts turn on moments of self-consciousness which are instinct with a satirical sense of foibles held up to a public scrutiny. Prufrock imagines a 'They' that Pooter does not need to imagine, since they can be found under his own roof. They each live out a different kind of parody of modern isolation, different ways to be lonely in a crowd.

If Eliot's poems occupy the imaginative terrain of the comic periodicals more often than is usually acknowledged, we can start to ask how far the parodic vein goes in Anglophone modernism, how narrow a gap might separate a *Punch* from a *Blast*. Ezra Pound, with his peculiar mix of irreverence and arch-seriousness, was in many respects a natural parodist, and composed occasional spoofs of poets throughout his career, such as his cod-Irish dig at Yeats:

> 'Neath Ben Bulben's buttock lies
> Bill Yeats, a poet twoice the soize
> Of William Shakespear, as they say
> Down Ballykillywuchlin way...[33]

---

[29] George and Weedon Grossmith, *The Diary of a Nobody*, ed. Kate Flint (Oxford: Oxford University Press, 1995), 2, 17.

[30] Arthur Symons, *The Symbolist Movement in Literature* (New York: E. P. Dutton, 1919), 304.

[31] Grossmith, *Diary of a Nobody*, 94.   [32] Eliot, *Complete Poems and Plays*, 14.

[33] Ezra Pound, *Pavannes and Divagations* (New York: New Directions, 1958), 228.

This, along with other parodies and 'lighter' pieces collected in 1958 as *Pavannes and Divagations*, points to an aspect of Pound's imagination which has been insufficiently read back into the wider canon of his work. Even the titles under which Pound's early poetry is presented hint powerfully at the deep engagement of his work with different aspects of the parodic: as riposte (*Ripostes*, 1912), as satirical broadside (*Blast*, 1914), and as imitation or emulation of voice (*Personae*, 1926). Sarah Davison has written persuasively of Pound as moving in an 'atmosphere of parody', of Imagism as a movement which grew up around a parodic impulse to spoof aspects of modern art.[34] And yet just as Prufrock's parody operates at a level of cultural satire, Pound's poetry is often most influenced by parody where parody is least distinguishable from influence. What is at stake in saying that 'Sestina: Altaforte' is a parody of Browning, rather than a poem in a Browningesque style?

> LOQUITUR: *En* Betrans de Born...
> Damn it all! all this our South stinks peace.
> You whoreson dog, Papiols, come! Let's to music![35]

The comic–satirical and savage–modernist strains of Pound's mind are too closely intertwined here to insist on that sharp demarcation between 'parody' and 'allusion', which has tended to line up with the demarcation between 'light' and 'serious' verse. When we question this division and start to read Pound's poems of the 1900s and 1910s as parodic, we can begin to hear more clearly the rough, abrasive humour in the early Poundian style. Moreover we can start to recognize the deeply ambivalent character of Pound's parodic modernism, which could accommodate sympathetic identifications with those poets he saw as like-minded (Yeats, Browning) as well as swinging satirical attacks on what he saw as stagnant or repellent in contemporary art. Pound's work points to the rude health of that culture of parody which animated his elder contemporaries Seaman and Beerbohm, as well as participating in its own modernist parody of culture—or, with the authentic Poundian mimicry, of 'kulchur'.

Coda: Beyond parody

'There may come a time', wrote Christopher Stone, at the conclusion to his short study *Parody* (1915), 'when the leather-strop upon which young men have sharpened their wits hitherto shall become a veritable scourge with which to rouse the

---

[34] See Sarah Davison, 'An "Atmosphere of Parody": Ezra Pound and Imagism', in Catherine Morley and Alex Goody (eds), *American Modernism: Cultural Transactions* (Newcastle upon Tyne: Cambridge Scholars, 2009), 143–64.

[35] Pound, *Personae: The Shorter Poems of Ezra Pound*, ed. Lea Baechler and A. Walton Litz (London: Faber, 1990), 26.

world.'[36] Stone's remarks went to press between the battles of the Marne and the Somme, and with historical hindsight an unintendedly revolutionary rhetoric begins to play around the identification of parody as a 'scourge' in the hands of the young. Elsewhere, during the years of the Great War, we find parodic techniques put to use to explore a growing sense of intergenerational conflict:

> Then Abram bound the youth with belts and straps,
> And builded parapets and trenches there,
> And stretchèd forth the knife to slay his son.
> When lo! an Angel called him out of heaven,
> Saying, Lay not thy hand upon the lad,
> Neither do anything to him, thy son.
> Behold! Caught in a thicket by its horns,
> A Ram. Offer the Ram of Pride instead.
>
> But the old man would not so, but slew his son,
> And half the seed of Europe, one by one.[37]

Like Stone's 'leather-strop', Owen's 'belts and straps' sound like weapons, or perhaps instruments of torture, as they are used to restrain Isaac for sacrifice (Owen's editor Jon Stallworthy notes the similarity between this phrase and 'a soldier's equipment'). The whole poem, though, turns itself back on the 'old man' as a different kind of weapon, a furious piece of political and moral satire.

'The most rigorous form of parody, or *minimal parody*', wrote Gérard Genette, 'consists . . . in taking up a familiar text literally and giving it a new meaning, while playing, if possible and as needed, on the words'.[38] Owen's 'Parable of the Old Man and the Young' is the most minimal kind of parody and one which, giving us so little in the way of self-conscious wit or technique, pushes the limits of what parody might be. Owen's retelling of the 'parable' works closely and responsively with his source text, changing the words of the King James Version 'as needed'. Owen's insistence on 'Abram' rather than 'Abraham' rewrites the broader Genesis narrative: 'Neither shall thy name any more be called Abram, but thy name shall be Abraham; for a father of many nations have I made thee' (Genesis 17:5). This 'Abram' is precisely *not* a father, but a slayer of nations. Owen's 'Parable', read against the long backdrop of parody and satire in the writing of the previous decades, comes to look like a point of departure, a redeployment of the tools of literary parody to a new purpose, bearing witness to a conflict that is in one sense beyond parody, and in another sense impossible to speak about in any other way.

---

[36] Stone, *Parody*, 62.
[37] Wilfred Owen, *The Complete Poems and Fragments*, ed. Jon Stallworthy (London: Chatto & Windus, 2013), 174.
[38] Gérard Genette, *Palimpsests: Literature in the Second Degree* (Lincoln, NE and London: University of Nebraska Press, 1997), 16.

At the beginning of Simon Dentith's study of parody, he cites the passage in *Middlemarch* in which Mr Brooke's stump speech is reduced to a farce by a member of the crowd holding up an effigy of the candidate 'within ten yards of him', and repeating his words in 'a parrot-like, Punch-voiced echo'.[39] Throughout the writing of the First World War, we find familiar voices—from the Bible, the Romantic poets, the working-class patter of Kipling's *Barrack-Room Ballads* (1892), the manly pessimism of Housman's *A Shropshire Lad* (1896), or the terrible ironies of Hardy's *Satires of Circumstance* (1914)—being echoed and transformed by the same satirical tendency to mimicry. 'Every war is ironic', wrote Paul Fussell in his landmark study of the literature of the First World War, 'because every war is worse than expected. Every war constitutes an irony of situation because its means are so melodramatically disproportionate to its assumed ends.'[40] For the writers who went to war the literary culture of their childhood supplied models of parody for dramatizing that irony, tools for survival as well as weapons for protest. Set against the long view of 1880–1920, Fussell's account helps indicate where the 'parrot-like, Punch-voiced echoes' of the turn of the century might go, and how they might emerge after 1920 with new and troubling inflections.

FURTHER READING

Cecil, David. *Max: A Biography* (London: Constable, 1964).

Davison, Sarah. 'An "Atmosphere of Parody": Ezra Pound and Imagism', in Catherine Morley and Alex Goody (eds), *American Modernism: Cultural Transactions* (Newcastle upon Tyne: Cambridge Scholars Publishing, 2009), 143–64.

Dentith, Simon. *Parody* (London: Routledge, 2000).

Fussell, Paul. *The Great War and Modern Memory* (New York: Sterling Publishing, 2009).

Genette, Gérard. *Palimpsests: Literature in the Second Degree* (Lincoln, NE and London: University of Nebraska Press, 1997).

Griffin, Dustin. *Satire: A Critical Reintroduction* (Lexington, KY: University Press of Kentucky, 1994).

Hall, N. John. *Max Beerbohm: A Kind of Life* (New Haven, CT and London: Yale University Press, 2002).

Hall, N. John (ed.) *Max Beerbohm: Caricatures* (New Haven, CT and London: Yale University Press, 2002).

Hutcheon, Linda. *A Theory of Parody: The Teachings of Twentieth-Century Art Forms* (London and New York: Methuen, 1985).

Rose, Margaret. *Parody: Ancient, Modern, and Post-Modern* (Cambridge: Cambridge University Press, 1993).

Stone, Christopher. *Parody* (London: Martin Secker, 1915).

---

[39] George Eliot, *Middlemarch*, ed. Rosemary Ashton (Harmondsworth: Penguin, 1994), 504.
[40] Paul Fussell, *The Great War and Modern Memory* (New York: Sterling, 2009), 7.

CHAPTER 32

LIFE WRITING

Biography, Portraits and Self-Portraits, Masked Authorship, and Autobiografictions

MAX SAUNDERS

Portraiture is founded on a wager of spatial mimesis. In its traditional incarnation, as with photography, its truth value is grounded on the exactness of its representation of surface, appearance, externals: its 'likeness' to an original at the moment of recording. Yet that hope of the coincidence of subject and representation in terms of space produces a dissonance between or splitting of the two in terms of time. The portraits or photographs freeze their subjects at a specific moment; but the subjects do not remain in that moment. They grow, age, transform, deteriorate, disappear. The meaning of 'a portrait of the artist as a young man' (to take an example of evident literary import) will depend on the age of the artist when he (or someone else) produced it; and his age when that phrase is used to describe the portrait. A self-portrait painted when the artist actually was a young man has a different valency from one reaching back in time to remember what he used to look like. The latter case is that of most autobiographies.

From one point of view, the central device of Wilde's *The Picture of Dorian Gray* is to reverse the terms of this contrast. Instead of the portrait fixing Dorian's appearance at the time of painting, and turning into a reminder of how he used to look, it is Dorian's appearance which becomes supernaturally fixed as a result of being portrayed; and it is the portrait which takes over the function of ageing. Wilde's novella is much more complex, of course. Dorian becomes his own portrait, shedding his soul onto the canvas—or, if you prefer, leaving the work of art as the arbiter of morality. Another truism of portraiture it plays with, then, is this idea that a portrait can represent external visual appearance so as to represent internal character. If this is the case when Basil Hallward paints Dorian's portrait, and Dorian's physical beauty is identical with his moral nature, by the end of the story, the gap between Dorian's appearance and the portrait's has become an abyss. In this case the picture actually changes, tracing the development of Dorian's 'inner life' over time (again, as in auto/biographical narratives). But one idea Wilde is playing off is that of the predictive power of portraiture. After many sittings with Gertrude Stein, Picasso found that the only way he could finish his portrait of her was to scrape away his attempts to paint her face from life, and replace them with an African-inflected mask-like face painted in her absence. When challenged that the result did not resemble Stein, he is famously supposed to have replied: 'Don't worry, it will.'[1] A post-impressionist or expressionist concentration on the planes produced by a sitter's bone structure may well result in a portrait looking more gaunt or haggard than the sitter does at the time; but one which will resemble him or her more closely as the flesh falls away. Picasso was confident enough probably also to have meant that his portrait had so transformed the conventions of portraiture that it would take time for everyone else to catch up with how to look at it.

Wilde's story, as is well known, is as much concerned with art as with life. It can be read as a working through of the idea he was articulating at the same time in 'The Decay of Lying', in which Vivian argues that 'Life imitates Art far more than Art imitates life.'[2] Rather than representing the truth of surface appearance that everyone can see, the portrait sees a truth no one else can see about Dorian. Rather than capturing him as he is now, it projects him into the future. *The Picture of Dorian Gray*, then, is as much an exploration of portraiture as it is a story of a young man's life (however that story is read: as about a homosexual counterculture, moral decline, degeneration, and so on). There are two further ways in which Wilde places the idea of the portrait on the easel in this story, both of which present further challenges to portraiture's mimetic aspiration. When Basil Hallward says 'every portrait that is painted with feeling is a portrait of the artist, not of the sitter', mimesis is split.[3] Mimesis of the artist is set against mimesis of the sitter. It might seem like a harmless, Romantic/expressive theory of art, according to which the work of art expresses the feelings of the artist. But it is more problematic when yoked to portraiture, the task of which had been conceived in terms of representing the sitter. Wilde then adds another twist in the Preface, writing: 'The highest as the lowest form of criticism is a mode of autobiography.'[4] The novella had already aroused controversy when published in *Lippincott's* magazine in 1890. In revising it for book publication the following year, Wilde doubtless wanted to fend off further attacks, by implying that any imputation of dirty-mindedness said more about the critic than the work. Perhaps he especially felt the need to insert this defence because he

---

[1] Howard Gardner, *Creating Minds: An Anatomy of Creativity Seen Through the Lives of Freud, Einstein, Picasso, Stravinsky, Eliot, Graham, and Gandhi* (New York: Basic Books, 2011), 155.

[2] See *Complete Writings of Oscar Wilde*, 10 vols (New York: Nottingham Society, 1909), VII, 33. Originally published in the January 1889 issue of *The Nineteenth Century*, 'The Decay of Lying' was revised for *Intentions* (1891). *The Picture of Dorian Gray* was first published in the July 1890 issue of *Lippincott's*, then revised for book publication in 1891, when the Preface was added.

[3] Oscar Wilde, *The Picture of Dorian Gray*, ed. Michael Patrick Gillespie (New York: Norton, 2006), 9.

[4] Ibid., 3.

realized that Basil's claim that a portrait expresses the artist could be taken to legitimize a reading of *The Picture of Dorian Gray* as about its artist: as being an allegory of Wilde's own autobiography. In short, then, the novella represents a multiple disturbance in the notion of portraiture. Not only is the nature of its representation of the sitter in question. Its mimetic function is also extended, on the one hand to the artist, on the other, to the viewer or reader.

The implications extend beyond Wilde's career. Jacques Rancière has argued that Western art needs to be understood in terms of three different 'regimes' governing what can be seen, represented, or understood. He calls these the 'ethical' (deriving from the Platonic conception of ideal forms and of the ethical basis of society); the 'representative' (drawing on the Aristotelian notion of mimesis, and codified in the neoclassicism of the seventeenth and eighteenth centuries); and finally the 'aesthetic' regime, emerging with romanticism as the social and mimetic order breaks down in the revolutionary period at the end of the eighteenth century.[5] That period also saw the emergence of modern autobiography, in works by Rousseau, Goethe, and Wordsworth—and indeed the appearance of the term 'autobiography' itself, first recorded in 1797. My argument is that the late nineteenth century witnessed another phase of transformation (whether one views it as a final triumph of the aesthetic regime or a new revolution ushering in modernism and postmodernism is beyond the scope of this chapter)[6]—a transformation in which those forms of life writing which had emerged in their modern types a century before, themselves began to disintegrate.

One index to this *fin-de-siècle* reconfiguration of life writing is the way the meanings of the adjectives 'autobiographical' or 'autobiographic' alter during the late nineteenth century. As I have argued elsewhere, although the *Oxford English Dictionary* (*OED*)'s definitions—'Belonging to, connected with, autobiography'; or 'of the nature of autobiography'—seem unsurprising, it is curious how almost all the dictionary's historical examples refer to works of autobiography or memoir. Throughout most of the nineteenth century it seemed natural to use the adjectives of works that were autobiographies. For example, when Carlyle wrote in 1834 of 'these Autobiographical times of ours', he meant it had become widespread for people to write autobiography.[7]

---

[5] Jacques Rancière, *The Future of the Image*, trans. Gregory Elliott (London: Verso, 2007). Hal Foster gives a good analysis of Rancière's position in 'What's the Problem with Critical Art?', *London Review of Books (LRB)* 35/19 (10 October 2013), 14–15.

[6] What is at stake here is whether the two centuries and more covered by Rancière's 'aesthetic' regime manifest enough coherence and continuity to warrant a unitary description. See Rancière's *Aisthesis: Scenes from the Aesthetic Regime of Art*, trans. Zakir Paul (London: Verso, 2013), for a closer focus on the developments across this period; Max Saunders's *Self Impression: Life-Writing, Autobiografiction and the Forms of Modern Literature* (Oxford: Oxford University Press, 2010) argues for a discontinuity as new, fictionalizing forms of life writing emerge in the late nineteenth century, but for a concomitant continuity between these *fin-de-siècle* experiments and modernism.

[7] Thomas Carlyle, *Sartor Resartus*, ed. Kerry McSweeney and Peter Sabor (Oxford: Oxford University Press, 1987), 73.

We are more likely now to use the adjective of something that is precisely *not* an autobiography, but written in another form: a poem, a novel, a painting. The *OED*'s first example of this later use is by the American poet James Russell Lowell, writing in the 1870s.

> The first remark to be made upon the writings of Dante is that they are all (with the possible exception of the treatise *De Vulgari Eloquio*) autobiographic, and that all of them, including that, are parts of a mutually related system, of which the central point is the individuality and experience of the poet.[8]

Even the allegorical and theological vision of the *Divine Comedy* contribute to this vision of the 'autobiographic'. Lowell is clearly using the term against the grain, to cover works it would not normally cover: works which are not autobiographies. This is the modern sense we use when we call a fiction 'autobiographical'. That the first instance recorded in the *OED* is from 1876 indicates that it is a later sense, which only begins to be used towards the end of the century.

By the turn of the century, this trope of calling things autobiographical that were not autobiography had become widespread, and manifested in more extreme forms. Dante is at least a first-person presence in the *Divine Comedy*, whereas innovative thinkers and writers like Nietzsche and Wilde were now arguing that even the least personal of discursive modes could be read autobiographically. Nietzsche wrote in *Beyond Good and Evil* (1886) that all philosophy is 'the confession of its originator, and a species of involuntary and unconscious auto-biography'.[9] As with Wilde's 1891 argument that criticism too can be read as autobiographical, it appeared to have become possible to read almost *any* utterance in that way.

The remainder of this chapter constellates two other cases of disturbance in the concept of portraiture alongside Wilde's: those of Walter Pater and of 'Mark Rutherford'. In 1878 Pater published an autobiographical short story called 'Imaginary Portrait: the Child in the House', in *Macmillan's Magazine*. He felt it expressed the spirit of the age, calling it 'the modern expression of a modern outlook'; and that it represented for him a form of imaginative autobiography, calling it 'the germinating, original, source, specimen, of all my *imaginative* work'.[10] It was certainly a model for much of his subsequent fiction. In 1887 he published a volume entitled *Imaginary Portraits*, consisting of four other pieces: 'A Prince of Court Painters'; 'Denys L'Auxerrois'; 'Sebastian Van Storck'; and 'Duke Carl of Rosenmold'. 'Emerald Uthwart' was published separately, but has been appended by subsequent editors, as

---

[8] James Russell Lowell, 'Dante', in *Among my Books*, 2nd ser. (London: Sampson Low, Marston, Searle & Rivington, 1876), 26.

[9] Friedrich Nietzsche, *Beyond Good and Evil*, trans. Helen Zimmern (London and Edinburgh: T. N. Foulis, 1914), 10.

[10] Quoted by William E. Buckler, *Walter Pater: Three Major Texts* (New York and London: New York University Press, 1986), 39.

have also occasionally 'The Child in the House', 'An English Poet', 'Apollo in Picardy', and even the longer portrait 'Gaston de Latour'.[11]

The imaginary portrait was thus central to Pater's conception of his work. What did he mean by the phrase? The four studies in the volume *Imaginary Portraits* are slightly different from 'The Child in the House'. They are cast as biographical studies, histories of figures who might have existed but just happened not to. As with Wilde's *Picture of Dorian Gray*, they inhabit the world of artists. In some ways they are a projection of Pater's response to the art of, say, the Flemish Golden Age ('Sebastian Van Storck') or of Watteau ('A Prince of Court Painters'). There is certainly an autobiographical reference in the latter, which focuses on Watteau's pupil, the Flemish painter Jean Baptiste Pater, 'whom the author regarded as his ancestor'.[12] In 'The Child in the House', though the narrative machinery goes through the motions of setting up the core narrative as other than autobiographical— an unnamed narrator tells the story of Florian Deleal, whose meeting someone on a walk sparks a dream about his childhood—the inwardness and authority of the dream narrative cannot but make us feel that Pater is recounting at least elements from his own memories of childhood. But in either of the two formats Pater adopts, the effect is to loosen the bond in portraiture between the picture and referential subject.

The Imaginary Portrait, that is, takes the genre which places the mimesis of individuality at its core—as opposed, say, to the portrayal of idealized or allegorized types in much Renaissance or neoclassical portraiture. It claims a paradoxical status. The work will be a portrait in form; but not of a sitter who existed objectively in the world. The Musée Fabre in Montpellier contains a number of portraits of the patron Alfred Bruyas. The most famous is the central figure in Courbet's masterpiece 'The Meeting', otherwise known as 'Bonjour Monsieur Courbet'. The portraits capture Bruyas at different ages, in different outfits, striking different poses in different places, and wearing different lengths and bushinesses of patriarchal beard. His marked cheekbones, aquiline nose, and fairly long red hair make him a striking figure, instantly recognizable across these differences of fashion and artistic style. The Imaginary Portrait dispenses with such real resemblance. Its portrait qualities require it to read as if it did, or could, refer to just such a specific individual. But any such reference is imaginary. At first sight it has some similarity to the situation of a Renaissance or neoclassical portrait of a religious or mythological subject. A picture of the virgin and child, or of Perseus, ostensibly claims a likeness to a person the

[11] 'Emerald Uthwart' was first published in the *New Review* 6 (1892), 708–22, and 7 (1892), 42–54; and included (together with 'The Child in the House' and 'Diaphaneitè') in *Miscellaneous Studies*, ed. Charles Shadwell (London: Macmillan, 1895). There was a separate publication with the subtitle *An Imaginary Portrait* (Portland, ME: Thomas B. Mosher, 1899). See for example *Imaginary Portraits by Walter Pater: A New Collection*, ed. Eugene J. Brzenk (New York, Evanston, IL and London: Harper and Row, 1964).

[12] Laurel Brake, Oxford *Dictionary of National Biography* (*DNB*) entry for Walter Pater.

painter cannot possibly have seen. At the same time, there is also probably an actual likeness, but to another person, whose identity is generally kept secret: that of the artist's model. The Paterian Imaginary Portrait suspends both these forms of likeness, substituting the possibility of autobiographical resemblance instead.

Many of these issues had been pressing in the mid-nineteenth century; nowhere more so than in Browning's poems about Renaissance artists such as 'Fra Lippo Lippi', who is piously reprimanded by his religious superiors:

> Your business is to paint the souls of men—
> …
> Give us no more of body than shows soul.
> Here's Giotto, with his Saint a-praising God!
> That sets you praising—why not stop with him?
> Why put all thoughts of praise out of our heads
> With wonder at lines, colours, and what not?
> Paint the soul, never mind the legs and arms!
> Rub all out, try at it a second time.
> Oh, that white smallish female with the breasts,
> She's just my niece… Herodias, I would say,—
> Who went and danced and got men's heads cut off…[13]

But Browning's *Men and Women* (1855) are often (as here) representations of actual historical individuals, a circumstance that gives such musings on the force of verisimilitude an added force. What is more, in its versification and characteristic verbal pyrotechnics, the style is unmistakably always Browning's, and the work unmistakeably his poem rather than Lippi's. There is no attempt to imitate an actual work of life writing. Browning knew his Vasari, and subsequent art historical scholarship. A poem like 'Fra Lippo Lippi' draws on the anecdotes and legends surrounding the painter's life. But the core of the poem is evidently Browning's riff on the nature of the paintings, and his imagining what their painter might have thought, felt, and done. The *portrait*, that is, is an imaginary one, in the sense of being the poet's act of imagination. But the *subject* is not.

Pater tells us of Florian Deleal:

> And it happened that this accident of his dream was just the thing needed for the beginning of a certain design he then had in view, the noting, namely, of some things in the story of his spirit—in that process of brain-building by which we are, each one of us, what we are.[14]

This 'story of his spirit' may seem to have affinities with the concept in Browning's poem of painting the soul. But whereas Fra Lippo Lippi's monks are disturbed by his too realistic evocations of the flesh, and want his pictures to express immaterial

---

[13] John Woolford, Daniel Karlin, and Joseph Phelan (eds), *The Poems of Browning*, 4 vols (London: Longman, 1991-), III, 540–1.

[14] Pater, 'The Child in the House', *Miscellaneous Studies*, 148.

things, in Florian's case, the 'brain-building' has been affected by the material of the house itself: its architectural 'design' and physical bricks-and-mortar building. Or rather, it has been affected by Florian's *impressions* of the house and its setting. For Pater is committed to an aesthetic of impressionism.[15] This has a paradoxical effect of, on the one hand, referring something as nebulous as subjectivity back to tangible material realities that have helped form it, such as domestic architecture; and, on the other, dispersing such apparent solidities themselves into an equally nebulous field of impressions. Florian's recollections of the top storey are representative of this combination of material specificity and impressionist tenuity:

> And on the top of the house, above the large attic, where the white mice ran in the twilight—an infinite, unexplored wonderland of childish treasures, glass beads, empty scent-bottles still sweet, thrum of coloured silks, among its lumber—a flat space of roof, railed round, gave a view of the neighbouring steeples; for the house, as I said, stood near a great city, which sent up heavenwards, over the twisting weather-vanes, not seldom, its beds of rolling cloud and smoke, touched with storm or sunshine. But the child of whom I am writing did not hate the fog because of the crimson lights which fell from it sometimes upon the chimneys, and the whites which gleamed through its openings, on summer mornings, on turret or pavement.[16]

The effect of both moves is a radical reconceptualization of the self. Rather than possessing the continuous identity of a 'soul' or a 'character'—which may be stable, or, if it changes, does so with a logic and intelligibility, the Paterian self is a dynamic process, subject to the advancing and receding of its contingent impressions. The effect on life writing is to leave the self deliberately unspecified. It is clear Florian is, like Pater, a writer, and that his formative memories are memories of what made him an artist. Clear too is the kind of artist—impressionist—he is. But the rest of his life is left all but un-sketched. We know nothing of his appearance, his body, its desires, his relationships or lack of them, his wealth, or even where he has lived since. The house of his memories, like his sensibility, seems middle class. But we would be hard pressed to recognize him if we ever met him in that milieu. As he put it in his most celebrated piece of writing, the Conclusion to *The Renaissance*:

> Experience, already reduced to a group of impressions, is ringed round for each one of us by that thick wall of personality through which no real voice has ever pierced on its way to us, or from us to that which we can only conjecture to be without. Every one of those impressions is the impression of the individual in his isolation, each mind keeping as a solitary prisoner its own dream of a world. Analysis goes a step farther still, and assures us that those impressions of the individual mind to which, for each one of us, experience dwindles down, are in perpetual flight...

---

[15] See Jesse Matz, *Literary Impressionism and Modernist Aesthetics* (Cambridge: Cambridge University Press, 2001), ch. 2, 53–78; Saunders, *Self Impression*, ch. 1, 29–70.

[16] Pater, 'The Child in the House', 149–50.

It is with this movement, with the passage and dissolution of impressions, images, sensations, that analysis leaves off—that continual vanishing away, that strange, perpetual weaving and unweaving of ourselves.[17]

Again, while that 'thick wall of personality' at first appears to pose the self as substantial and solid, it turns out to be a prison or a shell, within which the actual self is constantly being woven and unwoven. Such a vision of subjectivity is frighteningly destabilizing, especially to religious or empiricist sensibilities, in that image of 'unweaving'. But it also celebrates—in the image of 'weaving'—the self conceived as a dynamic process of continual creativity. A new notion of the self such as this requires new modes of auto/biography. The Imaginary Portrait seemed to provide Pater with an appropriate form to express his sense of subjectivity. The success of the portraiture was to be gauged not by external resemblance, but by the act of imagination. It is not hard to see why such a break with a realist verisimilitude appealed to the younger generation of emerging modernists. When W. B. Yeats edited *The Oxford Book of Modern Verse: 1892-1935*, he opened the selection—with scant regard for chronology, given that it had first been published in 1869—with an excerpt from Pater's chapter on Leonardo, audaciously re-lineated as if it were blank verse:

Mona Lisa

She is older than the rocks among which she sits;
Like the vampire,
She has been dead many times,
And learned the secrets of the grave;
And has been a diver in deep seas,
And keeps their fallen day about her;
And trafficked for strange webs with Eastern merchants;
And, as Leda,
Was the mother of Helen of Troy,
And, as Saint Anne,
Was[18] the mother of Mary;
And all this has been to her but as the sound of lyres and flutes,
And lives
Only in the delicacy
With which it has moulded the changing lineaments,
And tinged the eyelids and the hands.[19]

Yeats's rearrangement certainly brings out strikingly Pater's incantatory compound syntax with its series of rolling 'And's. But he cuts the quotation just before the two

---

[17] Walter Pater, 'Conclusion', *The Renaissance: Studies in Art and Poetry: The 1893 Text*, ed. Donald L. Hill (Berkeley, CA: University of California Press, 1980), 187–8.

[18] This second 'Was' is Yeats's interpolation: Pater, *The Renaissance*, 99.

[19] See Barrie Bullen, 'Walter Pater's "Renaissance" and Leonardo da Vinci's Reputation in the Nineteenth Century', *Modern Language Review* 74/2 (April 1979), 268. W. B. Yeats (ed.), *The Oxford Book of Modern Verse* (Oxford: Clarendon Press, 1936), 1.

sentences (more discursive, less verse-like) in which Pater stands back, and comments on the curious historical fantasy that licences this flowing across and between history, myth, and legend.

> The fancy of a perpetual life, sweeping together ten thousand experiences, is an old one; and modern philosophy has conceived the idea of humanity as wrought upon by, and summing up in itself, all modes of thought and life. Certainly Lady Lisa might stand as the embodiment of the old fancy.

This imagines a self woven from the many experiences of many lives across culture, in a way comparable to how the 'Conclusion' or 'The Child in the House' imagines a self woven from the many experiences of a single life. *Mona Lisa*, that is, represents for Pater an Imaginary Portrait writ large (or, as a less sympathetic critic might have it, he attempts to turn Leonardo's actual portrait into an imaginary one). Indeed, this passage is an imaginary portrait of a portrait itself long held to be mysterious. It is perhaps in this sense that Pater saw the Imaginary Portrait as the source of all his imaginative work. Writing 'The Child in the House' may have made him realize that what he had been writing in the chapters on artists in *The Renaissance* had already been, to an extent, imaginary portraits. True, the artists were real enough; but his approach to their imaginations through his own imaginary ruminations on their art signalled a departure from conventional biographical portraiture as from conventional art history. The year *Studies in the History of the Renaissance* first appeared, 1873, was also the year that Monet, Renoir, Pissarro, Sisley, Cezanne, and Degas organized the anonymous society of artists that would later take the name of Impressionists. Pater was more prescient than he could have known when, standing back from his impressionist reimagining of Leonardo's Renaissance secular icon, added that the Mona Lisa could equally stand as 'the symbol of the modern idea'. This was the remark that doubtless gave Yeats the idea to co-opt the passage as a precursor of what was 'modern' in verse; but it may also remind us of Pater's belief that his first Imaginary Portrait was 'the modern expression of a modern outlook'.

Pater's Imaginary Portraits are both biographical and autobiographical, then, but they are so in a new, impressionist way. And this novelty corresponds to radical shifts in the paradigms of selfhood, and where its traces can be deciphered. The turn of the century is also, famously, the period of the emergence of psychoanalysis. The tracing of unconscious or concealed or displaced autobiography in apparently non-autobiographical works is analogous to the Freudian project of tracing the unconscious in the apparently incoherent or insignificant material of dreams or slips. Pater's fantasia on *Mona Lisa* is not exactly free association, but shares something of that method's associative and accumulative process. The crucial point is that it welcomes fantasy into life writing, as Freud was to focus on dream, daydream, and fantasy in his metapsychology. In the less autobiographical Imaginary Portraits written after 'The Child in the House', Pater overtly welcomes fictionality into the narrative method as well. The notion of 'self expression' was evidently undergoing a paradigm shift during this period, as the Romantic aspiration to the possibility of full self-expression gives way to an aesthetic whereby the 'inner life' is understood as that which cannot be expressed directly, but only obliquely, discontinuously, through fragmentation, displacement, and condensation.

A perceptive young critic noticed the significance of this new form of hybridity, combining life writing and fiction. Stephen Reynolds is best known for his auto/ biographical book *A Poor Man's House* (1908), describing the period after he left literary London to live with struggling Devon fishermen. This has been received as a classic of labour history, and with justice. Yet a brilliant essay Reynolds published two years earlier suggests it might also have been something formally more experimental. This brief essay, titled with just the single portmanteau word 'Autobiografiction', argues for the recent development of a new hybrid mixing auto- biography, fiction, and the essay.[20] Reynolds distinguishes autobiografiction from on the one hand 'autobiographical fiction' (which he says is 'mainly reserved for fiction with a good deal of the writer's own life in it'), and on the other, 'those lapses from fact which occur in most autobiographies' (whether as a result of carelessness or mendacity he does not say). He goes on to define autobiografiction as 'a record of real spiritual experiences strung on a credible but more or less fictitious autobio- graphical narrative'—'spiritual experience' having been described, impressionisti- cally, as 'anything that reacts strongly on the mind . . . any emotion, beautiful thing, work of art, sorrow, religion, or love, which intensifies a man's existence'. Autobiografiction thus takes the *form* of an autobiographical narrative. But its con- tent is a paradoxical mixture of fictionalized narrative and psychological truth. Reynolds does not mention Pater, whose Imaginary Portraits are not autobiograph- ical enough in form to fit his definition. Nonetheless, he assembles a group of works experimenting with fictionalized autobiographical forms: three books then pub- lished anonymously, but later owned by A. C. Benson (*The House of Quiet: An Autobiography*, 1904; *The Thread of Gold*, 1905; and *The Upton Letters*, 1905); George Gissing's *The Private Papers of Henry Ryecroft* (1903); and, the earliest and most intriguing, *The Autobiography of Mark Rutherford, Dissenting Minister* (1881).

That title's mode of presentation may give us pause. Not just *Autobiography*, like John Stuart Mill's; or *The Autobiography*, like Margaret Thatcher's; not attributed to Mark Rutherford, figuring as author named above or below the title on the title page: as in 'Mark Rutherford: *Autobiography*'. The inclusion of the putative author's name as part of the title has precedents, especially for works not published by the authors themselves, but seen through the press posthumously, by family or friends— as with *The Autobiography of Benjamin Franklin*, for example. *The Autobiography of Mark Rutherford* appears to be such a volume, offered as 'Edited by his Friend,

---

[20] Stephen Reynolds, 'Autobiografiction', *Speaker* 15/366 (6 October 1906), 28, 30. For a more detailed account of the essay, and a case for its wider significance, see Saunders, *Self Impression*.

Reuben Shapcott'. It ends with an editorial note: 'Thus far goes the manuscript which I have in my possession. I know that there is more of it, but all my search for it has been in vain. Possibly some day I may be able to recover it.'[21] Yet the very paratextual material that seeks to assure us this is a genuine autobiography, rescued by a friend who can vouch for its authenticity and sincerity, is as likely to arouse suspicion as to reassure. The trope of the acquired manuscript, authenticated by paratexts, is as old as the English novel, and the subterfuge of the more fantastical of them, such as *Gulliver's Travels*.

According to the reviews quoted in an appendix to the third edition of 1889, the *Autobiography* was widely acclaimed as a non-fictional account of nonconformist religious doubt. With the publication of the sequel, *Mark Rutherford's Deliverance*, in 1885, again 'Edited by his Friend, Reuben Shapcott', reviewers were less certain. William Dean Howells, for example, assessing both volumes for *Harper's Magazine*, said the books 'may yet mark a new era in English fiction', only to add: 'We hardly know, indeed, whether to call them fiction, they carry so deep a sense of truthfulness . . .'.[22] He describes them as 'by an unknown hand'. Howells was clearly unaware that, two years earlier, the *Westminster Review* had revealed the identity of the author as being not Mark Rutherford, but William Hale White (1831–1913).[23] In fact White had been on the staff of the magazine. As Valentine Cunningham explains:

> John Chapman, 'editor' of the radical *Westminster Review* gave him work as a subscription tout and put him up in his raffish ménage at 142 The Strand. A momentous fellow lodger was the woman who actually ran the paper, Marian Evans, not yet the novelist known as George Eliot. Ever after Hale White...made her the type of all the sparky out-of-reach females who haunt the men of his stories.[24]

Nothing in the *Autobiography* may strike modern readers as requiring the protection of a fictionalized *nom de plume*; though its account of doubt and nervous breakdown certainly intimates anxieties customarily kept private before the First World War. Yet both Mark Rutherford and Reuben Shapcott are evidently fictional disguises. The narrative too has undergone a marked degree of fictionalization.[25]

---

[21] *The Autobiography of Mark Rutherford, Dissenting Minister* (London: Trübner, 1881), 176.

[22] *The Autobiography of Mark Rutherford and Mark Rutherford's Deliverance* (London: Trübner, 1889), 327–8. Howells's review (not attributed in the third edition of the *Autobiography*) is from his column 'The Editor's Study': 'Two Remarkable Examples of Sincerity in Fiction', *Harper's* 72 (1886), 485–6.

[23] Valentine Cunningham, Oxford *DNB* entry for Hale White. W. Robertson Nicoll, 'Memories of Mark Rutherford', in *A Bookman's Letters* (London: Hodder and Stoughton, 1913), 366–7, quotes from the *Westminster*: 'Not long ago Mr. Hale White published a remarkable little book, which attracted very much less attention than it deserved, *The Autobiography of Mark Rutherford, Dissenting Minister*'.

[24] Cunningham, Oxford *DNB* entry for Hale White. Also see Rosemary Ashton, *142 Strand: A Radical Address in Victorian London* (London: Chatto & Windus, 2006), 168–73.

[25] See Charles Swann, 'Autobiografiction: Problems with Autobiographical Fictions and Fictional Autobiographies. Mark Rutherford's Autobiography and Deliverance and Others', *Modern Language Review* 96/1 (2001), 21–37.

Hale White was not exactly a 'Dissenting Minister', for example, but had been expelled from theological college in 1851 for holding 'unsafe' views about scriptural authority, and entered the Civil Service instead when he was twenty-three (though he did sometimes preach in nonconformist chapels in the 1850s).[26] As his biographer C. Macdonald Maclean writes, 'While the first two books cannot be regarded as a "Confessions", still less can they be regarded as factual autobiography.'[27] Nonetheless, like many of its readers, she accords it truth value in terms remarkably similar to Reynolds's: 'Fictional though many of the events be, the delineation of the growth of a human soul is as faithful as that given in *The Prelude*.'[28] Such a claim may itself be too reassuring to reassure. She cannot possibly know the fidelity of something so private that by definition we only have the narrator's own word for it. But the attempt to reassure may bespeak an anxiety that, once you admit fictionalization to psychological confession, the reliability of the entire narrative comes under question.

When the two volumes of the *Autobiography* were combined into one, for the second edition of 1888, Hale White added a short narrative to the two chapters that had previously been appended to the *Deliverance*. The two chapters, 'Notes on the Book of Job' and 'Principles', clearly supplement the spiritual questions of the autobiography. The new addition is very different, and reinforces the idea of Hale White as another case of a writer exploring the problematics of portraiture, resemblance, identity, and fictionality in this period of ferment in auto/biographical forms. It is titled 'A Mysterious Portrait', and is more oblique in relation to the volume, resembling a short story.

It is cast as a reminiscence about a bachelor friend, who tells Rutherford the story of a portrait on his study wall of 'a singularly lovely woman'.[29] The bachelor has had two mysterious encounters with her. On both occasions she has disappeared before he can speak to her, in circumstances that suggest she might be a figment of his imagination. His obsession with what he calls his 'spectral friend—if spectre she was' comes to dominate his existence, and prevents him from further involvement with any other or actual woman.[30] Then he visits the Academy in London, and is amazed to find exhibited there a drawing of her face. He tracks down the artist to try to discover her identity. When he asks who sat for it, the artist replies: 'Nobody...it was a mere fancy sketch.'[31] The story can be seen as engaging with the idea of the Imaginary Portrait in several ways, the most obvious ones being the way

---

[26] The words 'Dissenting Minister' were silently removed from the title-page of the second edition of 1888.

[27] C. Macdonald Maclean, *Mark Rutherford: A Biography of William Hale White* (London: Macdonald, 1955), 276.

[28] Ibid., 276, 278.

[29] 'A Mysterious Portrait', in *The Autobiography of Mark Rutherford and Mark Rutherford's Deliverance* (London: Trübner & Co., 1888), 313.

[30] Ibid., 321.   [31] Ibid., 322.

in which both the bachelor and the artist can be said to have created one; the artist in his picture, the bachelor (possibly) in his head. That Hale White added it to the *Autobiography* the year after Pater's volume of *Imaginary Portraits* appeared may thus be more than coincidence.

Like a number of key autobiographical works from the long *fin de siècle*—Butler's *The Way of All Flesh*, Gosse's *Father and Son*, Joyce's *Portrait of the Artist*—*The Autobiography of Mark Rutherford* is a specific form of *Bildungsroman* charting the protagonist's move from the spiritual to the aesthetic life. One can view 'A Mysterious Portrait' as added for documentary or illustrative purposes, an example of his 'literary remains' which enables us to judge for ourselves the value of his choice of the artistic over the religious life. Yet from another point of view, its addition is more disturbing to the work's ontology.

At first it appears to be supplementing the *Autobiography* with more autobiographical material: a reminiscence of one of the author's friends. But as it becomes more fanciful and metaphysical it feels more like fiction, thus completing Reynolds's trio of autobiography, essay, and fiction—though ostensibly as a mixture of separate genres rather than a compound or hybrid. It also juxtaposes visual portraiture with verbal. However, the juxtaposition of the fictional with the autobiographical narrative raises a series of questions about the difference between the two kinds of narrative, and whether we can differentiate them. The title phrase—'mysterious portrait'—acquires an ambiguity within the tale. The conclusion seems to locate it as the actual drawing of an imaginary woman. But (as suggested) it could equally refer to the portrait in his imagination. Once we are alerted to this uncertainty we see how (as with Pater's examples) the portrait reflects back on the portraitist. The bachelor's possible imagining of the woman then becomes a portrait *of* his imagination. But, by the same token, the story is a portrait in words by Mark Rutherford of his friend; and so can be read, equally, as the self-portrait of *his*, Rutherford's, imagination. At this point, the ambiguity of reference can no longer be contained within the tale. It becomes a meta-narrative comment on the book which contains it. For, by the same token again, Rutherford's autobiography is offered to us as a picture of Rutherford, 'edited by his friend', Reuben Shapcott. The final ironic possibility offered by the tale is that Mark Rutherford's autobiography is itself a mysterious portrait. Which it is, precisely, since it is a compelling likeness of a person who didn't quite exist—one which, nevertheless, does shed light on the imagination of its real author too, William Hale White.

Autobiografiction such as this—or Reynolds's other examples by Gissing or Benson—is not just autobiographical fiction, but 'meta-autobiographic': fiction about autobiography. It appears akin to what Linda Hutcheon has famously defined as 'historiographic metafiction', of which she remarks: 'the very process of turning events into facts through the interpretation of archival evidence is shown to be a process of turning the traces of the past (our only access to those events today) into historical representation.'[32] When autobiografiction thematizes life writing documents—diaries, letters, essays, 'private papers', and the like—it might be labelled as 'autobiographic metafiction', which focuses on representations of individual portraits and life stories rather than on representations of more public historical upheavals. When Serge Doubrovsky coined the term 'autofiction' in *Fils* (1977), it was taken to be an exclusively postmodern hybrid. But, as the proponents of imaginary portraits and autobiografiction show, versions of it had appeared at least a hundred years earlier.

FURTHER READING

Beaujour, Michel. *Poetics of the Literary Self-Portrait*, trans. Yara Milos (New York: New York University Press, 1991).

Bizzotto, Elisa. 'The Imaginary Portrait: Pater's Contribution to a Literary Genre', in Laurel Brake, Lesley Higgins, and Carolyn Williams (eds), *Walter Pater: Transparencies of Desire* (Greensboro, NC: ELT Press, 2002), 213–23.

Eakin, Paul John. *Fictions in Autobiography: Studies in the Art of Self-Invention* (Princeton, NJ: Princeton University Press, 1985).

Jolly, Margareta (ed.). *Encyclopedia of Life Writing: Autobiographical and Biographical Forms*, 2 vols (London and Chicago, IL: Fitzroy Dearborn, 2002).

Lee, Hermione. *Biography: A Very Short Introduction* (Oxford: Oxford University Press, 2009).

Lejeune, Philippe. *On Autobiography*, ed. Paul John Eakin, trans. Katherine Leary (Minneapolis, MN: University of Minnesota Press, 1989).

Marcus, Laura. *Auto/biographical Discourses* (Manchester: Manchester University Press, 1994).

Matz, Jesse. *Literary Impressionism and Modernist Aesthetics* (Cambridge: Cambridge University Press, 2001).

Nalbantian, Suzanne. *Aesthetic Autobiography: From Life to Art in Marcel Proust, James Joyce, Virginia Woolf and Anaïs Nin* (New York: St Martin's Press, 1997).

Sanders, Valerie. 'Victorian Life Writing', *Literature Compass* 1/1 (2004), 1–17.

Saunders, Max. *Self Impression: Life-Writing, Autobiografiction and the Forms of Modern Literature* (Oxford: Oxford University Press, 2010).

Smith, Sidonie and Julia Watson. *Reading Autobiography: A Guide for Interpreting Life Narratives*, 2nd rev. edn (Minneapolis, MN: University of Minnesota Press, 2010).

Taylor, Charles. *Sources of the Self: The Making of the Modern Identity* (Cambridge: Cambridge University Press, 1989).

---

[32] Linda Hutcheon, *The Politics of Postmodernism* (London: Routledge, 1989), 57.

CHAPTER 33

JOURNALISM AND PERIODICAL CULTURE

FAITH BINCKES

In May 1887, Matthew Arnold published 'Up To Easter' in *The Nineteenth Century*. It was a substantial piece that dealt largely with 'Gladstone's dangerous plan of Home Rule' for Ireland.[1] In it, Arnold used the phrase the 'new journalism' to refer to another set of developments, in the modern media:

> We have had opportunities of observing a new journalism which a clever and energetic man has lately invented. It has much to recommend it; it is full of ability, novelty, variety, sensation, sympathy, generous instincts; its one great fault is that it is *feather-brained*. It throws out assertions at a venture because it wishes them true; does not correct either them or itself, if they are false; and to get at the state of things as they truly are seems to feel no concern whatever. Well, the democracy, with abundance of life, movement, sympathy, good instincts, is disposed to be, like this journalism, feather-brained; just as the upper class is disposed to be selfish in its politics, and the middle class narrow.[2]

Arnold's dismissal of the 'set of typographical and textual innovations that transformed the press' was explicitly connected to the changing conditions of the modern state, and to the association between that journalism and a newly enfranchised 'democracy'.[3] His praise of both was clearly double-edged, serving in part to accentuate their mutual failings. Nonetheless, 'Up To Easter' also registered Arnold's awareness that his authority resulted from, but was also challenged by, his age. 'As

---

[1] Matthew Arnold, 'Up To Easter', *Nineteenth Century* 21/123 (May 1887), 636.

[2] Ibid., 638.

[3] James Mussell, 'The New Journalism', in Laurel Brake, Marysa Demoor, and Margaret Beetham (eds), *The Dictionary of Nineteenth-Century Journalism:In Great Britain and Ireland* (London: British Library, 2009), 443. For a brief summary of this exchange, see Richard Salmon, *Henry James and the Culture of Publicity* (Cambridge: Cambridge University Press, 1997), 117–19; Laurel Brake, 'Journalism and Modernism Continued: The Case of W. T. Stead', in Ann Ardis and Patrick Collier (eds), *Transatlantic Print Culture, 1880–1940: Emerging Media, Emerging Modernisms* (Basingstoke: Palgrave Macmillan, 2008), 167–81.

I grow old, and profit, I hope, by the lessons of experience', he wrote, addressing himself to readers as one who 'is too old, of habits and tastes too formed, to wish to enter the House of Commons even if he could.'[4]

Opposing the waning power of the mid-Victorian sage stood the 'clever and energetic man' credited with the invention of this 'new journalism'—the pioneering investigative journalist, editor, and proprietor W. T. Stead. Stead had already used the phrase a year earlier, in a similarly lengthy article entitled 'The Future of Journalism', published in the *Contemporary Review* in November 1886. In this piece, he had attacked (to borrow Arnold's terms) the 'narrow' and 'self-interested' world of metropolitan papers, and the phony authority of their impersonal tone. In their place, he imagined a network comprising 'peripatetic apostles of the new journalism', operating as commercial travellers in information and opinion.[5] They would be men and women capable of accurately taking the temperature of 'the Demos' right across the country, and of feeding it back to a fourth estate unafraid of holding individuals, institutions, and governments to account. But Stead, like Arnold, understood the mechanisms of cultural authority. After the publication of 'Up To Easter', it was Stead who publicized Arnold's most negative summary of 'the new journalism' as *'feather-brained'*. Such re-contextualization appropriated Arnold's kudos, but also allowed Stead to call its patrician assumptions into question.[6] This dance between new and old, modernity and tradition, became something of a tradition in itself.

Another example was T. P. O'Connor's 'The New Journalism', published in *The New Review* in October 1889.[7] O'Connor argued that the kind of writing Arnold had criticized—lively and peppered with personal observations—had been the signature of notable historians such as Green, Macaulay, and Carlyle. The elements deemed worryingly 'new' in 'the new journalism' would be considered respectable and traditional if the cheap, large-circulation periodical were exchanged for a different form of print, and the name of a journalist was replaced by that of a canonical author. 'I should very much like to have been able to get the opinion of these three historians on the controversy between the New and the Old Journalism', O'Connor remarked.[8] In other words, the novelty of these developments was relative, not absolute, just as a figure Arnold considered a 'dangerous' revolutionary—Charles Stewart Parnell—was for O'Connor a distinguished parliamentarian, who might be set alongside Disraeli.

---

[4] Arnold, 'Up to Easter', 629–30.

[5] W. T. Stead, 'The Future of Journalism', *Contemporary Review* 50 (November 1886), 677.

[6] For an account of Stead's early career, and details of his management of Arnold's article, see Tony Nicholson, 'The Provincial Stead', in Laurel Brake, Ed King, Roger Luckhurst, and James Mussell (eds), *W. T. Stead: Newspaper Revolutionary* (London: The British Library, 2012).

[7] T. P. O'Connor, 'The New Journalism', *New Review* 1/5 (October 1889), 423–34.

[8] Ibid., 427.

This snapshot from the extensive debates surrounding 'the new journalism' offers a glimpse into the actual and symbolic significance of journalism and periodical culture towards the close of the nineteenth century and into the opening of the twentieth. In a period fascinated by newness—'the new journalism', 'the new woman', 'the new imperialism', and of course 'modernism'—periodicals revealed the tensions at work in the concept itself, and in their own identification with it. As it 'subtends modernity itself', Michael North has argued, yet is resistant to any solid definition, 'newness' or 'novelty' stands as both 'an indispensable concept and a serious problem'. Moreover, periodicals embody what North describes as a paradoxical 'tradition of the new', managing to be both 'routine' and 'revolutionary'.[9] Due to their processes of production and distribution, periodicals always run with the tide, cementing the relationship between the 'new' and 'news'—what is happening 'now'. But in another sense, they demonstrate the relativity of the term. 'New' not only directs the attention to an endlessly receding horizon, it indicates different, successive versions, reinventions, and variations upon a theme. The popularity of 'new' as a prefix in periodical titles stands as one of the most obvious signs of this contrary motion, which propels readers and producers into an immediate present while retaining them within frameworks familiar from the past.[10] Archibald Grove's *The New Review*, the venue for O'Connor's 'The New Journalism', is a good case in point. On one hand, the periodical was appropriately new, having been initiated in January of that year, 1889. On the other, it was the third publication titled *The New Review* to have been published in the United Kingdom that century, predecessors having appeared in 1813 and 1863.

It could be argued then, that in the years between 1880 and 1920, periodicals both told the story and were the story. Alongside the 'new journalism', with its connections to a more open and perhaps more populist press, ran the seemingly rarefied world of literary and artistic reviews and so-called 'little magazines'. With far smaller circulations, these publications advertised themselves as ideal venues for younger or more challenging writers and artists, whose work might not be considered acceptable for wider public consumption. The most influential of these were *The Yellow Book* (1894–7) and *The Savoy* (1896), very distinctive publications that shared the immediately identifiable visual signature of Aubrey Beardsley. But although this species of text was set up in opposition to the emerging mainstream, the points of contact between the two have been mapped in some detail.[11] *The Savoy*, edited by Arthur Symons, also attacked the literary and the social status quo, publishing George Bernard Shaw, Havelock Ellis, and Edward Carpenter as well as Yeats, Ernest Dowson, Paul Verlaine, Beardsley, and his own writing. Just as Stead

---

[9] Michael North, *Novelty: A History of The New* (Chicago, IL: Chicago University Press, 2013), 5, 9.

[10] Adrian Caesar, 'A Model for Myth-Breaking', in David Carter (ed.), *Outside the Book: Contemporary Essays on Literary Periodicals* (Sydney, NSW: Local Consumption Publications, 1991), 247.

[11] See, for instance, Peter McDonald, *British Literary Culture and Publishing Practice, 1880–1914* (Cambridge: Cambridge University Press, 1997).

publicized Arnold's criticism of his 'feather-brained' practices, so Symons publicized the more hostile elements of *The Savoy*'s reception. In an 'Editorial Note' to the second number he wrote: 'I wish to thank the critics of the press for the flattering reception which they have given to No. I. That reception has been none the less flattering because it has been for the most part unfavourable.'[12] These strategies, and their ironies, were equally central to the role periodicals played in the modernist drive to 'make it new'. In 2010 Robert Scholes and Cliff Wulfman could confidently assert that 'modernism began in the magazines'.[13] However, just as modernists self-consciously engaged with, and reworked, a range of texts and traditions, so periodical scholars have long acknowledged the debt modernist magazines owed to their *fin-de-siècle* forebears.[14]

Arnold's backhanded compliment on the 'novelty', 'variety', and 'sensation' of the new journalism is reminiscent of other ambivalent accounts of modernity from the turn of the nineteenth century: the cacophonous, cosmopolitan, fast-moving modern city, for instance. In 1893, Henri de Blowitz accused journalism of producing 'in the public mind a condition of uncertain kaleidoscopic eclecticism'.[15] And, despite the valiant efforts of over a century of indexing and cataloguing, the feeling that periodical texts are as disorientating as they are exciting does not seem to have changed as much as we might expect. In 1989, Linda Hughes pondered whether chaos theory, with its mixture of pattern and randomness, could help provide a model for the analytical challenges periodicals presented.[16] In 2006, Sean Latham and Robert Scholes's article 'The Rise of Periodical Studies' observed that magazines and newspapers 'create often surprising and even bewildering points of contact between disparate areas of human activity'.[17] When reviewing the first volume of the *Oxford Critical and Cultural History of Modernist Magazines* in 2010, Melba Cuddy-Keane congratulated the volume's editors for 'reconstructing this vibrant but unruly part of literary history'.[18] In this sense, it is difficult to separate the impact of the periodical press upon ideas of unruly and bewildering novelty from the way in which conditioned responses to newness shaped—and perhaps continue to shape—perceptions of periodicals as media. Since the turn of the twenty-first

---

[12] Arthur Symons, 'Editorial Note', *Savoy* 1/2 (April 1896), n. p.

[13] Robert Scholes and Cliff Wulfman, *Modernism in the Magazines: An Introduction* (New Haven, CT: Yale University Press, 2010), 73.

[14] For a summary of this scholarship, and a reading of one early modernist magazine's engagement with *fin-de-siècle* periodical traditions, see Faith Binckes, *Modernism, Magazines and the British Avant-Garde* (Oxford: Oxford University Press, 2010), 46–55.

[15] Henri de Blowitz, 'Journalism as a Profession', *Contemporary Review* 63 (January 1893), 39.

[16] Linda K Hughes, 'Turbulence in the "Golden Stream": Chaos Theory and the Study of Periodicals', *Victorian Periodicals Review* 22/3 (Fall 1989), 117–25.

[17] Sean Latham and Robert Scholes, 'The Rise of Periodical Studies', *Publications of the Modern Languages Association of America (PMLA)* 121/2 (March 2006), 528.

[18] Melba Cuddy-Keane, 'The Oxford Critical and Cultural History of Modernist Magazines: Vol. I', *Review of English Studies* 61/249 (2010), 323.

century, scholars have also considered the impact of another form of 'new media' on the periodical field of the late nineteenth and early twentieth centuries, as a series of digitization projects have revolutionized its study. But, in some cases, these 'new media' projects have served to re-illuminate questions that were familiar to producers and consumers of periodicals the first time around, connecting the period 1880–1920 back to our own critical moment. This chapter aims to maintain a similar double focus, exploring two very different publications and what they might tell us about both turn-of-the-century 'novelty' and its relationship to our own 'new periodical studies'.

My first example is *Le Petit Journal des Refusées*, published in California in 1896. It both conformed to and reinvented one of the standard narratives of periodical scholarship, demonstrating the widespread influence of late nineteenth-century aesthetic magazines, such as *The Yellow Book*, to which it alluded literally and visually. But this description fails to capture the wild inventiveness and ruthless self-reflexivity of the text. Its prime target was the performance of the 'new', and it took a scalpel to a whole suite of issues in play in the periodical field towards the end of the nineteenth century. These issues included the relationship between commercial and aesthetic culture, the circulation of cultural capital, and most particularly the role of women in advanced literary circles. In addition, *Le Petit Journal des Refusées* is particularly suitable for a chapter on twenty-first century approaches to Victorian and modern periodicals, as throughout the twentieth century it was largely absent from scholarship.[19] Johanna Drucker's 2010 article, which includes an account of her first encounter with the magazine while working as an assistant to the registrar at Oakland Museum in the 1970s, demonstrates why.[20] With miniscule print runs and status closer to that of a printed image, or even a sort of artist's book, these texts were more or less confined to the archives. Even in 1989, when Margaret Beetham imagined scholars building a discipline from the shelf-loads of periodicals crumbling away within their library bindings, it was not texts like this that she had in mind.[21]

Le Petit Journal des Refusées was an illustrated publication, published in San Francisco by Porter Garnett and the graphic artist and humourist Frank Gelett

---

[19] To compensate, there has been a surge of interest in the past five years. See Kirsten MacLeod, 'The Fine Art of Cheap Print: Turn-of-the-Century American Little Magazines', in Ardis and Collier (eds), *Transatlantic Print Culture*, 182–98; Johanna Drucker, 'Bohemian by Design: Gelett Burgess and *Le Petit Journal des Refusées*', *Connexions* (1 June 2009), http://cnx.org/content/m24320/1.1/; Johanna Drucker, '*Le Petit Journal des Refusées*: A Graphical Reading', *Victorian Poetry* 48/1 (Spring 2010), 137–69; Brad Evans, 'Introduction' to *Le Petit Journal des Refusées*', *Modernist Journals Project* (2009), http://www.modjourn.org/render.php?id=mjp.2005.00.119&view=mjp_object; Brad Evans, Review of *Le Petit Journal des Refusées*, *Journal of Modern Periodical Studies* 1/2 (2010), 229; and Brad Evans, 'Ephemeral Bibelots and the 1890s', in Peter Brooker and Andrew Thacker (eds), *The Oxford Critical and Cultural History of Modernist Magazines*, Volume 2: *North America, 1894–1960* (Oxford: Oxford University Press, 2012), 132–54.

[20] Drucker, '*Le Petit Journal des Refusées*: A Graphical Reading', 137.

[21] Margaret Beetham, 'Open and Closed: The Periodical as a Publishing Genre', *Victorian Periodicals Review* 22/3 (Fall 1989), 96.

Burgess. Gelett Burgess, a former draughtsman and furniture designer, had left Boston for California in the late 1880s and was already a veteran of similar very small magazines.[22] While the individual publications might have been tiny, the field was relatively large. Brad Evans estimates that two hundred or so similar publications were produced in the United States between 1895 and 1903, which were variously and unflatteringly labelled 'toy magazines', 'freak magazines', or 'fadzines'.[23] In 1897, the bibliographer F. W. Faxon provided them with the classification 'ephemeral bibelots'.[24] Faxon's 1903 bibliography catalogued well over two hundred—including another *The New Review*, published in Boston in 1894—in the process demonstrating the plurality and mobility of the category and the field. Two versions of *The Yellow Book* were listed, the London quarterly and a monthly magazine from New York, that ran between 1897 and 1898. Symons's *The Savoy* was also included, standing as contemporary with, not as an originator of, the North American publications flanking it.[25]

As Faxon's bibliography suggested, these 'bibelots' embraced European (and particularly French) artistic and print culture, but certainly did not show deference to it or reverence for it. The title *Le Petit Journal des Refusées* echoed the Parisian 'Salon Des Refusés', calling to mind its signal exhibition of 1863, when figures such as Edouard Manet found a forum for the aesthetics that shaped so much of the art of the later nineteenth and early twentieth centuries. But the word 'bibelot', which translates roughly as 'curio', also indicated an object resistant to tradition or classification, something anomalous or unusual. *Le Petit Journal des Refusées* emphasized both these qualities not only through its formal construction—it was crafted out of wallpaper and cut on a diagonal—but through its ambiguous relationship with reproducibility and periodicity. The 'journal' only ran to one number, and copies were not identical. Different patterns of wallpaper were used, and the contents were subject to rearrangement and substitution. The problem of how to categorize *Le Petit Journal des Refusées* did not stop there. It also toyed with the question of national identity. In addition to being particularly and generically international, it was also consciously local.[26] Drucker's close analysis of its graphic, as well as its textual, codes situated it firmly within a distinctive San Francisco literary and artistic scene, while the copious marginal illustrations brought together a range of very different visual cultures and styles. Many versions of the journal also included a

---

[22] Joseph Backus, 'Gelett Burgess of *The Lark* and *The Wave*', in Frank Gelett Burgess (ed.), *Behind the Scenes: Glimpses of Fin-de-Siècle San Francisco* (San Francisco, CA: The Book Club of California, 1968), 9–10.

[23] Evans, review of *Le Petit Journal des Refusées*, 229.

[24] Kirsten MacLeod, 'The Fine Art of Cheap Print: Turn-of-the-Century American Little Magazines', in Ardis and Collier (eds), *Transatlantic Print Culture*, 183.

[25] F. W. Faxon, *Ephemeral Bibelots: A Bibliography of Modern Chap-Books and their Imitators* (Boston, MA: Boston Book Company, 1903).

[26] MacLeod, 'The Fine Art of Cheap Print', 189–90. Johanna Drucker, '*Le Petit Journal des Refusées*: A Graphical Reading', *Victorian Poetry* 48/1 (Spring 2010), 144.

spoof advert with the wording 'Catchy "Ad" will turn a dollar quickly', a direct reference to the commercialism that so many little magazines cannily negotiated. Instead of the customary accompanying image of youth or beauty, Burgess provided a comically gothic drawing of a skeleton riding a bicycle.

As this final example suggests, *Le Petit Journal des Refusées* managed its series of balancing acts through one principal mechanism: humour. Humour is an important component of many periodicals, from the most popular to the most avant-garde, which enables and encourages a double consciousness within the reader. If used well, it can allow periodicals to participate in, analyze, and differentiate themselves from the surrounding field in a single complex gesture. We could think, for instance, of *BLAST*'s 'Blast' and 'Bless' lists (themselves a parodic tribute to Apollinaire's futurist manifesto) or of *The New Age*'s parodies, alongside recognizable and established comic publications such as *Punch*. Humour—and indeed the idea of 'the novelty' or 'the curiosity'—runs parallel with an element of the 'new' addressed by North at the very beginning of his study. 'Novelty', he noted, 'has a very shady reputation, being redolent of dime stores, corny songs, and practical jokes.'[27] And yet, I would suggest that this dime-store facade is part of the central, underlying question both then and now: what is this modernity, and how are we to address it? The role played by women in modern literary culture is a good example in point. The 'Refusées' of the title were a series of imaginary female authors, whose contributions had been rejected by at least three other magazines. On one hand, women—who contributed to and funded so many new periodical ventures during this period—were being mocked. But on the other hand, such women were also portrayed as principal agents of a new form of writing, perhaps even as active participants in the play of parodic self-reference. Certainly, the power and judgement of the male editor, who appeared as a dishevelled, childlike silhouette bearing the pompous title 'Rédacteur-en-Chef', was questioned throughout. Even the wider culture of the 'ephemeral bibelots' was subjected to critique. The most conspicuously self-referential example of this was an article titled 'Our Clubbing List', which alphabetically 'clubbed' together various attributes of the 'new' literary culture, in order to collectively 'club'—or bash—them.[28] 'F is for freak: see the great exposition / Of freak magazines—6 and 10 cents admission' ran one of the entries in 'Our Clubbing List'.[29] Was 'newness' at its heart the same as novelty, and the 'bibelot' the same as the curiosity? Once the tropes of the new were recognizable enough that they could be parodied, were they really so new any more?

Le Petit Journal des Refusées presented its version of, and commentary on, the 'little magazine' as vehicle for novelty by placing an ironic emphasis on recent

---

[27] North, *Novelty*, 1.
[28] Anne Southampton Bliss (pseudo.), 'Our Clubbing List', 11–16. Metzdorf version. *Modernist Journals Project*, http://www.modjourn.org/render.php?id=1349273909781251&view=mjp_object.
[29] Ibid., 9.

textual tradition, thus questioning the value and validity of the 'new'. This commentary was built into the material of the text, and its play upon the reproducible periodical as a unique object. It drew attention to parallel questions of value and validity in circulation, which, as Arnold and Stead's debates suggest, were more commonly associated with concerns about the volume of material. The idea that periodicals were both an innovative and a proliferating medium was not new. But although it was inherited, rather than invented, by the Victorians, the conditions of that inheritance were specific. For instance, the prospectus for the short-lived *New Review* in 1813 included the following reassurance:

> The consideration of the number of *Reviews*, Weekly, Monthly and Quarterly, offered to the Public, may produce wonder at the sight of a *Prospectus* for an additional periodical work; but the slightest examination of the nature of the new publication will make the wonder cease.[30]

The early nineteenth-century reader presented above experiences 'wonder'—surprise as well as perplexity—upon encountering yet another new publication, before assessing the field and understanding (or so the editors hope) where *The New Review* will fit, and why its existence is warranted. By the end of the century, while editors and proprietors remained optimistic that their new ventures would find a place in an increasingly crowded field, 'wonder' had to contend with a certain amount of anxiety. For one reviewer writing in 1885, the sheer number of periodicals in circulation caused even innocent holiday reading matter to take on a sinister aspect. Readers were informed that the 'extra Christmas numbers and annuals are assuming very menacing proportions', adding that 'it is quite impossible to do more than glance at those which are forwarded to us'.[31] As this example suggests, reservations about quantity were not necessarily prompted by concerns about quality. Rather, just as the material of later nineteenth-century newspapers encouraged some to consider them disposable or even self-destructing, so periodical texts accentuated parallels between writing and waste, challenging notions of literary value by providing a field too big to interpret.[32]

As Gelett Burgess had foregrounded the role of women in new periodical culture, so in *New Grub Street* (1891) George Gissing's character Marian Yule gave voice to anonymous female literary labour in this expanding and commodified marketplace. An able and intelligent writer working long hours to shore up the precarious family finances, Yule's reflection on her daily grind in the 'manufacture of printed stuff' was an observation both on the conditions of production and on the consequences of production. 'What was the use and purpose of such a

---

[30] Anon., 'Prospectus', *The New Review, or Monthly Analysis of General Literature* 1/1 (January 1813), 1.

[31] Anon., 'Extra Christmas Numbers and Annuals', *Birmingham Daily Post* (23 December 1885), 7.

[32] For more information on questions of paper deterioration, see Nicholson Baker's polemical study *Double Fold: Libraries and the Assault on Paper* (New York: Random House, 2001).

life as she was condemned to lead?', Marian asks herself, 'when already there was more good literature in the world than any mortal could cope with in his lifetime'. The same reverse alchemy that has turned what Marian considers the 'joy and privilege' of self-expression into something punitively mechanical threatens to reduce even 'good literature' to surplus 'stuff', because it risks being lost in 'a trackless desert of print'.[33]

The years from 1880 were witness to a series of attempts to address one element of this problem, through systems capable of bringing sense and order to the material. W. F. Poole produced the first volume of his retrospective subject index to periodicals in 1882, and in January 1890 Stead published his periodical study of recent periodicals, the *Review of Reviews*.[34] He introduced the publication with another striking image, this time of a disempowered modern reader who parallels Yule's alienated modern writer. This (male) figure 'wanders' rather than 'wonders', lost in a body of material as heterodox as it is voluminous:

> In the mighty maze of modern periodical literature, the busy man wanders confused, not knowing exactly where to find the precise article that he requires and often, after losing all his scanty time in the search, he departs unsatisfied.[35]

Unlike Gissing's 'trackless desert of print', Stead's image of the maze implied that confusion could be remedied by a different perspective, that if readers had access to the right sort of overview, they would be able to see order and pattern in its place.

Stead's image has retained its popularity into the twenty-first century, certainly with scholars considering the impact of digital 'remediations' of this periodical archive.[36] Such projects do not have the explicit social function of the *Review of Reviews*, but they do promise multiple routes through the maze and in doing so they generate equally important questions concerning the organization and accessibility of knowledge. Very recent work on nineteenth-century periodicals by James Mussell, or on twentieth-century magazines by Cliff Wulfman, has opened up a sort of second front, in which periodical scholars working with digital media interrogate the ways in which their working practices shape both fields, acknowledging

---

[33] George Gissing, *New Grub Street* (Oxford: Oxford University Press, 1993), 106–7.

[34] More properly, the *Review of Reviews* started as a joint venture between Stead and fellow periodical proprietor and publisher George Newnes. In 1882, the American librarian W. F. Poole published the first volume of his retrospective subject index to British and American periodicals, a monumental collaborative work that would generate a slew of additions and addenda. See W. F. Poole, 'Introduction' to *Poole's Index to Periodical Literature*. http://c19index.chadwyck.com/infoCentre/introvol1.jsp. As Poole notes, the first iteration of this project had been published far earlier, in 1852.

[35] James Mussell and Suzanne Paylor, '"Mapping the Mighty Maze": Nineteenth-Century Serials Edition', *19: Interdisciplinary Studies in the Long Nineteenth Century* 1 (2005), 1. http://www.19.bbk.ac.uk/index.php/19/article/view/437.

[36] The article by Mussell and Paylor from which the quotation above is drawn is just such a piece.

and analyzing the 'creative nature of bibliographic intervention'.[37] These biblio-graphic interventions have a number of significant angles, many of which refer to large-scale projects and the boundaries that must be drawn around them. But even small, individual texts can draw attention to the impossibility of a neutral 'new' window on the past. We can return to *Le Petit Journal des Refusées* for a brief exam-ple, as Drucker provided a specific context for her first meeting with the text:

> I had been hired for my typing skills, and such an encounter was as unlikely as it was life changing…The wallpaper cover, the trapezoidal shape, the strangely weird and wonderfully intriguing image on the front were so fascinating I could not keep myself from transgressing decorum and seizing the thing for examination. Questions imme-diately arose to drive my research.[38]

In highlighting that particular encounter, that particular moment, Drucker pro-voked questions of her own. The most conspicuous of these related to the power of the material object, which overwhelmed 'decorum' to demand both physical and intellectual 'examination'. However carefully the magazine was reproduced elec-tronically, clearly that experience was beyond replication. This, in turn, invites a consideration of the relationship between that largely inaccessible hard copy, and Drucker's 2009 digital edition, and its accompanying chapter.[39] In the same year, this digitized copy was joined by three others, mounted together as part of the *Modernist Journals Project*, with a further introductory chapter by Evans. These three copies were drawn from three separate collections, allowing readers to see for themselves the variance within its single number. Such differences were, as we have seen, crucial to *Le Petit Journal des Refusées*' play on its identity as a 'magazine'. But the differences in the framing of the text/s on its different platforms is equally revealing. Understandably given its remit, the *Modernist Journals Project* presented the magazine as essentially proto-modernist, its prefatory description arguing for its anticipation of the later avant-garde experiments of Dadaism and surrealism.[40] In the longer 'Introduction', Evans reasserted this, while noting the influence of Parisian publications of the later nineteenth century (such as *Le Chat Noir* and

---

[37] Mussell and Paylor, ibid., 2. James Mussell's *The Nineteeth-Century Press in the Digital Age* (Basingstoke: Palgrave, 2012) is the most subtle and comprehensive investigation of this period. Patrick Leary's 2005 article 'Googling the Victorians' is an engaging introduction to similar issues, and addresses Victorian print culture more generally, *Journal of Victorian Culture* 10/1 (Spring 2005), 72–86. Cliff Wulfman's *Blue Mountain Project* also engages with questions of remediation; see http://bluemountain.princeton.edu/conference for details of its October 2013 event. These texts could, and probably should, be viewed in tandem with work by Kathryn Sutherland and Marilyn Deegan. See *Transferred Illusions: Digital Technology and the Forms of Print* (Farnham: Ashgate, 2009).

[38] Drucker, '*Le Petit Journal des Refusées*: A Graphical Reading', 137.

[39] For anyone consulting this there is also a reminder of some of the vulnerabilities of our own 'new' media, and of the ongoing pressures of the publishing marketplace. Rice University Press, the original publishers, have now ceased to operate, and it has passed to the university's open access platform. For the edition, see: http://cnx.org/content/col10709/latest.

[40] See http://www.modjourn.org/render.php?view=mjp_object&id=1183478160359375.

L'Hydropathe) on the parodic nature of the 'bibelots' and of the movements that followed.[41] For Drucker on the other hand, one of the most significant aspects of the magazine was precisely its resistance to such positioning. She placed it as 'an exemplary instance of modern aesthetic activity, but one that cannot be absorbed into the orthodoxy of avant-garde theory'.[42] As readers with access to all these interpretations, one might choose to agree with one or another. Alternatively, through their juxtaposition, the character of such critical differences could be said to shift, and a new perspective on all positions might emerge.

Thus far then, a consideration of periodicals as the scene of the new has demanded a historically and materially sensitive perspective as self-aware as that of Burgess, Arnold, Stead, or O'Connor. Ideally, such explorations take the texture and the context of the media in question into account, and this includes whichever intellectual orthodoxies the 'new' modes of enquiry have inherited. One of the most pertinent of such divisions for studies of the periodical field between 1880 and 1920 is the historical divide between the 'Victorian' and the 'twentieth century' as discrete areas of study, despite widespread acknowledgement of their relatedness.[43] By way of demonstration, one might look at a text already touched upon above, the *Contemporary Review*. It occupies a different end of the spectrum from *Le Petit Journal des Refusées* in terms of duration, as its publication dates easily span the period 1880 to 1920. In fact, they are closer to 'mid-Victorian into the Present', as the first number appeared in 1866 and the magazine stopped appearing in print as recently as January 2013. It was initiated by Alexander Strahan as a response to Trollope's *Fortnightly Review*, and it engaged in both intellectual and ecclesiastical debate.

Throughout much of the period we are interested in, the journal was edited by Percy Bunting, a Liberal who held the role from 1882 until his death in 1911. The original ecclesiastical bias was never entirely lost, and the periodical continued to cover a series of theological, philosophical, and spiritual questions across its run, alongside extensive analysis of international affairs. As such, the *Contemporary Review* can be considered both as a 'Victorian' and as a 'modern' periodical. Yet, on the evidence of current scholarship, only the former designation currently applies. The publication makes sense in a series of agreed, noteworthy mid- to late-Victorian contexts, particularly those relating to the emerging periodical culture and the social changes discussed at the opening of this piece.[44] As we know, it was an

---

[41] Evans, 'Introduction', 10–14.

[42] Drucker, '*Le Petit Journal des Refusées*: A Graphical Reading', 148.

[43] As recently as 2013, in a Modern Language Association (MLA) roundtable on this topic, Ann Ardis drew attention to the persistence of the divide, and to 'disciplinary fragmentation' in general. However, she also expressed concerns about the potentially limiting effects of 'typological analysis', or the separation of periodical studies from the study of a larger 'media ecology of modernity'.

[44] The most recent scholarship available breaks from these narratives significantly, but retains a focus on the years 1877 to 1890, and has been published in *Victorian Periodicals Review*. See Katherine Malone, 'The Critical Work of the Notices Column: Remaking the *Contemporary Review* after 1877', *Victorian Periodicals Review* 46/2 (Summer 2013), 211–35.

important venue for Stead, who had known Bunting since 1885 and who placed both 'Government by Journalism' and 'The Future of Journalism' there in May and November 1886, respectively.

In the 1880s and 1890s the *Contemporary Review* published a number of notable female authors. These included the aesthetic theorist Vernon Lee and the feminist and anti-vivisectionist Frances Power Cobbe. Emily Crawford's article 'Journalism as a Profession for Women' appeared there in 1893, and can be read as a reply to de Blowitz's rather negative 'Journalism as a Profession'. Crawford, a successful Paris correspondent at that time, drew from her personal experience, and acquaintance with newspaperwomen from France and North America, portraying the life of a working female journalist in terms strikingly different from both Gelett Burgess's would-be decadents, or from Gissing's exhausted writing machine. 'It is impossible to doubt that women write well', Crawford asserted, wishing that 'Mrs Carlyle and Charlotte Brontë' had been commissioned to write about the Universal Exhibition, rather than 'dryasdust' men obedient to the dictates of the Old Journalism.[45]

For the *Contemporary Review*, the situation in the twentieth century is very different. It rarely appears as more than a footnote, despite an additional century of writing being available to readers with access to ProQuest's *Periodicals Archive Online*, with its comprehensive, full-text search facility. But what would we search for? We could look for references to 'modernism'. But when the *Contemporary Review* uses this term, it is more likely to be discussing theological rather than aesthetic innovation. We could look for 'big names', and would find W. B. Yeats, who placed 'Ireland Bewitched' and 'Literature and the Living Voice' there in 1899 and 1906.[46] But others are very thin on the ground: neither Conrad nor Joyce are mentioned until well after 1920, for instance, although the *Contemporary* does become interested in modernism after 1950 or thereabouts, which says something about the institutionalization of the term. High-profile women writers seem even more scarce. If we are interested in the material form of the text, in the role played by the seemingly more conservative 'review' format perhaps, then the fact that the digitized copies are all drawn from bound volumes limits our opportunities. From this perspective, the reason why the *Contemporary Review* has been left off the map of twentieth-century periodicals leads us back to similar questions about quantity and the marketplace to those that have already been addressed with reference to the 1880s and 1890s. With so many periodical texts from the period speaking directly to established and central disciplinary concerns, why turn to one that does not?

It is with one potential approach to this question that this chapter will close, choosing an angle suggested by *Le Petit Journal des Refusées* and its international

[45] Emily Crawford, 'Journalism as a Profession for Women', *Contemporary Review* 64 (September 1893), 362–3.

[46] W. B. Yeats, 'Ireland Bewitched', *Contemporary Review* 76 (July 1899), 388–404; 'Literature and the Living Voice', *Contemporary Review* 90 (July 1906), 472–82. Yeats also was reviewed in the journal.

networks of reference, its self-conscious play of the marginal against the central. Although the *Contemporary Review* occupies ground far closer to this 'centre', in the first half of 1912 alone it published articles on France, Germany, Hungary, Italy, India, Wales, Portugal, Ireland, Persia, Russia, Turkey, China, Libya, the West Indies, the Philippines, and Yucatan. A number of these pieces were contributed by a single author, the Dublin-born linguist and polymath E. J. Dillon. Dillon also worked as foreign correspondent for the *Daily Telegraph* for many years and held a university post in Russia.[47] This long-standing interest in Russia brought him, almost inevitably it seems, into close contact with Stead, who published his work frequently in the *Review of Reviews*. In the 1912 memorial number of this magazine, Dillon recalled not only his agreements and disagreements with Stead, but his familiarity with Tolstoy and his anonymous translation of *The Kreutzer Sonata*.[48] Glyn Turton has argued for Dillon's influence in the placing of works by Tolstoy in the *Contemporary* from the 1890s onwards, arguing that this exposure helped to cement Tolstoy's reputation in Britain and America.[49]

The *Contemporary Review* can, then, be considered as part of emerging twentieth-century debates on Russia, central not only to the global political environment, but also to the British literary and philosophical climate.[50] It could definitely be connected to the 'modes of identification Russian literature offered early twentieth-century English intellectuals, at a time when they were engaged in the remarkably intense process of self-identification that we think of as early modernism'.[51] There is another factor that must be taken into account. While Dillon might have been writing for established English periodicals, he was not English, in addition to which the *Contemporary* had a long-standing interest in Irish affairs, and particularly in Home Rule. It was as part of this tradition that in 'Literature and the Living Voice', Yeats had made a case for a modernity that eschewed a centralized, monocultural version of the 'new', finding novelty in the self-renewing traditions of an older, oral culture.[52] Between 1880 and 1920 the *Contemporary Review* may have been a hospitable venue for such diverse modernities, refracted not only through

---

[47] Anon., 'Obituary: Dr. E.J. Dillon', *The Times* (10 June 1933), 14. Kevin Rafter's chapter on Dillon, 'E.J. Dillon: Special Correspondent', provides a good short biography, and includes some information on Dillon's role at the *Contemporary Review*. See Kevin Rafter (ed.), *Irish Journalism before Independence: More a Disease Than a Profession* (Manchester: Manchester University Press, 2011), 91–103.

[48] E. J. Dillon, 'W. T. Stead as He Appeared to One who was often his Antagonist', *Review of Reviews: Memorial Number* 45/269 (May 1912), 483–4. In fact, Dillon claimed that his translation sparked the disagreement between Stead and Newnes that led to Stead's purchase of Newnes's share in the publication.

[49] Glyn Turton, *Turgenev and the Context of English Literature, 1850–1900* (London: Routledge, 1992), 141–2.

[50] See, for instance, Rebecca Beasley and Philip Ross Bullock (eds), *Russia in Britain, 1880–1940: From Melodrama to Modernism* (Oxford: Oxford University Press, 2013).

[51] Beasley, 'Russia and the Invention of the Modernist Intelligensia', in Brooker and Thacker (eds), *Geographies of Modernism: Literatures, Cultures, Spaces* (Abingdon: Routledge, 2005), 21.

[52] Yeats, 'Literature and the Living Voice', 472–3.

the metropolitan periodical culture criticized by Stead in 1886, but through the discursive and critical lenses they provided for one another. This version of the modern entirely suits the designation 'contemporary' in fact, suggesting not a single 'new', but set of interrelated modernities, sharing the same temporal and textual space.

This brief exploration of the possibilities offered by two periodical texts—one long-running, yet partially neglected, the other ephemeral, yet enjoying a surge of popularity—demonstrates the dialectical relationship between the 'new' and the 'old', which is unavoidable in the evolution of a discipline or of a form, and which seems to underpin North's novelty paradox. The dynamics of change create a circuitry in which newness shapes, and is shaped by, existing materials and the modes in which those materials can be presented. This process can be particularly visible in periodical studies, as periodicals can be its object (as in the 'new' reading of the *Contemporary Review* just sketched out), but it can also be their subject (as in O'Connor's discussion of modern journalism in *The New Review*). One can even encounter both ends of the process, as in *Le Petit Journal des Refusées*, with its highly refined self-reflexivity. Like the texts they study, twenty-first-century periodical analysis wrestles with critical questions. Now as then, the value of this still relatively understudied field lies in its capacity to stimulate and renew our understanding. In doing so, it has the power to enable us to remake even the most familiar past.

FURTHER READING

Brake, Laurel. *Subjugated Knowledges: Journalism, Gender and Literature in the Nineteenth Century* (Basingstoke: Macmillan, 1994).

Brooker, Peter and Andrew Thacker, Sascha Bru, and Christian Weikop (eds). *The Oxford Critical and Cultural History of Modernist Magazines*, 3 vols (Oxford: Oxford University Press, 2009–2013).

Churchill, Suzanne and Adam McKible (eds). *Little Magazines and Modernism: New Approaches* (Aldershot: Ashgate, 2007).

Collier, Patrick. *Modernism on Fleet Street* (Aldershot: Ashgate, 2006).

Gray, F. Elizabeth (ed.). *Women in Journalism at the Fin-de-Siècle: 'making a name for herself'* (Basingstoke: Palgrave Macmillan, 2012).

Mussell, James. *Science, Time and Space in the Late Nineteenth-Century Periodical Press: Movable Types* (Aldershot: Ashgate, 2007).

Palmegiano, E. M. *Perceptions of the Press in Nineteenth-Century British Periodicals* (London: Anthem, 2012).

Rubery, Matthew. *The Novelty of Newspapers: Victorian Fiction after the Invention of the News* (Oxford: Oxford University Press, 2009).

Waller, Philip. *Writers, Readers, and Reputations: Literary Life in Britain, 1870–1918* (Oxford: Oxford University Press, 2007).

CHAPTER 34

THE ILLUSTRATED BOOK

KAMILLA ELLIOTT

Called 'the Golden Age of Illustration' in the United States, the years 1880–1920 mark an age every bit as golden in Britain, even though it was abbreviated by the paper shortage of the First World War.[1] The years equally mark a golden age of illustration discourse, as the illustrated book became a prime locus for contesting the roles of literature and art, authors and artists, as well as their relative abilities to represent both 'reality' and each other. These discourses, which are the main focus of this chapter, extend beyond aesthetic, semiotic, and hermeneutic issues to engage philosophical, political, psychological, historical, technological, and scientific subjects. Some tap into age-old religious and classical disputes over words and images; others forge new ones, applying Darwinian theory to the consumption of illustrated books. Some take a Janus-faced view, looking back to undo aesthetic and technological 'progress', while aiming to forge socialist political 'progress'; others deem a modern, commercial, technological, popular illustrated press the best means of social and political democratization. Some illustrate older literature reverently and nostalgically; others do so irreverently and iconoclastically, amid critical accolades and fury.

Although many factors contributed to this golden age of illustration, it was inaugurated by the technology of photomechanical engraving, which allowed illustrations to be reproduced without the mediation of engravers, decreasing their costs, improving their quality, and expanding their variety.[2] In the wake of new technologies, new aesthetic styles developed, while older technologies and styles were revived. From black-and-white line drawings to painterly colour plates, from

---

[1] Critics of the 1890s designated the long 1860s the golden age of illustration in Britain. Gleeson White, *English Illustration: The Sixties, 1855–1870* (Westminster: A. Constable, 1897).

[2] Prior to the invention of this process, wood engraving involved the interpretive work of another artist between the initial drawing and the printed page, and a skilled woodcut could take many days to complete; photomechanical engraving reproduced artwork without the interpretive mediation of an engraver, photographing the drawing, exposing it to light-sensitive chemicals, and producing the etching used for printing mechanically.

photorealism to Impressionism and expressionism, from minimalist sketches to intricately detailed drawings, from medievalism to Futurism, from sentimental rural nostalgia to grotesque art nouveau, illustration flourished. There were illustrated books for all ages and classes, from the costly, handcrafted productions of William Morris's Kelmscott Press to the cheap, mass-produced Macmillan's Illustrated Classics and periodicals. In 1896, arts and crafts illustrator Walter Crane declared:

> Now for graphic ability, originality, and variety, there can be no doubt of the vigour of our modern black and white artists. It is the most vital and really popular form of art at the present day, and it, far more than painting, deals with the actual life of the people; it is, too, thoroughly democratic in its appeal, and, associated with the newspaper and magazine, goes everywhere—at least, as far as there are shillings and pence—and where often no other form of art is accessible.[3]

From 1900, mechanized colour processes brought colour illustrations to the masses as well.

The years 1880–1920 saw notable collaborations between contemporary authors and artists, including H. Rider Haggard and R. Caton Woodville (*Cleopatra*, 1889), Thomas Hardy and Hubert Herkomer (*Tess of the D'Urbervilles*, 1891), Charlotte M. Yonge and Kate Greenaway (*The Heir of Redclyffe*, 1864, reprinted multiple times until 1892; Figure 3), Oscar Wilde and Aubrey Beardsley (*Salome*, 1894; Figure 4), William Morris and Walter Crane (*The Story of the Glittering Plain*, 1894; Figure 5), Robert Louis Stevenson and Walter Paget (*Treasure Island*, 1899), Arthur Conan Doyle and Sidney Paget (stories in *The Strand Magazine*, 1891–1904), H. G. Wells and Claude A. Shepperson ('The First Men in the Moon', 1901–2; Figure 6), and J. M. Barrie and Arthur Rackham (*Peter Pan in Kensington Gardens*, 1906), while Rudyard Kipling illustrated his own *Just So Stories* in 1902.

Artists also illuminated the canon: C. E. Brock's work for *Gulliver's Travels* (1894), Walter Crane's for *The Faerie Queene* (1895), and William Strang's for *Paradise Lost* (1895: Figure 7). Thomas Sturge Moore produced an edition of Wordsworth in 1902, Shakespeare was illustrated by Joseph Noel Paton in1904, and Keats by Claude A. Shepperson in 1916 (Figure 8), while Edward Burne-Jones's magnificent hand-printed Kelmscott Edition of Chaucer came out in 1896. Hugh Thomson drew Jane Austen's novels between 1893 and 1898, and recently deceased authors were likewise commemorated: Thomas Carlyle by Edward J. Sullivan (1898; Figure 9), Alfred Tennyson by Edward J. Sullivan (1900), Elizabeth Gaskell by C. E. Brock (1904; Figure 10), and Christina Rossetti by Laurence Housman (*Goblin Market*, 1893). Complementing the illustration of new literature, the re-illustration of 'classic' British literature following each technological improvement not only extended the circulation

---

[3] Walter Crane, *Of the Decorative Illustration of Books Old and New* (London: George Bell & Sons, 1896), 169.

"Guy was pacing the terrace with Laura and Amabel."—*Page* 89.

Figure 3 Kate Greenaway, illustration for Charlotte M. Yonge's *The Heir of Redclyffe*, 1892 [1864]. (London: Macmillan, 1864; repr. 1892), between 88 and 89. Author's copy.

THE CLIMAX

Figure 4 Aubrey Beardsley, illustration for Oscar Wilde's *Salomé*, 1912 [1894]. (London: John Lane, 1894; repr. 1912), between 80 and 81. Author's copy.

Figure 5 Walter Crane, illustration for William Morris's *The Story of the Glittering Plain* (1894) (borders and capitals by Morris). (London: George Bell & Sons, 1894; repr, 1901), 190. Courtesy of Lancaster University Library special collections.

"'TRICKLE, TRICKLE,' WENT THE FLOWING LIGHT VERY SOFTLY."

Figure 6 Claude A. Shepperson, illustration for H. G. Wells's 'The First Men in the Moon', in *Strand* (1901). *The Strand Magazine* 21/123 (March 1901), 286. Author's copy.

of older writing, but also contributed to the shaping of a national canon—a trend epitomized by titles such as *The National Shakespeare* (illustrated by Paton, 1904).

New technologies and changing aesthetic fashions not only extended the consumption of older literature, they further reshaped its interpretation. As some artists illustrated new literature in old ways, others illustrated old literature in new ways, and still others forged new illustrative styles for new literature, so that new and old literary and illustration styles commingled and wrangled. In art and literary contexts where Impressionism was challenging realism,[4] black-and-white illustration reached a realist zenith (Figure 11), while colour plates ushered in new modes of illustrative realism (Figure 10). Yet black-and-white illustration was equally conducive to expressionism (Figure 6) and art nouveau (Figure 4), while colour technologies enabled Romantic and Impressionistic as well as realist effects (Figure 8).

Yet in spite of illustration's omnipresence in publications, most critics address the literature of this period as if it had never been illustrated,[5] and no theory of the

[4] The Impressionist movement in continental painting, pioneered by Claude Monet, Edouard Manet, Edgar Degas, and others, inspired authors such as Henry James, Joseph Conrad, Stephen Crane, and Ford Madox Ford to turn from realist to Impressionist techniques in prose. See, for example, Maria Elizabeth Kronegger, *Literary Impressionism* (New York: Rowman and Littlefield, 1973).

[5] Even J. L. Cranfield's 'Arthur Conan Doyle, H. G. Wells and *The Strand Magazine*'s Long 1901: From Baskerville to the Moon', *English Literature in Transition, 1880–1920* 56/1 (2013), 3–32, self-described as 'a close reading of the *Strand* between November 1900 and February 1902' (3), makes no mention of the illustrations by Paget and Shepperson. Of the 3,865 listings (excluding

Figure 7 William Strang, illustration for John Milton's *Paradise Lost*, 1905 [1895]. (London: George Routledge & Sons, 1895; repr. 1905), between 14 and 15. Author's copy.

dissertations) that address Thomas Hardy in the *Modern Language Association (MLA) International Bibliography*, only thirty-six address illustrations of his works. Similar statistics can be generated for other illustrated fiction, 1880–1920.

Figure 8 Claude A. Shepperson, illustration for *The Poetical Works of John Keats*, 1916.
The Poetical Works of John Keats, ed. Laurence Binyon (London: Hodder and Stoughton, 1916), between 136 and 137. Author's copy.

novel, poetry, or theatre takes illustrations into account. When art critics also accord illustration scant attention, deeming it more craft than art, illustration falls into a no-discipline's land. Although some critics have addressed illustration, and this chapter is indebted to them,[6] it remains marginalized in both literary and art studies, rarely occupying the central role that it held in the construction and reception of literature between 1880 and 1920.

Intriguingly, the seeds of illustration's subsequent neglect emerge in debates over illustrated books *within* the period. As authors and artists battled for cultural and representational supremacy, they increasingly carved out separate spheres for literature and art, disowning illustration *against* its prominence in cultural practice,

---

[6] In addition to this chapter's references and further reading, see also Percy Muir, *Victorian Illustrated Books* (London: Batsford, 1971); Gordon N. Ray, *The Illustrator and the Book in England from 1790 to 1914* (Oxford: Oxford University Press, 1976); Stuart Sillars, *Visualization in Popular Fiction 1860–1960: Graphic Narratives, Fictional Images* (London: Routledge, 1995); Catherine J. Golden (ed.), *Book Illustration: Text, Image, and Culture 1770–1930* (New Castle, DE: Oak Knoll Press, 2000).

THE REAL AND ITS IDEAL

Figure 9 Edward J. Sullivan, illustration for Thomas Carlyle's *Sartor Resartus*, 1900 [1898]. (London: George Bell & Sons, 1898; repr, 1900), 309. Author's copy.

Figure 10 C. E. Brock, colour illustration for Elizabeth Gaskell's *Cranford* (1904). (London: J. M. Dent & Co, 1904), between 54 and 55. Author's copy.

"I LEAPT UPON THEM LIKE A MADMAN."

(*See page* 246.)

Figure 11 Alfred Pearse, illustration for Knarf Elivas's *A Russian Experience*, in *Strand* (1897). *Strand* 13/75 (March 1897), 242. Author's copy.

until such theories and discourses *changed* cultural practices. Critics worked assiduously to displace pictorial illustration with that other etymological sense of 'illustration': verbal commentary.[7] Although these discourses and practices all but drove illustration out of adult fictive literature, illustration discourses resurfaced elsewhere, as the last section of this chapter details.

'The rivalry between art and literature'

Almost a decade on from the half-tone process that revolutionized illustration, P. G. Hamerton's 'Book Illustration' (1889) includes a conversation between a Poet, Artist, Scientist, and Critic concerning 'The Rivalry between Art and Literature'. The Critic, whom Hamerton indicates as himself 'purely and simply', declares: 'There cannot be a doubt that the question of rivalry between literature and art really exists.' The Scientist, who 'expresses what [Hamerton has] heard said by scientific men in real life', concurs: 'The conflict you speak of cannot be avoided. It is in the nature of things.' Hamerton's Poet, a literary purist who 'represents imaginative literature generally', and Artist, 'of the picturesque order and opposed to scientific views', manifest this rivalry. The Poet insists, 'A Poet needs no help from illustration'; the Artist retaliates, 'The Poet is jealous of the illustrator, and of the attention that the illustrator attracts to himself'.[8] The Poet deems the primary alliance of illustrated books not as one between artist and author but as 'a nefarious pact between artist and publishers. They plot together to get up a trade: they trade on illustrious [literary] names'. The Artist counters that often 'the illustrator perpetuates a poetical reputation that would perish without his help'.[9]

Illustrators were indeed attracting attention and establishing their own literally 'illustrious' reputations. Freed from the intermediary engravers, who often displeased artists with their lack of fidelity and finesse, prominent artists engaged more willingly in illustration. By 1896, *London Society* editor Henry Blackburn nominated illustrators 'painter-etchers', demanding that they receive 'recognition as original artists'.[10] Many became celebrities, commanding high earnings. Presses established series of illustrated classic fiction, in which famous illustrators rather than authors head the lists, as in this header to a 1904 advertisement:

Macmillan's
Illustrated Pocket Classics.
WITH ILLUSTRATIONS BY

---

[7] Kamilla Elliott, 'Prose Pictures', in *Rethinking the Novel/Film Debate* (Cambridge: Cambridge University Press, 2003), 31–76.

[8] Philip Gilbert Hamerton, 'Book Illustration', in *Portfolio Papers* (London: Seeley & Co, 1889), 293–301.

[9] Ibid., 298, 295.

[10] Henry Blackburn, *The Art of Illustration* (London: W. H. Allen, 1896), 3.

Hugh Thomson, Linley Sambourne, Randolph
Caldecott, Charles E. Brock, Chris Hammond, and others.[11]

The rising status and standard of illustration intensified inter-art rivalries. Hamerton's Poet indicates that 'if illustrations are appreciated for high artistic reasons[,] they are the more dangerous as rivals, and we who write have the stronger reasons for keeping them out'.[12] Twenty years on, in his preface to the New York edition of *The Golden Bowl* (1909), Henry James worried that 'the author of any text putting forward illustrative claims (that is producing an effect of illustration) by its own intrinsic virtue... [finds] itself elbowed, on that ground, by another and a competitive process'.[13]

Against such worries, aesthetic discourses maintain the axiomatic superiority of literature to art in the illustrated book, a superiority based on seniority, logophilia, iconophobia, and metaphysical aesthetic dualities that render the word spiritual, intellectual, universal, and profound and the image sensual, corporeal, local, and superficial. Although Hamerton's Critic envisions 'the arts of the draughtsman and the photographic reproducer... married to immortal verse' in the illustrated book, it is an unequal marriage.[14] Verse, immortal and singular, marries polygamously with plural arts, demoted by technical crafts and derivative technologies. Even advocates and producers of illustrated books accord illustration lesser value. A few years later, William Morris reflected:

> The picture-book is not, perhaps, absolutely necessary to man's life, but it gives us such endless pleasure, and is so intimately connected with the other absolutely necessary art of imaginative literature that it must remain one of the very worthiest things.[15]

Literature is 'absolutely necessary'; illustration is not, perhaps. Here in the shrine of 'ideal' illustrated books lie the seeds of illustration's subsequent optionality. Yet such discourses protest too much. Even as they elevate literature above illustration theoretically, they acknowledge that pictures dominate words in practice. The Scientist affirms 'that when literature and art are put together it is generally literature that suffers. People do not read splendidly illustrated editions'. Even the Poet admits that he is *himself* deterred from reading illustrated books: 'The mere material aspect of illustrated books is too much for me. I hate their superfine paper, their excessive margins, their obtrusively big and fine typography, their showy bindings'.[16]

---

[11] Jane Austen, *Northanger Abbey* and *Persuasion*, illustrated by Hugh Thomson (London: Macmillan, 1904), back matter, n. p.

[12] Hamerton, 'Book Illustration', 302.

[13] Henry James, *The Golden Bowl* (New York: Charles Scribner's Sons, 1909), x.

[14] Hamerton, 'Book Illustration', 294–5.

[15] William Morris, *The Ideal Book: A Paper by William Morris Read before the Bibliographical Society, London, 19 June 1893* (London: LCC Central School of Arts and Crafts, 1908), 13.

[16] Hamerton, 'Book Illustration', 298–301.

Such concerns reach beyond 1889 and editions *de luxe*. In 1914, Robert MacDougall complained similarly of cheap, mass market illustration: 'With the increasing dependence upon illustration the value of the text has correspondingly declined.'[17] The demise of triple-deckers, the rise of leaner prose and more elaborate illustrations all fed the changing balance of literary and artistic power. *Dalziels' Bible Gallery* (1881), illustrated by various artists, omits the sacred text entirely.

Illustrations were essential to the economic and popular value of literature; elitist literati therefore stressed competing 'higher' values, drawing on nineteenth-century middle-class ethics and Darwinian theories of evolution, as well as classical metaphysics and ancient Protestant-Catholic debates over words and images to devalue the consumption of pictures. When the Scientist asks, 'Why should pictorial art have this advantage over literature?', the Critic replies: 'The reason is simply because an engraving can be understood at a glance, whereas to read a page requires a little effort, and also a little time.'[18] Literature gains higher value than art through an intellectual work ethic. Implicitly and incongruously, the less literate labouring classes are charged with laziness in their consumption of literature. Other writers extend the critique to psychological atrophy: 'With pictures illustrating every phase and turn of a story, there is little left for imagination to do and...an undeveloped imagination means an undeveloped, or at least ill-developed, individuality.'[19] Illustrations, it seems, threaten middle-class individualism as well.

MacDougall turns to evolutionary theories of primitivism and regression to attack illustrated literature: 'In the stages of barbaric culture[,] picture and text are habitually associated... Among civilized peoples the picture drops back to a purely accessory position.'[20] In 1888, Felix L. Oswald testified patronizingly that his pet baboon 'will examine a picture-book, page for page, and occasionally use his fingers to verify the impression of a striking illustration.'[21]

Yet here again, critics protest too much. Illustrations mark not only mental failure, they also mark *literary* failure, as MacDougall admits: 'the introduction of pictures... marks a sense of insufficiency in the verbal medium.'[22] When Hamerton's Poet insists that illustrations 'pervert the author's conceptions by substituting others', the Artist retaliates that illustrators merely compensate for verbal deficiencies: only an illustrator can provide 'the true representation of costume and surroundings. Nobody without the help of an artist will imagine those correctly for any age except just his own.'[23] MacDougall agrees: 'Their service to the understanding is...twofold—they make clear to us relations too complex to be successfully conveyed by words... [and

[17] Robert MacDougall, 'The Picture and the Text', *Popular Science* 85/15 (September 1914), 278.
[18] Hamerton, 'Book Illustration', 301.
[19] William Jay Youmans, 'A Backward Movement', *Popular Science* 43/3 (July 1893), 415.
[20] MacDougall, 'Picture and Text', 275.
[21] Felix L. Oswald, 'Four-handed Sinners: A Zoological Study', *Popular Science* 34/1 (November 1888), 112.
[22] MacDougall, 'Picture and Text', 275.   [23] Hamerton, 'Book Illustration', 311–13.

they] bring before us a scene whose splendour and richness can not [*sic*] be successfully represented in imagination'. Yet he concludes: 'To need pictures in order to make the thought plain means...that the writer has not mastered his craft thoroughly and does not know how to use his tools.'[24]

By 1909, however, Henry James was rejecting even the '*service*' of illustrations: 'Anything that relieves responsible prose of the duty of being...pictorial enough, above all *in itself*, does it the worst of services, and may well inspire in the lover of literature certain lively questions as to the future of that institution.'[25] Joining discourses of pictorial regression, James raises a counterpointing evolutionary discourse of literary extinction.

'Their proper place'

Fearing extinction, writers pressed for a separation of spheres to minimize inter-semiotic competition, and marital metaphors turned to a rhetoric of divorce, class hierarchies, and territorial divisions. Hamerton's Poet wants 'the Fine Arts [to] keep to their proper place, and illustrate subjects of their own...I say nothing against pictorial art in its own domains...but I want to keep it out of ours'. The Artist agrees: 'the ordinary engraved letters under a print are an injury to it...I cannot see that painting gains much from literature'.[26]

Such separations are not limited to critical discussions: they are also evident in book illustration practice. In the 1900s and 1910s, re-illustrated literary 'classics' often separate illustrations from text, placing them on different pages in different paper, framed like paintings, with tissue further separating pictures from print (Figure 10). The mechanized colour processes that flourished from 1900 further heighten contrasts between black-and-white text and coloured pictures—all the more so as colour illustrators aspired to painterly effects (Figures 8 and 10). William Strang's photogravures for *Paradise Lost* (1905; Figure 7) and Claude A. Shepperson's colour illustrations to Keats's poems (1916; Figure 8) are even more separate, pasted onto and readily detached from their pages, prefiguring their subsequent detachment from adult fictive literature more generally. Against practices in mainstream periodicals that surrounded and interrupted text with illustrations, *The Yellow Book*'s first art editor, Aubrey Beardsley, and literary editor, Henry Harland, announced in an interview that there would be 'no connection whatever' between letterpress and pictures.[27] Text would be printed without illustration and title pages inserted before artwork, so that pictures appear on pages without words. Others

[24] MacDougall, 'Picture and Text', 276–7.
[25] James, *The Golden Bowl* (New York: Charles Scribner's Sons, 1909), x–xi (emphasis in the original).
[26] Hamerton, 'Book Illustration', 296, 302–3, 324–5.
[27] 'What the "Yellow Book" is to Be', *The Sketch* 5/1 (11 April 1894), 557–8.

went further to reject verbal *criticism* of illustrations. Crane ends his treatise thus: 'designs, to those who feel them, ought to speak in their own tongue for themselves more forcibly than any written explanation or commentary'.[28] In 1919, Malcolm C. Salaman called for illustrations to be 'entirely independent of... verbal interpretation'.[29]

Indeed, illustration's etymology, encompassing both pictorial and verbal commentaries, makes this the keener rivalry.[30] Hamerton's Scientist sees illustration as 'analogous to... a professor or commentator who draws attention to a great poet; but [is] a hundred times more efficacious because a hundred times more attractive than a prose commentator could ever be'.[31] As the twentieth century continued, literary critics won this battle, making their own 'nefarious pacts' with publishers, in which illustrated editions gave way to 'critical' editions, and critics displaced the pictorial 'commentaries' of frontispieces, illustrations, and decoration with their own verbal introductions, notes, and verbal commentaries.[32] Increasingly, the term 'illustrated books' was reserved for children's literature, following theories of pictorial primitivism. In Methuen's 'Catalogue of Books' (1898), 'Illustrated Books' refers only to titles for children. Yet adult books listed under other headings are lavishly illustrated—some 'with over 450 illustrations in the text and 12 photogravure plates'—and the catalogue appears at the back of a new edition of *The Pilgrim's Progress* 'with thirty-nine illustrations by Robert Anning Bell and an introduction by C. H. Firth'.[33] While such books combine critical and biographical 'illustrations' with pictorial illustrations, others maintain separate spheres. In the 1890s, Macmillan's Illustrated Standard Novels include illustrated poetry; in 1900, an advertisement for the unillustrated Aldine Edition of the British Poets, with its 'complete texts and scholarly introductions', claims to be 'something very different from the cheap volumes of extracts which are just now so much too common'.[34] Conversely, an advert for The Illustrated Pocket Library of Plain and Coloured Books inside Methuen's 1905 edition of *The Golden Bowl* describes it as 'A series, in small form, of some of the famous illustrated books of fiction and general literature. These are faithfully reprinted from the first or best editions *without introduction or notes*'.[35]

Although such discourses advance the separation of verbal and pictorial *signs*, the 1898 Methuen catalogue points to a further *disciplinary* separation of spheres reaching beyond literature and art. Scientific subjects, biographies, and travel books

[28] Crane, *Decorative Illustration*, 303.

[29] Malcolm C. Salaman, 'The Art of Claude A. Shepperson', *The International Studio* 76/268 (June 1919), 113.

[30] All dictionaries and many critics have attested to this. See, for example, Martin Meisel, *Realizations: Narrative, Pictorial, and Theatrical Arts in Nineteenth-Century England* (Princeton, NJ: Princeton University Press, 1983), 30.

[31] Hamerton, 'Book Illustration', 299.   [32] Elliott, *Novel/Film Debate*, 49–50.

[33] John Bunyan, *The Pilgrim's Progress* (London: Methuen, 1898), back matter, 10–11, 14, title page.

[34] Thomas Carlyle, *Sartor Resartus*, illus. Edmund J. Sullivan (London: George Bell & Sons, 1900), back matter, 29.

[35] Henry James, *The Golden Bowl* (London: Methuen, 1905), back matter, n. p. (emphasis added).

are almost always illustrated; books of philosophy, theology, politics, economics, psychology, ethics, social issues, and linguistics are not. Methuen's unillustrated subjects represent the chief disciplines that came to dominate literary criticism. Their own rejection of illustration carries over into their colonizing de-illustration of literature. Hamerton's Critic elucidates these trends: 'illustration becomes more and more unquestionably useful as it abandons the imaginative—and consequently the artistic—qualities to move in the direction of science'.[36] These discourses and practices serve to press illustration away from the imaginative domain of literary fiction towards the factual domain of science, and literature away from the concrete and material to the abstract and ideological.

'The Book Beautiful as a Whole'

Against such separations of spheres, arts and crafts bookmakers promoted a Romantic ideal of organic unity conjoining words, pictures, typography, binding, and paper. Under the final subheading of *The Ideal Book or Book Beautiful* (1902), 'The Book Beautiful as a Whole', T. J. Cobden-Sanderson writes:

> The Book Beautiful...should be conceived of as a whole...The proper duty of each Art within such limits is to co-operate with all the other arts, similarly employed, in the production of something which is distinctively Not Itself.[37]

Cobden-Sanderson followed Morris, who founded the Kelmscott Press in 1891. Although many Kelmscott books are decorated rather than illustrated, Morris's emphasis on typography, handmade paper, hand-pressed printing, and vellum bindings drew attention to the graphic dimensions of language and the materiality of books. Concomitantly, the arts and crafts preference for symbolic decoration over mimetic illustration draws attention to the symbolic dimensions of pictures, both of which broke down the distinctions between literature and art propounded by Hamerton and others. Returning to older word–image formats, such as medieval illuminated letters, further broke down such dichotomies.

Defying Hamerton's critique of pictorial primitivism, arts and crafts bookmakers turned from new technologies to older modes of production—to wood engraving, hand etching, and colour lithography. Further breaking down distinctions between past and present, regression and evolution, they sought socialist political progress through a return to the unalienated collective labour of cottage industry crafts; against views of illustrations as derivative and dependent, these technologies foregrounded illustrator invention and artistry.

---

[36] Hamerton, 'Book Illustration', 328.
[37] T. J. Cobden-Sanderson, *The Ideal Book or Book Beautiful: A Tract on Calligraphy Printing and Illustration* (London: Hammersmith Publishing Society, 1902), 8.

Yet in spite of his commitment to organic inter-semiotic unity, Morris also promoted separate disciplinary and representational spheres. While Hamerton and others *relegated* illustrations to books of science and material fact, Morris *excluded* 'a work on differential calculus, a medical work, a dictionary, a collection of a statesman's speeches, or a treatise on manures' from his candidates for ideal ornamentation: 'a book that must have illustrations...should...have no actual ornament at all, because the ornament and the illustration must almost certainly fight'. Above all, Morris precludes *art* books from decorative illustration: 'A work on Art, I think, bears less of ornament than any other kind of book', while imaginative literature is its prime candidate.[38] Thus even at the heart of organic theories of illustrated books, art and literature occupy separate spheres.

Realization and illustration

According to Martin Meisel, in Victorian inter-art discourse *realization* 'meant both literal re-creation and translation into a more real...more vivid, visual, physically present medium', while *illustration* 'carried a sense of enrichment and embellishment beyond mere specification; it implied the extension of one medium or mode of discourse by another, rather than materialization with a minimum of imaginative intervention'.[39] The arts and crafts Book Beautiful foregrounds 'enrichment and embellishment' and 'imaginative intervention' over literal and mimetic illustration. 'Imaginative intervention' also permeates the 'diabolic beauty'[40] of Aubrey Beardsley's art nouveau illustrations (Figure 4). In contrast to arts and crafts medievalism, Oscar Wilde's literary executor, Robert Ross, nominates black-and-white art nouveau illustration 'the most modern of the arts';[41] against arts and crafts collectivism, it asserts individual style and personality.

Art nouveau also challenged conventional dichotomies and hierarchies of literature and art, paradoxically giving rise to discourses that sought to reinscribe them. In 1913, Holbrook Jackson nominated Beardsley 'the most literary of the modern artists; his drawings are rarely the outcome of pure observation—they are largely the outcome of thought; they are thoughts become pictures'. But Jackson condemns such aspiration to the domain of the literary: 'He failed as an illustrator because his art was decoration in the abstract'.[42] If Jackson reasserts conventional separations of spheres, in which the abstract is reserved for literature, so do critics who praise Beardsley for his 'literary' qualities. Ross adduces: 'His art was, of course, intensely *literary*, to use the word hated of modern critics, but his expression of it was the

---

[38] Morris, *Ideal Book*, 2.   [39] Meisel, *Realizations*, 30.
[40] Arthur Symons, *The Art of Aubrey Beardsley* (London: Unicorn, 1898), 30.
[41] Robert Ross, *Aubrey Beardsley* (London: John Lane, 1909), 33.
[42] Holbrook Jackson, *The Eighteen Nineties: A Review of Art and Ideas at the Close of the Nineteenth Century* (London: Grant Richards, 1913), 99–100, 103.

legitimate literature of the artist, not the art peculiar to literature.'[43] Even as Ross disagrees with Jackson's assessment, he supports his separation of literary and pictorial spheres: Beardsley's 'designs must be judged independently, as they were conceived, without any view of interpreting or even illustrating a particular author. He was too subjective to be a mere illustrator'.[44]

Jackson further objects to the power of Beardsley's illustrations over the text they illustrate: 'His designs overpower the text—not because they are greater but because they are inappropriate, sometimes even impertinent... the *Salome* drawings seem to sneer at Oscar Wilde rather than interpret the play. *The Rape of the Lock* is eclipsed, not explained by Beardsley.'[45] Jackson is less concerned here with an illustrator's fidelity to authors and texts than with fidelity to *critics and criticism*: pictorial illustration, he determines, is to fill the same subservient functions as critical, verbal illustration.

'Mere illustration', often synonymous with mimetic realism, became increasingly disparaged as new modes of non-realist art gained ground. In 1896, Crane objected to the realist illustration enabled by photographic print processes because it 'concentrated artistic interest on the literal realization of certain aspects of superficial facts and instantaneous impressions, instead of ideas and the abstract treatment of form and line'.[46]

The brunt of critical opprobrium for 'literal realization' fell on mass media illustrated books and periodical literature. The latter is beneath even Herbert Spencer's 1902 attack on 're-barbarization' in literature, journalism, and art: 'I have deliberately avoided looking at the illustrated weekly journals.'[47] The following year, illustration critic Rose E. D. Sketchley attacks '[t]he ordinary illustrator, making drawings for cheap reproduction in the ordinary book' and insists that 'journalism is not literature, and picture matter-of-fact is not illustration, though it is convenient and customary to call it so'.[48]

In 1982, Edward Hodnett used a similar aesthetic hierarchy to justify scholarly neglect of mass media illustration: 'Much of the poor book work of these years appeared first in magazines or was by illustrators who were accustomed to work for magazines. Thus a number of productive and competent illustrators of the period... were omitted from this study'.[49]

These assessments are palpably unjust. While mimetic realism and photographs remained popular with the public, mass media illustrations were by no means limited to them, as even a single issue of *The Strand Magazine* attests. Its March 1901

[43] Ross, *Beardsley*, 34 (emphasis in the original).

[44] Ibid., 33.   [45] Jackson, *Eighteen Nineties*, 102.   [46] Crane, *Decorative Illustration*, 178.

[47] Herbert Spencer, 'Re-barbarization', in *Facts and Comments* (London: Williams & Norgate, 1902), 187.

[48] Rose E. D. Sketchley, *English Book Illustration of To-day: Appreciations of the Work of Living English Illustrators with Lists of Their Books* (London: Kegan Paul, Trench, Trübner & Co., 1903), 2–3.

[49] Edward Hodnett, *Image and Text: Studies in the Illustration of English Literature* (Aldershot: Scolar Press, 1982), 188.

issue features illustration styles ranging from mimetic realist half-tones to abstract painterly art, and from reverent medievalism to contemporary cartoon satire. Joining photographs and illustrations are illuminated letters, head and tailpieces, and decorative borders and embellishments. It contains both Sidney Paget's realist illustrations for Conan Doyle stories and Claude A. Shepperson's expressionist illustrations for H. G. Wells's 'The First Men in the Moon' (Figure 6); illustrations to other stories by less celebrated illustrators are intricately detailed, mobile, expressive, and dynamic (Figure 11). Conversely, *The Yellow Book,* a journal hailed for its avant-garde progressivism and aestheticism, includes photorealist art, most strikingly the image that illustrates the periodical's title (Figure 12).

To some extent, realist illustration of imaginative literature is an oxymoron, since it realizes what is not and has not been. Yet it is precisely for this reason that readers clamoured for pictorial realizations of it. The immensely popular Wig and Powder and Cranford schools of illustration brought realism to novels by Austen (Figure 13), Mitford, Goldsmith (Figure 14), Gaskell (Figure 10), and others in the forms of historically accurate costumes, architecture, and artefacts. And yet they also infused nostalgic sentimentality into their realism, illustrating the *yearnings* of producers and consumers for bygone, never-been fictions. In her analysis of Hugh Thomson, the Wig and Powder school's most famous illustrator, Sketchley's distinction between 'matter-of-fact' and 'feeling' illustrations breaks down, as 'his realization of the forms and manners of bygone times' presents 'a version of fact that has the farther charm of lavender-scented antiquity'.[50]

Such illustration—or more precisely, re-illustration—undoubtedly contributed to the formation of the British literary canon, recirculating old texts in new contexts with pictures that modelled the proper sentiments for contemporary readers, realizing national cultural ideologies along with material history. Realist illustration, then, was not limited to representing the matter-of-factual; it served to make fictive, affective, and ideological matter seem real.

Photography and photoplay editions

The taste for realism and realization was further reflected in the growing practice of photographic illustration. Both Henry Blackburn in 1893 and Joseph Pennell in 1896 identified photography as a major contributor to 'the collapsing role of, and the lack of respect for, the pictorial image, illustration, and the graphic artist'.[51] Photographs, then, joined prose in driving drawn illustrations from adult literature.

The practice was not limited to the popular press. While Hamerton's Critic decrees that 'a pure photograph from nature is out of place in any book whatever',[52]

---

[50] Sketchley, *English Book Illustration,* 80.
[51] Cited in Gerard Curtis, *Visual Words: Art and the Material Book in Victorian England* (Aldershot: Ashgate, 2002), 36.
[52] Hamerton, 'Book Illustration', 333.

Figure 12 Gertrude D. Hammond, 'The Yellow Book', *The Yellow Book* 6 (July 1895), 119.
Author's copy.

The messroom will drink Isabella Thorpe for a fortnight.

Figure 13 Hugh Thomson, illustration for Jane Austen's *Northanger Abbey*, 1904 [1897]. (London: Macmillan, 1897; repr. 1904), 127. Author's copy.

' " *Welcome, any way welcome, my dearest lost one—my treasure—*
to your poor old father's bosom ! " '

Figure 14 Hugh Thomson, illustration for Oliver Goldsmith's *The Vicar of Wakefield* (1914
[1892]). (London: Constable & Co, 1892; repr. 1914), 219. Author's copy.

surprisingly, after rejecting drawn illustration for *The Golden Bowl*, James allowed
A. L. Colburn to illustrate the novel with photographs, mitigating word and image
competition by declaring them 'a contribution in as different a "medium" as possible' from prose and insisting that any reference 'to Novel or Tale should exactly be

not competitive and obvious...expressions of no particular thing in the text, but only of the type or idea of this or that thing'.[53] Bestowing an uncharacteristic abstraction and symbolism upon photography for that period, James sought to establish a new hierarchy and separation of verbal and pictorial spheres.

James was short-sighted in believing that photographs would support the dominance of prose over visual representation. Film, photography's near relation and descendant, was to prove an even more formidable rival to prose's pictorial claims than illustration. Indeed, James was less prescient than Stephane Mallarmé, who, responding to a publisher's questionnaire about photographic illustrations in 1897, replied: 'I am in favour of—no illustration, since all that a book evokes must take place in the reader's mind; but, if you [use] photography, why not go straight to the cinematograph, whose unreeling will replace images and texts, many a volume, advantageously'.[54]

By the 1910s, worded films and illustrated books were in keen competition. To cite just two of numerous similar claims, a 1915 review of Edison's film of *Vanity Fair* decreed that 'the reels make a set of illustrations superior to the conventional pen-pictures of a deluxe edition',[55] while a 1921 *New York Times* article declared that film had trounced plays as well as illustrated books: this film is 'much more worth seeing than all the illustrated novels and plays turned out in a year'.[56] Such reviews set illustrated literature, spoken theatre, and titled films in new modes of competition as *hybrid* word–image arts, superseding earlier efforts to carve out separate spheres for words and pictures as pure arts.

Theatre and film not only rivalled illustrated books, they further *inhabited* them in 'photoplay editions'. From the 1880s, tie-in editions to celebrated plays contained photographs of stage productions. From the 1910s, the practice advanced to photoplay editions bearing *film* stills on their covers and within their pages, a practice that peaked in the 1920s and 1930s and continues to the present day. In 1915, *The Bookseller, Newsdealer and Stationer* observed that 'Grosset & Dunlap have ready a remarkable list of photoplay titles for 50 cents, and every one of the stories are appearing on films. The photoplay editions of the books...have illustrations from the popular screens'.[57] Just as illustrations had helped to sell books in the last part of

[53] *The Golden Bowl* (New York: Charles Scribner's Sons, 1909), x–xi (emphasis in original).

[54] Cited in and translated by Christophe Wall-Romana, 'Mallarmé's Cinepoetics: The Poem Uncoiled by the Cinématographe, 1893–98', *Publications of the Modern Language Association of America (PMLA)* 120/1 (2005), 132.

[55] *Boston Transcript*, 11 January 1916, cited in Robert A. Colby, '"Scenes of All Sorts...": *Vanity Fair* on Stage and Screen', *Dickens Studies Annual* 9 (1981), 178.

[56] Review of *Shattered*, 'Screen: Pictorial Efficiency', *New York Times*, 11 December 1921, sect. 6.3.

[57] *The Bookseller, Newsdealer, and Stationer* 43 (1915), 815. A. L. Burt also published numerous photoplay editions. The dominance by American publishers of both film and publishing markets at this time is the fallout from Britain's greater investment in the First World War.

the period, films were helping to sell books. For example, in 1920, *Publishers Weekly* announced:

> Working in conjunction with the moving picture people, the Harpers are soon to issue a photoplay edition of the Mark Twain classic. Representatives of the Famous Players are calling upon the booksellers in each town in which the pictures are to be released, supplying posters advertising both the picture and the book.[58]

Subsequently, historians of western book illustration assess that film fiction *replaced* illustrated fiction. In 1947, Philip James determined: 'Illustrated fiction, once a source of rivalry between all the great publishing houses and the illustrator's main occupation, has now given way to screen fiction loaded with all the overtones of photographic naturalism.'[59] The debates over printed prose and illustration with which this chapter began did not disappear, but found afterlives in contests over the relative values of other word and image arts. In the final analysis, the illustrated book of 1880–1920 was a richly variegated form, in which a wide array of technologies, tastes, ideologies, and narratives were innovatively produced and eagerly consumed. It gave rise to discourses and debates that are still being canvassed today in media studies, including the relative roles of art and science, progress and regress, social welfare and aesthetic pleasure, elitism and democracy, and the representational capacities of signs and media.

FURTHER READING

Crane, Walter. *Of the Decorative Illustration of Books Old and New* (London: George Bell & Sons, 1896).

Elliott, Kamilla. *Rethinking the Novel/Film Debate* (Cambridge: Cambridge University Press, 2003).

Felmingham, Michael. *The Illustrated Gift Book, 1880–1930* (Aldershot: Scolar Press, 1990).

Hamerton, Philip Gilbert. 'Book Illustration', in Philip Gilbert Hamerton (ed.), *Portfolio Papers* (London: Seeley & Co, 1889), 293–386.

Hodnett, Edward. *Image and Text: Studies in the Illustration of Englissh Literature* (Aldershot: Scolar Press, 1982).

Jackson, Holbrook. *The Eighteen Nineties: A Review of Art and Ideas at the Close of the Nineteenth Century* (London: Grant Richards, 1913).

Kooistra, Lorraine Janzen. *The Artist as Critic: Bitextuality in Fin-de-Siècle Illustrated Books* (Aldershot: Scolar Press, 1995).

Maxwell, Richard. *The Victorian Illustrated Book* (Charlottesville, VA: University of Virginia Press, 2002).

Meisel, Martin. *Realizations: Narrative, Pictorial, and Theatrical Arts in Nineteenth-Century England* (Princeton, NJ: Princeton University Press, 1983).

---

[58] *Publishers Weekly* 97/1 (1920), 639.

[59] Philip James, *English Book Illustration 1800–1900* (London: King Penguin, 1947), 9.

Morris, William. *The Ideal Book: A Paper by William Morris Read before the Bibliographical Society, London, 19 June 1893* (London: LCC Central School of Arts and Crafts, 1908).

Ray, Gordon Norton. *The Illustrator and the Book in England from 1790 to 1914* (London: Constable & Co., 1976).

Sketchley, Rose E. D. *English Book Illustration of To-day: Appreciations of the Work of Living English Illustrators with Lists of Their Books* (London: Kegan Paul, Trench, Trübner & Co., 1903).

Sullivan, Alvin (ed.). *British Literary Magazines: The Victorian and Edwardian Age, 1837–1913* (Westport, CT: Greenwood, 1984).

The Internet Archive (http://www.archive.org/index.php) is a free resource that offers scanned original editions with illustrations. It embraces periodicals as well as books cited in this chapter, including *The Strand Magazine* (although issue numbers are incorrectly referenced), *The Yellow Book*, the Kelmscott *Chaucer* (1896), and the Beardsley *Salomé* and *The Rape of the Lock*. Beardsley's *Lysistrata* illustrations can be viewed at the University of Adelaide's site: https://ebooks.adelaide.edu.au/b/beardsley/aubrey/lysistrata/.

PART VIII

TECHNOLOGIES

CHAPTER 35

THE COMING OF CINEMA

LAURA MARCUS

In December 1895, the Lumière brothers gave, to a Parisian audience, the first public exhibition of their Cinématographe, an event which is generally understood to mark the 'birth' of cinema. The presentation began with a projection of a stationary photograph on a screen which, to the audience's amazement, became an animated picture of, in the words of Georges Méliès, magician turned pioneer film-maker, 'the whole vitality of a street'.[1] The transmutation of still into moving image before the spectators' eyes crystallizes the motif of genesis: particularly apt, given the general understanding that the Cinématographe was, in a later film theorist's words, 'a recreation of the world in its own image'.[2] Audiences marvelled not only at the motion but also at the detail of the projected scenes, which seemed to represent a doubled reality.

While the sense of an entirely new phenomenon emerging into the world is a powerful one, a longer history of pre-cinematic technologies made this charged event possible. Historians of visual culture have traced this *longue durée* back to the optical shows and scientific instruments of earlier centuries (such as the *camera obscura* and the 'phantasmagoria'). In the last decades of the nineteenth century, there were a number of closer precedents to the Cinématographe, including the American inventor Thomas Edison's Kinetoscope. The central innovation of the Lumières' machine was that it could project images onto a screen for collective viewing, rather than for a single observer looking into a box or cabinet. The event taking place in December 1895 was thus public in a double sense.

Accounts from contemporary commentators have provided essential evidence for the cultural reception and conception of film at the turn of the century. Among the best known is that of Maxim Gorki, who was present at the first screenings of

---

[1] Quoted in Emmanuelle Toulet, *Birth of the Motion Picture* (New York: Abrams, 1995), 15.

[2] André Bazin, 'The Myth of Total Cinema', in *What is Cinema*, Vol. 1, ed. Hugh Gray (Berkeley, CA: University of California Press, 1967), 21.

the Lumières' films in Russia in 1896. 'Last night I was in the kingdom of the shadows', Gorki wrote, commenting on the uncanny dimensions of a projected world which was in every way life-like, but without sound and colour.[3] He pointed, as did so many early writers on film, to the moment of animation—'suddenly a strange flicker passes through the screen and the picture stirs to life'—and, at the film's close, to the 'vanishing' of the images from the edge of the screen. The mobile, shifting frame was a particularly marked dimension of the new medium for its early viewers.

While Gorki's article is a powerful evocation of the beginnings of cinema and its impact on its audiences, it also needs to be understood as the work of a writer seeking terms in which to represent the novelty of the moving pictures. His viewing of the films inspired him to write a short story dramatizing their impact: a prostitute watches one of the Lumière films ('The Family Breakfast') and its innocent image of family happiness leads her to wish to change her way of life. In broader terms, the incorporation of film and film viewing into the genre of the short story represents a significant interchange between literature and film in the early years of cinema and, indeed, in the years immediately preceding the Lumières' invention and its presentation. Stories appearing in magazines such as *The Strand* reveal the understanding of film as a device providing irrefutable evidence of crimes or love affairs. In other tales, apparently supernatural happenings—such as projections of light or uncanny images—are finally discovered to be the creation of cinematic devices.

Rudyard Kipling's 1904 'Mrs Bathurst'—perhaps the most powerful and complex of the short stories engaging with film in its early years—links the new medium ('The Cinematograph') and its representations with obsession, repetition, and absence. The present and the presence which film seems to deliver are chimera. Mrs Bathurst's look at the camera, which Vickery, the subject of the tale, misinterprets as a look at and for him, drives him to madness and to death. In this early story, Kipling alights on a concept of cinematic ontology which would, in the following decade, become central to an emergent film theory, as in Georg Lukács's 1913 'Thoughts Towards an Aesthetics of Cinema': '[T]here are only movements and actions of people—but *no people* . . . Through this the cinema images become uncannily lifelike.'[4]

Throughout the nineteenth century, writers had deployed such optical shows as magic lanterns and 'dissolving views' to represent states of consciousness and of dream states. George du Maurier's *Peter Ibbetson* (1891) used the analogy of the *camera obscura* to represent what the novel calls 'dreaming true': '[O]ne goes in and finds one's self in total darkness; the eye is prepared; one is thoroughly expectant and wide-awake. Suddenly there flashes on the sight the moving picture of the port

---

[3] Maxim Gorki, 'The Kingdom of Shadows', in Gilbert Adair (ed.), *Movies* (Harmondsworth: Penguin, 1999), 10–11.

[4] Georg Lukács, 'Gedanken zu einer Aesthetik des Kinos', *Frankfurter Zeitung* 10 Sept. 1913. Reprinted in Anton Kaes (ed.), *Kino-Debatte. Texte zum Verhältnis von Literatur und Film 1909–1929* (Tübingen: Max Niemeyer, 1978), 113.

and all the life therein, and the houses and cliffs beyond; and farther still the green hills, the white clouds, and blue sky.' His central characters, two separated lovers, meet every night in their dreams, moving, as apparitions, alongside their former selves and their ancestors.

The perception of film as capable of bringing the past into the present (and indeed the future) was central to Edison's vision of a future for his invention: '[G]rand opera can be given at the Metropolitan Opera House at New York without any material change from the original, and with artists and musicians long since dead.' It also became an inspiration for writers seeking to incorporate film into their narratives. A short story by the American writer and drama critic James Brander Matthews, 'The Kinetoscope of Time', published in *Scribner's Magazine* in December 1895, was a tale of mystery and imagination, in which the narrator enters a strange house and a chamber, empty apart from four 'curiously shaped narrow stands'.[5] Looking into one of these, he sees a blackness which emits 'warning sparks' before the darkness takes shape and a moving picture emerges. A sequence of scenes of dancing, separated by intervals of darkness, unfolds. Looking into the second cabinet, he sees scenes of battle. As all the sequences are described, it becomes clear that they are either drawn from works of literature (among them *The Scarlet Letter* and *Don Quixote*) or represent historical events. The narrator then becomes aware that he is being watched: a man introduces himself as the proprietor, 'glad always to show the visions I have under my control to those who will appreciate them'. He offers the narrator the opportunity to look into the two other viewing machines, which will show him his own past and his future, respectively: the price to be paid will be one year of his life, to be placed in the proprietor's service, for every ten years of his lifetime which is unfolded. The narrator refuses the pact and is escorted out of the chamber, finding himself in a busy urban street and 'the world of actuality'. Looking into a shop window, he sees a portrait which he recognizes as that of the man from whom he has just parted: 'Monsieur le Comte de Castiglione.'

The nature of the scenes viewed in the story is significant. Representations of the female dancing body, like those observed by the narrator in the first kinetoscope, became central to early cinematic technologies as the epitome of embodied motion, and played a significant role in literature of the late nineteenth and early twentieth centuries in which film, or proto-filmic devices, were represented. The French writer Villiers de l'Isle Adam's novel *L'Eve future* (1886), translated as *Tomorrow's Eve*, represents a fictionalized Thomas Edison, who creates a female android, Hadaly, through the new mechanical reproductive technologies of sound and vision. The novel also contains a depiction of 'the process of moving-picture technology'. In a chapter entitled 'Danse Macabre', the Edison character projects a 'film'

---

[5] James Brander Matthews, 'The Kinetoscope of Time', *Scribners Magazine* 18/6 (December 1895), 733–45. See also Helen Groth's excellent study *Moving Images: Nineteenth-Century Reading and Screen Practices* (Edinburgh: Edinburgh University Press, 2013).

showing an attractive young woman (Miss Evelyn Habal) dancing 'a popular Mexican dance'—'Her movements were as lively as life itself'—followed by a second filmstrip which reveals 'a little bloodless creature' singing an obscene song and dancing the same dance.[6] They are, it transpires, the same person. The woman who first appeared was an entirely manufactured product: *'the Artificial giving an illusion of life itself.'* The phrase was applied not only to femininity (as in Charles Baudelaire's concept of (female) artifice as modernity itself) but also, in turn-of-the-century contexts, to moving-image technologies. In Thomas Mann's *The Magic Mountain* (1924), to take a later example, the central characters (fellow patients at a sanatorium) visit a 'Bioscope Theatre', and watch scenes in which 'the phantasmagoria of the past' appears before them. One such scene represents 'a young Moroccan woman': 'the charming apparition...seemed to see and saw not....Its smile and nod were not of the present but of the past.'[7] Cinema, for all its conjuring of 'life', becomes viewed as a simulacrum operating on the side of death.

In Brander Matthews's story, the film scenes of the dances, drawn as they are from works of fiction, raise further questions of the relationship between the modes of picturing entailed in the act of reading (in 'the mind's eye') and the representations of the newly constituted 'moving picture' (which are at once actual and virtual). This bears on a striking aspect of the publication of Matthews's story in *Scribner's:* its use of illustrations. Many short stories in the magazine were illustrated extensively with drawings, but word and image tend to occupy distinct and separate parts of the page. In 'The Kinetoscope of Time', by contrast, the print is superimposed on the drawings, which are markedly perspectival, giving the appearance of three-dimensionality: drawn figures are not only adjacent to the printed words but are seen through and behind them (at some detriment to the legibility of the type). This mode of superimposition becomes a form of mingling indicative of the complex relationship between literature's conjuring up of mental images and the presentation of such images in the visual arts and media, to include not only drawing but film.

The nature of the second set of 'moving pictures' seen by the narrator in Matthews's story is also a telling one. The battle scenes, which show actual historical events, indicate the hope, or the fantasy, which became prominent among commentators in the early decades of the twentieth century, that 'history' could be taught through film, the medium endowed with the ability to capture events in all the detail of their reality and as they occurred. Film's 'objectivity' would banish the uncertainty and relativism, as well as the chronological yoke, of traditional historical enquiry. In 1912, the French film director Abel Gance wrote of cinema that it

---

[6] Villiers de l'Isle-Adam, *Tomorrow's Eve*, trans. Robert Martin Adams (Chicago, IL: University of Illinois Press, 1982), 9–10.

[7] Thomas Mann, *The Magic Mountain*, trans. H. T. Lowe-Porter (Harmondsworth: Penguin, 1960), 316–18.

was to be: 'A sixth art where we can evoke in minutes all the great disasters of history and extract from them an immediate objective lesson',[8] while in 1915 the American film pioneer D. W. Griffith suggested that the time would shortly come 'when the children in the public schools will be taught practically everything by moving pictures. Certainly they will never be obliged to read history again'. He envisaged a public library of the near future, in which there would be 'long rows of boxes of pillars, properly classified and indexed, of course. At each box a push button and before each box a seat'. Instead of having to wade through a

> host of books . . without a clear idea of exactly what did happen and confused at every point by conflicting opinions about what did happen, you will merely seat yourself at a properly adjusted window, in a scientifically prepared room, press the button, and actually see what happened. There will be no opinions expressed. You will be present at the making of history.[9]

The import of cinema's dual origins (often linked to Lumière and Méliès, respectively) in realism and in magic, in the film actuality and the fantastical film, in the evidential and the illusory, continued to be played out in the early years of cinema's development, reception, and representation in literary and cultural texts.

In September 1895, *Scribner's Magazine* published an article written by Alexander Black, cinema pioneer and novelist, in which he described his creation of a screen narrative, 'Miss Jerry'. In performances of this 'picture play', dissolving slides were projected against a fixed photographed background, so that the actors appeared to be in motion: Black spoke the voices for the different parts. The *Scribner's* article (which reproduced some of the photographs from 'Miss Jerry' and printed part of the accompanying dialogue) was titled 'Photography in Fiction'. Black explained the purpose of his 'picture play' invention: 'to illustrate art with life... bringing the living characters of my fictitious action against the actual life of the city'. With this mixed mode of fiction/reality, intended to create 'the illusion of reality', the 'text or monologue' was 'freed', for the most part, from the necessity of describing the appearance or actions of the characters, having 'to concern itself simply with their thoughts and words; and thus, in effect, a novelette which might require three hours to read, by this division of communication between the eye and the ear can be presented in an hour and a half or less time'.[10] Black's was a very particular mode of photographic storytelling—he later termed it the 'slow movie'—but it bears in important ways on more general imaginings of new and hybrid forms in the period, in which novel relationships were envisaged between word (printed or spoken) and

[8] Abel Gance, 'A Sixth Art' (1912), in Richard Abel (ed.), *French Film Theory and Criticism*, Vol. 1 (Princeton, NJ: Princeton University Press, 1988), 67.

[9] D. W. Griffith, 'Five Dollar "Movies" Prophesied', *The Editor* (24 April 1915), 407–10. Quoted in *Focus on D.W. Griffith*, ed. Harry M. Geduld (Englewood Cliff, NJ: Prentice Hall, 1971), 34–5.

[10] Alexander Black, 'Photography in Fiction', *Scribner's Magazine* 18/3 (September 1895), 348–60, esp. 348.

image. For Black, the photographic image would perform the work of 'the mind's eye', making the description of externals redundant and, in the process, speeding up the time formerly taken by reading alone.

The 'novelette' and the short story were seen to be particularly suitable for translation into such new visual/verbal media. Furthermore, and as I have suggested, representations of early cinematic devices emerged, in the literary sphere, most fully in the short story form. Writing some decades later, in the late 1930s, the novelist Elizabeth Bowen, introducing an anthology of modern short stories, wrote of the close affinities between the short story and the cinema: 'The short story is a young art... the child of this century... The cinema, itself busy with a technique, is of the same generation: in the last thirty years the two arts have been accelerating together.'[11] Early cinema, with its briefly projected images emerging from, and disappearing back into, the darkness, exemplifies modes of narrative compression and contingency which are closely paralleled in the genre of the short story. The magical qualities of the filmic medium, as it appeared to its first spectators, as well as its scientific/technological origins, also had their literary corollaries in the tales of the fantastic and in the science fictions and fantasies appearing around the turn of the century.

H. G. Wells and Joseph Conrad present two rather different modes of engagement by writers with early cinema. For Wells, whose early training was in the natural and physical sciences, cinema was a technology with the potential to represent new understandings of evolution, time, space, motion, and perception. For Conrad, the issues were more specifically literary ones, relating to modes of narration and the role of 'vision' in the production and reception of literary texts. Conrad's brief writings on the topic of cinema also point to the perceived relationship between film and mental life, which I touch on at the close of this chapter, and which became an increasingly important dimension of aesthetics, psychology, and phenomenology as the twentieth century progressed.

The moving image, with its powers to make manifest the speculative, became central to Wells's imaginative world and his writing. His earliest published novella, 'The Time Machine', was published in the mid-1890s, coincident with the first films and with the proto-cinematic apparatus of this period. The early film pioneer Robert Paul initiated a patent application for a 'time machine' based on Wells's fiction: the patent was for an arrangement of mobile platforms, from which the seated audience would 'move toward and away from a screen onto which still and motion pictures were to be projected' and which (as in one of the imaginings expressed in J. Brander Matthews's short story) would appear to carry spectators into the past and the future. The audience would be given, in Paul's words,

> the sensation of voyaging upon a machine through time... In order to increase the
> realistic effect I may arrange that after a certain number of scenes from a hypothetical

---

[11] Elizabeth Bowen, 'Introduction: The Short Story', in *The Faber Book of Modern Short Stories* (London: Faber, 1937), 7.

future have been presented to the spectators, they may be allowed to step from the buildings, and be conducted through grounds or buildings arranged to represent exactly one of those epochs through which the spectator is supposed to be travelling.[12]

Illusionism again operates in the service of 'the realistic effect', with a mingling of virtual and actual realities which was, at this time, also being envisaged for stage-craft and live performance.

Wells's fictions of the turn of the century were absorbed not only with time travel but also with spatial relations, and experiments with speed, motion, and perception. *The Invisible Man* (whose central trope, and the comic possibilities it engendered, became extremely popular in cinema in its first decades) plays with the relations of absence and presence, while the novel's focus on vision and optics introduces those scientific enquiries and technological experiments which had brought cinema into being. 'Visibility', Wells has his narrator proclaim, 'depends on the action of the visible bodies on light'. Many of his early short stories, including those published in 1899 as *Tales of Space and Time*, explore the conditions of vision and visibility, connecting them with optical technologies and instruments of vision. In 'The Remarkable Case of Davidson's Eyes', the eponymous protagonist suffers a laboratory accident which renders him not blind but confined to the perception of an alternative reality. After some weeks, the 'real world' begins to re-enter his vision in pieces, 'like a faint spectre of itself...It's like a hole in this infernal phantom world'.[13] 'At first', the narrator notes, 'it was very confusing to him to have these two pictures overlapping each other like the changing views of a lantern, but in a little while he began to distinguish the real from the illusory'. The story, Wells's narrator concludes, is perhaps 'the best authenticated in existence of real vision at a distance':[14] he invokes, sceptically, theories of relativity and the fourth dimension. In Wells's fictional frameworks, cinema (or to be more precise, its immediate antecedents) provides an explicit or implicit way of transmitting these scientific motifs.

Wells's writings at the beginning of the twentieth century show a particular concern with the representation of speed and locomotion. In his novel 'When the Sleeper Wakes' (1898) the central protagonist awakens after a two-hundred-year coma to discover himself in a world of perpetual machinic motion: Wells here represents the recent invention of the moving walkway and imagines it as the organizing principle of the future city. His narrator also discovers a version of television, based on the kinetoscope—'a little figure in white appeared, kinetoscope fashion on

---

[12] Quoted in John Barnes, *The Beginnings of the Cinema in England 1894–1901*, Vol. 1: *1895* (New York: Barnes and Noble, 1976), 38–9.

[13] H. G. Wells, 'The Remarkable Case of Davidson's Eyes', in *The Complete Short Stories of H.G. Wells*, ed. John Hammond (London: Phoenix Press, 1998), 69.

[14] Ibid., 70.

the dial, walking and turning'—and a larger-format version of sound film, video, or television, employing cylinders (in the manner of Edison's 'kinetophonograph').[15] Even in his realist fictions, such as his 'New Woman' novel of 1909, *Ann Veronica*, film would seem to have been a primary influence: *Ann Veronica* reads a little like one of Alexander Black's 'picture plays', with action and dialogue playing a significantly greater role than narration and description. In the first decades of the twentieth century, Wells became increasingly involved with film-making and the film industry. Among other activities, he wrote a synopsis for a prospective film, *The King Who Was a King*, and reviewed Fritz Lang's *Metropolis* (1928) very negatively— although, or perhaps because, it seemed to be so closely based on his earlier fictional works, in particular *The Time Machine* and *When the Sleeper Wakes*. In the 1930s Wells involved himself fully in Alexander Korda's film adaptation *Things to Come*. He was also seen as one of cinema's most important prophets. As Charlie Chaplin wrote of film in 1927: 'A giant of limitless power has been reared, so huge that no one quite knows what to do with it. I, for one, am hopeful that Mr. Wells shall settle the question for us in his next novel.'[16]

From the mid- to the late 1890s, film was certainly a medium Joseph Conrad could have encountered. It is, for one thing, likely, as the critic Steven Donovan has suggested, that he would have read a significant early response to the new medium in the pages of the *New Review*.[17] (It was here that Conrad's *The Nigger of the Narcissus* was published, with its famous assertion in the Preface that 'My task which I am trying to achieve is, by the power of the written word to make you hear, to make you feel—it is, before all, to make you *see*'.[18]) The article in question, 'The Cinematograph', was authored by O. Winter (about whom nothing seems to be known, other than that he contributed a further article on art history to the journal), and was published in the May 1896 issue. It has recently developed a place in the history of early cinema equivalent to that of Gorki's 'The Kingdom of Shadows'. O. Winter's article was an account of the February 1896 *Cinematograph* show in London, and many of Winter's responses are identical to Gorki's, including his description of the films as 'life stripped of colour and sound'. Winter's description of the 'white, inanimate screen' that 'quivers into being' and 'bustles with the movement and masquerade of tremulous life' (with the arrival of the train in the station) is also a significant commentary on the conventions of film exhibition and projection.

---

[15] Wells, *When the Sleeper Wakes* (1899) (London: Phoenix, 2004), 30.

[16] Charlie Chaplin, 'Foreword', in L'Estrange Fawcett, *Films: Facts and Forecasts* (London: Geoffrey Bles, 1927), v–vi.

[17] Steven Donovan, *Joseph Conrad and Popular Culture* (Basingstoke: Palgrave Macmillan, 2005), 58–9.

[18] Joseph Conrad, *The Nigger of the 'Narcissus': A Tale of the Sea* (Edinburgh and London: John Grant, 1925), x.

Winter's article has a rather broader remit than Gorki's, for his concerns are with modes of representation—visual and literary—and in particular the terms of realism, naturalism, and Impressionism, which particularly exercised the editor, and writers for the *New Review*. The journal took a strong stand against naturalism, associated particularly with the work of Zola. This was at the heart of Winter's critique of the new medium of film: he insisted upon the differences between human vision and the photographic lens. The one was capable of selecting and focusing, the other unable to choose or select what passes before it: '[T]he scene is forced to trickle upon our nerves with an equal effect; it is neither so quick nor so changeful as life...Man cannot see with the mechanical unintelligence of a plate, exposed forty times in a second.'[19]

'Both the Cinematograph and the Pre-Raphaelite', Winter wrote, 'suffer from the same vice. The one and the other are incapable of selection; they grasp at every straw that comes in their way; they see the trivial and important, the near and the distant, with the same fecklessly impartial eye' (509). By contrast:

> The eye of the true impressionist...is the Cinematograph's antithesis. It never permits itself to see everything or to be perplexed by a minute survey of the irrelevant...It is artistic, because it is never mechanical, because it expresses a personal bias both in its choice and in its rejection...Nature is its material, whereas Fred Walker [a Pre-Raphaelite painter] and his followers might have been inspired by a series of photographic plates.

Winter continues

> Literature too has ever hankered unconsciously after the Cinematograph. Is not Zola the M. Lumière of his art? And might not a sight of the Cinematograph have saved the realists from a wilderness of lost endeavour? As the toy registers every movement without any expressed relation to its fellow, so the old and fearless realist believed in the equal value of all facts. He collected information in the spirit of the swiftly moving camera, or of the statistician. (510)

The implication is not only that the realist (or naturalist) writer acts and records like a camera, but that the new medium of film had rendered the realist's enterprise redundant and also shown up the essential redundancy of the realist enterprise.

The article is significant not only because it describes the conditions of early film exhibition, but also because it engages so fully with the relationship of film to literature and painting. It extends debates that had been ongoing since the emergence of photography in the mid-nineteenth century and of literary naturalism in the same period. It has not previously been remarked, I believe, that a number of Winter's comments directly echo those of Max Nordau, in his highly influential study *Degeneration* (originally published as *Entartung* [1892]). Writing on 'Realism', and on Zola more particularly, Nordau criticized the writer who attempted merely

---

[19] O. Winter, 'The Cinematograph', *New Review* 14 (May 1896), 507–13, esp. 509.

a reflection or imitation of the world, rather than a subjectively determined selection and colouration of its aspects:

> To work absolutely in the method of a camera obscura and a sensitive plate would be only possible to a very obtuse handicraftsman, who, in the presence of the visible world, had no feeling for anything, no pleasure, no disgust, no aspirations of any kind… If the imaginative writer wished to transcribe the world phonographically or photographically, his work would no longer be a poem, even in a purely technical sense; it would not even be a book, to the extent that the work of the painter who only photographs still continues, in a purely technical sense, to be a picture; it would be something with neither form, sense, nor name.[20]

It does not diminish the historical and aesthetic interest of Winter's discussion to point to his indebtedness to Nordau: rather, it helps to clarify the ideological contexts in which it was written and would have been read.

If Winter's article should be read as a manifesto for the novel as much as a discussion of the Cinematograph, can Conrad's Preface to *The Nigger of the Narcissus* be understood as a manifesto for the novel in the face of the new medium? Negative responses to cinema (as well as more positive engagements) are an important dimension of writers' relationships to film. The literary aesthetics, as well as the literary texts, of the late nineteenth and early twentieth century would certainly seem to have been shaped by (or in opposition to) the new medium—or, at least, by what it seemed to represent—in relation, above all, to realism, the concept of the 'life-like', naturalism, and impressionism. These became, in the context of the *New Review* as elsewhere, an answer to the cinema's unselective recordings of the world that passed before it.

While there are scattered references in Conrad to film and photography in its early years, it is not until the 1920s that there is any very substantial commentary on it. Yet throughout the 1910s, Conrad was in touch with film companies interested in film versions of his novels and stories. In 1919, he received some US$20,000 for the sale of world cinema rights for *Victory*, *Chance*, *Romance* and *Lord Jim*: income that bought him his final home in Kent, Oswalds, and a Cadillac. As Gene Moore notes, 'the money to be made in film not only helped to improve Conrad's standard of living, but also affected the nature of his involvement with the new medium. Thereafter, whenever films were mentioned in his letters to [his agent] Pinker, he often mixed disdainful references with ironic allusions to the immense profits to be made'.[21]

In 1920, Conrad worked on a screenplay, with Pinker's help, of his short story 'Gaspar Ruiz', to be called 'Gaspar the Strong Man'. In 1915 Conrad had sent Pinker a 'Cinema Suggestion' noting 'the eminent fitness of *Gaspar Ruiz* for pictorial representation', adding that 'the story is simply crammed full of picturesque possibilities'.

---

[20] Max Nordau, *Degeneration* (Lincoln, NE: University of Nebraska Press, 1993), 477–8.
[21] Gene M. Moore (ed.), *Conrad on Film* (Cambridge: Cambridge University Press, 2006), 35.

Gene Moore gives a detailed account of the construction of the screenplay, noting Conrad's rudimentary filmic vocabulary, which allowed him only to distinguish between shots of dramatic action, which he called 'Picture', and written inter-texts (used to convey titles, narrative information, or dialogue) which he called 'Screen'. His only explicit direction for camera movement consists of suggestions that certain 'Pictures' should be taken 'Close-up'.[22] It is not, perhaps, surprising that in 1921 Famous Players–Lasky rejected the screenplay.

By the early 1920s, the issue of the relationship between the novel and the film had clearly become of some interest to Conrad. On occasion, he suggested that he would be more favourably disposed towards film than towards stage versions of his novels: referring to a proposed theatrical dramatization of 'The Arrow of Gold', he wrote to Pinker that 'the film deals only with the visual aspects, and as superficially as an illustration in a magazine; whereas the dramatisation cuts into the quick and may mangle the very heart of the thing'.[23] As Conrad started to work on the screenplay for 'Gaspar Ruiz', he wrote to the artist William Rothenstein:

> If one is to condescend to this sort of thing well then, all considered, I prefer Cinema to Stage. The Movie is just a silly stunt for silly people—but the theatre is more compromising since it is capable of falsifying the very soul of one's work on the imaginative and on the intellectual side—besides having some inferior poetics of its own which is bound to play havoc with that imponderable quality of creative literary expression which depends on one's individuality.[24]

While at one level these comments suggest little more than contempt for the cinema, it is important to note that they come in the context of the question of adaptation. Around the time Conrad was writing his letters, those most committed to and engaged with film were also expressing disenchantment with cinema's reliance upon literary texts. This emerges strongly in Virginia Woolf's 'The Cinema' (1926), discussed at the close of this chapter, in which Woolf envisages a future for the cinema once it has ceased to be parasitical upon works of literature.

In the spring of 1923, Conrad was preparing to travel to America, where he would be delivering public speeches. As he wrote in a letter to Eric Pinker (9 April 1923):

> I...have sketched out the outlines of a lecture, or rather of a familiar talk, on the (apparently) extravagant lines of the imaginative literary art being based fundamentally on scenic motion, like a cinema; with this addition that for certain purposes the artist is a much more subtle and complicated machine than a camera, and with a wider range, if in the visual effects less precise—and so on, and so on, for an hour; with a

---

[22] Ibid., 38.

[23] *The Collected Letters of Joseph Conrad*, Vol. 7, *1990–1922*, ed. Laurence Davies and J. H. Stape (Cambridge: Cambridge University Press, 2005), 15.

[24] Ibid., 163.

mixture of jocularity and intense seriousness (which *may* do). I intend to try it … with illustrative bits of reading from 'Victory'.

… (Don't imagine that I am going to be impertinent to the cinemas; on the contrary, I shall butter them up.)[25]

Conrad delivered his lecture at Garden City in New York, to the staff of his American publisher, Doubleday, Page, on 5 May 1923. Five days later he gave a more formal lecture and reading from *Victory* at the mansion home of the railroad industrialist Arthur Curtis James. 'This is Mr. Conrad's first appearance in public', Doubleday remarked in introducing Conrad to the audience, 'and please God, if I have anything to do with it, it will be his last'. (He was referring to Conrad's and his own nervousness before the occasion but, as an introduction, it seems to lack a certain grace.) Conrad's 'Notes for Speeches in America' include a section entitled 'Author and Cinematograph', in which he wrote:

> Long before the idea occurred to scientists and means devised by technicians that sun can make pictures, at first motionless and afterwards moving, the aim of the novelist has been (at least one of his aims) to present humanity in action on the background of the changing aspects of nature and a series of acted scenes exhibiting part of life in a connected series up to some appointed conclusion. But the author unlike the camera had the power to react not only to light, shades and colour but also to form … That general fundamental quality of visuality, of animation, applies to all the masters of creative art … fundamentally the creator in letters aims at a moving picture—moving to the eye, to the mind, and to our complex emotions which I will express with one word—heart.[26]

The 'Notes' continue with a brief discussion of the centrality of 'the human faculty of attention' for the realization of all forms of artistic representation of life, and of the appeal made by the picture screen to the eye, the stage to the sense of sight and the sense of hearing, and the different, perhaps greater, appeal of the book: '[T]he written word whether looked at on the printed page or even read aloud has a strange power both in its shape and in its sound of suggestion which the others somehow miss … [it] is born from introspection and bears the impress of one temperament'. Yet, Conrad suggested, speaking to an audience 'whose life's work is to disseminate the written word I don't mind confessing that many of my ambitions have been concentrated on the visuality and precision of images'. His powers, he argued, were not those of (literary) style but resided in his 'fidelity to the evocative power of the written word'.[27]

---

[25] *The Collected Letters of Joseph Conrad*, Vol. 8, *1923–1924*, ed. Lawrence Davies and Gene M. Moore (Cambridge: Cambridge University Press, 2008), 74–5.

[26] Joseph Conrad, 'Author and Cinematograph', quoted in Arnold T. Schwab, 'Conrad's American Speeches and His Reading from "Victory"', *Modern Philology* 62/4 (May, 1965), 342–7, esp. 345.

[27] Ibid., 347.

The 'Notes' by no means add up to a very developed argument, but they do offer an interesting return to the terms of the Preface to *The Nigger of the 'Narcissus'*, in their invocation of the relations of eye, mind, feeling. Conrad also suggested that literature's advantage lay in its possession not only of the impressionism of the camera—its reaction to 'light, shades and colour'—but also in the shaping brought into being by 'form', as well as the qualities of inwardness and subjective perception (we recall here the critic O. Winter's advocacy of the Impressionist's 'personal bias'). Most significant, however, was Conrad's argument that 'the creator in letters aims at a moving picture—moving to the eye, to the mind, and to our complex emotions'.[28] The play on the word 'moving' in its dual sense of 'motion' and 'emotion' occurs time and again in early commentary on the cinema. Conrad was not, however, simply translating 'motion' into 'emotion', but holding on to both terms at once, and continuing to emphasize the centrality of motion to his aesthetics.

One dimension of modernism's 'visual turn' has been the mapping of questions of modernist visuality onto optical technologies—in particular, photography and early film. Following Conrad's hints, however, it would be possible to reconsider the question of the novel as a 'moving picture'. Conrad's 'Notes' seem less concerned, at this stage, with the relationship between literature and film as a question of 'adaptation' than with the novel as (always having been) a form of cinema, whose motion and emotion are actualized by the reading process. The idea of continuous motion was clearly crucial to Conrad's conceptions of his novelistic practice, and colour many of his comments on visual media: 'When writing I visualize the successive scenes as always in motion—a flow of closely linked effects, so that when I attempt to arrest them in my mind at any given moment the first thought is always: that's no good.'[29] Similarly, his recorded comments on film nearly always come back to the issue of motion. The American portrait painter Walter Tittle's record of his conversations with Conrad in 1923, 'The Conrad who Sat for Me', detail another discussion of cinema. Conrad, Tittle writes, 'discovered to me a deep-seated aversion to the cinema' and a particular dislike of Chaplin. From this he launched into a real tirade against the films:

> They are absolutely the lowest form of amusement. I hate them!... They are stupid and can never be of real value. The cinema is not a great medium. It merely affords entertainment for people who enjoy sitting with thought utterly suspended and watching a changing pattern flickering before their eyes. Shadowgraphs in pantomime are much better .. There is no value in a gesture except at full speed.[30]

At least some of Conrad's alleged reservations towards the cinema seem to concern its alleged failure to represent a smooth flow of actuality in motion—hence his

---

[28] Ibid., 346.   [29] 16 August 1917, Conrad, *Collected Letters*, Vol. 6, 117.

[30] Walter Tittle, 'The Conrad who Sat for Me', *Outlook* (New York) CXL (1, 8 July 1925), 333–5, 361–2. Reprinted in *Conrad: Interviews and Recollections*, ed. Martin Ray (Iowa City, IA: University of Iowa Press, 1990), 161.

antipathy towards both slow motion and the speeding up of action through cutting. It is this antipathy, as well as Conrad's idealization of the literary 'moving picture' and his models of visualization and actualization, that suggest a model of what I am calling 'the cinema mind'. Conrad's relationship to the new medium appears to have underwritten, and competed with, both his 'visual' preoccupations and those of literary impressionism more generally. In impressionism, as some of its practitioners defined it, the writer's mind was viewed as a form of recording instrument. As Ford Madox Ford wrote in his study of Conrad: '[W]e saw that Life did not narrate, but made impressions on our brains.'[31]

Throughout Conrad's work, we see the play of shadow upon surface, shadow upon wall. One of the most striking occurrences of this effect comes at the close of *The Secret Agent*, in the seconds before Verloc is stabbed by his wife:

> He was lying on his back and staring upwards. He saw partly on the ceiling and partly on the wall the moving shadow of an arm with a clenched hand holding a carving knife. It flickered up and down. Its movements were leisurely. They were leisurely enough for Mr Verloc to recognize the limb and the weapon.[32]

The passage, and the action, is preceded by Winnie Verloc's nightmare envisionings—in which she translates overheard words into pictures—of her young brother Stevie's death, as the bomb he is unwittingly carrying detonates: 'She remembered now what she had heard, and she remembered it pictorially. They had to gather him up with the shovel...Mrs Verloc closed her eyes desperately, throwing upon that vision the night of her eyelids.'[33] Winnie Verloc, we are told, thinks in images: it is, in the terms of the novel, a mark of her limitations. The closing of her eyes to shut out the image of the shovel scraping up Stevie's shattered and scattered remains might be said to have the opposite effect to the one she intends: the inner surfaces of her eyelids in fact provide ('throwing upon that vision', or projecting) a night sky against which the 'pyrotechnic display' of Stevie's dismembering is spectacularly displayed. The relationship between the eye and the mind's eye ('before all, to make you *see*) is thus reinscribed.

For other modernist writers, including James Joyce and Virginia Woolf, cinema, perception, and consciousness would also become closely, and at times inextricably, intertwined. Writing to his patron Harriet Shaw Weaver, after one of the numerous eye operations he endured, Joyce wrote: 'Whenever I am obliged to lie with my eyes closed, I see a cinematograph going on and on and it brings back to my memory things I had almost forgotten.' Joyce's writings engaged with film in many different ways, as did Woolf's: in the context of the present argument, I would note the ways in which, from the short story 'The Mark on the Wall' (1917) to her novel *To the*

---

[31] Ford Madox Ford, *Joseph Conrad: A Personal Remembrance* (New York: Ecco Press, 1989), 194–5.
[32] Conrad, *The Secret Agent* (1907) (Oxford: Oxford University Press, 1983), 262.
[33] Ibid., 260.

Lighthouse (1927), Woolf represents the construction of screens or surfaces onto which images are projected, as a way of conceptualizing the processes of thought and memory. At the heart of her chapter 'The Cinema' (1926) is the image of an 'accidental' shadow on the screen: 'the emergence of an unexpected shadow', as she wrote in a draft version of the chapter, which, she suggests, might testify to 'a wind blowing about in us, a power of emotion which is still unharnessed to its proper object'.[34] Thus she gestured towards cinema as an art of the future which, because it was also an art at its beginnings, confounded the distinctions between old and new and returned the moderns to the very origins of representation.

FURTHER READING

Burch, Noël. *Life to These Shadows*, trans. and ed. Ben Brewster (London: British Film Institute, 1990).

Christie, Ian. *Early Cinema and the Birth of the Modern World* (London: British Film Institute, 1994).

Daly, Nicholas. *Literature, Technology and Modernity* (Cambridge: Cambridge University Press, 2004).

Gunning, Tom. 'The Cinema of Attractions: Early Film, its Spectator and the Avant-Garde', in Thomas Elsaesser (ed.), *Early Film: Space, Frame, Narrative* (London: British Film Institute, 1990), 56–62.

Higson, Andrew. (ed.) *Young and Innocent: The Cinema in Britain, 1896–1930* (Exeter: Exeter University Press, 2002).

Marcus, Laura. *The Tenth Muse: Writing about Cinema in the Modernist Period* (Oxford: Oxford University Press, 2007).

Plunkett, John and James Lyons (eds). *Multimedia Histories: From the Magic Lantern to the Internet* (Exeter: Exeter University Press, 2007).

Trotter, David. *Cinema and Modernism* (Oxford: Blackwell, 2007).

Williams, Keith. *H.G. Wells, Modernity and the Movies* (Liverpool: Liverpool University Press, 2007).

[34] Virginia Woolf, Draft 1 of 'The Movies', 135; held in the Henry W. and Albert A. Berg Collection of English and American Literature, The New York Public Library. The published version of the essay 'The Cinema' [1926] is in Andrew McNeillie (ed.), *The Essays of Virginia Woolf*, Vol. 4: *1925–1928* (London: Hogarth Press, 1994), 348–54; and in a variant edition as 'The Cinema'/'The Movies and Reality', 591–5.

CHAPTER 36

LITERATURE AND PHOTOGRAPHY

KATE FLINT

In 1888, Amy Levy published her short novel *The Romance of a Shop*. It tells the story of the London-based middle-class Lorimer sisters who, after they are orphaned, need to earn their living. In one of the relatively few novels that places photography right at the centre of its narrative Levy shows how they achieve this through launching a photographic business, after perfecting the necessary skills. Yet the studio trade described in Levy's novel is poised—although Levy could in no way have been aware of this fact—just before the nature of photography shifted hugely, and became a significantly more democratic pursuit. The invention of the Kodak camera in 1888, containing a roll of factory-loaded film that one sent off for developing ('You press the button—we do the rest' was its advertising slogan) was a transformation in portability. Cheaper and smaller still was the Pocket Kodak of 1895, followed by the Brownie in 1900. 'To Kodak' soon became a verb. The camera that Jonathan Harker carries on his Transylvanian business trip in *Dracula* (1897) is named as a Kodak—thus marking him as a man of the modern world. '"What an ass I was not to bring my Kodak!"', exclaims St John Hirst in Virginia Woolf's *The Voyage Out* (1915) on an excursion into the tropical jungle, revealing a decidedly tourist mentality.[1]

Levy's novel conveys an excellent sense of the material factors that determined the practice of photography itself at the beginning of our period, from the weight of camera equipment to the concern about light sources. But *The Romance of a Shop* is also an exemplary work, since it dramatizes several themes that run right through until the 1920s and beyond, including heated debates concerning the very status of photography. The Lorimer sisters use it primarily as a recording device, capturing the appearance of people, live and dead (the practice of post-mortem photography, and the attendant question of whether this is a suitable task for a woman, provides

---

[1] Virginia Woolf, *The Voyage Out* (Oxford: Oxford University Press, 2009), 326.

a significant hinge in the plot). They also provide a service for studio artists, photographing their oil paintings before they are sent out into the world for public exhibition. Knowledge of artworks, and memories of them, were increasingly mediated through photographic images: witness the packet of images that the tourist Lucy Honeychurch puts together at Alinari's shop in Florence in E. M. Forster's *A Room with a View* (1908), only to have them splashed with the blood of a murdered man. This image lodges in George Emerson's memory as surely as on a photographic plate. Yet even as photography served the established arts, its artistic status remained a controversial issue throughout this period. Arguments centred on whether or not this form could lay claim to significant aesthetic value; whether or not individual talent was involved in taking an image, or whether solely technical competence was required, and on how 'art photography' might be differentiated in appearance or function from images that provided—or were assumed to provide—a mere factual record. These distinctions were to be increasingly significant as photographs became an ever-expanding element of the visual habitus.

Knowledge of technological developments is essential for understanding the shifting contexts in which people encountered photographs, in life as well as in literature. New printing technologies, particularly the development of the half-tone process (initially introduced in 1875), meant that many more photographic images were made visible than previously. They began to appear regularly in newspapers and periodicals, and to illustrate biographies, works of travel, and even fiction. They expanded visual knowledge of the world. Indeed, the career of the newspaper illustrator, like Frank Jermyn in Levy's novel, was soon to be superseded. Other technological innovations made an impact, too, on the conditions under which photographs could be taken, especially the invention in 1887 of *blitzlichtpulver* ('lightning-light powder', or flash powder, which took image making indoors in an unprecedented way). In other words, photography became an increasingly ordinary form, was ever more portable, and was both found in and recorded a rapidly growing variety of occasions and locations.

Those photographers who made aesthetic claims for their work determinedly differentiated themselves from those who saw the camera as a purely instrumental device, let alone from hobbyists who used it to document family occasions and leisure hours. Antony Guest summed up this attitude, when he wrote in *Art and the Camera* (1907) that artistic photography should be thought of as the work of those who wish to give their

> personal impression of Nature's moods. Such an aspiration should engage sympathy, if only because of the afflicting capacity of the camera for recording the commonplace, its effrontery in stating platitudes, and its perversity in emphasising things of no importance. It has, in fact, certain of the qualities of a bore, and seldom fails to manifest them when left to its own devices.[2]

---

[2] Antony Guest, *Art and the Camera* (London: George Bell, 1907), 1.

Certain writers on photography borrowed language from the registers of literary criticism in order to suggest that photography could approach other arts in its capacity to provoke emotion and create affect. In his major theoretical contribution, *Naturalistic Photography for Students of the Art* (1889), P. H. Emerson, one of England's foremost practitioners of, and apologists for, pictorialist photography, attacked those who called any form of writing 'photographic'. He went on to distinguish between photographic images that convey 'sharp, common-place fact' and those that are 'full of truth and poetry'. There is, he emphasizes, 'a poetry of photography as there is of painting and literature'.[3] Yet because of the medium's associations with 'recording the commonplace', and because it was often assumed that operating a camera required little skill, the word 'photographic' was often, as Emerson complains, used in a demeaning way. It suggested that writers were merely transcribing the world around them without any exercise of selection or imagination. Thomas Hardy—despite his fascination, elsewhere, with the photograph as an object that may be invested with intense emotional power—distinguished human from mechanical observation, when he noted in 1882 that 'in life the seer should watch that pattern among general things which his idiosyncrasy moves him to observe, and describe that alone. This is, quite accurately, a going to Nature, yet the result is no mere photograph, but purely the product of the writer's own mind'.[4] This pejorative usage persisted: Forster, discussing H. G. Wells's characters in 1927, declared most of them to be 'as flat as a photograph', even as he allows that Wells agitates them 'with such vigour that we forget their complexities lie on the surface and would disappear if it was scratched or curled up'.[5]

This deployment of 'photographic' as a critical adjective carries an undertow of aesthetic elitism, unmistakably present in Hardy's use of the word 'mere'. However, challenges came from those who argued that photography possessed its own aesthetic powers. Charles Caffin, in *Photography as a Fine Art* (1901), described how the photographer, as opposed to the painter, can 'flash his meaning instantaneously upon our consciousness'—a concept underscored the following year by Bernard Shaw, himself a talented photographer, who distinguished photography from painting because of its ability to seize the moment when things in the world, and an artist's subjectivity, coincide.[6] It also ignores the important way in which photography can be seen as a democratic form: not in the sense that it comes to be practised by a wide social range of individuals, but one that can give (depending, of course,

[3] P. H. Emerson, *Naturalistic Photography for Students of the Art*, 2nd edn (London: Sampson Low, Marston, Searle & Rivington, 1890), 183, 251.

[4] Florence Emily Hardy, *The Early Life of Thomas Hardy, 1840–1891* (London: Macmillan, 1928), 198. Hardy also uses the vocabulary of photography to indicate the limitations of a scrupulously exact fidelity to detail in 'The Profitable Reading of Fiction' (1888) and 'The Science of Fiction' (1891).

[5] E. M. Forster, *Aspects of the Novel* (London: Penguin, 2005), 76.

[6] Charles H. Caffin, *Photography as a Fine Art: The Achievements and Possibilities of Photographic Art in America* (New York: Doubleday, Page, & Co., 1901), 175.

on composition, focus, and retouching) equal, indiscriminate weight to all that it contains. This had been recognized as 'one of the charms of photography' since the medium's inception, with Fox Talbot marvelling at how 'the operator himself discovers on examination, perhaps long afterwards, that he has depicted many things he had no notion of at the time'[7] (or as Virginia Woolf was to put it, much later, 'Isn't it odd how much more one sees in a photograph than in real life?'[8]). Such a bringing to visibility, plus what Walter Benjamin influentially termed the 'optical unconscious'—photography's revelation of that which cannot be seen without the camera's aid—contribute towards the photograph's role in what we might call 'secondary viewing'.[9] That is, seeing the world in a photographically mediated form.

Photography's democracy surfaces in another way. It increasingly comes to be mentioned in texts in passing—as part of the furniture, both literally and metaphorically. As befits a visual form often associated with the ephemeral, with the capturing of a brief moment, photographs often play a more prominent role in short stories than they do in longer fiction. Yet while rarely forming the pivot of a novel's plot, passing references to photographs act as constant reminders of their presence within daily life. Images of relatives or places or of classical sculpture hang on walls, pointing to familial and cultural ties. Photographs are used to form connections between people, whether we think of the plush covered albums indicating Constance's 'cult for photographs' in Arnold Bennett's *The Old Wives' Tale* (1908),[10] or the rather inappropriate bare-shouldered image of his fiancée Lily that William shares with his mother in D. H. Lawrence's *Sons and Lovers* (1913), or the obligations that are handed over from Kurtz to Marlowe along with a package of letters and the Intended's photograph, in *Heart of Darkness* (1899). They make occasional appearances as pornography: the window of Verloc's seedy shop in *The Secret Agent* (1907) 'contained photographs of more or less undressed dancing girls'.[11] Stephen Dedalus, in James Joyce's *A Portrait of the Artist as a Young Man* (1916), kept a 'sootcoated packet of pictures which he had hidden in the flue of the fireplace and in the presence of whose shameless or bashful wantonness he lay for hours sinning in thought and deed'.[12] What is more, and equally causally, knowledge of photography becomes such a part of everyday life that it provides a source of metaphor even when no actual images are involved. In Bennett's *Clayhanger* (1910), Edwin and Hilda shake hands early in their courtship, after which Edwin 'hastened away, with a delicate

---

[7] William Henry Fox Talbot, *The Pencil of Nature* (London: Longmans, 1844), 10.

[8] Virginia Woolf to Vita Sackville-West, 25 December 1935. See Nigel Nicolson and Joanne Trautmann (eds), *The Letters of Virginia Woolf 1932–1935*, 6 vols (London: Hogarth Press, 1975–80), V, 455.

[9] Walter Benjamin, 'The Work of Art in the Age of Mechanical Reproduction', in *Illuminations*, ed. Hannah Arendt and trans. Harry Zohn (New York: Schocken, 1969), 236.

[10] Arnold Bennett, *The Old Wives' Tale* (Oxford: Oxford University Press), 595.

[11] Joseph Conrad, *The Secret Agent* (London: Penguin, 2007), 3.

[12] James Joyce, *A Portrait of the Artist as a Young Man* (London: Penguin, 1992), 124.

photograph of the palm of her hand printed in minute sensations on the palm of his', while in Woolf's *The Voyage Out* (1915), she describes some guests watching out a storm in their tropical hotel: 'The flashes now came frequently, lighting up faces as if they were going to be photographed.'[13]

Whether perched on a mantelpiece, or carried in a wallet, photographs often serve the function of memento—'both a pseudo presence and a token of absence', as Susan Sontag puts it in *On Photography*.[14] They are revered, and on occasion desecrated. Frederick Locker-Lampson, one of many poets who saw something comic in the genre (thus demonstrating and consolidating its connection to the vernacular), has a speaker look back to the image his Di once gave him—'In *photo* we were group'd together; / She wore the darling hat and feather / That I adore'—but it passed into the hands of another:

> I've seen it in Smith's album-book!
> Just think! her hat – her tender look,
>   Are now that brute's!
> Before she gave it, off she cut
> *My* body, head, and lyrics, but
> She was obliged, the little slut,
>   To leave my Boots.[15]

Hardy's 'The Photograph' offers more serious and unsettling photographic destruction, playing with the idea that a photograph is, almost, the person themselves, and describing a quasi-erotic burning. 'The flame had eaten her breasts, and mouth, and hair', the speaker notes, before wondering whether, if the woman portrayed is still alive, she felt any visceral shudder at the moment of her virtual demise.[16]

A later poem by Hardy, 'The Son's Portrait', offers a more redemptive treatment of the discarded image, when a mother finds her dead son's photograph in a junk store:

> In burrowing mid this chattel and that,
> High, low, or edgewise thrown,
> I lit upon something lying flat –
> A fly-specked portrait,
> Framed. 'Twas my dead son's own.
>
> 'That photo? … A lady—I know not whence—
> Sold it me, Ma'am, one day,
> With more. You can have it for eighteen-pence:
> The picture's nothing;
> It's but for the frame you pay.'

[13] Bennett, *Clayhanger* (London: E. P. Dutton, 1910), 343; Woolf, *Voyage Out*, 429.
[14] Susan Sontag, *On Photography* (London: Penguin, 1979), 16.
[15] Frederick Locker-Lampson, 'Our Photographs', *London Lyrics* (London: Methuen, 1904), 154.
[16] Thomas Hardy, 'The Photograph', *Complete Poems* (New York: Macmillan, 1978), 469.

He had given it her in their heyday shine,
When she wedded him, long her wooer:
And then he was sent to the front-trench-line,
And fell there fighting;
And she took a new bridegroom to her.
I bought the gift she had held so light,
And *buried it*—as 'twere he.—[17]

Faces from home—and faces who were away from home—are poignant reminders in literature of travel and of war. Siegfried Sassoon, in 'Working Party', writes of a soldier who has just been killed: 'He was a young man with a meagre wife / And two small children in a Midland town; / He showed their photographs to all his mates.'[18] The very ordinariness of this counterbalances the unrepresentability of the emotional and visceral horrors of war—as Wilfred Owen wrote to Sassoon after the loss of his 'excellent little servant Jones'. 'Catalogue? Photograph? Can you photograph the crimson-hot iron as it cools from the smelting? That is what Jones's blood looked like, and felt like. My senses are charred.'[19] In many ways, however, this war's most notable legacy in terms of the links between literature and photography has come as writers look back on photographs that show young men with little concept of what they are about to encounter: Philip Larkin's 'MCMXIV', Ted Hughes's 'Six Men', George Szirtes's 'André Kertész: Latrine'.

It has become almost impossible to write about the nature of photography in relation to memory, loss, and pastness without falling back on Roland Barthes's *Camera Lucida* (1980). This slender work—simultaneously offering generalizations about photography while demonstrating that to write about the genre can be an intensely personal experience—has exercised a profound influence over the terms informing contemporary photographic scholarship. For Barthes, the photograph differs from all other images since it is a 'certificate of presence'; it refers to the '*necessarily* real thing which has been placed before the lens, without which there would be no photograph', and it gains its particular poignancy from the fact that 'it is literally an emanation of the referent'. 'From a real body, which was there,' Barthes continues, 'proceed radiations which ultimately touch me, who am here; the duration of the transmission is insignificant; the photograph of the missing being, as Sontag says, will touch me like the delayed rays of a star'.[20]

The absolute truth of this was challenged almost as strongly by Victorian composite printing, and by practices of darkroom retouching, as it has been by the possibilities of digital manipulation. But Barthes links this sense of immanence, a

[17] Hardy, 'The Son's Portrait', *Complete Poems*, 862.
[18] Siegfried Sassoon, 'Working Party', *The War Poems of Siegfried Sassoon* (London: Faber, 1983), 27.
[19] Wilfred Owen to Siegfried Sassoon, 10 October 1918. See Wilfred Owen, *Collected Letters*, ed. Harold Owen and John Bell (London: Oxford University Press, 1987), 581.
[20] Roland Barthes, *Camera Lucida*, trans. Richard Howard (New York: Farrar, Straus, and Giroux, 1981), 87, 76, 80–1.

tie to the image's material origins, with an intense longing for the past. *Camera Lucida*, written just after his mother's death, is shot through with an unfulfillable desire for people and worlds that have irrevocably disappeared. It both enacts and declares the idea that responses to photographs may themselves be highly personal. What speaks to one person may carry no resonances at all for another. For this reason, Barthes refuses to include the 'Winter Garden' photograph of his mother, 'the treasury of rays which emanated from my mother as a child'. Unbearably poignant to him, he cannot bear the thought that for 'you, it would be nothing but an indifferent picture, one of the thousand manifestations of the "ordinary"'.[21]

As Barthes recognized (and as practitioners of spirit photography were ready to exploit), we project our own desires, emotions, and memories onto what we see. We believe—or choose to believe—that what is shown in a photograph is true, or real. This, at any rate, is the premise behind very many of the photographs that are mentioned, in passing, in the fiction of this period. In this vein, the 'imaginative woman' at the heart of Thomas Hardy's 1894 short story of that name fantasizes about the rapport that she imagines must exist between her and a male poet whom she never meets in person. Both poems and, crucially, the image of his 'striking countenance' with its large dark eyes convince her of this.[22] Christian Metz has outlined some of the features that make a photograph a readily fetishizable object: it is small, portable, touchable; one can keep it in a private place and enjoy close, private communion with it.[23] Ella's behaviour certainly exemplifies this: 'As she gazed long at the portrait she fell into thought, till her eyes filled with tears, and she touched the cardboard with her lips.'[24] She is devastated when, shortly later, she hears that he has committed suicide. Nine months later, she bears a child; she dies, exhausted, shortly after. Later still, her husband comes upon the photograph of the deceased poet and, musing, compares its features with those of his little boy. 'By a known but inexplicable trick of Nature there were undoubtedly strong traces of resemblance to the man Ella had never seen; the dreamy and peculiar expression of the poet's face sat, as the transmitted idea, upon the child's, and the hair was of the same hue'.[25]

Hardy borrows from folklore that maintains that a pregnant woman who experiences a strong shock may end up imprinting its record onto her foetus. But the idea that there is something akin to magic in photography's powers is found in numerous other cases, from the horror in a dead man's eye that is somehow caught on a camera plate in Rudyard Kipling's 'At the End of the Passage' (1890), to the strange sequence of pictures taken of a prisoner in Richard Marsh's 'The Photographs' that show a woman who had been invisible to the naked eye—images that prove that the man who was the ostensible subject had been wrongfully sentenced.

---

[21] Ibid., 82, 73.

[22] Hardy, 'An Imaginative Woman', in *Life's Little Ironies* (London: Macmillan, 1912), 16.

[23] Christian Metz, 'Photography and Fetish', *October* 34 (Autumn 1985), 81–90.

[24] Hardy, 'Imaginative Woman', 16.   [25] Ibid., 31.

Underlying all these tales of the supernatural is the camera's claim to veracity. ' "It is a well-authenticated fact that the camera cannot lie. On this occasion it has seen something which was concealed from our less sensitive vision" ', explains a doctor in Marsh's narrative.[26] A ghost tale by E. G. Swain, published in 1912, is in the tradition of the 'magic picture' story—as are a significant number involving photography. In this case, a photograph of a rectory lawn temporarily stirs into motion to show the perpetrator of a century-old murder: the explanation rests on the premise that the very workings of photography are still somewhat mysterious. 'Doubtless there is more in our photography than we yet know of', the narrator portentously tells us.

> The camera sees more than the eye, and chemicals in a freshly prepared and active state, have a power which they afterwards lose. Our units of time, adopted for the convenience of persons dealing with the ordinary movements of material objects, are of course conventional. Those who turn the instruments of science upon nature will always be in danger of seeing more than they looked for.[27]

These stories, and many others, pivot on a crucial dichotomy between the evidentiary and the indexical, on the one hand, and the uncanny, the supernatural, and the unreliable, on the other. The two facets, however, are completely intertwined. Were it not for the habitual association of the camera's eye with a mechanical exactitude, a fidelity to fact, plots that feature photographs that have been tampered with—let alone those that possess strange powers of their own—would lose their force. Literary photographs provoked, and were deliberately used to invoke, questions of authenticity, reliability, veracity, and gullibility.

For on the one hand, to possess a photograph of something is a form of evidence—or it would be, if only one had one's camera with one. 'If only I had thought of a Kodak!', laments H. G. Wells's 1895 time traveller. 'I could have flashed that glimpse of the Under-world in a second, and examined it at leisure.'[28] A number of Arthur Conan Doyle's Sherlock Holmes stories pivot on photographic evidence, something increasingly used in real-life police work.[29] In 'The Man with the Twisted Lip', the beggar Hugh Boone is identified as 'the missing man...I know him from the photograph'.[30] In 'The Yellow Face', the mystery surrounding a masked child is solved when Holmes discovers a miniature photo of his father, 'bearing unmistakable signs upon his features of his African descent'.[31] Notably, photography often carries

---

[26] Richard Marsh, 'The Photographs', in *The Seen and the Unseen* (London: Methuen, 1900), 29.

[27] E. G. Swain, 'The Man with the Roller', in *The Stoneground Ghost Tales* (Cambridge: W. Heffer & Sons, 1912), 54.

[28] H. G. Wells, *The Time Machine* (London: Penguin, 2005), 54.

[29] See Ronald R. Thomas, *Detective Fiction and the Rise of Forensic Science* (Cambridge: Cambridge University Press, 2004).

[30] Arthur Conan Doyle, 'The Man with the Twisted Lip', in *The Penguin Complete Sherlock Holmes* (London: Penguin, 2009), 242.

[31] Conan Doyle, 'The Yellow Face', in *Complete Sherlock Holmes*, 361.

some rather negative associations in these stories, too. It provides an occupation for the criminals in 'The Red-Headed League' and 'The Adventure of the Copper Beeches'. It furnishes a sinister record for the predatory Baron Gruner in 'The Adventure of the Illustrious Client', who collects women 'as some men collect moths or butterflies. He had it all in his book. Snapshot photographs, names, details, everything about them'.[32] Although in this last case, the Baron's motivations are more erotic than strictly illegal, it is surely the openness of the medium to deception that allies it with villainy.

Such deliberate deception is dramatized by Hardy in *A Laodicean* (1881). The unscrupulous William Dare tries to stifle the romantic interest that the heiress Paula Power is showing towards another of her suitors, and lets drop a *carte de visite* upon the floor.

> It was a portrait of Somerset; but by a device known in photography the operator, though contriving to produce what seemed to be a perfect likeness, had given it the distorted features and wild attitude of a man advanced in intoxication. No woman, unless specially cognizant of such possibilities, could have looked upon it and doubted that the photograph was a genuine illustration of a customary phase in the young man's private life.

Of all the thoughts that passed through Paula's mind, the narrator tells us, 'the thought that the photograph might have been a fabrication was probably the last. To them the picture of Somerset had all the cogency of direct vision'.[33] In such a context of photo reception, Conan Doyle's own credulity with regard to the spirit world, his susceptibility to images of fairies, and to contacts with deceased members of his family, is decidedly telling: if one strongly desires an image to show something in which one believes, one may lose rational judgement about how that image might have been constructed. The response of Hardy's Paula is completely credible within a culture that readily wanted to believe that photographs tell the truth; the testimony of *A Laodicean*, like that of so many other literary works, warns one against making that assumption.

Photographs are not solely important to literary culture as objects that are represented or referenced in poetry or prose. They had their own material functions. Increasingly, they were used as illustrative devices, whether interleaved with fiction, or functioning as frontispieces—like those that accompanied the 1912–14 Wessex Edition of Hardy's work. They carried documentary roles; they accompanied discursive writing on literature. Photography was central to the development of a celebrity culture around authorship, via illustrated articles, frontispieces, *cartes de visite*, and postcards. Authors started to be stalked as celebrities; had their images retouched in flattering ways; posed in locations that emphasized their cultural

---

[32] Conan Doyle, 'The Adventures of the Illustrious Client', in *Complete Sherlock Holmes*, 976.
[33] Hardy, *A Laodicean* (London: Penguin, 1998), 281, 283.

credentials.[34] In turn, the increasing physical presence of photography within many texts enhanced the sense of photography as an everyday visual commodity.

Photography played a role in literary tourism from its beginnings. Fox Talbot's second photo-book, *Sun Pictures in Scotland* (1845), for example, contained an image of the ruined Dryburgh Abbey holding Sir Walter Scott's tomb. Ease of reproduction consolidated its role. Hardy's friend, Hermann Lea, traced and photographed the original settings for many of the fictional scenes in *Thomas Hardy's Wessex* (1912), capturing many thatched cottages and sleepy-looking towns with a sensibility akin to the contemporary archival work being done by the photographic survey movement, commemorating a disappearing England.[35] Frederick Treves's *The Country of 'The Ring and the Book'* (1913) tempers the experimental style of Browning's epic by bringing 'the actual incidents of the narrative into immediate association with the places of their happening'.[36]

Perhaps nowhere was as familiar an overseas photographic cliché as Venice. 'Every one has been there, and every one has brought back a collection of photographs', wrote Henry James, with cultivated weariness, at the beginning of his section on Venice in *Italian Hours* (1909).[37] He complains that there is nothing new to be said about the city; it is already familiar. Venice stands as an example of a place that is extraordinary, but has been rendered peculiarly quotidian through photographic repetition. As James had already put it, in an 1875 chapter published in *Transatlantic Sketches*, '[t]he broad glare of photography has dissipated so many of the sweet mysteries of travel'.[38]

So if Venice was already, by the turn of the century, a photographic cliché, what was a photographer to do when called to illustrate works set in the city, when the author in question—Henry James—quite pointedly tells him to avoid choosing 'the pompous and obvious things that one everywhere sees photos of'?[39] The photographer in question was Alvin Langdon Coburn. Coburn's work was entwined with the literary in a number of ways. His two volumes of photographic portraits, *Men of Mark* (1913) and *More Men of Mark* (1923), include numerous authors—all male—ranging from Bernard Shaw, G. K. Chesterton, and Andrew Lang, through W. B. Yeats, Roger Fry, and Robert Bridges, to Thomas Hardy, Joseph Conrad, and Ezra Pound. For the most part soft focus, printed in browny-black sepia, and usually, though not invariably, of the head alone, they suggest the solitary mind of the

[34] For an excellent and detailed summary of the development of the author-as-celebrity photograph, see Ch. 8, 'Product Advertising and Self-Advertising', in Philip Waller, *Writers, Readers, and Reputations: Literary Life in Britain, 1870–1918* (Oxford: Oxford University Press, 2006), 329–63.

[35] See Elizabeth Edwards, *The Camera as Historian: Amateur Photographers and Historical Imagination, 1885–1918* (Durham, NC and London: Duke University Press, 2012).

[36] Frederick Treves, *The Country of 'The Ring and the Book'* (London: Cassell, 1913), vii.

[37] Henry James, *Italian Hours* (London: Penguin, 1995).

[38] James, *Transatlantic Sketches* (Boston, MA: James R. Osgood, 1875), 25.

[39] Alvin Langdon Coburn, *Alvin Langdon Coburn, Photographer: An Autobiography* (New York: Praeger, 1966), 56.

writer set against a deep black darkness, an impenetrable well of inspiration and imagination.

But the images would not have had the same power—according to Coburn, at least—if they had not been the product of a connection between sitter and photographer. Indeed, Coburn maintains that a photographic portrait requires even more of a rapport than that which develops between painter and subject. 'The camera is all recording and very sensitive to the slightest gradation of expression of the personality before it', and because of this, 'the impression that I make on my sitter is as important as the effect he has on me'.[40] Such an impression may not, however, be entirely capturable by the camera. Coburn wished that he could have made his portrait of Lang surrounded by the books with which he spent much of his time, but the need for good light obliged him to take the photograph in the garden. 'My mental portrait of him is there, however, as I last saw him, lovingly turning the pages of a favourite author, or showing me some rare manuscript'.[41]

This comparison of the memory to the camera's recording plate was already well established by the late nineteenth century, and it is found time and again, mostly in passing references, but sometimes in a more sustained form.[42] Jennifer Green-Lewis has discussed photography's impact on the nineteenth century, and its symbiotic connection to 'a crisis of memory, a heightened fear of forgetting in the Victorian period, stimulated...by the emergence onto the plate of the mind of too many things to remember'.[43] She attributes this in part to the unprecedented expansion of knowledge, and to the importance of the detail and the particular, when it came to constituting and recording this knowledge. She links this fear of forgetting, too, to the heightened consciousness of the vastness of time and space created by contemporary paths in scientific and evolutionary theory. All of this, Green-Lewis maintains, created anxiety about the capacity of the human mind to remember a proliferation of specifics, and concomitant admiration for the power of the daguerreotype (notable for its capacity to record minute detail) and photographs to capture and retain images of the material world. Photographs, she explains, acted both as substitutes and as prompts for human memory, helping one set up 'a kind of resistance to the oblivion that surrounds life and into which the better part of it disappears. To remember is to do one's duty in affirming the significance of one's fellow human beings and the history they have made'.[44]

---

[40] Coburn, *Men of Mark* (London: Duckworth, 1913), 21.

[41] Ibid., 11.

[42] Douwe Draaisma, in *Metaphors of Memory: A History of Ideas about the Mind* (Cambridge: Cambridge University Press, 2001), provides an exceptionally rich account of the evolution of this metaphor in the latter half of the nineteenth century. He places it, in turn, within a long history of attempts to find analogues within the material world for the ways in which the mind records experience and perceptions.

[43] Jennifer Green-Lewis, 'Not Fading Away: Photography in the Age of Oblivion', *Nineteenth-Century Contexts* 22/4 (2001), 264.

[44] Ibid., 569.

Photography is elided with memory in, for example, *Recalled to Life* (1891) by the journalist, popular novelist, and physiologist Grant Allen. This sensational detective novel pivots on the connection between traumatic memory loss and the circumstances that led to six flashlight prints being taken of a murder.[45] Fred White's 1901 short story 'The Black Narcissus' describes Inspector Darch, of Scotland Yard, as 'a man with a gliding step and a moist grey eye, that took the whole room and the trim garden beyond and eke the novelist in like the flash of a camera, and held the picture on the mental gelatine for all time'.[46] Coburn himself projected the conceit onto Henry James, as he describes their collaborations in producing the frontispieces to the twenty-four volumes of James's Collected Works.[47] He quotes from the Preface to the first volume of *The Golden Bowl*, in which James recounts their work together.

> Both our limits and the very extent of our creation, however, lay in the fact that, unlike wanton designers, we had not to 'create', but simply to recognize—recognize, that is, with the last fineness. Mr James, although he is not literally a photographer, must have, I believe, sensitive plates in his brain with which to record his impressions. He always knew exactly what he wanted, and what we did was to browse diligently until we found such a subject.[48]

Two of the images that Coburn provided were of Venice. They are emphatically *not* tourist images—and nor, in any obvious sense, are they illustrations. As James stated clearly in the Preface to *The Golden Bowl*, he intended the frontispieces to bear a reference 'to Novel or Tale [which] should exactly be *not* competitive and obvious, should on the contrary plead its case with some shyness, that of images always confessing themselves mere optical symbols or echoes, expressions of no particular thing in the text, but only of the type or idea of this or that thing'.[49] Yet rather than leaving Coburn to roam Venice's *calle* looking for locations that might spark his own associations with James's prose, the novelist issued the photographer with very precise instructions. One set of directions led him to the Palazzo Barbaro, long-time centre of American art and social life in Venice and commemorated, inside and out, by many artists. James stayed here between 1869 and 1907, and borrowed it for the Palazzo Leporelli, Milly's death palace in *The Wings of the Dove* (1902). Coburn's image, cropped into a long straight frame, offers no sense of the

---

[45] The most extended and thoughtful treatment of Grant Allen's *Recalled to Life* is in Anne Stiles, *Popular Fiction and Brain Science in the Late Nineteenth Century* (Cambridge: Cambridge University Press, 2012), 85–115.

[46] Alan K. Russell, *Rivals of Sherlock Holmes: Forty Six Stories of Crime and Detection from Original Illustrated Magazines* (Secaucus, NJ: Castle Books, 1981), 233.

[47] See Ira B. Nadel, 'Visual Culture: The Photo Frontispieces to the New York Edition', in David McWhirter (ed.), *Henry James's New York Edition: The Construction of Authorship* (Stanford, CA: Stanford University Press, 1995), 90–108.

[48] Coburn, *Men of Mark*, 19.

[49] James, Preface to *The Golden Bowl*, in *Novels, 1903–1911* (New York: Library of America, 2010), 438.

opulence within, 'hung about with pictures and relics'.[50] Rather, the face-on facade gives nothing away about the palazzo's interior: an apt visual analogue for the novel's sustained concern with privacy, secrets, and not-knowing.

For the other image that he wanted, James sent Coburn off to Ca' Capello, his model in *The Aspern Papers* (1888) for 'a dilapidated old palace on an out-of-the-way canal'.[51] Here Miss Bordereau and her niece Tita (niece, or maybe daughter—the story offers the faintest hint of this possibility) live very, very quietly indeed—avoiding what the querulous narrator terms this modern age of 'newspapers and telegrams and photographs and interviewers'. Again, it is a house of concealment, which the narrator is determined to read even into its architectural detail: its 'motionless shutters became as expressive as eyes consciously closed'.[52] Yet his desire to bring the poet Aspern's past 'to the light'—the rhetoric of exposure—aligns him, however, with this modern world at the same time as he affects to despise it. After all, as he puts it, harking back to Aspern's day, 'when Americans went abroad in 1812 there was something romantic, almost heroic in it, as compared with the perpetual ferryings of the present hour, when photography and other conveniences have annihilated surprise'.[53] James writes of his narrator that he is—like himself—preoccupied with the idea of a 'visitable past' which, although the parallel is not expressly made, is precisely the promise inherent in the idea of photography's capture of the 'now'.[54]

So—how to convey this in a photograph? By refusing any standard tourist view of Venice, Coburn's image is a determined departure from convention. It does not even deliver what James had asked for: a shot of the large Sala in the house, which would at least have suggested a faded past. Rather, it shows a small corner of the garden: plain, dusty, ordinary. Its effectiveness in suggesting not just the secrets that are literally and deliberately concealed in the house, but also the infuriating narrator's almost wilful self-blindness, depends on its own illegibility. If tourist photography depends on instant recognition and on site celebration, Coburn's image, in all its understatedness, refutes the Venetian commonplace. Indeed, it barely seems to be *of* Venice at all: apposite, indeed, since the house's inhabitants seem barely aware that they live there. It is a photograph that is irrefutably of the unglamorous, everyday present, or maybe 'timeless', but only in the sense that it conveys no patina of history, no lament for a Venice in decay. Yet its impact depends on all those other, familiar images of Venice that have rendered this extraordinary city *ordinary* through constant exposure. Coburn's brilliant interpretive gesture is to remind us to look elsewhere than at the 'pompous and the obvious'. If this is, in the first instance,

[50] James, *The Wings of the Dove*, in *Novels, 1901–02* (New York: Library of America, 2006), 507.
[51] James, 'The Aspern Papers', in *Complete Stories, 1884–1891* (New York: Library of America, 1999), 228.
[52] Ibid., 231, 255.   [53] Ibid., 255, 258.
[54] James, Preface to 'The Aspern Papers', in James, *Literary Criticism,* ed. Leon Edel and Mark Wilson, 2 vols (New York: Library of America, 1984), I, 1177.

a reinforcement of James's constant push to get us to look beneath the surface, it is also, at the level of visual culture, a reminder to look at ordinary things—and in doing so, make one's sense of an already known city fresh again. Even more provocatively, and in a broader context, it points to a way in which photographs may play an interpretive, interrogative role, working in partnership with a text, rather than occupying a subordinate position. Coburn's frontispieces suggest new possibilities for the relationship between language and image, and also that art photography and the apprehension of the everyday need not, by any means, be seen as unrelated.[55]

Coburn's interest in making things new was soon to take a very different turn. Ezra Pound was one of the authors whom he photographed in 1913, using his customary soft focus technique. He was drawn into Pound's fascination with representation, with pattern, arrangement, abstraction, and created a 'Vortoscope' using three of the poet's shaving mirrors. These, when attached to a camera, worked as a prism, warping and fragmenting whatever was in front of the lens—the corner of a room, a window, Pound himself—into kaleidoscopic shards. In these, as Pound himself wrote in his Introduction to the exhibition at which Coburn showed them, 'THE CAMERA IS FREE FROM REALITY'.[56] What the Vortoscope does is to allow the recognition of beautiful form, decoupling photographic technology from accurate or even evocative reproduction of the external world.

Yet at the same time as Pound praises this photographic innovation, he also relegates it to a subordinate position among the other 'vorticist arts', calling it 'an art of the eye, not of the hand and eye together'. If its potential rescues art photography from being 'stale and suburban',[57] as Pound would have it (yet more vernacular photography seems to be beneath his notice altogether), it is still, for him, very much a lesser art form. Even by the end of this period, photography—despite the experimental, the subtle, and the conceptually provocative ends to which it might be put—still occupied an uncomfortable aesthetic position. It remained commonly, and understandably, associated with the instrumental, with the factual, and with mass culture. Some photographers continued to make strong claims for the original and evocative nature of their images. A number of writers of poetry and fiction drew upon certain of photography's key properties—properties that were to be given articulate voice by such later commentators as Barthes, Walter Benjamin, Siegfried Kracauer, and Susan Sontag—in order to enhance the imaginative resonances of their texts. Yet, as Ezra Pound's comments make very clear, photography still had a long way to go before it would cease to be regarded automatically as a lesser form than other arts, including literature itself. Moreover, it was because of the long-standing

---

[55] Coburn also collaborated with H. G. Wells, producing similarly suggestive photographs to illustrate *The Door in the Wall* (1911).

[56] Ezra Pound, 'The Vortographs', for the February 1917 Camera Club exhibition of *Vortographs and Paintings* by Coburn. See Harriet Zinnes (ed.), *Ezra Pound and the Visual Arts* (New York: New Directions, 1980), 155.

[57] Ibid., 156.

and enduring hierarchy of aesthetic forms that photography, together with its most significant contribution to modernity, went undervalued. For as writers of imaginative prose and poetry recognized, photography played a new role in allowing us to notice, appreciate, and interrogate the ordinary. Through this, rather than through any trickery with mirrors, photography, together with writing about this visual form, began to call into question precisely what we do, and do not, see.

FURTHER READING

Armstrong, Nancy. *Fiction in the Age of Photography: The Legacy of British Realism* (Cambridge, MA: Harvard University Press, 2002).

Bogardus, Ralph. *Pictures and Texts: Henry James, A. L. Coburn, and New Ways of Seeing in Literary Culture* (Ann Arbor, MI: UMI Research Press, 1984).

Green-Lewis, Jennifer. *Framing the Victorians: Photography and the Culture of Realism* (Ithaca, NY and London: Cornell University Press, 1996).

Groth, Helen. *Victorian Photography and Literary Nostalgia* (Oxford: Oxford University Press, 2003).

Harker, Margaret E. *The Linked Ring: The Secession in Photography, 1892–1910* (London: Heinemann, 1979).

Henisch, Heinz K. and Bridget Ann Henisch. *The Photographic Experience, 1839–1914: Images and Attitudes* (Philadelphia, PA: Pennsylvania University Press, 1994).

Humm, Maggie. *Modernist Women and Visual Cultures: Virginia Woolf, Vanessa Bell, Photography and Cinema* (Edinburgh: Edinburgh University Press, 2002).

Jay, Bill and Margaret Moore (eds). *Bernard Shaw on Photography* (Salt Lake City, UT: Gibbs Smith, 1989).

Novak, Daniel A. *Realism, Photography, and Nineteenth-Century Fiction* (Cambridge: Cambridge University Press, 2008).

Rabb, Jane M. (ed.). *Literature & Photography, Interactions 1840–1990: A Critical Anthology* (Albuquerque, NM: University of New Mexico Press, 1995).

Shloss, Carol. *In Visible Light: Photography and the American Writer, 1840–1940* (Oxford: Oxford University Press, 1987).

Smith, Graham. *'Light that Dances in the Mind': Photographs and Memory in the Writings of E. M. Forster and his Contemporaries* (Oxford: Peter Lang, 2007).

Thomas, Ronald R. *Detective Fiction and the Rise of Forensic Science* (Cambridge: Cambridge University Press, 2004).

CHAPTER 37

ELECTRICITY, TELEPHONY, AND COMMUNICATIONS

SAM HALLIDAY

Introduction

Towards the end of D. H. Lawrence's *The Rainbow* (1915), Ursula Brangwen receives a letter from Anton Skrebensky that reignites the pair's romance. When she posts her own letter in reply, Lawrence comments, 'the world became a very still, pale place, without confines'.[1] A few paragraphs later, Ursula recalls a conversation in which her science teacher has imparted advice that now, in the wake of Skrebensky's letter, seems hollow and insensible: ' "I don't see why we should attribute some special mystery to life", the teacher has said. ' "We don't understand it as we understand electricity...but that doesn't warrant our saying that it is something special...May it not be that life consists in a complexity of physical and chemical activities, of the same order as the activities we already know in science?" ' By her current perturbation's lights, this view strikes Ursula as soul-denyingly materialistic. While Lawrence doubtless shares these reservations (as an insistent if inconsistent critic of science's alleged explanatory overreach), this does not stop him describing Ursula herself, later in the novel, as 'vibrat[ing] like a jet of electric, firm fluid' under her lover's touch.[2] So electricity *is*, apparently, a factor in the quickening and experience of 'life'. Thus, two characters that postal communications help bring together end up enjoying physical encounters partially described in terms of science.

---

[1] D. H. Lawrence, *The Rainbow*, ed. Mark Kinkead-Weekes (Harmondsworth: Penguin, 2007), 407.
[2] Ibid., 408, 442. For the vicissitudes of Lawrence's attitude to science, see Jeff Wallace, *D. H. Lawrence, Science and the Posthuman* (Houndmills: Palgrave, 2005). Lawrence's de facto concession to the science teacher here complicates any reading of him as anti-materialist or, in his period's terms, commensurately pro-vitalist. Whilst electricity does indeed appear in vitalist discourses of the period—including, at times, at Lawrence's own hands—it just as often appears in anti-vitalist alternatives.

Published just under twenty years earlier, Bram Stoker's *Dracula* (1897) takes a rather different view of electricity. Here, another scientist, Van Helsing, explains: ' "there are things done today in electrical science which would have been deemed unholy by the very men who discovered electricity—who would themselves not so long before have been burned as wizards. There are always mysteries in life." '[3] By contrast to Lawrence's scientist, then, Stoker's does not see 'mysteries' as being solved or rendered moot by electricity; rather, Van Helsing sees electricity as itself mysterious. Correlatively, Stoker's scientist does not regard science as sowing up phenomena in neat explanatory bundles, but as extending a duly philosophic person's sense of what science cannot yet (but maybe one day will) explain. Not coincidentally, Van Helsing and his colleagues make prolific use of electrical technologies throughout *Dracula*. The telegraph, especially, proves vital to their arranging of meetings and exchanges of information. And on one occasion, one of Van Helsing's colleagues is assisted by someone using a newer technology, the telephone, to find out about a cargo unloaded at a railway station. As a direct consequence of the telephone call, the labourers responsible for unloading this cargo are directed to the enquirer to impart further information, face to face. When this meeting takes place, the labourers impart further information still, in the form of a waybill and other documents.[4]

Electricity and telephony are not integral merely to the plot of *Dracula*, however. The transmission of messages and information is also conceptually significant for the novel. Despite its lack of overt interest in telephony, *The Rainbow* is likewise illustrative of this trend. For when Ursula experiences the world as a place 'without confines', Lawrence has his readers understand the power that all types of communication may have to draw disparate persons and places into relation. That these powers are not specific to any one communications medium acting alone is another lesson we may derive from *Dracula*. On the evidence of that one telephone episode, we see how one conversation over distance might prompt another, face to face, and how relatedly, the telephone provides information cognate with that conveyed by handwriting or print. Similarly, in *The Rainbow* a written communication resonates in the mind alongside a remembered conversation. Van Helsing pursues vampires with the help of interdependent conduits for information—post, telegraph, telephone, and newspaper.

This is why, when I return to *Dracula* briefly in the final section, Communications, of the present chapter, I will do so under the sign of 'media ecology', a term now widely used by literary scholars as well as communications theorists to emphasize how media are best seen as interdependent and not self-contained.[5] If literary texts

[3] Bram Stoker, *Dracula*, ed. Maurice Hindle (Harmondsworth: Penguin, 1993), 247.

[4] Ibid., 292.

[5] See, for example, Joseph Tabbi and Michael Wutz (eds), *Reading Matters: Narrativity in the New Media Ecology* (Ithaca, NY: Cornell University Pres, 1997).

often depict such ecologies, they are also part *of* such ecologies, by virtue of their dependence on technologies—not least, print—for the dissemination of words. Before seeing this, however, we must first address the physical phenomenon underwriting many of the newer communications media at the turn of the century: electricity.

Electricity

Electricity rose to prominence in the late eighteenth and early nineteenth centuries, principally as a result of a series of discoveries linking it to inorganic matter and organic life.[6] Thereafter, it was deployed in such technologies as the electric telegraph (first used in Britain in 1838); electric light (commercially successful from the 1880s onwards); large-scale power generation and transmission (another development, mainly, of the 1880s); telephony (1876); and radio (first known under the name of Guglielmo Marconi, who patented it in 1897). Recent scholarship has stressed the diversity of significations electricity acquired correlatively with such applications: Paul Gilmore, for instance, has noted how electricity articulated opposed responses to early nineteenth-century American democracy.[7] Peter Bowler's *Science for All*, meanwhile, documents the extent to which electrical and other kinds of scientific knowledge were diffused among the laity well into the early twentieth century via an array of literary genres.[8]

Within literature itself, an abiding link was forged early in the nineteenth century between electricity and 'life'. This link extends from the very famous (if actually fleeting and oblique) reference to electricity in Mary Shelley's *Frankenstein* (1818, rev. 1831), in which the titular scientist animates a quasi-human creature. Within the 1880–1920 period, two film adaptations of *Frankenstein* were made, the first (*Frankenstein*, dir. J. Searle Dawley, 1910) under the aegis of electrical inventor Thomas Edison (1847–1931). Though it was not until James Whale's 1931 film adaptation that Frankenstein's life-bringing technique was explicitly linked to the electrical phenomenon of lightning, any reader of Shelley's novel might have drawn this inference in the interim. It is presumably Shelley's novel that Lawrence is thinking of by naming the science teacher in *The Rainbow* Dr Frankstone.

Further to this link with 'life', another persistent literary tradition links electricity with sexuality. Lawrence is again exemplary of this: nowhere more so than in

[6] Perhaps the best survey of these developments remains Andrew Cunningham and Nicholas Jardine (eds), *Romanticism and the Sciences* (Cambridge: Cambridge University Press, 1990).

[7] Paul Gilmore, *Aesthetic Materialism: Electricity and American Romanticism* (Stanford, CA: Stanford University Press, 2009), 104.

[8] Peter Bowler, *Science for All: The Popularization of Science in Early Twentieth-Century Britain* (Chicago, IL: University of Chicago Press, 2009).

Women in Love (1920), his sequel to *The Rainbow*. In anticipation of his affair with 'Pussum', Gerald Crich feels 'delightfully conscious of himself, of his own attractiveness. He felt full of strength, able to give off a sort of electric power'. This 'power' soon enough draws Pussum into bed, in terms that bear out that braggartly and misogynistic way of putting it. For Gerald himself, if not (perhaps) for Lawrence, Pussum is 'a victim. He felt that she was in his power, and he was generous. The electricity was turgid and voluptuously rich, in his limbs. He would be able to destroy her utterly in the strength of his discharge'.[9] 'Discharge' here equates electricity with phallic potency, in ways implicitly identifying one potential sexual effect of men on women with death by electrocution. And this, indeed, is no coincidence, given *Women in Love*'s obsessive interest in what seems to it the ineluctably adversarial nature of heterosexual relationships. How does Lawrence think one might find relief from such relationships? Through physical engagement with persons of one's own sex, as in the novel's famous wrestling scene, where wrestling itself appears as a thinly disguised proxy for sex between men. Electricity features again here, with Rupert Birkin remarking of Japanese people (in relation to a previous wrestling partner) that 'when they are hot and roused, there is a definite attraction—a curious kind of electric fluid—like eels'.[10]

Despite its evident importance to *Women in Love*'s thinking about sexuality (and race), however, there is something curiously and even wilfully atavistic about all this. Take the term 'fluid' in the passage quoted immediately above, a relic of an understanding of electricity *as* a fluid long abandoned by science at the novel's time of writing. In literary language, such terminology is redolent of nineteenth-century American writers like Melville and Whitman, whom Lawrence much admired and wrote about in *Studies in Classic American Literature* (1923).[11] Other aspects of Lawrence's representation of electricity are, however, more clearly related to electrical technologies taking root in his own lifetime. Elsewhere in *Women in Love*, he references electric power and lighting and, in *Fantasia of the Unconscious* (1921), asserts that between any 'individual and any external object with which he has an affective connection, there exists a definite vital flow, as definite and concrete as the electric current whose polarized circuit sets our tram-cars running and our lamps shining, or our Marconi [i.e. radio] wires vibrating'.[12] The 'affective' inclinations of an Ursula or a Gerald might thus be likened to the workings of the machines amid which these characters abide.

Lawrence was by no means alone in his attraction to electrical tropes. Henry Adams's *The Education of Henry Adams* (1907) famously links the electric dynamo

---

[9] Lawrence, *Women in Love* (Ware, Herts: Wordsworth, 1992), 53.   [10] Ibid., 233.

[11] More closely contemporary sources for Lawrence's thinking can be identified, however: see Andrew Harrison, *D. H. Lawrence and Italian Futurism: A Study of Influence* (Amsterdam: Rodopi, 2003), ch. 4.

[12] Lawrence, *Fantasia of the Unconscious; And, Psychoanalysis and the Unconscious* (Harmondsworth: Penguin, 1971), 131.

to the awesome idea of the Virgin Mary in the minds of medieval Christians. Electric lighting, meanwhile, illuminates a railway station in Rudyard Kipling's *Kim* (1901); a dockyard in Joseph Conrad's *The 'Nigger' of the Narcissus* (1897); a laboratory and a bedside in Richard Marsh's *The Beetle* (1897); and the streets of New York in Henry James's 'The Jolly Corner' (1908). Perhaps the most striking literary treatment of electric lighting appears in William Dean Howells's *A Hazard of New Fortunes* (1890), where another New York setting—an entire cityscape, illuminated both by gaslight and electric light itself—forms an 'incomparable perspective'. What a shame it is, Howells's narrator says, that in 'a city full of painters', this 'superb spectacle' should go unpainted. But we should not take this narrator at his word: part of Howells's covert wager, here and throughout his novel, is that he is creating just the 'painting[s]' he ostensibly laments the lack of, with his words.[13]

The final associative link we must consider in this section connects electricity with communication. This link owes most to the electric telegraph, but was given further impetus in this period by telephony and radio. It is the latter that seems uppermost in Lawrence's mind throughout the string of questions he poses to the titular fauna of his poem, 'Bare Almond Trees' (1923):

> What are you doing in the December rain?
> Have you a strange electric sensitiveness in your steel tips?
> Do you feel the air for electric influences
> Like some strange magnetic apparatus?
> Do you take in messages, in some strange code,
> From heaven's wolfish, wandering electricity...[14]

Radio *was*, in fact, used to exchange coded messages prior to (and after) its emergence as a largely unencrypted medium—a process, incidentally, well underway at this poem's time of writing. That Lawrence should imagine trees as de facto radio receivers is therefore fitting, given his poem's overall premise that whatever communication almond trees may (or may not) be involved in is imperceptible and thus occult to humans. But radio is not the only technology Lawrence is thinking of here. A few lines after those quoted above, he asks his trees: 'Do you telephone the roar of the waters over the earth?'[15] This is the point, then, at which to turn our own focus to telephony itself.

---

[13] William Dean Howells, *A Hazard of New Fortunes*, ed. Philip Lopate (New York: Penguin, 2001), 65. One of *A Hazard*'s plots concerns an illustrated literary journal, whose selling point is an apparently novel way of combining text with images. Given this, it is tempting to view the novel as a whole as an attempt to recapitulate this plot-point at the level of its text—an attempt to 'be' (or at least be a surrogate for) the thing its plot imagines.

[14] Lawrence, *The Complete Poems of D. H. Lawrence*, ed. Vivian de Sola Pinto and Warren Roberts, 2 vols (London: Heinemann, 1962), I, 301.

[15] Ibid., 301.

Telephony

While not as prominent as in writing of the late 1920s and after, the telephone's appearances in turn-of-the-century literature are instructive. Take the following episode from Theodore Dreiser's *Sister Carrie* (1900), where Hurstwood walks the streets of Chicago, trying to figure out how he can flee across the US border into Canada accompanied by both the money he has stolen from the safe of his employer and (though he only thinks of this belatedly) his mistress Carrie:

> At the first drug store he stopped, seeing a long-distance telephone booth inside. It was a famous drug store and contained one of the first private telephone booths ever erected.
>
> [...]
>
> 'Give me 1643,' he called to Central, after looking up the Michigan Central Depot number. Soon he got the ticket agent.
>
> 'How do the trains leave here for Detroit?' he asked.
>
> The man explained the hours.
>
> 'No more tonight?'
>
> 'Nothing with a sleeper. Yes, there is too,' he added. 'There's a mail train out of here at three o'clock.'
>
> 'All right,' said Hurstwood.
>
> He was thinking, if he could only get there and cross the river into Canada [...]
>
> 'Mayhew won't open the safe till nine,' he thought. 'They can't get on my track before noon.'
>
> Then he thought of Carrie. With what speed must he get her, if he got her at all. She would have to come along. He jumped into the nearest cab standing by.[16]

At least three features of this passage demand attention. First, it is striking that what the phone is used to talk about here is *travel*—specifically involving trains, an echo of that earlier discussed fictional representation of telephony in *Dracula*. This suggests a material truth about all telecommunications: that because these typically connect correspondents disparate in space, they are especially congenial for planning and verifying movements *over* space, by these correspondents themselves or others. Shortly after finishing his phone call, Hurstwood boards a cab, the call having apprised him of how little time he has in which to get aboard a given train. Here, as in many instances involving both transport and communication technologies, usage or invocation of one technology dovetails with that of another.

---

[16] Theodore Dreiser, *Sister Carrie*, ed. Neda M. Westlake et al. (New York: Penguin, 1986), 271–2.

The second point to note of Hurstwood's use of the telephone is its hybrid private–public character. On the one hand, he makes his call inside a 'private' booth; on the other, this booth is in a public space (a drugstore). Moreover, Hurstwood is connected to the person he wants to speak to only by the similarly private–public imbricating agency of the telephone operator whom Dreiser invokes under the sign of a 'Central' switchboard station where that operator works (such stations were a feature of almost all early telephony, and involved operators manually 'matching' callers to receivers). Intermediation by such agents meant that telephone users of this period could never be entirely sure whether what they said would end up audible only to those they intentionally addressed or to operators as well. Thus the third point to take from telephony in *Sister Carrie*: the fact that this 'will-I-be/won't-I-be-overheard?' dialectic, as it were, is reflected in the very form of Dreiser's text. A shift in the narration of Hurstwood's conversation with the ticket agent juxtaposes the two alternatives concerned. When Dreiser writes, 'The man explained the hours', the reader does not 'overhear' the agent's speech; when he writes ' "Nothing with a sleeper" ' (and so on), however, the reader *does*. The shift in Dreiser's narration shunts the reader into the same position, vis-à-vis the speaker, as that of an eavesdropping operator.[17]

Mark Twain's 'A Telephone Conversation' (1880) explores the comic potential of such 'eavesdropping'. The reader is invited to bear witness to 'that queerest of all the queer things in the world', another person's telephone conversation, of which, not being on the telephone oneself, one can only hear 'half'. As Twain explains: 'You hear questions asked; you don't hear the answer. You hear invitations given; you hear no thanks in return. You have listening pauses of dead silence, followed by apparently irrelevant and unjustifiable exclamations of glad surprise, or sorrow, or dismay. You can't make head or tail of the talk'.[18] Contrary to this last assertion, however, Twain proceeds to cite a one-sided conversation whose 'audible' half so clearly bears semantic traces of its missing counterpart that his reader *can* reconstruct more or less the entire conversation. Though the humour Twain attempts to derive from this effect is disappointing, the effect itself is striking, demonstrating how not only this but any text may throw a kind of 'shadow' of itself, suggesting things it does not contain. To similar effect, Wyndham Lewis's *The Ideal Giant* (1914) resituates Twain's 'queer' experience within a stage play, a stage direction indicating that when a character listens to someone speaking on the telephone, he '*inclines his head and listens crossly. The voice speaking in his ear evidently annoys him*'.[19] Body language thus becomes an index for audience members to interpret—a visual trace of what is to them a 'silent' sound.

[17] On electricity in *Sister Carrie*, meanwhile, see Tim Armstrong, *Modernism, Technology and the Body: A Cultural Study* (Cambridge: Cambridge University Press, 1998), 21–6.

[18] Mark Twain, 'A Telephonic Conversation', in Twain, *Collected Tales, Sketches, Speeches, and Essays, 1852–1890*, ed. Louis J. Budd (New York: Library of America, 1992), 738.

[19] Wyndham Lewis, *The Ideal Giant, The Code of a Herdsman, Cantelman's Spring-Mate* (privately printed for the London Office of the *Little Review*, 1917), 21 (emphasis in original).

Echoes of both Twain's and Dreiser's representations of telephony coincide in Robert Frost's 'Snow' (1920), perhaps the most satisfying meditation on the technology of the period. Like Twain, Frost presents a one-side-only-'audible' telephonic conversation, effectively forcing readers to infer what the 'absent' speaker must be saying (and what she *doesn't* say: one thing we are told is that she avoids the words 'Good night'). Like Dreiser, Frost presents a telephone conversation concerning movement over space: ' "I called you up to say Good night from here" ', a caller tells his wife, ' "Before I went to say Good morning there" '.[20] In a move that trumps both Twain and Dreiser, however, Frost features more than one telephone conversation in his text, and in the process shows how these may variously provoke and comment on each other. Thus, the poem's final telephone call brings confirmation that a traveller has reached his destination, and so effectively 'completes' the first.

Despite the relative success of telephonic communications in this instance, most writers of the 1880–1920 period who do address telephony associate the medium with communicative opacity, anxiety, and even outright failure.[21] When H. G. Wells describes a voice as like one 'heard in a badly connected telephone' (in his 1902 novel *Ann Veronica*), for instance, he suggests the extent to which telephone users of his time could find the device more obstructive than conducive to mutual intelligibility.[22] Similarly, Dorothy Richardson's *The Tunnel* (1919; volume 4 of *Pilgrimage*) features a call from someone whose 'far-off faint' and 'angry voice' is only barely heard amid the 'uproar' of the telephone's own apparatus.[23] But if the telephone in this instance is annoying, in Ford Madox Ford's '4629 Padd' (1908) it is positively terrifying, by virtue of its phenomenological properties and the way these lend themselves to certain forms of social pressure.[24] In this story, a caller phones a woman's house knowing that it is likely to be answered by a man who is not the woman's husband; when that man does indeed pick up, the answerer finds not only that he is forced to betray his own identity—and thus his implication in circumstances that suggest adultery—but also that the caller's identity remains a mystery to *him*. Of decisive importance here is telephony's division of the auditory from the visual: whereas the caller knows to whom he is talking, the receiver finds that he cannot put the voice to a face. Thus the receiver's eventual madness, brought about

[20] Robert Frost, *Complete Poems of Robert Frost* (London: Jonathan Cape, 1951), 168.
[21] David Trotter, *Literature in the First Media Age: Britain between the Wars* (Cambridge, MA: Harvard University Press, 2013), 47; Kate McLoughlin, 'Interruption Overload: Telephones in Ford Madox Ford's "4629 Padd" ', 'A Call', and 'A Man Could Stand Up', *Journal of Modern Literature* 36/3 (Spring 2013), 50–68. See also Sam Halliday, *Science and Technology in the Age of Hawthorne, Melville, Twain and James: Thinking and Writing Electricity* (New York: Palgrave, 2007), ch. 5.
[22] H. G. Wells, *Ann Veronica* (London: Virago, 1980), 159.
[23] Dorothy Richardson, *Pilgrimage*, 4 vols (London: Virago, 2002), II, 45. A biographical link between Wells and Richardson may be noted here: both *Ann Veronica* and *Pilgrimage* fictionalize features of their affair.
[24] For an extended discussion of this and related texts by Ford, see McLoughlin, 'Interruption Overload'.

by unassuaged anxiety about the identity of the person who has called and who may (presumably) go on to blackmail or disgrace him.

As David Trotter's *Literature in the First Media Age* (2013) argues, when telephony *does* feature more regularly in literature, from around 1929 onwards, it brings with it a 'significantly enhanced…status of dialogue', commensurate with post-1920s telephony's increased sound quality, reliability, and social diffusion.[25] By contrast, fiction and other literature of the 1880–1920 period is more heavily reliant on written letters and telegraphy, two older media that are crucial to the way the whole period thinks about the nature of communication.

Communications

What is communication? For Charles Horton Cooley, writing in 1894, it is essentially 'psychical', by contrast to the 'physical' activity of transport.[26] However, psychical and physical are constantly spilling over into and reflecting one another, just as are communication and transport themselves. Hence Cooley's observations that in a 'modern railway service…psychical rather than physical processes' such as 'discussion', and 'decision' are almost as important as the physical things to which they relate, and that on the psychical side, communication itself depends on 'physical means', including 'signs and gestures, spoken language, letters…telegraphs and telephones'.[27] Thus the psychical can only become socially effective by means of physical embodiment and mediation.

These reflections lead us back to the concept of 'media ecology' cited in my introduction. For not only may transport and communication technologies interact; communication technologies may do so with one another. We have seen how *Dracula* features a telephone call about a railway cargo, and can now observe the more pervasive way in which that novel's many featured diaries, letters, telegrams, newspaper cuttings, and phonograph recordings pass in and out of one another. At a crucial juncture in the novel's action, all instantiations of these media generated up to that point are collated and transcribed within a single typescript, so that they appear to characters as a 'whole connected narrative'.[28] What the typist achieves here is what the contemporary theorists Jay David Bolter and Richard Grusin call 'remediation'—the representation in one medium of others.[29] According to its

[25] Trotter, *Literature in the First Media Age*, 38.

[26] Charles Horton Cooley, 'The Theory of Transportation', *Publications of the American Economic Association* 9/3 (May 1894), 70.

[27] Ibid., 67.   [28] Stoker, *Dracula*, 289.

[29] Jay David Bolter and Richard Grusin, *Remediation: Understanding New Media* (Cambridge, MA: MIT Press, 1999).

own conceit, Stoker's novel *is* this typescript, mass-produced and bound. *Dracula* remediates remediation.[30]

Dracula aside, three other texts are more squarely representative of the primarily 'postal', text-centred (rather than image- or sound-centred) media ecology of the 1880–1920 period: Henry James's *The Ambassadors* (1903), E. M. Forster's *Where Angels Fear to Tread* (1905), and Oscar Wilde's *De Profundis* (composed in 1897).[31] James's novel concerns Lambert Strether's 'embassy' in Paris, where Strether has been sent from the United States by Mrs Newsome to retrieve her putatively errant son Chad. Mrs Newsome is Strether's most prolific correspondent—four letters from her await Strether in Paris when he arrives, and thereafter he expects no less than 'several a week' and sometimes 'more than one by each mail'.[32] Commensurately, Strether sends many letters in return, on one occasion telling Chad that he has been writing to Chad's mother 'perpetually'. At times, these letters are supplemented by telegrams, especially in situations of perceived urgency, where Strether 'communicat[es] with a quickness with which telegraphy alone would rhyme'. A certain telegram refers *to* letter writing.[33] Clearly, in this novel, posted letters and telegrams form an integrated complex, yet its articulations are not always amicable. As doubts about Strether's fidelity to his mission grow (not least within Strether himself), the correspondence in which he is involved becomes both more socially circuitous and less substantively transparent. The telegram referred to immediately above responds to news that other 'ambassadors' are being sent, which Strether hears of via Chad, who himself receives the news as a telegram from his mother that misses Strether out. One telegram Mrs Newsome does send directly to Strether betrays the fact that, as Strether infers, another person has been communicating with Mrs Newsome behind his back. Yet another telegram from Mrs Newsome prompts Strether to compose an especially long letter that he then tears into pieces without sending.[34] Communication is thus placed under the sign of conflict.

This is also the case in my second exemplary 'postal' text. The main events of *Where Angels Fear to Tread* are precipitated by a letter from Lilia Herriton to her dead husband's family announcing her intention to remarry. Having read this letter, the enraged Mrs Herriton destroys it and then sends a telegram in response—signally, to someone other than Lilia herself (the woman with whom Lilia is travelling). Lilia's second marriage proves unhappy, prompting both Lilia and her husband Gino to interestingly contrastive 'postal' responses. Whereas Gino opts not to write to friends on the grounds that '[f]riends cannot travel through the post', Lilia is

---

[30] Among many discussions of *Dracula's* media, perhaps the most germane to the current discussion is Jennifer Fleissner's 'Dictation Anxiety: The Stenographer's Stake in Dracula', *Nineteenth Century Contexts* 22/3 (2000), 417–55.

[31] I take the term 'postal' from Kate Thomas's *Postal Pleasures: Sex, Scandal and Victorian Letters* (Oxford: Oxford University Press, 2012). The fact that James, Forster, and Wilde are all identifiable with homosexuality lends circumstantial weight to Thomas's thesis that postal media are 'queer'.

[32] Henry James, *The Ambassadors* (Harmondsworth: Penguin, 2001), 53–4.

[33] Ibid., 103, 92, 214.   [34] Ibid., 214, 209, 201.

driven to write a lengthy letter to her daughter Irma, the child of her first marriage, who is now living with Mrs Herriton.[35] Here is Forster's narration of this letter's origin and fate:

> [Lilia] wildly took up paper and pen and wrote page after page, analysing [Gino's] character, enumerating his iniquities, reporting whole conversations, tracing all the causes and the growth of her misery. She was beside herself with passion, and though she could hardly think or see she suddenly attained to magnificence and pathos which a practiced stylist might have envied. It was written like a diary, and not till its conclusion did she realize for whom it was meant.

> 'Irma, darling Irma, this letter is for you...It will make you unhappy, but I want you to know everything...God bless you, my dearest, and save you. God bless your miserable mother.'

> Fortunately Mrs Herriton was in when the letter arrived. She seized it and opened it in her bedroom. Another moment, and Irma's placid childhood would have been destroyed for ever.

As a direct result of this communication, Mrs Herriton sends Lilia a note 'forbidding direct communications between mother and daughter'.[36] Again, communications in this novel pass between people other than those addressed by the initial communication of a given series. Also significant is the way Lilia's intent to write this letter does not initially announce itself as such, but rather as the impulse to write something 'like a diary': as a result, thematic and stylistic features of the diary genre pass into and become entangled with the letter form. Forster's text, like Stoker's, remediates the text that it imagines; in this instance, via the paragraph Forster 'quotes' from Lilia's letter.

Novels aside, it is a non-fictitious letter that represents perhaps the most striking depiction of postal relations in the period—a depiction all the more striking for the fact that it is not *just* a depiction but also an actual part of the postal series it describes. *De Profundis* is originally a private letter sent by Oscar Wilde to Lord Alfred Douglas, 'Bosie', subsequently published (in excised form) in 1905.[37] Famously, the text dissects Wilde and Bosie's disastrous relationship; less famously, it does so largely through extensive discussion of the couple's correspondence. One thing Wilde dilates on is Bosie's 'mania for writing revolting and loathsome letters'.[38] Wilde recalls one such occasion: 'You went sullenly after luncheon, leaving one of your most offensive letters behind with the butler to be handed to me after your departure.' In Wilde's account, Bosie excels at manipulating the relation between his presentation in person and by pen. He also excels at using all the postal media available: elsewhere, we hear of Bosie's use of telegrams and postcards.[39]

---

[35] E. M. Forster, *Where Angels Fear to Tread*, ed. Oliver Stallybrass (Harmondsworth: Penguin, 2007), 11.

[36] Ibid., 49.   [37] Richard Ellmann, *Oscar Wilde* (London: Hamish Hamilton, 1987), 551.

[38] Oscar Wilde, *Plays, Prose Writings and Poems* (London: Everyman's Library, 1991), 551.

[39] Ibid., 554, 583–84, 629.

But it is in recounting how Wilde and Bosie's correspondence became entwined with that of *other* correspondents that Wilde's account becomes what one can only call sublime. One lengthy paragraph of *De Profundis* offers an inventory and chronology of letters and telegrams sent over a certain period between not only Wilde and Bosie, but also Bosie and his mother, between Bosie's mother and Wilde, Bosie and Wilde's wife, and Wilde's wife and Wilde. All these communicative dyads, save the first, appear in Wilde's account as mere prompts, and attempts, to influence the first. Wilde relates: 'Finally you actually telegraphed to my wife begging her to use her influence with me to get me to write to you.'[40] As in *The Ambassadors*, stressed relations between pairs turn 'triangular'. More broadly, we may again observe how here, as in so many texts addressed above, communications provoke and comment on each other.

And what, finally, of Wilde's own communications, of which *De Profundis* is an instance? '[R]eal letters', Wilde comments at one point, 'are like a person talking to one'—a formula suggesting the criteria against which Wilde would have his own letter judged.[41] According to these criteria, letters are best when they suspend a reader's consciousness of both their 'sent-ness' and 'written-ness'—that is, when they become evocative of speech under conditions of *immediacy*. As John Durham Peters writes, however, such immediacy only becomes thinkable in the 'shadow' of its mediated counterpart. Historically, it is the experience of mediated communications, including postal ones—with all the potential for failure and discord which the present chapter has shown these as involving—that installs immediacy as a regulatory ideal.[42] Wilde's gloss on 'real' letters thus exemplifies the too-quick privileging of this immediacy that Peters sets out to criticize. Despite this, however, *De Profundis* ultimately accepts its mediated status, just as it ultimately affirms the postal culture of which it is part. The very first, and in some respects most egregious fault it finds with Bosie is not writing to Wilde in two years. Towards the letter's end, Wilde advises Bosie of how he should reply. And as a correlative of all this, Wilde's text foregrounds its own materiality. 'You must take [the letter] as it stands,' Wilde tells Bosie: 'blotted in many places with tears, in some with the signs of passion or pain, and make it out as best you can, blots, corrections and all.'[43] The psychic is revealed through matter's ruin, matter's flaw.

FURTHER READING

Armstrong, Tim. *Modernism, Technology and the Body: A Cultural Study* (Cambridge: Cambridge University Press, 1998).

Halliday, Sam. *Science and Technology in the Age of Hawthorne, Melville, Twain and James: Thinking and Writing Electricity* (New York: Palgrave, 2007).

---

[40]   Ibid., 558.   [41]   Ibid., 591.

[42]   John Durham Peters, *Speaking into the Air: A History of the Idea of Communication* (Chicago, IL: University of Chicago Press, 2000), 6.

[43]   Wilde, *Plays, Prose Writings and Poems*, 545, 648, 638.

Masten, Jeffrey, Peter Stallybrass, and Nancy J. Vickers (eds). *Language Machines: Technologies of Literary and Cultural Production* (New York: Routledge, 1997).

Mattelart, Armand. *The Invention of Communication*, trans. Susan Emanuel (Minneapolis, MN: University of Minnesota Press, 1996).

Menke, Richard. *Telegraphic Realism: Victorian Fiction and Other Information Systems* (Stanford, CA: Stanford University Press, 2008).

Peters, John Durham. *Speaking into the Air: A History of the Idea of Communication* (Chicago, IL: University of Chicago Press, 2000).

Tabbi, Joseph and Michael Wutz (eds). *Reading Matters: Narrativity in the New Media Ecology* (Ithaca, NY: Cornell University Press, 1997).

Trotter, David. *Literature in the First Media Age: Britain between the Wars* (Cambridge, MA: Harvard University Press, 2013).

Thomas, Kate. *Postal Pleasures: Sex, Scandal and Victorian Letters* (Oxford: Oxford University Press, 2012).

Wallace, Jeff. *D. H. Lawrence, Science and the Posthuman* (Basingstoke: Palgrave, 2005).

CHAPTER 38

THE RESIDUE OF MODERNITY

Technology, Anachronism, and Bric-à-Brac in India

ALEXANDER BUBB

The eighty-day sprint around the globe imagined by Jules Verne in 1873 was enabled by a cluster of transportation breakthroughs. In May 1869, Leland Stanford drove a golden railway spike at Promontory, Utah, to herald the opening of direct traffic across the North American continent. Six months later the Empress Eugénie became the first passenger to transit the Suez Canal. The final threshold was attained in March 1870 when, as the *Morning Chronicle* informs Phileas Fogg at the Reform Club, the main trunk line was completed between Bombay and Calcutta.[1] Hastened partly by the demand at Manchester for Indian cotton, this event represented the first large-scale penetration of Asian markets by European-owned railway companies. As he approaches Allahabad three weeks later, however, Fogg discovers that his implicit trust in the London press was misplaced: there is a gap in the line. Separating the two railheads spreads fifty miles of jungle, and an interlude in which Fogg enlists the services of an elephant, and his factotum Passepartout rescues a young *sati* from the funeral pyre. Such detours into the picaresque, precipitated by erring machinery, are almost generic to satires of modern travel. Since Verne's protagonist is a fastidiously punctual Englishman, moreover, India is the obvious location in which his elite travellers are to be ejected from the comfort of their Pullman car, and forced to negotiate the old world at its own pace. It is notable that this technical miscarriage, however, not only breaks up a narrative bound by schedule, but triggers a series of anachronistic juxtapositions. Fogg's mount first provides more than facile local colour. It is a war-elephant, the trained pet of rajas who no longer conduct wars.[2] Following the disorienting interlude, which thrusts the reader into a

---

[1] Jules Verne, *Around the World in Eighty Days*, trans. William Butcher (Oxford: Oxford University Press, 1995), 19.

[2] The elephant was, moreover, a common element in the anachronistic heraldry of British India. One was pictured with a locomotive, for example, on the crest of the Great Indian Peninsula Railway.

bygone genre of Indian romance, the fledgling industry and smoking chimneys of Monghyr's foundries are made to appear newly strange. From an Allahabad Jew, Passepartout supplies his *sati* with a second-hand cloak and otter-skin pelisse—incongruous, lost objects of unexplained provenance. And at Calcutta, charged with trespassing in a temple, he is confronted with his discarded leather boots.[3]

In this chapter, I wish to examine literary passages—usually carefully crafted vignettes within larger narratives—that position European technologies and manufactures within discrepant Indian settings. My argument will take in the large-scale, infrastructural phenomena that have often engaged scholars of empire writing, but will also follow the turn led by David Arnold, in the study of colonial material culture, towards objects of everyday technology. My focus is the anachronism as a device in three Anglo-Indian writers at the turn of the century,[4] specifically those many appearances of incongruous, often discarded technological paraphernalia that mark the uneven frontier of material progress. Each of these authors was drawn repeatedly to the rough outer edges where Western technology is introduced to, and finds a tenuous niche within narrow localities. Rudyard Kipling's journeys to the edge of the railway and telegraph networks is the focus of the first section, while the second considers Flora Annie Steel's observations of everyday technologies imported into the Indian household. Treated as uncanny or as absurd, it is right to term these encounters anachronistic—for though they involve *misplaced* items, India is understood as a space in which separate eras jar against one another, disrupting the order of time.[5] This is particularly true of Edmund Candler's writings, treated in the third section, which figure modern material culture as jumbled refuse or 'lumber'.

The technologies in question are sometimes integral to plot and action, such as the 'devil-carriage' or tricycle that allows Kipling's all-seeing policeman Yunkum Sahib to stalk his errant native constables with disconcerting quietness in 'At Howli Thana'. More often they are eloquent simply by their presence. Even so, they do not merely populate the material background of the Anglo-Indian sketch, but form points of descriptive focus. As Jeremy Tambling remarks in his treatise *On*

Conflating the two, a locomotive fashioned in the shape of an elephant conveys Verne's travellers in his subsequent *The Steam House* (*La Maison à Vapeur*)—in which Nana Sahib plots to destroy the GIPR.

[3] Ibid., 70, 74, 78.

[4] By Anglo-Indian, I mean writers drawn from the British community resident in colonial India. Edwin Arnold (b. 1832) and Alfred Lyall (b. 1835) were precursors to Steel (b. 1847) and Kipling (b. 1865), who casts a long shadow over later authors like Candler (b. 1874). Hector Munro ('Saki', b. 1870) also had a brief career in South Asia, while Leonard Woolf (b. 1880) and George Orwell (b. 1903) were outsiders in the British community and grew to loathe its values.

[5] Anne McClintock originally described the colony as 'anachronistic space'. 'Imperial progress across the space of empire', she writes, 'is figured as a journey backward in time'. See *Imperial Leather: Race, Gender and Sexuality in the Colonial Context* (New York and London: Routledge, 1995), 40. Rather than the fetishizing of the East's antique curiosities, my focus is on objects from 'the future' displaced in the colonial context, and the use of such anachronism as a distinct literary device.

Anachronism, cultures habitually make use of anachronistic conceits—neo-Gothic architecture, for example—either to differentiate theirs from a prior era, or to draw analogies with the past. Of greater significance than the practice itself is whether the discrepancy is occluded and smoothed over, or openly performed. To deploy anachronisms self-consciously, Tambling argues, is the behaviour of a present culture 'confident' in its relationship to the past.[6] A selective reading of *The Unveiling of Lhasa* (1905) would bear this out, the inventory of stray technologies that Candler accumulates amounting to a deliberate, if grim, tally of material progress. Candler's marked overuse of the word 'anachronism' itself, however, points to a particularly bitter sense of personal alienation, which he understood not in terms of being in the wrong place, but in the wrong time. Viewed in the context of an imperial culture that frequently did draw ingenuous emblematic links with the past (such the medievalist trappings of Lord Lytton's 1877 Durbar, itself a colonial outgrowth of neo-Gothic sensibilities), these writers' acknowledged mismatchings can be seen to probe sceptically at official myths. Because anachronism can operate both forwards and backwards in time, their tricycles and boots—modern objects mislaid in the past—cut against the feudal bric-à-brac unearthed and exported to the present by the 1877 Durbar. They disrupt the continuity implied by that glib transition, and put the future in doubt. Last, the anachronisms of the past that do attract Kipling, Steel, and Candler are drawn not from indigenous history, but from their own, eighteenth-century Anglo-Indian heritage. As the final section will discuss, a sense of colonial belatedness affects all three writers. Counterpointed with the prematurely decaying, junked residue of the latter-day Raj, the awkward ephemera and obsolete infrastructure of the Company period becomes a touchstone for this nostalgia.

The gap in the line: Kipling's frayed technological networks

When the Great Indian Peninsula Railway finally met its counterpart, the East Indian line at Jabalpur, Lord Mayo put aside his silver-plated hammer and declared his ambition that 'the whole country should be covered with a net-work of lines on a general and uniform system'.[7] Like David Lloyd George's metaphor for the Indian Civil Service, 'the steel frame', this remark warrants more than a cursory reference to the *stahlhartes Gehäuse* of Max Weber.[8] The 'iron cage' connotes above all centralized and comprehensive rationalization, and the viceroy's implication was that

---

[6] Jeremy Tambling, *On Anachronism* (Manchester: Manchester University Press, 2010), 9.

[7] *Times of India*, 12 Mar 1870, 3.

[8] Quoted in Phiroze Vasunia, *The Classics and Colonial India* (Oxford: Oxford University Press), 193; Max Weber, *The Protestant Ethic and the Spirit of Capitalism*, trans. Stephen Kalberg (Chicago, IL: Roxbury, 2001), 123, 245.

the state-guaranteed Indian lines would contrast favourably with those that emerged from the speculative chaos of Britain's 1840s 'Railway Mania', or with the variant gauges used by the poorly coordinated Australian colonies. The grid was still patchy, however, and solid black ink did not guarantee the existence of what engineers, nudged out to Canada and India by the decline in British construction, called with new, purposeful emphasis 'the permanent way'.

Verne's gap in the line was exaggerated, but by no means unprecedented. Engineers were slow to scale the escarpment of the Western Ghats and, until the end of the century, rail journeys would also have been frequently interrupted by river crossings. The narrator of Kipling's 'In Flood Time' (1888) listens to the tale of an elderly ford keeper while waiting for high waters to subside, and in one article he described crossing between two railheads via a pontoon bridge traversed by a rickety tramway. The core trunk routes had taken shape during Kipling's childhood and, in 1870, his family had made use of the new Bombay–Calcutta line to holiday in Nashik.[9] Following the Russian attempt on Herat in 1885, bridging the Punjab's eponymous five rivers became a defence priority and, as a Lahore journalist, he was sent to report on these iron statements of a government that 'does not approve of interference with its frontier communications'.[10] In March 1887 he saw the aforementioned tramway replaced by a fixed link over the Sutlej at Ferozepur, and two months later attended the opening ceremony of another crossing on the Jhelum. Both were named for the Queen-Empress.

The first and larger structure left the most abiding impressions. 'The Sutlej Bridge' opens by celebrating the vast scale of an unprecedented, alien object which has transformed the landscape for miles around. Excavators have built up two vast embankments at either bridgehead, and created artificial islands to bear the immense brick piers. The revolution is social as well as physical: cosmopolitan villages have sprung up on the mudflat to house the workmen, who 'hang and cluster like bees' on the superstructure. Rope specialists from Gujarat man the winches, while Caribbean creoles supervise the piledriver.[11] Always capitalized, the Bridge becomes an ungodly idol tended by a vortex of worshippers. As the chapter proceeds, however, a harsh, inhuman quality begins to emanate from the ironwork and infect its surroundings.

> The inclination to smile does not come over the unprofessional mind till it is out of the range of the influences of the Bridge—out of the bitter chill shade, the keen dry wind that twangs like a strained wire as it hurries over the sand…out of the hearing of the clang of the riveters, the straining and clanking of the cranes, and the grumble of the concrete-blocks shot over the barge sides into the river—till it is disconnected, in fact, from the terribly eager, restless, driving life that fills the river-bed, and falls back once more on everyday existence.[12]

[9] Andrew Lycett, *Rudyard Kipling* (London: Phoenix, 2000), 42–3.
[10] Thomas Pinney (ed.), *Kipling's India: Uncollected Sketches, 1884–88* (London: Papermac, 1987), 207.
[11] Ibid., 214.   [12] Ibid., 212.

Such experiences in India do much to explain the faintly sinister quality, mingled with admiration, which persisted in all of the inscrutable murmuring engines that Kipling later pictured—universally quarrying, irrigating, and levelling the earth. It was, likewise, his colonial upbringing that shaped his peculiarly *networked* understanding of modernity. The impress technology makes on everyday life through generic interlocking structures was a process to which he was acutely sensitive. Moreover, just as in our own time uni-linear understandings premised on exploitation and hegemonic knowledge have given way to a more nuanced perception of how colonial societies adapted to and repurposed foreign technology, Kipling did not see modernity purely as a penetrative, despoiling influence. Indeed, as Elleke Boehmer has argued in respect of 'the te-rain' in *Kim* (1901), his mature fictions persuasively depict the 'iron cage' enmeshed with and undergirding Indian social exchange.[13] In one of his rare press interviews, in October 1891, Kipling told a New Zealand reporter about the need for swifter express trains to satisfy provincial demand. Pilgrimages were now made by rail, he noted, and extra services scheduled for festivals. Furthermore, the industrial division of labour had been ratified into castes by the Indian labour force, ranging from drivers and brass-fitters to embankment coolies. But while this dynamic adaptation represented what he called 'a marvellous departure from the old traditions and ways', the apparatus of the railway remained a strange and 'monolithic' imposition.[14] Constructed by a militarist state, its fortified stations were marked by banal precision, Kipling's imagery recalling the surreal, pinched perspective of a de Chirico painting. His remarks in 1891 closely echoed a scene in his new novel, *The Naulahka*, in which the enterprising American Tarvin arrives dismayed at a dusty railhead in Rajasthan.

> It was final, intended, absolute. The grim solidity of the cut-stone station-house, the solid masonry of the empty platform, the mathematical exactitude of the station name-board looked for no future. No new railroad could help Rawut Junction. It had no ambition. It belonged to the Government.[15]

The journey off the rails and across the desert that awaits Tarvin was modelled after Kipling's own Rajasthani assignment of 1887, in which he abandoned the railway and its 'globetrotters' in favour of the overland mail. It was commonplace, in late nineteenth-century India, to equate a visit to the princely states—realms of anachronism embedded in a modern polity—with time travel. To meet an elephant of the royal 'fighting stud' plying the streets here, wrote Candler, is 'an anachronism

---

[13] Elleke Boehmer, 'Global and Textual Webs in an Age of Transnational Capitalism; Or, What Isn't New About Empire', *Postcolonial Studies* 7/1 (2004), 11–26. I have discussed *Kim*'s rail journey in greater depth in 'The Provincial Cosmopolitan: Kipling, India and Globalization', *Journal of Postcolonial Writing* 49/4 (2013), 399 and 'Beneath the Skin: Kipling and Contemporary British Understanding of the Colonial Relationship', *British Politics Review* Norway 8/4 (Autumn 2013), 16–17.

[14] *Otago Witness*, 22 October 1891, 33.

[15] Rudyard Kipling and Wolcott Balestier, *The Naulahka: A Story of East and West* (London: Macmillan, 1915), 57.

which no custom can stale', while Kipling described the kingdoms in one story as delicately poised between non-contiguous centuries, 'touching the Railway and the Telegraph on one side, and, on the other, the days of Harun-al-Raschid'.[16] But although Lord Lytton's Durbar took its appearance largely from the design of his own father Lockwood, the princedoms' superannuated trappings typically operated less strongly upon Kipling's imagination than anachronisms projected in the opposite direction: that is, modern technology displaced, or dumped, into the past. On reaching his destination, Tarvin sets about dispatching a telegram home to Colorado and is directed towards a 'desecrated mosque'. Looking about dispiritedly for the blue and white sign of the Western Union, he tries an unmarked door, 'disclosing a flight of steps eighteen inches wide'.

> Up these he travelled with difficulty, hoping to catch the sound of the ticker. But the building was as silent as the tomb it had once been. He opened another door, and stumbled into a room, the domed ceiling of which was inlaid with fretted tracery in barbaric colours, picked out with myriads of tiny fragments of mirrors. The flood of colour and the glare of the snow-white floor made him blink after the pitchy darkness of the staircase. Still, the place was undoubtedly a telegraph-office, for an antiquated instrument was clamped upon a cheap dressing-table. The sunlight streamed through the gash in the dome which had been made to admit the telegraph wires, and which had not been repaired.[17]

Rather than pursuing romantic, antique purity, Kipling is attracted by places to which modern technology has just partially penetrated—not as fully as Jaipur's street lighting and hydraulic cotton-press, which he termed 'raw' and 'aggressive', but in an attenuated form that has been untidily subverted to local conditions.[18] The frayed edge of a fine-spun, tenuous network seems to particularly engage him, and to epitomize his ever-ambiguous attitude towards imperial modernity. Enabling rapid global communication, the telegraph testifies to the modern project of bringing India up to date, uniting the regions of the world in homogeneous time. As a token of what Trotsky termed uneven development, however, the episode undermines this project, implying that Rajasthan will remain at a chronological remove which technology will serve only to emphasize. The province's continued isolation today from India's centres of commerce notwithstanding, Rhatore's 'antiquated instrument' is a specimen of a technology that was still expanding in South Asia, but which in the West was undergoing the accelerated obsolescence characteristic of mass production. The Naulahka was published in the same year that Alexander Graham Bell made the first New York to Chicago telephone call, while telegram

---

[16] Edmund Candler, The Mantle of the East (Edinburgh and London: William Blackwood and Sons, 1910), 38; Kipling, Wee Willie Winkie and Other Stories (London: Macmillan, 1895), 198.

[17] Kipling and Balestier, The Naulahka, 77–8.

[18] Kipling, From Sea to Sea and Other Sketches: Letters of Travel, 2 vols (London: Macmillan, 1900), I, 23.

services were finally suspended in India only in 2013.[19] Anticipating the industrial nostalgists who hunt out rusty tramcars and Clyde-built steamboats in today's South Asia, therefore, in 1891 Kipling began to perceive deposits of residual modernity. Already tarnished, the Rhatore telegraph has commenced its own long, colonial obsolescence. It is undergoing the same dusty, premature decay that afflicts the English salesmen who await Tarvin at the *daak* bungalow, or the sleepy clerk whom he takes initially for a corpse. A visitor from the future in 1890s Rajasthan, the 'ticker' will survive to be an anachronistic relic of the past.[20]

Flora Annie Steel and the anachronistic object in Indian material culture

'Clamped upon a cheap dressing-table', the nondescript instrument also recalls another mechanical import which, if not yet ubiquitous, had attained its distinct niche within the cottage industry of urban India. The first Singer sewing machines were imported in 1875, although as David Arnold points out the machine's impact was felt in the domestic sphere often as absence rather than foreign presence, as the stitching once carried out by the household *darzi* was increasingly executed in local workshops.[21] Hence it is to the familiar whirr and odour of 'the sewing-machines of the bazar' that Kim compares the unfamiliar gadget—a phonograph—with which Lurgan Sahib attempts to frighten him during his first night at Simla.[22] The shift in recent scholarship towards the 'everyday technology' manifested in such objects has been, in part, a turn away from a prior fixation on railways, industry, and other 'big technology'. A more malleable understanding of colonialism, furthermore, less constrained by Marxist economics and by the hegemonic paradigm established by Said, has fastened on European mechanical commodities as sites for the negotiation and domestication—or, as Frank Dikötter terms it in his study of modern China, the 'appropriation'—of European products by their colonial customers.[23] In their introduction to a 2012 special issue of *Modern Asian Studies* devoted to the topic, David Arnold and Erich DeWald propose that 'technological modernity might

---

[19] *Times of India*, 14 July 2013, available at http://timesofindia.indiatimes.com/city/pune/Pune-sends-its-last-telegram-citizens-mourn-death-of-163-year-old-medium/articleshow/21065238.cms.

[20] The moment at which American time and Indian time are made, comically, to jar is on the delivery of Tarvin's stray telegram (its addressee—whose purpose in Rhatore is to loot a necklace—has been mis-transcribed as 'Turpin'). Resembling recent films in which a time-travelling hero pre-empts disaster by depositing a warning message for himself further back in history, the clerk 'dive[s]' into his drawer and excavates from it an envelope 'covered with dust'.

[21] David Arnold, 'Global Goods and Local Usages: The Small World of the Indian Sewing-Machine, 1875–1952', *Journal of Global History* 6/3 (2011), 412–14.

[22] Kipling, *Kim* (Oxford: Oxford University Press, 2008), 151.

[23] Frank Dikötter, *Things Modern: Material Culture and Everyday Life in China* (London: Hurst, 2007), 9.

be—and often was—something far more pragmatic, mundane, and experiential than many current and rather grandiose interpretations of modernity would seem to suggest.'[24]

Like Kipling, the author and educationist Flora Annie Steel was attentive to the eloquence of objects. The masterful opening scene of *On the Face of the Waters* (1896), her novel of the 1857 Rebellion, imagines the British annexation of Awadh as the public dismemberment of one material culture by another, as the Nawab's chattels are auctioned for a pittance on the riverbank at Lucknow.

> 'Going! Going! Gone!' What was going? Everything, if tales were true; and there were so many tales nowadays. Of news flashed faster by wires than any, even the gods themselves, could flash it; of carriages, fire-fed, bringing God knows what grain from God knows where! Could a body eat of it and not be polluted? Could the children read the school books and not be apostate?[25]

This broad sweep of transformation and derangement, news-wire and fire-carriage, is of a piece with the authoritative vista of the grand historical novel, with its 1850s setting and its dramatic antithesis of clashing civilizations. Steel's own Indian career, however, spanned the years 1867 to 1889, during her husband's tenure in the Indian Civil Service. This was a period in which, following the opening of the Suez Canal, the Anglo-Indian family unit girded itself with modern conveniences, medicines, and wistful décor (Steel was perhaps best known in her lifetime as author of *The Complete Indian Housekeeper and Cook*). More pertinently, through her teaching, folklore-collecting, and interviews with Punjabi women, Steel became a close observer of the integration, and even repurposing, of European manufactures within Indian domestic economy and social practice.

Arnold and DeWald suggest that the hitherto prevailing focus by historians on 'big technology' was prompted in part by passages like that above, or more particularly by Kipling's use of infrastructure to aggrandize or justify paternalist, utilitarian rule.[26] Scholars, they note, have not been 'altogether immune' from a tendency to follow the authors of empire and 'identify technology in its grander forms with the ideological aspirations, the political priorities, and economic exigencies of the colonial state'. If so, this susceptibility has been insensitive to Kipling's ambivalence, as well as to Steel's and Candler's pronounced interest in the everyday technological object. By following the same lead, however, we can also perceive why commodified technologies—sewing machines, bicycles, and phonographs—have also been viewed chiefly in uni-linear terms that describe the capture of colonial markets as outlets for European products. Steel shared with Kipling a concern for artisanal traditions and their erosion by cheap imports, a process on which her

---

[24] David Arnold and Erich DeWald, 'Everyday Technology in South and Southeast Asia: An Introduction', *Modern Asian Studies* 46/1 (January 2012), 9.

[25] Flora Annie Steel, *On the Face of the Waters: A Tale of the Mutiny* (New York: Macmillan, 1896), 11.

[26] Arnold and DeWald, 'Everyday Technology', 3–5.

much more prolonged residency in India gave her a fuller perspective.[27] Her contribution, in 1905, to a series on foreign countries and industry published by Adam & Charles Black laid particular emphasis on crafts. If the domination of the cloth market by Manchester imports was a matter of common knowledge, Steel identified mass-produced aniline dyes as more effectively fatal to inherited finesse in Indian fabric making, while the Nasmyth steam hammer put its uniform stamp on cheap jewellery.

> In the old days, from one end of the village street to the other, in house and workshop, nothing was to be found save village manufactures. Now it is otherwise, and, even in the most remote, Birmingham and Berlin is writ clear on many things exposed for sale, paraffin is burnt everywhere, and the peasant going to his fields lights his *hukka* with matches.[28]

'Writ clear', the Berlin trademark typifies Edwardian anxieties: to use once again the example of the sewing machine, the German firm Pfaff more than quintupled its Indian market share between 1900 and the First World War. 'Our rivals in commerce' are likewise stealing a march in cottons, Steel noted, explaining the Indian customer's preference with the tellingly emphatic phrase 'because the *measure is always right*'.[29] The use however, or reuse, of European containers for Indian consumables was already a well-established trope in her fiction. In the 1893 story 'Gunesh Chund', a village headman celebrates the birth of his child by distributing 'a few flat baskets of sweets, covered with penny-halfpenny Manchester pocket-handkerchiefs printed in the semblance of a pack of cards'. When an unwanted girl is delivered, the handkerchiefs are presumably among the betrothal gifts which the doomed Gunesh packs for his second wife, committing them 'to the broad white road that carried Western civilization, in the shape of a post-bag'. In Steel's domestic fictions, incongruous details like these are carefully staged and embroidered with minute ironies. The playing card motif counterpoints Gunesh Chund's marital tragedy with the trivial complacency of English households and, as an omen of the fatal dynastic game subsequently played by his scheming mother, associates the cheap English product with bad faith and false fronts. The echo of prevailing trade patterns (Indian staples exported in foreign vessels) is stronger in 'At a Girls' School' (1893), in which the sisters Fâtma and Hoshiaribi drink tea from ceramic basins emblazoned 'with an English flag, and "Union is Strength" upon them in gay colours'. Once again, the product's charmless ornament glibly predicts the discord and separation that is to follow, although the 'sickly sweet, cinnamon-flavoured' tea the sisters pour into their cups, accompanied by a vernacular

[27] Thomas Pinney (ed.), *The Letters of Rudyard Kipling*, 6 vols (London: Macmillan, 1990–2004), II, 56.
[28] Mortimer Menpes and Flora Annie Steel, *India* (London: Adam and Charles Black, 1905), 106, 117, 15.
[29] Arnold, 'Global Goods and Local Usages', 412; Menpes and Steel, *India*, 94–5.

proverb, highlights Indian adaptation of Europe's imports and sublime indifference to the cruder messages encoded within them.[30]

'In a Citron Garden' (1893) also describes orient liquor decanted into base vessels, by an aged parfumier who harvests shaddock blossom under the eyes of a young girl.

> The first time she saw the yellow mash which was left after the sweetness had trickled into the odd assortment of little bottles the old distiller brought with him, she had cried bitterly. But a whole bottle of orange-flower water as her very own had been consoling, and the fact that the label proclaimed her treasure to be '*Genuine, Old, Unsweetened Gin*' did not disturb her ignorance.

Steel's interest in incongruous branding is particularly clear in this story and, by the age of sixteen, the girl has collected a row of bottles 'labeled "*Encore*," "*Dry Monopole*," "*Heidsiecker*," and "*Chloric Ether Bitters*"'.[31] Rendered meaningless in their new surroundings, the garish labels are subject to a gross bathos: perfume sharpens and refines desire (pleasure and its deferral is the chief theme of the story), but the bottles formerly contained no such aphrodisiac for the benumbed Western sensibility. For the reclusive inhabitant of the citron garden, fated to a lifetime of widowhood, they are also receptacles for unfulfilled desire. The reposing of cloistered, often female longings in a foreign, half-understood object of dubious provenance is a theme that recurs in 'Music Hath Charms' (1897). Steel's most eloquent study of modern technology describes a crowded family mansion, where the widow Râdha gazes on her dead husband's photograph, hanging between two German prints of the Madonna and Salome (substitutes for the infant Krishna and demon-slaying Durga). The story hinges around a second-hand church harmonium—an anachronism of the future when housed beneath the parlour's smoke-blackened beams, but a wheezing relic in the eyes of the London-returned barrister. The latter eventually breaks the instrument while attempting to play *God Save the Queen*, thus forever depriving the family's blind music master of 'a noise which somehow or other seemed to set you free, and yet kept you longing for something more'.[32] The scenario is highly reminiscent of Tagore's novel *Ghare Baire* (*The Home and the World*), in which so much hangs on the imported furniture which cumbers an ancestral Bengali home—not least the shrill gramophone by which the Bara Rani, a widow who sublimates her frustrated motherhood into worship of the infant Krishna, dwells on the lewd ballads of the Calcutta stage. In both works, the domestic modernity and Victorian companionate marriage promised by these acquisitions—values imaged in the products' Indian advertisements—remain unconsummated or, like the economic modernity heralded by Kipling's telegraph, are betrayed into insubstantiality.[33]

---

[30]   Steel, *From the Five Rivers* (London: Heinemann, 1893), 12, 40, 162.   [31] Ibid., 186.

[32] Steel, *In the Permanent Way* (London: Macmillan, 1897), 392–3, 289–90.

[33] Rabindranath Tagore, *The Home and the World* (London: Macmillan, 1919), 298; for advertisements picturing the gramophone within the Indian bourgeois household, see Gerry Farrell, 'The Early

Edmund Candler and imperial detritus

In keeping with Tambling's proviso, it is not the mute testimony of European objects in the texture of Steel's fiction, but their deliberate staging—sometimes merely as ironic incongruity, but often within the conventions of anachronism—which is significant. This trope becomes especially pronounced in the work of Edmund Candler, the schoolmaster and journalist best known today for his novel *Siri Ram— Revolutionist* (1914). As one of the last authors of note to spend their writing life in colonial India, Candler knew himself inescapably overshadowed by Kipling, and hampered in his social reconnaissance by the nationalist animosity of which his predecessor had suffered only a foretaste. Candler's years in India (1895–1921) coincided with the large-scale import of everyday mechanical commodities—the bicycle from the 1890s onwards, the gramophone after 1902. Moreover, their enumeration—often, indeed, listing—in his stories bears out Arnold and DeWald's remark that such technologies should be understood as arriving and functioning in 'clusters'.[34] In respect to British residents, the Anglo-Indian domesticity that Steel had observed was, with the lapse of another twenty years, ripe for anachronistic satire. In 'The Testimony of Bhagwan Singh' (1911), for example, the engineer Carpendale brings his bride home to an appropriated Mughal tomb. He has defaced the building with wooden partitions and a veranda roofed with galvanized iron, and fitted the interior with bells, electric light, and 'an ice and a soda-water machine'.[35] Candler often substitutes for the unseen British their lumpen material culture, using this device to imply a creeping Decadence and widening insulation of the sahibs from the people whom they administer. In one sketch he contrasts the 'intricately involved' alleyways of Benares's old city with the gridwork streets of its cantonment, where 'detached from one another by walled compounds, live that other half of the Aryan stock whose practical evolution is symbolised by the club, the Spectator, the bicycle, the galvanised iron bath, and the Bible.'[36]

Candler takes a largely one-sided view of what Arnold and DeWald term the 'mobility' of the sewing machine or bicycle which, 'weaving its way between the native town, the cantonment, and the civil lines', tends to elide rather than reify racial difference.[37] The aspirational meanings it may have held for its Indian users do not interest him. But its undetected, insinuating movement through the subcontinent is

Days of the Gramophone Industry in India: Historical, Social and Musical Perspectives', *British Journal of Ethnomusicology* 2 (1993), 46.

[34] Arnold and DeWald, 'Cycles of Empowerment? The Bicycle and Everyday Technology in Colonial India and Vietnam', *Comparative Studies in Society and History* 53/4 (October 2011), 974; Farrell, 'Early Days of the Gramophone', 34; Arnold and DeWald, 'Everyday Technology', 15.
[35] Candler, *The General Plan* (Edinburgh and London: William Blackwood and Sons, 1911), 191.
[36] Candler, *The Mantle of the East*, 6.
[37] Arnold and DeWald, 'Everyday Technology', 16.

a mystery on which he dwells repeatedly—made more mysterious by fact that the bicycle which he meets in *The Unveiling of Lhasa*, gone to ground on the city's outskirts, is without wheels. Candler spent 1904 in Tibet as the *Daily Mail* correspondent attached to the Younghusband Expedition, and his account abounds with incongruous manufactures which, by crossing the Himalayan threshold, have also travelled in time. Like the bicycle which rusts nearby, 'a sausage-machine made in Birmingham' appears to have found its way to Lhasa of its own accord. Such anomalous scraps have filtered into Tibet haphazardly, squeezed through its closed borders as if by the sheer pressure of modernity in British Bengal. Younghusband's oversized column also leaves in its wake a trail of miscellaneous refuse. In the Chumbi Valley local women scavenge their camp site for tin cans and old newspapers, giggling over the fashion plates in Oscar Wilde's magazine *The Lady*.[38] Candler's attitude to all this discarded and re-harvested bric-à-brac is one of ambivalent disgust and periodic self-loathing.[39] The opening of Tibet to free trade was the expedition's stated objective and, as a literary carpetbagger bent on 'romance', Candler too is guiltily implicated in the country's despoil and disenchantment. Lashing out in other passages, technological anachronisms become instruments of his own vengeful antipathy to the xenophobic and backward lamas, who (the refusal of dialogue always infuriates Candler) decline to parley with 'the mission'.[40]

In the most carefully rehearsed of his vignettes, Candler relishes the blasphemous whine of a soldier's gramophone. 'It is destined, I hope, to resound in the palace of Potala, where the Dalai Lama and his suite may wonder what heathen ritual is accompanied by "A jovial monk am I", and "Her golden hair was hanging down her back."'[41] In the event, upon reaching the holy city he discovers that the Nepalese Ambassador has already presented a so-called 'voice without a soul' to the Thirteenth Dalai Lama, who is said to have found it distinctly unappealing.[42] Once again, Candler could not even begin to consider the significance sound recording might hold for the Indian drawing room. Only fifteen months beforehand, Fred Gaisberg had made his first recordings in Calcutta on behalf of 'His Master's Voice'—a cultural transaction which also began with a grating rendition of 'And her Golden Hair was Hanging Down her Back', but which ended with the voice of the *tawaif* Gauhar Jaan, whose mother had sung for the deposed Nawab of Awadh, being pressed onto shellac at a plant in Hanover. Lurgan Sahib is similarly short-sighted in dismissing Kim's

---

[38] Candler, *The Unveiling of Lhasa* (London: Thomas Nelson & Sons, 1905), 339, 60.

[39] For David Trotter's argument that litter in modern fiction signifies contingency, chance, and regret in human life, see *Cooking with Mud: The Idea of Mess in Nineteenth-Century Art and Fiction* (Oxford: Oxford University Press, 2000), 110, 26.

[40] In his autobiography, for instance, Candler resents the sullen reserve of his politicized Bengali students. See *Youth and the East: An Unconventional Biography* (Edinburgh and London: William Blackwood and Sons, 1924), 224.

[41] Popular numbers from *La Poupée* (1897) and *The Shop Girl* (1894), respectively. For the latter, see Sos Eltis, Chapter 29 in this volume.

[42] Candler, *Unveiling of Lhasa*, 54, 321.

phonograph as a raja's toy, when rather it was into the urban bourgeois home that records transmitted the courtly music of a vanishing era.[43]

Nonetheless, it is notable that Kipling, Tagore, and Candler were all drawn to the detached babble of the record player—for children a repository of spirits, for adults of displaced longings. Candler chose again to deploy the gramophone, in gothic mode, in 'The Testimony of Bhagwan Singh'. Pleased with his other improvements, Carpendale too amuses himself by profaning a hallowed space with English popular songs (the tomb is that of a Mughal poet). Instead, the uncanny machine brings the living into rapport with the dead, ghost summoning ghost.

> Then he felt the urge to do something absurd, something which sensible folk would laugh at...He turned on the gramophone. He put it on a chair by his side so that he might keep it going. But the awe of the moment cowed the thing. Its silly jokes appeared to come from infinitely far off, its humour was a child's profanity. The cracked laughter mocked his precautions, not his fear. The earth-walker appeared in the whir between two recitations. It passed solemnly by Carpendale's chair without regarding him. Its passage was a long-drawn wound; it left a great cicatrice. The roof and floor of his faith fell together, Alpha upon Omega.[44]

It is, appropriately, to the railway tracks that the restless shade of Bhagwan Singh leads the white man, indicating the spot where his murdered lover lies buried. The simultaneous cutting and clapping together of a wound, leaving a scar, is an image which testifies to the disorienting potential of anachronism. The man who thinks himself custodian of the past is instead made its instrument, in an experience which renders not merely his light bulbs and icebox papery and superficial, but also the bloodless marriage which they prop. Like the pages from *The Lady* scattered on the Tibetan steppe, records are the facsimile product of a replicatory culture, caught in the imitation of itself and beset with an anxiety of running out of time. Steel's photographs in 'Music Hath Charms' perform the same function, as does indeed the sausage machine at Lhasa, and when buried in the midden such objects amount to perhaps the most radically cynical thought in Candler's oeuvre: the use of rubbish as a synecdoche for empire.

Conclusion: Eighteenth-century relics and Anglo-Indian belatedness

Candler's volume of travel sketches *The Mantle of the East* (1910) ends, like Fogg and Passepartout's adventure off the rails, in a junk shop. Sheltered by a 'web of suspended telephone wire', Candler's narrator surveys 'shredded horse-hair chairs',

[43] Farrell, 'Early Days of the Gramophone', 32–4, 39.
[44] Candler, *The General Plan*, 194–95.

once-garish ottomans, and a miscellany of untraceable—possibly colonial—objects littering a Covent Garden side street. While the discarded 'lumber' of the West is immediately contrasted with the unencumbered lifestyle of the tropics, however, this passage was published only a few years after a more disconcerting encounter with Indian bric-à-brac.[45] In his autobiography, Candler describes his short-lived appointment as private tutor to a wealthy zamindar's son, who inhabited a frayed and faded palace stuffed with 'glazed oleographs' and 'cut-glass chandeliers of a distressing brilliancy', housing in its magenta-cushioned reception room 'a museum of antiquated clocks'. Most '*criard*' of all, however, was the family coach.

> … if it was less like the ark, the reason was that it was *ante*-diluvian. It was embarrassing to drive in it through the streets of Calcutta behind the Kumar's coachman in his bright orange turban and his parroqueet-coloured livery. The anachronism filled the Chowringhee.[46]

'Anachronism' is a somewhat over-used word in Candler's oeuvre, appearing three times in *The Mantle of the East* alone. He uses it nearly always to denote a relic of the past lingering into the modern day, such as the aforementioned war-elephant (which he mentions directly after discussing gnomons, yantras, and other venerable technologies with Jaipur's royal astronomer). He was instead drawn at least as frequently, as we have seen, to modish gadgets abandoned in the past. But to conclude, it is worth enquiring why the antediluvian coach should be a source of personal embarrassment to Candler. Clearly he was reluctant to advertise his employment in an Indian household, lacking even the semi-official position of schoolmaster. Was this anxiety not accentuated, however, by being thus pantomimically cumbered with the trappings of the eighteenth century?

The carriage was presumably of a similar vintage to the high dog cart driven by Alice Gissing in Steel's *On the Face of the Waters*. The brewer's wife climbs into her vehicle attended by an ostentatious crowd of grooms, 'old-fashioned' even in 1850s Lucknow, 'with silver crests in their pith turbans and huge monograms on their breastplates'. Steel devotes careful description to the up-to-date Anglo-Indian home of the time, with its prim nostalgia and painstakingly cultivated English annuals. But the boxwallah Gissings are, like Candler, of nebulous standing, and in their home 'there was no cult of England. Everything was frankly, staunchly of the nabob and pagoda-tree style; for the Gissings preferred India, where they were received into society, to England, where they would have been out of it'. The heavy furniture favoured by bellicose and gluttonous East India Company merchants, it is made clear, owes nothing to Eastern design. Nonetheless, newcomers to the household find them un-English. In an odd phrase, a young officer is struck by 'a strange unkennedness about their would-be

[45] Candler, *The Mantle of the East*, 298.
[46] Candler, *Youth and the East*, 229.

familiarity.[47] His surprise is prompted first by anachronism, but second by the success with which the deployers of that anachronism have drawn an analogy with the past. In contrast to the wilting pansies and other fetishes of English authenticity, nabobish taste bespeaks a more adaptive, Indianized sensibility. The vignette anticipates the distinction the novel goes on to draw repeatedly between those characters, like Alice Gissing, who are able to face the Mutiny with a command of 'vernacular' languages, and those who are not.

Nostalgia for the technologies, infrastructure, and household lumber of the Company period runs through late-Victorian Anglo-Indian writing. In Kipling's networked imagination, this meant the Grand Trunk Road he evoked in a much-quoted passage from *Kim*, and the overland mail—slenderest and yet most dependable bar of the colonial iron cage—that traverses it. A grimy authenticity even clung to the fetid daak bungalow—like that haunted, in 'My Own True Ghost Story' (1888), not by long-dead billiard players but by the writer's own phantom nostalgias. In Steel's closely textured domestic scenarios, such objects exist in a state of prolonged concurrence. They are touchstones harking back to an era of coeval time, when Indian and European encountered one another as contemporaries. For Candler, however, the sense of discrepancy was too pronounced to permit such affect. In place of the incipient techno-nostalgia that enfolds Kipling's telegraph, ranged eighteenth-century clocks only intensify his sense of alienation. Reduced to rubbish, eloquent objects are not allowed to speak. Understanding his geographical and social displacement always in terms of temporal miscarriage, he is the most solipsistically acute witness to Anglo-Indian belatedness, and hence the most sceptical augur for the future of British India. When he chose to apply the word so often at the tip of his pen to a latter-day item dropped into a bubble of past time, it was at a place—Angkor Wat—which testified to the fatuity of all imperial projects, and it was to himself.

> For this place, so peaceful and remote, is haunted more than any other place on earth with the sense of dead strife, titanic labourings to no lasting purpose, it seems, save a casual holocaust of human lives... With these epic fragments in my head and confused moralisings I fell asleep, a huddled anachronism, on the *zayat* floor.[48]

FURTHER READING

Colonial technology and material culture, and Bric-à-Brac

Arnold, David and Erich DeWald. 'Everyday Technology in South and Southeast Asia: An Introduction', *Modern Asian Studies* 46/1 (January 2012), 1-17.

---

[47] Steel, *On the Face of the Waters*, 57, 52, 55.
[48] Candler, *The Mantle of the East*, 215.

Chua Ai Lin. ' "The Modern Magic Carpet": Wireless Radio in Interwar Colonial Singapore', *Modern Asian Studies* 46/1 (January 2012), 167–91.

Dikötter, Frank. *Things Modern: Material Culture and Everyday Life in China* (London: Hurst, 2007).

McClintock, Anne. *Imperial Leather: Race, Gender and Sexuality in the Colonial Context* (New York and London: Routledge, 1995).

Taylor, J. G. 'The Sewing-Machine in Colonial-Era Photographs: A Record from Dutch Indonesia', *Modern Asian Studies* 46/1 (January 2012), 71–95.

Trotter, David. *Cooking with Mud: The Idea of Mess in Nineteenth-Century Art and Fiction* (Oxford: Oxford University Press, 2000).

Kipling and 'Big' technology

Aguiar, Marian. *Tracking Modernity* (Minneapolis, MN: University of Minnesota Press, 2011).

Bubb, Alexander. 'The Provincial Cosmopolitan: Kipling, India and Globalization', *Journal of Postcolonial Writing* 49/4 (2013), 391–404.

Davies, Laurence. 'Science and Technology: Present, Past and Future', in Howard J. Booth (ed.), *The Cambridge Companion to Rudyard Kipling* (Cambridge: Cambridge University Press, 2012).

Harvie, Christopher. ' "The Sons of Martha": Technology, Transport, and Rudyard Kipling', *Victorian Studies* 20/3 (Spring 1977), 269–82.

Candler, Steel, and Anglo-Indian writing

Krishnaswamy, Revathi. *Effeminism* (Ann Arbor, MI: University of Michigan Press, 1998).

Morton, Stephen. *States of Emergency* (Liverpool: Liverpool University Press, 2013).

Parry, Benita. *Delusions and Discoveries: India in the British Imagination, 1880–1930*, 2nd edn (London: Verso, 1998).

Procida, Mary A. *Married to the Empire* (Manchester: Manchester University Press, 2002).

Roy, Anindyo. *Civility and Empire: Literature and Culture in British India, 1822–1922* (London and New York: Routledge, 2005).

Tickell, Alex. *Terrorism, Insurgency and Indian-English Literature, 1830–1947* (London: Routledge, 2013).

Walsh, Judith E. *Domesticity in Colonial India* (Oxford: Rowman & Littlefield, 2004).

CHAPTER 39

ACTORS AND PUPPETS

From Henry Irving's Lyceum to Edward Gordon Craig's Arena Goldoni

OLGA TAXIDOU

'To save the Theatre, the Theatre must be destroyed, the actors and actresses must all die of the plague... They make art impossible!'[1]

The above epigram acts as an appropriate introduction to Edward Gordon Craig's hugely influential essay of 1909, 'The Actor and the Übermarionette'. Delivered in the aphoristic and eschatological tone of many a modernist anti-theatrical tract by Eleanora Duse, herself an actress whom Craig was later to direct, it enacts all the contours of the debates surrounding acting of the period, its aesthetic and political efficacy. Indeed many of the general debates about the 'retheatricalisation' of the theatre, Cocteau's 'poetry *of* the theatre' and 'poetry *in* the theatre',[2] are centred round the representational efficacy of the human form. Martin Puchner calls the actor 'the scapegoat of modernism',[3] and the above quotation, steeped as it is in the imagery of sacrifice and resurrection, enacts the basic dramatic structure of the debate itself.

From Plato onwards most discussions about the representational efficacy of the human form also include puppets and marionettes. In many ways, the debates about theatricality and the ways they are mapped onto to the performing body can be seen as a modernist rehearsal of the oldest of aesthetic debates: that between

---

[1] Eleanora Duse quoted in *The Mask*, Vol.1, 22 (Florence, 1909).

[2] Jean Cocteau, 'Preface' (1922) to *The Wedding on the Eiffel Tower* (1921), trans. Michael Benedikt, in *Modern French Plays: An Anthology from Jarry to Ionesco* (London: Faber and Faber, 1964), 96–7.

[3] Martin Puchner, *Stagefright: Modernism, Anti-theatricality and Drama* (Baltimore, MD and London: Johns Hopkins University Press, 2002).

poetry and philosophy, where poetry is read through theatricality. The 'Ancient quarrel', as Plato calls it,[4] is read through specific interpretations of the function of theatre. It is this theatrical paradigm that is radically reworked within the modernist experiments in stagecraft. More often than not these experiments are located within the physical, semantic/representational, and ideological contours of the performing body.

These experiments with the performing body can be read within the broader radical changes that theatre was undergoing during the late nineteenth and early twentieth centuries, both within the Anglophone and the European context. The impact of naturalism and Ibsen on the modernist stage,[5] the impact of the emerging movement of feminism,[6] and the shift from the actor–manager system to the notion of the modernist director cannot be overestimated.[7] The more strictly literary 'high modernists' like W. B. Yeats, T. S. Eliot, and Ezra Pound engage actively with the stage and view it as a way of embodying modernist aesthetics. Yeats pronounces his aphoristic 'After us the savage God', after viewing the first rehearsal on Alfred Jarry's *Ubu Roi* in 1896.[8] He also works very closely with Craig, whose famous screens were first materialized as a way of conceptualizing scenic space for The Abbey Theatre's production of *The Hour Glass* (1911). T. S. Eliot praises The Ballets Russes in 'A Dialogue on Dramatic Poetry' (1928), and, of course, writes plays heavily influenced by the charismatic group of Cambridge scholars known as 'The Cambridge Ritualists'.[9] Pound's long-standing relationship with the theatre, from his early interest in the Noh to his late translations of classical Greek plays, informs every aspect of his work.[10] Crucially, in all these cases the concern is not solely with the function of the poetic word, but with the nature of stagecraft itself.

In this context the work of Craig can be read as a bridge between the late-Victorian actor—manager system and the more modernist inflected 'director' figure. His own

---

[4] Plato, *Republic* (607b5–6). For a recent reflection on this quarrel as representing two distinct philosophical traditions and its repercussions on philosophy from Socrates to Bakhtin, see Raymond Barfield, *The Ancient Quarrel between Poetry and Philosophy* (Cambridge: Cambridge University Press, 2011).

[5] See Kirsten Shepherd-Barr, *Ibsen and Early Modernist Theatre, 1890-1900* (Westport, CT: Greenwood Press, 1997); Thomas Postlewait (ed.), *William Archer on Ibsen: The Major Essays, 1889–1919* (Westport, CT: Greenwood Press, 1984).

[6] See Penny Farfan, *Women, Modernism and Performance* (Cambridge: Cambridge University Press, 2004).

[7] See Edward Braun, *The Director and The Stage* (London: Methuen, 1982).

[8] W. B. Yeats, 'The Tragic Generation' (1914), in *Autobiographies* (London: Macmillan, 1955), 279–349, esp. 348–9.

[9] T. S. Eliot, *Selected Essays* (London: Faber and Faber, 1951), 46; also see Robert Crawford, *The Savage and the City in the Work of T. S. Eliot* (Oxford: Clarendon Press, 1990); Martha C. Carpentier, *Ritual, Myth and the Modernist Text: The Influence of Jane Ellen Harrison on Joyce, Eliot, and Woolf* (Amsterdam: Gordon and Breach, 1998).

[10] See Sophocles, *Women of Trachis, A Version by Ezra Pound* (London: Faber and Faber, 19560; R. Reid (ed.), *Elektra—A Play by Ezra Pound* (Princeton, NJ: Princeton University Press, 1992).

biography can been seen as almost literally enacting a shift from Henry Irving's Lyceum, where he worked as a young actor with his mother Ellen Terry, to the Arena Goldoni in Florence, which became the stage for all his experiments in stagecraft.

Craig's manifesto on acting is part of a long and distinguished Romantic European tradition that from Kleist onwards re-conceptualizes theatrical movement (acting *and* dance) in relation to puppets, but also results from the late nineteenth-century and Victorian fascination with puppets and masks. As early as 1888 William Archer, the great supporter of Ibsen, writes a treatise on acting entitled *Masks or Faces*,[11] where he debates the merits and pitfalls of both stylization and expressiveness in response to Diderot's famous *Le paradoxe sur le comédien* (1773).[12] Again Irving is used as the prime example of the power of the 'expressive' actor, 'who combines the electric force of a strong personality with a mastery of the resources of his art and must have a greater power over his audiences than the passionless actor who gives a most artistic simulation of the emotion he never experiences'.[13] In many ways, this is exactly the type of acting that Craig saw as psychological, narcissistic, distorting of reality, and manipulative towards its audience. Despite this seeming contradiction Craig still hails Henry Irving as the finest example of his 'masked-marionette' actor:

> I consider him to have been the greatest actor I have ever seen, and I have seen the best in Italy, France, Russia, Germany, Holland and America.
>
> But you who are younger, and who never saw Irving, will see him now...a figure solemn and beautiful like an immense thought in motion. If you will be an Actor in such a day as this, and if you are an English man, take but one model...the masked marionette.[14]

It is fascinating that Craig, whose work by 1918 already had a huge impact across Europe, goes back to Irving as a prototype of acting that is at once historical and modern. Craig's championing of the Übermarionette, not so much as a substitute for the actor, but as a kind of hyper-actor, free from psychology, personality, and narcissism, sits somewhat uncomfortably with the image we have of Irving as a kind of actor/demiurge, as an actor who can transfix and *mesmerize*. Still, Craig manages to reconcile Irving's mesmerizing, entrancing acting, with the kind of stylized, non-psychological acting that was embodied by the figures of the mask and the marionette. This is less of a contradiction and more endemic to the ways the whole anti-theatrical tradition is rehearsed within modernism, where the traits and languages

---

[11] William Archer, *Masks or Faces: A Study in the Psychology of Acting* (London: Longman, Green, 1888).

[12] See Joseph R. Roach, *The Player's Passion: Studies in the Science of Acting* (Newark, DE: University of Delaware Press, 1985), on Diderot's essay and its impact on modernist theories of acting.

[13] See Archer, *Masks or Faces*, 212.

[14] Edward Gordon Craig, *The Marionette*, Vol. 1, No. 6 (Florence, 1918), 170.

of the theatre itself are conscripted in the attempt to create a modernist theatrical aesthetic. In this context it does not seem incongruous that the greatest Victorian actor, Henry Irving, is heralded as the prototype for the modernist actor, in Craigian terms, the 'masked marionette'. Interestingly this appears in Craig's other journal, *The Marionette*, that he published in Florence during the difficult years of 1918–19, when *The Mask* had to cease publication. *The Marionette* was less ambitious than *The Mask* and appeared more as a leaflet rather than a full-blown journal. The image of Irving projected through its pages—the 'masked marionette'—manages to act as an emblem both for acting and possibly for his combined magazines as well.

Irving as a 'masked marionette' also points towards the ways that the radical modernist experiments in stagecraft are a continuation of the Victorian stage and not simply a break from it. Another figure that is crucial in this transition is Isadora Duncan. The American dancer was also entranced by Irving, and had a huge impact on Craig, both personal and artistic. Again Duncan's experiments in dance can be seen as part of the fascination with theatrical presence in general, a presence that relies formally on modes of performance that borrow from and experiment with stylized and expressive acting but also with dance.

Duncan's debut on the London stage in March 1900 at the New Gallery can be read as bringing together many of these concerns and in its both critical and artistic reception had a huge influence on ideas about stagecraft of the period. Her first appearance was curated by the gallery owner Charles Hallé,[15] and the guest list reads like a roll call of leading British writers, artists, and academics—all of whom were to play a significant role in that heady transitional period from aestheticism to modernism—but Hallé's coup was to invite the classicist Jane Harrison to recite extracts from Theocritus to accompany Duncan's dance. A few nights later Duncan was taken to Henry Irving's Lyceum Theatre to watch him perform in the notorious production of *The Bells*. There she also watched a performance of *Cymberline* with Ellen Terry, a production that included her son Edward Gordon Craig. Again Irving acts as a type of mediating figure between Craig and Duncan. Duncan's experiments in dance that brought together her background in the Delsarte system[16] and combined it with a vitalist, even nostalgic Hellenism, all filtered through her particular feminism, might be seen initially to be far removed from both Irving and Craig. Her brand of female expressiveness that focused on the female body of the dancer may appear to be the exact opposite of Craig's Übermarionette. However, these two apparently extreme positions mirror each other and dance is as central to these as is Craig's more stylized, mechanized super-puppet.

---

[15] See Fredrika Blair, *Isadora: Portrait of the Artist as a Woman* (Wellingborough: Thorsons, 1987), 33–49.
[16] See Carrie Preston, *Modernism's Mythic Pose: Gender, Genre and Solo Performance* (Oxford: Oxford University Press, 2011).

The grouping of Isadora Duncan and Jane Harrison is also iconic in bringing together the visionary scholar/theorist and the equally visionary dancer/practitioner. Also present that evening was Andrew Lang, the pioneer of the so-called British School of Anthropology. Part of a charismatic and radical group of thinkers, fuelled by the work of James Frazer, they merged classicism, sociology, and anthropology in a heady cocktail that proposed an evolutionary model for the study of human culture.[17] Opposed to reading myth and religion simply through philology and narrative, the principles of ritual and rhythm became central. Indeed, it was these very principles that seem to have been embodied by Isadora Duncan's dance and punctuated by Jane Harrison's text. Harrison was yet to write her monumental *Themis* (1912), but it is clear that the encounter with Duncan will also have had an impact on the aesthetics and politics of this central figure of Sapphic modernism.

The Cambridge Ritualists (Jane Ellen Harrison, 1850–1928; Francis M. Cornford, 1874–1943; Gilbert Murray, 1866–1957) created a new approach to the 'Greeks' heavily influenced by Darwin and Frazer—based on rhythm rather than narrative, on embodiment and vitalism rather than texuality—that helped to construct a distinctively modernist Hellenism. Modernist experiments in acting and dance will regularly draw on this new Hellenism in search for models of the performing body and its relation to theatrical space. The Cambridge Ritualists were to have a huge impact on the theatrical experiments of the period, from the direct textual influences on T. S. Eliot, W. B. Yeats, and Ezra Pound, to the experiments in stage movement and design by Duncan and Craig. So, when Craig quotes Plato and Aristotle to frame his Übermarionette manifesto, he is exercising a similar modernist Hellenism that at once revives the ancient quarrel in terms of the philosophical anti-theatrical legacy, but also sees in the 'Greeks' a performance practice for his understanding of the art of the actor and scenic space. For Craig all these forces came together in his Greek-inspired designs for Eleanora Duse as Electra and in his collection of 'Black Figures', including designs of Iphigenia, Helen, and the chorus that explored the performer's physicality and mobility in relation to the mask and the puppet.[18]

That Irving should also act as a link between Duncan and Craig is not surprising within the general interest from the late nineteenth century onwards in the 'science' of acting. As Joseph Roach has shown, this period is significant in redefining the art of acting both in response to Diderot's *paradox* and also fuelled by Darwinism. In general there seems to be an equal concern with formulating a scientific language for the stage as there is in its poetics and theatricality. This redefining of stagecraft is also concerned with modes of spectatorship. In *Stage Presence* (2008) Jane Goodall

---

[17] See Robert Ackerman, *The Myth and Ritual School* (New York and London: Garland, 1991). For a bibliography of the group's work see Arlen Shelley, *The Cambridge Ritualists: An Annotated Bibliography* (Metuchen, NJ and London: Scarecrow, 1990).

[18] Lindsay Mary Newman (ed.), *Black Figures of Edward Gordon Craig* (Wellingborough: Christopher Skelton, 1989).

argues that in 'the discourse surrounding stage presence in western modernity' there is 'an ambivalent relationship between the cultures of science and poetics'.[19] And this ambivalence can be found in the work of Anton Mesmer (1734–1815), who studied astronomy and medicine at Vienna and whose name coined the term 'mesmerism'. Mesmer's work on the relationships between magnetic fields and personality, influence and hypnotism had a huge impact on theories of acting. Goodall writes:

> One of Mesmer's unintentional legacies was the injection of a new kind of significance into the relationship between performer and audience. The actor had never been so powerful, and the later nineteenth century was a period in which the stage star acquired an aura of supernatural energy. There was also a growing interest in psychological power as a subject for dramatic exploration.[20]

Again Henry Irving is mentioned as the example of an actor who quite consciously applies these techniques of mesmerism. His famous performance in *The Bells*, much written about and lauded for its haunting, supernatural qualities, can be read as an exercise in mesmerism. Although Craig complained that the power of this performance was impossible to capture in words, he proceeded throughout his life to provide various accounts of it, especially when formulating his own theories on acting. He invariably characterizes it as 'mesmeric in the highest degree', as 'supernatural', and as a 'dance'. Through detailed reminisces such as this Craig provides us with a useful account of the *mechanics* of mesmerism and how this impacts on the audience. The emphasis on the eyes as 'the means by which the mesmerist generates a contagious interiority', as Goodall claims,[21] is underlined as a chief trait. This is acting as trance, as channelling, and the actor's psycho-motoric functions are all enlisted to create this effect, an effect that was also influenced by the introduction of electricity to the stage. Henry Irving's haunting dance–acting, where the body of the actor itself becomes a mechanism for the creation of affect, is later echoed in the writings of Vsevolod Meyerhold and Antonin Artaud, where the actor is conceptualized as a kind of electric conductor or a laboratory that offers glimpses into scientific, political, and aesthetic truths. And this link between these categories of the metaphysical and the scientific, the political and the aesthetic, is provided or channelled through the performing body. Despite the initial contradiction, or even the biographical context, we can see what attracted Craig to Irving.

This attraction to Irving need not be read in opposition to Craig's fascination with puppets, but as parallel to it, as a kind of double in the Artaudian sense where the interest in the modes of stylization and abstraction offered by the puppet is almost always haunted and shadowed by the 'liveness' of the performing body. It is a doubleness that may also have contributed to Craig's inability actually to construct

---

[19] Jane Goodall, *Stage Presence* (London and New York: Routledge, 2008), 100.
[20] Ibid., 101.   [21] Ibid., 106.

an Übermarionette. For, as we know, his phantasmic hyper-puppet remained unrealized and probably unrealizable; rather than this being viewed only as a failure or as a shortcoming it may also be read as part of the utopian aspiration of much of modernist stagecraft.

This aspiration itself is not uniquely modernist as it feeds directly off the nineteenth-century aesthetic and Symbolist 'cult of the puppet'. In the Anglophone tradition, Arthur Symons, Walter Pater, and Oscar Wilde all write passionate tracts exalting the puppet as the ultimate art form. This was a legacy also continued by many modernist writers who are not readily associated with ideas of theatre and performance, at once underlining the centrality of the theatrical paradigm for modernist experimentation in general and the particular attention paid to the performing body in this context. The high priest of aestheticism himself, Walter Pater, also contributes to the man or marionette debate, reiterating the platonic strand of the argument. The actor, corrupted and weakened by the act of mimesis itself, subsequently becomes unsuitable material for art. The power of the stage to act as a contaminating agent, spreading social and moral disease, is elaborated on by Pater:

> The stage in these volumes presents itself indeed not merely as a mirror of life, but as an illustration of the utmost intensity of life, in the fortunes and characters of players. Ups and downs, generosity, dark fates, the most delicate goodness, have nowhere been more prominent than in the private existence of those devoted to the public mimicry of men and women. Contact with the stage, almost throughout its history presents itself as a kind of touchstone, to bring out the *bizzarrerie*, the theatrical tricks and contrasts of the actual world.[22]

Like any body or object that has been ordained with the power to *stand in for* somebody or something else, the stage and the actor acquire magical, almost totemic qualities. It is this ritualistic power of acting (as both poison and cure, a *pharmakon*) that makes it unsuitable for humans. The puppets, on the other hand, seem ideal. On a lighter note Oscar Wilde comments that puppets 'are admirably docile and have no personalities at all'.[23]

The lack of personality is a huge attraction in puppets and is again echoed in much of the writing of the time. As the stage is trying within modernism to articulate a language distinct to its own modes of production, the puppet is conscripted into the argument that tries to maintain the power of the playwright. It becomes the purest form of mediation for the playwright's voice. This, of course, is not the sole interpretation of the role of the puppet. As it is, however, in the Anglophone tradition, puppet theatres present a kind of absolute aesthetic totality that is linked directly to the power of the artist's aesthetic will. They acquire a very special aura,

[22] Walter Pater, 'Another Estimate of the Actor's Character', rpt. in *The Mask*, Vol. 3, nos 10–12 (Florence, 1911), 174.
[23] Rupert Hart-Davis (ed.), *The Letters of Oscar Wilde* (London: Harcourt, 1962), 311, from a letter to the editor of *The Daily Telegraph*, 19 February, 1982.

as they are seen as propagating this role. In particular, the Petit Théâtre des Marionettes in Paris, with Maurice Bouchor as its director at the Galerie Vivienne from 1889 to 1894, becomes one of those modernist sites, like the Cabaret Voltaire later on, to attract many visitors and much attention. Oscar Wilde records in a letter from the same period (the same letter as the one quoted above), after watching a performance of *The Tempest* at the Petit Théâtre, that 'Miranda took no notice of the flowers I sent her after the curtain fell'.[24]

Many such puppet theatres throughout Europe became the centre of aesthetic and sometimes political experimentation. They managed to act as magnets for the cosmopolitan and sometimes internationalist outlook of much of the modernist experiment in the theatre. Arthur Symons asks after such a visit to a theatre in Rome, 'why we require the intervention of any less perfect medium between the meaning of a piece, as the author conceived it, and that other meaning which it derives from our reception of it'.[25] Symons possibly hints at the ways that puppets also help to redetermine the relationships between playwright, actor, and director.

Most of the puppet theatres of Italy, however, were of the traditional kind. Maurice Bouchor's Petit Théâtre des Marionettes was already a specific reading of puppet theatre. Inspired by symbolism, Bouchor wrote a number of original plays for his puppets (*Tobias; Noël, or The Mystery of the Nativity; The Story of Christmas; The Legend of Saint Cecile; Devotion to Saint Andrew; The Dream of Kheyam; The Mysteries of Eleusis in Four Acts and Verse*) that were inspired by biblical or mythological themes and staged medieval mysteries and plays by Hrostwitha. These were all very successful and caused a stir despite the short life of the Petit Théâtre (1889–93). Bouchor himself emerges as a major theorist of puppetry of the period.[26]

Bouchor's conception of marionettes and their expressive abilities is in line with the slightly mystical and heightened use proposed of them by Symbolism. Indeed, Maeterlinck's first collection of plays for marionettes appears in 1894. Like Bouchor's adaptations, alongside which they were staged, these are highly stylized pieces with metaphysical undertones. And the Belgian's experiments with the use of marionettes were to be hugely influential all over Europe and Russia.

This centrality of puppets for the 'retheatricalisation' of the stage and for the general thinking about representation provides a further link between the Anglophone experiments of the stage *and* on the page with those of the historical avant-garde, where the allure of the puppet also works both ways. On the one hand it represents the utter utopian faith in technology as the emancipatory force of modernity, as seen in the Futurist robot plays or in Vsevolod Meyerhold's appropriation of puppetry in the formation of his biomechanics, while on the other it can represent

[24] Ibid., 311.

[25] Arthur Symons, 'Apology for Puppets', *The Mask* 5/2 (Florence, 1912), 103.

[26] Quoted in Segel, *Pinocchio's Progeny*, 83, from Maurice Bouchor, *Mystères bibliques et chrétiens* (Paris: Ernest Flammarion, n.d.), 7–8.

the bleakest, most technophobic aspects of the same project, as seen in Karel Čapek's *RUR* (*Rossum's Universal Robots*), published in 1920 (and featuring the first use of the term 'robot').

The utopian and somewhat uncritical acceptance of technology as almost inherently emancipatory and critical by the Russian/Soviet constructivists is matched by the utter dystopian and apocalyptic tone of the Czech work, where the robots take over and apocalypse is imminent. *RUR* does end on a somewhat Kleistian note, where the robots, after revolting against the humans and killing all of them except Alquist—a builder, hence like a robot—finally turn into 'better' versions of their original human creators. The last robots/new humans go forth into the world to the tune of 'Go, Adam. Go, Eve—be a wife to him. Be a husband to her, Primus'.[27] This technophobic use of puppets, marionettes, and robots can be read as a direct descendant of the Romantic, even gothic tradition of the monstrous machine. Like *Frankenstein*, this narrative is fully equipped with uncontrollable reason gone wild, anxieties about gender and reproduction, and dubious relationships with parent figures.

Although the puppet inhabits the modern world with its anxieties about mechanization and its fears about an ever-decreasing humanism, it also firmly resides within the oral and popular tradition. The puppets such as Punch and Judy deriving from the *Commedia dell'Arte*, popular shadow puppets like Karagiozis from the Balkans, Turkey, and Greece, the Petrushka tradition in Russia, all attract interest and inspire imitation. This is a tradition that is seen as having somehow escaped the all-encompassing and humanizing impact of the Enlightenment. It is viewed cheerfully as blasphemous and anti-theological, offering modernist artists, like Kandinsky and Picasso, paradigms for imitation and homage. The attitude that most theatre practitioners and theorists of the period share towards the oral tradition of puppetry in some ways mirrors a similar attitude towards the so-called Theatres of the Orient. This almost invariably permeates with Romantic undertones about its authenticity, its naivety, its uniqueness, and its unquestionable anti-authoritarianism. It is this view of orality and the popular tradition as almost inherently radical, a somewhat uncritical attitude to all things oral, popular, and folk, and the puppet seems to successfully represent all three. Puppets deriving from the *Commedia dell'Arte* or from the Petrushka tradition come to represent the defiant body of the people against the overwhelming impact of Christianity, the Church, and the State. As such they can become either the actors or the models of the actors for the new societies, envisaged by their puppet masters/directors.

Craig's Übermarionette can be seen as drawing on all these traditions, forming a complex network of relationships. It connects his work to the visionary and somewhat idealist Romanticism of Kleist, while also paying homage to the theatrical

---

[27] Karel Čapek, *RUR (Rossum's Universal Robots)*, trans. Claudia Novack-Jones, in Peter Kussi (ed.), *Toward the Radical Centre: A Karel Čapek Reader* (Highland Park, NJ: Catbird Press, 1990), 109.

traditions of the past (which he considered 'great'). His Arena Goldoni in Florence housed puppet collections from East and West; *The Mask* featured articles on the puppet traditions of the *Commedia dell'Arte*, the Wayang and Bunraku traditions among others. His hyper-puppet also allowed him to theorize the newly emergent role of the director (his 'Artist of the Theatre'). However, Craig was more interested in sketching out the imaginative and aesthetic potential of such a 'creation/creature' than exploring the mechanics of its production. The Übermarionette, for Craig, acquires a *phantasmic* quality, never meant actually to be constructed, perhaps always meant to provide 'the ghost in the machine'.

The actual technology of production for these modernist puppets/automata/robots was of little or no interest to Craig. Rather, his view and his writings on the Übermarionette create the notion of a creative, imaginative space, a kind of theoretical 'laboratory'. The actual empirical act, the process of construction—so crucial for the theatres of the historical avant-garde—is totally absent from his writings. Instead, what transpires, in a rhetorical trope that utilizes the Platonic dialogue, is a highly reflective—one could even claim philosophical—mode of writing that hails the Übermarionette as an almost utopian site: a notional, creative, imaginative sphere that reconfigures the representational contours of the human form. Again one could claim that this utopian aspect of Craig's project continues the long and distinguished tradition of Platonism.[28] This phantasmic quality of his Übermarionette could be read as part of its utopian aspiration. It is not coincidental in this context that the term 'future' appears so central in Craig's writing ('The Artist of the Future', 'The Theatre of the Future', etc.). And this future refers not solely to Craig's immediate epigones and the huge impact that his writings have had on later generations of theatre makers, but in a sense gestures towards all the futures to come. The subsequent 'success' of the Übermarionette from modernism onwards could be at least partly due to Craig's 'failure' to actually construct one. Rather than view this as a shortcoming we might, with the benefit of hindsight and the future itself, view it as creating a 'potentiality',[29] a space that allows both his contemporaries and future generations of theatre makers to experiment with the representational efficacy of the human form.

In its reception the Übermarionette has sometimes been read in opposition to the more technologically inflected and materialist legacies of the historical avant-garde. However, this is a binary that, following Jane Goodall's work, I believe is problematized through the workings of theatricality itself. For the main issue on a philosophical level is that of 'presence', a matter that from Martin Heidegger[30] through to Jacques Derrida has been highly contentious. This 'metaphysics of

[28] See Puchner, *The Drama of Ideas: Platonic Provocations in Theatre and Philosophy* (Oxford: Oxford University Press, 2010).

[29] For an analysis of this view of 'potentiality', see Giorgio Agamben, *The Coming Community*, trans. Michael Hardt (Minnesota, MN: University of Minnesota Press, 1993).

[30] See among other works, Martin Heidegger, 'The Turning', in *The Question Concerning Technology and Other Essays*, trans. William Lovitt (New York: Harper and Row, 1977).

presence' has been associated with concerns about false consciousness, ideology, manipulation, and oppression, even when it comes to reception. In other words much of the thinking about presence can also be read as rehearsing some of the basic tenets of the anti-theatrical tradition in philosophy. However, as this analysis suggests, this very anti-theatrical tradition is radically reworked through these modernist experiments, centred around the presence of the human form.

In this sense Craig's Übermarionette need not be read in opposition to the more technologically savvy experiments of the Italian Futurists or the German Bauhaus. It might be more a case of experiments taking place along a similar trajectory, in many ways reflecting the collaborations of the artists themselves. Although Oscar Schlemmer's work on the Theatre of the Bauhaus may provide a different way of conceptualizing stage presence, informed by technology, it is still concerned with similar issues, folding back onto the human form Craig's thinking about the Übermarionette. Utilizing a more modernist vocabulary Moholy-Nagy's conceptualization of the actor as the 'Mechanized Eccentric' can itself be read as revising and reworking Craig's view of Irving as the 'masked marionette'.[31]

For Schlemmer and Nagy, like Craig, the human form is not the most appropriate material for art. Following a different direction from Craig, the Bauhaus artists opt for presence rather than absence, a presence that is facilitated by technology. However, the two tropes are not mutually exclusive. As Joseph Roach claims, 'Theatrical performance is the simultaneous experience of mutually exclusive possibilities— truth and illusion, presence and absence, face and mask'.[32] In this context it does not appear as such a stretch of the imagination to view Irving himself and his contribution to theories of acting as a predecessor of the Mechanized Eccentric.

The Mechanized Eccentric is called upon not only in terms of its ability to restructure the representation of the human form but also as a way of creating the very desirable and very modern response of estrangement. This reading of presence, as articulated by Schlemmer, rather than creating identification, empathy, and what we could call homeliness, presents itself almost in the Heidegerian terms of the 'unhomely'. Here Schlemmer is quite consciously reworking an opposition— between abstraction and empathy—that was formulated by Wilhelm Worringer, while also somewhat revising its aestheticism.[33] Citing Kleist, Schlemmer comments on theatre as expressing both 'the new mathematics of relativity' and 'a yearning for synthesis' with the 'promise of total art'.[34]

---

[31] Maholy-Nagy, in Walter Gropius (ed.), *The Theatre of the Bauhaus*, trans. Arthur Wensinger (Baltimore, MD and London: Johns Hopkins University Press, 1996), 54.

[32] Roach, 'It', *Theatre Journal* 56 (2004), 559. Also quoted in *Stage Presence*, 6.

[33] Wilhelm Worringer, *Abstraction and Empathy: A Contribution to the Psychology of Style*, trans. Michael Bullock (1908; repr. New York: International Universities Press, 1967), 24.

[34] Oscar Schlemmer, *The Letters and Diaries of Oscar Schlemmer*, selected and ed. Tut Schlemmer, trans. Krishna Winston (September 1922; repr, Middletown, CT: Wesleyan University Press, 1972), 126–7.

The fascination with science, something that was to also characterize the Brechtian project, coupled with the very psycho-physical act of yearning, makes for a very interesting reading of the Mechanized Eccentric, less as a programmatic emotionless piece of metal, and more as a desiring machine, there to channel the hopes and aspirations for a total theatre. Like the Übermarionette, the Mechanized Eccentric enacts a utopian gestus, one where presence and absence do not negate each other but coexist.

Like Oskar Schlemmer's, the Russian visionary theatre director Vsevolod Meyerhold's[35] work may be said to be characterized by a similar yearning of marrying the modern and the technological with the traditional and the organic. This is clear in the coinage of the term *biomechanics*, the technique for training actors that he formulated. Meyerhold's work and life can be read as comprising one of the boldest and most utopian projects of the historical avant-garde. His biomechanics occupies a central position as it brings together, in an inspired fusion, the Symbolist legacy, the oral tradition of puppetry, and the modernist fascination with technology. Although this formed a heady cocktail of 'high' and 'low' traditions, precise technology, and Symbolist stylization, it culminated in a series of concrete applications: *études* as Meyerhold called them. In many ways all these projects start from the same position: the arbitrariness of the human form and its inappropriateness as raw material for the art of the theatre. This is a concern that permeates much Russian Symbolist writing on theatre.[36] It also is important to underline the fact that despite their political differences (Meyerhold's utopian Marxism and Craig's fellow-travelling fascism) both men were trying to provide solutions to similar problems and both initially work within similar theoretical frameworks. Craig's first dialogue had been pirated and published in Russia by 1906 and he was very influential within the group of 'decadent' Symbolists who published similar manifestos, mostly on acting. Fyodor Sologub himself declared his debt to Craig in 1909:

> It is remarkable that in the very first year of this new century E. G. Craig flung a challenge to the naturalistic theatre…therefore, this young Englishman is the first to set up initial guideposts on the new road of the Theatre.[37]

Craig's Übermarionette was to also be part of this 'new road of the theatre'. However, together with its posture towards the future, Craig's phantasmic creature also pays homage to the past. That immediate past for Craig is Henry Irving and the type of acting he embodied. In this sense the Übermarionette could be said to haunt both

---

[35] See Robert Leach, *Vsevolod Meyerhold* (Cambridge: Cambridge University Press, 1989).

[36] Fyodor Sologub, 'The Theatre of a Single Will', in Laurence Senelick (ed. and trans.), *Russian Dramatic Theory from Pushkin to the Symbolists: An Anthology* (Austin, TX: University of Austin Press), 132–48.

[37] Quoted in Senelick, 'Moscow and Monodrama: The Meaning of the Craig-Stanislavsky Hamlet', *Theatre Research International* 6 (1981), 109–24, 114.

Irving's Lyceum in Victorian London and Craig's Arena Goldoni in modernist Florence.

Craig's 'masked marionette', Moholy-Nagy's 'mechanized eccentric', the Futurist robot plays, and Meyerhold's biomechanics can all be read as experimenting with ideas of presence and absence in relation to the performing body within the broader context of modernist stagecraft. This context itself allows for both the metaphysical yearnings and the technological innovations in a scheme of things where body and machine are not mutually exclusive. And the puppet emerges as the most apt model for these sometimes conflicting but creative discourses. At once modern and ancient, carrying within it the wisdom of the people but also making itself available to the wonders of technology, the puppet can be seen as a paradigm of the work of art itself. It shares in the vital and organic nature of the oral tradition while also celebrating the artificiality of its mechanics of production. It also points towards the centrality of the theatrical paradigm for modernism more generally in providing that very material but also illusive link between textuality and physicality, between the word and the body.

FURTHER READING

Ackerman, Alan and Puchner, Martin. *Against Theatre: Creative Destructions on the Modernist Stage* (Basingstoke and New York: Palgrave Macmillan, 2007).

Berghaus, Günter. *Theatre, Performance and the Historical Avant-garde* (Basingstoke and New York: Palgrave Macmillan, 2010).

Goodall, Jane. *Stage Presence* (London and New York: Routledge, 2008).

Leach, Robert. *Makers of Modern Theatre* (London: Taylor & Francis, 2004).

Puchner, Martin. *Stagefright: Modernism, Anti-theatricality and Drama* (Baltimore, MD and London: Johns Hopkins University Press, 2002).

Puchner, Martin. *The Drama of Ideas: Platonic Provocations in Theatre and Philosophy* (Oxford and New York: Oxford University Press, 2010).

Reilly, Kara. *Automata and Mimesis on the Stage of Theatre History* (Basingstoke and New York: Palgrave Macmillan, 2011).

Roach, Joseph. R. *The Player's Passion: Studies in the Science of Acting* (Newark, DE: University of Delaware Press, 1985).

Segel, Harold B. *Pinocchio's Progeny: Puppets, Marionettes, Automatons, and Robots in Modernist and Avant-Garde Drama* (Baltimore, MD and London: Johns Hopkins University Press, 1995).

Taxidou, Olga. *The Mask: A Periodical Performance by Edward Gordon Craig* (London: Harwood Academic Publishers, 1998).

Taxidou, Olga. *Modernism and Performance: Jarry to Brecht* (Basingstoke and New York: Palgrave Macmillan, 2007).

Walton, J. Michael (ed.). *Craig on Theatre* (London: Methuen, 1983).

INDEX